www.wadsworth.com

wadsworth.com is the World Wide Web site for Wadsworth and is your direct source to dozens of online resources.

At *wadsworth.com* you can find out about supplements, demonstration software, and student resources. You can also send email to many of our authors and preview new publications and exciting new technologies.

wadsworth.com
Changing the way the world learns®

From the Wadsworth Series in Mass Communication and Journalism

General Mass Communication

Biagi, Shirley, *Media/Impact: An Introduction to Mass Media,* 5th ed.

Bucy, Erik, *Living in the Information Age: A New Media Reader*

Craft, John, Frederic Leigh, and Donald Godfrey, *Electronic Media*

Day, Louis, *Ethics in Media Communications: Cases and Controversies,* 3rd ed.

Dennis, Everette E., and John C. Merrill, *Media Debates: Great Issues for the Digital Age,* 3rd ed.

Fortner, Robert S., *International Communications: History, Conflict, and Control of the Global Metropolis*

Gillmor, Donald, Jerome Barron, and Todd Simon, *Mass Communication Law: Cases and Comment,* 6th ed.

Gillmor, Donald, Jerome Barron, Todd Simon, and Herbert Terry, *Fundamentals of Mass Communication Law*

Hilmes, Michele, *Only Connect: A Cultural History of Broadcasting in the United States*

Jamieson, Kathleen Hall, and Karlyn Kohrs Campbell, *The Interplay of Influence,* 5th ed.

Kamalipour, Yahya K., *Global Communication*

Lester, Paul, *Visual Communication,* 2nd ed.

Lont, Cynthia, *Women and Media: Content, Careers, and Criticism*

Sparks, Glenn G., *Media Effects Research: A Basic Overview*

Straubhaar, Joseph, and Robert LaRose, *Media Now: Communications Media in the Information Age,* 3rd ed.

Zelezny, John D., *Communications Law: Liberties, Restraints, and the Modern Media,* 3rd ed.

Zelezny, John D., *Cases in Communications Law,* 3rd ed.

Journalism

Adams, Paul, *Writing Right for Today's Mass Media: A Textbook and Workbook with Language Exercises*

Anderson, Douglas, *Contemporary Sports Reporting,* 2nd ed.

Bowles, Dorothy, and Diane L. Borden, *Creative Editing,* 3rd ed.

Catsis, John, *Sports Broadcasting*

Chance, Jean, and William McKeen, *Literary Journalism: A Reader*

Dorn, Raymond, *How to Design and Improve Magazine Layouts,* 2nd ed.

Fischer, Heintz-Dietrich, *Sports Journalism at Its Best: Pulitzer Prize–Winning Articles, Cartoons, and Photographs*

Fisher, Lionel, *The Craft of Corporate Journalism*

Gaines, William, *Investigative Reporting for Print and Broadcast,* 2nd ed.

Hilliard, Robert L., *Writing for Television, Radio, and New Media,* 7th ed.

Kessler, Lauren, and Duncan McDonald, *When Words Collide,* 5th ed.

Klement, Alice M., and Carolyn Burrows Matalene, *Telling Stories/Taking Risks: Journalism Writing at the Century's Edge*

Laakaniemi, Ray, *Newswriting in Transition*

Rich, Carole, *Writing and Reporting News: A Coaching Method,* 3rd ed.

Rich, Carole, *Workbook for Writing and Reporting News,* 3rd ed.

Photojournalism and Photography

Parrish, Fred S., *Photojournalism: An Introduction*

Public Relations and Advertising

Hendrix, Jerry A., *Public Relations Cases,* 5th ed.

Jewler, Jerome A., and Bonnie L. Drewniany, *Creative Strategy in Advertising,* 7th ed.

Newsom, Doug, and Bob Carrell, *Public Relations Writing: Form and Style,* 6th ed.

Newsom, Doug, Judy VanSlyke Turk, and Dean Kruckeberg, *This Is PR: The Realities of Public Relations,* 7th ed.

Sivulka, Juliann, *Soap, Sex, and Cigarettes: A Cultural History of American Advertising*

Woods, Gail Baker, *Advertising and Marketing to the New Majority: A Case Study Approach*

Research and Theory

Babbie, Earl, *The Practice of Social Research,* 8th ed.

Baran, Stanley, and Dennis Davis, *Mass Communication Theory: Foundations, Ferment, and Future,* 2nd ed.

Rubenstein, Sondra, *Surveying Public Opinion*

Rubin, Rebecca B., Alan M. Rubin, and Linda J. Piele, *Communication Research: Strategies and Sources,* 5th ed.

Wimmer, Roger D., and Joseph R. Dominick, *Mass Media Research: An Introduction,* 6th ed.

LIVING

in the

INFORMATION AGE

A New Media Reader

Erik P. Bucy
Indiana University

Australia • Canada • Mexico • Singapore • Spain
United Kingdom • United States

WADSWORTH

THOMSON LEARNING

Publisher: Holly J. Allen
Assistant Editor: Nicole George
Editorial Assistant: Mele Alusa
Marketing Manager: Kimberly Russell
Marketing Assistant: Neena Chandra
Signing Representative: Lori Grebe
Project Manager, Editorial Production: Mary Noel
Print/Media Buyer: Rebecca Cross

Permissions Editor: Joohee Lee
Production Service: G&S Typesetters, Inc.
Copy Editor: Elliot Simon
Cover Designer: Annabelle Ison
Cover Image: Ryan McVay/PhotoDisc
Cover Printer: Webcom, Ltd.
Compositor: G&S Typesetters, Inc.
Printer: Webcom, Ltd.

For permission to use material from this text,
contact us by
 Web: http://www.thomsonrights.com
 Fax: 1-800-730-2215
 Phone: 1-800-730-2214

Library of Congress Cataloging-in-Publication Data
  Living in the information age : a new media reader / edited
by Erik P. Bucy.
    p. cm. — (Wadsworth series in mass communication and
    journalism)
  Includes bibliographical references and index.
  ISBN 0-534-59049-7 (pbk.)
  1. Mass media. 2. Information society. I. Bucy, E. Page,
    1963– II. Series.
P91.25 .L58 2001
302.23—dc21   2001046511

Wadsworth/Thomson Learning
10 Davis Drive
Belmont, CA 94002-3098
USA

For more information about our products, contact us:
Thomson Learning Academic Resource Center
1-800-423-0563
http://www.wadsworth.com

International Headquarters
Thomson Learning
International Division
290 Harbor Drive, 2nd Floor
Stamford, CT 06902-7477
USA

UK/Europe/Middle East/South Africa
Thomson Learning
Berkshire House
168-173 High Holborn
London WC1V 7AA
United Kingdom

Asia
Thomson Learning
60 Albert Street, #15-01
Albert Complex
Singapore 189969

Canada
Nelson Thomson Learning
1120 Birchmount Road
Toronto, Ontario M1K 5G4
Canada

Brief Contents

Detailed Contents

Preface

From Silicon Valley to Madison Avenue, it's no longer a prediction or distant vision: The vaunted Information Age is here. The rise of networked computing and digital media over the past three decades has brought about a communications revolution and inalterably changed the way traditional media do business. Gatekeeping roles are eroding, storytelling techniques are transforming, and new media entrepreneurs are challenging established industry players and practices. The credo for a new millennium: Embrace the hive that is the World Wide Web or be left behind. And just as the media industries are not immune from Moore's Law—the tendency for computer processing power to double every 18 months to 2 years—so citizens of the information society cannot escape the forces unleashed by technological advancement. Consumers are reaping the rewards of revolution, but access to new technology remains uneven and many adopters, notably of computers, abandon their complicated machines after a period of initial, frustrating use. Digital media clearly do not benefit everyone equally.

In this time of rapid transformation, two developments in particular are revolutionizing the media and telecommunications industries: the transition from analog to digital systems, and the rapid expansion in the reach, capabilities, and user-friendliness of the Internet through the World Wide Web. These developments have far-reaching social, economic, and professional implications and are fundamentally changing the way audiences approach and utilize media. Increasingly, media consumers are seen as active *users* of communication technologies rather than passive *receivers* of content. At the same time, content providers are retooling their operations to remain viable in a media environment characterized by increased competition, program experimentation, and audience restiveness. Needless to say, the dynamism of this theory/practice interface offers students of new media ample opportunity for intellectual exploration and engagement.

PURPOSE AND ORIENTATION

Living in the Information Age offers students of new media focused articles that illuminate the social, psychological, and professional impact of communication technologies. Much of the allure of digital media revolves around the latest hardware and software developments. Yet however much the "new, new thing" may attract our attention, ultimately it is counterproductive to weigh the meaning and consequences of new media technologies exclusively from the standpoint of current applications. In an era of seamless change, narrowly focusing on the latest programs and applications only delivers transient knowledge—information with a short shelf life. Instead, readers stand to benefit over the long term by considering broader trends, issues, and patterns in the evolving information and entertainment ecology.

The articles comprising *Living in the Information Age* have thus been selected on the basis of their conceptual import *and* industry relevance. Included are readings that illuminate important information-age issues (e.g., digital copyright controversies and the Napster file-sharing phenomenon) while incorporating more explanatory pieces describing the broader, enduring role of communication technology in society. Developments addressed in this reader include, among others, the following trends.

- How multitasking and the accelerating pace of everyday life can be viewed as byproducts of both computer efficiency and seemingly harmless devices like the remote control
- How the Internet can be profitably thought of as a *communication* medium that enables different levels of social and professional interaction
- How interactivity made possible by networked computing also increases opportunities for surveillance and incursions on personal privacy

To assist learners in a classroom setting, each reading is prefaced by a short introduction and three questions for critical thinking and discussion. The questions are offered to encourage in-depth consideration of the issues raised in the readings and spark spirited discussion of the material. Following each article are suggestions for performing relevant follow-up searches using the InfoTrac® College Edition full-text article database.

As any instructor of information-age topics knows, courses in new media are themselves under continuous revision, reflecting the dynamism of the industries and processes they are dedicated to explaining. Prior to digital convergence—the merging of once-separate media technologies into new hybrid forms—courses in communication, journalism, and media studies all but ignored the impact of computing, while offerings in computer and information science programs routinely overlooked mass media. Given the transition to a digital society, however, information-age topics are rapidly moving to the center of debates about mass media and their volatile future. In the coming decade, information-age approaches will become even more central to general mass communication courses as more media become computer reliant and digitally based. Inasmuch as trends in computer culture tend to foreshadow and predict developments in the broader consumer culture, information-age issues that may still seem peripheral today could very well occupy the mainstream of media studies tomorrow.

ORIGIN AND ORGANIZATION

The idea for *Living in the Information Age: A New Media Reader* grew out of an introductory telecommunications course I have taught for the past several years at Indiana University. Reflecting the organization of this course, *Living in the Information Age* is divided into six major thematic sections that trace the development of, survey the literature on, and explore the impact of new technologies on the media landscape, examining both conceptual and practical aspects of life in an information society. The articles included in this reader examine the utopian promises of technology's true believers as well as the dystopian views of technology's critics, all the while exploring how the media industries are being transformed through digital convergence and corporate concentration. *Living in the Information Age* thus provides students of new media with a broad understanding of the impact of new communication technologies while encouraging original thinking about media, both analog and digital, in relation to theory.

From an educational standpoint, *Living in the Information Age* is intended to enhance college-level courses addressing media and technology, social informatics, cyberculture studies, new communications technologies, or mass communication and society, with an emphasis on the changing media environment. Dozens of courses are beginning to emerge in this area—indeed, new media offerings are currently catalogued by the Resource Center for Cyberculture Studies (http://www.com.washington.edu/rccs)—but despite growing student and scholarly interest in new media, there are few satisfactory texts.

Living in the Information Age is designed to help bridge this gap. Note, however, that even this reader has its limits; there are few articles, for example, on business uses of the Internet. The emphasis throughout this collection is on the social/psychological implications and professional impact of new media, not on the dynamics of e-commerce per se. On the other hand, the media ethicist should feel quite at home contending with the legal and moral dilemmas presented by the issues discussed in many of these readings.

Although it may be used as a primary text, *Living in the Information Age* is intended to serve as a supplementary resource for introductory communication courses that have a new media orientation. Specifically, *Living in the Information Age* is designed as a companion volume for the Wadsworth textbooks *Media Now* (3rd ed.) by Joseph Straubhaar and Robert LaRose, *Electronic Media in the Information Age* by Robert LaRose and Joseph Straubhaar, and *Electronic Media* by John Craft, Frederic Leigh, and Donald Godfrey. Unlike traditional textbooks, which are obliged to offer a broad historical overview of the different media industries, *Living in the Information Age* focuses on topical issues that can serve as the basis of individual class discussions. In larger classes, the readings in *Living in the Information Age* can be used to inform main lectures as well as smaller discussion sections. Whether packaged with a more traditional textbook or assigned separately, *Living in the Information Age* presents a variety of intriguing vantage points from which to examine the new media landscape.

The organization of the reader roughly follows the general outline of *Media Now* (3rd ed.) and *Electronic Media in the Information Age*. The first part of *Living in the Information Age* consists of articles dealing with the evolution of the information society and overviews a set of theories relevant to understanding new media. The next section examines issues pertaining to convergence and concentration in the various media and telecommunications industries. The third section highlights interesting issues "at the interface" of new media and society, exploring new technologies, the self, and social life as well as media acceleration and the increasing velocity of everyday life. The fourth section addresses social and economic impacts of networked computing as well as dystopian views of information technology. The fifth section delves into issues surrounding electronic democracy and uneven access to the Internet, commonly referred to as the "digital divide." The last section raises concerns about copyright, privacy, and computer hacking—legal and ethical dilemmas that are perhaps unique to our Information Age.

While this reader covers a broad range of topics, some issues important to readers may have been overlooked. Related topics that could be further addressed in future editions include (but are by no means limited to) e-commerce, information overload, wearable computing, cyberpunk fiction, information warfare, transborder data flow, digital crime, online ethics, cultural biotechnology, sex and morality in cyberspace, and continuing explorations of the impact of new technology on specific media industries and practices. I welcome any comments or suggestions readers may have in response to the current selection of articles as well as ideas regarding future editions of *Living in the Information Age*.

ACKNOWLEDGMENTS

Any attempt on my part to organize the literature of new media would not be complete without acknowledging John Newhagen, who focused my thinking about media and new technology while I was at the University of Maryland, and Thom Gillespie, whose impromptu, brainstorm discussions in the hallways at Indiana University allow me to continuously revise my outlook on interactivity and immersive environments. I wouldn't trade these real-life influences for any amount of virtual collaboration.

I am also especially grateful to those authors who recognized the educational value of this project and permitted their work to be reprinted in this collection, either at a nominal fee or free of charge.

Sharing knowledge and freely circulating ideas is the essence of the educational enterprise and provides students and professors alike with the intellectual raw materials necessary to arrive at new insights.

The editorial team in Wadsworth's communication division was instrumental in making this project happen and deserves special praise for their enthusiasm and support. I thank in particular Karen Austin, who recognized the value of this reader early on and advocated for its development even when the permissions fees mounted. Lori Grebe also played a pivotal contact role during the book's nascent stages. Gretchen Otto and the helpful professionals at G&S Typesetters brilliantly managed the production aspects of this project.

I thank also those who reviewed the manuscript: David Atkin, Cleveland State University; Ronald C. Bishop, Drexel University; Robert H. Bohle, University of North Florida; Phillip G. Clampitt, University of Wisconsin—Green Bay; Paul D'Angelo, Villanova University; Joseph Dominick, University of Georgia; Junhao Hong, State University of New York—Buffalo; Dorothy Kidd, University of San Francisco; Rebecca Ann Lind, University of Illinois—Chicago; Linda Lumsden, Western Kentucky University; Maclyn McClary, Humboldt State University; Stephen McDowell, Florida State University; John E. Newhagen, University of Maryland; Maurice Odine, Tennessee State University; Paula Otto, Virginia Commonwealth University; Arthur A. Raney, Florida State University; Brad L. Rawlins, James Madison University; David Silver, University of Washington; and Danney Ursery, St. Edward's University.

Finally, my deepest appreciation is reserved for Betsi Grabe, who inspires me daily with her style, grace, and thoroughgoing unconventionalism.

Erik P. Bucy, Ph.D.
Indiana University, Bloomington
ebucy@indiana.edu

The New Information and Entertainment Ecology

This section establishes a foundation for examining the development and consequences of the new information and entertainment ecology. The use of the word *ecology* to describe the information landscape evokes the environmental nature of today's communications media; in many ways, media serve as a primary source of sensory stimulation, knowledge gain, and need satisfaction. Information technologies and entertainment media literally saturate modern life, to the point where it has become difficult to imagine life *without* them. The readings in Chapter 1 explain the origins and development of the information revolution, highlighting the developments that made our current mediated existence possible. The convergence of digital technology and enhanced telecommunications systems since the early 1980s has resulted in the explosive growth of new media in recent years, yet the trends that set this process in motion were long in the making. The readings in Chapter 2 present several theoretical approaches relevant to studying new media, including *mediamorphosis*, which describes the process of media evolution as well as how new technologies diffuse or spread throughout society, and *medium theory*, which explains how mass media don't merely convey information but actively shape the social environment. Additionally, readings on two audience-centered theories of media use are presented, the first on *uses and gratifications*, addressing the needs that media fulfill and the sources of need satisfaction that media compete with, and the second on *parasocial interaction*, the experience of social intimacy with an on-air radio or television personality, albeit at a distance.

1

The Communication Revolution

Reading 1-1

The Roots of Revolution

Frances Cairncross

EDITOR'S NOTE

In the first of these two excerpts from The Death of Distance: How the Communications Revolution Will Change Our Lives, *Frances Cairncross discusses the major changes that have occurred since 1980 to the three communications technologies most important to the Information Age—the telephone, television, and networked computer. In the second excerpt, "The Trendspotter's Guide to New Communications," she offers thirty predictions for how the "death of distance"—her term for the ability to reach anyone in the world at any moment through electronic media—will shape the future.*

CONSIDER

1. What important advances in communications technology have occurred since 1980?

2. In your opinion, do the transformations that have taken place in communications technologies deserve to be called "revolutionary"?

3. Which predictions do you *agree* with in "The Trendspotter's Guide to New Communications"? Which do you *disagree* with, and why?

It is easy to forget how recently the communications revolution began. All three of today's fast-changing communications technologies have existed for more than half a century: the telephone was invented in 1876; the first television transmission was in 1926; and the electronic computer was invented in the mid-1940s.[1] For much of that time, change has been slow, but, in each case, a revolution has taken place since the late 1980s. In order to approach the future, we need first to ask why the really big changes have been so recent and so far-reaching.

THE TELEPHONE

Since the 1980s, the oldest of the three technologies has undergone two big transformations—an astonishing increase in the carrying capacity of much of the long-distance network and the development of mobility. They result, in the first case, from the use of glass fibers to carry digital signals, and, in the second, from the steep fall in the cost of computing power.

For much of its existence, the telephone network has had the least capacity for its most useful service: long-distance communication. A cross-Atlantic telephone service existed early on: indeed, by the 1930s, J. Paul Getty could run his California oil empire by telephone from European hotels, in which he chose to live because their switchboard operators could make the connections he needed.[2] But even in 1956, when the first transatlantic telephone cable went online, it had capacity for only eighty-nine simultaneous conversations between all of Europe and all of North America.[3] Walter Wriston, former chairman of Citibank, recalls the way it felt to be an international banker in the 1950s and 1960s: "It could take a day or more to get a circuit. Once a connection was made, people in the branch would stay on the phone reading books and newspapers all day just to keep the line open until it was needed."[4]

Since the late 1980s, capacity on the main long-distance routes has grown so fast that, by the start of 1996, there was an immense and increasing glut, with only 30 to 35 percent of capacity in use.[5] The main reason for this breathtaking transformation was the de-

velopment of fiber-optic cables, made of glass so pure that a sheet seventy miles thick would be as clear as a windowpane. The first transatlantic fiber-optic cable, with capacity to carry nearly 40,000 conversations, went online only in 1988. The cables that will be laid at the turn of the century will carry more than 3 million conversations on a few strands of fiber, each the width of a human hair.

Meanwhile, new cables are being laid; new satellites, which carry telephone traffic on less popular routes, are due to be launched; and a range of low-orbiting satellites may eventually carry international traffic between mobile telephones. In addition, new techniques are starting to allow many more calls to travel on the same fiber. It is as though an already rapidly expanding fleet of trucks could suddenly pack several times as many products into the same amount of space as before.

This massive growth in capacity is increasingly reflected in tariffs. MCI's generous Mother's Day gesture [of free long-distance calls in 1995 and 1996] cost the firm plenty, but would have been impossible without the growth in capacity on the American network, where the traffic on that day is probably the heaviest of any day, anywhere in the world. Already, international and long-distance call rates have been falling, changing our mental map of the world. But the cost of carrying an extra telephone call across the Atlantic and on many other long-distance routes has fallen much further and now approaches zero. This fall in rates is the drive behind the death of distance.

By the middle of 1997, the threat of a glut had receded. The reason was the enormous increase in demand created by the Internet, which carries messages of many sorts at prices that ignore distance. When distance carries no price penalty, people communicate more, and in new ways. In the future, the lavish plans to build more capacity and ingenious technologies to compress signals will continue to push prices down, until it costs no more to telephone from New York to London than to the house next door.

While capacity has been increasing, the telephone has become mobile. Cellular communication, which dates back to the period immediately following World War II, became commercially viable only in the early 1980s, when the collapse in the cost of computing made it possible to provide the necessary processing power at a low enough cost.

Now, the mobile telephone may arguably be the most successful new way of communicating that the world has ever seen—already, more than one telephone subscription in seven is to a mobile service. Mobile telephony's share will continue to rise: in 1996, it accounted for 47 percent of all new telephone subscriptions.[6] For conversations, people will come to use mobile telephones almost exclusively.

They will be able to communicate from every corner of the globe: in the course of 1996, two stranded climbers on Mount Everest used mobile telephones to call their wives. One wife, 2,000 miles away in Hong Kong, was able to arrange her husband's rescue; the other, sadly, could merely say a last farewell.[7]

The mobile telephone also allows better use of the most underused chunk of time in many peoples' lives: traveling time. People will use their commuting time more fully, but other benefits may be even greater: passengers can be checked in for flights during the bus ride to the airport, for example, and maintenance staff can schedule visits more efficiently, knowing exactly when equipment in transit will arrive. The mobile telephone thus raises productivity by using previously idle time.

THE TELEVISION

At the end of the Second World War, a mere 8,000 homes worldwide had a television set. By 1996, that number had risen to more than 840 million—two-thirds of the world's households.[8] The basic technology of television sets has not changed over those fifty years, but the transmission of programs has been revolutionized by the development of communications satellites. Now another revolution—in channel capacity—has begun.

In fall 1963, people around the world witnessed for the first time an important but distant political event as it was taking place. The 1962 launch of Telstar, the first private communications satellite, had made possible the live global transmission of the funeral of President John F. Kennedy.[9] The psychological impact was huge: this unprecedented new link among countries would change perceptions of the world, creating the sense that the world's peoples belonged to a global, not merely local or national, community.

The 1988 launch by PanAmSat of the first privately owned commercial international (as opposed to domestic) satellite constituted another milestone, cutting the cost of transmitting live television material around the world. As recently as the 1970s, more than half of all television news was at least a day old. Today, almost all news is broadcast on the day it occurs.[10] Big

events—the fall of the Berlin Wall, the Gulf War, the O. J. Simpson trial verdict—go out to billions of viewers as they happen.

Until recently, most television viewers around the world have had access to perhaps half a dozen television channels at most—and often to only two or three. The main reason is purely physical: analog television signals are greedy users of spectrum. Only in the United States and a handful of other countries, and mainly only since the 1980s, have cable-television networks—less constrained by the limits of spectrum—brought people real viewing choice.

Now choice is expanding with breathtaking speed. Toward the end of the 1980s, communications satellites began to broadcast directly to a small dish attached to people's homes, thus inexpensively distributing multichannel television. Suddenly, more viewers had more choice than ever before.

In the mid-1990s came another revolutionary change: broadcasters began to transmit television in digital, not analog, form, allowing the signal to be compressed and, consequently, far more channels to be transmitted, whether from satellite, through cable, or even over the air. Like the long-distance parts of the telephone network, a service that had been constrained by capacity shortage for most of its existence has suddenly begun to build more capacity than it knows what to do with.

The result will be a revolution in the nature of television. For those who want it (most of us), the old passive medium will remain, a relaxing way to pass the evening after a day spent at work. But television—the business of transmitting moving pictures—will develop many more functions, including new roles in business. The finances of television will also change, and in a way that many viewers will resent. The scarcest thing in television is not transmission capacity, but desirable programs, especially live programming. In the future, these will rarely be available at no cost to viewers. Increasingly, viewers will pay directly for what they most want to watch.

THE NETWORKED COMPUTER

The newest of the three building blocks of the communications revolution, the electronic computer, has evolved fastest. In 1943 Thomas Watson, founder of IBM, thought that the world market had room for about five computers.[11] As recently as 1967, a state-of-the-art IBM, costing $167,500, could hold a mere thirteen pages of text.[12]

Two key changes have altered this picture: First, computing power has grown dramatically. As a result, the computer can be miniaturized and has become a consumer durable, with computing power embedded in everything from automobiles to children's toys. The main processor on Apollo 13 contained less computing power than does a modern Nintendo games machine.[13] Second, computers are increasingly connected to each other. The Internet, essentially a means of connecting the world's computers, makes apparent the spectacular power of such networked computers.

The increase in computing power has followed a principle known as "Moore's Law," after Gordon Moore, cofounder of Intel, now the world's leading maker of computer chips, the brains of the modern computer. In 1965, Moore forecast that computing power would double every eighteen months to two years. So it has done for three decades, as engineers have found ways to squeeze ever more integrated circuits of transistors onto chips—small wafers of silicon. A 486 chip, standard in a computer bought around 1994, could perform up to 54 million numerical calculations per second. A Pentium chip, the standard three years later, could perform up to 200 million calculations per second. And Moore's law continues to apply. By 2006, according to Intel forecasts, chips will be 1,000 times as powerful and will cost one-tenth as much as they did in 1996.[14]

As the power of the chip has multiplied, the price of computing power has fallen, computer size has decreased, and computer capacity has risen. This has had implications for many aspects of communications: the development of mobile telephones, for example, and of the "set-top boxes" that decode encrypted television signals. A landmark occurred in 1977, when Steven Jobs and Stephen Wozniak, two young computer enthusiasts, launched the Apple II, opening the way for the computer to become a household good. Today, 40 percent of homes in the United States contain a computer.

Meanwhile, responding to the limitations of computers in the 1960s, when they were large, expensive, and scarce, the American Defense Department's Advanced Research Projects Agency (ARPA) backed an experiment to connect computers across the country as a way to exchange messages and share their processing power. This effort yielded a nationwide network that initially linked only university computers. Because different computers in those early days had different operating standards, a common standard, or *protocol*, became a fundamental requirement of the network. In response, Transmission Control Protocol/Internet Protocol (TCP/IP) was developed and, since the early 1980s, has provided the format for packaging all data sent over the Internet.

TCP/IP is the essence of the Internet. It provides an electronic Esperanto: a common language and a set of rules through which computers all over the world can talk to one another, regardless of whether they are PCs or Apple Macs, whether they are vast university mainframes or domestic laptops. Through the Internet, any number of computer networks can connect with one another and behave as a single network.

Although the use of the Internet grew rapidly in the 1980s and early 1990s, doubling every year, its transformation into a popular success dates only from about 1993 to 1994. At that point, the World Wide Web made it possible to accommodate online graphics, sound, and moving pictures, rather than just text, making the Internet more versatile and more interesting to look at. This was thanks to Marc Andreessen, a young programmer, and his colleagues at the University of Illinois. They developed the most successful graphical Web browser, which allowed navigation fairly easily from one screenful (or "page") of information to another, even if that second page was held on a different computer in another part of the world, simply by using a handheld "mouse" control to point and click on a shaded word on the screen.

These transformations have had three main consequences. First, they vastly increased the world's computing power. Even if Moore's law stopped grinding inexorably along, the Internet has the potential to allow immense multiplication of computing power simply by linking many different computers. Second, the Internet has emerged, almost by accident, as the first working model of the "global information superhighway" that politicians and big communications companies talked so much about in the early 1990s.[15] It has become not only a new global means of communicating but also a new global source of information on a gigantic scale. Third, the Internet has given birth to a vigorous new industry dedicated to developing ways to use it and services to sell across it. Only in 1994 did the number of commercial computers connected to the Internet overtake the number of academic computers. Now, tens of thousands of companies, many of them small start-ups, are racing to find profitable uses for this new technology. Never in history have so many entrepreneurs attempted, in so short a space of time, to develop uses for an innovation.

The Internet is thus a global laboratory, allowing individuals as well as the marketing departments of multinationals and academics in top universities to pioneer uses for communications technology. Already it carries telephone and video conferences as well as live television and radio broadcasts. All sorts of communications experiments, carried out on the Internet, will feed through into the other media, changing and developing them. The Internet thus functions as both a prototype and a testing ground for the future of communications. Watching its evolution, we can catch a glimpse of what lies ahead.

NOTES

1. Melvin Harris, *ITN Book of Firsts*. London: Michael O'Mara Books, 1994, pp. 108, 124, 162.

2. John Pearson, *Painfully Rich: J. Paul Getty and His Heirs*. London: Macmillan, 1995, p. 68.

3. A cable from the mainland United States to Hawaii that went online the following year had only 91 such "voice paths." See Gregory C. Staple (Ed.), *TeleGeography 1995: Global Telecommunications Traffic Statistics and Commentary*. Washington, DC: TeleGeography, 1995, p. 84.

4. Walter B. Wriston, *The Twilight of Sovereignty: How the Information Revolution Is Transforming Our World*. New York: Scribner's, 1992, p. 36.

5. Gregory C. Staple (Ed.). *TeleGeography 1996–97: Global Telecommunications Traffic Statistics and Commentary*. Washington, DC: TeleGeography, 1996, p. xv.

6. International Telecommunication Union. *International Telecommunication Union Database*, Geneva, May 1997.

7. Stephen Goodwin, "Trapped on Everest? I'm on My Mobile," *London Independent*, April 27, 1996, p. 3.

8. International Telecommunication Union. *World Telecommunication Development Report 1996/97*, Geneva, 1997.

9. *Defining Moments*. London: A. T. Kearney, 1996, p. 46.

10. Robert H. Frank and Philip J. Cook, *The Winner-Take-All Society: How More and More Americans Compete for Ever Fewer and Bigger Prizes, Encouraging Economic Waste, Income Inequality, and an Impoverished Cultural Life*. New York: Free Press, 1995.

11. Quoted in Victor Navasky, "Tomorrow Never Knows," *New York Times Magazine*, September 29, 1996, p. 216.

12. *Defining Moments*.

13. Christopher Anderson, personal communication, February 1997.

14. "Computer Power and Data Storage Capacity," *Screen Digest*, December 1996, p. 287.

15. Christopher Anderson, "The Accidental Superhighway: A Survey of the Internet," *The Economist*, July 1, 1995, p. S3.

Reading 1-1 (continued)

The Trendspotter's Guide to New Communications
Frances Cairncross

How will the death of distance shape the future? Here are some of the most important developments to watch.

1. *The Death of Distance*. Distance will no longer determine the cost of communicating electronically. Companies will organize certain types of work in three shifts according to the world's three main time zones: the Americas, East Asia/Australia, and Europe.

2. *The Fate of Location*. No longer will location be key to most business decisions. Companies will locate any screen-based activity anywhere on earth, wherever they can find the best bargain of skills and productivity. Developing countries will increasingly perform online services—monitoring security screens, running help-lines and call centers, writing software, and so forth—and sell them to the rich industrial countries that generally produce such services domestically.

3. *The Irrelevance of Size*. Small companies will offer services that, in the past, only giants had the scale and scope to provide. Individuals with valuable ideas, initiative, and strong business plans will attract global venture capital and convert their ideas into viable businesses. Small countries will also be more viable. That will be good news for secession movements everywhere.

4. *Improved Connections.* Most people on earth will eventually have access to networks that are all switched, interactive, and broadband: "switched," like the telephone, and used to contact many other subscribers; "interactive" in that, unlike broadcast TV, all ends of the network can communicate; and "broadband," with the capacity to receive TV-quality motion pictures. While the Internet will continue to exist in its present form, it will also be integrated into other services, such as the telephone and television.

5. *More Customized Content.* Improved networks will also allow individuals to order "content for one"; that is, individual consumers will receive (or send) exactly what they want to receive (or send), when and where they want it.

6. *A Deluge of Information.* Because people's capacity to absorb new information will not increase, they will need filters to sift, process, and edit it. Companies will have greater need of boosters—new techniques—to brand and push their information ahead of the competition's.

7. *Increased Value of Brand.* What's hot—whether a product, a personality, a sporting event, or the latest financial data—will attract greater rewards. The costs of producing or promoting these commodities will not change, but the potential market will increase greatly. That will create a category of global super-rich, many of them musicians, actors, artists, athletes, and investors. For the successful few and their intermediaries, entertaining will be the most lucrative individual activity on earth.

8. *Increased Value in Niches.* The power of the computer to search, identify, and classify people according to similar needs and tastes will create sustainable markets for many niche products. Niche players will increase, as will consumers' demand for customized goods and services.

9. *Communities of Practice.* The horizontal bonds among people performing the same job or speaking the same language in different parts of the world will strengthen. Common interests, experiences, and pursuits rather than proximity will bind these communities together.

10. *Near-Frictionless Markets.* Many more companies and customers will have access to accurate price information. That will curtail excessive profits, enhance competition, and help to curb inflation,

resulting in "profitless prosperity": it will be easier to find buyers, but hard to make fat margins.

11. *Increased Mobility.* Every form of communication will be available for mobile or remote use. While fixed connections such as cable will offer greater capacity and speed, wireless will be able not just to send a signal over a large region, but to carry it fixed point to users in a relatively small radius. Satellite transmission will allow people to use a single mobile telephone anywhere, and the distinctions between fixed and mobile receiving equipment (a telephone or a personal computer) will blur.

12. *More Global Reach, More Local Provision.* While small companies find it easier to reach markets around the world, big companies will more readily offer high-quality local services, such as putting customers in one part of the world directly in touch with expertise in other places, and monitoring more precisely the quality of local provision.

13. *The Loose-Knit Corporation.* Culture and communications networks, rather than rigid management structures, will hold companies together. Many companies will become networks of independent specialists; more employees will therefore work in smaller units or alone. Loyalty, trust, and open communications will reshape the nature of customer and supplier contracts: suppliers will draw directly on information held in databases by their customers, working as closely and seamlessly as an in-house supplier now does. Technologies such as electronic mail and computerized billing will reduce the costs of dealing with consumers and suppliers at arm's length.

14. *More Minnows, More Giants.* On one hand, the cost of starting new businesses will decline, and companies will more easily buy in services so that more small companies will spring up. On the other, communication amplifies the strength of brands and the power of networks. In industries where networks matter, concentration may increase, but often in the form of loose global associations under a banner of brands or quality guarantees.

15. *Manufacturers as Service Providers.* Feeding information on particular buyer's tastes straight back to the manufacturer will be easier and so manufacturers will design more products specially for an

individual's requirements. Some manufacturers will even retain lasting links with their products: car companies, for instance, will continue electronically to track, monitor, and learn about their vehicles throughout the product life cycle. New opportunities to provide services for customers will emerge, and some manufacturers may accept more responsibility for disposing of their products at the end of the cycle.

16. *The Inversion of Home and Office.* As more people work from home or from small, purpose-built offices, the line between work and home life will blur. The office will become a place for the social aspects of work such as celebrating, networking, lunching, and gossiping. Home design will also change, and the domestic office will become a regular part of the house.

17. *The Proliferation of Ideas.* New ideas and information will travel faster to the remotest corners of the world. Third World countries will have access to knowledge that the industrial world has long enjoyed. Communities of practice and long-distance education programs will help people to find mentors and acquire new skills.

18. *A New Trust.* Since it will be easier to check whether people and companies deliver what they have promised, many services will become more reliable and people will be more likely to trust each other to keep their word. However, those who fail to deliver will quickly lose that trust, which will become more difficult to regain.

19. *People as the Ultimate Scarce Resource.* The key challenge for companies will be to hire and retain good people, extracting value from them, rather than allowing them to keep all the value they create for themselves. A company will constantly need to convince its best employees that working for it enhances each individual's value.

20. *The Shift from Government Policing to Self-Policing.* Governments will find national legislation and censorship inadequate for regulating the global flow of information. As content sweeps across national borders, it will be harder to enforce laws banning child pornography, libel, and other criminal or subversive material and those protecting copyright and other intellectual property. But greater electronic access to information will give people better means to protect themselves. The result will be more individual responsibility and less government intervention.

21. *Loss of Privacy.* As in the village of past centuries, protecting privacy will be difficult. Governments and companies will easily monitor people's movements. Machines will recognize physical attributes like a voice or fingerprint. People will thus come to embody their identity. Civil libertarians will worry, but others will accept the loss as a fair exchange for the reduction of crime, including fraud and illegal immigration. In the electronic village, there will be little true privacy—and little unsolved crime.

22. *Redistribution of Wages.* Low-wage competition will reduce the earning power of many people in rich countries employed in routine screen-based tasks, but the premium for certain skills will grow. People with skills that are in demand will earn broadly similar amounts wherever they live in the world. So income differences within countries will grow; and income differences between countries will narrow.

23. *Less Need for Immigration and Emigration.* Poor countries with good communications technology will be able to retain their skilled workers, who will be less likely to emigrate to countries with higher costs of living if they can earn rich-world wages and pay poor-world prices for everyday necessities right at home. Thus inexpensive communications may reduce some of the pressure to emigrate.

24. *A Market for Citizens.* The greater freedom to locate anywhere and earn a living will hinder taxation. Savers will be able to compare global investment rates and easily shift money abroad. High-income earners and profitable companies will be able to move away from hefty government-imposed taxes. Countries will compete to bid down tax rates and to attract businesses, savers, and wealthy residents.

25. *Rebirth of Cities.* As individuals spend less time in the office and more time working from home or traveling, cities will transform from concentrations of office employment to centers of entertainment and culture; that is, cities will become places where people go to stay in hotels, visit museums and galleries, dine in restaurants, participate in civic events, and attend live performances of all kinds. In contrast, some poor countries will

stem the flight from the countryside to cities by using low-cost communications to provide rural dwellers with better medical services, jobs, education, and entertainment.

26. *The Rise of English.* The global role of English as a second language will strengthen as it becomes the common standard for telecommunicating in business and commerce. Many more countries, especially in the developing world, will therefore adopt English as a subsidiary language. It will be as important to learn English as to use software that is compatible with the near-universal MS-DOS.

27. *Communities of Culture.* At the same time, electronic communications will reinforce less widespread languages and cultures, not replace them with Anglo-Saxon and Hollywood. The declining cost of creating and distributing many entertainment products and the corresponding increase in production capacity will also reinforce local cultures and help scattered peoples and families to preserve their cultural heritage.

28. *Improved Writing and Reading Skills.* Electronic mail will induce young people to express themselves effectively in writing and to admire clear and lively written prose. Dull or muddled communicators will fall by the information wayside.

29. *Rebalance of Political Power.* Since people will communicate their views on government more directly, rulers and representatives will become more sensitive (and, perhaps, more responsive) to lobbying and public-opinion polls, especially in established democracies. People who live under dictatorial regimes will make contact more easily with the rest of the world.

30. *Global Peace.* As countries become even more economically interdependent and as global trade and foreign investment grow, people will communicate more freely and learn more about the ideas and aspirations of human beings in other parts of the globe. The effect will be to increase understanding, foster tolerance, and ultimately promote worldwide peace.

 RELATED LINKS

- Bell Labs Innovations (http://www.bell-labs.com/technology)
- International Telecommunication Union (http://www.itu.int/home/index.html)
- TeleGeography, Inc. (http://www.telegeography.com)

 FOR FURTHER RESEARCH

To find out more about the topics discussed in this reading, use InfoTrac College Edition. Type in keywords and subject terms such as "communications revolution," "fiber-optic networks," and "networked computing." You can access InfoTrac College Edition from the Wadsworth/ Thomson Communication Cafe homepage: http://communication.wadsworth.com.

Reading 1-2

Beyond the Information Revolution
Peter F. Drucker

EDITOR'S NOTE

Peter F. Drucker is known throughout the world for his trenchant analyses of economic trends and pioneering management practices. True to form, as the original preface to this article from The Atlantic Monthly *noted, he uses history in this read-*

ing to gauge the significance of e-commerce—a "totally unexpected development"—and throw light on the future of the knowledge worker, *a term Drucker himself coined in 1959 to mark the emergence of information-based skills that require a good deal of formal education and the ability to apply analytical knowledge.*

CONSIDER

1. Why was e-commerce, which has taken the business world by storm, a "totally unexpected development," according to Drucker?

2. In what ways are the impacts of the Information Revolution similar to those of the Industrial Revolution of the late eighteenth and early nineteenth centuries?

3. What are some of the implications of the global reach of the Internet, on which e-commerce is based?

The truly revolutionary impact of the Information Revolution is just beginning to be felt. But it is not "information" that fuels this impact. It is not "artificial intelligence." It is not the effect of computers and data processing on decision making, policymaking, or strategy. It is something that practically no one foresaw or, indeed, even talked about ten or fifteen years ago: *e-commerce*—that is, the explosive emergence of the Internet as a major, perhaps eventually *the* major, worldwide distribution channel for goods, for services, and, surprisingly, for managerial and professional jobs. This is profoundly changing economies, markets, and industry structures; products and services and their flow; consumer segmentation, consumer values, and consumer behavior; jobs and labor markets. But the impact may be even greater on societies and politics and, above all, on the way we see the world and ourselves in it.

At the same time, new and unexpected industries will no doubt emerge, and fast. One is already here: biotechnology. And another: fish farming. Within the next fifty years fish farming may change us from hunters and gatherers on the seas into "marine pastoralists"—just as a similar innovation some 10,000 years ago changed our ancestors from hunters and gatherers on the land into agriculturists and pastoralists.

It is likely that other new technologies will appear suddenly, leading to major new industries. What they may be is impossible even to guess at. But it is highly probable—indeed, nearly certain—that they will emerge, and fairly soon. And it is nearly certain that

few of them—and few industries based on them—will come out of computer and information technology. Like biotechnology and fish farming, each will emerge from its own unique and unexpected technology.

Of course, these are only predictions. But they are made on the assumption that the Information Revolution will evolve as several earlier technology-based "revolutions" have evolved over the past 500 years, since Gutenberg's printing revolution, around 1455. In particular the assumption is that the Information Revolution will be like the Industrial Revolution of the late eighteenth and early nineteenth centuries. And that is indeed exactly how the Information Revolution has been during its first fifty years.

THE RAILROAD

The Information Revolution is now at the point at which the Industrial Revolution was in the early 1820s, about forty years after James Watt's improved steam engine (first installed in 1776) was first applied, in 1785, to an industrial operation—the spinning of cotton. And the steam engine was to the first Industrial Revolution what the computer has been to the Information Revolution—its trigger, but above all its symbol. Almost everybody today believes that nothing in economic history has ever moved as fast as, or had a greater impact than, the Information Revolution. But the Industrial Revolution moved at least as fast in the same time span, and had probably an equal impact if not a greater one. In short order it mechanized the great majority of manufacturing processes, beginning with the production of the most important industrial commodity of the eighteenth and early nineteenth centuries:

textiles. Moore's Law asserts that the price of the Information Revolution's basic element, the microchip, drops by 50 percent every eighteen months. The same was true of the products whose manufacture was mechanized by the first Industrial Revolution. The price of cotton textiles fell by 90 percent in the fifty years spanning the start of the eighteenth century. The production of cotton textiles increased at least 150-fold in Britain alone in the same period. And although textiles were the most visible product of its early years, the Industrial Revolution mechanized the production of practically all other major goods, such as paper, glass, leather, and bricks. Its impact was by no means confined to consumer goods. The production of iron and ironware—for example, wire—became mechanized and steam-driven as fast as did that of textiles, with the same effects on cost, price, and output. By the end of the Napoleonic Wars the making of guns was steam-driven throughout Europe; cannons were made ten to twenty times as fast as before, and their cost dropped by more than two-thirds. By that time Eli Whitney had similarly mechanized the manufacture of muskets in America and had created the first mass-production industry.

These forty or fifty years gave rise to the factory and the "working class." Both were still so few in number in the mid-1820s, even in England, as to be statistically insignificant. But psychologically they had come to dominate (and soon would politically also). Before there were factories in America, Alexander Hamilton foresaw an industrialized country in his 1791 *Report on Manufactures*. A decade later, in 1803, a French economist, Jean-Baptiste Say, saw that the Industrial Revolution had changed economics by creating the "entrepreneur."

The social consequences went far beyond factory and working class. As the historian Paul Johnson has pointed out, in *A History of the American People* (1997), it was the explosive growth of the steam-engine-based textile industry that revived slavery. Considered to be practically dead by the Founders of the American Republic, slavery roared back to life as the cotton gin—soon steam-driven—created a huge demand for low-cost labor and made breeding slaves America's most profitable industry for some decades.

The Industrial Revolution also had a great impact on the family. The nuclear family had long been the unit of production. On the farm and in the artisan's workshop husband, wife, and children worked together. The factory, almost for the first time in history, took worker and work out of the home and moved

them into the workplace, leaving family members behind—whether spouses of adult factory workers or, especially in the early stages, parents of child factory workers.

Indeed, the "crisis of the family" did not begin after the Second World War. It began with the Industrial Revolution—and was in fact a stock concern of those who opposed the Industrial Revolution and the factory system. (The best description of the divorce of work and family, and of its effect on both, is probably Charles Dickens's 1854 novel *Hard Times*.)

But despite all these effects, the Industrial Revolution in its first half century only mechanized the production of goods that had been in existence all along. It tremendously increased output and tremendously decreased cost. It created both consumers and consumer products. But the products themselves had been around all along. And products made in the new factories differed from traditional products only in that they were uniform, with fewer defects than existed in products made by any but the top craftsmen of earlier periods.

There was only one important exception, one new product, in those first fifty years: the steamboat, first made practical by Robert Fulton in 1807. It had little impact until thirty or forty years later. In fact, until almost the end of the nineteenth century more freight was carried on the world's oceans by sailing vessels than by steamships.

Then, in 1829, came the railroad, a product truly without precedent, and it forever changed economy, society, and politics.

In retrospect it is difficult to imagine why the invention of the railroad took so long. Rails to move carts had been around in coal mines for a very long time. What could be more obvious than to put a steam engine on a cart to drive it, rather than have it pushed by people or pulled by horses? But the railroad did not emerge from the cart in the mines. It was developed quite independently. And it was not intended to carry freight. On the contrary, for a long time it was seen only as a way to carry people. Railroads became freight carriers thirty years later, in America. (In fact, as late as the 1870s and 1880s the British engineers who were hired to build the railroads of newly Westernized Japan designed them to carry passengers—and to this day Japanese railroads are not equipped to carry freight.) But until the first railroad actually began to operate, it was virtually unanticipated.

Within five years, however, the Western world was engulfed by the biggest boom history had ever seen—

the railroad boom. Punctuated by the most spectacular busts in economic history, the boom continued in Europe for thirty years, until the late 1850s, by which time most of today's major railroads had been built. In the United States it continued for another thirty years, and in outlying areas—Argentina, Brazil, Asian Russia, China—until the First World War.

The railroad was the truly revolutionary element of the Industrial Revolution, for not only did it create a new economic dimension but also it rapidly changed what I would call the *mental geography*. For the first time in history human beings had true mobility. For the first time the horizons of ordinary people expanded. Contemporaries immediately realized that a fundamental change in mentality had occurred. (A good account of this can be found in what is surely the best portrayal of the Industrial Revolution's society in transition, George Eliot's 1871 novel *Middlemarch*.) As the great French historian Fernand Braudel pointed out in his last major work, *The Identity of France* (1986), it was the railroad that made France into one nation and one culture. It had previously been a congeries of self-contained regions, held together only politically. And the role of the railroad in creating the American West is, of course, a commonplace in U.S. history.

ROUTINIZATION

Like the Industrial Revolution two centuries ago, the Information Revolution so far—that is, since the first computers, in the mid-1940s—has only transformed processes that were here all along. In fact, the real impact of the Information Revolution has not been in the form of "information" at all. Almost none of the effects of information envisaged forty years ago have actually happened. For instance, there has been practically no change in the way major decisions are made in business or government. But the Information Revolution has routinized traditional processes in an untold number of areas.

The software for tuning a piano converts a process that traditionally took three hours into one that takes twenty minutes. There is software for payrolls, for inventory control, for delivery schedules, and for all the other routine processes of a business. Drawing the inside arrangements of a major building (heating, water supply, sewerage, and so on) such as a prison or a hospital formerly took, say, twenty-five highly skilled draftsmen up to fifty days; now there is a program that enables one draftsman to do the job in a couple of days,

at a tiny fraction of the cost. There is software to help people do their tax returns and software that teaches hospital residents how to take out a gall bladder. The people who now speculate in the stock market on-line do exactly what their predecessors in the 1920s did while spending hours each day in a brokerage office. The processes have not been changed at all. They have been routinized, step by step, with a tremendous saving in time and, often, in cost.

The psychological impact of the Information Revolution, like that of the Industrial Revolution, has been enormous. It has perhaps been greatest on the way in which young children learn. Beginning at age four (and often earlier), children now rapidly develop computer skills, soon surpassing their elders; computers are their toys and their learning tools. Fifty years hence we may well conclude that there was no "crisis of American education" in the closing years of the twentieth century—there was only a growing incongruence between the way twentieth century schools taught and the way late twentieth century children learned. Something similar happened in the sixteenth century university, a hundred years after the invention of the printing press and movable type.

But as to the way we work, the Information Revolution has so far simply routinized what was done all along. The only exception is the CD-ROM, invented around twenty years ago to present operas, university courses, a writer's oeuvre, in an entirely new way. Like the steamboat, the CD-ROM has not immediately caught on.

THE MEANING OF E-COMMERCE

E-commerce is to the Information Revolution what the railroad was to the Industrial Revolution—a totally new, totally unprecedented, totally unexpected development. And like the railroad 170 years ago, e-commerce is creating a new and distinct boom, rapidly changing the economy, society, and politics.

One example: A mid-sized company in America's industrial Midwest, founded in the 1920s and now run by the grandchildren of the founder, used to have some 60 percent of the market in inexpensive dinnerware for fast-food eateries, school and office cafeterias, and hospitals within a hundred-mile radius of its factory. China is heavy and breaks easily, so cheap china is traditionally sold within a small area. Almost overnight this company lost more than half of its market. One of its customers, a hospital cafeteria where someone went "surfing" on the Internet, discovered a European manufacturer that offered china of apparently better quality at a lower price and shipped cheaply by air. Within a few months the main customers in the area shifted to the European supplier. Few of them, it seems, realize—let alone care—that the stuff comes from Europe.

In the new mental geography created by the railroad, humanity mastered distance. In the mental geography of e-commerce, distance has been eliminated. There is only one economy and only one market.

One consequence of this is that every business must become globally competitive, even if it manufactures or sells only within a local or regional market. The competition is not local anymore—in fact, it knows no boundaries. Every company has to become transnational in the way it is run. Yet the traditional multinational may well become obsolete. It manufactures and distributes in a number of distinct geographies, in which it is a *local* company. But in e-commerce there are neither local companies nor distinct geographies. Where to manufacture, where to sell, and how to sell will remain important business decisions. But in another twenty years they may no longer determine what a company does, how it does it, and where it does it.

At the same time, it is not yet clear what kinds of goods and services will be bought and sold through e-commerce and what kinds will turn out to be unsuitable for it. This has been true whenever a new distribution channel has arisen. Why, for instance, did the railroad change both the mental and the economic geography of the West, whereas the steamboat—with its equal impact on world trade and passenger traffic—did neither? Why was there no "steamboat boom"?

Equally unclear has been the impact of more-recent changes in distribution channels—in the shift, for instance, from the local grocery store to the supermarket, from the individual supermarket to the supermarket chain, and from the supermarket chain to Wal-Mart and other discount chains. It is already clear that the shift to e-commerce will be just as eclectic and unexpected.

Here are a few examples. Twenty-five years ago it was generally believed that within a few decades the printed word would be dispatched electronically to individual subscribers' computer screens. Subscribers would then either read text on their computer screens or download it and print it out. This was the assumption that underlay the CD-ROM. Thus any number of newspapers and magazines, by no means only in the United States, established themselves online; few, so far, have become gold mines. But anyone who twenty years ago predicted the business of Amazon.com and barnesandnoble.com—that is, that books would be sold on the Internet but delivered in their heavy, printed form—would have been laughed off the podium. Yet Amazon.com and barnesandnoble.com are in exactly that business, and they are in it worldwide. The first order for the U.S. edition of my most recent book, *Management Challenges for the 21st Century* (1999), came to Amazon.com, and it came from Argentina.

Another example: Ten years ago one of the world's leading automobile companies made a thorough study of the expected impact on automobile sales of the then-emerging Internet. It concluded that the Internet would become a major distribution channel for used cars, but that customers would still want to see new cars, to touch them, to test-drive them. In actuality, at least so far, most used cars are still being bought not over the Internet but in a dealer's lot. However, as many as half of all new cars sold (excluding luxury cars) may now actually be "bought" over the Internet. Dealers only deliver cars that customers have chosen well before they enter the dealership. What does this mean for the future of the local automobile dealership, the twentieth century's most profitable small business?

Another example: Traders in the American stock market boom of 1998 and 1999 increasingly buy and sell online. But investors seem to be shifting away from buying electronically. The major U.S. investment vehicle is mutual funds. And whereas almost half of all mutual funds a few years ago were bought electronically, it is estimated that the figure will drop to 35 percent next year and to 20 percent by 2005. This is the opposite of what "everybody expected" ten or fifteen years ago.

The fastest-growing e-commerce in the United States is in an area where there was no "commerce" until now—in jobs for professionals and managers. Almost half of the world's largest companies now recruit through Web sites, and some 2.5 million managerial and professional people (two-thirds of them not even engineers or computer professionals) have their résumés on the Internet and solicit job offers over it. The result is a completely new labor market.

This illustrates another important effect of e-commerce. New distribution channels change who the customers are. They change not only how customers buy but also *what* they buy. They change consumer behavior, savings patterns, industry structure—in short, the entire economy. This is what is now happening, and not only in the United States but increasingly in the rest of the developed world, and in a good many emerging countries, including mainland China.

LUTHER, MACHIAVELLI, AND THE SALMON

The railroad made the Industrial Revolution accomplished fact. What had been revolution became establishment. And the boom it triggered lasted almost a hundred years. The technology of the steam engine did not end with the railroad. It led in the 1880s and 1890s to the steam turbine, and in the 1920s and 1930s to the last magnificent American steam locomotives, so beloved by railroad buffs. But the technology centered on the steam engine and in manufacturing operations ceased to be central. Instead the dynamics of the technology shifted to totally new industries that emerged almost immediately after the railroad was invented, not one of which had anything to do with steam or steam engines. The electric telegraph and photography were first, in the 1830s, followed soon thereafter by optics and farm equipment. The new and different fertilizer industry, which began in the late 1830s, in short order transformed agriculture. Public health became a major and central growth industry, with quarantine, vaccination, the supply of pure water, and sewers, which for the first time in history made the city a more healthful habitat than the countryside. At the same time came the first anesthetics.

With these major new technologies came major new social institutions: the modern postal service, the daily paper, investment banking, and commercial banking, to name just a few. Not one of them had much to do with the steam engine or with the technology of the Industrial Revolution in general. It was these new industries and institutions that by 1850 had come to dominate the industrial and economic landscape of the developed countries.

This is very similar to what happened in the printing revolution—the first of the technological revolutions that created the modern world. In the fifty years after 1455, when Gutenberg had perfected the printing press and movable type he had been working on for years, the printing revolution swept Europe and completely changed its economy and its psychology. But the books printed during the first fifty years, the ones called incunabula, contained largely the same texts that monks, in their scriptoria, had for centuries laboriously copied by hand: religious tracts and whatever remained of the writings of antiquity. Some 7,000 titles were published in those first fifty years, in 35,000 editions. At least 6,700 of these were traditional titles. In other words, in its first fifty years printing made available—and increasingly cheap—traditional information and communication products. But then, some sixty years after Gutenberg, came Luther's German Bible—thousands and thousands of copies sold almost immediately at an unbelievably low price. With Luther's Bible the new printing technology ushered in a new society. It ushered in Protestantism, which conquered half of Europe and, within another twenty years, forced the Catholic Church to reform itself in the other half. Luther used the new medium of print deliberately to restore religion to the center of individual life and of society. And this unleashed a century and a half of religious reform, religious revolt, religious wars.

At the very same time, however, that Luther used print with the avowed intention of restoring Christianity, Machiavelli wrote and published *The Prince* (1513), the first Western book in more than a thousand years that contained not one biblical quotation and no reference to the writers of antiquity. In no time at all *The Prince* became the "other best seller" of the sixteenth century, and its most notorious but also most influential book. In short order there was a wealth of purely secular works, what we today call literature: novels and books in science, history, politics, and, soon, economics. It was not long before the first purely secular art form arose, in England—the modern theater. Brand-new social institutions also arose: the Jesuit order, the Spanish infantry, the first modern navy, and, finally, the sovereign national state. In other words, the printing revolution followed the same trajectory as did the Industrial Revolution, which began 300 years later, and as does the Information Revolution today.

What the new industries and institutions will be, no one can say yet. No one in the 1520s anticipated secular literature, let alone the secular theater. No one in the 1820s anticipated the electric telegraph, or public health, or photography.

The one thing (to say it again) that is highly probable, if not nearly certain, is that the next twenty years will see the emergence of a number of new industries. At the same time, it is nearly certain that few of them will come out of information technology, the computer, data processing, or the Internet. This is indicated by all historical precedents. But it is true also of the new industries that are already rapidly emerging. Biotechnology, as mentioned, is already here. So is fish farming.

Twenty-five years ago salmon was a delicacy. The typical convention dinner gave a choice between chicken and beef. Today salmon is a commodity, and is the other choice on the convention menu. Most salmon today is not caught at sea or in a river but grown on a fish farm. The same is increasingly true of trout. Soon, apparently, it will be true of a number of other fish. Flounder, for instance, which is to seafood what pork is to meat, is just going into oceanic mass production. This will no doubt lead to the genetic development of new and different fish, just as the domestication of sheep, cows, and chickens led to the development of new breeds among them.

But probably a dozen or so technologies are at the stage where biotechnology was twenty-five years ago—that is, ready to emerge.

There is also a *service* waiting to be born: insurance against the risks of foreign-exchange exposure. Now that every business is part of the global economy, such insurance is as badly needed as was insurance against physical risks (fire, flood) in the early stages of the Industrial Revolution, when traditional insurance emerged. All the knowledge needed for foreign-exchange insurance is available; only the institution itself is still lacking.

The next two or three decades are likely to see even greater technological change than has occurred in the decades since the emergence of the computer, and also even greater change in industry structures, in the economic landscape, and probably in the social landscape as well.

THE GENTLEMAN VERSUS THE TECHNOLOGIST

The new industries that emerged after the railroad owed little technologically to the steam engine or to the Industrial Revolution in general. They were not its "children after the flesh"—but they were its "children after the spirit." They were possible only because of the mind-set that the Industrial Revolution had created and the skills it had developed. This was a mind-set that accepted—indeed, eagerly welcomed—invention and innovation. It was a mind-set that accepted, and eagerly welcomed, new products and new services. It also created the social values that made possible the new industries. Above all, it created the "technologist." Social

and financial success long eluded the first major American technologist, Eli Whitney, whose cotton gin, in 1793, was as central to the triumph of the Industrial Revolution as was the steam engine. But a generation later the technologist—still self-taught—had become the American folk hero and was both socially accepted and financially rewarded. Samuel Morse, the inventor of the telegraph, may have been the first example; Thomas Edison became the most prominent. In Europe the "businessman" long remained a social inferior, but the university-trained engineer had by 1830 or 1840 become a respected "professional."

By the 1850s England was losing its predominance and beginning to be overtaken as an industrial economy, first by the United States and then by Germany. It is generally accepted that neither economics nor technology was the major reason. The main cause was social. Economically, and especially financially, England remained the great power until the First World War. Technologically it held its own throughout the nineteenth century. Synthetic dyestuffs, the first products of the modern chemical industry, were invented in England, and so was the steam turbine. But England did not accept the technologist socially. He never became a "gentleman." The English built first-rate engineering schools in India but almost none at home. No other country so honored the "scientist"—and, indeed, Britain retained leadership in physics throughout the nineteenth century, from James Clerk Maxwell and Michael Faraday all the way to Ernest Rutherford. But the technologist remained a "tradesman." (Dickens, for instance, showed open contempt for the upstart ironmaster in his 1853 novel *Bleak House*.)

Nor did England develop the venture capitalist, who has the means and the mentality to finance the unexpected and unproved. A French invention, first portrayed in Balzac's monumental *La Comédie Humaine*, in the 1840s, the venture capitalist was institutionalized in the United States by J. P. Morgan and, simultaneously, in Germany and Japan by the universal bank. But England, although it invented and developed the commercial bank to finance trade, had no institution to finance industry until two German refugees, S. G. Warburg and Henry Grunfeld, started an entrepreneurial bank in London, just before the Second World War.

BRIBING THE KNOWLEDGE WORKER

What might be needed to prevent the United States from becoming the England of the twenty-first century? I am convinced that a drastic change in the social mind-set is required—just as leadership in the industrial economy after the railroad required the drastic change from "tradesman" to "technologist" or "engineer."

What we call the Information Revolution is actually a Knowledge Revolution. What has made it possible to routinize processes is not machinery; the computer is only the trigger. Software is the reorganization of traditional work, based on centuries of experience, through the application of knowledge and especially of systematic, logical analysis. The key is not electronics; it is cognitive science. This means that the key to maintaining leadership in the economy and the technology that are about to emerge is likely to be the social position of knowledge professionals and social acceptance of their values. For them to remain traditional "employees" and be treated as such would be tantamount to England's treating its technologists as tradesmen—and likely to have similar consequences.

Today, however, we are trying to straddle the fence—to maintain the traditional mind-set, in which capital is the key resource and the financier is the boss, while bribing knowledge workers to be content to remain employees by giving them bonuses and stock options. But this, if it can work at all, can work only as long as the emerging industries enjoy a stock market boom, as the Internet companies have been doing. The next major industries are likely to behave far more like traditional industries—that is, to grow slowly, painfully, laboriously.

The early industries of the Industrial Revolution—cotton textiles, iron, the railroads—were boom industries that created millionaires overnight, like Balzac's venture bankers and like Dickens's ironmaster, who in a few years grew from a lowly domestic servant into a "captain of industry." The industries that emerged after 1830 also created millionaires. But they took twenty years to do so, and it was twenty years of hard work, of struggle, of disappointments and failures, of thrift. This is likely to be true of the industries that will emerge from now on. It is already true of biotechnology.

Bribing the knowledge workers on whom these industries depend will therefore simply not work. The key knowledge workers in these businesses will surely continue to expect to share financially in the fruits of their labor. But the financial fruits are likely to take much longer to ripen, if they ripen at all. And then, probably within ten years or so, running a business with (short-term) "shareholder value" as its first—if not its only—goal and justification will have become counterproductive. Increasingly, performance in these new knowledge-based industries will come to depend on running the institution so as to attract, hold, and motivate knowledge workers. When this can no longer be done by satisfying knowledge workers' greed, as we are now trying to do, it will have to be done by satisfying their values, and by giving them social recognition and social power. It will have to be done by turning them from subordinates into fellow executives, and from employees, however well paid, into partners.

RELATED LINKS

- Internet Modern History Sourcebook: The Industrial Revolution (http://www.fordham.edu/halsall/mod/modsbook14.html)

- Telecommunications in an Information Age (http://usinfo.state.gov/products/pubs/archive/telecomm/homepage.htm)

- Troy: Networking for Innovation (http://www.troynet.net/networkinnovation/networks/networks.html)

FOR FURTHER RESEARCH

To find out more about the topics discussed in this reading, use InfoTrac College Edition. Type in keywords and subject terms such as: "e-commerce," "Information Revolution," and "knowledge worker." You can access InfoTrac College Edition from the Wadsworth/Thomson Communication Cafe homepage: http://communication.wadsworth.com.

Reading 1-3

Harmonic Convergence

Ted Greenwald

EDITOR'S NOTE

This list, a multimedia timeline of new communications technologies, was compiled in 1999, so the entries beginning with the year 2000 either are based on projections or consist of pure speculation. In one telling speculation, for 2015, Yahoo! buys Turner Networks for an undisclosed sum and announces that all future Turner content will be available exclusively online. Fact proved stranger than fiction when, in January 2000, America Online announced that it was acquiring Time Warner (which already owned Turner Networks) for $165 billion. Sorry Yahoo! (For more on the AOL Time Warner merger, see Reading 5-3). Note in the timeline how the pace of technological change accelerates throughout the twentieth century.

CONSIDER

1. Which of the predictions about the future of media (those toward the end of this list) do you think will come true, and why?

2. What other predictions can be made about the media landscape? How can you be sure?

3. Other than the printing press, which communications invention in your opinion has had the greatest impact on society, and why?

How we got here and where we're going: a multimedia timeline.

- **1436** Johannes Gutenberg debuts printing press in Germany.

- **1790** U.S. Copyright Act establishes basic parameters of copyright in United States.

- **1841** *Folsom v. Marsh* introduces doctrine of fair use.

- **1844** Samuel Morse transmits first message by telegraph, from Washington, DC, to Baltimore.

- **1857** Transatlantic cable, laid by Cyrus W. Field and John Pender, connects U.S. and Europe.

- **1876** Alexander Graham Bell demonstrates telephone in U.S.

- **1877** Thomas Edison records and plays "Mary Had a Little Lamb" on tinfoil cylinder phonograph.

- **1894** Guglielmo Marconi transmits wireless telegraph signals.

- **1895** Louis and Auguste Lumière project movies on a screen in public demonstrations in France.

- **1905** Jukebox is introduced.

- **1909** U.S. Copyright Act revised to address media categories beyond literature, especially music.

- **1931** Alan Blumlein invents stereo audio recording.

- **1938** John Logie Baird transmits color television signal.

- **1948** Columbia Records introduces 33$\frac{1}{3}$-rpm 12-inch vinyl LP.

- **1949** Jay Forrester at MIT invents magnetic computer memory.

- **1951** Nagra's Stephan Kudelski develops portable audiotape recorder.

- **1952** Recording Industry Association of America (RIAA) is founded to represent interests of record companies.

- **1955** Narinder Kapany invents fiber optics in England.

- **1956** Prerecorded, stereo, open-reel audiotapes hit market. Video recording is developed in U.S. by Ray Dolby and Charles Ginsburg of Ampex. IBM markets RAMAC 305 hard-disk drive, which stores 5 Mbytes on 50 disks 2 feet wide.

- **1958** Stereophonic records are introduced.

- **1959** Xerox debuts photocopier.

- **1963** Philips demonstrates compact audiocassette. Sony launches consumer open-reel videotape recorder.

- **1965** Eight-track audiotape cartridges developed by William Lear. Computers at MIT and System Development Corporation in Santa Monica, California, communicate via 1200-bps connection.

- **1966** Xerox markets first fax machine.

- **1967** Ampex introduces the portable videotape deck.

- **1969** Sony releases U-Matic videocassette in Japan.

- **1971** Project Gutenberg begins digitizing major literary works.

- **1972** Intel introduces 8008 CPU running at 200 kHz.

- **1973** File-transfer protocol (FTP) specification is developed for uploading and downloading digital files between nodes on a network.

- **1974** Sony launches Betamax videocassette format in U.S.

- **1975** First personal computer developed, the MITS Altair 8800.

- **1976** Intel 8085 CPU runs at 5 MHz. U.S. Robotics markets PhoneLink 300, a modem that operates at 300 baud. VHS videocassette format launched by JVC. Universal and Disney sue Sony for encouraging copyright infringement via Betamax.

- **1979** Walkman portable audiocassette player introduced by Sony.

- **1982** Philips and Sony introduce CD digital audio format. Intel 80286 processor runs at 6, 10, and 12 MHz, processing 16-bit rather than 8-bit words.

- **1984** Apple introduces Macintosh computer. Number of Internet hosts exceeds 1,000. Philips and Sony develop CD-ROM format with 650-Mbyte capacity. Motorola 68020 CPU runs at 16 MHz. Sony introduces Discman portable CD player.

- **1985** U.S. Robotics Courier 2400 modem operates at 2400 bps. AOL goes online. Microsoft releases Windows 1.0.3.

- **1987** DAT is introduced in Japan. Number of Internet hosts exceeds 10,000. Fraunhofer Institute begins work on new audio codec, later formalized as MP3.

- **1988** AT&T installs first transatlantic fiber-optic cable.

- **1989** Number of Internet hosts exceeds 100,000. Barry Shein founds World.std.com, which soon becomes the first commercial dialup ISP.

- **1992** Number of Internet hosts exceeds 1 million. U.S. Robotics Sportster 14,400 fax modem operates at 14.4 kbps. U.S. Congress enacts Audio Home Recording Act. The Moving Picture Experts Group approves MPEG-1 video and audio data-compression spec, including Audio Layer 3, or MP3. Apple releases QuickTime 1 for Windows.

- **1993** Intel Pentium CPU runs at 66 MHz.

- **1994** Under the name Netscape Communications, Marc Andreessen and Jim Clark release Navigator 1.0. Rob Glaser founds Progressive Networks (renamed RealNetworks in 1997). U.S. Robotics ships 28.8-kbps modem. MPEG finalizes MPEG-2 spec for video and audio data compression.

- **1995** Progressive Networks releases RealAudio 1.0. @Home Network is founded to provide broadband Net access via cable modem.

- **1996** MCI upgrades Net backbone, adding 13,000 ports and boosting effective speed from 155 Mbps to 622 Mbps.

- **1997** David Bowie releases five tracks in Real-Audio 3.0 format. U.S. Robotics ships modems capable of 56-kbps performance over twisted pair. RealNetworks ships RealVideo 1.0. Encoding.com founded by Martin Tobias, Alex Tobias, David Conover, and Adam Berman. MP3.com founded by Michael Robertson. Audible Inc. ships Audible MobilePlayer.

- **1998** Microsoft releases Windows Media Player. Diamond Multimedia announces Rio PMP300 portable MP3 audio player. RIAA applies for temporary restraining order to halt shipment of Rio PMP300. U.S. District Court for Central District of California allows Diamond Multimedia to ship Rio PMP300. MPEG approves preliminary version of MPEG-4. RealNetworks releases RealSystem G2. Intel Pentium II Xeon processor runs at 450 MHz. U.S. Congress passes Digital Millennium Copyright Act. RIAA announces Secure Digital Music Initiative.

■ **1999** Audible begins offering MP3-encoded content. AT&T releases beta version of DjVu image-compression technology. Intel Pentium III Xeon processor runs at 550 MHz. IBM unveils Madison Project, a digital audio-distribution platform. Microsoft releases Windows Media Technologies. RealNetworks acquires Xing Technology, pioneer in MPEG streaming. RealNetworks releases RealJukebox. Universal Music partners with InterTrust to develop technology for selling music online. Hollywood motion picture premieres on the Net—available for three days only.

■ **2000** MPEG approves MPEG-4 spec. TiVo delivers a Diamond Rio for television programming.

■ **2001** Motion Picture Association of America (MPAA) proposes the Secure Digital Motion Picture Initiative to create a downloadable-video file format that incorporates copyright protection.

■ **2002** MPEG approves MPEG-7 encompassing multimedia search, filtering, management, and processing.

■ **2003** Handheld wireless Net radios receive streaming audio on demand. Handheld wireless TVs use cheap LCD screens to deliver streaming video on demand.

■ **2004** Chinese film students crack Paramount's intranet and post entire contents to Beijing University server. For 79 hours, Net users have free access to streaming 800-kbps MPEG-2 versions of innumerable movie classics.

■ **2008** New codecs deliver HDTV resolution on Net. Cable modems and DSL phone services achieve 50 percent penetration in U.S.

■ **2009** ABC debuts a Net-only soap opera, aimed at office workers.

■ **2015** Yahoo! Media buys Turner Networks for an undisclosed sum. Yahoo! Media announces that all future Turner content will be available exclusively online.

■ **2016** Interactive sitcom My.Friends grips nation.

■ **2024** Fiber optics to home available to 50 percent of U.S. public.

RELATED LINKS

■ The Computer Museum History Center (http://www.computerhistory.org)

■ Jones Telecommunications and Multimedia Encyclopedia (http://www.digitalcentury .com/index.html)

■ Multimedia: From Wagner to Virtual Reality (http://www.artmuseum.net/w2vr/ project.html)

FOR FURTHER RESEARCH

To find out more about the topics discussed in this reading, use InfoTrac College Edition. Type in keywords and subject terms such as "media technology," "future of media," and "technological change (pace of)." You can access InfoTrac College Edition from the Wadsworth / Thomson Communication Cafe homepage: http://communication.wadsworth.com.

2

New Media Theory

Principles of Mediamorphosis

Roger Fidler

EDITOR'S NOTE

The emergence of new media rarely precipitates the death of old media; instead, existing media forms evolve and adapt to the changing communication environment, in a gradual process comparable in some ways to the evolution of species. In this reading Roger Fidler introduces a unified way of thinking about media transformation and adaptation, a process he calls mediamorphosis. *Instead of studying each new media form separately, mediamorphosis regards all media as constituent elements of an interdependent system. By studying the communication system as a whole, Fidler asserts, it becomes clear that new media do not arise spontaneously and independently—they emerge gradually from the metamorphosis of old media.*

CONSIDER

1. Why, to better understand technological change, must we first discard most of our commonly held assumptions, particularly about the pace of change?

2. What are the dangers of *technomyopia?* How do inflated short-term hopes distort initial expectations for new media and cause us to treat future growth phases with skepticism?

3. How can the six principles of mediamorphosis be used to predict what will happen in the next stage of media evolution?

21

Change is not something most people look forward to or are particularly good at predicting. Even for the inventors and innovators who stimulate technological and social changes, visualizing the future presents an enigmatic problem. Yet, despite the anxieties often caused by change, humans seem to have a remarkable propensity for rapidly assimilating new ideas, products, and services once they are perceived to fit into their personal and cultural definitions of reality. While no one, it seems, is ever completely prepared for change or able to accurately predict outcomes, we can all begin to discern probable shapes of the future by learning to recognize the historic patterns and mechanisms of change. This chapter introduces several frameworks for assessing change and evaluating new media technologies.

YESTERDAY'S FUTURE, TODAY'S PAST

Much of what is now taken for granted has, in fact, only recently emerged. Just one human generation ago, at the beginning of the 1970s, electronic pocket calculators were just starting to compete with slide rules and mechanical adding machines; computers were big and impersonal; and AT&T was still a monopoly that leased nearly all private telephones in the United States. Portable communicators and voice interaction with computers only existed in the imaginary twenty-third century universe of the original *Star Trek* television series.

Twenty-five years ago, electronic media were confined to broadcast radio and television. Lasers and fiber-optic networks, miniature video cameras and handheld television sets, compact disc players and music CDs, digital fax machines, cellular phones, and laptop computers were all unknown outside of a few research and development laboratories.

Information retrieval was something one only did in libraries with printed books and periodicals, or microfilm, using pencils and paper. The Internet and electronic mail (e-mail) were still confined to the rarefied and generally secret world of defense-related research.

Newspapers and magazines had just begun converting their newsrooms from mechanical typewriters

to electronic text-editing systems and their composing rooms from hot-type to cold-type technologies. Few journalists then could have imagined the electronic news-gathering and production technologies that are common today or foreseen desktop publishing and the explosion of news graphics made possible by personal computers.

A mere decade ago, few people could have imagined that by the mid-1990s digital fax machines, electronic mail services, and miniature cell phones would be routinely used to communicate just as easily and inexpensively with individuals in distant countries and rural communities as within large cities and office buildings. In the mid-1980s, most publishers abandoned consumer online services (then called videotex) after collectively losing several hundred million dollars and promptly declared that electronic publishing would not emerge as a viable business until well into the next century. Who then would have envisioned the frenzy of activity that now surrounds consumer online services and the World Wide Web?

THE 30-YEAR RULE

While we may never be able to foretell the outcomes of technological change with a high degree of precision, we can sharpen our focus. To do so, we must first enlarge our perspective and discard most of our commonly held assumptions, particularly about the speed of change.

Changes may seem to be occurring more rapidly in the world today, but studies of historical records have shown that this is a common misconception. Paul Saffo, a director at the Institute for the Future in Menlo Park, California, posits that the amount of time required for new ideas to fully seep into a culture has consistently averaged about three decades for at least the past five centuries. He calls this the 30-year rule.

As a new media forecaster, Saffo has learned from experience that our short human memories all too often confuse surprise with speed. When it comes to emerging technologies, he finds that the slowness of change is the rule rather than the exception. Most ideas take much longer to become "overnight successes" than anyone is ever prepared to admit.

The reason life feels so much more rapid today, Saffo contends, is not that individual technologies are accelerating at a faster rate or that things are happening more quickly than they have in the past. What's actually occurring is that "more technologies are coming up at the same time. It is the unexpected cross-impact of maturing technologies that creates this powerful acceleration that we all feel."[1] Cross-impacts are also the variables, he says, that make new media forecasting so difficult.

STAGES OF DEVELOPMENT

There is, however, a relatively consistent pattern of accelerated development that takes place as each new technology moves from laboratory to marketplace. Saffo has identified three typical stages within the 30-year rule. "First decade: lots of excitement, lots of puzzlement, not a lot of penetration. Second decade: lots of flux, penetration of the product into society is beginning. Third decade: 'Oh, so what?' Just a standard technology and everybody has it."[2]

Which Development Stage Are We In?

As we attempt to peer into the future of communications, it would seem, therefore, that the critical question to be asked with regard to emerging media technologies is, Which development stage are they in? But, as we will discover, the answer to such an apparently simple question is not always obvious. To know the stage, we must also have some idea of when the clock started, and how innovations are likely to be affected by other technological and social developments, which are not easily determined in the midst of change.

Example: Xerox's Alto

When the first personal computer designed specifically for nontechnical users was switched on at the Xerox Palo Alto Research Center (PARC) in the early 1970s, most of the underlying ideas and technologies had been under development for one to three decades. The scientists who created the Alto, as this early computer was called, believed they were already in the second stage and that their invention could quickly penetrate the office market, but the company's senior executives and market researchers were unconvinced.[3]

While Xerox's decision not to immediately begin marketing Alto systems is often held up as an example of corporate incompetence, it may have been based on a more accurate assessment than the pundits have acknowledged. With the benefits of hindsight, we can now see that personal computing in the 1970s was still in its first stage. Beyond a small cadre of scientists and amateur enthusiasts, few people then were ready to believe they might soon have a practical use for their own desktop computer. Additionally, many of the component and manufacturing technologies needed to make personal computers affordable to general consumers were not yet available.

Another decade would pass before a personal computer system comparable to the Alto would enter the consumer marketplace. And even in the 1980s there was uncertainty as to which stage personal computers were in. Many financial bets were made on the assumption that they were then in the third stage, only to be lost when the market for home computers faltered toward the middle of the decade. What we can see only now is that the cross-impacts of video game, electronic mail, online information, and Internet technologies coupled with faster and cheaper telecommunications and a growing home office market in the 1990s finally thrust personal computers into the third stage.

RESTATING THE RULE

The 30-year rule may not be foolproof, but it does put the development of new technologies into a more realistic perspective. We need to remember, however, that this rule is not intended to fix a precise time frame for the widespread adoption of new technologies. Saffo's essential point is that impressions of spontaneous technological advancements are generally wrong. This rule can be restated in two different ways: (1) Laboratory breakthroughs and discoveries nearly always take longer than anyone expects to become successful commercial products or services. (2) Technologies that appear to have suddenly emerged as successful new products and services have been under development for much longer than anyone admits.

THE DANGERS OF TECHNOMYOPIA

While the time required for new technologies to migrate from laboratories to store shelves may span several decades, Saffo also cautions industry leaders against complacency. History, he says, shows that once consumers perceive a new technology to be useful and affordable, widespread adoption can take place rather quickly. Yet, despite the frequent repetition of this pattern, he has found that people are still nearly always caught by surprise.

The relatively flat, slow ramp followed by a steep, rapid climb is the growth model upon which most start-up companies build their business plans. But that model can be misleading. The actual pattern for enterprises attempting to exploit new technologies rarely conforms to a smooth ascending curve. More often than not, the typical, real-life trend line resembles a roller coaster. Several moderate ups and downs generally precede the final grand ascent to market success, although there are never any assurances that there will, in the end, be a final grand ascent. This tendency to undergo several initial ups and downs may contribute to the surprise factor when a new technology finally does take off. Typically, a great deal of publicity will follow the announcement of a discovery or new invention. But when the first rush of excitement is dampened by disappointments and setbacks, we usually treat future growth phases with skepticism. Saffo calls this affliction technomyopia:

> [Technomyopia] is a strange phenomenon that causes us to overestimate the potential short-term impacts of a new technology. And when the world fails to conform to our inflated expectations, we turn around and we underestimate the long-term implications. First we overshoot and then we undershoot.[4]

Example: The Video Game Roller Coaster

The development of video game technology illustrates this phenomenon. Beginning in 1972 with two simple ball-and-paddle games called Odyssey and Pong, video games quickly captivated the minds, and wallets, of teenagers and young adults. A steady stream of popular video arcade games, such as Pac-Man and Space Invaders, followed in the late 1970s. Within ten years, Americans were spending more money on home video game systems and at video arcades than they spent on movies and music—a total of more than $11 billion. Then, even more suddenly, the market collapsed. By 1985 total sales of home video game systems had dropped from more than $3 billion at its peak to only $100 million.[5]

The crash forced nearly all U.S. video game companies into other computer businesses or bankruptcy. Most industry executives and analysts saw this as a sign that video games were merely a fad. But just as the U.S. market was collapsing, Nintendo, a Japanese toy company, introduced a new game system in Japan called Famicon. And two years later, Nintendo swept across the Pacific with the speed and power of a tsunami. Armed with a wider selection of fast-action games that incorporated sophisticated graphics, Nintendo quickly revived interest among those who had become bored with earlier systems and attracted a new generation of players as well. By 1989 Nintendo controlled 80 percent of the U.S. video game market, which had recovered to its $3 billion precrash level. By the beginning of the 1990s, one out of every five U.S. households owned a Nintendo set.

TECHNOLOGICAL ACCELERATORS AND BRAKES

Rogers's diffusion theory is perhaps the simplest model for visualizing the historic adoption patterns of established technologies, but it only partially explains why a new media technology will suddenly diffuse into the general consumer market and attain a dominant position. Early adopters may encourage others to try a new technology, but they alone have not been shown to provide the energy needed for rapid acceleration, or to have sufficient influence to significantly affect the introduction and diffusion of a technology.

Diffusion theory cannot adequately explain, for example, why FM radio (which was invented in the early 1930s and provided a far superior means of broadcasting than the original AM radio technology) floundered for three decades and then, in less than 10 years, managed to dethrone its rival all across North America. What was the accelerator? And what had applied the brakes for so long? These are the questions that Brian Winston, a journalism professor at the University of Wales, has attempted to answer.[6]

Winston blends a strong cultural perspective with the history of media technologies to arrive at a comprehensive explanation of how new media are born and developed. His ideas are based on the following convictions:

- Social, political, and economic forces play powerful roles in the development of new technologies.

- Inventions and innovations are not widely adopted on the merits of a technology alone.

- There must always be an opportunity as well as a motivating social, political, or economic reason for a new technology to be developed.

SUPERVENING SOCIAL NECESSITIES

In Winston's view, the accelerators that push the development of new media technologies are what he calls *supervening social necessities*. He defines these as "the interfaces between society and technology." They derive from the needs of companies, requirements of other technologies, regulatory or legal actions, and general social forces. In the case of FM radio, the supervening social necessities that emerged in the 1960s fit into all four categories.

Needs of Companies

Competition with television was cutting deeply into the profits of large, established AM stations, and their future seemed in doubt. By contrast, the dramatically lower costs associated with FM broadcasting made the operation of smaller stations that targeted niche audiences quite profitable and appealing to media companies, entrepreneurs, and investors. Manufacturers were also attracted to FM because it created a new and potentially even larger market for radios.

Requirements of Other Technologies

Advances in recording and playback technologies, significant improvements in home equipment, and the growing popularity of hi-fi and stereo recordings created the need and demand for high-quality broadcasting technology, which FM readily provided. Stereo, introduced on FM in 1961, offered radio audiences yet another incentive to switch. The miniaturization of electronic components also made it possible for radio manufacturers to combine AM and FM technologies in more compact receivers, which, in turn, increased the demand for FM stations and new equipment.

Regulatory and Legal Actions

The resolution in the mid-1960s of patent infringement suits finally removed a serious legal impediment to FM's development. But even more important was the 1967 Public Broadcasting Act. This regulatory action established National Public Radio (NPR) as a production center for educational and public affairs broadcasting and reserved space on the FM dial for new public radio stations.

General Social Forces

However, FM owes a great deal of its ultimate success to rock 'n roll music and to teenagers in the late 1950s and 1960s. Because of AM's broad reach and large un-differentiated audiences, stations tended to broadcast only Top 40 popular music and avoid so-called underground recordings, such as rock, jazz, and blues. The smaller FM stations could afford to target niche audiences, which allowed them to satisfy the musical tastes of teenagers and to provide an outlet for small, independent recording studios.

The increasing popularity of FM music stations among teenagers helped drive demand for new portable and car radios with FM receiver technology. It also attracted advertisers who were trying to reach the affluent young audience, which was rapidly becoming a social and economic force to be reckoned with. By 1969, the average FM listener was about 10 years younger than the average AM listener, and more than half of all Americans listening to radio were tuned to FM stations.

THE LAW OF SUPPRESSION OF RADICAL POTENTIAL

The law of suppression of radical potential, in Winston's view, applies the brakes that slow the disruptive impact of a new technology upon the social or corporate status quo. Brakes arise from the same four broad categories identified with supervening social necessities. The [suppression] law helps us understand why FM radio took so long to succeed in the general consumer market despite its obvious technical and economic superiority over AM broadcasting.

Needs of Companies

In 1933, when Howard Armstrong demonstrated his FM prototype to David Sarnoff, president of the powerful Radio Corporation of America (RCA), AM radio was already well established and generating high profits for manufacturers and broadcasters. Sarnoff recognized that FM represented a revolutionary new radio technology that was far better than AM, but he was not eager to disrupt RCA's substantial profits from AM radio, especially in the midst of the Great Depression.

Requirements of Other Technologies

In the 1930s RCA was also investing heavily in the development of television, and many of the company's patents involved using the same portion of the radio spectrum that Armstrong was proposing for FM radio. Sarnoff saw television as RCA's next great opportunity and marshaled the company's resources to protect its position.

Regulatory and Legal Actions

When Armstrong realized that RCA would not back his invention, he decided to push its development on his own. After the Federal Communications Commission (FCC) allocated a small range of the radio spectrum for FM broadcasting, he secured licenses to build several stations and begin manufacturing FM radios. Buoyed by his early success, he confidently predicted in 1940 that the existing AM broadcast system would be largely superseded by FM within five years.

But, however farsighted he was about technology, Armstrong underestimated the interest Sarnoff and other broadcasters had in maintaining the status quo, as well as their political clout, particularly with the FCC.[7] At the insistence of RCA and the network broadcasters, the FCC began hearings in 1944 into the appropriate spectrum allocations for television and other broadcast technologies that were poised to take off as soon as the war ended. Using dubious evidence to justify its decision, the FCC in 1945 approved the recommendations of the broadcasters to move FM to a different location in the radio spectrum and give TV broadcasters the portion previously allocated to FM.

With this one ruling, the FCC rendered all of Armstrong's installed FM broadcast equipment and radios obsolete and useless. At the time, there were more than fifty FM broadcast stations and half a million FM radios in operation in the United States.

General Social Forces

The 1929 stock market crash and subsequent global depression significantly reduced consumer demand for new radio sets and caused a shakeout in the radio manufacturing business. Enthusiasm for a new radio technology that would require replacement of existing sets and broadcast equipment was understandably low.

However, even with the financial constraints posed by the Depression, Armstrong managed to attract a credible number of early adopters and investors. Unfortunately, just as FM broadcasting was poised to take off, its commercial development and expansion were abruptly halted by the United States' entry into World War II. After the war, FM technology still had a strong following, but the obsolescence caused by the FCC's change of radio spectrum allocations seriously inhibited continuing support. Moreover, by the end of the 1940s, TV was already rapidly drawing consumer and investor attention away from both AM and FM radio.

THE MEDIAMORPHIC PROCESS

While the preceding hypotheses are integral to the process I call mediamorphosis, they only provide general insights into the pacing and timing of technological developments. Before we can even begin to make reasonable judgments about emerging technologies and the future of mainstream media, we need to acquire a broad, integrated knowledge of human communications and the historic patterns of change within the overall system. This knowledge is central to our understanding of the mediamorphic process, which I have defined as: *the transformation of communication media, usually brought about by the complex interplay of perceived needs, competitive and political pressures, and social and technological innovations.*

Mediamorphosis is not so much a theory as it is a unified way of thinking about the technological evolution of communication media. Instead of studying each form separately, it encourages us to examine all forms as members of an interdependent system, and to note the similarities and relationships that exist among past, present, and emerging forms. By studying the communication system as a whole, we will see that new media do not arise spontaneously and independently—they emerge gradually from the metamorphosis of old media. And that when newer forms of communication media emerge, the older forms usually do not die—they continue to evolve and adapt.

The example of FM's delayed success and radio's transformation from a mass-audience medium to a niche-audience medium can also be used to illustrate this key principle of mediamorphosis. As TV began its grand ascent, general-audience radio went into a steep decline that led some analysts to predict the imminent death of the medium. But radio didn't die. Nor was AM entirely subsumed by FM. Instead, AM adapted and through the adoption of new technologies and marketing strategies has steadily become more competitive with FM. Since the beginning of the 1990s, AM radio has been showing strong signs of revival in the United States and elsewhere.

The rapid diffusion of TV also brought about significant transformations within the newspaper, magazine, and film industries. Each was declared a dying medium without the capacity to compete with TV's immediacy and compelling images, yet each proved to be more resilient and adaptable than expected. This also illustrates an important corollary to the metamorphosis principle: Established forms of communication media *must* change in response to the emergence of a new medium—their only other option is to die. The metamorphosis principle, as well as several other key principles of mediamorphosis, derives from three concepts—coevolution, convergence, and complexity.

COEVOLUTION

All forms of communication are, as we shall see, tightly woven into the fabric of the human communication system and cannot exist independently from one another in our culture. As each new form emerges and develops, it influences, over time and to varying degrees, the development of every other existing form. Coevolution and coexistence, rather than sequential evolution and replacement, have been the norm since the first organisms made their debut on the planet. The wealth of communication technologies we now take for granted would not have been possible if the birth of each new medium had resulted in the simultaneous death of an older medium.

Communicatory Codes

Specific forms of media, as with species, have life cycles and eventually do die out, but most of their defining traits will always remain part of the system. Just as biological characteristics are propagated from one generation to another through genetic codes, media traits are embodied and carried forward through communicatory codes that we call languages. Languages have been, without compare, the most powerful agents of change in the course of human evolution.

The development of spoken language and written language brought about two great transformations, or mediamorphoses, within the human communication system. Each of these two classes of language has been responsible for reordering and greatly expanding the human mind in ways that made modern civilization and culture possible. Countless transforming technologies affecting all aspects of human life and communication have been inspired and energized by these two agents of change.

Now a third great mediamorphosis resulting from the recent development of a new class of language is poised to once again radically influence the evolution of communication and civilization. For the past two centuries, industrial-age and information-age technologies have been conjointly contributing to the rapid development and spread of this language, which has only become known to most people in the past two decades. This new class of language is called *digital*

language. It is the *lingua franca* of computers and global telecommunication networks.

CONVERGENCE

Nearly every personal computer sold today offers users the ability to play CD-ROMs that blend text and still images with audio and video clips, as well as the opportunity to conveniently dial into global networks and access vast stores of textual and audio/visual information. This is just one of the more obvious examples of the concept known as *media convergence*. The idea that diverse technologies and forms of media are coming together now seems almost commonplace, but not so long ago it was considered quite visionary.

In 1979, when Nicholas Negroponte began popularizing the concept in his lecture tours to raise funds for a building to house the Media Lab at the Massachusetts Institute of Technology, few people had any comprehension of convergence. Audiences were often astonished by Negroponte's revelation that "all communication technologies are suffering a joint metamorphosis, which can only be understood properly if treated as a single subject."[8] To illustrate this concept, Negroponte drew three overlapping circles labeled "broadcast and motion picture industry," "computer industry," and "print and publishing industry" (see Figure 1). Since then, the notion that these industries are coming together to create new forms of communication has shaped much of the thinking about the future of mass media and human communications.

Multimedia Forms of Communication

Negroponte and others at MIT are credited with being among the first to recognize that this convergence of media industries and digital technologies would ultimately lead to new forms of so-called multimedia communication. *Multimedia,* or *mixed media* as it is also known, is generally defined as any medium in which two or more forms of communication are integrated.

Within the broadest definition of the term, most printed newspapers and magazines qualify as forms of multimedia because they convey information through a blend of written words, photography, and graphics displayed on a paper medium. However, the visions of multimedia popularized in the past two decades have tended to dismiss paper as an "old" medium. The preferred "new" medium for displaying blended content is the electronic screen. With an electronic display medium, such as a computer monitor or television screen,

1978

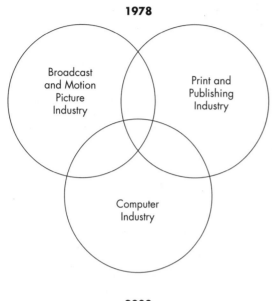

2000

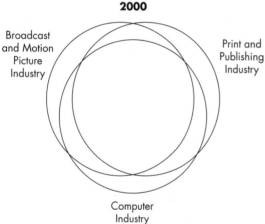

FIGURE 1. The MIT Media Lab's construct of convergence.

new multimedia systems are capable of conveying information through various blends of full-motion video, animation, and sounds, as well as still images and written words.

COMPLEXITY

During periods of great change, such as we are now experiencing, everything around us may appear to be in a state of chaos and, to a large extent, it is. Chaos is an essential component of change. Without it, the uni-

verse would be a dead place and life would be impossible. Out of chaos comes the new ideas that transform and vitalize systems.

Chaos Theory

A central tenet of contemporary chaos theory is the notion that seemingly insignificant events or slight initial variations within chaotic systems, such as the weather and the economy, can trigger cascades of escalating, unpredictable occurrences that ultimately lead to consequential or catastrophic events. This aspect of the theory is often illustrated by the example of a butterfly flapping its wings in China and causing a hurricane to develop off the coast of Florida.

Chaotic systems are essentially anarchistic. That is, they exhibit nearly infinite variability with no predictable long-term patterns, which explains why precise long-range weather and national economic forecasts are all but impossible. It also explains why no one will ever be able to accurately predict which specific new media technologies and forms of communication will ultimately succeed and which will fail.

The importance of chaos to our understanding of mediamorphosis and the development of new media is actually less in the theory than in its connection to another related concept—complexity. In this context, *complexity* refers to the events that take place within certain apparently chaotic systems.

Chaos and order, like birth and death, are opposite extremes of all complex, or so-called *living systems*. According to physicist Mitchell Waldrop, the edge of chaos is "where new ideas and innovative genotypes are forever nibbling away at the edges of the status quo."[9]

Complex, Adaptive Systems

As scientists studied the behavior of complex systems, they discovered that the richness of the interactions that occur within living systems allows them to undergo *spontaneous self-organization* in response to changing conditions. In other words, Waldrop observes, complex systems are *adaptive,* in that "they don't just passively respond to events the way a rock might roll around in an earthquake. They actively try to turn whatever happens to their advantage."

By recognizing that the human communication system is, in fact, a complex, adaptive system, we can see that all forms of media live in a dynamic, interdependent universe. When external pressures are applied and new innovations are introduced, each form of communication is affected by an intrinsic self-organizing process that spontaneously occurs within the system. Just as species evolve for better survival in a changing environment, so do forms of communication and established media enterprises. This process is the essence of mediamorphosis.

PRINCIPLES OF MEDIAMORPHOSIS IN PERSPECTIVE

This discussion furnishes a number of general insights into the adoption and implementation of new media technologies that can guide our thinking about the next stage in the transformation of mainstream media and emerging computer-mediated communications. The following *six fundamental principles of mediamorphosis* flow from the preceding discussion:

1. *Coevolution and coexistence:* All forms of communication media coexist and coevolve within an expanding, complex adaptive system. As each new form emerges and develops, it influences, over time and to varying degrees, the development of every other existing form.

2. *Metamorphosis:* New media do not arise spontaneously and independently—they emerge gradually from the metamorphosis of older media. When newer forms emerge, the older forms tend to adapt and continue to evolve rather than die.

3. *Propagation:* Emerging forms of communication media propagate dominant traits from earlier forms. These traits are passed on and spread through communicatory codes called languages.

4. *Survival:* All forms of communication media, as well as media enterprises, are compelled to adapt and evolve for survival in a changing environment. Their only other option is to die.

5. *Opportunity and need:* New media are not widely adopted on the merits of a technology alone. There must always be an opportunity, as well as a motivating social, political, and/or eco-

nomic reason for a new media technology to be developed.

6. *Delayed adoption:* New media technologies always take longer than expected to become commercial successes. They tend to require at *least* one human generation (20–30 years) to progress from proof of concept to widespread adoption.

By combining the principles of mediamorphosis with an understanding of the attributes that have shaped the development of communication media in the past, we can gain valuable insights into the new forms that may emerge as well as the ways in which existing forms may adapt and continue to evolve.

NOTES

1. "Paul Saffo and the 30-Year Rule," *Design World, 24*, 1992, p. 18.

2. Ibid.

3. The story of Xerox's development of the first personal computer system is told by Douglas K. Smith and Robert C. Alexander in *Fumbling the Future: How Xerox Invented then Ignored the First Personal Computer*. New York: Morrow, 1988.

4. "Paul Saffo and the 30-Year Rule," p. 18.

5. Steven Lubar, *InfoCulture: The Smithsonian Book of Information Age Inventions*. Boston: Houghton Mifflin, 1993, p. 274.

6. Brian Winston, "How Are Media Born and Developed?" In John Downing, Ali Mohammadi, and Annabelle Sreberny-Mohammadi (Eds.), *Questioning the Media: A Critical Introduction*. Thousand Oaks, CA: Sage Publications, 1995, pp. 54–74.

7. Tom Lewis, *Empire of the Air: The Men Who Made Radio*. New York: HarperCollins, 1991, pp. 300–301.

8. Quoted in Stewart Brand, *The Media Lab: Inventing the Future at MIT*. New York: Viking Penguin, 1987, p. 11.

9. M. Mitchell Waldrop, *Complexity: The Emerging Science at the Edge of Order and Chaos*. New York: Touchstone, 1992, p. 12.

RELATED LINKS

- The Poynter Institute's New Media Timeline (http://poynter.org/research/nm/timeline/index.htm)

- Remediation: Understanding New Media (http://www.lcc.gatech.edu/%7Ebolter/remediation/index.html)

- Xerox Palo Alto Research Center (http://www.parc.xerox.com/parc-go.html)

FOR FURTHER RESEARCH

To find out more about the topics discussed in this reading, use InfoTrac College Edition. Type in keywords and subject terms such as "mediamorphosis," "media evolution," and "new technology adoption." You can access InfoTrac College Edition from the Wadsworth / Thomson Communication Cafe homepage: http://communication.wadsworth.com.

Reading 2-2

Medium Theory
Joshua Meyrowitz

EDITOR'S NOTE

When a new medium such as television or the Internet is introduced into society, scholars and critics formulate assessments of its social and psychological impact. Medium theorists examine the potential influences of communication technologies by looking at the overall characteristics of a medium rather than its specific content elements (for example, sexual or violent programming). From their perspective, mass media don't merely convey information—they actively shape the social environment. As this reading points out, this big-picture approach to media influence can yield important historical insights about information technology's role in transforming society.

CONSIDER

1. Who were the two most important first-generation medium theorists, and what were their major contributions?

2. How can the history of civilization be told from a medium-theory perspective, and what are the broad outlines of this history?

3. If print media emphasize words and ideas and electronic media emphasize sounds and images, what likely effects do these differences have on media users?

Most of the questions that engage media researchers and popular observers of the media focus only on one dimension of our media environment: the content of media messages. Typical concerns center on how people (often children) react to what they are exposed to through various media; how institutional, economic, and political factors influence what is and is not conveyed through media; whether media messages accurately reflect various dimensions of reality; how dif-

Adapted from *Communication Theory Today,* edited by David Crowley and David Mitchell, with the permission of the publishers, Stanford University Press, 1994, pp. 50–77. This collection copyright © 1994 Polity Press. Each collection copyright the author. Originating publisher: Polity Press, Cambridge, U.K.

ferent audiences interpret the same content differently; and so on. These are all very significant concerns, but content issues do not exhaust the universe of questions that could, and should, be asked about the media.

A handful of scholars—mostly from fields other than communications, sociology, and psychology—have tried to call attention to the potential influences of communication technologies in addition to and apart from the content they convey. I use the singular "*medium* theory" to describe this research tradition in order to differentiate it from most other "media theory." Medium theory focuses on the particular characteristics of each individual medium or of each particular type of media. Broadly speaking, medium theorists ask: What are the relatively fixed features of each means of communicating and how do these features make the medium physically, psychologically, and socially different from other media and from face-to-face interaction?

Medium theory examines such variables as the senses that are required to attend to the medium, whether the communication is bidirectional or unidirectional, how quickly messages can be disseminated, whether learning how to encode and decode in the medium is difficult or simple, how many people can attend to the same message at the same moment, and so forth. Medium theorists argue that such variables influence the medium's use and its social, political, and psychological impact.

Medium questions are relevant to at least two social levels: the micro, individual-situation level, and the macro, cultural level. On the micro level, medium questions ask how the choice of one medium over another affects a particular situation or interaction (calling someone on the phone versus writing them a letter, for example). On the macro level, medium questions address the ways in which the addition of a new medium to an existing matrix of media may alter social interactions and social structure in general. The most interesting—and most controversial—medium theory deals with the macro level.

The analyses of the medium theorists are often more difficult to test and apply than the results of studies of media content, but they are of significance because they suggest that media are not simply channels for conveying information between two or more environments, but rather shapers of new social environments themselves.

FIRST-GENERATION MEDIUM THEORISTS

The best-known and most controversial medium theorists are two Canadians, Harold Adams Innis and Herbert Marshall McLuhan. Trained as a political economist, Innis adapts the principles of economic monopolies to the study of information monopolies. He argues that one way in which social and political power is wielded is through control over communication media (such as a complex writing system controlled by a special class of priests). Information monopolies can be broken, however, by new media. Innis suggests that the medieval Church's monopoly over religious information, and thereby over salvation, was broken by the printing press. The printing press bypassed the Church's scribes and allowed for the wider

availability of the Bible and other religious texts. The same content, the Bible, therefore, had different effects in different media.

Innis argues that elites can more easily control some media than others. A medium that is in short supply or that requires a special encoding or decoding skill has more potential to support the special interests of elite classes because they have more time and resources to exploit it. On the other hand, a medium that is easily accessible to the average person is more likely to help democratize a culture.

Innis also argues that most media of communication have a "bias" either towards lasting a long time or towards being moved easily across great distances. He claims that the bias of a culture's dominant medium affects the degree of the culture's stability and conservatism as well as the culture's ability to take over and govern a large territory. "Time-biased" media such as stone hieroglyphics, he argues, lead to relatively small, stable societies because stone carvings last a long time and are rarely revised, and their limited mobility makes them poor means of keeping in touch with distant places. In contrast, messages on light, "space-biased" papyrus allowed the Romans to maintain a large empire with a centralized government that delegated authority to distant provinces. But papyrus also led to more social change and greater instability. The Romans conquered and administered vast territories, but then their empire collapsed when they lost their supply of papyrus from Egypt.

In his densely written *Empire and Communications* and *The Bias of Communication,* Innis rewrites human history as the history of communication technologies. His overview begins with the cradle of civilization in Mesopotamia and Egypt and ends with the British empire and the Nazis.

Among the people Innis influenced was a literary scholar, Herbert Marshall McLuhan. Extending aspects of Innis' perspective, McLuhan's work adds the notion of "sensory balance." He analyses each medium as an extension of one or more of the human senses, limbs, or processes. McLuhan suggests that the use of different technologies affects the organization of the human senses and the structure of the culture. He divides history into three major periods: oral, writing/printing, and electronic. Each period, according to McLuhan, is characterized by its own interplay of the senses and therefore by its own forms of thinking and communicating. McLuhan also suggests that each medium requires its own style of behavior, so that an intense performance that works well on the "hot" medium of radio might seem very stiff and wooden on the "cool" medium of television.[1]

Walter Ong, Edmund Carpenter, Tony Schwartz, and Daniel Boorstin have looked at the ways in which electronic media have altered thinking patterns and social organization.[2] Carpenter and Schwartz are generally McLuhanesque in content, method, and style, but they add many fresh insights and examples. Ong and Boorstin present more traditional scholarly analyses that support McLuhan's basic arguments but also go beyond them. Ong describes the similarities and differences between the "primary orality" of preliterate societies and the "secondary orality" that results from the introduction of electronic media into literate societies. He looks at the spiritual, sensory, and psychological significance of the return of "the word," as a spoken event, in an electronic form. Boorstin describes how new media "mass-produce the moment," make experience "repeatable," and join many other recent technological inventions in "leveling times and places." He also compares and contrasts political revolutions with technological revolutions and discusses the impact of new technologies, including electronic media, on our conceptions of history, nationality, and, progress.

THE HISTORY OF CIVILIZATION
FROM A MEDIUM-THEORY PERSPECTIVE

Each of the medium theorists mentioned above covers different territory, takes a different approach, and reaches somewhat different conclusions. Yet when their arguments and analyses are taken together, a surprisingly consistent and clear image of the interaction of media and culture emerges. Broadly speaking, these theorists' works cohere into a shared image of three phases of civilization matched to three major forms of communicating: the move from traditional oral societies to modern print societies (via a transitional scribal phase), to an electronic global culture.

Global Electronic Culture

Ironically, print culture comes to its full power just as the seeds of its destruction are planted. The late nineteenth century sees the drive toward universal literacy, but during the same years the first electronic media begin to be widely used: the telegraph and the telephone herald the future age of radio, television, and beyond. The use of electronic communication, like other media, takes time to develop and ripen before having dramatic, visible impact on social structure in the mid-twentieth century.

Electronic media bring back a key aspect of oral societies: simultaneity of action, perception, and reaction. Sensory experience again becomes a prime form of communicating. Yet the orality of electronic media is far different from the orality of the past. Unlike spoken communication, electronic communication is not subject to the physical limitations of time or space. Electronic messages can be preserved, and they can be experienced simultaneously by large numbers of people regardless of their physical locations.

Electronic media bypass traditional "literary circles," group associations, and national boundaries and give us a new worldview by thrusting us among people who have not read what we have read, have not shared our territory, and may not even speak our language.

While print allows for new ways of sharing *knowledge*, and industrialization enables the wide-scale sharing of *products*, electronic media tend to foster new types of shared *experience*.

As a result of the widespread use of electronic media, there is a greater sense of personal involvement with those who would otherwise be strangers—or enemies. The seemingly direct experience of distant events by average citizens fosters a decline in print-supported notions of delegated authority, weakening the power of political parties, unions, and government bureaucracies. The sharing of experience across nations dilutes the power of the nation state.

While written and printed words emphasize ideas, most electronic media emphasize feeling, appearance, mood. There is a decline in the salience of the straight line—in thinking, in literary narrative, in human-made spaces and organizations. There is a retreat from distant analysis and a dive into emotional and sensory involvement. The major questions are no longer "Is it true?" "Is it false?" Instead we more often ask, "How does it look?" "How does it feel?"

Electronic Conceptions of Group Identity, Socialization, and Hierarchy

The telephone, radio, and television make the boundaries of all social spheres more permeable. One can now "witness" events without being physically present; one can communicate "directly" with others without meeting in the same place. As a result, physical structures no longer fully mold social identity. The walls of the family home, for example, no longer wholly isolate the home from the outside community. Family members at home now have access to others and others have access to them. Now, where one is has less to do with who one is.

We still live in and interact in segregated physical locales. But television and other electronic media have broken the age-old connection between where we are and what we know and experience. Children may still be sheltered at home, but television now takes them across the globe before parents give them permission to cross the street. Through television, women—once isolated in the domestic sphere—have been exposed to places and activities men used to tell them they should know nothing about. And while few of us actually travel to see our leaders in the flesh, television now shows us our politicians close up—stammering and stumbling in living color. Television blurs the line between public and private by bringing the public sphere into the home, and by emphasizing the personal and emotional dimensions of public actions through its intimate close-ups of human faces.

Television has lifted many of the old veils of secrecy between children and adults, men and women, and politicians and average citizens. By blurring "who knows what about whom" and "who knows what compared to whom," television has fostered the blurring of social identities, socialization stages, and ranks of hierarchy. The electronic society is characterized by more adult-like children and more childlike adults; more career-oriented women and more family-oriented men; and by leaders who act more like the "person next door," just as average citizens demand to have more of a say in local, national, and international affairs.

As we move forward, our society also spirals backwards. The middle and upper classes are moving towards the behaviors once associated with the illiterate lower classes. Premarital sex, high illegitimacy rates, "shacking up," and drug use spread upward through all levels of society. As recently as the early 1970s, differences in teenage sexuality could still be predicted accurately on the basis of race, socioeconomic status, religion, and residence. But many of these distinctions have largely disappeared. These changes violate the print industrial society's belief in "Progress." Yet they support the view that we are retreating from "literate forms" and returning to "oral forms" of behavior.

The relatively shared information environment fostered by electronic media does not lead to identical behaviors or attitudes. Far from it. While the world is more homogenized on the macro, societal level, the experience on the micro, personal level is the opposite: the individual's world becomes more heterogeneous,

a world filled with more variety, more choices. Just as traditional differences among people of different ages, sexes, status, families, neighborhoods, and nationalities are blurring, people of the same age, sex, status, families, neighborhoods, and nationalities are becoming less similar to each other.

While the print social order segregated people in their "special spheres" in order to homogenize individuals into interchangeable elements of a larger social machine, the electronic society integrates all groups into a common sphere with a new recognition of the special needs and idiosyncrasies of individuals. What people share is not identical behavior, but a common set of options.

But sharing of options is too weak a bond to hold people together. Metaphors aside, one cannot consider the whole country or world as one's "neighborhood" or "village." Another outcome of the homogenization of information networks, therefore, is the development of many new, more superficial, more shifting groupings that form against the now relatively unified backdrop of common information. People traditionally united and divided into groups that corresponded primarily to social class, ethnicity, race, education type and level, religion, occupation, and neighborhood. But current groupings also develop on the basis of wearing similar clothes, participating in similar sports, listening to the same type of music, or attending the same class.

Nations evolved from feudal systems of local alliances when local membranes and arteries of communication were superseded by national ones. Now, new arteries and membranes are bypassing nations and fostering the rise of a system of quickly changing, neo-feudal ties and alliances on a global scale. Here, too, there is both unification on the macro level and fragmentation on the micro level. Old boundary lines fade in significance as distinct European countries join into a single economic unit and as once taken-for-granted differences between East and West blur. But new boundary lines are created as earlier unions—Soviet, Yugoslav, Czech/Slovak—splinter.

RELATIVE STRENGTHS AND LIMITS OF MEDIUM THEORY

Unlike content research, the "effects" that medium theorists look for are generally difficult to demonstrate through "social-scientific" methods. For the most part, medium theory, especially macro-level medium theory, relies heavily on argument, historical analysis, and large-scale pattern identification. Although the best studies weigh evidence carefully and search for disconfirming as well as confirming examples, most medium theory is not supported by systematic quantitative analyses. For some people, this makes medium theory much more exciting and interesting than traditional content analysis; to others, it makes medium theory frustrating and "unscientific."

Just as traditional content approaches tend to obscure important differences among media, medium approaches tend to overlook the significance of content. Generally, medium research is most helpful when looking at broad structural patterns over a long period of time. But medium theory is not terribly useful in short-term analyses of how to use a communication technology and whether and how to regulate it. A parent who is angry about the violent and advertising-saturated programs his or her children see will find cold comfort in a medium perspective that argues that TV in general weakens the print-supported sphere of innocent childhood and returns us to a world where, to control what children know, parents must either censor their own experience or isolate themselves from their children. Similarly, a woman faced with a daily stream of often demeaning gender images on television may have difficulty focusing on the encouraging medium-theory argument that television, more than print, includes women in many all-male spheres of the culture. Rather than leaving such situations at the medium-theory level, we also need to look at the institutional and economic forces that shape media content. And, if we want to change the current media systems, we need to look at the available political options for doing so.

Medium theorists' focus on the characteristics of media has tended to lead to another weakness. Most medium theory begins with the invention and use of a medium and has tended to ignore the institutions that have important political and economic stakes in the development of some technologies over others. A political and economic system that is interested in stimulating consumption of goods and ideology, for example, is likely to foster the development of unidirectional mass communication technologies such as broadcast radio and television. Other technologies or similar technologies used differently—such as ham radio or interactive community television—may receive much less support and encouragement. Medium theory has also tended to ignore vast cultural differences that mute and alter the development, use, and perception of various communication technologies.

The relative strengths and weaknesses of content and medium perspectives are often most visible when we look to the past. Neither approach in isolation, for example, would have told us the full story of the impact of the spread of printing in the sixteenth and seventeenth centuries. A content/institutional approach probably would have led researchers to conclude that books had two major influences: (1) the fostering of religion (most early books were religious texts); and (2) the further empowering of central monarchical and religious authorities (who controlled most of what was printed). Yet most analysts would now agree that in the long term the printing press fostered the opposite: the weakening of religion with the growth of science and the decline of monarchs with the development of constitutional systems.

With respect to these long-term consequences, medium theory clearly wins. But one cannot discount the implications of content control over those people who actually lived through the initial years of printing. The medium-theory analysis of the long-term tendencies of printing would give little comfort to the family of William Carter, who, after printing a pro-Catholic pamphlet in Protestant-dominated England in 1584, was promptly hanged. Similarly, our current information environment is choked by the way television content is controlled—regardless of the "inherent characteristics" of the medium.

The medium-theory view of the unique features of global electronic media gives us tremendous insight into the power and potential of our new technologies. But the content/institutional perspective allows us to observe how the selective use and foci of the global spotlight intersect with issues of power, ideology, economics, and journalistic conventions. We need to study all these things if we are to understand our media world.

Ultimately, medium theory is most helpful when it is used not to supplant content concerns but to add another dimension to our understanding of the media environment. What is needed is a better integration of medium theory with other perspectives.[3]

NOTES

1. See, e.g., Marshall McLuhan, *The Gutenberg Galaxy: The Making of Typographical Man*. Toronto: University of Toronto

Press, 1962; and McLuhan, *Understanding Media: The Extensions of Man*. New York: McGraw-Hill, 1964.

2. Daniel J. Boorstin, *The Americans: The Democratic Experience*. New York: Random House, 1973, pp. 307–410; Daniel J. Boorstin, *The Republic of Technology: Reflections on Our Future Community*. New York: Harper & Row, 1978; Edmund Carpenter, *Oh, What a Blow That Phantom Gave Me!* New York: Holt, Rinehart & Winston, 1973; Edmund Carpenter and Ken Heyman, *They Became What They Beheld*. New York: Outerbridge & Dienstfrey/Ballantine, 1970; Tony Schwartz, *The Responsive Chord*. Garden City, NY: Anchor, 1974; Tony Schwartz, *Media: The Second God*. Garden City, NY: Anchor, 1983; Walter J. Ong, *The Presence of the Word: Some Prolegomena for Cultural and Religious History*. New Haven, CT: Yale University Press, 1967, pp. 17–110, 259–262,

287–324; Ong, *Interfaces of the Word: Studies in the Evolution of Consciousness and Culture*. Ithaca, NY: Cornell University Press, 1977, pp. 82–91, 305–41; Ong, *Orality and Literacy: The Technologizing of the Word*. Ithaca, NY: Cornell University Press, 1982, pp. 79–81, 135–138.

3. As I have argued elsewhere, content approaches and medium approaches should be combined with at least one other approach, media "grammar" studies, in order to explore the media environment more fully. See Joshua Meyrowitz, "The Questionable Reality of Media." In John Brockman (Ed.), *Ways of Knowing: The Reality Club*. New York: Prentice-Hall, 1991, pp. 141–160; Joshua Meyrowitz, "Images of Media: Hidden Ferment—and Harmony—in the Field." *Journal of Communication, 43* (Summer 1993), pp. 55–66.

RELATED LINKS

- The CIOS/McLuhan Web Site (http://www.cios.org/encyclopedia/mcluhan/m/m.html)
- The Media and Communication Studies Site (http://www.aber.ac.uk/media/Functions/mcs.html)
- Media Ecology Association (http://www.media-ecology.org/)
- *Media Ecology: A Journal of Intersections* (http://raven.ubalt.edu/features/media_ecology)

FOR FURTHER RESEARCH

To find out more about the topics discussed in this reading, use InfoTrac College Edition. Type in the names of key theorists such as: "Harold Innis," "Marshall McLuhan," and "Joshua Meyrowitz." You can access InfoTrac College Edition from the Wadsworth/Thomson Communication Cafe homepage: http://communication.wadsworth.com.

Reading 2-3

Uses of the Mass Media
Werner J. Severin and James W. Tankard, Jr.

EDITOR'S NOTE

Conceptions of the media audience are changing. Increasingly, media consumers are seen as active users of communication technologies rather than passive receivers of content. From a uses and gratifications perspective, they always were. Rather than ask what media do to people, uses and gratifications research turns the question on its head and asks what people do with media. Different people, it turns out, can use the same media message for very different purposes. As this reading by Werner Severin and James Tankard illustrates, uses and gratifications is the area of communication study that most directly acknowledges the active audience.

CONSIDER

1. Conventional wisdom assumes that media audiences are generally passive. What is the evidence that members of the media audience are, in fact, quite active?

2. What specific uses and gratifications do you derive from your media use? Do different uses and gratifications vary according to different media? If so, how and why?

3. Are new communication media such as the Internet providing uses and gratifications that the old media did not, or are they just satisfying user needs in different ways?

Many of us, both in the media and out of the media, tend to think of the media "acting" upon their viewers, listeners, and readers. Subconsciously we often continue to accept the model of the media as a hypodermic needle or a bullet directed to a passive target. But audiences are not always passive; one classic study, titled "The Obstinate Audience," pointed out that the audience is often quite active (Bauer, 1964). Other researchers (Bryant & Street, 1988) echo the statement: "The notion of 'the active communicator' is rapidly achieving preeminent status in the communication discipline" (p. 162). Rubin (1994) has argued that audience activity—the deliberate choice by users of media content in order to satisfy their needs—is the core concept of the *uses and gratifications approach*.

Along similar lines, one group of authors suggested that the term "audience" be replaced with the idea of an active "reader" of mass communication content (Gamson, Croteau, Hoynes, & Sasson, 1992). These authors stress that much mass media content is rich in meaning and open to multiple readings.

The uses and gratifications approach involves a shift of focus from the purposes of the communicator to the purposes of the receiver. It attempts to determine what functions mass communication is serving for audience members. In at least one respect the uses and gratifications approach to the media fits well with the Libertarian theory and John Stuart Mill's notions of human rationality. Both stress the potential of the individual for self-realization.

BEGINNINGS OF THE USES AND GRATIFICATIONS APPROACH

The uses and gratifications approach was first described in an article by Elihu Katz (1959) in which he was reacting to a claim by Bernard Berelson (1959) that the field of communication research appeared to be dead. Katz argued that the field that was dying was the study of mass communication as persuasion. He pointed out that most communication research up to that time had been aimed at investigating the question "What do media do to people?"

Katz suggested that the field might save itself by turning to the question "What do people do with the media?" He cited a few studies of this type that were already done. One of them was, curiously enough, by Berelson (1965). It was his "What 'Missing the Newspaper' Means," a 1949 study conducted by interviewing people about what they missed during a newspaper strike.

During this two-week strike of delivery workers, most readers were forced to find other sources of news, which is what they overwhelmingly said they missed the most. Many read because they felt it was the socially acceptable thing to do, and some felt that the newspaper was indispensable in finding out about world affairs. Many, however, sought escape, relaxation, entertainment, and social prestige. These people recognized that awareness of public affairs was of value in conversations. Some wanted help in their daily lives by reading material about fashion, recipes, weather forecasts, and other useful information.

Another example cited by Katz (1959) was Riley and Riley's study (1951) showing that children well integrated into groups of peers use adventure stories in the media for group games, while children not well integrated use the same communications for fantasizing and daydreaming. This example illustrates a basic aspect of the uses and gratifications approach—different people can use the same mass communication message for very different purposes. Another study (Herzog, 1944) examined the functions radio soap operas fulfilled for regular listeners. Some listeners found emotional release from their own problems. For others, listening provided escape, while a third group sought solutions to their own problems.

USES AND GRATIFICATIONS IN AN ELECTION CAMPAIGN

Blumler and McQuail (1969) used the uses and gratifications approach as the overall research strategy in a study of the 1964 general election in Britain. The central aim of their study was "to find out why people watch or avoid party broadcasts; what uses they wish to make of them; and what their preferences are between alternative ways of presenting politicians on television" (pp. 10–11). Part of their aim was to answer the challenging question posed by earlier election studies that indicated mass media election campaigns had little effect on voters: If voters are not influenced by mass media election programming, why do they follow it at all? Also, the researchers expected that classifying viewers according to their motives for viewing might disclose some previously undetected relationships between attitude change and campaign exposure and, thus, might tell us something about effects after all.

Blumler and McQuail began the task of determining people's motives for watching political broadcasts by using open-ended questions to interview a small sample. On the basis of the responses to these questions, they drew up a list of eight reasons for watching political broadcasts. This list was used in subsequent interviewing with a large sample survey. On the basis of this interviewing, the researchers determined the frequency with which each reason was cited. The three most frequently mentioned reasons reflect a desire for what Blumler and McQuail call "surveillance of the political environment." These reasons, each cited by more than half the respondents, indicate that people used the political broadcasts as a source of information about political affairs. Other data from the survey indicated that one of the specific purposes of this surveillance was to find out about campaign promises and pledges. Only about a third of the respondents chose "to remind me of my party's strong points," a reason that would indicate the political broadcasts were being used for reinforcement of existing attitudes. This casts

some doubt on the indication from some earlier research that people turn to the mass media primarily for reinforcement.

CLASSIFYING INDIVIDUAL NEEDS AND MEDIA USES

A few years later, in a paper that summarized work in the field to that time, Katz, Blumler, and Gurevitch (1974) pointed out that the studies were concerned with: (1) the social and psychological origins of (2) needs, which generate (3) expectations of (4) the mass media or other sources, which lead to (5) differential patterns of media exposure (or engagement in other activities), resulting in (6) need gratifications and (7) other consequences, perhaps mostly unintended ones (p. 20).

They cited two Swedish researchers who in 1968 proposed a "uses and gratifications model" that included the following elements:

1. The audience is conceived of as active, that is, an important part of mass media use is assumed to be goal directed.

2. In the mass communication process much initiative in linking need gratification and media choice lies with the audience member.

3. The media compete with other sources of need satisfaction (pp. 22–23).

The uses and gratifications literature has provided several ways of classifying audience needs and gratifications. Some have spoken of *immediate* and *deferred* gratifications (Schramm, Lyle, & Parker, 1961); others have called them *informational-educational* and *fantasist-escapist* entertainment (Weiss, 1971).

McQuail, Blumler, and Brown (1972), based on their research in England, suggested the following categories:

1. *Diversion*—escape from routine and problems; emotional release.

2. *Personal relationships*—social utility of information in conversations; substitute of the media for companionship.

3. *Personal identity* or *individual psychology*—value reinforcement or reassurance; self-understanding; reality exploration, and so on.

4. *Surveillance*—information about things which might affect one or will help one do or accomplish something.

In 1975, Mark R. Levy (1978b) examined the cross-national applicability of the McQuail, Blumler, and Brown typology with a sample of 240 adults living in Albany County, New York. He found that their four groupings or clusters of items from England were reduced to three substantially overlapping dimensions in the United States. All three clusters contained surveillance items, and the other two clusters were equally mixed. Levy speculated that the differences may be caused by several factors, including the greater availability of television news in the United States, the fact that Americans may rely on it for a greater variety of needs, and the differences [between countries] in the style and presentation of television news.

In a more complete report of the same research Levy (1978a) concluded that besides informing viewers, television news also tests their perceptions and attitudes on "fresh" events and personalities. However, the participation is at a distance with reality "sanitized" and made safe by the celebrity newsreader. Many viewers, he says, "actively" choose between competing newscasts, "arrange their schedules to be near a television set at news time, and pay close, albeit selective, attention to the program" (p. 25).

Katz, Gurevitch, and Haas (1973) see the mass media as a means used by individuals to connect themselves with others (or disconnect). They listed thirty-five needs taken "from the (largely speculative) literature on the social and psychological functions of the mass media" and put them into five categories:

1. *Cognitive needs*—acquiring information, knowledge, and understanding.

2. *Affective needs*—emotional, pleasurable, or aesthetic experience.

3. *Personal integrative needs*—strengthening credibility, confidence, stability, and status.

4. *Social integrative needs*—strengthening contacts with family, friends, and so on.

5. *Tension release needs*—escape and diversion (pp. 166–167).

In a study comparing computers with other means of satisfying needs, Perse and Courtright (1993) identified eleven needs that might be satisfied by mass, interpersonal, or computer-mediated communication:

to relax; to be entertained; to forget about work or other things; to have something to do with friends; to learn things about myself and others; to pass the time away (particularly when bored); to feel excited; to feel less lonely; to satisfy a habit; to let others know I care about their feelings; and, to get someone to do something for me.

NEW TECHNOLOGY AND THE ACTIVE AUDIENCE

Researchers have only begun to study the ways that cable television and other new media offering expanded user choices relate to the user's pursuit of uses and gratifications. A few studies done so far provide clues concerning the impact of new technology on how people use the mass media.

Cable television provides new and diverse opportunities for the audience to become active. With cable, the number of channels can increase from the ten or fewer available with broadcast television to over 100. Cable viewers adopt various strategies to cope with this increased number of choices. One strategy is to narrow one's regular watching to a subset of the available channels that correspond to one's interests. This subset has been called an individual's "channel repertoire" (Heeter & Greenberg, 1985). Viewers differ in their awareness of available cable options. To some extent, viewers appear to be overwhelmed by the number of programs and channels now available. One survey of users of a thirty-five-channel cable system found viewers were able to correctly identify an average of only nine channels by their number or location on the channel selector (Heeter & Greenberg, 1985).

About half the time, cable viewers have a program in mind when they turn on the television set. The other half of the time, programs are chosen at the time of viewing. Viewers use a variety of scanning strategies to decide which programs to watch. These strategies differ in whether they are *automatic* (going from channel to channel in the order that they appear) or *controlled* (going from one selected channel to another on the basis of some desired goal); *elaborated* (involving all or most channels) or *restricted* (involving a limited number of channels); and, *exhaustive* (searching all channels before returning to the best choice) or *terminating* (stopping when the first acceptable option is located). The most active viewers of cable television tend to use controlled, elaborated, and exhaustive searching strategies. They tend to be young adults (Heeter & Greenberg, 1985).

The videocassette recorder also gives the television viewer opportunities to be a more active viewer. It offers the user greater flexibility in terms of times for viewing and it increases the choices of available content. Levy (1980) argues that using a VCR to time-shift programs is a demanding task and that viewers who take the trouble to do it must be among the most active members of the television audience.

Several studies have looked at the uses to which people put computers as communication devices. Perse and Courtright (1993) found in a 1988 survey that computers ranked lowest among twelve types of mediated and interpersonal communication for satisfying communication needs such as relaxation, entertainment, self-awareness, and excitement. The picture changed a few years later, however. Another survey (Perse & Dunn, 1995) looked particularly at the use of computers to communicate with others through information services and the Internet, or what the authors called *computer connectivity.* People using computers for electronic communication were satisfying the following needs: learning, entertainment, social interaction, escapism, passing the time, and out of habit. Use of computers hooked to networks or information services for reasons of passing time or out of habit suggests a ritualistic use, not a use aimed at the gratifications provided by specific content. The authors suggest that this ritualistic use of computers for connectivity might actually lead some users of computer networks or information services to become addicted. [For further discussion about the effects of computer use, see Reading 11-4.]

The uses and gratifications approach may be particularly useful in helping us understand how people use the World Wide Web, e-mail, and other aspects of cyberspace.

RECENT DEVELOPMENTS IN USES AND GRATIFICATIONS RESEARCH

One recent development has been a movement away from conceptualizing audiences as active or passive to treating activity as a variable (Rubin, 1994) That is, sometimes media users are selective and rational in their processing of media messages, but at other times they are using the media for relaxation or escapism. These differences in type and level of audience activity might also have consequences for media effects. For instance, cultivation effects of the type proposed by George Gerbner and his associates might be most likely to occur when audience members are viewing television for diversion or escape.

Another new direction has been to focus on media use for satisfying particular needs. For instance, one possible use of the mass media is to relieve loneliness. Canary and Spitzberg (1993) found evidence supporting this use, but the relationship depended on the extent of loneliness. They found the heaviest use of the media to relieve loneliness was in the *situationally lonely,* or those who were temporarily lonely. They found less use of the media to relieve loneliness in the *chronically lonely,* or those who have felt lonely for a period of years. The explanation seems to be that the chronically lonely attribute their loneliness to internal factors and so do not believe that communication in itself will provide relief.

Film scholars have begun to use an active audience approach to help us understand the viewing of extremely violent motion pictures. Why do people watch films such as *Reservoir Dogs, Pulp Fiction, True Romance, Natural Born Killers, Man Bites Dog, Henry, Portrait of a Serial Killer, Bad Lieutenant,* and *Killing Zoe?* And what kinds of active cognitive processing strategies might they use to make the violence more tolerable? Hill (1997) studied focus groups of viewers of brutal films and found that they responded with *portfolios of interpretation*—particular methods of response that they brought to the viewing experience. Factors within the portfolio included a conceptualization of fictional violence as entertaining, anticipation of upcoming violence and readiness to choose methods of self-censorship, and establishing individual thresholds for acceptable violence.

CONCLUSIONS

The uses and gratifications approach reminds us of one very important point—people use the media for many different purposes. This approach suggests that to a large extent, the user of mass communication is in control. The uses and gratifications approach can serve as a healthy antidote to the emphasis on passive audiences and persuasion that has dominated much earlier research.

The uses and gratifications approach may make a significant contribution to our understanding of media effects as we move further into the digital age and media users are confronted with more and more choices. It is obvious that the media user dealing with cable television with as many as 500 channels or with a videocassette recorder that allows time-shifting, archiving, and repeated viewing of television content is a much more active audience member than the traditional media consumer of a few years ago. The uses and gratifications approach should eventually have some things to say about the users of these new media. After all, it is the single area of theory that has attempted most directly to deal with the active audience.

At the very least, the uses and gratifications approach should direct our attention to the audience of mass communication. Brenda Dervin (1980) recommended that the development of information campaigns should begin with study of the potential information user and the questions that person is attempting to answer in order to make sense of the world. The same lesson probably applies to the producers of much of the content of the mass media. Media planners in many areas should be conducting more research on their potential audiences, and the gratifications those audiences are trying to obtain.

REFERENCES

Bauer, R. A. (1964). The obstinate audience: The influence process from the point of view of social communication. *American Psychologist, 19,* 319–328.

Berelson, B. (1959). The state of communication research. *Public Opinion Quarterly, 23,* 1–6.

Berelson, B. (1965). What "missing the newspaper" means. In W. Schramm (ed.), *The Process and Effects of Mass Communication* (pp. 36–47). Urbana: University of Illinois.

Blumler, J. G., & D. McQuail (1969). *Television in Politics: Its Uses and Influence.* Chicago: University of Chicago Press.

Bryant, J., & Street, R. L., Jr. (1988). From reactivity to activity and action: An evolving concept and Weltanschauung in mass and interpersonal communication. In R. P. Hawkins, J. M. Wiemann, and S. Pingree (eds.), *Advancing Communication Science: Merging Mass and Interpersonal Processes* (pp. 162–190). Newbury Park, CA: Sage.

Canary, D. J., & Spitzberg, B. H. (1993). Loneliness and media gratifications. *Communication Research, 20,* 800–821.

Dervin, B. (1980). Communication gaps and inequities: Moving toward a reconceptualization. In B. Dervin and M. J. Voight (eds.), *Progress in Communication Sciences, Vol. 2* (pp. 73–112). Norwood, NJ: Ablex.

Gamson, W. A., Croteau, D., Hoynes, W., & Sasson, T. (1992). Media images and the social construction of reality. *Annual Review of Sociology, 18,* 373–393.

Heeter, C., & Greenberg, B. (1985). Cable and program choice. In D. Zillmann and J. Bryant (eds.), *Selective Exposure to Communication* (pp. 203–224). Hillsdale, NJ: Lawrence Erlbaum.

Herzog, H. (1944). Motivations and gratifications of daily serial listeners. In W. Schramm (ed.), *The Process and Effects of Mass Communication* (pp. 50–55). Urbana: University of Illinois Press.

Hill, A. (1997). *Shocking Entertainment: Viewer Response to Violent Movies.* Luton, Bedfordshire, England: University of Luton Press.

Katz, E. (1959). Mass communication research and the study of popular culture: An editorial note on a possible future for this journal. *Studies in Public Communication, 2,* 1–6.

Katz, E., Blumler, J. G., & Gurevitch, M. (1974). Utilization of mass communication by the individual. In J. G. Blumler and E. Katz (eds.), *The Uses of Mass Communications: Current Perspectives on Gratifications Research* (pp. 19–32). Beverly Hills, CA: Sage.

Katz, E., Gurevitch, M., & Haas, H. (1973). On the use of the mass media for important things. *American Sociological Review, 38,* 164–181.

Levy, M. R. (1978a). The audience experience with television news. *Journalism Monographs, 55.*

Levy, M. R. (1978b). Television news uses: A cross-national comparison. *Journalism Quarterly, 55,* 334–337.

Levy, M. R. (1980). Home video recorders: A user survey. *Journal of Communication, 30*(4), 23–25.

McQuail, D., Blumler, J. G., & Brown, J. R. (1972). The television audience: A revised perspective. In D. McQuail (ed.), *Sociology of Mass Communications* (pp. 135–165). Harmondsworth, UK: Penguin.

Perse, E. M., & Courtright, J. A. (1993). Normative images of communication media: Mass and interpersonal channels in the new media environment. *Human Communication Research, 19,* 485–503.

Perse, E. M., & Dunn, D. G. (1995, August). *The utility of home computers: Implications of multimedia and connectivity.* Paper presented at the annual meeting of the Association for Education in Journalism and Mass Communication, Communication Theory and Methodology Division, Washington, DC.

Riley, M. W., & Riley, J. W., Jr. (1951). A sociological approach to communications research. *Public Opinion Quarterly, 15,* 445–460.

Rubin, A. M. (1994). Media uses and effects: A uses-and-gratifications perspective. In J. Bryant and D. Zillmann (eds.), *Media Effects: Advances in Theory and Research* (pp. 417–436). Hillsdale, NJ: Lawrence Erlbaum.

Schramm, W., Lyle, J., & Parker, E. B. (1961). *Television in the Lives of Our Children.* Stanford, CA: Stanford University Press.

Weiss, W. (1971). Mass communication. *Annual Review of Psychology, 22,* 309–336.

RELATED LINKS

- Mass Media: Uses and Gratifications (http://www.cultsock.ndirect.co.uk/MUHome/cshtml/media/ugdetail.htm)

- Uses and Gratifications of the Web Among College Students (http://www.ascusc.org/jcmc/vol6/issue1/ebersole.html)

- Why Do People Watch Television? (http://www.aber.ac.uk/media/Documents/short/usegrat.html)

FOR FURTHER RESEARCH

To find out more about the topics discussed in this reading, use InfoTrac College Edition. Type in keywords and subject terms such as: "uses and gratifications," "the active audience," and "need satisfaction (sources of)." You can access InfoTrac College Edition from the Wadsworth/Thomson Communication Cafe homepage: http://communication.wadsworth.com.

Reading 2-4

Mass Communication and Parasocial Interaction: Observations on Intimacy at a Distance

Donald Horton and R. Richard Wohl

EDITOR'S NOTE

Shortly after television became the dominant mass medium in the early 1950s, media observers Donald Horton and Richard Wohl identified one of the defining characteristics of its appeal: the ability of on-air personalities to offer the illusion of a face-to-face relationship with the audience. In this now-classic article, they describe how effective television and radio personalities are able to cultivate intimacy at a distance, a process known as parasocial interaction. *Note the many parallels that can be drawn between the techniques of pioneering talk show host Steve Allen and today's late night hosts (especially David Letterman).*

CONSIDER

1. In what important ways do parasocial relationships differ from real-life relationships? Which media personalities do you like? Which do you dislike?

2.   To facilitate the illusion of intimacy, what performance and social roles must the persona, audience, and supporting cast play?

3.   How do many of the techniques that Horton and Wohl described in 1956 still apply to television shows (especially late night and talk shows) today?

———————————

One of the striking characteristics of the new mass media—radio, television, and the movies—is that they give the illusion of face-to-face relationship with the performer. The conditions of response to the performer are analogous to those in a primary group. The most remote and illustrious men are met *as if* they were in the circle of one's peers; the same is true of a character in a story who comes to life in these media in an especially vivid and arresting way. We propose to call this seeming face-to-face relationship between spectator and performer a *parasocial relationship*.

In television, especially, the image which is presented makes available nuances of appearance and gesture to which ordinary social perception is attentive and to which interaction is cued. Sometimes the "actor"—whether he is playing himself or performing in a fictional role—is seen engaged with others; but often he faces the spectator, uses the mode of direct address, talks as if he were conversing personally and privately. The audience, for its part, responds with something more than mere running observation; it is, as it were, subtly insinuated into the program's action and internal social relationships and, by dint of this kind of staging, is ambiguously transformed into a group which observes and participates in the show by turns. The more the performer seems to adjust his performance to the supposed response of the audience, the more the audience tends to make the response anticipated. This simulacrum of conversational give and take may be called *parasocial interaction*.

Parasocial relations may be governed by little or no sense of obligation, effort, or responsibility on the part of the spectator. He is free to withdraw at any moment. If he remains involved, these parasocial relations provide a framework within which much may be added by fantasy. But these are differences of degree, not of kind, from what may be termed the *ortho-social*. The crucial

difference in experience obviously lies in the lack of effective reciprocity, and this the audience cannot normally conceal from itself. To be sure, the audience is free to choose among the relationships offered, but it cannot create new ones. The interaction, characteristically, is one-sided, nondialectical, controlled by the performer, and not susceptible of mutual development. There are, of course, ways in which the spectators can make their feelings known to the performers and the technicians who design the programs, but these lie outside the parasocial interaction itself. Whoever finds the experience unsatisfying has only the option to withdraw.

What we have said so far forcibly recalls the theatre as an ambiguous meeting ground on which real people play out the roles of fictional characters. For a brief interval, the fictional takes precedence over the actual, as the actor becomes identified with the fictional role in the magic of the theatre. This glamorous confusion of identities is temporary: the worlds of fact and fiction meet only for the moment. And the actor, when he takes his bows at the end of the performance, crosses back over the threshold into the matter-of-fact world.

Radio and television, however—and in what follows we shall speak primarily of television—are hospitable to both these worlds in continuous interplay. They are alternately public platforms and theatres, extending the parasocial relationship now to leading people of the world of affairs, now to fictional characters, sometimes even to puppets anthropomorphically transformed into "personalities," and, finally, to theatrical stars who appear in their capacities as real celebrities. But of particular interest is the creation by these media of a new type of performer: quiz-masters, announcers, "interviewers" in a new "show-business" world—in brief, a special category of "personalities" whose existence is a function of the media themselves. These "personalities," usually, are not prominent in any of the social spheres beyond the media.[1] They exist for their audiences only in the parasocial relation. Lacking an appropriate name for these performers, we shall call them *personae*.

THE ROLE OF THE PERSONA

The persona is the typical and indigenous figure of the social scene presented by radio and television. To say that he is familiar and intimate is to use pale and feeble language for the pervasiveness and closeness with which multitudes feel his presence. The spectacular fact about such personae is that they can claim and achieve an intimacy with what are literally crowds of strangers, and this intimacy, even if it is an imitation and a shadow of what is ordinarily meant by that word, is extremely influential with, and satisfying for, the great numbers who willingly receive it and share in it. They "know" such a persona in somewhat the same way they know their chosen friends: through direct observation and interpretation of his appearance, his gestures and voice, his conversation and conduct in a variety of situations. Indeed, those who make up his audience are invited, by designed informality, to make precisely these evaluations—to consider that they are involved in a face-to-face exchange rather than in passive observation. When the television camera pans down on the performer, the illusion is strong that he is enhancing the presumed intimacy by literally coming closer. But the persona's image, while partial, contrived, and penetrated by illusion, is not fantasy or dream; his performance is an objectively perceptible action in which the viewer is implicated imaginatively, but which he does not imagine.

The persona offers, above all, a continuing relationship. His appearance is a regular and dependable event, to be counted on, planned for, and integrated into the routines of daily life. His devotees "live with him" and share the small episodes of his public life—and to some extent even of his private life away from the show. Indeed, their continued association with him acquires a history, and the accumulation of shared past experiences gives additional meaning to the present performance. This bond is symbolized by allusions that lack meaning for the casual observer and appear occult to the outsider. In time, the devotee—the "fan"—comes to believe that he "knows" the persona more intimately and profoundly than others do; that he "understands" his character and appreciates his values and motives.[2] Such an accumulation of knowledge and intensification of loyalty, however, appears to be a kind of growth without development, for the one-sided nature of the connection precludes a progressive and mutual reformulation of its values and aims.[3]

The persona may be considered by his audience as a friend, counselor, comforter, and model; but, unlike real associates, he has the peculiar virtue of being standardized according to the "formula" for his character and performance which he and his managers have worked out and embodied in an appropriate "production format." Thus his character and pattern of action remain basically unchanged in a world of otherwise disturbing change. The persona is ordinarily predictable, and gives his adherents no unpleasant surprises. In their association with him there are no problems of understandings or empathy too great to be solved. Typically, there are no challenges to a spectator's self—to his ability to take the reciprocal part in the performance that is assigned to him—that cannot be met comfortably.

THE BOND OF INTIMACY

It is an unvarying characteristic of these "personality" programs that the greatest pains are taken by the persona to create an illusion of intimacy. We call it an illusion because the relationship between the persona and any member of his audience is inevitably one-sided, and reciprocity between the two can only be suggested. There are several principal strategies for achieving this illusion of intimacy.

Most characteristic is the attempt of the persona to duplicate the gestures, conversational style, and milieu of an informal face-to-face gathering. This accounts, in great measure, for the casualness with which even the formalities of program scheduling are treated. The spectator is encouraged to gain the impression that what is taking place on the program gains a momentum of its own in the very process of being enacted. Thus Steve Allen is always pointing out to his audience that "we never know what is going to happen on this show." In addition, the persona tries to maintain a flow of small talk which gives the impression that he is responding to and sustaining the contributions of an invisible interlocutor. Dave Garroway, who has mastered this style to perfection, has described how he stumbled on the device in his early days in radio.

Most talk on the radio in those days was formal and usually a little stiff. But I just rambled along, saying whatever came into my mind. I was introspective. I tried to pretend that I was chatting with a friend over a highball late in the evening. . . . Then—and later—I consciously tried to talk to the listener as an individual, to make each listener feel that he knew me and I knew him. It seemed to work pretty well then and later. I know that strangers often stop me on the street today, call me Dave and seem to feel that we are old friends who know all about each other.[4]

In addition to creating an appropriate tone and patter, the persona tries as far as possible to eradicate, or at least to blur, the line which divides him and his show, as a formal performance, from the audience both in the studio and at home. The most usual way of achieving this ambiguity is for the persona to treat his supporting cast as a group of close intimates. Thus all the members of the cast will be addressed by their first names, or by special nicknames, to emphasize intimacy. They very quickly develop, or have imputed to them, stylized character traits which, as members of the supporting cast, they will indulge in and exploit regularly in program after program. The member of the audience, therefore, not only accumulates a historical picture of "the kinds of people they really are," but tends to believe that this fellowship includes him by extension. As a matter of fact, all members of the program who are visible to the audience will be drawn into this by-play to suggest this ramification of intimacy.

Furthermore, the persona may try to step out of the particular format of his show and literally blend with the audience. Most usually, the persona leaves the stage and mingles with the studio audience in a question-and-answer exchange. In some few cases, and particularly on the Steve Allen show, this device has been carried a step further. Thus Allen has managed to blend even with the home audience by the maneuver of training a television camera on the street outside the studio and, in effect, suspending his own show and converting all the world outside into a stage. Allen, his supporting cast, and the audience, both at home and in the studio, watch together what transpires on the street—the persona and his spectators symbolically united as one big audience. In this way, Allen erases for the moment the line which separates persona and spectator.

All these devices are indulged in not only to lure the attention of the audience, and to create the easy impression that there is a kind of participation open to them in the program itself, but also to highlight the chief values stressed in such "personality" shows. These are sociability, easy affability, friendship, and close contact—briefly, all the values associated with free access to and easy participation in pleasant social interaction in primary groups. Because the relationship between persona and audience is one-sided and cannot be developed mutually, very nearly the whole burden of creating a plausible imitation of intimacy is thrown on the persona and on the show of which he is the pivot. If he is successful in initiating an intimacy which his audience can believe in, then the audience may help him maintain it by fan mail and by the various other kinds of support which can be provided indirectly to buttress his actions.

THE ROLE OF THE AUDIENCE

The general outlines of the appropriate audience role are perceived intuitively from familiarity with the common cultural patterns on which the role of the persona is constructed. These roles are chiefly derived from the primary relations of friendship and the family, characterized by intimacy, sympathy, and sociability. The audience is expected to accept the situation defined by the program format as credible, and to concede as "natural" the rules and conventions governing the actions performed and the values realized. It should play the role of the loved one to the persona's lover, the admiring dependent to his father-surrogate; the earnest citizen to his fearless opponent of political evils. It is expected to benefit by his wisdom, reflect on his advice, sympathize with him in his difficulties, forgive his mistakes, buy the products that he recommends, and keep his sponsor informed of the esteem in which he is held.

Other attitudes than compliance in the assigned role are, of course, possible. One may reject, take an analytical stance, perhaps even find a cynical amusement in refusing the offered gambit and playing some other role not implied in the script, or view the proceedings with detached curiosity or hostility. But such attitudes as these are, usually, for the one-time viewer. The faithful audience is one that can accept the gambit offered; and the functions of the program for this audience are served not by the mere perception of it, but by the role-enactment that completes it.

THE COACHING OF AUDIENCE ATTITUDES

Just how the situation should be defined by the audience, what to expect of the persona, what attitudes to take toward him, what to "do" as a participant in the program, is not left entirely to the common experience and intuitions of the audience. Numerous devices are used in a deliberate "coaching of attitudes," to use Kenneth Burke's phrase.[5] The typical program format calls for a studio audience to provide a situation of face-to-face interaction for the persona, and exemplifies to the home audience an enthusiastic and "correct" response. The more interaction occurs, the more clearly is demonstrated the kind of man the persona is, the values to be shared in association with him, and the kind of support to give him. A similar model of appropriate response may be supplied by the professional assistants who, though technically performers, act in a subordinate and deferential reciprocal relation toward the persona. The audience is schooled in correct responses to the persona by a variety of other means as well. Other personae may be invited as guests, for example, who play up to the host in exemplary fashion; or persons drawn from the audience may be maneuvered into fulfilling this function. And, in a more direct and literal fashion, reading excerpts from fan mail may serve the purpose.

Beyond the coaching of specific attitudes toward personae, a general propaganda on their behalf flows from the performers themselves, their press agents, and the mass communication industry. Its major theme is that the performer should be loved and admired. Every attempt possible is made to strengthen the illusion of reciprocity and rapport in order to offset the inherent impersonality of the media themselves. The jargon of show business teems with special terms for the mysterious ingredients of such rapport: ideally, a performer should have "heart," should be "sincere"; his performance should be "real" and "warm." The publicity campaigns built around successful performers continually emphasize the sympathetic image which, it is hoped, the audience is perceiving and developing.

The audience, in its turn, is expected to contribute to the illusion by believing in it, and by rewarding the persona's "sincerity" with "loyalty." The audience is entreated to assume a sense of personal obligation to the performer, to help him in his struggle for "success" if he is "on the way up," or to maintain his success if he has already won it. "Success" in show business is itself a theme which is prominently exploited in this kind of propaganda. It forms the basis of many movies; it appears often in the patter of the leading comedians and in the exhortations of MCs; it dominates the so-called amateur hours and talent shows; and it is subject to frequent comment in interviews with "show people."[6]

VALUES OF THE PARASOCIAL ROLE FOR THE AUDIENCE

In addition to the possibilities we have already mentioned, the media present opportunities for the playing of roles to which the spectator has—or feels he has—a legitimate claim, but for which he finds no opportunity in his social environment. This function of the parasocial then can properly be called compensatory, inasmuch as it provides the socially and psychologically isolated with a chance to enjoy the elixir of sociability. The "personality" program—in contrast to the drama—is especially designed to provide occasion for good-natured joking and teasing, praising and admiring, gossiping and telling anecdotes, in which the values of friendship and intimacy are stressed.

It is typical of the "personality" programs that ordinary people are shown being treated, for the moment, as persons of consequence. In the interviews of nonprofessional contestants, the subject may be praised for having children—whether few or many does not matter; he may be flattered on his youthful appearance; and he is likely to be honored the more—with applause from the studio audience—the longer he has been "successfully" married. There is even applause, and a consequent heightening of ceremony and importance for the person being interviewed, at mention of the town he lives in. In all this, the values realized for the subject are those of a harmonious, successful participation in one's appointed place in the social order. The subject is represented as someone secure in the affections and respect of others, and he probably senses the experience as a gratifying reassurance of social solidarity and self-confidence. For the audience, in the studio and at home, it is a model of appropriate role performance—as husband, wife, mother, as "attractive" middle age, "remarkably youthful" old age, and the like. It is, furthermore, a demonstration of the fundamental generosity and good will of all concerned, including, of course, the commercial sponsor. But unlike a similar exemplification of happy sociability in a play or a novel, the television or radio program is real; that is to say, it is enveloped in the continuing reassurances and gratifications of objective responses. For instance, there may be telephone calls to "outside" contestants, the receipt and acknowledgment of requests from the home audience, and so on. Almost every member of the home audience is left with the comfortable feeling that he too, if he wished, could appropriately take part in this healing ceremony.

EXTREME PARASOCIABILITY

For the great majority of the audience the parasocial is complementary to normal social life. It provides a social milieu in which the everyday assumptions and understandings of primary group interaction and sociability are demonstrated and reaffirmed. The "personality" program, however, is peculiarly favorable to the formation of compensatory attachments by the socially isolated. The persona himself is readily available as an object of love—especially when he succeeds in cultivating the recommended quality of "heart." Nothing could be more reasonable or natural than that people who are isolated and lonely should seek sociability and love wherever they think they can find it. It is only when the parasocial relationship becomes a substitute for autonomous social participation, when it proceeds in absolute defiance of objective reality, that it can be regarded as pathological.

The existence of a marginal segment of the lonely in American society has been recognized by the mass media themselves, and from time to time specially designed offerings have been addressed to this minority. In these programs, the maximum illusion of a personal, intimate relationship has been attempted. They represent the extreme development of the parasocial, appealing to the most isolated, and illustrate, in an exaggerated way, the principles we believe to apply to a whole range of "personality" programs. The programs which fall in this extreme category promise not only escape from an unsatisfactory and drab reality, but try to prop up the sagging self-esteem of their unhappy audience by the most blatant reassurances. Evidently on the presumption that the maximum of loneliness is the lack of a sexual partner, these programs tend to be addressed to one sex or the other, and to endow the persona with an erotic suggestiveness.

Such seems to have been the purpose and import of *The Lonesome Gal,* a short radio program which achieved such popularity in 1951 that it was broadcast in ninety different cities. Within a relatively short time, the program spread from Hollywood, where it had originated, across the country to New York, where it was heard each evening at 11:15.[7]

The outline of the program was simplicity itself. After a preliminary flourish of music, and an identifying announcement, the main and only character was ushered into the presence of the audience. She was exactly as represented, apparently a lonesome girl, but without a name or a history. Her entire performance consisted of an unbroken monologue unembarrassed by plot, climax, or denouement. On the continuum of parasocial action, this is the very opposite of self-contained drama; it is, in fact, nothing but the reciprocal of the spectator's own parasocial role. The Lonesome Gal simply spoke in a throaty, unctuous voice whose suggestive sexiness belied the seeming modesty of her words.[8]

From the first, the Lonesome Gal took a strongly intimate line, almost as if she were addressing a lover in the utter privacy of some hidden rendezvous:

> Darling, you look so tired, and a little put out about something this evening. . . . You are worried, I feel it. Lover, you need rest . . . rest and someone who understands you. Come, lie down on the couch, relax, I want to stroke your hair gently. . . . I am with you now, always with you. You are never alone, you must never forget that you mean everything to me, that I live only for you, your Lonesome Gal.

At some time in the course of each program, the Lonesome Gal specifically assured her listeners that these endearments were not being addressed to the hale and handsome, the clever and the well poised, but to the shy, the withdrawn—the lonely men who had always dreamed, in their inmost reveries, of finding a lonesome girl to comfort them.

The Lonesome Gal was inundated with thousands of letters tendering proposals of marriage, the writers respectfully assuring her that she was indeed the woman for whom they had been vainly searching all their lives.

As a character in a radio program, the Lonesome Gal had certain advantages in the cultivation of parasocial attachments over television offerings of a similar tenor. She was literally an unseen presence, and each of her listeners could, in his mind's eye, picture her as his fancy dictated. She could, by an act of the imagination, be almost any age or any size, have any background.

The new mass media are obviously distinguished by their ability to confront a member of the audience with an apparently intimate, face-to-face association with a performer. Nowhere does this feature of their technological resources seem more forcefully or more directly displayed than in the "personality" program. In these programs a new kind of performer, the persona, is featured whose main attribute seems to be his ability to cultivate and maintain this suggested intimacy. As he appears before his audience, in program after program, he carries on recurrent social transactions with his adherents; he sustains what we have called parasocial interaction. These adherents, as members of his audience, play a psychologically active role which, under some conditions, but by no means invariably, passes over into the more formal, overt, and expressive activities of fan behavior.

As an implicit response to the performance of the persona, this parasocial interaction is guided and to some extent controlled by him. The chief basis of this guidance and control, however, lies in the imputation to the spectator of a kind of role complementary to that of the persona himself. This imputed complementary role is social in character, and is some variant of the role or roles normally played in the spectator's primary social groups. It is defined, demonstrated, and inculcated by numerous devices of radio and television showmanship. When it has been learned, the persona is assured that the entire transaction between himself and the audience—of which his performance is only one phase—is being properly completed by the unseen audience.

Seen from this standpoint, it seems to follow that there is no such discontinuity between everyday and parasocial experience as is suggested by the common practice, among observers of these media, of using the analogy of fantasy or dream in the interpretation of programs which are essentially dramatic in character. The relationship of the devotee to the persona is, we suggest, experienced as of the same order as, and related to, the network of actual social relations. This, we believe, is even more the case when the persona becomes a common object to the members of the primary groups in which the spectator carries on his everyday life. As a matter of fact, it seems profitable to consider the interaction with the persona as a phase of the role-enactments of the spectator's daily life.

In this connection, it is relevant to remark that there is a tradition—now of relatively long standing—that spectators, whether at sports events or television programs, are relatively passive. This assertion enjoys the status of an accredited hypothesis, but it is, after all, no more than a hypothesis. If it is taken literally and uncritically, it may divert the student's attention from what is actually transpiring in the audience. We believe that some such mode of analysis as we suggest here attunes the student of the mass media to hints *within the program itself* of cues to, and demands being made on, the audience for particular responses. From such an analytical vantage point the field of observation, so to speak, is widened and the observer is able to see more that is relevant to the exchange between performer and audience.

In essence, therefore, we would like to expand and capitalize on the truism that the persona and the "personality" programs are part of the lives of millions of people, by asking how both are assimilated, and by trying to discover what effects these responses have on the attitudes and actions of the audiences who are so devoted to and absorbed in this side of American culture.

NOTES

1. They may move out into positions of leadership in the world at large as they become famous and influential. Frank Sinatra, for example, has become known as a "youth leader." Conversely, figures from the political world, to choose another example, may become media "personalities" when they appear regularly. Fiorello LaGuardia, the late Mayor of New York, is one such case.

2. Merton's discussion of the attitude toward [radio personality] Kate Smith of her adherents exemplifies, with much circumstantial detail, what we have said above. See Robert K. Merton, Marjorie Fiske, and Alberta Curtis, *Mass Persuasion: The Social Psychology of a War Bond Drive.* New York: Harper, 1946; especially Chapter 6.

3. There does remain the possibility that over the course of his professional life the persona, responding to influences from his audience, may develop new conceptions of himself and his role.

4. Dave Garroway as told to Joe Alex Morris, "I Lead a Goofy Life," *The Saturday Evening Post*, February 11, 1956, p. 62.

5. Kenneth Burke, *Attitudes Toward History, Vol. 1.* New York: New Republic, 1937, p. 104.

6. The "loyalty" which is demanded of the audience is not necessarily passive or confined only to patronizing the per-

sona's performance. Its active demonstration is called for in charity appeals, "marathons," and "telethons"; and, of course, it is expected to be freely transferable to the products advertised by the performer. Its most active form is represented by the organization of fan clubs with programs of activities and membership obligations, which give a continuing testimony of loyalty.

7. This program apparently evoked no very great amount of comment or criticism in the American press, and we are in-

debted to an article in a German illustrated weekly for details about the show, and for the verbatim quotations from the Lonesome Gal's monologue which we have retranslated into English. See "Ich bin bei dir, Liebling . . . ," *Weltbild* (Munich), March 1, 1952, p. 12.

8. This is in piquant contrast to the popular singers, the modesty of whose voice and mien is often belied by the sexiness of the words in the songs they sing.

RELATED LINKS

- Oprah.com (http://www.oprah.com)
- Parasocial Interaction (http://www.indiana.edu/~hotmedia/psi)
- Steve Allen Online! (http://www.steveallenonline.com/)
- The Late Show with David Letterman (http://www.cbs.com/latenight/lateshow)
- The Rosie O'Donnell Show (http://rosieo.warnerbros.com/pages/rosieo/home.jsp)
- The Tonight Show with Jay Leno (http://nbctv.nbci.com/tonightshow)

FOR FURTHER RESEARCH

To find out more about the topics discussed in this reading, use InfoTrac College Edition. Type in keywords and subject terms such as: "parasocial interaction," "illusion of intimacy," and "media persona." You can access InfoTrac College Edition from the Wadsworth/Thomson Communication Cafe homepage: http://communication.wadsworth.com.

SECTION II

Convergence and Concentration in the Media Industries

This section surveys the different ways in which the media and telecommunications industries are coping with digital convergence and corporate concentration. The readings in Chapter 3 address the print world's struggle to "get the Net," beginning with a merciless salvo from *Wired* aimed at the moribund newspaper industry. The contrasting styles and relative success of the leading online magazines, *Slate* and *Salon,* are examined in a reading that highlights the gains made by the tradition-bound journalism profession in recent years. Chapter 4 explores the impact of digital technology on the radio, television, and film industries. Thanks to streaming media, radio is experiencing a rebirth on the Web, resulting in a broader range of channel choice and content diversity for online listeners. In television and filmmaking, new programming formats, recording technologies, and editing software are revolutionizing the production process, making it faster, easier, and less costly to put together a professional-quality production. On the consumer side of the equation, high-definition television, or HDTV, promises to measurably enhance the viewing experience and transform the way we relate to the screen. In the telecommunications industry, readings in Chapter 5 report, mergers and spin-offs continue to redefine and restructure the future of broadband media, bringing together unlikely industry partners—phone companies, cable networks, entertainment conglomerates, and Internet service providers—and raising questions about the desirability of corporate concentration. Advertising and public relations, the classic media support fields, are also undergoing radical transformation, owing, among other reasons, to the precision accountability of the Web, as addressed by the readings in Chapter 6. Rather than spelling the end of old media, digital convergence signals a new era of media cross-fertilization. Concerns remain, however, that the recent wave of media mergers may stifle innovation and hinder access to the content in cyberspace, issues raised by the readings in Chapter 7.

3

Print Media

Reading 3-1

Online or Not, Newspapers Suck
Jon Katz

EDITOR'S NOTE

For media writer Jon Katz, newspapers are perhaps the most staid and unchanging of all the traditional media. Relentlessly one-way, noninteractive, and smug, papers, Katz asserts, are "the biggest and saddest losers in the Information Revolution." In this provocative rant against media conventionalism from Wired *magazine, Katz asks how any industry that regularly pulls* Doonesbury *comic strips for being too controversial can possibly hope to survive online. Though leveled in 1994 during the World Wide Web's infancy, many of the criticisms this article raises remain valid today. Katz's observations thus serve as a benchmark against which to measure the newspaper industry's online progress.*

CONSIDER

1. To what extent, and in what ways, do online newspapers provide an alternative to their print counterparts?

2. In what sense do online newspapers offer the illusion of interactivity but not the reality? Where is real editorial power located, according to Katz?

3. How has the explosion of new media actually made newspapers and journalists more vital, necessary, and useful than ever?

For millions of Americans, especially young ones, newspapers have never played a significant role. That's why it's sometimes hard to know, recall, or even imagine that there's almost no media experience sweeter—at the right time, in the right place, with the proper accessories—than poring over a good newspaper. In the quiet morning, with a cup of coffee—so long as you haven't yet turned on the TV, listened to the radio, or checked in online—it's as comfortable and personal as information gets.

Delivered to your door daily, newspapers are silent, highly portable, require neither power source nor arcane commands, and don't crash or get infected. They can be stored for days at no cost and consumed over time in small, digestible quantities. They can also be used to line trashcans and train pets. They're recyclable. At their best, they have been fearless, informative, and heroic—exposing corrupt practices and crooked politicians, delving into health care and other complex issues. They can be deliciously quirky, useful, even provocative—filled with idiosyncratic issues and voices.

They're under siege, of course. Newspapers have been foundering for decades, their readers aging, their revenues declining, their circulation sinking, their sense of mission fragmented in a world where the fate of presidents is slugged out on MTV, *Donahue,* and *Larry King Live.* Television has stolen much of their news, magazines their advertisers and best writers, cable many of their younger readers. And the digital revolution has pushed them still closer to the wall, unleashing a vigorous flow of news, commentary, and commerce to millions and millions of people. CNN and [the Web] ensure that newspapers are stale before they're tossed on the trucks. With the possible exception of the comics, everything a newspaper used to do somebody else is doing more quickly, more attractively, more efficiently, and in a more interesting and unfettered way.

The newspaper industry has never liked change, viewing it rather the way a Temperance Lady viewed speakeasies. For a long time, papers have demonstrated an unerring instinct for making the wrong move at the wrong time. At heart, newspapers are reluctant to change because of their ingrained belief that they are the superior, serious, worthwhile medium, while things electronic are trivial or faddish.

Over the past decade, newspapers have made almost every kind of radical move except transforming themselves. It's as if they've considered every possible option but the most urgent—change.

That makes newspapers the biggest and saddest losers in the Information Revolution. With the possible exception of network-TV newscasts, papers are now our least hip medium, relentlessly one-way, noninteractive, and smug. We all know the formula: Plopped on the doorstep once a day. Breaking national and international news up front, local news next, stories broken up and jumping inside. Grainy, mostly black-and-white photos. Culture, features, TV, listings, recipes, and advice columns in the back. Stentorian voices on the editorial page. Take it or leave it, and if you don't like it, write us a letter.

But the growing millions of people sending and receiving news and their opinions of it to one another via modem is another story. Digital news differs radically from other media. No other medium has ever given individual people such an engaged role in the movement of information and opinion or such a proprietary interest in the medium itself. The computer news culture fosters a sense of kinship, ownership, and participation that has never existed in commercial media.

Meanwhile, after years of newspapers' ignoring computers or relegating them to the far corners of the business sections, you can't pick up a paper any longer without reading the words *e-mail, Internet,* or *cyberspace.* The media, burned so often by techno-hype, are belatedly realizing that this time it's not all fantasy.

You can practically hear them shrieking "OK, we get it!" So-called electronic publishing is the hottest thing in newspaper publishing since cold type, and one of the last great hopes for a reeling industry that is trying to preserve a vital role for itself.

One of the best arenas in which to watch the newspaper and computer cultures collide is America Online, where much of the nation's elite traditional media are scrambling to catch the train. There, side by side, two profoundly different information structures clunk into one another, new next to old, diverse next to homogeneous, Washington pundits one icon away from Smashing Pumpkins fans, the powerful few alongside the voluble and suddenly empowered many.

"Online or Not, Newspapers Suck," by Jon Katz. From *Wired,* September 1994, pp. 50–58. Copyright © 1994 by Jon Katz. Reprinted with permission of the author.

The online explosion has caught newspaper publishers' attention, and what's left of their imaginations, blasting them off their self-important butts. This is where they are making their stand, haunted by the ghosts of cathode-ray tubes past. This time, publishers say, they're not going to be left behind, cut out of all those profits, isolated from young markets, watching their influence erode.

But watching sober, proper newspapers online stirs only one image: that of Lawrence Welk trying to dance at a rap concert. Online newspapers are unnatural, even silly. There's too much baggage to carry, too much history to get past.

The *New York Times* is partly hamstrung by the fact that it can't offer most of its past articles and reviews, having sold its electronic archival rights to Mead Data Central's Nexis a decade ago, when most of the media thought computer users were credit card thieves and national security risks.

So far, at least, online papers don't work commercially or conceptually. With few exceptions they seem to be just what they are, expensive hedges against onrushing technology with little rationale of their own. They take away what's best about reading a paper and don't offer what's best about being online.

Online papers pretend to be seeking and absorbing feedback, but actually offer the illusion of interactivity without the reality, the pretense of democratic discussion without yielding a drop of power. The papers seem careful about reading and responding to their e-mail, but in the same pro forma way they thank readers for writing letters. They dangle the notion that they are now really listening, but that's mostly just a tease—the media equivalent of the politically correct pose. The real power, as always, lies not in online exchanges but in daily story conferences among a few editors who don't read e-mail. In fact, the familiar newspaper model lurks behind every icon: You can write us as many letters as you want, in a faster way than before, and we'll read them. But we're still going to decide what's important, and then we'll tell you. And we'll do it in a format that's even less pleasant, portable, and convenient than the paper itself.

To read the *San Jose Mercury News* or any other newspaper at home or work, you have only to spread it over your desk and read what catches your eye or intrigues you.

Reading a newspaper online is difficult, cumbersome, and time consuming. There is none of the feel of scanning a story, turning pages for more, skipping easily back to the beginning. The impact of seeing a picture, headline, caption, and some text in one sweep is completely lost. With news glimpsed only in fragments and short scrolls, the sense of what the paper thinks is important disappears. You can't look at a paper's front page to absorb some sense, however limited, of the shape your town, city, or world is in. You can't skip through a review for the paragraph that tells you whether to see the movie or not or skim through movie listings for show times. Much of what still works about a paper—convenience, visual freedom, a sense of priorities, a personal experience—is gone. Online, papers throw away what makes them special.

The online culture is as different as it's possible to be from the print press tradition. Outspoken and informal, it is continuously available, not delivered once a day. It is so diverse as to be undefinable, a home to scientists, hackers, pet owners, quilters, swingers, teenagers, and homemakers. Online, there is the sense of perpetual conflict, discovery, sudden friendship, occasional hostility, great intensity, lots of business being transacted, the feeling of clacking through your own world while whole unseen galaxies rush above and below you. You log on never quite knowing what discussion or argument you'll be drawn into, which new people you'll meet, or who from your past will mystically appear. The experience bears no relationship to reading a newspaper. In fact, one of the major selling points of a paper is its organizational and informational predictability. The weather, sports, and TV listings are always in the same place, or ought to be.

It doesn't have to work this way. These two media can coexist and complement one another.

To read *Time* online and offline is to sense that the new information culture is actually changing the magazine. Rather than simply shoveling *Time* online, the magazine's editors and writers have gone to considerable lengths and expense to understand and adapt to it.

For one thing, *Time* now covers new media better than its competitors. Not too long ago, it wouldn't have approved much of the freewheeling online communication style, complete with flaming, dirty words, and diverse opinions. Once it would have published a cover story just like *Newsweek*'s silly "Men, Women and Computers" (in the May 16, 1994, issue), which stereotyped computer men as macho dirtballs and women as nurturing, delicate cybermoms. Now it wouldn't.

Time Online's issues boards have become vigorous and democratic civic forums, with thousands of subscribers slugging it out around the clock about everything from Clinton's sex life to gays in the military. Anyone interested in journalistic accountability should drop by to watch *Time*'s once-Olympian editors receive electronic drubbings from irate members of the National Rifle Association, retirees furious about coverage of entitlement programs, devout Catholics defending the Vatican's latest pronouncement.

One such thumping occurred following publication of the June 27, 1994, issue of the magazine. *Time*'s Managing Editor Jim Gaines went online to face a record number of visitors—*Time* officials estimated the number to be at least 70,000—including many outraged readers demanding to know why the magazine had altered a photograph of O. J. Simpson to make the picture appear darker than it was. The notion that a *Time* managing editor would face so many readers live is the media equivalent of cows learning how to fly.

From the start, *Time* seemed to grasp that online communications required a different ethic than a Letters to the Editor column, perhaps partly because *Time* had hired as consulting editor Tom Mandel, a professional futurist and a longtime member of the WELL, and chosen Senior Writer Philip Elmer-DeWitt, who covers the digital world, as its editorial guiding force. The pair seems to have brought with them the right combination of the values and traditions of both journalism and the Net. Mandel, whose own online style is to be ubiquitous and sometimes aggressive, understands that real interactivity transcends Feedback icons.

But the more telling impact of *Time*'s online experiment is the intense, sometimes furious back-and-forth between *Time Online* subscribers and *Time*'s writers and editors. Discussions in *Time Online* have also influenced stories in the magazine, Mandel said.

Time has gained only a handful of new subscribers from its online project and doesn't expect many. But it has gained more than a foothold online: it has become a part of the culture.

Newspapers, by contrast, seem to have missed the real lesson of the past half-century. Their mistake wasn't that they didn't invest in television or put their stories on screens, it was that they refused to make any of the changes that the rise of television should have mandated.

TV meant that breaking news could be reported quickly, colorfully, and—eventually—live. Live TV supplanted the historic function of the journalist. Cable TV meant a whole new medium with the time and room to present breaking and political news, entertainment news, live trial coverage. Computers meant that millions of people could flash the news to one another. All of these changes have given newspapers a diminished role in the presentation of news.

But the explosion of new media needn't eliminate the traditional journalistic print function. Quite the opposite, it could make newspapers more vital, necessary, and useful than ever.

The more complicated the gadgets become, and the more new media mushroom, the more we need what newspapers have always been—gatekeepers and wellheads, discussion leaders on politics and public policy questions, distributors of horoscopes, sports listings, and comics. They're not going to have a monopoly any more, and they don't get to tell us only what they think we should know. They'll have to chuck the stern schoolmarm's voice. They'll also have to really listen to us, not just pretend.

If newspapers could do with more interactivity, they might not need as much as bulletin boards offer. Everybody can't be talking to everyone at the same time. We need distinct voices standing back, offering us detached versions of the best truth they can find in the most factual way. We need fair-minded if less arrogant fact-gatherers and opinion makers to help us sort through the political, social, and cultural issues we care about but need help in comprehending.

We need something very close to what a good newspaper is but with a different ideology and ethic: a medium that gives its consumers nearly as much power as its reporters and editors have. A medium that isn't afraid of unfettered discussions, intense passions, and unashamed opinion. A medium that recognizes we've already heard the headlines a dozen times.

Online publishing seems to reinforce the idea that newspapers should look to the past, not the future, for help in figuring out how to respond to all this competition and pressure. What newspapers need to change isn't the delivery technology—it's the content of their papers. Even if they get all interactive and smart about going online, it's a marginal solution to a fundamental problem, and a diversion of resources that could be put to much wiser use.

The *San Francisco Chronicle* is never going to beat the WELL at its own game anymore than the WELL could become a successful print daily, nor should it.

Online services provide breaking news, are intrinsically interactive, and know much more about computers and technology.

Newspapers might begin to think about reversing their long-standing priorities, recognizing that everyone with electricity has access to more breaking news than they provide, faster than they provide it. They should, at last, accept that there is little of significance they get to tell us for the first time. They should stop hiding that fact and begin taking advantage of it. What they can do is explain news, analyze it, dig into the details and opinions, capture people and stories in vivid writing—all in greater depth than other media. They should get about the business of doing so.

Newspapers remain one of the few elements of modern media that refuse to bid for talent. As a result, they've long ceded many of their best writers and editors to publishing or magazines. Newspapers now have little original or distinctive writing: when newspaper reporters do have something extraordinary to say, they are often forced to go outside their medium to give their stories the treatment they merit and to gain full impact. Papers ought to reclaim this territory, seeking out provocative writers, giving them freedom, paying to keep them.

And the newspaper industry's relentless alienation of the young is the corporate equivalent of a scandal. Big city papers have almost no young staffers, now that it takes years to work through elaborate hiring structures and rigorous trials to get to urban metro desks. In addition, papers have trashed almost every significant part of youth culture for decades—from rock to radio to TV to rap and video games—portraying each as stupid, violence-inducing, and dangerous. Hackers were mostly portrayed as weirdos while newspapers dozed through the arrival of another new medium that the nerds were piecing together in basements and bedrooms.

Newspaper publishers then hold regular conventions at which they wring their hands in bewilderment at the loss of younger readers and despair even more at those lost advertising dollars. Kids' tastes are no great mystery, not to cable TV or to a whole new generation of magazines. The young are busy and mobile. They like their media with attitude and lots of point of view. They especially like media that is full of informality and self-mockery—the much reviled *Beavis & Butt-Head* being a classic example. Interactive media, from Nintendo to computer games to call-in talk shows—even

channel zapping—is not a futuristic notion but the only kind of media they know, the kind they patronize and expect.

There's more.

Real investigative reporting, something few other media can do as effectively as newspapers, has almost vanished from mainstream media. Op-ed pages are almost universally soporific. Papers are still astonishingly primitive graphically, many still running black-and-white photographs 24 hours after we saw the real events live and in color. Papers have clearly lost touch with much of the public on issues as diverse as race, crime, and political coverage. A Gallup Poll found that journalism ranks far below banks and cops in terms of public confidence—and that the number of people who rate journalists highly in terms of ethics and honesty has dropped from an already dismal 31 percent in 1985 to 22 percent in 1993.

The institutions of journalism seem in desperate need of some mechanism for reconnecting with an alienated public, and they needn't transform themselves into online publications to do it. An e-mail address on every reporter's stories would help. And gain journalists countless news sources as well.

If newspapers are going to invest heavily in anything, perhaps it ought to be in younger, more talented, more diverse staffs. The newspaper industry fails to take into account the dreary toll corporatization and chain ownership—the great fears of online users have taken on newspapers' voice, vibrancy, and relevance. Founded by hell-raisers, papers too often have been cautious, tepid, and pompous. A century ago newspapers were markedly more opinionated, fractious, and provocative than the corporate chain–produced dailies of today. Newspapers are drunk on information highway coverage and gee-whiz stories about the Internet, and their readers have to be overdosing.

There's more to come.

Roger Fidler, director of new media development for Knight-Ridder, told the Newspapers and Telecommunications Opportunities conference last year that he's working on yet another futuristic fantasy: an electronic publication combining the traditional look of a paper with full-motion, full-color video and sound on a portable notebook–sized display. Newspapers somehow never seem at home with techno-hype or fantasies. It's not in their history or tradition, not a natural part of their culture. They have always been at their finest rooting out, shaping, and helping us define the great issues of the day. And writing about and mirroring our lives closer to home.

Maybe Fidler's tablet will work and help papers finally catch up. But it's hard to see why we need it or why Knight-Ridder wouldn't be better off hiring a couple of hundred bright young reporters instead. The answers to newspapers' problems might be much closer to home and much simpler.

"People have not stopped reading newspapers because of the latest high-tech gadgets," said Peter Thieriot, president of The Chronicle Publishing Company's newspaper division, last year. "People have stopped reading newspapers because newspapers became less relevant."

 RELATED LINKS

- *The Mercury News* (http://www0.mercurycenter.com)
- *The New York Times* on the Web (http://www.nytimes.com)
- *San Francisco Chronicle* (http://www.sfgate.com/chronicle)
- Newsweek.MSNBC.com (http://www.msnbc.com/news/NW-front_Front.asp)
- Time.com (http://www.time.com/time)

 FOR FURTHER RESEARCH

To find out more about the topics discussed in this reading, use InfoTrac College Edition. Type in keywords and subject terms such as "electronic journalism," "online newspapers," and "reader interaction." You can access InfoTrac College Edition from the Wadsworth/Thomson Communication Cafe homepage: http://communication.wadsworth.com.

Reading 3-2

Net Gain: Journalism's Challenges in an Interactive Age
J. D. Lasica

EDITOR'S NOTE

The original preface to this series of articles, which served as a wake-up call to the profession, said it aptly: A great many Internet users consider old media's practice of top-down, father-knows-best journalism to be clunky, obsolete, and irrelevant to their lives. While demanding accuracy, fairness, and other timeless journalistic values, digital news junkies also want to engage in a dialogue about the news. Perhaps journalists need to trade in their traditional gatekeeper role and instead make readers partners in the news process.

CONSIDER

1. What will be the role of journalists when anyone with a computer and an Internet connection can lay claim to being a reporter, an editor, and a publisher?

2. Will professional journalists even be needed in an era when people can get their news "unfiltered" by the editorial process?

3. What about the audience? Given the decline of traditional editorial gatekeeping, do news consumers now have the responsibility to be smarter in their search for information?

Michael Crichton stood before a lunchtime crowd at a National Press Club banquet in April 1993 and delivered a simple message to the movers and shakers of journalism: Change your news culture, or become fossils. Adapt to the new digital realities, or become museum relics.

The author of *Jurassic Park* called upon news organizations to reinvent themselves, to abandon sensationalistic "junk-food journalism" in favor of a sensitive, informed, responsive approach that empowers the reader and removes the artificial filters that distort or trivialize the news.

He issued a warning: "To my mind, it is likely that what we now understand as the mass media will be gone within 10 years—vanished, without a trace."

Since that day, a lot of bits have passed under the virtual bridge. Consider:

The Internet has exploded in popularity, attracting an estimated [175] million users in North America, many of whom spend every free moment cruising the World Wide Web.

Almost overnight, new breeds of information-providers—from niche-news purveyors, like AT&T and C|NET: The Computer Network, to more broad-based efforts from competitors like Microsoft—have jumped into the news pool, siphoning off subscribers, advertisers, and employees from Old Media.

In response to that impending threat, newspapers have stampeded onto the Web. The number of online newspapers has soared from a handful to over 1,300 [by 1996; as of December 2000 there were 3,400 online newspapers in the United States and 2,000 internationally] according to AJR/NewsLink.

So does Crichton approve of the news media's efforts to jump into the electronic frontier? "I think the major media are more out of touch than ever. And doing a worse job than ever. And receiving more public disdain than ever," he said in an e-mail interview.

It's a conclusion many Americans would seem to endorse, according to public opinion polls. Slamming

the media is a sport that's particularly popular in many quadrants of cyberspace.

On the Net, the level of discourse fluctuates wildly, from the thoughtful discussions on the WELL (an electronic conferencing service based in Sausalito, California) to the electronic food fights of Usenet. But a common theme is that Old Media's practice of top-down, father-knows-best journalism is tired, clunky, and obsolete.

"A tremendous power shift is under way, and it's about our ability to connect with each other in new ways," Internet pioneer and author Howard Rheingold said in a telephone interview. "A personal computer plugged into a telephone creates a new communication medium, with unique properties and powers. The fact that you don't have to own a newspaper or TV station to broadcast what you think to anyone anywhere in the world is a significant political shift.

"The day the *New York Times* tells us 'all the news that's fit to print' is over. Its era of dominance has passed because the world changed."

What remains uncertain is what this new world heralds. While there have been entire forests of newsprint cleared for articles written about the new technologies, there has been scant attention paid to the question of how the new media are transforming the message.

UNFILTERED NEWS: ONE APPROACH

The old joke in newsrooms was that "MTV News" is an oxymoron. But the joke's not so funny anymore now that many young people get their news from non-traditional sources—including MTV—rather than from their local paper or TV newscast.

MTV's secret? It doesn't talk down to the young. It doesn't dismiss their interests as unimportant. It presents information in an eye-catching way. And recently it has begun to let its viewers participate in the news.

A few summers ago MTV ran promos touting its new first-person news program, news told through the lens of a participant in the story. The network was deluged with 12,000 calls.

Steven Rosenbaum, the creator of *MTV News Unfiltered,* says: "Part of what's changing in society is this

"Net Gain: Journalism's Challenges in an Interactive Age," by J. D. Lasica. From *American Journalism Review,* November 1996, pp. 20–33. Copyright © 1996 American Journalism Review. Reprinted with permission.

top-down model where the media decide what's important and spoon-feed it to a docile, accepting public. That's becoming obsolete, and a lot of people in journalism find that threatening. But all that's really happening is we're allowing the audience to participate in the news. That doesn't make us any less important, it just changes our role."

Rosenbaum's staff of story coordinators sorts through viewers' phone calls, about 2,500 a week. They green-light forty of the most promising subjects, help focus the story with each caller, then send out forty camcorders so viewers can produce their own stories in the field. From that pool, the producers pick six to eight segments per show to air.

Rosenbaum admits the show's title shouldn't be taken literally. "We have a half hour. Call it what you will—a funnel, a strainer—there is a selection process. But all the segments chosen are important, insightful stories that would never find a place in the conventional news media."

The show, which runs once a month, is rough and raw but real. It has won critical praise and "fantastic" viewer response, Rosenbaum says.

He recalls one segment in which a teenage girl proposed a story about a friend's suicide. "One of our producers wanted to know why this kid killed himself. Well, that's not what the girl wanted to do. It would have been very easy for us to use our expertise as journalists as a cudgel to say, 'You're not getting the story right, Missy.' Instead, we let her do her own piece, a very moving, strong piece of television about how this teen's suicide affected this group of 14-year-olds. . . . When we showed it at a screening for a group of broadcast executives, four of them were in tears. If just a few kids in the audience saw the depth of despair in the piece and learned something from it, then it was worth it."

Rosenbaum has fought a running battle with broadcasters over the notion of news. "Before MTV signed us, I had three offers to do the show elsewhere, including one of the networks. But we turned them down because nobody would call it news. That word was so sacred that no one was willing to say that what the audience had to say was equally important to what we in the profession considered news."

Rosenbaum says Old Media had better get used to the idea. "A lot of us have gotten hung up on the rules of balance and objectivity we learned in journalism school. I've been described as the devil incarnate because we run stories where those things don't come into play. We think the audience is sophisticated

enough to tell the difference between an objective and subjective story. To me, the idea of storytelling as a profession that best not be tried in your own home is a dangerous and sad state of affairs."

He has this parting advice: "When all is said and done, *Unfiltered* is based on the simple act of answering the telephone and interacting with your viewers. With the Internet, the online services, and the potential for interactive television, viewers are going to have a channel into newsrooms."

GOODBYE, GUTENBERG?

It should come as no surprise that a large number of Net users have manned the virtual ramparts against Big Media's incursion into cyberspace. This is, after all, a medium that was built from the grassroots up. No corporate financing [initially]. No silver-maned publishers, broadcasters, or cable bigwigs calling the shots.

Journalists cling to the conceit that we're at the center of the media universe. But the harsh reality is that, for many, the press is expendable. Increasingly, citizens are bombarded with news and information from all directions: TV talk shows, talk radio, newsletters. And now the Net.

The digital age is turning middlemen everywhere into endangered species. Already, travel agents, stock brokers, traders, real estate agents, bank tellers, and insurance brokers are polishing up their resumes. Some believe that journalists may be next.

For diehard Netheads who want to play reporter, the Internet is the ultimate news-you-can-use machine. It's a worldwide library (even if all the books are on the floor), filled with tens of thousands of specialty nooks and niches. Experts in the fields of law, the economy, education, politics, and the arts are all accessible online.

Even for breaking news, many people turn not to the mainstream media but to the Usenet, Internet Relay Chat, and other wired forums.

Art Nauman, ombudsman for the *Sacramento Bee*, says he has encountered an entirely new class of readers since going online—younger, well-educated, and avid news junkies. "There are an awful lot of people out there who can do without us very nicely," he says, pointing to declining newspaper readership figures in most of the major markets. "Clearly, it's not just the uninformed who aren't picking us up. For growing numbers of young people especially, we're not relevant."

So is it time to close up shop and ask cousin Charlie about that job opening in PR? Not so fast.

"Newspapers and broadcast media will be with us for a very long time," says Kevin Kelly, executive editor of *Wired* magazine. "The Net doesn't obliterate Old Media, it merely redefines it. It will liberate newspapers from some of their stale habits and enable them to try new, more creative approaches to communicating with their readers.

"The real phenomenon of the Net is micropublishing, microaudiences, micromarkets. Whatever obsession you have—taboo sites, roadkill sites, the most socially unacceptable things you can imagine—you can find somebody out there who's doing it. . . . The Web won't replace Old Media. But it will add greatly to the diversity of viewpoints."

Rheingold agrees. "The Internet changes the media equation, and it's very simple: If you want to publish a newspaper, you need trucks, barrels of ink, big printing machines, capital. If you just want to publish the news, all you need is a computer and a telephone, and you can go online and provide an eyewitness account of the massacre at Tiananmen Square. The Internet puts the 'masses' back in 'mass media.'

"Does that mean that the Hearsts and Murdochs and Turners of the world will wither away and disappear? No way. But they won't have a monopoly on the news either. If you're a writer or playwright or restaurateur, the newspaper of record can make you or break you. That kind of dominance is a scary thing. To my mind, a multiplicity of voices is far, far healthier."

WHAT JOURNALISM CAN BRING TO THE NET

Journalists in television and radio have long wrestled with the immediacy of their mediums, weighing the harm of broadcasting unconfirmed reports against the public's right to know. What is different, as we step onto this new turf, is that we are entering a medium that has a set of operating principles already in place.

If cyberspace has a First Commandment, it is this: Information wants to be free. But that mantra, which dovetails nicely with journalists' First Amendment proclivities, also has a downside: It's difficult to separate fact from wild rumor and hearsay.

MTV's Rosenbaum says, "I assume that everything I read on the Net is half true." And that is precisely the problem.

"When you get into cyberspace, you get an awful lot of misinformation," says media scholar Stephen Hess of the Brookings Institution. "'Unmediated news' may be harmless when you throw it back and forth across the backyard fence. But when it goes out into the ether, it takes on a life of its own. At least journalists are quasi-professionals who have some training and a code of ethics and some rules of the road."

Cyberspace has become particularly fertile ground for conspiracy theories. After the crash of TWA flight 800 [in July 1996], the Net lit up with rumors that the airliner was downed by a missile accidentally fired by a U.S. Navy warship. By September the rumor—repeated and magnified via endless e-mails and Usenet postings—had taken on such authority that FBI and Navy officials took pains to denounce it as an "outrageous allegation" at a press briefing. Similar rumors of government plots and cover-ups surfaced after White House counsel Vincent Foster's suicide and the bombing of the federal building in Oklahoma City.

Increasingly, online users are looking to journalists to bring their truth-telling tools to cyberspace. Indeed, that is what spurred a group of writers, editors, and Net analysts to found the Internet Press Guild, a nonprofit group devoted to promoting accuracy in reporting on and about the Internet.

Says online journalist Kline: "We're beginning to see a new theme emerge on the WELL. Because of the unreliable, un-factchecked nature of the Net, people are starting to realize they need vetted information. With total information glut, more and more people are asking, 'Which of these sources is true, good and reliable?'

"The more time people spend online, the more they appreciate what good old-fashioned journalism can do for them."

Online journalists interviewed for this article disagreed about the specific changes journalism must undergo if it is to succeed in cyberspace, but all agreed that journalists need to hold onto such time-honored values as truthfulness, trustworthiness, accountability, and credibility. And nearly all agreed that restraint and perspective should be the yardstick by which Net journalism is measured.

"The Net is crawling with people who call themselves journalists," says Stephen Pizzo, an award-winning investigative print reporter who was senior editor of *Web Review,* a multimedia magazine that folded before reopening as an industry news product. "There's a guy in Reno who publishes his pieces in a dozen or so newsgroups dedicated to politics and conspiracy theories. His stories have a dateline, and the syntax is what you would expect of a straight news story. He has published a series on the death of Vince Foster, claiming unnamed intelligence sources have told him that Foster and Hillary Clinton were selling nuclear launch codes to the Israelis, and Foster was murdered by Mossad while he was having oral sex performed on him by Dee Dee Myers. I kid you not.

"The fact is, there are plenty of people out there who can be captured by that kind of phony journalism. There's no way to stop it, so we have to educate the reader. Readers will have to become much more discerning news consumers. The Internet is the biggest fact-checking tool in history. It's a poor man's Lexis-Nexis. If you have a question, bore into a subject and find out if that reporter is telling you the truth. You can't be a lazy reader anymore."

We also need journalists to point out information we didn't know we wanted to know. "Part of the value of newspapers is the serendipity," said James Fallows, [then] editor of *U.S. News & World Report* and author of *Breaking the News: How the Media Undermine American Democracy,* in an e-mail interview.

"The drawback of computer 'search agents' is that they presumably wouldn't be able to find articles that might otherwise surprise us or catch our fancy . . . ," Fallows added. "The historic function of the news includes understanding what your audience cares about and thinks—but also telling them things they may not know are important to them."

Michael Hallinan, a journalist-turned-online editorial administrator at USA Today Information Systems, adds: "The value of online journalists will be seen in their skills in sifting through documents, asking difficult questions, and getting the 'who, what, when, why and how' right. Also, there remains a need for skilled reporters to ferret out information that no one wants you to know.

"But beyond just-the-facts-ma'am reporting and investigative pieces, the most important thing newspapers can bring to the Net is context to make sense of it all."

The question is, do online newspapers make sense?

WHAT THE NET CAN BRING TO JOURNALISM

If journalism brings great things to the table—fact-checking skills, a certain level of credibility and trust—

it also brings a lot of baggage. Newspapers, TV, and radio stations are, at bottom, businesses first.

Kline points out: "There's a core conflict of values between the basic nature of the Internet and the demands of large businesses. The Net is free, it's egalitarian, decentralized, open and peer-to-peer, autonomous, and anarchic. Now contrast that to the vocabulary of commercialism: profit-oriented, hierarchical, bureaucratic, closed, organized, reliable."

It's little wonder, then, that critics like Jon Katz, media writer for *Wired,* suggest that online newspapers are inherently untenable. "I think newspapers don't have much business being online at all," he says from his home in suburban New Jersey. "Newspapers online disappear into the great electronic maw. Cyberspace is a different culture; it's not what newspapers are about."

Katz's 1994 article in *Wired,* "Online or Not, Newspapers Suck" [see Reading 3-1], remains the unofficial treatise for the legions of Old Media bashers in the digital nation. In it he wrote, "Watching sober, proper newspapers online stirs only one image: that of Lawrence Welk trying to dance at a rap concert."

Katz hasn't been swayed by the progress some online newspapers have made from those awkward early efforts. "Most newspaper Web sites are ugly, clunky, present unoriginal, outdated information, and reflect corporate traditions that emphasize tepid opinion, stuffy writing, and middle-of-the-road banality," he says. "That's not what people go online for. Young people, especially, like strong point of view, attitude, graphics, in-depth pop culture coverage—all the things that newspapers won't do. It's this inability to change and take risks that is the real Achilles' heel of newspapers."

Katz is surely right about our shortcomings. Too many newspapers are guided by the maxim "Bland is beautiful." *Editor & Publisher* columnist Steve Outing, who's no bomb-thrower, says, "Newspapers today are homogenized, have little personality, and tend to look like all of their corporate siblings."

But perhaps Katz underestimates the potential value of online newspapers. News publications can bring a historical sweep and depth to events. Context is not confined to the front page of a Web site; it's hidden in the rich layers of information that each user can ferret out.

If online newspapers evolve into what they should become, they will provide far more than a screenful of electronic headlines, photos, and recycled stories. A next-wave online publication will be an indispensable resource tool, a round-the-clock service that not only checks facts and prioritizes the news, but also provides a community encyclopedia of sorts—a navigation device for exploring the news universe.

Newspapers can succeed in cyberspace, but only if they're willing to leave behind conventions that no longer make sense in the digital world. The Net provides a fantastic opportunity for newspapers to reinvent themselves and to hold onto the things that make them vital to our lives, but also to let go of stale and suffocating habits.

In short, we need to approach this young medium with a fresh set of eyes.

A TWO-WAY WINDOW

One of the most hallowed traditions of journalism is the veil of secrecy that newsrooms cast over the news-gathering process. That mystique—wrapped up in inaccessibility and arrogance—has hurt. It feeds the public's mistrust of large institutions. It gives ammunition to the conspiracy theorists and creates doubts even among loyal readers. And it gives us a far too comfortable insulation from the public's ire when we fail to live up to our standards.

"I've always said the great untold story of journalism is journalism itself," says Nauman, the *Sacramento Bee*'s ombudsman. "Too many readers mistrust us. We need to show that there isn't some evil genius sitting in the cockpit pulling the levers. It's a collegial process where decisions and mistakes are made at any number of levels."

Opening up the process will give readers more confidence in what we do. Giving them a window into the newsroom will instill a sense of trust that news judgments are made honestly and responsibly. Interactive journalism is that window.

The Internet, at heart, is much less a publishing medium than a two-way communication medium. The zeitgeist of the Net—its unifying principle—is centered in interaction and interconnectedness, not "I-will-publish, you-will-accept." The Net is not a megaphone. The Net is a conversation.

At present, it's a noisy conversation, but noise is the price we pay for the signal. As news publications climb online, they should resist the temptation to give in to the Net's slicker, baser instincts—the cheap attitude, the smug hipness of the Irony Zines that pose as official arbiters of all things cool. Newspapers should look at the tools of multimedia not as a chance to jazz up their sites with dancing electrons, but to engage in a true give-and-take with their readers, to grasp the Net's unparalleled opportunities for making us all more informed and more connected.

Readers don't want pixel pyrotechnics—not in the long run. They want humanity. They want intimate, passionate journalism that's grounded in facts.

Journalism needs to look at the Net not as a threat but as an opportunity to repair our strained public relations. But it goes beyond image repair; we need to change the way we do business.

"Unless certain newspaper practices are reconsidered, there's no amount of explaining to the public that will help," says Richard Harwood, president of The Harwood Group, a public issues research and innovation firm in Bethesda, Maryland. "People aren't much interested in the technology, whether it's new media or old media. In all the studies we've done, people keep coming back to the same themes: context, perspective, meaning."

Adds Fallows: "We need to make ourselves more accountable to our readers. Not become lackeys to that audience, but find ways to respond to and respect their real concerns about thoroughness and fair-mindedness."

The Net has the potential to be the greatest First Amendment tool in history. As we adapt to the new technologies, it's up to us to hold on to the timeless values of journalism and discard the ink-on-dead-trees baggage.

At bottom, this is the secret of journalism: To those of us in the field, it's not about marketing, or business earnings, or technology. It's about a reporter going out into the night to live a story and bringing the reader along to share the experience.

Journalism, at its core, is an interaction between a writer and a reader. The Net brings those two closer together. And that's something to celebrate.

RELATED LINKS

- *American Journalism Review* Newslink (http://ajr.newslink.org)
- *Columbia Journalism Review* (http://www.cjr.org)
- *Online Journalism Review* (http://ojr.usc.edu)
- *The Quill Magazine* (http://spj.org/quill)

FOR FURTHER RESEARCH

To find out more about the topics discussed in this reading, use InfoTrac College Edition. Type in keywords and subject terms such as "journalistic values," "news gatekeeping," and "cyber journalism." You can access InfoTrac College Edition from the Wadsworth/Thomson Communication Cafe homepage: http://communication.wadsworth.com.

Reading 3-3

Slate vs. *Salon:* The Leading Online Magazines Struggle to Get the Net
Nicholas Stein

EDITOR'S NOTE

Slate *and* Salon, *the two leading online news and opinion magazines, face the same challenge as other electronic publications: transferring the core principles of print journalism onto the Internet. But that's where the similarities end. As this article explains, these two well-regarded magazines—one published by Microsoft* (Slate), *the other launched with seed money from Apple Computer* (Salon)—*are evolving quite different visions of what an online magazine can and should be. Pioneers of Internet-only content, they are both struggling to become financially independent while carving out an audience niche for their unique editorial visions.*

CONSIDER

1. How do *Slate* and *Salon* differ in terms of their journalistic approach and editorial content? With this in mind, how do you think the audiences for *Slate* and *Salon* might differ?

2. Why does *Salon* editor David Talbot call his magazine a "smart tabloid"?

3. *Slate* editor Michael Kinsley describes his work as "building a medium as well as a magazine." Is this an overstatement?

For Michael Kinsley, the world has become a raging sea of content, its inhabitants floundering in an endless

news cycle. What they need is a filter, and as the editor of the online magazine *Slate,* Kinsley is trying to provide one—a tool to help his readers navigate the political, technological, and cultural issues of the Information Age.

For David Talbot, the editor and CEO of the competing online magazine *Salon,* the world is awash instead in commentary: opinion dispensed by wise men who comment passively from the shore. What readers need is more reporting. Wading into the currents, *Salon* relishes introducing new topics to The Conversation, with the expectation that its readers will construct filters of their own.

Other Internet-only publications have claimed their own positions along this reporter–pundit continuum, but *Slate* and *Salon* have become defining editorial visions of the medium. What fascinates is how different are these two evolving visions of what an online magazine can and should be.

EVOLUTION

In the summer of 1996, around the time the Internet began to emerge as a populist medium—and some observers began to forecast the death of print—Microsoft entered the world of online publishing with the launch of *Slate*. The fiscal might of its owner, coupled with the reputation its editor had built during his battles with Pat Buchanan on CNN's *Crossfire* and his editorships at *Harper's* and *The New Republic,* gave *Slate* the lavish media attention necessary to pierce the public's consciousness.

"The basic test was to show that serious magazine journalism can succeed on the Web," says Kinsley. "We tried to develop features that are both suited to the Web and useful to our readers." In his attempt to execute this combination, Kinsley has seen his views about online journalism change dramatically, and *Slate* has changed with him.

In its inaugural issue, June 24, 1996, *Slate* ran a 2,218-word article by Nicholas Lemann titled "Jews in Second Place: When Asian-Americans Become the 'New Jews,' What Happens to the Jews?" A profile of Bob Dole in the same issue added another 1,648 words. Italicized word counts appeared below the headlines, taunting those who claimed that traditional magazine-length pieces couldn't succeed on the Internet. In fact, Kinsley consciously modeled his mix of political commentary and arts criticism on a magazine that helped to define the tradition—*The New Yorker.*

Nearly three years later, long features have all but disappeared. "One thing we feel we just cannot do on the Web is *New York Times Magazine–New Yorker*-type articles," says Kinsley. Instead, *Slate* has developed a stable of what he calls "meta-features"—intelligent and readable syntheses of news events and issues of the moment. "Our meta-features are intended to couple understanding with a little bit of wit," he says. "To save you the time and trouble of reading something you don't want to, and to direct you to what you do."

Slate has faced the same challenges as other online publications: to transmogrify the principles of print journalism onto the Internet. It has adapted by molding itself into an observer that distills and comments on the political, social, and cultural affairs of the day.

In November 1994, while the *San Francisco Examiner* was embroiled in a bitter labor dispute, its arts and features editor David Talbot, and several of his colleagues—including Gary Kamiya (now *Salon*'s executive editor), Andrew Ross (its vice president of business and strategic development), Scott Rosenberg (its technology senior editor), and Mignon Khargie (its design director)—left the paper for the unknown world of Internet publishing. Launched in late 1995 with about $100,000 in seed money from Apple Computer, Inc., *Salon* delivered, in a distinctly irreverent voice, a biweekly mix of cultural criticism, social and political commentary, book reviews, and author interviews. The *New York Times* described it as "an interactive magazine of books, arts, and ideas."

But soon Talbot began to notice an Internet phenomenon: "Readers came back only as long as we had new material—especially material tied to the day's news." Based on this discovery, Talbot began, in early 1997, to produce an issue every weekday. Traffic rose nearly 40 percent, to more than 400,000 unique visitors (from distinct Internet addresses) per month.

Salon also increased emphasis on breaking news, notably after the death of Princess Diana. Her accident occurred during Labor Day weekend, 1997, when many media organizations were on cruise control. The *Salon* staff's newspaper background enabled it rapidly to translate breaking news into fluid articles, like Jonathan Broder's "Blood on Their Hands," one of the first to implicate the paparazzi in Diana's death. *Salon* posted eleven pieces on the subject between August 31 and September 8, producing further readership gains. Encouraged, Talbot began to divert resources—and space—from the cultural commentary of *Salon*'s past to the investigative stories and breaking news he was certain were its future.

On September 16, 1998, only a month after publishing an attention-grabbing five-part series alleging a conspiracy between chief Whitewater witness David Hale, right-wing mogul Richard Mellon Scaife, and independent counsel Kenneth Starr, Talbot published an account of a 5-year extramarital affair between House Judiciary Committee chairman Henry Hyde (who was 41 years old at the time) and a married women with three children.

The story, about a 29-year-old affair, had been rejected by many other media outlets, and Talbot's decision to publish drew fire from politicians and media figures alike. One of his harshest critics was *Salon*'s own Washington bureau chief Jonathan Broder, who offered to resign after publicly questioning the decision—despite instructions from his bosses not to do so. Talbot accepted the resignation.

These kinds of high-octane stories brought *Salon* a giant leap in readership, from 620,000 to more than 1 million visitors a month. Three months later, *Salon* had retained half of those new viewers, and its readership was estimated to be about 850,000 visitors a month.

CONTENT

"I don't think the world needs more scoops," says Kinsley, defending his decision to curtail original reporting. *Slate*'s content can be divided into three categories: summaries, features, and dialogues.

In Today's Papers, Scott Shuger highlights the leading stories in the *New York Times, Washington Post, Los Angeles Times, USA Today,* and *Wall Street Journal.* Other Magazines distills the views of *Time, Newsweek, U.S. News & World Report, The Economist, The New Yorker,* and *The Weekly Standard.* International Papers touches on some of the lead stories from English, French, German, Spanish, and other papers.

Slate also includes several sections that comment upon the news itself. In The Week / The Spin, William Saletan looks at the top stories, and how the involved parties have spun them to their respective advantage. In Frame Game, Saletan promises "20 spins you'll hear from partisan flacks." At The Breakfast Table, a weekly duo, usually a pair of writers, "dissect the day's news via e-mail." More careful analysis can be found in Chatterbox, Pundit Central, and Explainer.

In the issue just before the November elections, almost half of *Slate*'s pages were devoted to commentary in some form. Some have faulted *Slate* for this emphasis. *Vanity Fair* media columnist James Wolcott describes the publication as a journalistic echo chamber, a place in which reviewing and reporting have been replaced by "a lot of writers with too much free time."

Slate also features "electronic discourses"—lightly edited e-mail exchanges between writers. "The most interesting discussions of my life are with the half dozen close friends I e-mail with every day," says Kinsley, who envisions the discourses as "writing with the spontaneity of speech." In *Slate,* these pieces take one of two forms: e-mail discussions between two writers (The Book Club, The Music Club, and The Breakfast Table) and individual journal entry prose (Diary).

Unfortunately, many of these reveal nothing more than the mundane details of daily life, legitimized by the reputation of the writer. "Started the morning with a good swim in the beautiful Bel Air pool," begins the February 12, 1998, entry of architect Moshe Safdie. "At 9 A.M. I'm at the Skirball Cultural Center for a full board of trustees meeting."

When these pieces work, however, they achieve a gripping immediacy. "I want people to read me for the first time as though they were reading me for the second," writes André Aciman in his Diary entry on November 4. "I want them to feel that they've heard all this before, though they can't remember where, because every word they read is stalked by a pre-existing shadow seemingly originating from their own experience, not mine."

Talbot calls his magazine a "smart tabloid," and concedes that the headlines sometimes take artistic license. But readers drawn in by headlines like Microsoft .orgy (July 21, 1998), about an embarrassing mishap with Microsoft's video conferencing software, will often find that the articles themselves contain intelligent, well-written prose. "We live in an environment where even smart, educated people need to be gripped," he says.

Salon is not above gripping them with sex, using such columnists as Camille Paglia, the contrarian, lesbian, academic; Susie Bright, who dispenses advice in her weekly Sexpert Opinion; and until her abrupt, unexplained departure, relationship guru Courtney Weaver, whose more than 100 Unzipped columns (now languishing in *Salon*'s Discontinued Features archive) tapped into the dating-scene zeitgeist. In October 1998, the magazine introduced Urge, a column that has included articles about a debauched bachelor party and the newly celebrated phenomenon of black homoerotic fiction.

Yet *Salon* reaches far beyond the bedroom— to breaking news (Newsreal), technology (21st), the media (Media), academia (Ivory Tower), business (Money), and parenting issues (Mothers Who Think). Many of these include substantial reporting and run a couple of thousand words or longer—a tactic frowned upon by many of the Net's talking heads. But, argues

Talbot, "the Internet is a deep medium. People want to make up their own mind. If they are interested in a subject, they want to read a lot, to go deep, and to have links to other sources of information."

While coverage of politics has increased, *Salon* has not abandoned its movie, music, and television reviews. It has increased coverage of books, with reviews, author interviews, listings of author events, and an annual *Salon* Book Awards.

OUTLOOK

Kinsley admits that *Slate* probably will never be able to survive on advertising dollars alone. Readership fell dramatically after *Slate* introduced a $19.95 annual subscription fee in the spring of 1998. Paid circulation hovers in the high 20,000s. Yet in October, *Slate's* Front Porch, the free section of its site, received almost 400,000 visitors. The vast discrepancy between visitors and subscribers clearly must be attributed to the cost.

"It will be a few years before we reach profitability, if we ever do," Kinsley says. "Yet people forget that it took *Sports Illustrated* almost 10 years to turn a profit." In reality, *Slate's* continued viability depends on the whims of its corporate parent. Despite the red ink, Microsoft CEO Bill Gates continues to praise the magazine.

Talbot estimates that *Salon* is still 4 years from turning a profit. It has attracted more than 120 advertisers, half long-term, who make up some of that shortfall. But most of the magazine's funding—$11 million as of November 1998—has come from four major investors: the software giant Adobe; venture capital firm Hambrecht & Quist; the Japanese computer concern ASCII; and borders.com, which until recently had an e-commerce arrangement with the magazine: a percentage of each book bought on *Salon's* site went to the magazine. *Salon* has since switched its e-commerce allegiance to barnesandnoble.com, which may buy Borders' investment.

In an imaginative way to charge for editorial content on the Internet, *Salon* began in October '98 to sell "memberships." For $25 a year, members will get a *Salon* T-shirt, access to a members' lounge (a chat area that features exclusive discussions with *Salon* writers, editors, and special guests), and a CD-ROM reproduction of the first edition of John Milton's *Areopagitica*. Promotion letters compare the membership fee to contributions listeners and viewers give to NPR and PBS. Those networks, however, are nonprofit. Though Talbot admits "some readers have balked at supporting us because we accept advertising," he says the income from the club is "above what our projections were."

Attempting to extend *Salon's* franchise, Talbot plans to launch European editions, financed jointly by *Salon* and European media partners. Eventually he hopes that these new editions will provide more international content to the U.S. edition.

SLATE AND *SALON*

Both Kinsley and Talbot hesitate to comment on each other's publication, though Kinsley does acknowledge his rival's visual superiority. "Their design and presentation is very attractive. They suck you in and lead you from article to article better than we do."

"For us, we are building a medium as well as a magazine," explains Kinsley. "That's what makes it fun. In 10 years, all of this will be defined."

"We have an opportunity with our medium to provide a real mix of popular content with insightful, investigative journalism," says Talbot. "There is lots of room between Matt Drudge and the *New York Times*."

RELATED LINKS

- *Harper's* (http://www.harpers.org)
- *The Nation* (http://www.thenation.com)
- *The New Republic Online* (http://www.thenewrepublic.com)
- *Salon* (http://salon.com)
- *Slate* (http://slate.msn.com)

FOR FURTHER RESEARCH

To find out more about the topics discussed in this reading, use InfoTrac College Edition. Type in keywords and subject terms such as "online magazines," "interactive writing," and "magazine journalism." You can access InfoTrac College Edition from the Wadsworth/Thomson Communication Cafe homepage: http://communication.wadsworth.com.

Reading 3-4

It's Time to Turn the Last Page

Steven Levy

EDITOR'S NOTE

Book publishing is about to be overtaken by e-books—digital texts displayed by a handheld device with an ultrasharp display. Two obstacles remain, however: high-speed wireless bandwidth to shorten download times, and screen technology that is physically as well as visually pleasing. In the long run, concludes Newsweek *technology columnist Steven Levy in this forward-looking reading, the e-book's most startling impact won't be technological but will involve what goes* between *the virtual covers. With vastly reduced distribution costs, Levy predicts, the book-publishing industry will experience a return to literary quality.*

CONSIDER

1. Do you agree with the assessment that when pundits look back on the twenty-first century, they'll remember it as the last century of the book?

2. How might the self-publishing of e-books over the World Wide Web by brand-name authors create opportunities for so-called "midlist" writers?

3. Will the predicted death of traditional books, which this reading claims will happen in this century, necessarily mean the *disappearance* of books, or something else?

No one is calling the 1900s the Century of the Book. But you could make a case for it. For most of those years, the heavy hitters in our culture landed their big punches between the covers of bound boards: Joyce, Freud, Proust, Salinger, Orwell . . . even Bill Gates weighed in, twice. Sure, television eventually mesmerized the nation and the globe, but the number of books printed in the fading century surely dwarfed the production of all previous eras. And when e-commerce began, what did its flagship, Amazon.com, sell? Duh.

Still, when Y3K pundits look back on our time, they'll remember it as the Last Century of the Book. Why? As a common item of communication, artistic expression, and celebrity anecdote, the physical object consisting of bound dead trees in shiny wrapper is headed for the antique heap. Its replacement will be a lightning-quick injection of digital bits into a handheld device with an ultrasharp display. Culture vultures and bookworms might cringe at the prospect, but it's as inevitable as page two's following page one. Books are goners, at least as far as being the dominant form of reading.

Most of the pieces are already in place: fast chips, long-lasting batteries, capacious disk drives, and the Internet. Only two things, really, hold us back from having reading devices that are just as felicitous as the dust-jacketed packages we know and love. One is high-speed wireless bandwidth, so that the devices can be quickly loaded. Fixing that is a no-brainer. No one doubts that such a big digital transmission system will show up early in the millennium.

The second is a screen whose output is as sumptuous as the current book's, which engage not only our minds but our sense of touch. Oh, and having it cost so little that we won't hesitate to drag the thing to the beach or grab it on the way to the loo. In other words, cheap enough to lose.

What are the odds of that happening? Let's see. In the last 50 years, we've made computers thousands of times more powerful, while shrinking them from the size of a basketball court to something you can cradle in your palm. All while dropping the price tag from millions of bucks to a few hundred. Does it really seem plausible that sometime next century we can't make a device that approximates the size and heft of a book or magazine, with a screen that's every bit as easy on the eyes as the Modern Library edition of *Sense and Sensibility*? Unless the world's computer scientists suddenly get struck stupid, we're going to get those devices, and they'll probably cost so little that we'll pay nothing for them—they'll be given away by content moguls so that we can buy more twenty-first-century news, pictures, and literature. The cards have been dealt, says Microsoft e-book czar Dick Brass. The only difference is how fast people will play the hand.

Skeptics focus on the failings of the current generation of e-books. These are paperback-size readers with fairly clear type but backlit screens that don't compare with the things routinely shelved at the local Barnes and Noble. Still, I recently polished off a Stephen King novel in e-book form, an adventure tale involving a little girl lost in the woods. After a few screens' worth of King-speak, I was sufficiently sucked into the tale to pretty much forget about the medium, and I finished the novel in a few hours. I doubt that I would have gotten any more or less from it if I'd paged through the hardback.

Bottom line: you can use those things, even as unattractive and uncool as they are now. And within 5 years, promises NuvoMedia CEO Martin Eberhard, we'll have front-surface technology that doesn't require you to read behind glass. So it's easy to see how, when the reading experience gets better, e-books will overwhelmingly swamp the objections of book mavens like Sven Birkerts, a literary critic whose book *The Gutenberg Elegies* eloquently sheds tears over the coming purge. The loss will be important, but it's elusive to specify, he says. We'll miss the culture of the book, the envelope of associations.

An understandable complaint. But once we get past the question of whether the e-book will dominate, we can ponder a more interesting issue: what are the changes that will accompany the shift? The first big upheaval will come, of course, in the business of publishing. When publishers no longer have to focus on moving pulped forests to distributors, the business model will go bananas. The turning point is going to come when one of the brand-name authors actually bolts and goes direct to readers, says one executive at a major publishing house, who even ventures a guess who that author might be: Stephen King. The master of horror is not only a perennial best seller, but a roll-the-dice kind of guy who's previously pulled headline-grabbing book-release stunts (like dribbling out *The Green Mile* in six easy pieces). So what's to stop him from selling *The Dead Again Zone* or some other 2004 thriller exclusively by $12 downloads in e-book format from StephenKing.com—and raking in a 100 percent royalty, after the relatively minimal expenses of formatting the book and maintaining the server? Such only-available-in-bit books would be the sort of killer app that spikes sales of e-readers. And after King does it, will Clancy, Grisham, and Tom Wolfe be far behind?

When—not if—that happens, there will be widespread panic on book row. After all, the profits of big-time book publishing these days involve shipping tons of would-be blockbusters and hoping that they don't come back unsold. Brand-name authors minimize the risk and reap the biggest profits. But if every brand-name author had the wherewithal to make it on his or her own by self-publishing e-books, the publishers might have to look elsewhere.

This could have a salutary effect on the business, and not just for authors and readers. For years we've been hearing about how publishers neglect the serious novels and nonfiction on what is known as the midlist. These are books launched with moderate advances on interesting subjects. Unlike tell-alls by murderers' girlfriends, memoirs of professional wrestlers, and philosophical insights from stand-up comedians, these are the books that enable editors to look themselves in the mirror at night. Freed from fretting about the mechanics of distributing blockbusters, those editors might find time to carefully nurture books of quality—and be more aggressive in helping those books find their audiences. They'll have a great tool at hand: the Internet, perfect for identifying even the most obscure niches.

And if publishers don't concentrate their efforts on selling those midlist books more effectively? Then they could say goodbye to those authors, who will migrate to a new breed of electronic booksellers who will do just that.

In the long term, the e-book's most startling effect will involve what goes between the virtual covers. After all, the most notable feature of these new reading devices will be that all of them will be connected to the Internet. That simple fact will trigger profound changes.

First, watch for a change in the way we read. Physical books are discrete objects that open up to small worlds; connected e-books will offer the world. Only a few pokes on the touchscreen, and you're no longer in the middle of the novel you've been devouring—you're in the middle of some other book, or a critic's gloss on your reading material. Or maybe you're grooving to some streaming-audio tune. We may see the literary equivalent of channel surfing. It will depreciate the author, laments Birkerts.

Finally, watch for the works themselves to change. Some kinds of books will instantly disappear. (Why would you want a static travel guide when you can instantly access all the up-to-date dope on any place in the world?) Familiar creative forms will slowly evolve to conform to the new medium. The novel, after all, fits neatly into the covers of physical books: long enough to be worth buying, but not too bulky to drag around. Without being confined by those physical limitations—and with the ability to include other kinds of digital media—creative minds will inevitably find new forms of expression. Will authors satisfy us with shorter stories? Lengthy tales that make *The Magic Mountain* look like a molehill? Soundtracks? Linguistic samplings that interweave new prose with previous classics or even random gatherings like ad copy or cartoons? Who knows? Just trust that every new medium finds its exploiters.

Meanwhile, true bibliophiles shouldn't get too broken up. The death of books won't necessarily mean the disappearance of books. Microsoft's Brass echoes the view of most observers when he says those of us raised on the pleasures of page turning and shelf browsing will ensure that all the world's volumes won't go up in one big *Fahrenheit 451* bonfire. Books will persist because they're beautiful and useful, he says. They're like horses after the automobile—not gone, but transformed into a recreational beast.

Feel better?

RELATED LINKS

- Amazon.com (http://www.amazon.com)
- Barnes & Noble.com (http://www.bn.com)
- eBook Home (http://www.nuvomedia.com)
- The Official Stephen King Web Presence (http://www.stephenking.com)

FOR FURTHER RESEARCH

To find out more about the topics discussed in this reading, use InfoTrac College Edition. Type in keywords and subject terms such as "e-books," "digital publishing," and "NuvoMedia." You can access InfoTrac College Edition from the Wadsworth/Thomson Communication Cafe homepage: http://communication.wadsworth.com.

4

Radio/TV/Film

Reading 4-1

The World Streaming In
Bill McKibben

EDITOR'S NOTE

As with other media, radio is experiencing a rebirth through the Internet and World Wide Web, resulting in a broader range of channel choices and content diversity. At the same time, online listeners, no longer bound by local station formats and schedules, are free to select programming that appeals to their own interests and tastes. On the content side of the equation, would-be radio commentators the world over can now record and edit broadcast-quality audio for relatively little cost, allowing new stories to be told. From Newark to New Zealand, the industry is undergoing a dynamic period of digital transition and experimentation, including the roll-out of commercial-free satellite radio. The bottom line: free, easy-to-use software can turn any multimedia PC into the best global radio receiver there ever was.

CONSIDER

1. Commercial radio suffers from an overabundance of prepackaged program formats, resulting in a homogenized sound. To what extent will digital radio open new audio horizons?

2. In what ways are the Internet and World Wide Web revolutionizing the way radio is transmitted, produced, and experienced?

3. How has digital recording and editing technology opened creative possibilities for radio commentators everywhere?

Your taste for serendipity will be tested over the next few years. Radio turns out to mate easily with digital technology, opening up whole new worlds. Just this morning, for instance, I've listened to a (terrible) band called Salmonella Dub on station bFM from Auckland, New Zealand; a weather forecast for Alberta; the top-forty from São Paulo; jazz from Newark. But you can also use the technology to narrow your world and make sure you'll never hear anything disconcerting again—a use that might endanger public, college, and community radio stations, all that good stuff at the left end of the dial. What you look for will depend on the value you place on the local, the particular, the immediate—on the funky in all its forms.

The only tool you need is a copy of RealPlayer or Windows Media Player, software that more than 100 million people already use (and that is free in its basic versions; the upgrades that RealPlayer encourages you to buy don't seem to add much to the free version). Once you've got one of these programs, you can listen to any audio on the Web—sound, unlike video, requires only limited bandwidth. Hundreds of "Internet only" radio stations have sprung up, including gogaga.com, WWW.com, and NetRadio.com, which boasts 120 "channels" subdivided into remarkably narrow segments. Classical fans can baroque around the clock or concentrate on chant; rock fans can decide between "Fab '60s" and "Pre-Fab '60s." You listen through the speakers on your desktop computer—this is music for cubicles. And it is fast becoming music for cars. Sirius Satellite Radio will soon be standard in many Fords, using satellites to "stream" channels playing nothing but New Age, opera, blues, country, alternative. For a monthly fee you'll be able to push the button preset for opera and hear endless arias, uninterrupted by commercials.

The sound quality will be unimpeachable—no fading in and out as you crest hills. In fact, you may very well stop listening to classical music on your local public-radio station, which means that you won't be tuned in at fundraising time, which means the station might go out of business. The thought has certainly occurred to National Public Radio, which has agreed to provide programming for two nationwide NPR channels over Sirius Satellite Radio but has refused to license the two biggest ones, *Morning Edition* and *All Things Considered,* for fear of losing too many listeners.

All reggae all the time exacts another cost: although it's efficient to listen to the kind of music or talk you already know you like and nothing else, it's also a little dull, or at least parochial. That is to say, one of the glories of public radio, as of any neighborhood, is its inefficiency—the fact that because it offers all sorts of things to all sorts of people, it obliges you to expose yourself to the tastes of the people around you. Maybe you'll hear something about the local schools, or the local nursing home; maybe you'll hear zouk music before opera comes on. Commercial AM and FM have already achieved near-total homogenization. A distributor in Texas or California, say, sends prepackaged oldies or conservative bluster or "adult contemporary" out across thousands of stations—satellite radio with commercials. With regular broadcast radio there weren't enough opera fans in Boston or Louisville to support an all-opera station, so Pavarotti fans sometimes had to suffer through Joshua Redman. Now they won't unless they want to.

Digital radio can widen your world as well as narrow it. To imagine how far, you perhaps need to have hovered over a shortwave set in your childhood, trying to coax in the distant signals of Radio Luxembourg, intrigued by the idea that there were other, perhaps more interesting, places you could conjure up out of the ether. There's no more waiting for nightfall, worrying about sunspots, stringing antennas out the window—all of a sudden the computer has turned into the greatest shortwave set there ever was. Visit a site called comfm.com and you can choose from 3,619 stations (by the time you try it, the number will doubtless have topped 4,000). About 2,000 of these broadcast from the United States, but you can also hear Armenian, Azerbaijani, and Tanzanian broadcasts. Radio Mostar and Radio Slon stream in live from Bosnia. Click on RSI in Singapore and you can choose live programming in English, Tamil, Malay, Mandarin, or Japanese. Click on All India Radio and music from Bollywood surges through your speakers. What you hear is local radio, not the propaganda broadcasts that governments send out over shortwave.

Aurally, anyone can now live in, say, Boston, which has a dozen college stations, three of them great: WMBR, at the Massachusetts Institute of Technology (check out Sunday evening's *R&B Jukebox*); WERS, at Emerson College (*Gyroscope* offers three hours of world music every weekday afternoon); and WHRB, at Harvard, locally famous for the exam-period "orgies" it broadcasts twice a year (last winter every note Bach wrote, continuously for ten days). If your local public-radio station plays nothing but classical music, you can now tune in KCRW, the NPR outlet in Santa Monica, which offers *Morning Becomes Eclectic*— perhaps the most gorgeously idiosyncratic music program in the country (Beck, Cassandra Wilson, Jacques Brel, back to back)—and also lots of original radio drama, not to mention satire from Harry Shearer.

What makes this programming wonderful is that it's local, made for particular people in particular places—or, to put it the other way around, that it's not made for everyone everywhere, like TV. Radio is cheap to produce. *This American Life,* the weekly documentary show from WBEZ, in Chicago, that beats anything else on the public-radio schedule, costs less than $20,000 an hour to produce and transmit—a sum that will buy just half the opening credits for any TV show. Because it is cheap, radio allows you either to make a great deal of money selling commercials—urban licenses routinely go for tens of millions of dollars—or, if you don't care about profit, to make whatever kind of program you want. There's no need to gather a vast audience: with some of a school's student activities fee or a few thousand loyal, pledging listeners, you can cover the costs of a radio station. The Internet is cheap too. WarpRadio.com, for instance, will Webcast a station's signal in exchange for only 2 minutes of advertising time a day. For very little incremental cost any local station can suddenly reach a global audience.

Ever since Marshall McLuhan coined the term, people have taken "global village" to mean that there would one day be a single planetary culture. Indeed, that's what came about as TV spread around the world, doing its best to create a global American suburb. Even TV's "local news" looks as if it were filmed and beamed out from some central studio.

The Internet, combined with radio, offers the possibility of a different model—many communities you can look in on from time to time. You wouldn't want to spend all your time in them: Tamil radio doesn't, in the end, have that much to do with how you live. But there is something delightful about hearing what interests local people in far-flung places. It's the difference between staying in a bed-and-breakfast and staying in a hotel-resort.

The digital revolution has another gift to offer radio. It changes not only the way radio is transmitted but also the way it is made. Say you want to produce a small report for a radio station, the way people have always written columns for their local newspapers. In the past this was complicated. Even if you were doing a straightforward commentary, you usually had to either travel to the station (sound suffers as it comes across the phone lines) or mail in a tape. To do anything more elaborate—lay in music in the background, piece together quotations from your neighbors—you needed an elaborate suite of editing equipment and the almost mystical ability to cut tape with razor blades and piece it back together, removing the *ums* and preserving the words you wanted. Five years ago the walls of the control room in any good local public-radio station were covered with segments of tape waiting to be spliced into essays. Now in the same control room there are instead a couple of Gateways or Macs. Tape is nearly dead.

My daughter and I spent several weeks last year interviewing our neighbors in the Adirondack Mountains, in New York, recording hailstorms and waterfalls, interrogating each other as we climbed high peaks. Our Sony MZ-R55 recorder, no bigger than a pack of playing cards, weighs a few ounces, and all of our summer's work fit on a dozen mini-discs (think of them as compact compact discs) that can be fed into any computer equipped with a sound card, using a $2 cable from RadioShack. With software you can download for a small fee, you can edit the sound almost as easily as you can edit words in a word processing program (try the shareware program CoolEdit 2000 or, for Macs, Sound Studio).

When you're finished, you can convert your meditation on the summer's first swim into an MP3 file and e-mail it to your local station; it will emerge sounding as crisp and clear as anything else on the radio. In the past, when high-quality equipment was expensive and the required skills arcane, there were very few prominent radio producers. Anyone who listens to *All Things Considered* will recognize their names: Jay Allison, David Isay, the Kitchen Sisters. But now, at least in theory, the technical obstacles have diminished enough that anyone who loves the sound of the human voice and owns a computer built in the past 5 years can join the ranks. Already you can hear the results on our local public-radio station: freed of cutting tape, correspondents turn out more—and more daring—work, and new voices crop up. Jay Allison is inaugurating a new Web site, Transom.org, that invites anyone to send in an attempt at making radio; a rotating group of pros will critique the pieces, award prizes to the best ones, and send as many of them as possible on to *All Things Considered* and other national shows. "We're going to use the Net to cast a net," Allison says. "There are so many stories out there just waiting to be told."

Done on the cheap, TV looks terrible—the garish, shabby amateur hour that is public-access cable in any city in the country, unwatched except by friends and family. Radio can't be done *except* on the cheap, and with a $150 microphone (try the Electro-Voice 635A) anyone can make it sound just fine. If you want to make it sound magnificent, you need the insight of a good writer, and a few technical tricks besides. Ira Glass, the man behind *This American Life,* last year pro-

duced a comic book designed for tyro producers: *Radio: An Illustrated Guide*. It covers everything from story structure to how to make people comfortable when you're sticking a mike in their faces. It ends with a note from Glass, the man who made the airwaves safe for normal voices: "Radio is boring when the people on the air just want to sound like everyone else. The people who are the most fun to listen to—from Paul Harvey to Terry Gross—they sound only like themselves. Everyone should try it."

RELATED LINKS

- comfm (http://www.comfm.com)
- National Public Radio (http://www.npr.org)
- netradio.com (http://www.netradio.com/index.asp)
- Real.com (http://www.real.com)
- WindowsMedia.com (http://windowsmedia.msn.com/mg/home.asp)

FOR FURTHER RESEARCH

To find out more about the topics discussed in this reading, use InfoTrac College Edition. Type in keywords and subject terms such as: "streaming technology," "satellite radio," and "Internet radio." You can access InfoTrac College Edition from the Wadsworth/Thomson Communication Cafe homepage: http://communication.wadsworth.com.

Reading 4-2

Radio Squeezes Empty Air Space for Profit

Alex Kuczynski

EDITOR'S NOTE

Thanks to a new digital time-compression device, radio stations can wedge in more minutes of commercials per day by truncating sounds and pauses in talk programs. The technology even caught conservative radio personality Rush Limbaugh by surprise when listeners started asking why there were more commercials than normal on his 3-hour talk-radio program. Radio stations are profiting, but, as this reading reveals, there is a limit to the amount of advertising listeners will tolerate. Even as stations attempt to find the optimal balance between an acceptably paced broadcast and an overcrowded one, there are some in the industry who feel the clutter has already gotten out of control.

CONSIDER

1. Do you agree with the author's assessment that commercials, which once punctuated the cultural landscape, now dominate it? What do you think of this trend?

2. Why is the problem of commercial clutter much more apparent in radio than on television?

3. How does the Cash time-compression system create more space for commercials during a radio broadcast?

Rush Limbaugh said he noticed it about 2 months ago. Listeners to his daily radio show were sending in e-mail messages by the thousands, asking why there were more commercials on his 3-hour talk-radio program.

"At first I didn't know what they were talking about," Mr. Limbaugh said. "I was talking for the same amount of time every day."

He may have been speaking for the same amount of time, but his words were, without his knowledge, being sucked into a temporal never-never land. A new kind of digital technology was literally snipping out the silent pockets between words, shortening the pauses and generally speeding up the pace of Mr. Limbaugh's speech.

In New York City, listeners to WABC heard the accelerated version of Mr. Limbaugh's program, causing Mr. Limbaugh to complain about it during a broadcast.

With no fanfare, the digital program—called Cash, in the direct manner of software nomenclature, because that's what it makes—has recently established a foothold in the radio industry. General managers at about fifty radio stations across the country are using it, to quicken talk programs so that they can wedge in more commercials. Radio stations are adding as many as 4 minutes of commercial time an hour—or eight 30-second commercials. At one point, some stations added as many as 6 minutes of commercials, the maximum allowed by the technology, but eventually pulled back.

While the radio industry has previously used devices to speed up programming, this is the first time that time compression has been applied on live programming to expressly make room for more advertising. And the new device has angered radio denizens like Mr. Limbaugh, who says he uses pauses for emphasis much like an actor raises an eyebrow on stage. He spared no hyperbole when he spoke in an interview of its potential impact on radio: "I think it is potential doom for the radio industry," he said.

Mr. Limbaugh may be accustomed to predicting doom, but in an economy where advertising dollars are plentiful and radio stations can, as a result of deregula-

tion, run as many commercials as listeners will tolerate, some say the radio industry is like a hungry child staring at an open cookie jar.

While radio executives say the impact of the Cash technology is often imperceptible to consumers, advertising executives complain that there is already too much clutter on the dial, making each commercial less effective. Other critics point to a larger issue: that the growth in commercials in recent years, combined with listeners drifting toward other media, may be helping to eat away at the radio audience.

Shrinking radio's content reflects the growing impulse to cram in advertising wherever and whenever possible. Once punctuating the cultural landscape, commercials now dominate it, from the flashing computer screens at the local deli cash register to the piped-in advertisements on corporate telephone lines to airport baggage carousels and supermarket floors.

Critics say that jamming too many ads on radio is one of the first places commercial overload becomes swiftly apparent. James Duncan, president of Duncan's American Radio, a Cincinnati-based broadcasting industry consulting group, said that as deregulation has loosened the industry's limits on commercials, their number has jumped to twenty commercials an hour, from about a dozen. That typically represents a rise of about 10 minutes an hour to, in some programs, as much as 30 minutes.

Since 1990, the total time Americans have spent listening to radio programming has shrunk by 12 percent, Mr. Duncan said. According to figures from Arbitron, the independent research agency that tracks radio ratings, time spent listening has indeed fallen in the last decade, to 21 hours 15 minutes a week, from 23 hours 45 minutes a week—a decline of 10.5 percent.

"We are throwing way too many commercials at our listeners," Mr. Duncan said. "I think stations will slowly realize that there is a maximum that listeners can stand, and if they don't they will seriously downgrade their listenership."

But expanding commercial time has proved too tempting for the radio industry, which is experiencing boom times thanks to the healthy economy but also partly because the industry is now owned by a small cluster of giants like Clear Channel Communications, which has a pending deal to buy AMFM; the Infinity

Broadcasting division of CBS; *and* Walt Disney's Capital Cities/ABC Broadcast Group. As the industry has consolidated, the economics of radio management have become more efficient, streamlining ad sales and centralizing programming.

The Radio Advertising Bureau estimates that radio sales will have reached $15.5 billion for 1999. Advertising revenue was up 14 percent on the local level and 27 percent on the national level through October 1999, compared with the same period the previous year, the bureau said.

When Cash became available last spring, it seemed a natural outgrowth of the advertising boom. Prime Image, a Silicon Valley technology company, introduced it after its device for television stations—the Time Machine, which compresses audio and visual signals to make more time for commercials on live programming—caught the eye of a radio station owner in Philadelphia.

The notion of time compression began to take hold in television about a decade ago, and has been used to moderately shrink syndicated programming like talk and game shows. But the time-compression equipment was not aggressively marketed as devices to create extra time for commercials until about 3 years ago.

The promotional literature for the Time Machine, for example, reads in part: "Use the Time Machine to add commercials to your program schedule and profits to your bottom line." Bill Hendershot, the president of Prime Image, said that more than 250 television stations—affiliates from NBC, CBS, ABC, and Fox, several owned and operated stations, and a handful of cable networks—own the Time Machine. The Inspirational Network in Charlotte, North Carolina, has used it to speed up sermons and religious programming.

Use of time-compression devices on television generally creates less time for extra advertising, so the impact on the bottom line is proportionally less than for radio. Because television viewers and executives are much more sensitive to commercial clutter, the quantity of commercials on television has not reached the numbers of those on radio.

To squeeze in those vast numbers of commercials, Cash works on live radio by digitally recording the entire broadcast. It begins by recording the first couple of minutes of live radio—depending on how many commercials the manager wants to insert—then replays it, condensing the silent parts throughout the rest of the broadcast. It is used primarily by local radio stations that apply it to syndicated programs.

For example, one day last month, WWDB-FM in Philadelphia, which broadcasts Mr. Limbaugh's national program every day at noon, sought to gain almost 3 extra commercial minutes in 1 hour. The engineer inserted a 1-minute commercial block at noon, and Cash silently recorded Mr. Limbaugh during that minute. At 12:01 P.M., the program began to play Mr. Limbaugh's now not-exactly-live broadcast; during the next 21 minutes, the digital program eliminated pockets of silence between Mr. Limbaugh's words and also removed what is known as "redundant" data from within words—for example, shortening a long syllable. The station gradually earned back the 1 minute lost at the top of the broadcast.

The impact of Cash is minimized by Phil Boyce, the program director of New York's WABC-AM, who experimented with Cash on Mr. Limbaugh's show in November 1999—until Mr. Limbaugh complained about it during a broadcast, a contretemps reported in the *New York Post*.

Mr. Boyce said that he had not yet decided if he would continue to use Cash. "Yes, you can shoehorn more commercials in," Mr. Boyce said. "But it really wouldn't be noticeable with the naked ear unless some station was using it to its maximum capacity by removing 5 or 6 minutes an hour."

But that is already happening. Dennis Begley, the general manager of WWDB-FM, has squeezed as many as 6 extra commercial minutes from an hour of Mr. Limbaugh's program, prompting complaints from listeners. But, he said, the benefits outweigh the disadvantages. "When I first heard about this thing, I knew we had to get it," he said, "because I knew the money-making potential was ridiculous."

But because listeners complained, he said, these days he aims to squeeze no more than 4 minutes an hour.

Mr. Boyce of WABC, the only New York station to experiment with Cash, said that the station used Cash because there was an unprecedented demand for commercial inventory.

"When you're in a sold-out situation, you look for any way possible to manage more advertising," Mr. Boyce said. Because of sensitivity to listeners and Mr. Limbaugh, WABC has suspended its use of Cash for the time being.

And that feast for radio stations has turned out to be a famine of sorts for advertisers, who are becoming sensitive to the quantity of commercials on radio. Jackie Davenport, a vice president and broadcast supervisor at Lowe Lintas & Partners Worldwide, an advertising agency in New York, said that the problem of clutter was much more apparent in radio than in television. Unlike television, where they closely watch how many minutes they will devote to commercial time, "radio will just add more minutes when the demand increases," she said. "The clutter has gotten out of control."

Ms. Davenport said advertisers had become wary of getting lost in a long commercial block, so that not only price but placement had become part of the negotiating process.

The compression technology has certainly given radio purists pause—or maybe a lack thereof. Michael Harrison, the editor in chief of *Talkers,* a weekly magazine that chronicles the talk-radio industry, said that compression reflects trends in both radio and in the commercial-polluted American culture at large.

"It's a syndrome of our times," Mr. Harrison said. "We have no patience for anything that might seem superfluous. We're at a time when we're so caught up in

speed and greed that we have no qualms about bastardizing artistic integrity."

Kraig T. Kitchin, the president and chief operating officer of Premiere Radio Networks, the subsidiary of Clear Channel that distributes *The Rush Limbaugh Show,* said he had studied Cash to see if its speed had any adverse affects on Mr. Limbaugh's ratings and found that it did not. He called Cash's innovation inevitable.

"In life, everything moves faster now," Mr. Kitchin said. "You get more e-mails and voice mails than you can keep up with. But you still have the same number of hours in the day."

Even Mr. Limbaugh's complaints are not all tied to purist motives. Mr. Limbaugh, who receives a percentage of the advertising revenue raised during his program, said he was concerned about advertisers' perception of Cash.

"Nobody is going to listen to a radio program where 30 of every 60 minutes is advertising," Mr. Limbaugh said. "And no advertiser wants to be sandwiched in between six other commercials. But of course, to the technology nerds, this is a fascinating device."

RELATED LINKS

- Arbitron (http://www.arbitron.com)
- Prime Image, Inc. (http://www.primeimageinc.com)
- Radio Advertising Bureau (http://www.rab.com)
- The Rush Limbaugh Show (http://www.rushlimbaugh.com)

FOR FURTHER RESEARCH

To find out more about the topics discussed in this reading, use InfoTrac College Edition. Type in keywords and subject terms such as "radio advertising," "time compression," and "advertising overload." You can access InfoTrac College Edition from the Wadsworth / Thomson Communication Cafe homepage: http://communication.wadsworth.com.

Reading 4-3

Television's New Voyeurism Pictures Real-Life Intimacy
Bill Carter

EDITOR'S NOTE

In addition to expanding channel choices, the character of much television programming is changing. With the success of COPS, Jerry Springer, *and* MTV's The Real World, *more and more reality-based shows are arriving on the scene. Now, direct from Europe, a new wave of voyeuristic formats is invading American TV. Second-generation shows like* Survivor *and* Big Brother *play to the participants' sense of vanity by documenting their every move while satisfying the audience's strange desire to observe the intimate details of other people's lives at a safe distance. The newest reality shows push the limits of voyeurism and, some would say, good taste but continue to attract audiences and participants eager for their 15 minutes of fame. The network prime-time ratings race is more Darwinian than ever.*

CONSIDER

1. What is the basic appeal of shows based on real-life experiences? Why are audiences so drawn to them?

2. For the television industry, what are the economic advantages of reality shows over scripted series? Whose careers do these shows hurt?

3. What is the relationship that appears to be emerging between European and American television?

The European invasion began with *Who Wants to Be a Millionaire,* which transformed the competitive landscape of network television. Now a new wave of formats, all based on real-life experience voyeuristically captured on camera, is coming from abroad.

The shows range from examinations of people trying to survive on a desert island to people trying to get along while locked together in various settings of forced intimacy—in a house, on a bus or a tourist vacation, in a home set up to match conditions 100 years ago.

The shows, many of which will have ambitious Internet components, have been described as various combinations of MTV's cinéma vérité show *The Real World,* the syndicated talk show *Jerry Springer,* and, of course, *Who Wants to Be a Millionaire,* which came from Britain. One show makes its Orwellian aura overt: It is called *Big Brother.*

Virtually all the shows have been significant hits in European countries. *Big Brother* is a phenomenon in Holland, even spawning a second series, a talk show where the events on the show are exhaustively discussed.

It is the chance for the networks—which have been losing viewers to cable television for at least a decade—to create the kind of phenomenon in this country that ABC did with *Who Wants to Be a Millionaire,* which is driving network executives to pursue the other inventive European television formats that break the mold of comedies, dramas, and news programs.

In fact, the bidding for the American version of *Big Brother* reached a fever pitch last week, with prices escalating to a point where one senior network executive labeled the process "totally nuts."

CBS, which will carry the first two examples of this [new voyeuristic] genre, is already deep into its planning for a thirteen-episode summer series called *Survivor*—a giant hit in Sweden—in which sixteen people will be stranded on an island off Borneo in the Pacific Ocean, charged with finding ways to survive. Cast members will be eliminated each week by vote of the other contestants until one is the final survivor, winning $1 million. *Survivor* has lined up eight sponsors, and they will be given product-placement opportunities. For example, Reebok is a sponsor; the contestants will most likely be wearing Reebok shoes.

Leslie Moonves, president of CBS Television, said the move toward these wilder formats reflected the network's conclusion that tried-and-true television, like situation comedies on brightly lit Hollywood sound stages, now leaves many American viewers cold.

"What's happening is people are realizing you need to be different," Mr. Moonves said. "You can't go with the same old meat and potatoes anymore. You've got to shake things up. And clearly people are realizing it's a big world out there and shows really can come from the other side of the Atlantic."

The reality shows have an economic advantage over scripted series: They do not employ vast numbers of writers and they have no expensive stars at all. That points to a downside for Hollywood. Mr. Moonves said that every game show in prime time cost the industry 100 jobs. Producers have already complained that the proliferation of news magazines and game shows are radically shrinking prime-time opportunities.

"There's no question that if the reality shows take off there will be a contraction in the business," he said. "There could be a real shift in who's working and not working."

More than anything, the move toward the European shows reflects the effect of *Millionaire,* which has transformed the network prime-time ratings race, pulling ABC from a likely third place for the season to a near-certain first-place finish.

Millionaire has already fathered a brood of game shows. Last year there were no game shows on network prime time. Now there are eight hours of games each week. Because *Millionaire* emerged from Britain as a fully developed hit, network executives have started looking at other European shows.

One agent who has been in the middle of many of the negotiations for these new programs, Ben Silverman, head of international packaging for the William Morris Agency, lived for more than 4 years in England.

"I scoured the TV listings all over Europe looking for shows that sounded interesting," Mr. Silverman said. "The European producers don't come from the American system. They don't have this track record that leads them to reject certain ideas. They also don't

have the infrastructure to support shows full of writers and stars. So they have to find innovative stuff."

Mr. Silverman, along with a William Morris partner in Los Angeles, Greg Lipstone, represented the British company Celador in negotiations with ABC for *Millionaire,* which was supposed to be nothing more than a summer series. After it became a hit, Mr. Silverman started getting calls about other European properties he had already lined up.

Even PBS called, securing the rights to a show produced by a British company called Wall to Wall. This one, *1900 House,* involves bringing a family into a home with cameras and making them live just as they would have a century ago—without, for example, television.

But *Big Brother,* owned by the Dutch company Endemol Entertainment, is currently the hottest property in this genre. Mark Itkin, the senior vice president of William Morris for reality programs, said: "I had no idea the bidding would be so hot. But the show has so many elements, from being on 100 days in a row to an Internet component that is especially attractive to networks."

Mr. Silverman first believed only a cable network would make the commitment to Endemol's format: 100 consecutive nights of *Big Brother.* But after *Millionaire,* three big broadcast networks jumped into the bidding, each promising to broadcast *Big Brother* essentially every single night over summer.

Big Brother throws a group of ten people, mostly in their 20s, into a new house constructed with cameras and recording equipment everywhere to document their every move. In Holland that included everything from showers to sex, though an American version is clearly not going to go that far.

In Holland, the Internet helped drive the show because users could log onto the show's Web site, pick out certain characters and cameras, and literally watch 24 hours a day.

Each week one cast member is voted out, with viewers participating by phone and Internet. The last cast member standing in Holland won 250,000 guilders, about $111,000.

Many of the elements are similar to *Survivor,* so similar, that Mark Burnett, who is producing *Survivor* for CBS, said the show's British originators had filed suit against Endemol.

Mr. Burnett described *Survivor* as "a little bit of *The Truman Show* and *Lord of the Flies,* with an edgy *Gilligan's Island* thrown in."

Currently Mr. Burnett is whittling down the hundreds of applicants for *Survivor,* using, among other things, a battery of psychological tests. He hopes to avoid the unfortunate outcome of the show's first edition in Sweden, when one cast member committed suicide after being rejected by his comrades.

And that was in a format that was softer than the American version. In Sweden, cast members decided by voting whom they wanted to remain on the island. Mr. Burnett acknowledged that the American version would be far more Darwinian. Individuals will be voted *out* by the group.

Though CBS may lead this trend, program executives at the other networks are likely to try to come up with their own, similar formats.

Mike Darnell, executive vice president of special programs for Fox, has been highly inventive in the reality arena, coming up with the concepts for everything from the game show *Greed* to *When Good Pets Go Bad.* He was also the man behind the now-scrapped idea to crash a Boeing 747 live in the desert.

Mr. Darnell's latest brainstorm is a special called *Who Wants to Marry a Millionaire,* in which fifty female contestants will be whittled down by beauty pageant–like contests and extensive interviewing to five finalists, all in wedding gowns, one of whom will be proposed to and married on the air, live, by a willing millionaire.

"All these shows are voyeuristic," Mr. Darnell said. "After a while they become soap operas. That's why casting is so important. The people you pick will determine whether you're a hit or a bomb."

Robert Thompson, founder of the Center for the Study of Popular Television at Syracuse University, called the trend toward voyeurism shows an inevitable confluence of advances in technology and basic human interest.

"Popular culture is beginning to catch up with our real behavior," Mr. Thompson said. "We all talk about family values, but that's not how most of us operate as human beings. In some ways, this is the programmers discovering what TV was always so great at in the first place. This is 'Peeping Tom' to the max."

RELATED LINKS

- Fear Factor (http://home.nbci.com/LMOID/bb/fd/0,946,-0-5676-headless,00.html)
- MTV's The Real World (http://www.mtv.com/mtv/tubescan/rw10)
- Survivor (http://www.cbs.com/primetime/survivor2)
- Temptation Island (http://www.fox.com/temptation)
- Who Wants to Be a Millionaire? (http://abc.go.com/primetime/millionaire/millionaire_home.html)

FOR FURTHER RESEARCH

To find out more about the topics discussed in this reading, use InfoTrac College Edition. Type in keywords and subject terms such as "reality-based television," "viewer voyeurism," and "experimental TV formats." You can access InfoTrac College Edition from the Wadsworth/Thomson Communication Cafe homepage: http://communication.wadsworth.com.

Reading 4-4

HDTV Demystified
Dean Mermell

EDITOR'S NOTE

High-definition television, or HDTV, is about to transform the way we relate to the screen. Properly displayed in a high-resolution, wide-screen format, HDTV images are so sharp and clear that many first-time viewers say they have the impression of gazing through a window rather than looking at a televised picture. More than enhanced image quality, digital television also carries high-fidelity audio and surround sound. But before HDTV becomes commonplace, offering more than twice the resolution of traditional analog television, two things must happen: the industry must convert its analog signals to digital broadcasts, and the price of consumer HDTV sets needs to drop dramatically. For early adopters of HDTV, television images will seem almost real, but the cost will be considerable. Nevertheless, the transition to a digital platform represents the most significant change in television technology since the introduction of color.

CONSIDER

1. Why does the transition to a digital platform represent the most significant change in television technology since the introduction of color in the 1950s?

2. What are the key differences between analog television and digital television in terms of image resolution, sound quality, aspect ratio, and signal transmission?

3. How might the *experience* of watching television change when high-definition sets become affordable and widely available? What are some potential ramifications for the viewer and for the motion picture and television industries?

Change is scary. Only 70 years ago the whole idea of sending image and sound across vast distances seemed preposterous. On September 7, 1927, in a makeshift laboratory in a loft on Green Street in San Francisco, a young inventor named Philo Taylor Farnsworth demonstrated an invention to his eager investors. He was able to transmit the image of a thick white line painted on a glass slide from a wireless transmitter, which was received by a device with a tiny, round, glass viewing screen. He could rotate the slide and the line would change its orientation simultaneously to the receiving end. This one act and the brilliance that led up to it put Farnsworth ahead of everyone with similar intentions and commenced a two-decades-long legal battle with

RCA for the origin of the patent, which Farnsworth ultimately won.

Farnsworth had a vision of people the world over being able to send and receive televised signals, but he could never have imagined the scope of the industry his invention would spawn. Our present change-over to digital television seems like a minor upgrade, compared with selling the whole idea. Imagine trying to get people to buy televisions when there was no programming available! Farnsworth's first broadcasts were from a funky Philadelphia studio featuring talent-show-level ˜entertainers, sent over short distances using a low-wattage transmitter to the early television engineers, who had test sets in their homes a few miles away.

Although Farnsworth and his assistants came up with a few prototypes and early sets that were actually marketed, the ultimate production and distribution of television sets fell to companies like RCA and Philco. These early devices were typically housed in cabinets that looked like small wardrobes, with tiny windows into a magical world. The technology for these black-and-white sets quietly evolved into bigger, clearer pictures, and eventually in the 1950s, a technique for carrying color information in the signal led to the first and only real significant change in the receiver end of the technology since its inception: color TV sets. But the signal still carried the same amount of resolution (about 400 lines per frame), the same kind of sound (weak), and the same box-shaped picture it always had.

EARLY TELEVISION AND THE LETTERBOX FORMAT

The shape, or aspect ratio, of the traditional television screen has its roots in the early development of motion-picture film. It was developed by W. K. L. Dickson, an inventor in Thomas Edison's lab in the late 1800s. Working with a motion-picture camera called a Kine-scope (a variation of which is still used today to transfer video to film), Dickson, who made his own film, settled on a frame size of 1 inch wide and ¾ inches high, or 4 units by 3 units. When the industry adopted this aspect 4:3 ratio as the standard, everything concerning the viewing of film and television images, from initial production to final viewing, whether on a big or small screen, took on that shape. And so it remained for over half a century.

But the shape of things eventually changed. In the 1950s Hollywood began to feel threatened by the sudden popularity of television. Between rock and roll and family night around the tube, people weren't going to the movies anymore. So the studio moguls went to their engineers and said, "Give us something *big!*" which led to film formats like Cinerama, Cinemascope, and VistaVision. There are more film formats with similarly colorful names, but the common thread is that all these pictures are wider than 4 by 3. They're not a box. They're stretched out wide, like a landscape picture, into a 16 by 9 aspect ratio. Shooting film (and now video) in this frame shape offers more compositional possibilities and more closely reflects the way we naturally see the world.

Today there are two formats in which to view motion pictures and television productions: letterbox and "pan and scan." Watch a rented video and chances are you'll see the message "this film has been formatted to fit your screen" at the beginning of the tape; this means the movie has been panned and scanned. An editor has gone through the entire film, often with the original director or producer present, and isolated the "action frame" of the movie, essentially cutting out those images deemed nonessential to the picture. A letterboxed production has literally been trimmed at the sides to fit onto a 4:3 TV screen. Without such careful editing, that touching scene of the lovers in the far corner would end up being just voices with a shot of an empty room. Of course, the cinematographer and director never thought any part of their film was nonessential, but these are the realities of marketing for the television and home-video markets. HDTV will change that, and soon your favorite movie, which was only video released in a letterboxed or formatted version, may become available in its native 16 by 9 format.

WHY DIGITAL?

Aside from the obvious advantages of the shape, there are significant advantages to the way a high-definition digital picture is produced. To begin with, everything about digital is either on or off. In other words, a digital signal doesn't weaken over distance like an analog signal. If you can receive it at all, you generally receive it perfectly. A digital picture isn't subject to ghosting, hazing, and interference of the kind you get through nondigital equipment and service. This is because the picture is actually reconstructed inside a digital TV set's decoder (which is either part of your set or integrated into a separate tuner) and then displayed on screen. But to get there, the signal must first be compressed. Digital signals can be compressed much easier than analog signals and take up far less bandwidth. The compression scheme for digital television is called MPEG-2, the same one used to create DVDs.

All compression is a compromise. The highest-quality digital video is uncompressed, but that takes an incredible amount of data (equal to about 27 floppy discs per second!), and that kind of bandwidth may never be available on anything outside of a local network. To accommodate digital signals through available transmission channels, a picture with about four times the resolution of a nondigital environment is compressed as much as 55 to 1. But not uniformly because MPEG-2, though not perfect, is marvelously good at knowing what to compress. It takes advantage of how the eye perceives color variations and motion. Inside each frame, an MPEG-2 encoder records just enough detail to make it appear as if nothing is missing from the picture. The encoder also compares adjacent frames and only records those sections of the picture that have moved or changed. The result is such that a true high-definition broadcast is as clear as gazing through a window.

The compression process allows for more than a superior picture. Digital audio can also be encoded through the leftover bandwidth, radically changing the home entertainment experience. And true surround sound may immerse the viewer as much as an improved picture. This new level of sonic quality opens up possibilities for audio programming that could change the role of radio in our lives as well. Multicasting, or the ability to receive more than one signal at a time, will also become commonplace. Although the signals for multicasting are analog, they're high quality. Finally, digital transmission allows us to surf the Web and creates opportunities for video conferencing and Internet communication.

Perhaps the most significant component of HDTV is the lowly pixel, or picture element. In analog TV, the pixels, which display red, green, and blue color information, are rectangular, standing upright like little obelisks. You can see the red, green, and blue components of each pixel in the output of many older projection TVs. But HDTV displays pictures the way computer screens do, with square pixels, and they're over four times smaller than analog TV pixels. These smaller picture elements yield much finer detail with far less of the fuzziness associated with analog broadcasts.

Picture resolution differs dramatically for digital (computer-like) screens and analog (TV) monitors. Picture resolution refers to the way pixels are arranged across the screen, both vertically and horizontally. The total number of lines that can be resolved on an analog television monitor (sometimes known as NTSC) are 720 vertical lines by 486 horizontal lines. HDTV, which is capable of resolving as many as 1920 vertical by 1080 horizontal lines, can produce a significantly sharper, crisper, and more color-saturated image.

HDTV STANDARDS

There are currently 18 different standards for digital television. However, for purposes of consumer products, a high-definition television set must be capable of displaying either a 720p (progressively scanned) or 1080i (interlaced scanned) signal in a 16 by 9 format to

be considered HDTV. Progressive scanning and interlaced scanning are discussed below. For the most part all HDTVs coming out today will play both 720p and 1080i. And depending on the broadcaster, both 720p and 1080i signals are being broadcast today.

An argument over whether 1080i is better than 720p is one you should probably stay out of at your next dinner party. There are lots of variables in this mix, and the two formats really shouldn't be compared with each other; they really are different systems. The 1080i standard offers more horizontal resolution, while 720p is free of "ghosting" and other image artifacts. The standard that eventually wins out will be determined by the visual quality of the subject matter on the screen, as well as the quality of the encoded MPEG-2 signal. Considering high-definition TV in relation to analog television may help clarify questions about image quality.

HDTV will usually make analog content look better. However, keep in mind that television programming not produced digitally with HDTV specifications needs to go through a conversion process to be displayed with the newer technology. This is called up-conversion. Before delving into the specifics of up-conversion, it is important to first understand how standard television receives its signal. Standard television's signal is beamed across the airwaves at a rate of thirty frames per second. Each of these frames is broken down into two fields for a total of sixty fields per second. These fields alternate every other resolution line, giving viewers the fluid "interlaced" picture we see on TV today. But while interlacing offers smoother motion than frames alone, analog pictures are subject to fuzziness, ghosting, and other image artifacts, that is, distortion, shadows, or weird shapes in the picture.

HDTV, on the other hand, takes these sixty fields and up-converts them to a progressively scanned picture. In other words, the lines of the picture are transmitted consecutively, one solid line after another, rather than two slightly overlapping fields. This is how computer monitors display information. There is some debate as to whether this type of display in its lower resolutions of 480p (progressive) qualifies as a high-definition format or should instead be called something like "enhanced definition." Another up-conversion process possible with some digital sets enhances the resolution of an analog picture to 1080i, or 1080 interlaced lines of resolution. This is accomplished by the process of line doubling. When watching an analog broadcast such as a daytime soap and a prompt pops onto the screen announcing "you're watching digital television," you're actually seeing a line-doubled image, not true HDTV.

RECEPTION DECEPTION

A common misconception is that digital cable is required to receive digital or HDTV signals; it's not. In fact, digital cable is presently *incompatible* with digital television signals and only improves the delivery of analog programming. Instead of digital cable, HDTV can be received through a satellite dish, ordinary cable, or even old-fashioned "rabbit ears." Current high-definition programming is, for now, only available at night (Jay Leno, many pay-per-view movies and movie channels, some HBO, and much of *Monday Night Football*). What you see during the day being advertised as digital television is presently up-converted

from standard definition to 1080i. Over the next year or two, as the broadcasters pay the big bucks for the equipment switchover and more high-definition content becomes available, true HDTV will gradually become available.

In the foreseeable future cable may hold an advantage via cable modems, which may merge television and the Internet into one GUI (graphical user interface), where any viewer/user is only two button clicks away from any television show ever produced. If the cable companies can find a way to use digital cable for HDTV signal distribution, we'll have both a better picture and more programming choices. Keep your eye on what AOL and Time Warner do now that they've merged. Satellite dish services are another way to receive HDTV broadcasts. RCA is currently marketing an HDTV satellite dish and receiver, with other industry players scheduled to follow suit.

RELATED LINKS

- HDTV Magazine (http://www.web-star.com/hdtvmagazine/menu.html)
- PC-Webopaedia: HDTV (http://www.pcwebopaedia.com/TERM/H/HDTV.html)
- What is HDTV? (http://www.howstuffworks.com:80/hdtv1.htm)

FOR FURTHER RESEARCH

To find out more about the topics discussed in this reading, use InfoTrac College Edition. Type in keywords and subject terms such as "HDTV," "digital broadcasting," and "digital television (DTV)." You can access InfoTrac College Edition from the Wadsworth/Thomson Communication Cafe homepage: http://communication.wadsworth.com.

Reading 4-5

1999: The Year That Changed Movies
Jeff Gordinier*

EDITOR'S NOTE

From a creative standpoint, the last year of the millennium was a watershed for the movie industry. As Jeff Gordinier observes in this article from Entertainment Weekly, *in 1999, "All the old, boring rules about cinema started to crumble." Movies like* The Matrix, Fight Club, *and* Being John Malkovich *seemed to embody the cut-and-paste sensibility of video games, while* The Blair Witch Project *redefined what is possible to do on a $60,000 budget. New filmmakers are shunning the prevailing orthodoxy, drawing their inspiration from music or other creative sources. Indie films are in; dull, formulaic scripts are out. And new technology is hastening conventional wisdom's demise. Hollywood may never be the same.*

CONSIDER

1. What accounts for the dart-and-weave character of the new style of filmmaking?

2. Do you agree with *Being John Malkovich* producer and R.E.M. front man Michael Stipe that "Hollywood narrative film is in its death throes . . . and people are looking for something else"?

3. Why do moviemakers feel increasingly obliged to "keep the thrills coming"? Do cinematic pageants like *The English Patient* and *Shakespeare in Love* have a future?

You can stop waiting for the future of movies. It's already here. Someday, 1999 will be etched on a microchip as the first real year of twenty-first-century filmmaking. The year when all the old, boring rules about cinema started to crumble. The year when a new generation of directors—weaned on cyberspace and COPS, Pac-Man, and Public Enemy—snatched the flickering torch from the aging rebels of the 1970s. The year when the whole concept of "making a movie" got turned on its head.

Skeptical? Consider the evidence: The whirling cyberdelic Xanadu of *The Matrix.* The relentless, rapid-fire overload of *Fight Club.* The muddy hyperrealism of *The Blair Witch Project.* The freak show of *Being John Malkovich.* The way time itself gets fractured and tossed around in *The Limey* and *Go* and *Run Lola Run.* The spooky necro-poetry of *American Beauty* and *The Sixth Sense.* The bratty iconoclasm of *Dogma.* The San Fernando Valley sprawl of *Magnolia.* Were you prone to theatrical pronouncements, you might say that not since the *annus mirabilis* of *The Wizard of Oz, Gone With the Wind,* and *Stagecoach* has Hollywood brought so many narrative innovations screaming into the mainstream. "It's like 1939," marvels director Alexander Payne, whose dark satire *Election* represents yet another escape from the fuddy-duddy format. "There's a bumper crop of movies that, even if they're not perfect, are interesting and intelligent."

And fearless. If Hollywood's old guard tends to kneel before the Ten Commandments of screenwriting ("Thou shalt insert a plot point on page 27"), the new guard behaves with blissful sacrilege—even when it comes to the laws of physics. In these new films there's no such thing as death. (Lola takes a bullet to the heart 30 minutes into *Run Lola Run,* but that barely slows

down her kinetic dash through the streets of Berlin.) Time doesn't move in a straight line. (*The Limey* casually skips and flutters between days and decades.) And why get hung up on logic? If you want John Malkovich to slide down a slimy tunnel into the cerebral cortex of John Malkovich, what's stopping you?

Nothing. Like Keanu Reeves' hero in *The Matrix* (aptly named Neo), members of this new breed—backed by stars like Tom Cruise, Brad Pitt, Bruce Willis, and Cameron Diaz—are wondering whether the rules that have governed the silver screen for nearly a century amount to little more than an illusion. "Hollywood narrative film is in its death throes right now and people are looking for something else," declares R.E.M.'s Michael Stipe, who produced *Being John Malkovich.* Which doesn't mean the studios are going to cease and desist from giving us *Random Hearts* and *Runaway Bride*—flicks like those often make money—but only that *Random Hearts* and *Runaway Bride* are starting to look as clueless and wheezy as a Bing Crosby movie in the year of *Bonnie and Clyde.*

"Everybody knows that we're hitting the limits of traditional filmmaking because it's becoming so perfectionistic," says Tom Tykwer, the German director of *Run Lola Run.* "You are seeing films that are so perfect you don't even connect to them anymore. A film like *Malkovich* is an invitation to do something completely different. Even *The Matrix,* because it still serves all of our traditional desires in cinema, but it plays with your mind in a very strange way. Ten years ago, I don't think people would have even been ready for it."

They are now: *The Matrix* gobbled up $171 million at the ticket booth and has become a blockbuster behemoth—the best-selling movie ever in the aggressively Neo DVD format. "At the risk of sounding a little bit dramatic, I think there is a new age of cinema upon us," says Ricky Strauss, 33, senior VP of production at Columbia. "With the dawn of the millennium, there's definitely this set of really exciting young artists who have their own voices."

Don't think the artists haven't noticed—especially in a year when esteemed vets like Stanley Kubrick

---

"1999: The Year That Changed Movies," by Jeff Gordinier. From *Entertainment Weekly,* November 26, 1999, cover, pp. 38–49. Copyright © 1999 Entertainment Weekly, Inc. Reprinted with permission.

*Additional reporting by Daniel Fierman and Troy Patterson.

and Martin Scorsese gave us DOA duds like *Eyes Wide Shut* and *Bringing Out the Dead*. "The previous 'A list' of directors are running on empty now," says a director of one major Class of '99 movie. "It's not like we're looking at Oliver Stone's latest and going 'Oh, it's gonna be great.' Or Rob Reiner. Or Sydney Pollack. Or even Scorsese, you know? All these guys feel like they're running on empty, and we're all gaining. We're inspired."

"This is our screen," says Darren Aronofsky, flipping a switch in a vast rec room.

Aronofsky is the director of *[Pi]*—1998's frantic parable of cerebral meltdown—and this is Protozoa, his New York City production compound. Protozoa doesn't look like the outpost of a revolution. Aside from a few hints of youthful clutter—a Chemical Brothers sticker, a woozily lettered flier that says "No sex causes bad eyes"—Protozoa is a warren of white walls and computer nooks, almost as tidy and sleek as one of those utopian vistas in *The Matrix*.

A massive movie screen comes gliding down from the ceiling. "We put the PlayStation away when we have journalists come over," Aronofsky laughs. "But playing it on the big screen is really awesome."

He's not joking. If the last wave of Hollywood rebels (Coppola, Scorsese, Rafelson) drew their creative sustenance from the global titans of the art house (Fellini, Truffaut, Kurosawa), the new brigade is just as likely to find Parnassus in a Game Boy. Films of the new guard dart and weave; they reflect the cut-and-paste sensibility of video games, the Internet, and hip-hop. "It's about figuring out ways to entertain people who have been bombarded by billions upon billions of images," Aronofsky says. Your average movie has 600 or 700 cuts; Aronofsky's next, *Requiem for a Dream,* has over 2,000. Images riff on themselves in a kind of synaptic spray. "We call them 'hip-hop montages,'" he says.

"If you're growing up cutting and pasting constantly on your laptop or your home computer, yes, then you look at visual information and visual storytelling that way," says Bill Block. Block is the president of Artisan Entertainment, the indie renegade most readily identified with the new wave: Artisan's slate includes *[Pi], The Blair Witch Project, The Limey, The Cruise,* and *Requiem for a Dream*. "You look at scenes as just chunks—data chunks. To play with and move around. PlayStation Cinema, you could call it."

Block might be the most theory-minded Hollywood player ever to score a hot table at Mortons—let the guy go and he'll actually start talking about "compression algorithms"—but he's not the only one who believes that Hollywood needs to catch up with the human brain. You don't "watch" a film like *Fight Club;* you mainline a deluge of visual and sonic information (including a hefty chunk of the IKEA catalog) straight into your cranium. The director, David Fincher, remembers telling one of his producers: "Don't worry, the audience will be able to follow this. This is not unspooling your tale. This is downloading."

These days, the jumble of data chunks may be the very meat of the story—the hallowed Beginning, Middle, and End. The film *Go* takes off from Quentin Tarantino's clockwork manipulations in *Pulp Fiction:* It keeps rewinding to the same moment—and then skittering off in weird directions. "Audiences are a lot better now at understanding that," says *Go's* screenwriter, John August. "One thing that channel flipping has taught us is how to catch up to things really quickly. A lot of times you come into something halfway through and you have to think, 'Well, why are Ross and Rachel fighting about this?'"

Which leads to *The Blair Witch Project*. A year ago, if you had told a studio suit that a murky, herky-jerky, starless $60,000 horror flick would wind up trouncing Tom Cruise at the summer box office, he'd have set you up on a blind date with Andy Dick. "I'm grateful for its existence," says documentary director Bennett Miller, "because it reminded Hollywood that it doesn't know everything."

The key lesson: Kids are wired funny. *Blair Witch* might've induced motion sickness in many a potbellied boomer, but it felt as cozy as a Pikachu plush toy to any tot raised on a steady diet of *When Animals Attack*. "Kids today are growing up with camcorders in their house," says Aronofsky. "I'm sure a lot of kids run around their neighborhoods making horror films and stuff, and they saw something in *Blair Witch* that they could really connect to." It's no accident that Wes Bentley's sensitive brooder in *American Beauty* had a camera permanently attached to his palm.

For years, the prevailing wisdom about the PlayStation Generation could be summed up in one slur: vidiots. Critics presumed that these kids would soil the Temple of Cinema; instead, it now looks like the kids might be bringing the congregation back to life. "Once you get in the habit of seeing the world that way, it's very hard to readjust to that old-fashioned way of seeing it—to the sluggish, sedate way of seeing it," says director James Toback, whose movie release *Black and White* is created from a series of supercharged improvisations. "Right now you could not get a young audience to sit through David Lean."

So what's the remedy when your audience views every "normal" movie as a 4-hour Richard Attenborough epic on NyQuil? *Speed.* Watch *Run Lola Run* and you can lap up the biography of a cameo character within 8 seconds: Every time Lola encounters a bystander, you get a lightning blast of footage showing you the rest of that bystander's life. The movie itself sprints along like a video game: Every time Lola fails to win the prize—game over!—she just starts running again. "It starts to be in your blood. It becomes your language," Tykwer says. "In computers you can always open new doors. The Internet—you can just go and go and go; there's a new door and there's another door. This is something that a whole generation is completely used to. If you do films in the old way, they just don't offer this kind of perception."

The old way. If *Fight Club* and *Being John Malkovich* and *Dogma* have anything in common (and from an aesthetic standpoint, they don't), it's a nagging impatience with the old way. Plenty of art forms—the novel, chamber music, painting—have gone through a series of stylistic earthquakes over the past century. Although Hollywood has absorbed creative shocks from the likes of John Cassavetes, Andy Warhol, Robert Altman, Jim Jarmusch, and David Lynch, the bedrock form of a mainstream movie has stayed pretty much the same. Agents and producers still preach the Gospel According to Syd Field; budding hacks clutch tattered copies of Field's *Screenplay* and *The Screenwriter's Workbook,* handy guides that boil down classics like *Chinatown* into the sort of paradigm charts you'd study in a Harvard Business School efficiency seminar. Ever watch a movie and get the feeling that you know exactly what's going to happen? Well, you're supposed to. A teacher and lecturer, Field isn't famous for writing any landmark scripts of his own, just for telling Hollywood how to do it. "These movie-executive people and producers—bad producers—I think they're aware of the silliness of Syd Field, and they like to think that they are breaking out of that mold," says *Boogie Nights* director Paul Thomas Anderson. "But all they are doing is propagating it."

Familiarity, after all, breeds contempt. M. Night Shyamalan remembers fiddling with the script for *The Sixth Sense.* "I was four or five drafts in," says the writer-director, "and I just felt like this movie was comparable to other movies that I had seen, and that was not good enough. It felt familiar. So I sat down and said, 'What will raise this to another level above everybody else?'" Shyamalan's clever solution—let's give the lead character a creepy secret—helped convert a standard spook-fest into the twelfth-highest domestic gross of all time.

Hollywood's never going to abandon the three-act structure—it's been around since Aristotle's mega-pic deal with DreamWorks—but it's amazing to hear how many filmmakers are bored stiff with the dogma. "The whole school of Act 1/Act 2/Act 3 is destructive to a thriving, growing cinema," says *Election's* Payne. "I think that for the last 20 years American films have lived under ideological restrictions which are as stringent as—if not more stringent than—the restrictions on Eastern European films under Communism. You know, the hero has to triumph. The lovers have to reunite. The so-called liberal freethinkers running Hollywood are extremely conservative."

A lot of young directors just keep their eyes wide shut to the orthodoxy. "I've never read a screenwriting book," Anderson says flatly. When he was composing the arc of *Magnolia,* Anderson borrowed a model from an unlikely source: the Beatles. "I had a really ridiculously ambitious and presumptuous goal: I looked to *Sgt. Pepper* and the *White Album* for inspiration," he says. "I tried to structure my movie after "A Day in the Life," how it would sort of build build build build build build—fall off a cliff, and then start building back up again. I took more structurally from that song than from any movie I've seen."

Magnolia even throws out one of the holiest tenets of Hollywood's book of common prayer: Thou shalt get the ball rolling fast. "You can just imagine Joel Silver or any one of these big producers saying 'You've gotta suck 'em in the first 5 minutes!'" Anderson says. "I wanted to create a prologue that to a certain extent has nothing to do with the movie." Indeed, *Magnolia* kicks off with a trio of vignettes—and then veers off into territory that's totally unrelated to them. "The most important thing that a film can do is to get an audience to ask the question, 'What is going to happen next?'" Anderson says. "But to keep an audience asking 'What is going to happen next?' makes them uncomfortable. In other words, it makes studio executives uncomfortable. And it doesn't result in very good test scores. They want to be smarter than the movie, and it's a little frustrating when the movie's smarter than you."

It's easy to hear this new brigade slipping into one of Conan O'Brien's deadpan "In the Year 2000" routines: In the year 2000, people will make movies without a film crew! But a lot of the zaniest blurts from the crystal ball have already come true. Take *The Cruise,* a documentary about a New York City tour guide. The sole crew member on *The Cruise?* Bennett Miller, the director. By shooting on digital video—"There are cameras out there that are not much bigger than your fist," he says—Miller could deal with all the tasks that are usually juggled by an army of grips, techies, and assistants. "I have either a neurological or pathological disorder that prohibits me from collaborating with people. This technology was made for me," Miller says. "At my own pace, according to my own whims and instincts, I could pick up a camera and shoot without even speaking to anybody."

Making a cheap indie used to mean that your movie would look like it was shot by a crackhead with a 7-Eleven surveillance camera. Not anymore. "Right now, I can go through a feature film and turn every blue sky into a green sky," Aronofsky says. "I can create a world that's never been on the screen. It's becoming cheaper and cheaper and easier and easier to do that."

As he says this, Aronofsky is squinting into a computer. On the screen, Marlon Wayans is pressed up against the bars of a jail cell. *Requiem for a Dream* is based on a hallucinatory 1978 novel by Hubert Selby, Jr.; in the book, Wayans' character watches a prisoner turn into a rat. "There's no way I can afford to do that," Aronofsky says. "So how can I convey that he feels surrounded by rats? This was a crazy idea that I had." As Wayans hovers at normal speed, you watch a frenzy of rodent snouts sniffing and scurrying behind him. They're actually people wearing rat masks, but the sorcery of digital technology allows Aronofsky to make them move really fast, thereby creating a piece of persuasive, pricey-looking wigginess. Directors from Orson Welles to Tim Burton have dazzled us with such optical magic. What's radical is that Aronofsky's doing it on less than a $5 million budget.

All this technical stuff is cool, but it doesn't explain why any studio executive would interrupt his tantric Hopi aroma therapy class to worry about it. ("We're gonna have a big hit, Barry, if we can just rock the kids with those compression algorithms!") After all, the movie industry "is the most fake-reckless institution ever devised," Toback says. "It's filled with a bunch of incredibly cautious people who like to talk about themselves as gamblers and freewheelers. And in fact they're the most cowardly, cautious lot imagin-

able. They have the mentality of insurance clerks."

Which is why the savviest members of the new guard have a nice little insurance policy: movie stars. Big ones. Brad Pitt is in *Fight Club,* Tom Cruise is in *Magnolia,* and Cameron Diaz is in *Being John Malkovich.* (Trust us, she is—she's the frizzy-haired woman who gets stuck in the cage with the chimp.) You think you watch a lot of boring movies? Actors have to slog through 100 times as many dull, formulaic scripts. "The smart stars, the ones who tend to have long careers, realize they have to push and stretch themselves, so that means taking on different and sometimes difficult material," says Fox president Tom Rothman. "The fantastic thing about Cameron Diaz is that she's a bold actress. She's very willing to challenge her own image in the marketplace."

A star can get an executive to snap to, but even that's no guarantee when you're making a movie that involves puppets, lesbian lust, and psychic portals. "It was a total fluke that this movie got made. It was a struggle up until the very end, even with this cast," says *Being John Malkovich*'s producer Sandy Stern. "There was a studio head who asked us, 'Can it be *Being Tom Cruise?*'" Charlie Kaufman cranked out the script 5 years ago, but he still remembers the knee-jerk reactions from the Hugo Boss contingent: "'This is very funny. This is the funniest thing we've ever read. This is too weird. This will never be made.' That was the conventional wisdom."

Now that *Malkovich* has become an indie smash—grossing $6 million in 2 weeks and sending conventional wisdom flushing down a chute behind a file cabinet—Kaufman and director Spike Jonze have become the Hollywood equivalent of Web site designers whose IPO just went bonkers on the NASDAQ. ("One day this conformist mob of mediocrity is on top," Miller marvels. "The next day you've got some aberrant genius kid like Spike Jonze who manages to pull something off.") Kaufman's got a whole bunch of scripts just as bizarre as *Malkovich,* but what's even stranger is, they're hot. Mike Myers and Sean Penn are reportedly duking it out over *Confessions of a Dangerous Mind,* Kaufman's Dada-noir saga of *Gong Show* host Chuck Barris and his fantasized career as a CIA hitman. Jonathan Demme is shepherding along *Adaptation*—which is both an adaptation of Susan Orlean's book *The Orchid Thief* and the story of Charlie Kaufman's struggles to adapt Susan Orlean's book *The Orchid Thief.* (Got that?) Patricia Arquette is attached to *Human Nature;* she'll play a woman with a hormonal problem that causes her body to be covered in hair. (Robin Williams presumably had scheduling problems.) "It's a whole new world out there," observes *Malkovich* producer Steve Golin. "People are calling me up saying 'Can you get me in on that Charlie Kaufman project?'"

Naturally, the birth of every new world renders another one musty. The "indie versus studio" dogma may have dominated the first half of this decade, but that's old hat now. These days, it's wired versus tired. Miramax looked like Hollywood's maverick court of the Medicis in the early '90s, thanks to indie landmarks like *Pulp Fiction, Clerks,* and *The Crying Game.* But now that the major studios are waltzing with the avant-garde—Fox did *Fight Club,* Columbia did *Go,* Warner did *The Matrix*—Miramax's Bob and Harvey Weinstein are starting to look like the guards outside Buckingham Palace, marching in step with Oscar-friendly pageants like *The English Patient* and *Shakespeare in Love.* "The Weinsteins are getting to a place like Sam Raimi is," says up-and-coming director Jude Weng. "They all want to become respectable now." When Aronofsky went to the Sundance Film Festival in 1998, *[Pi]* became Artisan's first acquisition. "I recognized that Miramax was sort of out of the business of doing films like *[Pi],*" he says diplomatically. "And I recognized that there was a vacuum, because I want to see films like that."

Artisan has rushed in to fill that vacuum, but so have the majors. "When there is that odd, quirky type of material, agents aren't afraid anymore to send that into the studio," says Columbia VP of production An-drea Giannetti. "Before, a lot of times we wouldn't even see it."

"Ten years ago, *Being John Malkovich* wouldn't have been set up somewhere," says Columbia's Strauss.

"Even 5 years ago," says Giannetti.

Which suggests that 5 years from now, we might wind up getting lost in a forest of cruddy shaky-cam movies narrated by puppeteers and dead people. "Always in Hollywood, it comes down to what's going to sell," says Weng. "I go to a lot of meetings, and people are always like, 'Oh, I'm looking for the next *American Beauty,* I'm looking for the next *Being John Malkovich.*' It's going to get tapped out. Like teen films were huge, and that got tapped out." Indeed, just because the Neo Turks have awesome technology at their fingertips doesn't mean they'll all be talented enough to do something awesome with it. "I think there's going to be this wonderful, explosive glut of mediocrity," Miller chuckles. "It's going to be horrible. You know, big ideas without a lot of preparation. The technology invites a certain carelessness, because it's easy to let your guard down and not be disciplined."

Then again, we might wind up with a masterpiece or two. "I grew up in Coney Island, with the Cyclone, which is one of the oldest standing roller coasters in America," says Aronofsky, suddenly sounding more than a bit like one of those old-guard masters who came of age in the postwar boom. "I grew up on that. That was my main form of entertainment. And the one thing that taught me was, you've gotta keep the thrills coming."

RELATED LINKS

- Atom Films (http://www.atomfilms.com)

- iFilm: The Internet Movie Guide (http://www.ifilm.com)

- Hollywood.com (http://www.hollywood.com)

- The Internet Movie Database (http://www.us.imdb.com)

FOR FURTHER RESEARCH

To find out more about the topics discussed in this reading, use InfoTrac College Edition. Type in keywords and subject terms such as "independent filmmaking," "cinematic conventions," and "screenwriting." You can access InfoTrac College Edition from the Wadsworth/Thomson Communication Cafe homepage: http://communication.wadsworth.com.

5

Telecommunications

Reading 5-1

Hooking Up the Nation: AT&T-TCI Merger Is Driven by the Internet

Saul Hansell

EDITOR'S NOTE

The corporate marriage between phone giant AT&T and cable giant TCI in June of 1998, announced with much fanfare, helped solidify AT&T's position as a dominant player in the coming era of broadband communications. As this reading suggests, the TCI merger was not so much driven by a grand vision of digital fecundity as it was a competitive move to keep pace with other major industry players intent on providing high-speed Internet access. Little did anyone know at the time that AT&T's cable acquisitions and the attempted move into broadband services would not prove popular with investors, as the next reading makes clear. Somewhat tellingly, AT&T first courted America Online, which remained independent until acquiring Time Warner 18 months later.

CONSIDER

1. What was AT&T's motivation for acquiring Tele-Communications Inc. (TCI), and how was the acquisition supposed to help AT&T retain its position as a leading provider of integrated communications?

2. How does the merger illustrate the trend toward convergence in the telecommunications industry?

3. In terms of high-speed Internet access, what are the unique advantages of cable networks? What remains desirable about traditional telephone networks?

A telephone giant agrees to acquire the cable company Tele-Communications Inc. in a bold move that promises to redefine the communications landscape. Sound familiar?

It should. Nearly 5 years ago, another big phone company, Bell Atlantic, struck a merger agreement with the same cable giant. But that deal, which soon unraveled, was based on the vague plan of morphing telephone and cable networks into an "information highway" with 500 channels of interactive television—something no one could be certain consumers even wanted.

So what is different now that that would prompt AT&T to spend $48 billion to buy TCI? In two words: the Internet.

By agreeing to merge, AT&T and TCI are not so much gambling on a vague vision of the future but betting they can help satisfy the proven public demand for high-speed connections to the global Internet.

Though few would have predicted it back in 1993, the Internet and its multimedia World Wide Web have become that vaunted information highway—and the main vehicle for driving it is not a television set but an increasingly TV-like computer.

These days, tens of millions of households are regularly surfing the Web to download text, images, sound, and video clips and to chat on America Online or other Internet access services.

So important has the Internet become to so many people's lives, in fact, that the average amount of time Americans spent watching television declined in 1997 for the first time since television's invention. And for the first time, more messages were sent via electronic mail than through the post office.

"Nobody wanted 500 channels," said Eric Paulak, a telecommunications analyst for the Gartner Group. "Today, what people do want is Internet access."

Rather than chasing an elusive vision, then, AT&T and TCI are scrambling to keep pace with a race to use phone networks, cable networks, and other means

---

"Hooking Up the Nation: AT&T-TCI Merger Is Driven by the Internet," by Saul Hansell. From *The New York Times,* June 25, 1998, p. A1. Copyright © 1998 The New York Times Company. Reprinted with permission.

to provide consumers and businesses with connections to the Internet—a race that involves not only other cable titans like Time Warner and ambitious phone companies like MCI-WorldCom, but also competitors like America Online that were barely visible 5 years ago.

Indeed, even as AT&T began talking to TCI, the phone company was still trying to arrange a merger with America Online, which decided to remain independent—at least for the time being.

"Just as the home computer caused a whole lot of changes over the last 10 years, there is going to be a new revolution in telecommunications," said Barry Schuler, the president of creative development at America Online. "When you are chatting with someone on AOL, you will be able to click a button and your phone will ring and you can talk to them by voice."

AT&T, primarily a long-distance telephone carrier, with 90 million customers, and TCI—still mainly a cable company, serving 13 million homes—are already dabblers in Internet service.

AT&T's generic Worldnet Internet access service has attracted about 1 million customers on the strength of its brand name and an initial offering of a year of free service.

TCI owns about 40 percent of the @Home Network, which is developing technology and information and entertainment content for high-speed Internet access over television cables. While phone networks have the advantage of being able to route traffic virtually anywhere on the system, cable networks have a much higher carrying capacity—which on the Internet translates to higher speed.

Yet both companies know the network future lies not in today's telephone-network or cable-system technologies but in providing consumers and businesses with high-speed network access based on Internet technology—whether for data transfers, voice conversations, or, yes, eventually even TV-quality video.

While Internet traffic can flow over phone wires or cable lines or even wireless radio waves, the Internet itself employs a transmission format that is far more efficient and flexible than conventional telephone or cable systems and seems destined eventually to render those conventional systems obsolete.

"There is going to be no difference between local and long distance, between voice and data, between voice mail and e-mail," said Howard Anderson of the Yankee Group, a telecommunications consulting firm.

Indeed, such a network is so flexible, that everything from thermostats to refrigerators to door locks are being designed that can be linked to the Internet so they can be controlled remotely by the owners.

But the many billions of dollars that will be required for the communications industry to update its networks for a future all-Internet format must come from the revenues of current customers. That is why the first battles in the long war over who provides Internet access to the home will probably be over local voice telephone service.

After all, nearly every household, whether it subscribes to cable service or even has a personal computer, requires phone service—which remains the one surest way to establish a direct relationship with an individual household.

AT&T has not had a direct line into most consumer's homes since it was banished from the local telephone business by the Bell System breakup in 1984. But the company, freed to return to the local phone business by the Telecommunications Act of 1996, now hopes to offer customers a complete package that includes local, long-distance, and wireless telephone service along with cable television and Internet access all on one monthly bill.

Even before the TCI deal, AT&T had been assembling pieces of that capability. In January 1998, it agreed to pay $11.3 billion for Teleport Communications Group, which provides local phone and data services—mainly to businesses.

And it has been trying to develop an affordable wireless system for local calls from the home that would bypass the local telephone companies, by tapping into the vast cellular network it acquired with the purchase of McCaw Cellular. It has been expanding and modernizing that network ever since.

But in the local markets in which TCI operates, the deal merging AT&T with TCI would give AT&T direct wires into homes.

There is no guarantee that AT&T and TCI will succeed in their joint quest, of course. The competition is simply too fierce to predict the winners, as players in all areas of the telecommunications industry are rapidly moving into one another's markets.

America Online, in an effort to fend off phone company competition, for example, has signed up 1 million people for its low-cost long-distance service, offered through Tel-Save Holdings.

Local telephone companies, meanwhile, are creating technology that would enable them to offer high-speed Internet connections over conventional phone wires. And Sprint, the long-distance company, already a big provider of Internet transport services to other network operators, has spent $2 billion to reconfigure its entire network to use Internet-format technology rather than traditional phone-network circuitry.

And all the while, the industry urge to merge grows stronger on the assumption that victory ultimately will go the companies with the greatest size and geographic reach. Thus WorldCom has a pending deal to acquire MCI, the Baby Bell SBC Communications has agreed to buy another Bell, Ameritech, and so on. All of which has put pressure on AT&T to respond.

"The WorldCom/MCI deal will make the resulting company the most important worldwide supplier of communications," said Jerry Michalski, a computer industry consultant. "AT&T had to do something in order to avoid slipping out of contention as the major platform for worldwide, integrated communications."

It is only when a company can offer a full range of services that it can hope to recoup the cost of building an advanced, Internet-ready network.

"It will cost $500 to $600 per house to offer Internet, telephone and cable services," said David Dorman, the chief executive of the Internet company Pointcast and a former top executive of one of the original Baby Bells, Pacific Telesis. "If a household spends $100 to $200 a month for all those services, it doesn't sound like a terrible payback."

But as Paulak of the Gartner Group points out, only the affluent will be able to afford these new offerings.

"At $100 a month for telephone and high-speed Internet access, that rules out the half of the population that earns less than $35,000 a year," he said. "And it will mainly benefit the 12 percent who earn more than $100,000."

What is more, TCI, lumbering under a huge debt burden, has been much slower than its competitors to modernize its network.

"TCI is big hat, no cattle," said Anderson of the Yankee Group, who estimates that AT&T will have to invest $10 billion in TCI's network to be able to de-

Table 5.1

1993

Investor	Investment	Size	Rationale
*Bell Atlantic	TCI	$23 billion	Have a path for video, voice, and data, but the deal fell apart.
*AT&T	McCaw Cellular	$12.6 billion	Buy a cellular phone system to get a toehold in local markets.
†U.S. West	Time Warner Cable	$2.5 billion	Finance part of a joint cable TV venture.

1995

Investor	Investment	Size	Rationale
*Disney	ABC/Capital Cities	$19 billion	Package name-brand content with a network delivery system.
*Time Warner	Turner Broadcasting	$7.5 billion	Offer traditional media content over cable and TV networks.
*Westinghouse	CBS	$5.4 billion	Even a faltering network has value.

1996

Investor	Investment	Size	Rationale
*Bell Atlantic	Nynex	$25.6 billion	Bigger is better in the local phone service market.
*British Telecom	MCI	$19 billion	Attempt at a transatlantic phone linkup; deal fell through.
*SBC	Pacific Telesis	$16.7 billion	Another bigger-is-better acquisition.
*WorldCom	MFS Communications	$14 billion	Buy a bigger piece of the Internet.
*U.S. West	Continental Cablevision	$5.3 billion	Own more of the wires going into every home; the deal was closed but the company was spun off the next year.

1997

Investor	Investment	Size	Rationale
*WorldCom	MCI	$37 billion	Achieve control over most of the Internet backbone.
†Microsoft	Comcast	$1 billion	A provider of high-speed access to the Internet via cable.
*Microsoft	WebTV	$400 million	Another link to the Internet, this time through a TV service.

1998

Investor	Investment	Size	Rationale
*SBC	Ameritech	$62 billion	Become an even bigger local telephone company.
*AT&T	Teleport Communications	$12.9 billion	Buy a local phone company to get back in the business.
*Northern Telecom	Bay Networks	$7.7 billion	Get into selling data equipment for network traffic.
*Tellabs	Ciena	$6.9 billion	Making network equipment for phone and data services is big business.

*Planned acquisition.

†Investment.

liver all the new services it is promising. And AT&T better start writing big checks immediately, Anderson added, because the winner in the market will be decided early.

"The first person to provide high-speed Internet access with voice and data wins," he said, "because if customers are satisfied, they are never going to switch."

EXTENDING THEIR REACH

The AT&T and TCI deal is the latest in a string of agreements between telecommunications businesses intended to increase their reach, either within their own fields or to extend their businesses into other services. Table 5.1 (on the previous page) shows some of last decade's most significant deals.

RELATED LINKS

- AT&T (http://www.att.com)
- @Home (http://www.home.com/index_flash.html)
- MCI (http://www.mci.com)
- WorldCom (http://www.worldcom.com/main.phtml?loc=bmh)

FOR FURTHER RESEARCH

To find out more about the topics discussed in this reading, use InfoTrac College Edition. Type in keywords and subject terms such as "telecommunications mergers," "broadband communications," and "high-speed Internet access." You can access InfoTrac College Edition from the Wadsworth/Thomson Communication Cafe homepage: http://communication.wadsworth.com.

Reading 5-2

AT&T: Breaking Up Again

Seth Schiesel

EDITOR'S NOTE

American Telephone & Telegraph, or AT&T, dominated the telephone business to such an extent in the early 1980s that government regulators stepped in and used the antitrust laws to break the company into seven smaller regional phone systems (known as the "Baby Bells") and restricted AT&T to long-distance services. With the passage of the Telecommunications Act of 1996, AT&T was freed to expand into new areas and spent over $100 billion acquiring cable television systems TCI and MediaOne, hoping to become the nation's first one-stop shop for long-distance, wireless, cable TV, and broadband Internet services. Now, facing a high debt burden and flagging stock value, AT&T, under the direction of Chairman C. Michael Armstrong, has decided to break itself into four parts. This time, instead of government scrutiny, the overhaul was prompted by market pressures. As Armstrong took a chisel to the company, consumer advocates expressed concern about the breakup and investors were left wondering which pieces of the telecommunications giant could succeed on their own.

CONSIDER

1. Do you agree with AT&T Chairman Armstrong that the company's self-initiated breakup was the only way for it to remain competitive in today's economy? Why or why not?

2. Is it realistic to think that a single company will be able to provide a "one-stop shop" for long-distance, wireless, cable TV, and broadband Internet services across the nation as a single package with a single bill? Is such an arrangement even desirable?

3. Among AT&T's four new spin-off companies—AT&T Consumer Services, AT&T Business Services, AT&T Broadband Services, and AT&T Wireless Services—which do you think will be the most competitive and which the most vulnerable? Why?

Running out of time with impatient investors, AT&T pulled back from an expensive 3-year effort to become the first one-stop shop selling long-distance, wireless, cable television, and Internet services across the nation as a single package with a single bill. It announced that instead it would break itself into four parts.

The nation's eighth-largest company, which only two decades ago dominated the telephone business and ranked with General Motors and Mobil among the nation's very largest companies, will become four much smaller businesses competing against many formidable, and sometimes larger, rivals.

AT&T announced that it would create three companies with four publicly traded stocks. Under the plan, for which AT&T will seek shareholder approval, it will spin off its cable television operation, the nation's biggest, and its wireless unit, among the nation's biggest, as separate companies over the next 2 years. It will leave control of most of the company's global communications network and the unit that serves business customers in the hands of the core AT&T. That company will also control AT&T's consumer unit, which is dominated by its shrinking long-distance business. The consumer business will then have its own publicly traded stock.

AT&T aimed its announcement at the investment world—AT&T's stock is among the most widely held. The company made less mention of the plan's effect on its millions of customers. But it is clear that AT&T's units, operating separately but all using the AT&T brand, would deliver just about the same range of services. And customers could benefit as the newly freed AT&T units begin to compete against one another and to expand their product lines, possibly offering better prices and new choices for services, including residential high-speed Internet access.

AT&T's customers are unlikely to notice much immediate change as the plan becomes reality. The AT&T name on their bills will stay the same, at least for a few years, and their services will not change in the short run. Prices are not likely to change quickly, either.

Some consumer advocates worried that the breakup would leave too much power in the hands of the Bell phone companies—BellSouth, Qwest, SBC, and Verizon—which still dominate local communications markets in most of the nation and which have begun to enter the long-distance arena.

Investors in AT&T were not delighted. Concerns about the plan, especially the fact that the separated units would pay a lower combined dividend than the company does now, were one reason. Also, while AT&T announced earnings for the third quarter that exceeded predictions, it released forecasts for the fourth quarter that fell short of analysts' expectations.

AT&T's roots stretch to 1887, when Alexander Graham Bell founded the Bell Telephone Company. In 1984, under pressure from the Justice Department, the company divested its local phone holdings as seven "Baby Bells." In 1996, the company spun off its communications equipment operation as Lucent Technologies.

Deregulation in 1996 allowed new competition, and the proliferation of the Internet and other new technologies created a race in which communications companies have scrambled to get bigger.

AT&T wanted to top them all by offering customers everything they needed in communications services. AT&T has spent more than $90 billion since

---

C. Michael Armstrong took over as chairman 3 years ago to become the nation's biggest cable company. The idea was to use cable systems to deliver phone service and high-speed Internet access as well as interactive television. Coupled with the wireless unit, the cable systems gave AT&T a broader portfolio than any other communications carrier.

In the end, however, financial markets did not appear to support that strategy, or at least its execution. AT&T's stock has languished recently. The plan announced is based on the notion that those operations would be worth more on their own than as a whole.

With $62.4 billion in revenue for 1999, AT&T ranked eighth on *Fortune* magazine's most recent list of the nation's biggest companies. Without the cable, wireless, and consumer units, AT&T would have ranked forty-first.

The new plan is as potentially complex as the 1984 breakup. But in the 1980s, because the overhaul was forced by antitrust pressure, the government oversaw carefully crafted ground rules and timetables to try to reduce consumer confusion.

This time, with the overhaul prompted by market pressures, the government will not manage the process. Few, if any, regulatory hurdles appear to stand in the way of AT&T's plan. But that reflects the fact that in important ways, the communications landscape is much different now. Back in 1984, AT&T and its seven Baby Bell spin-offs had few competitors. Now, the rise of competition means that consumers have a variety of alternatives, and many people have become used to choosing among them.

Some consumer advocates expressed concerns about the plan.

"This is a cataclysmic marketplace event that reflects the failure of deregulation policy; it's terrible for consumers," said Gene Kimmelman, codirector of Consumers Union's Washington office. "There will not be a unified AT&T wire to carry local, long-distance, cable, and broadband services. Nobody in long-distance has come up with a viable, cost-effective strategy to challenge the Bells. This restructuring truly demonstrated that the long-distance market and local market, for the majority of consumers, will be ceded to the Bell monopolies."

But Mr. Armstrong, in a statement, said the deal "creates a family of four national service providers that will be even better equipped to bring American families and businesses a new generation of broadband communications and information services."

AT&T said that the consumer unit would begin trials in 2001 of high-speed Internet access over standard telephone wires using a technology known as digital subscriber lines, or DSL. AT&T has mostly shunned such systems in the past, partly because DSL is the main competitor to cable modem technology. AT&T, as the biggest cable company, had a big interest in cable modems' success.

AT&T held up the DSL initiative as an example of the benefits that the units' new independence could hold for consumers. Ultimately, however, AT&T seemed more focused on investors than on consumers. The company highlighted the potential business benefits of the plan.

Most important, AT&T expects investors to give the separate units a higher value on their own than they did when the units were part of AT&T. That is because some of AT&T's diverse units are typically judged by investors by different financial results. Mature operations, such as the long-distance telephone business, are generally valued based on their earnings per share. Newer units that are growing more quickly, like cable and wireless, are generally valued by their cash flow, or earnings before interest, taxes, depreciation, and amortization.

Aside from any particular quarter's results, the larger financial problem that AT&T's plan is meant to solve is that investors have appeared to judge the company mostly by its earnings per share (as well as revenue growth), denying the company full credit for the cash flow growth in the cable and wireless businesses. AT&T is hoping that on their own, the cable and wireless businesses will be compared with their industry peers and will thus enjoy greater favor with investors.

Nonetheless, some communications experts said the overhaul plan was misguided.

"This is one of the silliest reorganizations in communications," said Howard Anderson, founder of the Yankee Group, a communications research firm, and senior managing director of YankeeTek, a venture capital firm based in Boston. "They have essentially genuflected to the financial markets when in reality staying the course would have gotten them to where they want to be. AT&T would have been in much more horrible straits had they not done the cable mergers, had they not done wireless. They have the pieces. It belongs as one company. They have listened to the wrong angel here talking about shareholder value."

Mr. Armstrong himself agrees that AT&T's expansion into the cable market was essential. But he sees the plan as part of the same overall strategy that he has had all along.

In an interview, Mr. Armstrong said: "Once I got here and realized that we needed a strategy, I realized that the challenge was really whether there would be an AT&T. That was what the risk was. And here I was at the helm of an American icon and the outcome of everything could be no AT&T."

He added, "It's the outcome that will count. And the thing that keeps me charged up, smiling, and hopefully rising above it is that I'm convinced the outcome is going to be successful."

THE AT&T INCUBATOR

AT&T's court-ordered breakup in 1984 spawned seven regional local telephone companies. Since then, many of those companies have combined or merged with other companies and AT&T has spun off other businesses, creating an eclectic group of offspring in the telecommunications industry. The announcement that AT&T will spin off more companies will broaden the mix further.

- Pre-1984: AT&T offers local and long-distance service in the U.S.

- 1984: spins off into seven regional local telephone companies, including US West, Bell Atlantic, Nynex, BellSouth, Ameritech, Southwestern Bell, and Pacific Telesis

- 1991: acquires NCR (computer company)

- 1996: spins off NCR and equipment business as Lucent Technologies

- 1998: acquires Tele-Communications, Inc. (cable TV system)

- 1999: acquires MediaOne (cable TV system)

- 2000: announcement of breakup into four separate units:

  AT&T Consumer Services

  AT&T Business Services

  AT&T Broadband Services

  AT&T Wireless Services

RELATED LINKS

- AT&T Consumer (http://www.att.com/home/index_js.html)

- AT&T Business (http://www.att.com/business)

- AT&T Broadband (http://www.attbroadband.com)

- AT&T Wireless (http://www.attwireless.com)

FOR FURTHER RESEARCH

To find out more about the topics discussed in this reading, use InfoTrac College Edition. Type in keywords and subject terms such as "AT&T breakup," "telecommunications restructuring," and "digital subscriber line (DSL)." You can access InfoTrac College Edition from the Wadsworth/Thomson Communication Cafe homepage: http://communication .wadsworth.com.

Reading 5-3

AOL Time Warner: How Blind Alleys Led Old Media to New

Amy Harmon

EDITOR'S NOTE

The $165 billion merger between America Online (AOL) and Time Warner—the largest in media history—turned the communications world upside down when it was announced in January 2000. Once a small and content-poor Internet community, AOL emerged in recent years as the largest paid online service, with over 20 million subscribers. The combined company, AOL Time Warner, is a force to be reckoned with in the lucrative future of broadband media. As this reading reveals, both companies stand to benefit from the deal by harnessing their respective strengths—access to audiences and control over content. The merger is already placing incredible competitive pressure on rival television networks and content providers.

CONSIDER

1. What are the harms and benefits of the AOL Time Warner merger, from the consumer's perspective as well as that of the companies involved?

2. What was America Online's motivation for acquiring Time Warner, and why did Time Warner, a traditional media giant, agree to be acquired by the online service?

3. What does the merger say about the competitive environment of broadband media in a digital age?

In the fall of 1994, when America Online, with just about a million subscribers, lagged behind its competitors—and when the smart money was betting that the free World Wide Web would quickly eclipse the paid online services—Time Warner unveiled a site that aspired to be the emerging Web's prime destination.

Gerald M. Levin, Time Warner's chairman and chief executive, proclaimed that the Web site, called Pathfinder, would turn the company's magazines into an indispensable daily electronic information guide.

That, of course, was one of the things that America Online was trying to be, and its chairman and chief executive, Stephen M. Case, did not fail to take notice. In 1995, as Case's company suddenly surged past its online rivals Prodigy and CompuServe, he even discussed a joint venture with Pathfinder executives.

"We thought Pathfinder was a good idea," Case recalled in an interview. "Thankfully, it was poorly executed. I thought they had a great opportunity, but for them at the time the Internet was a curious peripheral. For us, it was the be-all, end-all."

The story of why Pathfinder ultimately failed—alongside the story of Case's unending focus—goes a long way toward explaining how it happened that the media world with this proposed merger turned upside down.

The agreement by America Online, known for dive-bombing the nation with free diskettes of its software, to acquire Time Warner, whose cartoon characters and magazines are some of the most recognizable icons of popular culture, has been seen as a startling triumph of the new media over the old. At $165 billion, it would be the biggest merger ever.

But on some grounds, the deal shouldn't have been all that startling. A close look at Time Warner's history of earnest efforts to harness the digital media business shows a predictable set of obstacles, underscoring why virtually no traditional media brands are central players in today's frothy Internet industry.

Despite a longstanding commitment by Levin to digital technology, Time Warner was stymied by corporate politics, distracted by other, more profitable ventures and was unrealistic about how quickly it could harness the technology to suit its needs. Moreover, it was focused on promoting its editorial and entertainment products, while America Online pursued Case's belief that connecting people was the Internet's most addictive application.

Time Warner's mixed experience in the digital realm also explains how the company came to appreciate its own weaknesses and see the benefits of the merger.

Asked why Time Warner, with all its resources and reach, did not simply start its own online service, Ted Turner, the company's vice chairman, said simply: "It's not that easy to build an AOL."

Even so, it may be simplistic to label the deal a triumph for America Online. Case's eagerness to make an acquisition—at a huge premium—that will surely slow the momentum of his company's stock is an indication that he expects the formula of America Online's success to change radically in the coming years.

As the Internet becomes available over television, telephone, and particularly over high-speed networks, Case believes that content, even more than community-building, will grow in importance. That is where his company has stumbled in the past. And at $21.95 a month, its main service faces new competition from several fast-growing free Internet services. Case sees the need to diversify.

"We went from 1 million to 20 million subscribers in the last 5 years. That's great, but a billion people watch CNN," Case said. "We've gone from members spending an average of 1 hour a week to 1 hour a day on the service—but there are 23 other hours in a day. This is the reality of how consumers live their lives, and if we really want to have an impact, we have to paint on the broadest possible canvas."

The most obvious benefit of the deal to America Online is that, in buying Time Warner, it is acquiring the nation's second-largest cable provider. Without guaranteed access to the cable modems that will increasingly enable subscribers to surf the Internet at fifty times today's average speed, America Online could have been shut out of a big chunk of what looks to be the lucrative future of broadband service.

But whether the two companies will be able to find other kinds of synergies—ways of serving up Time

Warner's rich media brew to America Online's loyal users—may ultimately depend on how much they have learned from their past successes and failures.

In many ways, Steve Case and Gerald Levin were both ahead of their time.

In 1981, Case, just out of college, took a job at Procter & Gamble, in large part because it was in Cincinnati, one of two places in the country where interactive television was being tested. But the neighborhood in which he chose to live did not have access to the service, called Qube—which happened to be provided by a company, Warner Amex Cable, that was a venture of a predecessor to Time Warner.

At a friend's house, his excitement dimmed as he repeatedly used the service. Clunky interactive quiz shows somehow were not what he had in mind. Instead, Case bought a computer, connected it to a phone line, and began exploring the early versions of online communities.

Levin's fascination with interactive television was not so quickly put aside. As a rising star at Time Inc. in the early 1970s, Levin had built an early satellite network for the company's HBO movie channel.

By the time he became chief executive in 1992, Time had merged with Warner Communications and its cable division had won a special Emmy Award for entwining thick coaxial cable with slender fiber-optic strands so that cable subscribers could both send and receive information.

That meant a lot of things, theoretically. It meant that you could order a pizza through your cable system, pay your bills through your cable system, shop through your cable system. But the main thing it meant—theoretically—was what cable executives came to call "video on demand." The fantasy of having millions of cable subscribers pay to summon up any movie they wanted, at any time, blinded much of the industry to the lack, or exorbitant cost, of the technology to make it happen.

Many cable companies sponsored interactive television tests, but none as lavish as the one Time Warner rolled out in Orlando, Florida. After a small trial in New York City, Levin was so taken with the idea that he authorized tens of millions of dollars to be spent on proprietary equipment for the project, which was announced in December 1994 to a gathering of 450 journalists from ten countries.

In the spring of 1997, having garnered a total of 4,000 subscribers, Time Warner shut the network down, declaring it a valuable trial for a system that could be extended nationally once the technology became less expensive.

But the company's plans to make such Jetsonian technology available to its millions of cable subscribers were delayed as upgrading its systems with fiber took longer than expected, and the price of the complicated set-top boxes remained exorbitantly high.

Attention then turned to the Internet as the source for interactive activities. It is just now, as Time Warner prepares to merge with an Internet company, that it has started to offer interactive television in Honolulu and is on the cusp of being able to provide it on a much wider scale.

"We had hoped it would happen faster for sure," said Jim Chiddix, chief technical officer for Time Warner Cable. "There was a theory that interactive TV would have been the way this all happened. In hindsight that wasn't realistic."

Still, Levin's conviction that his company needed to be retrofitted for the digital age was growing only stronger. In 1994, a month before the introduction of the Orlando project, he announced Pathfinder, a Web site that allowed Internet users to read articles of Time Inc. magazines, including *Time, Life,* and *Sports Illustrated.* The idea was to make it the first Web portal, a free competitor to services like America Online that would earn its keep through advertising, magazine subscriptions, and other products.

From the start, however, Pathfinder was criticized by insiders and outsiders alike as chronically failing to live up to its promise. Not only were the company's music and film divisions not interested in taking part, but the magazines themselves didn't have much incentive to contribute resources to a project that, at least initially, showed no sign of generating any cash in return.

Levin, who was busy buying cable franchises against the better judgment of many investors—in addition to overseeing the rest of the Time Warner empire—seemed to have neither the clout nor the attention to carry out his vision. A year after Pathfinder's introduction, it was famously dubbed a "black hole" by Time Inc.'s executive editor, Don Logan, at a magazine conference.

Several key executives left: Walter Isaacson, a *Time* editor who lent the project credibility as its managing editor, fled back to the print world as soon as he was offered the job of managing editor at *Time.*

Paul Sagan, once Time Inc.'s president of new media, is now president of a high-profile Internet start-up called Akamai Technologies, with a stake worth hundreds of millions of dollars.

James Kinsella, the founding managing editor of Pathfinder, who is now president of MSNBC.com, recalls the frustration of trying to get the company's disparate divisions to work together on a centralized online service.

"It was all such a struggle," Kinsella said. "You didn't have a strong leader saying, 'We're going to make this our core.' They all wanted to have their own titles and own look and feel, so it was clearly a hodgepodge of stuff."

In April 1999, after pouring more than $100 million into Pathfinder with little to show for it, Time Warner announced it was disbanding that service, too. Since then, the individual magazines have been fending for themselves on the Web, developing advertising deals across both media in what Time Inc. executives contend is likely to be a far more lucrative business model. The online division of Warner Brothers, meanwhile, has developed a well-received entertainment site called Entertaindom. What America Online will do with all that has yet to be seen.

Time Warner executives say Pathfinder's costs were less than those of many an Internet start-up, but they agree that the corporate setting wasn't always an advantage.

"I never lost my zeal," Levin said in an interview. "But Pathfinder never became the central focus of the company."

The slower pace of decision making in a large company also frustrated efforts by other Time Warner outposts to make money from the Internet. One former manager at CNN recalled a plan 3 years ago to create a search and directory portal like Yahoo!, called Gotwo, for Time Warner Online. Despite support from Levin, the plan went nowhere.

"We sometimes felt on the team like we were preparing for one of those G-7 summit meetings," said the former manager. "You had to go make your case to the publishing guys, the film guys, the cable guys. You had to waste a lot of time. It ultimately got studied to death."

Perhaps nobody was more frustrated than Levin. Over the summer, he moved to impose his long-held views on the importance of digital technology. He created a new division called Time Warner Digital Media and appointed his chief financial officer, Richard Bressler, to run it.

In October, however, Levin received a phone call from Case. And Levin attributes his receptiveness to his own long history of digital experimentation.

"I am not defensive about any of this," Levin said in an interview. "Every one of these experiences enhanced my consciousness level about what the right thing to do is. It helped me recognize why this merger made sense. You won't find too many CEOs that would do it."

You might not find too many chief executives who would propose such a merger, either. But Case's well-known single-mindedness may be the key to America Online's unlikely success.

While more-established competitors like Compu-Serve still doled out e-mail addresses composed of long strings of digits, and Prodigy offered neither e-mail nor online chat, America Online's service was easy to navigate and encouraged interaction. "We believed the soul of the medium was people interacting with each other," Case said.

Yet early on, Case learned the value of content, too. A contract with *Time* magazine in 1993 helped legitimize AOL in the eyes of traditional media companies, he said. With a sharp focus on the consumer, as opposed to the technology, along with a heavy-duty marketing campaign, the company began to add subscribers quickly.

There were plenty of stumbles and recoveries along the way. From 1985, when Case helped form AOL's predecessor company, until about 1992, he developed almost no market for his service. But by the mid-1990s, rather than competing with the Internet, America Online simply incorporated it into its own offerings.

In late 1996, America Online switched to a flat-rate pricing plan, but failed to account for its popularity, resulting in well-publicized busy signals for many customers. The company apologized, then furiously added capacity.

But America Online has never quite mastered the creation of its own original content. AOL programming—like Entertainment Asylum, which Case now characterizes as "just another entertainment site"—has not performed well.

"We realize it's hard; it requires a different kind of culture," Case said. "We were always better at building the community brands that rely on people contributing content."

Hence the deal with Time Warner, Case said. But rather than reviewing how his company came so far, he would rather spin a story about the virtues of convergence among all forms of communication: "I understand the need to talk about the past, but I'd rather talk about the future."

Case may prefer to take the long view in part because the stock market's more immediate response last week was less than enthusiastic. The market may have been reacting to the merger's long-term risks. Whatever the two companies have learned from their pasts, they will be confronting a new and shifting series of obstacles in the future.

As chairman of a huge media conglomerate, Case will no longer have a founder's unique power to rally troops around his message. And as chief executive of an Internet company, Levin will face for the first time the brutal pace of change and expectations of rapid growth.

Other questions abound. If America Online's strength has been its dogged pursuit of online subscribers, what happens when it merges with a company that is so notoriously scattered?

"AOL has been built really on just one idea, making it easy for people to get online," said John Battelle, publisher of *The Industry Standard,* a technology trade publication. "Time Warner is a company with almost indecipherable conflicts of interest. It will be interesting to see how AOL sorts out the priorities."

And if one of America Online's chief virtues has been ease of use, what happens when consumer electronics manufacturers begin marketing devices that make it far simpler to tap the Internet?

"If the Internet was about bringing an appliance home, plug it in, get on and go, that's a threat to the core of AOL," said Paul Saffo, director of the Institute for the Future in Menlo Park, California. "They have this marvelous community of users, but one could see the world changing where all those people are lured away in other directions."

As the four executives on the AOL Time Warner "integration team" ordered in Chinese food to America Online's board room to discuss the merger, a range of other opinions asserted themselves on new message boards that America Online had set up. "Think maybe now we can switch screen names faster?" asked one user, referring to online aliases. "Big is not always better," wrote another, while yet another said, "Good only if monthly fee comes down."

Typing in www.pathfinder.com still brings users to the *Time* magazine site. No message boards on the subject of the merger appeared there [when it was announced], although those interested could vote in a poll on whether or not it was good for the Internet.

RELATED LINKS

- America Online (http://www.aol.com)
- AOL Time Warner (http://www.aoltimewarner.com)
- Time.com (http://www.time.com/time)
- Warner Bros. (http://www2.warnerbros.com/web/main/index.jsp)

FOR FURTHER RESEARCH

To find out more about the topics discussed in this reading, use InfoTrac College Edition. Type in keywords and subject terms such as: "AOL Time Warner," "media acquisitions," and "telecommunications networks." You can access InfoTrac College Edition from the Wadsworth/Thomson Communication Cafe homepage: http://communication.wadsworth.com.

Reading 5-4

The Threat to the Net
Pat Aufderheide

EDITOR'S NOTE

In this cautionary commentary about the future of broadband networks, Pat Aufderheide, a professor in the School of Communication at American University, warns that the recent wave of media mergers and acquisitions (notably AOL and Time Warner, and AT&T and TCI) may partition a large part of the Internet with a costly commercial fence, stifling innovation and hindering access. Given that the future of high-bandwidth media depends on broadband networks, Aufderheide sees the actions of the cable industry as the front line in the battle to keep access to the Internet open and free. At stake, she argues, is not just whose voice gets heard in cyberspace but the stifling of opportunity—political, social, economic—before it's even imagined.

CONSIDER

1. In your opinion, do the mergers of America Online and Time Warner and of AT&T and TCI threaten freedom of access to the Internet? Why or why not?

2. Why is the debate over broadband networks not just about the future of the Internet but about the future of communication media generally?

3. If the cable companies succeed in becoming the dominant Internet service providers, will the innovation and creativity that have characterized the Web until now vanish?

Who owns the Internet? If you think the answer is "nobody," you're right—for now. That's why it has been such an astonishing innovation that has flourished so vibrantly at the grassroots. But this pioneering era may end badly, with an all-too-familiar finish: Big business tames a giddy and experimental phenomenon and turns it into a nice, tidy, and ever-so-profitable money maker. And why not? That's what happened with phones, with radio, with TV. The difference this time may be that too many people have sampled an open information environment to settle for less.

The thugs of the story, who want to fence in the Internet, are the cable companies, led by communications conglomerates like AT&T. They now have something many of us want: broadband Internet service. But they plan to make us pay for it in more ways than one. And the stakes have risen dramatically since the largest of the Internet Service Providers, America Online (AOL), announced a merger with Time Warner.

The fight is about closed access versus open access to broadband.

"Broadband" means faster transmission of more data. For Web users, that's a lot. It's the Internet squared: no waiting, no loading. With broadband, Web pages fly by like the flicked pages of a book, and Web video looks just like TV. In fact, it may be TV, and your phone, and your spreadsheet program, and your fax, and anything else that can attach to the sophisticated transmission system. That's because broadband is not simply the future of the Internet. It's the future of our communications systems.

Now, as cable companies are beginning to offer broadband, local governments are demanding open access: the ability to get on the broadband using any Internet Service Provider on the same terms as anyone else's. The cable companies are fighting for closed access: They want to force everyone who uses their broadband service to go through their preferred Internet Service Providers.

Until the announced merger, America Online had been one of the leaders in the battle for open access. But, with its merger [now approved], that could change. Time Warner, along with owning TV networks, movie studios, magazines, and music companies, is also the second-largest cable operator. AOL executives proudly pledged their continued commitment to open access. But if the merger goes through [which it did], AOL Time Warner will have to decide whether it's still for open access or whether it will opt instead for closed access.

What AT&T does may be very important in that story. It's now the largest cable provider in the country, as well as the largest long-distance phone company in the world. Back when AT&T was Ma Bell, before 1982, the phone company was an easy target for resentment. It's an easier target now. It became the largest cable company in the world last year when it bought TCI, which has had its own image problems. Before

the merger, TCI was the largest cable company in the United States. Now the two reviled giants are joined at the bottom line [see Readings 5.1 and 5.2].

Almost two decades after government lawyers broke up the old phone monopoly and AT&T abandoned local service, the company owns a pathway to many of us again.

Cable wires reach out and touch three-quarters of U.S. homes. They also pass almost all of them, and digital cable wires could handle phone traffic. AT&T has gone on to buy other cable systems and awaits Federal Communications Commission (FCC) approval of a merger with the third-largest cable company, Media-One. Factor in MediaOne's 25 percent interest in—you guessed it!—Time Warner, and AT&T has access to more than half of America's homes once more. AT&T may even be interested in joining forces with AOL Time Warner in some formal way down the line.

What these mergers do is threaten the freedom to access the Internet.

Today, you can choose from thousands of Internet Service Providers, and you can make that decision based on whether they offer quick hookups or whether they design nice chat rooms or whether they're run by your neighbor's teenager. If you want broadband service, though, cable companies will steer you to their own Internet Service Providers (AT&T's is Excite@Home).

Cable companies want to determine the speed at which any user might send information or receive it, and the Internet hardware company Cisco Systems is already selling the equipment to let them do so. AT&T, for instance, won't let you send more than 10 minutes of video at a time via Excite@Home.

Since cable companies like AT&T are the first ones out of the chute with broadband, they are in a position to set terms. And they want to discourage potential competition by strangling it at birth. They have no interest in allowing anyone else to offer the equivalent of a channel over their cable lines on the same terms they offer to their own Internet Service Providers. They want people to come to cable itself for that content or to the Internet for that content, as long as it's through their system.

Content providers—be they Disney, Fox, progressive news groups, the PTA, or consumer guide services—all may lose an opportunity to reach citizens on the Net directly and to create programming that would find its own audience without paying a gatekeeper and submitting to that gatekeeper's terms.

The content providers that stand to lose the most are those without financial clout, and especially the nonprofit organizations that keep our civic culture alive. They could become second-class citizens on the Web. Their material could be transmitted at a slower speed or not at all. And if the cable companies succeed, the grassroots innovation and creativity that has characterized the Web may vanish.

Today, the Net environment is pretty chaotic, and many consumers have become accustomed to using search engines and portals and filters to find their way around. You choose the selectors; you can pick a provider that simply hauls your data around and lets you go where you want to go, or you can hook up with a more commercialized provider.

But are you ready for an Internet where you have no choice but to go through a provider that tailors your searches according to the profit-sharing deals it can cut? And are you ready to hand over to the cable company the power to determine whether to deliver your material and at what speed?

This is not some science fiction story. The battle for control over the Internet is already raging. And it is taking place on the unlikely field of local regulation, as cities and counties face off against the cable companies. Free speech and public interest advocates, along with the Internet Service Providers, joined forces to support these local officials, who confront cable companies as they apply to open or renew local franchises.

What's at stake here is not just the kinds of problems we face with cable services. That would be bad enough. On cable today, we have content problems, like having them decide for us which channels are on our systems, which news services they'll carry, and whether we can see C-SPAN II. We also have monopoly pricing problems. Cable companies give us stations we don't want and make us pay for the whole bundle. If we get only the broadband services that cable companies find it convenient and lucrative to give us, we'll certainly have these problems.

But we may have a much bigger problem: the killing of opportunity—political, social, economic—before it's even been imagined.

No one imagined the burgeoning of freedom of expression on the Net, or the skyrocketing of Net businesses, or the way that Internet communication has changed the operations of nonprofit groups, which can now instantly alert members to a zoning hearing or create an online public record of parents' complaints about school issues or post their grant applications on the Net.

The original design of the Web was responsible for its dynamism, and if the cable companies are allowed to dictate the design of broadband, the Web will take a much different shape in the future.

Why foreclose futures that stimulate competition, benefit consumers, foster innovation, boost the economy, and nurture civic life?

"The reason the Internet has been such an engine for creativity and growth is the way it was built, its architecture," Lawrence Lessig, a Harvard law professor, explained at a briefing in Washington, DC, held by public interest advocates and underwritten by what was then America Online. Lessig's book, *Code and Other Laws of Cyberspace* (Basic Books, 1999), explains the link between this architecture and politics. Closed access services, by the way, can easily discourage unprofitable transactions. If you had wanted to see a video transmission of Lessig's presentation (which was available through nogatekeepers.org), you couldn't do it on Excite@Home.

The Internet was designed for researchers to be able to work together cheaply and easily, so it was open to any use by any user. The Net is really nothing more than the set of open and public agreements among computers about how to reach each other's code. Any computer can use the same simple software to "speak" to any other, often sending its packets of digitized data over phone lines. So long as your machine knows how to talk to all the other machines, and it has a pathway to send its data, you're part of the network. You're on the Net. You are the Net. Users make the Net; and the system evolves with the users.

When most of that data was in the form of simple text, phone lines worked perfectly to get ordinary users hooked up to the Net. Voice takes ten times as much space as data does, so there was lots of extra room.

"We've been lucky. Today's Internet ecology required no effort of design," Lessig explained. But images, especially moving images, take up gargantuan amounts of space when turned into digital code, and the great wads of data they send clog up the whole system.

So the next stage of the Net can't piggyback on existing networks. It must be built. And the way it is built will determine how it is used, and what it is used for. AT&T wants to design the system so that it controls the technology, making it closed from the start.

Broadband is not entirely the province of cable companies. In fact, local phone companies are developing what are called DSL (digital subscriber line) services—vastly speeded-up data transmission over phone lines. They are legally required to make their facilities available to anyone who wants to provide DSL service. But they are lumbering far behind in offering rapid Internet service, partly because they aren't any more eager for competition than the cable companies are, and partly because the cost of laying new wires is high.

Cable companies, which have no legal requirement to share their broadband, have told policymakers that they've paid a lot for these systems, so why should they give access away free? As Daniel Somers, the new head of AT&T's cable operations, said recently, the company didn't spend $56 billion to get into cable "to have the blood sucked out of our vein."

Portland, Oregon, has led the way for open access. But the battle with AT&T, which began in late 1998, took City Commissioner Erik Sten by surprise. He's in charge of utilities, and he went head-to-head with AT&T.

"In Portland, we had two cable companies: Paragon and TCI, and AT&T bought both of them," Sten recalls. "When they came to us for approval of their franchise license, we said that they had to offer open access, which is also called nondiscriminatory broadband service. There are about 100 Internet Service Providers in the Portland area, and we wanted them to be able to offer access to broadband on the same terms as Excite@Home. If you don't have competition with Internet Service Providers, you ultimately hand over control of the Internet to AT&T. Plus, our 100 local companies, which pay local taxes, would go out of business."

But there's more to it than that. "Access to the Internet should be as open and reasonably priced as possible," he says. "Allowing AT&T to have closed access would be just one more step in the homogenization of the information industry. It goes against the free flow of ideas, and it doesn't allow competitive pricing."

Sten attended the briefing in Washington with Professor Lessig and explained the decision to confront AT&T. "This did not look like a tough issue for us," he said. "We thought the question was, why *wouldn't* you require open access? I was astonished at AT&T's reaction. We had an amicable hearing, we saw nothing to stop us from requiring open access, we laid out the reasons, and AT&T's response was: 'We hope you have a large legal budget.'"

Sten didn't. But the city of Portland still won its first court battle. Since then, eleven other local jurisdictions have followed suit. But in Portland, rather than knuckle under and actually provide broadband service,

AT&T has ordered its lawyers to appeal. And AT&T has plenty of money to spend.

To Ron Sims, the county executive who stared down AT&T in the Seattle area, the issue is uncomplicated. It's about control of content; it's about free speech; it's about choice. "No single entity should control content," he says. "We live in the heartland of high-tech development. We know high-speed access is the doorway to innovation. Don't slam that door."

But how long will the door stay open? Part of the answer depends on the fate of AOL and Time Warner.

Part of the answer also lies with AT&T. It could move toward open access itself. As a result of pressure from regulators and activists, AT&T signed an agreement in principle with the large Internet Service Provider MindSpring, permitting access to AT&T's broadband service in Seattle.

The FCC has the authority to decide whether cable should provide open access, and it has a new opportunity to advise the Federal Trade Commission and the Justice Department about the AOL Time Warner merger.

Unfortunately, with AT&T, it has declined to decide. Instead, it has adopted a policy of "watchful waiting," in the words of [former] FCC chairman, Bill Kennard.

"The real sad thing is that the FCC has just sat on its hands while a big company is trying to buy up something that should be publicly available," says Sten.

The problem with "watchful waiting," says Lessig, is that not mandating open access comes down to supporting closed access. And if the cable industry gets to build closed systems, it will be expensive and perhaps impossible to crack open later or to nurture the innovation that has been stifled. It's like saying you don't need to use seat belts, Lessig told the FCC, because people can always go the emergency room if they get hurt.

Under the 1996 rewrite of the nation's basic communications law, the FCC is required to streamline its regulations and phase out any that aren't conducive to competition. The FCC has argued that any regulation will stop broadband deployment. This is just what the biggest cable-telecom companies want it to say.

While the FCC treats AT&T like a tender flower of innovation, local officials are aggressively pursuing its competitors. "Innovative broadband companies are coming to Portland now, in spite of the fact that we're a pretty small market," Sten says. "That's a result of our open access decision."

Sten worries that the AOL Time Warner merger could just mean another giant with its own closed access system. "From the open access perspective, that's not any better," he says. "We should have a federal policy role here."

And the message that regulators need to hear is simple: Protect what we've got, and make sure we can build on it. Make open access the terms of doing business.

RELATED LINKS

■   Civil Rights Forum on Communications Policy (http://www.civilrightsforum.org/home.htm)

■   Federal Communications Commission (http://www.fcc.gov)

■   Media Access Project (http://www.mediaaccess.org)

■   Lawrence Lessig (http://cyberlaw.stanford.edu/lessig/content/index.html)

■   Patricia Aufderheide (http://www1.soc.american.edu/aufderheide/Books/intrfin.htm)

FOR FURTHER RESEARCH

To find out more about the topics discussed in this reading, use InfoTrac College Edition. Type in keywords and subject terms such as "nondiscriminatory broadband service," "Internet regulation," and "open Internet access." You can access InfoTrac College Edition from the Wadsworth/Thomson Communication Cafe homepage: http://communication.wadsworth.com.

Reading 5-5

Get Wireless: Spectrum Is the Real Estate on Which the Wealth of the 21st Century Will Be Built
Catharine Lo

EDITOR'S NOTE

Over the next few decades, the true leaps in connectivity will not come from the ground—through wires strung around the globe—but from the airwaves or electromagnetic spectrum that makes communication among vast networks of space satellites possible. The new wireless infrastructure, this reading proposes, will augment the existing wired infrastructure and envelope the world "in cheap, high-bandwidth, ubiquitous connectivity." Indeed, this is happening already. The rise of new personal communications technologies outlined here suggests that the future of media may indeed be wireless.

CONSIDER

1.   Why does the electromagnetic spectrum represent the next frontier of the digital revolution?

2.   In what two ways does digitization of data, sound, and video make more space available in the wireless spectrum?

3.   Why is it difficult to answer the question "Who owns the airwaves?"

Air. You need to know about air. Not for breathing, but for something almost as elemental—for communicating. The airwaves, the electromagnetic spectrum—this truly is the next frontier of the Digital Revolution.

We've done wires. We've got wires buried and strung around most of the globe. There may be plenty of work left in filling out that wired infrastructure, beefing up bandwidth, upgrading to fiber optics, and laying the last few feet into every room of every home. Yet the real action is happening not on the ground, but in the air. That's where the true leaps in connectivity will come.

In the twentieth century analog world, you needed separate devices for separate communication functions, and you needed to transmit the signals on exclusive channels. Only radios picked up broadcast radio signals. Only TVs picked up television signals. In the twenty-first century digital world, data, sound, and video will have been reduced to the same binary bits, which can be picked up by a variety of devices and transmitted in any order over similar territory in the spectrum. This technological change has sent a chain reaction reverberating through the world of wireless communications.

Digitization expands the amount of space available in the spectrum in two ways. Internally, it allows more layers of information to be transmitted simultaneously—and more efficiently—in the same frequencies we used before. Externally, advances in digital technology promise to push the boundaries into parts of the spectrum once considered useless. However, along with the new space come new applications and services that push up demand. The more space we gain, the more crowded we get.

The problem in the United States boils down to this: we're still trapped in an analog world. Everyone thought in terms of analog devices when the spectrum was doled out. Now we're watching the first big digital projects being launched and facing up to the idea that everything eventually will go digital. The federal government has slowly begun to react. Congress finally passed the Telecommunications Act of 1996 to supersede legislation devised in 1934. And the Federal Communications Commission began to put parts of the spectrum up for public auction. More radical reallocation of the airwaves may come soon.

"Get Wireless: Spectrum Is the Real Estate on Which the Wealth of the 21st Century Will Be Built," by Catharine Lo. From *Wired,* April 1997, pp. 142–147. Copyright © 1997 by Catharine Lo. Reprinted with permission of the author.

So you need to know about air and space. For one, because you own large portions of it as a U.S. citizen—and the government is giving a lot of it away. A lot of very powerful people are spending billions of dollars to buy licenses to the airwaves early—while some, in the case of digital television, are finagling ways to get those same rights for free.

Within the next decade, that air grab will be over. The new wireless infrastructure—the complement to our wired infrastructure—will be well on its way to completion. Vast networks of antennas will be constructed on the ground. Even more vast networks of space satellites will arch overhead. If all goes well, you'll be enveloped in cheap, high-bandwidth, ubiquitous connectivity. Everywhere on the planet. If all does not go well, you'll be paying big bucks for patchy service. So tune in now.

WHO OWNS THE AIRWAVES?

Tough question. Who will own them is tougher still.

Who owns the airwaves is a difficult question to answer. The same frequency can be owned by different organizations in every major city. That's why TV channel 2 belongs to NBC in one city and CBS in another. And, according to Broadcast Investment Analysts, that's why the television industry is composed of 696 companies that own 1,366 commercial broadcast stations.

The key point is that two kinds of companies own the airwaves: content providers, like TV and radio, and conduit providers, the raw infrastructure concerns that offer cellular phone services and the like. Monopolies among content providers are considered more dangerous to society at large because they can stifle the free flow of ideas. Monopolies in infrastructure companies can bring beneficial economies of scale—as long as they feel pressure to keep prices down.

The Telecommunications Act of 1996 loosened the ownership restrictions among broadcast networks. Radio broadcasters can now own up to eight stations in a single market and up to 50 percent of a market, depending on the size of the region. The new law allows TV broadcast networks to increase their slice of the national audience from 25 percent to 35 percent, and lifts the twelve-station ownership cap, though each company may still operate only one station in a given market.

Does this change allow single corporations to control too much content? Doubtful. These broadcasters face even more content competition from the cable, computer, and telephone industries. And in truth, the bottom has fallen out of the prime-time audience of the traditional Big Three TV networks. According to a 1996 *Media Studies Journal* article, audience share plummeted from 92 percent in 1976 to 53 percent in 1996.

THE AUCTION OPTION

Who will own the spectrum is another—very unfinished—story. Given the laws of physics and current technological restraints, the amount of usable spectrum is limited. Just as two cars cannot occupy the same parking space at the same time, two licensees cannot share the same spectrum space simultaneously. In that sense, spectrum is scarce. However, spectrum cannot be depleted like other natural resources. In that sense, it is infinite.

Historically, the FCC has distributed licenses to operate within a designated frequency for a period of time, at essentially no cost. This often has been a very political process—dependent on who you know. Since 1994, the agency has experimented with auctioning off licenses. Acquiring spectrum has become a very expensive process—dependent on how much money you hold. It's also been very lucrative for the government. By the end of January, the Feds had raised $24 billion in ten major auctions of the airwaves, with more auctions to come. The success has led to some radical ideas for the free-market allocation of spectrum: auctioning much of it to the highest bidders and allowing them to decide what services to provide in response to consumer demand. An FCC study in 1991, for example, showed that a single UHF TV channel in Los Angeles could be worth $8 billion over eight years—if used for cellular phone services.

THE MANHATTAN OF SPECTRUM REAL ESTATE

As on the ground, success in the air boils down to three things: location, location, location.

The electromagnetic spectrum encompasses the broad range of all frequencies that travel in waves. It extends from the lower levels of audible sounds to the midreaches of visible light to the higher planes of cosmic rays. Within that vast range of spectrum, only a portion of the radio spectrum is suitable for use in wireless communications: the subset of frequencies from 3 kHz to 300 GHz. But the really valuable portion of that radio spectrum can be narrowed down even further, ranging from 30 MHz to 30 GHz. With the exception of AM radio, almost all the real action in the telecommunications world takes place there.

Spectrum is not completely interchangeable. Some services need particular frequencies. The FCC has orchestrated the allocation of spectrum by determining where airwaves can be put to best use. There is a mind-numbing number of spectrum allocations, ranging from military communications to astronomical research. You won't see them here. The guide below cuts through the clutter and points out where the first digital projects are taking off and where the most intense telecom activity is. It describes the frequencies most relevant to the wired—or, more to the point, wireless—world.

THE PUBLIC/PRIVATE SPLIT

Spectrum is considered a natural resource that belongs to the people. The American people, through the federal government, license companies to use that resource. So all the usable spectrum is divided into three categories: *government-exclusive,* or terrain that only the government can use (including defense and public safety); *nongovernment-exclusive,* or terrain that businesses or private citizens use; and *shared.*

Technically, 6 percent of the radio spectrum is assigned for exclusive use by the private sector, 1.7 percent for exclusive government use. This leads to the erroneous conclusion that 92 percent of the spectrum is "shared." As the rules stand now, the Feds define two categories of users in the shared space, with secondary users deferring to primary users—and the private sector is secondary to government. So although it appears the private sector has access to a shared region, it often is precluded by the government. In reality, according to the Reason Foundation, only 10.6 percent of the shared spectrum is accessible to the private sector, while 81.6 percent is not.

Cordless Telephones

- 43.69–46.6 MHz   base stations (channels 1 to 15)

- 46.6–47 MHz   base stations (16 to 25)

- 47–49.6 MHz   handsets (1 to 15)
- 49.6–50 MHz   handsets (16 to 25)

When cordless phones were first introduced, they saturated the airwaves, leading to cross talk, interference, and eavesdropping. Random radio signals from other phones led to spontaneous ringing and weird squawking noises. Then in April 1995, the FCC allocated more frequencies for cordless phones and required that phones operating in these new frequencies have interference-prevention mechanisms. Now a new generation of even higher-quality cordless phones is moving to the 902- to 928-MHz and 1920- to 1930-MHz bands.

Baby Monitors

- 49.82–49.90 MHz

Have a cordless phone and a baby monitor? Don't be surprised if your kid butts into the conversation. Both devices operate within the same frequency and baby monitors often cause interference.

Broadcast Television

- 54–72 MHz   VHF TV channels 2, 3, and 4
- 76–88 MHz   VHF TV channels 5 and 6
- 174–216 MHz   VHF TV channels 7 to 13
- 470–512 MHz   UHF TV channels 14 to 20
- 512–608 MHz   UHF TV channels 21 to 36
- 614–806 MHz   UHF TV channels 38 to 69

While broadcast TV is familiar to channel surfers everywhere, see Digital Television [below] to glimpse the next wave. No transmissions are permitted on channel 37 [608–614 MHz], a scientific band reserved for radio astronomy.

Specialized Portable Radios

- 72.44–75.6 MHz

Instant replay: special portable radios rented at stadiums or golf courses can pick up broadcasts of sporting events.

Remote-Control Toys

- 72–73 MHz
- 75.4–76 MHz

Toy story: remote-control freaks can choose from fifty channels for model airplanes and thirty channels for model boats and cars.

News Satellite Trucks

- 161.625–161.775 MHz

Back to you, Tom: This is how those TV reporters on location get a signal from the van with the telescoped antennae back to the station.

FBI Communications Channel

- 173.075 MHz

Car thieves, beware: The Stolen Vehicle Recovery Service uses this FBI channel to activate a tracking beacon installed inside vehicles. Developed by Lo-Jack Corp., these beacons will contact specially equipped police cars, which are easily identified by their four vertical antennas.

Digital Television

- 174–216 MHz   VHF channels 7 to 13
                     (proposed)
- 470–698 MHz   UHF channels 14 to 51
                     (proposed)

Digital TV will allow transmission of a new generation of high-definition pictures and CD-quality sound. Digitizing the signals without upgrading the video and audio will enable up to six analog-style programs to be transmitted simultaneously over the same channel where one traveled before. One of the most difficult tasks facing the FCC this year will be orchestrating the transition from analog to digital broadcasting. Last July, Congress rejected an FCC proposal to auction off a portion of the spectrum, estimated to be worth $11 billion to $70 billion, for digital TV. Instead, broadcasters will be lent an additional 6-MHz channel at no cost to simulcast in both analog and digital until enough viewers have purchased digital receivers. Upon completion of this 10- to 15-year transition, the broadcasters will return their original analog channel to the government.

Police Tracking Transmitters

- 219–220 MHz

Now, this is hot money. ETS, the electronic tracking subsidiary of ProNet, has developed transmitters that are hidden in money or other valuables so police can later track them down.

Remote Controls, Car Alarms, Air Force One

- 303.8, 315, 318 MHz

Mixed signals: While these frequencies are commonly used for remote controls and car alarms, they also carry high-powered transmissions from Air Force One. The president has been known to open garage doors throughout neighborhoods in his flight path.

Talking Toy Animals

- 470–512 MHz

Forget Elmo. Now we've got stuffed animals that can talk in response to data signals sent on this frequency from television sets.

Specialized Mobile Radio

- 800-MHz SMR   806–821 MHz mobile-to-base frequencies
                 851–866 MHz base-to-mobile frequencies
- 900-MHz SMR   896–901 MHz mobile-to-base frequencies
                 935–940 MHz base-to-mobile frequencies

Out of the auctions emerged another formidable challenger in the wireless industry: specialized mobile radio (SMR). Plain old SMR services have been targeted to users who need to dispatch mobile units, such as those in the construction and transportation industries. But new digital SMR services are poised to compete with cellular phones and PCS [personal communications services] for voice and data mobile communications. Nextel Communications, the leading SMR licensee, now offers an attractive mobile service free of roaming charges and is hoping to build a digital network that will cover 85 percent of the U.S. population.

Personal Communications Services (Narrowband)

- 901–902 MHz
- 930–931 MHz
- 940–941 MHz

This narrowband PCS spectrum was the subject of the first license auction ever held by the FCC, in July 1994. This is the terrain for paging and messaging giants Mtel, AT&AMPT Wireless, AirTouch, Mobile-Comm, and PageNet, among others. These advanced networks can accommodate two-way paging devices and one-way alphanumeric messaging.

Wireless Barcode Readers, Child Monitoring Systems

- 902–928 MHz

This is the realm of a variety of services, including wireless barcode readers. Another, the Newchild monitoring system, locates lost children in amusement parks and zoos; the child wears a transponder that bounces signals to fixed transmitter sites in the park.

Personal Communications Services

- 1850–1990 MHz   Broadband PCS
- 1910–1930 MHz   Unlicensed PCS

The Guinness Book of Records declared the sell-off of PCS spectrum the largest auction in history. FCC chair Reed Hundt called it "one of the most important sales of public property since Napoleon sold almost half of the west of this country to Jefferson's United States." Total broadband PCS auctions raised upward of $20 billion for the federal government. Driving the explosive growth in the wireless industry are the champions of PCS: PrimeCo Personal Communications (a partnership of Bell Atlantic, Nynex, AirTouch, and US West), Sprint Spectrum, AT&AMPT Wireless, and NextWave Personal Communications. These nascent broadband personal communications services are becoming fierce competitors to their cellular phone siblings, offering rates up to 20 percent lower than cellular services. PCS devices employ digital transmission, which results in better sound quality, reliability, and security.

Digital Audio Radio Services

- 2320–2345 MHz

Music normally heard crackling over local radio stations soon will be coming in crystal clear on new digital channels. This spring, American Mobile Radio, CD Radio, Direct Broadcasting Satellite Corp., and Primosphere (formed by the managers of several pop stars, including Bruce Hornsby and Def Leppard) will vie in an auction for two slots allocated for digital audio satellite broadcasting. The satellites will beam 50 to 100 channels of specialized, CD-quality national programming to compete with ground-based radio broadcasters. A study by Mitre Corp. shows that 47 percent of surveyed consumers are willing to pay $5 to $16 per month for such services. But not everyone is enthused. Edward Fritts, president of the National Association of Broadcasters, declared that this "plethora of new technologies will be the death knell of local stations."

AM Radio Broadcasting

- 535–1605 kHz

AM radio is the granddaddy of wireless telecommunications hot-shots. Back in its day, the action of the wireless world took place way down the spectrum block in the lower frequencies—so low that AM radio doesn't even map onto the chart of hot spots today.

Unlicensed National Information Infrastructure

- 5.15–5.35 GHz
- 5.725–5.875 GHz

In the spirit of keeping some of the public airwaves public, the FCC has allocated open space for devices using this band. These devices will provide an economical means for classrooms, hospitals, libraries, and other public institutions to be linked to advanced networks without the need for wires. Rural areas can become part of the National Information Infrastructure cost-effectively, bringing us one step closer to the ideal of universal access. Separate efforts—by Apple Computer and WINForum, a group of mostly computer and communications hardware firms—to develop wireless local-area networks (NII Band and SUPERNet, respectively) can now proceed. These networks will enable digital transfer of data, video, and imaging to occur at the rate of up to 20 million bits per second. WINForum claims SUPERNet will be able to transmit a 1,000-page, single-spaced document in a little more than 3 seconds.

Direct Broadcast Satellites (DBS)

- 12.2–12.7 GHz   DBS Downlinks
- 17.3–17.8 GHz   DBS Uplinks

DBS can broadcast 175 channels of specialized programming, including CD-quality audio channels and pay-per-view movies, to 18-inch satellite dishes. With more than 4 million current subscribers, DBS has quickly become a powerful new competitor to cable television. In January 1996, MCI outbid TCI for the second-to-last available DBS orbital spot for the United States, paying $682.5 million for a spectrum license so they can then build a $1 billion satellite broadcast system. MCI joins DirecTV, U.S. Satellite Broadcasting, and EchoStar as a provider in the rapidly growing market for DBS services.

FM Radio Broadcasting

- 88–108 MHz

While the world of classic rock and drive-time celebs is still a very analog place, some digital experimentation is beginning—spurred by the expected arrival of satellite-based digital audio radio services.

Cellular Phones

- 824–849 MHz
- 869–894 MHz

During the mid-1980s, the FCC decided to reallocate a portion of what was formerly UHF-TV spectrum (channels 70 to 83) to mobile services, jumpstarting the wireless industry. The analog cellular standard is known as AMPS (advanced mobile phone service), first developed by AT&AMPT in 1970. Today, there are more than 40 million analog cell phone users in the United States. The cellular industry is developing digital equipment to keep up with new, advanced digital communications services like PCS, which have invaded the wireless market. AT&AMPT recently introduced a digital cellular service that will provide digital paging, voicemail, and Caller ID. As analyst Mark Lowenstein puts it, "This is really the beginning of the digital wars."

Multiple Address Systems

- 928–929 MHz
- 932–932.5 MHz
- 941–941.5 MHz
- 952–960 MHz

Here's one you run into every day but never knew was there. Multiple address systems (MAS) involve communications between a central master station and surrounding remote stations. Utilities and pipelines use MAS to monitor distribution systems; airports use it to control runway lights; banks use it for ATM transactions; retailers use it for credit card verification; and restaurants and offices use it to play elevator music. MAS spectrum is very congested and the FCC allocated new space in the 932- and 941-MHz bands to accommodate increased use. However, MAS operators are still waiting for the FCC to act on licenses pending since 1992.

Prayers Heavenbound

- 930–931 MHz

A Vermont company's radio service, called Prayers Heavenbound, sends religious messages into space—for a fee.

Geostationary Mobile Satellite Service

- 1525–1530 MHz   Lower L-band
- 1530–1544 MHz   Lower L-band
- 1626.5–1645.5 MHz   Lower L-band
- 1545–1559 MHz   Upper L-band
- 1646.5–1660.5 MHz   Upper L-band

Hovering at a stationary point 22,320 miles above the earth, geostationary satellites transmit signals for weather, television, and telecommunications services. Geostationary satellites, which travel in a geosynchronous orbit, could offer global service, but because the satellite is so far away, there is a slight delay of 1 or 2 seconds in signal transmission. The only geostationary satellite licensee in the United States is American Mobile Satellite Corp., whose $500 million satellite was launched in April 1995, offering voice, data, and fax services. The International Mobile Satellite Organization, aka Inmarsat, links these satellites to telecommunications networks through ground stations operated in each country by a designated signatory. The U.S. signatory is Comsat Corp.

Extraterrestrial Monitoring Frequencies

- 1420–1660 MHz

The Search for Extraterrestrial Intelligence League monitors this band for The Signal that will prove we're not alone.

Nongeostationary Mobile Satellite Service

- 1610–1626.5 MHz   NGSO/MSS (Big LEO) Uplinks
- 2483.5–2500 MHz   NGSO/MSS (Big LEO) Downlinks

Known as Big LEOs (for their low earth orbit), nongeostationary mobile satellites orbit about 800 miles above the earth. The *nongeostationary* part of the name refers to the moving satellite; the *mobile* part of the name refers to the moving devices on the ground receiving the signals.

There are three licensed Big LEOs: Motorola's $3.7 billion Iridium, a sixty-six-satellite system; TRW's $1.8 billion Odyssey, a twelve-satellite system; and Loral/Qualcomm's $1.5 billion Globalstar, a forty-eight-satellite system. Big LEOs will provide worldwide digital wireless communications services (voice, data, paging, fax). The development of a "world phone" for ubiquitous telecommunications will be especially useful in rural areas and in countries with remote villages and limited wired networks. The end result: You'll be in touch wherever you are on the planet.

Microwave Ovens

- 2450 MHz

There are more than 100 million ovens in the U.S. pumping out microwaves in this frequency. Let's hope they cause no harm.

Wireless Cable

- 2500–2655 MHz
- 2655–2690 MHz

Wireless cable is not an oxymoron—it's a method of moving cable television programming through microwaves. Using a microwave technology known as multichannel multipoint distribution service (MMDS), wireless cable operators can deliver up to thirty-three channels of programming to viewers who receive the signals with rooftop antennas and set-top boxes. CAI Wireless Systems Inc., the largest wireless cable operator, recently received approval from the FCC to begin two-way voice, video, and data transmission. MMDS operators—especially the RBOCs [regional Bell operating companies]—hope that these new digital systems, which increase the number of channels and offerings available to subscribers, will make them more competitive with cable and satellite broadcasters.

General Wireless Communications Service

- 4.66−4.685 GHz

Slated for auction this year are 875 licenses to provide general wireless communications service, which represents an important milestone in the industrywide push for spectrum flexibility. Those who secure the licenses will be permitted to offer virtually any wireless service: two-way interactive data transmission, cellular phone, microwave, dispatch, whatever. Only public broadcasting, radar systems, and satellite services are off limits. Practical applications of this latest breed of wireless communications might include in-flight airline entertainment.

Teledesic

- 18.8−19.3 GHz
- 28.6−29.1 GHz

This massive $9.55 billion nongeostationary fixed satellite project plans to launch 840 satellites (at the cost of $5.5 million apiece), creating a global "Internet in the sky." At a capacity equivalent to 20,000 simultaneous T1 lines, the Teledesic network will offer voice channels, videoconferencing, and interactive multimedia channels to fixed devices on the ground at transmission speeds sixty times faster than today's modems. Operation is expected to begin by 2002. Cofounders Bill Gates and Craig McCaw, each of whom owns a third of the company, want to do nothing less than seamlessly link people and businesses anywhere on the planet. "I think this has the potential to change the world as much as the first transcontinental railway," says an admittedly biased observer, Teledesic CEO David Twyver.

Fixed Satellite Service

- 17.7−18.8 GHz   Downlinks
- 19.7−20.2 GHz   Downlinks
- 28.35−28.6 GHz   Uplinks
- 29.5−30 GHz   Uplinks

These fixed satellite systems are not to be confused with the Big LEO (low earth orbit) mobile satellite systems like Iridium and Globalstar, which are being developed for global portable phones. These geostationary satellites will provide high-speed, Internet-like services, including e-mail, database access, software distribution, videoconferencing, and financial transactions to fixed equipment on the ground. In that respect, they will compete with Teledesic, which is classified as a nongeostationary fixed satellite service. A lot of big players are lining up to develop communications services that can be reached from all over the planet. GE American Communications has proposed a system of nine satellites. Hughes Communications Galaxy has proposed a twenty-satellite system. Other big system developers include AT&AMPT, Lockheed Martin, Comm Inc., and EchoStar. Many believe that these fixed satellite systems will have a tremendous social and economic impact in the next century. We'll see.

K-Band Police Radar

- 24.15 GHz

Beware the cop with the K-band police radar. He's operating in this frequency.

RELATED LINKS

- CITA's World of Wireless Communications (http://www.wow-com.com)
- Mobile Computing Online (http://www.mobilecomputing.com)
- NASA's Electromagnetic Spectrum Site (http://imagine.gsfc.nasa.gov/docs/science/know_l1/emspectrum.html)

FOR FURTHER RESEARCH

To find out more about the topics discussed in this reading, use InfoTrac College Edition. Type in keywords and subject terms such as "wireless infrastructure," "digitization," and "electromagnetic spectrum." You can access InfoTrac College Edition from the Wadsworth/Thomson Communication Cafe homepage: http://communication.wadsworth.com.

6

Advertising and Public Relations

Reading 6-1

Is Advertising Finally Dead?

Michael Schrage

EDITOR'S NOTE

The world of twenty-first century telecommunications spawns myriad ways to sell products and learn about consumers. This article by MIT Media Lab fellow and Adweek *columnist Michael Schrage explores what the next generation of consumer-driven advertising might look like and how genetic information may provide advertisers with useful marketing cues. Despite the reading's provocative title, advertising isn't dead, Schrage argues; it's being reborn. Indeed, the future of advertising is in many ways the future of media. Soon, Schrage says, advertising, information, and transactions will begin to blur; increasingly, "advertisements will feel and play like visual conversations, video games, and simulations." Being sold to has never been more entertaining.*

CONSIDER

1. How is the ongoing explosion of personal and portable media creating new kinds of opportunities for advertising, sponsorships, and promotions?

2. What role might games play in the new advertising environment? How are games, in a sense, "dual purpose"?

3. How are the discoveries and innovations in biotechnology of potential benefit to advertisers and marketers?

Wherever there are audiences, there will be advertisers. As media evolve, so do audiences. Time and geography—more than human nature—separate the captive crowds at the Roman Coliseum [in ancient times] from user lists on the Internet.

Make no mistake—as surely as today's PBS features endless pledge nights and corporate advertisements masquerading as public service announcements—tomorrow's digital advertising will be inextricably woven into networks and VR fabrics. The digital David Ogilvy may not have materialized yet, but cyberspace's commercial future is inevitable. There will be billboards along the Information Superhighway.

Pop media, of course, have a rich tradition of subsidy: In the nineteenth century, advertising brought mass affordability to the daily newspaper with the "penny dreadfuls"; in the twentieth century, commercial sponsorship turned radio and then television into dominant media. The ongoing explosion of personal and portable media—imbued with ever-growing quantities of bandwidth and processing power—is creating opportunities for new kinds of advertisements, sponsorships, and promotions. Can the comfortable clichés of Speedy Alka-Seltzer, Mr. Whipple, and the Bud Bowl see what's coming?

Already, a Sega/Nintendo video game offers innovative advertisers potential levels of customer interaction no traditional 30-second spot could dream of. What better way to burn a sales message directly onto the synapses of an impressionable teenager than to craft an exciting, high-speed video game around it? Maybe the Trix rabbit, Cap'n Crunch, and Honey Bear can be turned into kinder, gentler video games for the wee ones. . . .

The fashionable, faux futurism predicts that this time will be different, that this time new media technology will guarantee the individual the upper hand over the advertiser. Maybe; maybe not. More likely, we'll see these new media renegotiate the power relationships between individuals and advertisers. Yesterday, we changed the channel; today, we hit the remote; tomorrow, we'll reprogram our agents/filters. We'll interact with advertising where once we only watched; we'll seek out advertising where once we avoided it. Advertising will not go away; it will be rejuvenated.

"Is Advertising Finally Dead?" by Michael Schrage. From *Wired*, February 1994, pp. 71–74, 124–126. Copyright © 1994 by Michael Schrage. Reprinted with permission of the author.

WHAT DOES THIS NEXT GENERATION OF ADVERTISING LOOK LIKE?

Obviously, the rise of smart networks and programmable agents/filters means that advertisements will become more targeted and selective. Databases will drive many ads over the Net, with smart databases responding to queries by curious consumers. Advertisers and buyers will negotiate for information over the Net. Indeed, *Wired* senior columnist and MIT Media Lab Director Nicholas Negroponte has argued that the future of advertising will see a total inversion of traditional practice: Instead of advertisers soliciting response, they'll respond to solicitations by potential customers.

But what about the nature of the advertisements themselves? Are ads destined to be little more than the shards of targeted databases mating with personal agents and ingenious viruses infecting the Net? More likely, we'll see advertisements imitate the principles that have enabled Nintendo and Sega to redefine American pop culture. Advertisements will feel and play like visual conversations, video games, and simulations.

Ads would become software seducers, enticing and guiding customer interaction. Advertising, information, and transaction would all begin to blur. Interactive ads can evolve into compelling direct-response environments—informative, intimate, and immediate.

The same holds true for games. Sega already offers a video game featuring the 7-Up Spot as the lead character, but that's merely using the medium for promotion.

Think instead of designing games that blend the properties of the medium with the advertising message. It's easy to imagine McDonald's producing an educational video game called, say, Burger Hunt, for its kiddie customers. Ronald McDonald gives the player a random quantity of "McDollars" and the child has to maneuver, Mario-like, through mazes of Hamburglars and other McDonald-Land obstacles to buy and bring back just the right number of burgers, fries, shakes, and McNuggets—plus change—to win.

Such a game would literally reward kids for buying virtual McBurgers. No doubt, PCMCIA card versions of the game will print out redeemable McDonald's coupons and gift certificates, or plug directly into McDonald's cash registers. The point is simple: Games are dual purpose—they create compelling experiences and get customers even more involved with the product. Coca-Cola, Toys R Us, PepsiCo, and Nabisco may all ultimately design games to imprint their products onto the neurons of their younger customers. What advertising on MTV was to the youth market of the last decade, video game advertising will be to the youth market of the next.

Similarly, Chrysler or Toyota might develop VR driving games for adolescents and adults to promote their cars. If for no other reason than to differentiate themselves, sophisticated advertisers will invest more capital and creativity in high-involvement media.

American Express, Fidelity, and other financial go-betweens have an enormous stake in garnering high-net-worth investors. Imagine interactive ads built around expert systems that offer custom-calibrated investment advice. A potential customer might answer a series of questions—or be confronted with a set of investment options—and the responses would lead to a digital description of the investor's risk profile. Based on that profile, the appropriate financial vehicles would be put on display: venture capital and small-cap stocks for the major risk seekers, mutual funds and municipal bonds for the more financially faint-of-heart. Tap on the keyboard or utter the right voice command and the transaction is complete. This type of expert-systems model would easily translate to travel planning or finding that perfect wedding present.

So, the focus of advertising design shifts: Ads become a medium of collaboration between potential buyer and potential seller. Indeed, if the interaction and information is crafted appropriately, even the term "advertisement" becomes passé, replaced by a new genre of commercial communication.

IS THERE A SHOPPING GENE?

As sweeping and pervasive as the media technology revolution may be, the pace of discovery and innovation in biotechnology is even more startling. The University of Minnesota studies of identical twins—in which identical twins separated at birth frequently smoke the same brand of cigarettes and buy the same brands of clothing—strongly indicate that understanding the human genome could offer insights into the marketplace.

Is it bizarre to envision a time when advertisers and marketers conduct focus groups filled with people of certain genotypes to test their predisposition toward certain advertising campaigns? Wouldn't an advertiser want to know if shy customers respond more openly to male or female salespeople or quiet versus noisy advertising campaigns? In an era of targeted marketing, might not the human genome be the best database of all?

Of course, the real future of advertising and marketing may rest in the new ecology and the interrelationship between genes and memes. The term "meme" was invented over 15 years ago by Oxford zoologist Richard Dawkins as an ingenious way to explain cultural change.

Even though the concept of memes represents the boldest and most provocative theory of how new ideas spread, the word has somehow managed to avoid capture by the advertising, media, and marketing communities. That's too bad: Memetics offers a new paradigm to explain pop culture. Apparently, more agencies are comfortable drawing inspiration from a double martini than a double helix.

"Examples of memes are tunes, ideas, catchphrases, clothes fashions, ways of making pots or of building arches," Dawkins writes in *The Selfish Gene*. "Just as genes propagate themselves in the gene pool by leaping from body to body via sperm or eggs, so memes propagate themselves in the meme pool by leaping from brain to brain."

What are the memes that urge us to purchase and consume? How do you splice two or three seemingly disparate memes? What is the appropriate medium to transmit certain memes? VCR? TV? CD? Radio? Do some cultures diffuse advertising memes more efficiently than others? These are the kinds of questions that the meme paradigm will force advertising agencies and their clients to address explicitly. Forget demographics and psychographics. Think memegraphics.

Indeed, the future of advertising may draw design inspirations less from the emerging networks of new media technology than from the powerful metaphors of genetic and memetic engineering.

RELATED LINKS

- AdCritic.com (http://www.adcritic.com)
- *Advertising Age* (http://www.adage.com)

- The Center for Interactive Advertising (http://www.ciadvertising.org)
- ITV Report (http://www.itvreport.com)

 FOR FURTHER RESEARCH

To find out more about the topics discussed in this reading, use InfoTrac College Edition. Type in keywords and subject terms such as "interactive advertising," "memetics," and "commercial communication." You can access InfoTrac College Edition from the Wadsworth/Thomson Communication Cafe homepage: http://communication.wadsworth.com.

Reading 6-2

Bye-Bye: The Net's Precision Accountability Will Kill Not Only Traditional Advertising, But Its Parasite, Big Media. Sniff.
Randall Rothenberg

EDITOR'S NOTE

Most media observers view the trend toward media consolidation and bigness as an ominous development (see Chapter 7 on Media Concentration). Author Randall Rothenberg, however, thinks the Internet's precision accountability might just spell the end of big media as we know it. Once advertisers start seeing results from their online marketing efforts and are able to pinpoint what worked and when on the basis of click-throughs, vague assurances about the old media regime's effectiveness will seem like so much hot air. The winners in this new advertising order? Consumers will no longer have to endure spurious ads but instead will receive commercial information only about products and services they are interested in purchasing. Rothenberg suggests a power shift may not be far behind.

CONSIDER

1. What is the "knowability paradox," and why does Rothenberg suggest it is important to understanding the coming disintegration of big media?

2. Unlike traditional mass media, the Net is accountable—how so?

3. What is the difference between image advertising and retail advertising? How might new media technologies gradually erode this distinction?

It was as luminous as L.A. gets at eight in the morning. Studio chiefs. Production company heads. Bernard Weinraub, entertainment reporter for the *New York*

Times. Peter Bart, editor of *Variety.* Burt Manning, chair of the J. Walter Thompson advertising agency, had flown his bearded self in from La Côte Droite. The only person missing, it seemed, was Merv Griffin. But his picture was everywhere. He owned the hotel where these hundreds of mediarati were juicing and schmoozing.

They'd come this May morning in 1995 to bear witness as the most formidable of their number—

Michael Ovitz of Creative Artists Agency; former CBS head Howard Stringer; and Ray Smith, Ivan Seidenberg, and Phil Quigley—of Bell Atlantic, Nynex, and Pacific Telesis, respectively—announced the formation of a $300 million joint venture in interactive television, which they dubbed Tele-TV.

The air was thick with anticipation. Eighteen months earlier, Nynex had sunk $1 billion-plus into Viacom. The result: nothing. *Time*'s prediction of a "brave new world" of interactive multimedia was already a year old. But Stringer—beloved for his hard-times stewardship of the greatest of broadcast networks, and the highest-profile deserter to new media—was exultant. Media, marketing, and interactivity were about to unite. "You are no longer restrained by the constraints of time!" he rejoiced, his accent a refreshing mix of Wales, Oxford, and New York. "Time as you know it is gone."

Today, Stringer is gone—as are most of his partners. Having succeeded in their various real goals (a large finder's fee, a desperately needed new job, scaring competitors away), they've found better things to do: for Ovitz, the brief presidency of (and $100 million buyout from) the Walt Disney Company, a conventional media conglomerate; for Stringer, the presidency of Sony, a conventional entertainment company; and for Smith, Seidenberg, and Quigley, a merger focused on conventional telephony.

One doesn't have to be a genius to detect the self-interest that has lurked beneath the development of new media. And from the day Absolut put a URL on a NoHo billboard to signal its hipness to New York's downtowners, advertisers and their agencies have been feeding the hype and then exploiting the buzz of the Web.

Were it not for the fact that the media world knows no shame, the shamelessness of it all would be astonishing. Last year, I heard Jupiter Communications head Gene DeRose guess that Web advertising would hit $4 billion to $6 billion by 2000—a mere 400 to 600 percent jump in 4 years. Not to be outdone, Mark Kvamme of the CKS Group, the most successful of the interactive-advertising start-ups, estimated that it could reach $100 billion. "That's madness," a Wall Street analyst sitting next to me whispered.

Madness with a mission. Soon after CKS completed its auspicious initial public offering, it acquired an established agency that specializes in—guess what?—old-fashioned print and broadcast advertising. A marketing executive at a large broadcasting company once told me that his Web site's profitability was based en-

tirely on using the promise of front-page banner placement to lure advertisers into buying more commercials on his network.

Marketing in the Information Age is, in short, a form of gamesmanship. Playing on advertisers' valid fear that conventional print and electronic media have exhausted their ability to attract consumers, ad agencies, research firms, trade publications, and the digital dominion have been willing new media into existence, building it upon a foundation of swagger and fabrication.

But here's the beauty of it: They are stitching together a Frankenstein that will, that must, inevitably destroy them all.

To understand the coming disintegration of Big Media—the *Los Angeles Times* and *New York Times*, *60 Minutes* and *20/20*, Howard and Rush, *Glamour* and *Slate*—you've got to grasp the Knowability Paradox.

It was not a foregone conclusion that advertising would become the dominant force in the development of American media. In Europe, royal support, state sponsorship, and political-party assistance helped guarantee the primacy of specific manufacturers and certain media institutions well up to the present.

But in the U.S., starting in the early nineteenth century, something curious happened: the media abandoned the Old World models and wrapped itself—contextually as well as financially—around advertising. The move was driven partly by mass manufacturers' need to brand commodity goods, partly by the vastness of our continental marketplace, and partly by a presumption of class mobility that made us want to sell, earn, acquire, and display.

A newfound "objectivity" in news reporting arose from publishers' desire to draw the largest audience with the least offense. What historian Daniel Boorstin has labeled *pseudo-events*—news conferences, press releases, and stunts that "someone has planned, planted, or incited"—were concocted to fill the print space and broadcast time that increased year by year as advertisers sought to satiate a growing middle class. For the three decades between commercial radio's first appearance in Pittsburgh and the TV quiz show scandals of the '50s, advertising agencies produced not only the ads, but also the programs themselves.

But this massive edifice has always been undergirded by a contradiction: No one understands how, or even if, advertising works. Because the system of production, distribution, sales, and communications is so large and complex, attempting to isolate the effectiveness of a single element—advertising content—is all but impossible.

Advertising agencies exploited this confusion by urging clients to buy more pages, more spots, more billboards. The agencies became more profitable, which in turn led to the creation of more media. But to forestall uncomfortable scrutiny by a business culture addicted to scientism and certitude, agencies were always on the lookout for new services. Copywriting, market research, psychological research, sales promotion, public relations, even the procurement of prostitutes for clients—all were gimmicks designed to draw attention away from advertising's inscrutability and toward the unverifiable but desperate need for *more*.

Hence the Knowability Paradox: The less we have known about how advertising and the media work, the more advertising and media there have been. Conversely, the more advertising and media there have been, the more they have shaped the culture they saturate. Sitcoms, docudramas, advertorials, celebrity covers, radio shock jocks, drive time—the forms and conventions that are as familiar and invisible as the air we breathe—owe their existence to the fact that we don't know what works to attract consumers, or why. Hence the continual hammer of innovation against the hard shell of tradition.

So too in the agency business proper. Advertising's creative revolution in the '60s sprang from the unprovable belief of Bill Bernbach—guru of the groundbreaking Doyle Dane Bernbach agency—that "advertising is fundamentally persuasion and persuasion happens to be not a science, but an art." Led by Doyle Dane, an entertainment impulse engulfed the ad industry, providing consumers with Borscht Belt blackouts (Alka-Seltzer's "I can't believe I ate the whole thing" campaign) and cinematic sentimentality (Coca-Cola's "I'd like to teach the world to sing"), culminating with what some believe to be the greatest TV commercial ever produced, Chiat/Day's stirring, neo-constructivist "1984" spot for Apple's introduction of the Macintosh.

The postmodern wave that's swept over advertising during the 1990s—self-referential, mediacentric, and coy—is also impelled by the Knowability Paradox. Its hallmark is the self-conscious admission: Hey, we're only doing an ad here; we *know* that you can see right through us. While the roots of this are planted firmly in the '50s—in *Mad* magazine's scathing indictment of advertising ballyhoo—the cynicism, pastiches, and layered meanings of postmodernism have blossomed into the core currency of the media culture. They are evi-

dent in Oliviero Toscani's political tracts for Benetton; in ABC's current TV-rots-your-brain promotional campaign; and, most famously, in virtually everything produced by Portland's Wieden & Kennedy, whether it's Spike Lee proclaiming the transubstantiating power of Michael Jordan's shoes or Robert Goulet warbling the virtues of ESPN. Using sly social commentary as a vehicle for marketing—or is it the other way around?—is only the latest of the innovations bequeathed to us by a media-spindustrial complex that simply doesn't know its own strengths.

If it has any. For evidence abounds that people just aren't paying attention. The phenomenal growth of a few megabrands like Nike can't disguise the fact that, despite a 70 percent increase in U.S. advertising spending between 1986 and 1996—from $102 billion to $175 billion—more people than ever believe that most products in most categories are exactly alike. A contemporary television blockbuster like *Seinfeld* draws only one-third the audience, as a percentage of the total, that saw 1960s network hits like *The Beverly Hillbillies*. Unsurprising, because Nielsen's People Meters (a more accurate viewer sampling technology than the Audimeters it replaced) have shown far fewer people watching television in toto than TV executives previously believed.

By the dawn of the 1990s, it was clear that new gimmicks were needed, equal in their subversive power to marketing's earlier gimmicks. So advertisers and their media supplicants have tried ever-more ham-handed ways of blurring the line between advertising and content. BMW tied the launch of a new car to its paid placement in a James Bond flick. The *Los Angeles Times* recently reorganized its news division around Procter & Gamble's brand-management model, putting marketing executives on an equal footing with editors. Media giants set up or acquired new narrowcast cable networks, the better to reach consumers with preidentified interests, all primed for the targeted sell—Chop TV for martial-arts enthusiasts, The Recovery Network for 12-step aficionados, et cetera.

Great ideas, but all subject to external tension. Newspaper readership continues to drop, by 10 percent in the past 4 years. Sports sponsorships by tobacco companies invite government scrutiny. Even heavily promoted new networks like MSNBC and Fox News top out with an average daily viewership of between 20,000 and 100,000 households, probably not much more than the circulation of your local weekly newspaper. By the time the recession began to lift in 1992, a much better gimmick was needed if advertising-as-we-know-it (witty copy, brilliant graphics, extravagant productions, superstar pitchmen, long lunches, houses in the Hamptons) was to survive.

The Internet happened at exactly the right time.

The Net, though, is different. Different from the 30-second spot, the classified ad, and the four-color double-truck. Different from product placement, Nascar logos, and rock-tour sponsorship. Different from Leo Burnett's Middle American corn, David Ogilvy's sophisticated imagery, and Phil Dusenberry's boffo productions.

The Net is accountable. It is knowable. It is the highway leading marketers to their Holy Grail: single-sourcing technology that can definitively tie the information consumers perceive to the purchases they make. No less an institution than Procter & Gamble, perhaps the most influential force in advertising this century, recognized this when it announced that P&G would compensate its online media outlets on the basis of click-throughs—by the number of people who push the button and choose to read an ad.

Some, notably Yahoo!, complied. But it's telling that the old guard of advertising and media reacted to the proposal with a mixture of indignation and fear. After all, if Procter's recommendation were to be adopted industrywide, it would destroy the very basis of advertising and the media it supports: imperfect research (like broadcasting's Nielsen and publishing's Simmons, which project total audiences from small and often flawed samples); pass-along readership, out-of-home viewers, and similar numbers-game chimeras; and ad-agency creative "geniuses" and their fulminations about unique selling propositions, power copy, and like hokum. With accountability, they all must wither and die.

Accountability, of course, has existed for generations. It's called direct marketing, and responses to it can be tabulated and, to a great degree, controlled. As far back as 1923, Claude C. Hopkins, the president of the Lord & Thomas agency, was writing that, because of direct marketing, "the time has come when advertising in some hands has reached the status of a science. We know what is most effective, and we act on basic laws."

Marketers have certainly been tantalized. During the past quarter century or so, direct marketing—which encompasses such disciplines as junk mail and infomercials—and other "below the line" marketing functions, have grown to constitute some two-thirds of all marketing-communications spending, with con-

ventional advertising accounting for the rest. That's a reversal of the historic ratio and a clear sign of trouble for Madison Avenue.

But direct marketing was always hobbled by a few facts and a lot of fancy. The facts: It's enormously expensive to send missives through the mail, the lag time between call and response is too long, and it's still too damned inefficient, a 2 percent response being akin to nirvana. The fancy: You can never build a brand through direct marketing; there'll always be a difference between image advertising and (ugh!) retail advertising.

The new media technologies, by drastically reducing production and distribution costs and making possible almost continual and instantaneous refinements in message, promise to increase the efficiency of accountable advertising so that its widespread adoption, not as an ancillary medium but as the primary communications choice, becomes inescapable. That powerful brands will be built by such means is as certain a fact as primitive junk mail created L. L. Bean and the antediluvian infomercials spawned the Psychic Friends Network. The spurious distinction between image advertising and retail advertising will erode, then disappear, as each advertisement, every product placement, all editorial can be tied to transactions.

This is no futuristic fantasy. Consider one upcoming innovation: a combination barcode scanner/smartcard reader that can be hidden in a TV remote control. When viewers see a commercial they like, they can point the zapper at the screen, read an offer embedded in the ad, and download a coupon into a smartcard, which can be used the next time they go shopping. The response will then be registered for review by the manufacturer and retailer.

In other words, just as the billion-channel universe descends upon us, knowability will wipe away marketing and media as we know them. Communications conglomerates—Rupert Murdoch's News Corporation, Sumner Redstone's Viacom, and the fractious Time Warner—will lose their oligopolistic control of a limited media shelf space. The conventional media forms they produce and dominate will diminish in influence as audiences are drawn to thousands of new variations whose ability to entertain, inform, and induce transactions will be knowable and known. Marketers will marshal their resources, spending only as much on a given venue as their returns can justify. If quality information and entertainment are to survive, the consumer will have to make up the difference.

Once advertising's Knowability Paradox is solved, the era of Big Media and the coddled audience will be over.

In early 1995, having returned from 18 months abroad to a city, a country, a culture ablaze with Internet fever, I called an old acquaintance with a plaintive request for help. He was one of Silicon Alley's rising stars, an expert on the fortunes and presumptions of this fresh medium, and I just couldn't understand all the 'zine start-ups, the friends transferring from "old" to "new" media jobs, and the gallant affirmations of an advertising inflow that would surely topple the structure of New York's Communications Corridor. As we

hunched over beers and cheeseburgers at one of Greenwich Village's more venerable literary pubs, I asked him where all the rosy projections were coming from.

"We make them up," he said. "Everyone does."

I had dinner again this fall with the same friend. We talked about Net hoopla, the shakeout in the 'zine market, and the failure of some recent interactive media IPOs. I couldn't help but wag a self-righteous finger at him. "The reason all these things went down," I said, with inquisitorial satisfaction, "is because you and your pals inflated the figures."

"Oh, we don't do that any more," he responded. "Now we know this thing can't be stopped."

RELATED LINKS

- Forrester Research (http://www.forrester.com)
- Leo Burnett (http://www.leoburnett.com)
- TBWA/Chiat/Day (http://www.chiatday.com)
- J. Walter Thompson (http://www.jwtworld.com)
- Jupiter Media Metrix (http://wreportus.mediametrix.com/clientCenter.html)
- Measuring User Action: The Click-Through (http://www.emediaplan.com/Internet/clickthroughs.asp)
- Nielsen Media Research (http://www.nielsenmedia.com)

FOR FURTHER RESEARCH

To find out more about the topics discussed in this reading, use InfoTrac College Edition. Type in keywords and subject terms such as "direct marketing," "click-throughs," and "Web advertising." You can access InfoTrac College Edition from the Wadsworth/Thomson Communication Cafe homepage: http://communication.wadsworth.com.

Reading 6-3

Public Relations
Douglas Rushkoff

The truth never hurts you, unless the truth hurts, and then you don't use it.
    —Howard Rubenstein

EDITOR'S NOTE

Contemporary public relations techniques leave little to chance and bear considerable resemblance to coercive strategies used by military strategists and intelligence operatives. So argues Douglas Rushkoff, best-selling author of Media Virus, *in this ex-*

cerpt from his recent critique of consumer society, Coercion. *Understanding the relationships between reality perceptions, irrationality, emotional triggers, and belief systems has enabled skilled practitioners to pace mass audiences for centuries, allowing them to move public opinion in a desired direction. Even in a digital age, tapping primal fears can prove very persuasive.*

CONSIDER

1. Celebrated public relations consultant Howard Rubenstein uses the media not to fool the public into believing lies but to "change the truth." How does he accomplish this feat?

2. Why is merely paying lip service to an issue no longer sufficient to restore one's public image in the midst of a crisis?

3. How do public relations specialists, according to Rushkoff, seek to mirror the conscious and unconscious concerns of their "targets" in order to change their perceptions of reality?

The scandal had made the headlines by the time Howard Rubenstein got the call from Kathie Lee Gifford's attorneys.

"Everyone had seen the story break," Rubenstein explained to me from his office overlooking midtown Manhattan. "It got tremendous play. They had portrayed her as a knowing participant in sweatshop manufacturing for clothing, and it was awful."

In April 1996, the *Daily News, New York Post,* and just about every other newspaper in town reported that clothing being sold nationally under Kathie Lee's name had actually been made by people working under atrocious conditions in Honduras. America's sweetheart turned out to be a character straight out of the pages of Upton Sinclair. Worse, as far as Rubenstein was concerned, a labor union that had long been looking for a media hook to publicize its underreported cause had finally found one in the famous television star. "They had what they thought was a pigeon." And without Rubenstein to guide her, Kathie Lee was fluttering out of control.

"She went on the air, and she attacked the critics. She attacked the union that was in back of it. She was stunned very badly and lashed out at her critics." That's when Kathie Lee and her lawyers called for help.

Howard Rubenstein, founder of Rubenstein and Associates Public Relations, is a man to have on your side in a crisis. He'll make you apologize, he'll make

---

you work, and he'll make you pay for your mistakes— but you'll end up smelling like roses.

In Kathie Lee's case, Rubenstein used his time-tested technique of putting the embattled client on the offensive. In terms of storytelling, his job was to change her from a villainous antagonist into an active protagonist. He knew that this fiasco would probably associate Kathie Lee with sweatshops for the rest of her life. So why not turn this situation to her advantage? What Jerry Lewis is to muscular dystrophy, Kathie Lee would be to sweatshops.

"The first thing I wanted to know was if it was true," Rubenstein says. "She was adamant in saying she didn't know about it. So I said, 'You have a clear path on what you have to do: you have to lead the fight against sweatshops. And be serious about it.'"

Within hours, Rubenstein was on the phone with the angry union, offering them something they wanted even more than a pigeon: a celebrity-fronted publicity campaign. With Kathie Lee's face and Rubenstein's contacts, it was easy.

"We made several moves," Rubenstein told me. "We had dinner with [Labor] Secretary [Robert] Reich, and came to an understanding of her position. We met with the governor of New York State, George Pataki, and also said we'd help him in getting through anti-sweatshop legislation, which happened. I called Cardinal O'Connor and asked if he would help, and he said 'Absolutely.'"

By the time Rubenstein had finished working, Kathie Lee Gifford was standing next to Bill Clinton in the White House Rose Garden, unveiling a program to help manufacturers certify that their garments had not been produced in sweatshops. Eventually, the Smithsonian Institution included Kathie Lee in its display on sweatshops as a leader in the fight against them. The original story—Kathie Lee revealed as an exploiter—had been spun into a different narrative entirely. The villain became the *ingenue,* as Kathie Lee—a symbol of American naiveté—learned the hard lesson that the Third World is a dark and dangerous place for its oft-victimized inhabitants. Drawn into battle, she would adopt their plight as hers, forever carry the torch of freedom and dignity for these oppressed people.

"It started with her inaccurately being portrayed as the sponsor of sweatshop clothing, and at the end of the line being praised as leading the fight against them. . . . What I tried to do was first tell the story that she was not a bad person and did not encourage sweatshops. The second thing, we tried to galvanize government and the private sector to a real fight against sweatshops. We took charge of the story."

Howard Rubenstein is not a devious man. Quite to the contrary, the sixty-something Harvard Law dropout ("I got bored") prides himself on the integrity of his campaigns, as evidenced by the fact that journalists rarely feel the need to double-check the assertions he makes in press releases. Although he is famous for taking on "crisis" clients like Marv Albert and George Michael, he spends most of his time managing the long-term images of corporate icons such as Rupert Murdoch and George Steinbrenner. He has become the most respected public relations man in the business, not because he knows how to fool the public into believing lies but because he understands how to use the media to change the truth.

Rubenstein has survived in a fast-changing business because his storytelling strategy is always based in reality. "I try to find out what happened, I try to get somebody to say 'I did wrong—here are the reasons I did,' maybe, and 'I shouldn't have done it, and I apologize to you, now.' And then I try to correct the thing that has been wronged. Visibly correct the error."

Like the many public relations specialists who preceded him, Rubenstein crafts his campaigns to fit the requirements of his audience. For today's sophisticated television public, this means admitting one's mistakes and then taking charge of the story by leading the media in its quest for retribution. Even though Kathie Lee had indirectly violated our sense of morality, she seemed to more than make up for it with her highly visible campaign to end improper labor practices around the world.

Rubenstein admits to focusing on visibility. When the Department of Labor busted a sweatshop manufacturing clothes for Kathie Lee in midtown Manhattan, Rubenstein made sure her husband, Frank Gifford, was photographed by a multitude of journalists as he handed envelopes of cash to the confused laborers as compensation. For Rubenstein's clients, such photo-ops are always backed by a genuine commitment to help solve the problem with which they have become associated. As far as the clients are concerned, this may or may not be because they wish to do the right thing. More often than not it's because paying lip service to an issue is no longer sufficient to restore one's public image in a crisis.

At the core of Rubenstein's strategy is a technique that public relations artists have been using for centuries: figuring out what the target audience believes, finding the inconsistencies in those beliefs, and then leveraging those inconsistencies into a new story. For Rubenstein, the new story will always more accurately depict the reality of the situation. He feels he is correcting public misperception, and he knows he wouldn't get away with a fallacious cover story for very long. In the age of the Internet and 24-hour news, Rubenstein's style of follow-through is costly and time-consuming, but mandatory for getting the job done. It wasn't always this way.

For many of Rubenstein's predecessors, the new and improved stories created for the target audience bore no more relationship to the truth than the story the public already believed. Still, the essential methodology involved—pacing the audience in order to gain control of the narrative, and then rewriting the story to lead the audience to a new conclusion—remains the same.

Like salesmen, public relations specialists seek to mirror the conscious and unconscious concerns of their targets in order to change their perception of reality. Just as a car dealer sizes up his walk-in clientele, researchers working for governments, public relations firms, and corporations expend a great deal of effort sizing up their constituencies on a regular basis. Once they understand our belief system and, more important, where the irrationality and emotional triggers lie in those beliefs, they can work to move us in a different direction. "Closing the sale" in these cases might mean gaining public support for a war, changing an industry's reputation as a polluter, or simply restoring voters' trust in a president who has lied to them.

Instead of focusing on one prospect at a time, however, the PR man [or woman] must work on a target that consists of thousands or even millions of people. In order to pace and lead such a large group the practitioners of mass communications must reduce their entire target population to a single, malleable mass— much in the way the promoters of spectacle aspire to transform a stadium filled with thousands of individual, thinking adults into a single, surging body.

ALIEN NATIONS

Mass communications find their historical foundations in centuries of imperialist cultural coercion. Funded mostly by their governments, well-meaning (and a few not-so-well-meaning) anthropologists developed methods for analysis and redirection while studying "primitive" peoples from foreign cultures. Whether or not they were aware of their sponsors' intentions, these anthropologists laid the groundwork for subsequent military invasions.

The early Christian missions of the fifteenth and sixteenth centuries, for example, served as the first outposts for the European troops that would eventually invade South America. These missions were not generally sponsored by the church but by the monarchy. As a result, the visiting missionary served the dual role of converter and intelligence gatherer. Ultimately, both functions simply prepared the target population to be taken by force.

The procedure for cultural domination invariably followed the same three steps used by public relations specialists today: First, learn the dominant myths of the target people and, in the process, gain their trust; second, find the gaps or superstitions in their beliefs; and third, either replace the superstitions or augment them with facts that redirect the target group's perceptions and allegiance.

Christian missionaries to the New World first studied the indigenous people in order to appraise their pantheistic belief system and to gain their trust. They observed local rituals to learn about particular beliefs associated with each god. Then they converted people by associating local gods with the closest corresponding Catholic saints or deities. The native god for animals, the people were taught, is really just Saint Francis. The drinking of chicken's blood is really just a version of the communion. And so on, until a local, hybridized version of Christianity evolved.

In the 1500s, Franciscan brothers studied the language and religion of the people of Tenochtitlan before choosing to build the hilltop basilica of the Virgin of Guadalupe on the site of an Aztec temple dedicated to the earth goddess Tonatzin. In its new incarnation, the mountaintop church became an homage to Mary, who is pictured stepping on the stars and moon, the symbols of her pagan predecessor. She overlooks what is now called Mexico City. The missionaries used their target audiences' devotion to local gods to sell them the saints.

This is the two-millennium-old process by which Christianity absorbed the rituals and beliefs of the peoples it converted. The Christmas tree began as part of a solstice ritual practiced by Germans to light the darkest night of the year. Smart missionaries of the time realized that this ritual had developed in connection to people's fear of the darkness of winter. The tannenbaum exposed the Germans' deepest fear—and the missionaries understood that it thus represented the most fertile ground for conversion. By identifying the tree with the holy cross and the birth of Christ, the Christians augmented the pagan ritual and redirected its sense of hope toward their own messiah.

Although business interests eventually replaced the church as the dominant force behind imperialist expansion, the techniques of population analysis and coercion—pacing and leading the target audience—remained the same. The British East India Company, for example, was formed in 1600 and given a "perpetual charter" from the British monarchy for trade in the East Indies and, later, China. In a series of well-funded wars spanning centuries, the company used a private army to effectively annex India for the British Monarchy, and Queen Victoria eventually became empress of India in 1876. Instead of using pure military might, the imperialists exploited researched tensions between the Indian Moghul emperors and their constituencies. After successfully breaking down Moghul rule, the smaller factions were easily conquered.

What remains a little less known about these efforts is that they involved active intelligence-gathering and social-influence techniques. After learning of the Indian people's respect for architecture, the British built a tremendous train station in Bombay dedicated to the new empress, Victoria Terminus, with vaulted Gothic ceilings and other construction techniques that demonstrated British technological superiority. The structure, an imported version of London's own cultural icon, Victoria Station, was not-so-coincidentally erected on the site of a former shrine to Indian goddess

Mumba Devi. The motif included both Western and Indian imagery, to imply that Indian society had been incorporated into the culturally dominant West.

In the early twentieth century, science replaced economic liberty as the cloak for governments seeking to extend their territorial reach. The United States funded dozens of research expeditions to the Far East and the South Pacific, all in the name of anthropology. While the young anthropologists of the 1920s may have had scientific inquiry in their hearts, military strategists looking for insights into the indigenous peoples of these territories often exploited the intelligence they gathered. The work of Margaret Mead, in particular, with its focus on the traditions and values of the natives of the South Pacific islands of New Guinea and Bali, came in handy when the regions were contested by the Japanese in World War II.

How was anthropological data used in war? For one, it offered insights into winning local support for the establishment of military bases and for convincing townspeople to inform on neighbors who might be working for the enemy. During the Vietnam War, the United States printed comic books and other propaganda that displayed a sensitivity for native customs, while they attempted to sway native loyalty.

In military decision making, it was also crucial to have a handle on the local or national psyche. For example, although Franklin Roosevelt had considered assassinating the emperor of Japan to force the nation's surrender, his advisors learned through anthropological research that such a move would surely backfire. With no emperor, there would be no one with the authority to surrender. Moreover, the attack on the emperor would so infuriate the people that they would likely fight until the last man was standing. Only a tremendous humiliation—such as that endured at Hiroshima—was deemed sufficient to force the Japanese emperor to admit defeat.

After World War II, Air Force Brigadier General Edward G. Lansdale emerged as the preeminent "counterinsurgency" strategist for the CIA. Over a period of three decades, he developed a wide range of intelligence and propaganda theories that were employed and refined in the field.[1] For example, in the 1950s, as part of his counterinsurgency campaign against the Huk rebels of the Philippines, Lansdale conducted research into local superstitions. He learned that the Huk battleground was believed to be inhabited by an *asuang,* or vampire figure. To capitalize on this mythology, his "psywar" units would follow Huk patrols and then qui-

etly ambush the last man on the trail. They would kill the soldier by means of two punctures on the neck, drain him of his blood, and then leave him to be found the next morning. On encountering the victim, the Huks in the area would retreat for fear of further vampire attacks.

By the 1980s, such psywar techniques had been catalogued by the CIA in a volume called *Counter Intelligence Study Manual,*[2] which was used mainly in Central American conflicts. The psyops book provides as clear a depiction of the kinds of graphic research and influence techniques used by public relations experts as you're likely to find.

To gather information on the target population, agents mix in among the population at "pastoral activities, parties, birthdays, and even wakes and burials" to learn of their beliefs and aspirations. Psyops officers also organize "discussion groups" to gauge local support of planned actions.

Once influence is to be exerted, the agents identify and recruit "established citizens" to serve as role models for cooperation by giving them jobs in "innocuous" but highly visible areas. Their next task is to smooth over difficult or irrational concepts with simple slogans. As a rationale for carrying guns, for example, guerillas are instructed to say, "Our weapons are, in truth, the weapons of the people, yours." Whatever the guerilla group actually intends, they are required to "make the people feel that we are thinking of them." In cases where CIA interests are irreconcilably opposed to those of the people, the manual suggests creating a "front organization" with a set of stated goals very different from what will be the movement's real agenda. Finally, all efforts at conversion are fine-tuned to the preexisting propensities of the target group: "We should inculcate this in the people in a subtle manner so that these feelings seem to be born of themselves, spontaneously."

For a culture as "alien" as that of the Huk rebels, the mythologies and superstitions fueling their emotional triggers are easy to locate. The more foreign the belief system is from that of the anthropologist, the more easily it can be observed with some measure of distance and objectivity. Besides, the trick only needs to work long enough to win (or avoid) a war. Even if the "truth" emerges sometime later, at least the primary objective has already been achieved. At the very worst, the enemy won't be fooled as readily in the future.

It is much harder for anthropologists to identify and exploit the emotional inconsistencies in their own cultures. That's why when American corporate and governmental interests adopted these techniques for use against the American people, they needed to cloak their assault in a seemingly benign manifestation: the focus group. About ten "average" members of a target population are brought into a room and asked to discuss an issue while a team of researchers, clients, and a camera record their responses from behind a one-way mirror. A researcher stays in the room with the subjects, asking them questions and pushing them in new directions. The focus group offers a laboratory in which interactions and discussions between real human beings are dissected and analyzed for their inconsistencies and leverage points.

Bob Deutsch, an anthropologist who worked for the Department of Defense before offering his services to the private sector, has conducted at least a thousand focus groups during his career. He is well known in the advertising and public relations industries for his ability to extract material from his subjects that no one else seems to be able to get. His secret, as he tells it, is to let the subjects speak freely until they stumble on their own faulty logic.

I first encountered Deutsch when he was giving a lecture to advertising researchers on how to lead and analyze focus groups. He showed a videotape of himself on ABC's *Nightline,* in which he led focus groups revealing Americans' irrational beliefs about Japan. "You want to uncover in your audience what I call a 'spasm of sentiment,'" he explained. "It's their illogic—their emotional logic." He told us how in focus groups with average American citizens, he learned that most people still associate the Japanese with Pearl Harbor: "People say, for example, 'Japan took our lives in 1941, and they took our livelihoods in 1991.'" Because Japan disrupted America's self-mythology of being invincible, the nation would never be forgiven in the irrational American sentiment.

A few months later, I found myself consulting to the same advertising agency as Deutsch—and, although I was initially wary of his self-consciously gurulike manner, I came to realize the brilliance of his work, as well the innocent sense of inquiry with which he performs it. To prepare me for a study on cult branding, the agency let me review videotapes of focus groups Deutsch had conducted with the Hells Angels about their extreme affinity for Harley-Davidson motorcycles.

On the tapes, he walks into a room filled with scary tattooed and leather-jacketed motorcycle thugs, sits down arrogantly, and says, "Tell me something: Why can't you buy a simple fucking Jap bike and live happily ever after?"

The bikers are immediately charged up, and the biggest one challenges him: "Who the hell are you to ask that?"

"I'm just a guy that asked you to come and you came," he replies. "For a lousy hundred dollars. So don't fuck around!"

"I don't want this videotaped," another burly biker protests.

"Why not?" Deutsch asks.

"Well, I just escaped from Rikers Island," the biker answers.

Again, Deutsch stands his ground, telling the ex-con to live with the camera or leave.

Instead of becoming violent with Deutsch, the bikers delivered one of the most revealing focus groups he had ever conducted. Deutsch's provocative tactics not only earned him the Hells Angels' trust but also engaged them in a genuine emotional conflict. What he learned, he later told me from his temporary office at another agency—the plush, pop-art filled DDB Needham headquarters on Madison Avenue—was that "they are protecting themselves. That's what their core story is about. Images are created to defend loss, not maximize gain."

Deutsch discusses his subjects with an air of detachment, a scientist's objectivity that he derived from his upbringing. As a child, Deutsch always felt out of place in America, where "99 percent of the linguistic universe was stereotypes." He was attracted to primitive cultures and became an anthropologist precisely so he could live and work among them. "These people live in the same world I do. They live in a world of emotion, nature, storytelling, and mythology."

On returning to the United States, he had the "magnificent insight" that the farther away our modern experience takes us from our mythological routes, the more we long for media, ideas, and images that help us to reconnect to them. "We're living at the subterranean level, anyway." While he adamantly opposes the putative goals of public relations, calling it a "charlatan profession," he is absolutely dedicated to focus groups for what they can reveal about a given population's connection to metaphor and archetype. "The mind is an organism that will make patterns. It doesn't care if there are no real patterns to be had. We make conclusions to stories all by ourselves."

In identifying these patterns, however, whether Deutsch likes it or not, he is revealing trigger points in our reasoning that can be exploited. During a focus group about Ronald Reagan, one of Deutsch's participants confessed, "I like the way President Reagan handled that conflict. I've forgotten which one." While many researchers would discard such a statement for its irrelevance to any real data, Deutsch sees such illogical statements as the goal of his inquiry: "It's not a stupid statement!" he told me, banging his hand on his borrowed designer desk. "It is literally prelinguistic. Noncontingent on any attributes—it cannot be justified even by the person who holds the opinion. Everything else just falls away. What I'm trying to do is understand the subjectivity of the audience in its full complexity and contradiction and illogic."

Once Deutsch has discovered the emotional core of his audience's mythology, he can begin to construct what he calls the "grand narrative," the overriding story of the group in relation to the subject being studied. It is the framework they use to organize their perception of the world. Because such mythologies are emotionally based and devoid of rationality, they are particularly vulnerable to reengineering from the outside.

While Deutsch limits such engineering to clever advertising campaigns (he came up with the "Q" campaign for Compaq based on his insight that computer users value good questions more than the "solutions" offered by IBM's marketers), others hope to capitalize on our irrational beliefs for much bolder efforts. Take the following anecdote as an example: "I volunteered at the al-Addan hospital. . . . I saw the Iraqi soldiers come into the hospital with guns, and go into the room where fifteen babies were in incubators. They took the babies out of the incubators, took the incubators, and left the babies on the cold floor to die."

Does that story sound familiar? It was offered as testimony to the House Human Rights Caucus by a 15-year-old Kuwaiti girl, first known only as Nayirah. Presented in late 1990, the story helped the United States muster domestic support for its entrance into the Gulf War. The incubator tale made the headlines and evening-news shows across the nation. The never-photographed image of Kuwaiti babies being hauled from their incubators has stayed with us to this day.

Less known, of course, is that the anonymous 15-year-old Kuwaiti girl presenting the American people with this arresting image was the daughter of Sheikh Saud Nasir al-Sabah, Kuwait's ambassador to the United States. The girl's story, which has subsequently proven impossible to corroborate, was prepared by a public relations firm called Hill & Knowlton as part of an $11 million campaign financed by the Kuwaiti government.[3] (Though the firm has since apologized for and distanced itself from the capaign, it still demonstrates their mastery of the coercive story.)

What better image to select for the American public than babies being ripped from their incubators? In the early 1990s, abortion was even more of a hot-button issue than it is today. Further, television news surveys have shown that the abuse or death of first-world babies is the most compelling story one can broadcast. If the 15-year-old had told us that babies had been taken from their homes, they still might have seemed foreign to the American public. Kuwait is an Arab country whose customs are unknown to us. We might have imagined the babies living in primitive stone huts or tents. By depicting them in incubators, Hill & Knowlton made the babies seem not only more helpless but more like members of the technologically advanced West. The image also resonated with an American public who feared that its own technological superiority—largely a product of a free-flowing supply of oil from the Middle East—was threatened by Arab barbarians.

Once we were fully engaged in the Gulf War, the Bush administration adopted slogans and symbols designed to stifle reasoned debate. As if following the CIA manual's suggestions for smoothing over dissonance with easy slogans, Bush's public relations people created meaningless mottoes specifically crafted to replace thought with emotion. The response to any question about the appropriateness of our military action was reduced to "Support our troops." Do we support our troops? Well, of course we do. They are our sons and daughters—but that's not the point. As Noam Chomsky explained:

> Support our troops. Who can be against that? Or yellow ribbons. Who can be against that? The issue was, Do you support our policy? But you don't want people to think about that issue. That's the whole point of good propaganda. You want to create a slogan that nobody's going to be against, and everybody's going to be for. Nobody knows what it means because it doesn't mean anything. Its crucial value is that it diverts your attention from a question that does mean something: Do you support our policy? That's the one you're not allowed to talk about. So you have people

arguing about support for the troops? "Of course I don't not support them." Then you've won.[4]

Public relations efforts of this kind amount to a systematic assault on our ability to make rational decisions. The idea is to blur any real policies in emotional platitudes or in evocative storytelling, based on research into the target group's mostly unconscious triggers. This is a delicate science, and it can easily backfire.

"PR is bullshit," Deutsch told me when I pressed him for information about how his own work might be applied by governments. "It's a very short-term deal and it's superficial. I don't know how to do public relations. I'm not that smart." Perhaps no one is.

Hill & Knowlton's efforts at promoting the Gulf War worked in the short run but ultimately served only to confuse Americans when George Bush refused to "finish" the war and kill Saddam Hussein. When the press revealed Nariyah to be an ambassador's daughter and the majority of domestic coverage as having been spun by Hill & Knowlton, America's relationship to the Gulf War and its propaganda abruptly changed. The public relations firm's reputation was irreparably compromised.

Stung by the bitter lessons of tinkering with a public's mythologies, public relations experts have found a new cloak for their emotional arguments: facts and figures. By appearing to remove themselves from the influence equation, they create the illusion that they are simply telling us how it is. In this way, they can make the irrational seem rational.

NOTES

1. Peter Watson, *War on the Mind: The Military Uses and Abuses of Psychology,* excerpted at Psywar Terror Tactics Web site. [Available: http://www.parascope.com]

2. Central Intelligence Agency, *Counter Intelligence Study Manual* LN 324–91, released through the Freedom of Information Act, and available from the National Archives.

3. John Carlisle, "Public Relationships: Hill & Knowlton, Robert Gray, and the CIA," *Covert Action Quarterly* (Spring 1993).

4. Noam Chomsky, *Media Control: The Spectacular Achievements of Propaganda.* Westfield, NJ: Open Magazine Pamphlet Series, 1991.

RELATED LINKS

- Counterintelligence Study Manual (http://www.derechos.net/soaw/manuals/ci-toc.html)
- Douglas Rushkoff (http://www.rushkoff.com)
- Frontline: The Merchants of Cool (http://www.pbs.org/wgbh/pages/frontline/shows/cool)
- Frontline: Douglas Rushkoff (http://www.pbs.org/wgbh/pages/frontline/shows/cool/rushkoff)
- Shadow Warrior: Howard Rubenstein's Life in Conflict (http://www.newyorkmag.com/page.cfm?page_id=918)

FOR FURTHER RESEARCH

To find out more about the topics discussed in this reading, use InfoTrac College Edition. Type in keywords and subject terms such as "image handler," "psychological coercion," and "social influence techniques." You can access InfoTrac College Edition from the Wadsworth/Thomson Communication Cafe homepage: http://communication.wadsworth.com.

Reading 6-4

Spin Sisters: Why Is PR the Only High-Tech Field That Women Run?

Janelle Brown

EDITOR'S NOTE

One of the least discussed aspects of the digital revolution and the new information-based economy is the underrepresentation of women in the high-tech industry. As this reading from the online magazine Salon *discusses, public relations is perhaps the only field where women seem to have real opportunity for executive advancement. Questions remain, however, about whether public relations is considered marginal to an organization's central operations and whether PR represents a type of "pink-collar ghetto" to which women are relegated not so much by choice but by circumstance.*

CONSIDER

1. How is the traditional role of public relations changing? How has the Internet affected the day-to-day rules of public relations?

2. Why is public relations one of the few areas in the high-tech industry where women seem to have real opportunity for executive advancement?

3. Is public relations simply the first high-tech sector to witness gender equity, or does PR represent a type of "pink-collar ghetto"—the only place where women *can* pursue management opportunities?

Last month [November 1998], *Upside* released its annual 100 Digital Elite list. Disappointingly, but perhaps not surprisingly, only eight women were included on this list of Silicon Valley muckety-mucks, with another five straggling in via a group of around fifty "honorable mentions."

That women are vastly underrepresented in the upper ranks of the high-tech industry is nothing new—even the more eclectic *Wired* 25 list the same month included only three women (none, incidentally, actually in technology). But what was notable about *Upside's* Digital Elite feature was exactly where the women appeared in its seventeen categories: Of the eight women listed, three were listed in the "PR Pros" category, as were two of the five honorable mentions. By comparison, of the ninety-two men on the list, only one was a public relations exec.

The debate about the underrepresentation of women in the technology industry has raged for years, with some feminists arguing that the geeky engineering focus of the industry excludes women, and other women maintaining that the industry's youth and lack of conventionality provides more of an opening for women to advance. There are certainly some women leaders in technology businesses—CEOs like Kim Polese of Marimba, Katrina Garnett of CrossWorlds, and Carol Bartz of Autodesk, or chief technology officer Judy Estrin of Cisco, venture capitalist Ann Winblad, Palm cofounder Donna Dubinsky, and ubiquitous pundit Esther Dyson.

But within the technology industry, public relations is already a stronghold of female executives; it's the only area, actually, where the plaudits go more often to women than men. Thanks to public relations, women are not only entering the executive boardrooms of Silicon Valley, but also are often credited with wielding powerful industrywide influence. Women like Pam Edstrom (executive vice president of Microsoft's PR firm Waggener Edstrom), Pam Alexander (president of Alexander Ogilvie), and Andy Cunningham (Cunningham Communications) now have recognized names and high-powered clients in every corner of the technology industry.

As Jody Peake, cofounder and executive vice president of Waggener Edstrom, puts it, "I get so intellectually stimulated when I get to sit next to senior-level people making changes in how the world operates, and go vicariously through all the things you do at a very high executive level in business."

But are women merely participating in the industry, as Peake put it, "vicariously"? Public relations may be the first visible stronghold of women in the technology industry, but does it mean that they are getting a seat at the table? Or is it, as some are concerned, becoming a "pink-collar ghetto"—the default career for women in the digital world because they aren't given the opportunity to do anything else?

PR—IT'S NOT JUST A JOB, IT'S A PROFESSION!

"I have this uneasy feeling that the reason there are so many women in PR is that it's a form of journalism that's less respected and therefore easier for them to get ahead," says Richard Brandt, editor-in-chief of *Upside*. "But I have also seen the profession increase its role, its influence, and its importance very dramatically over the last couple of decades. And at the same time that's when a lot of women have gotten into it."

The Bureau of Labor Statistics has tagged public relations as one of the three fastest-growing industries in the United States (No. 1 is computer and data-processing services, and No. 2 is health services). High tech, in turn, is the fastest-growing sector of PR. According to Glen Broom, a professor at the School of Communications at San Diego State University who has been tracking the growth of public relations, the industry has doubled in size in the last 15 years; today, he says, there are an estimated 350,000 public relations professionals in the United States.

Increasingly, those employees come complete with a formal degree in public relations: There are now 300 colleges in the United States that offer some sort of undergraduate or graduate degree in public relations. Most of those PR graduates are women—70 percent of all graduates, according to most estimates, with some schools boasting an 80-20 split.

Larissa Grunig, a public relations professor at the University of Maryland who studies the feminization of PR, believes that part of the reason public relations is such a popular field for women is because there are accessible management positions—but that they're accessible only because they're not considered as important.

"Companies consider PR as marginal to organization function, not central like finance or marketing. They're not afraid to give women a shot at PR because the risk factor is low," says Grunig. "This is a place where companies traditionally hire women within the executive ranks. If an organization pays lip service to affirmative action and the importance of hiring women, but doesn't trust women to be as effective in management, PR seems like a safe place to put women."

Even though large numbers of men also flock to the field, communications, marketing, and PR are still stereotyped as "female," and therefore less important, tasks. Communication and relationship nurturing may be important to the growth of a company, but we still live in a world where CEOs [chief executive officers] and CFOs [chief financial officers] are put on a pedestal for number crunching and strategic planning.

And though there are plenty of women in executive PR roles, Grunig and Broom agree, there aren't as many as there should be, given the huge preponderance of women in the overall PR ranks. "Women traditionally in PR have been held to more of a technician's role, hired and paid to do the work of PR—the craft, the writing, the media relations, the special events," explains Grunig. "Women are overrepresented in technicians' ranks, and underrepresented in management."

But the suggestion that women might not be getting equal play in decision making doesn't sit well with the female executives in the industry. Jonelle Birney, the new CEO of the female-helmed PR firm Blanc & Otus, has a small forest of photos and awards in her office from her last job as vice president of public relations at MCI. There's a plaque awarding her the Silver Anvil award for excellence in public relations, snapshots of her sipping wine with the top (male) executives at MCI, and a framed photo of her at the press conference announcing the MCI merger with BT [British Telecom]. She has, she insists, always been given a seat at the decision-making table with the men.

"At MCI the senior people appreciated the role of public relations—I always felt I was treated like an equal and respected. It was never 'she's the woman,' and I was always in the room," she says. Since she graduated in 1980 with a degree in PR, she says, she's watched her industry become increasingly respected by executives. "Public relations has grown to mean so much, and enough things have gone wrong in the past that corporations have started to realize that they have to take this seriously and be proactive."

What, though, does public relations "mean"? Traditionally, it's been seen as a matter of just sending out press releases—but the women who are helming these positions say that this is changing. Even if public relations truly is a "ghetto," it is one that is wielding increasing power.

Public relations has existed as long as individuals have tried to manipulate their image in the public eye. As American industry has grown since World War II, so have pressures on businesses from activists, journalists, and consumer groups, and the public relations industry has exploded as a result. "Flacks" can be found everywhere from the White House to newspapers themselves—anywhere a company wants to make itself look good in the press.

But the role of public relations is changing, thanks in part to leaders like Andy Cunningham, CEO of Cunningham Communications, who are consciously trying to make public relations into a sexier industry that involves more than fielding calls from reporters. Cunningham, who began her career in trade journalism in the 1980s and ended up publicizing the launch of the first Macintosh, currently has 140 employees in three offices, and is working to invent what she calls the "new public relations."

THE INTERNET HAS CHANGED ALL THE RULES OF PUBLIC RELATIONS

"Public relations has always been an afterthought: 'We screwed up as a company, get those PR people out there to make the journalists go away, manipulate the press, make it all OK.' PR people have always been on the outskirts of the company, being pooper scoopers. You don't get a lot of respect in that kind of a field," Cunningham says. "Now we're becoming part of the inner circle of the company. We're now bringing a perspective and a database of knowledge about markets into the decision-making room. You just can't get away with shit anymore as a company. If you want an image as a company—you want positive brand and momentum—you better understand what you're doing, because within 2 minutes on the Internet you are going to get found out."

The Internet, apparently, *has* changed all the rules of public relations: Not only is competition being ac-

celerated by technology that changes faster than the speed of light, but the media is growing and consumers are becoming more vocal. Business success is increasingly due to what PR agents call "mindshare"—getting the right kind of attention in the vast morass of competitive products and accelerating news headlines. As a result, the role of public relations in the technology field is expanding.

Today's public relations professionals say they no longer merely peddle their company's image to journalists (though that is still part of their jobs), but advise on positioning, work with market analysts, help organize conferences, instruct their clients on how to align their images and their practices and suggest business strategy. The most influential PR companies are trying to build a family roster or "keiretsu" of prestige clientele, similar to that of venture capital firms like Kleiner Perkins Caufield and Byers. Pam Alexander, for example, is a major force within industry conferences and publications—among her numerous clients are Tech-Net, TED, Qwest, Hewlett-Packard, Ziff Davis, and the Red Herring—and the parties Alexander Ogilvie throws at Comdex and E3 are lavishly studded with both shrimp and industry bigwigs.

"It was never my goal to be a PR person," explains Pam Alexander. "I thought of myself as a market researcher and educator, which I think is the best kind of technology specialist. You're always reading about what's happening in the industry and thinking about what the implications are, and then you teach that to your clients."

The changing image and function of public relations may be partly due to its increasingly academic roots, as well as the influx of former journalists to the position. Countless public relations professionals have backgrounds in journalism and, in fact, the growth of public relations as a career seems to be at the expense of journalism. At the Medill School of Journalism at Northwestern, for example, the number of applicants to the Integrated Marketing Communications program has risen 15 percent in recent years, while the number of students applying to the traditional journalism program has dropped an equivalent amount. Only 20 percent of all recipients of journalism and mass communications bachelors degrees in 1997, according to a survey by Lee Becker of the University of Georgia, found work in some reporting, writing, or editing capacity; nearly 21 percent took jobs in public relations.

The forces responsible for these trends are easy to locate. Public relations jobs currently pay significantly more than, say, a newspaper job and the growing industry is snatching up students as fast as they graduate. But public relations also entices young careerists with its management potential and the opportunity to learn business skills—plus it's a flexible career that can be used as an entryway to any industry, from entertainment to high tech.

"I think a lot of people look at high tech and say, 'How can I get in that? The Net, the Net—how do I get involved in it?'" says Tara Suan, who since her graduation from U.C. Berkeley in 1994 has worked as a high-tech publicist at Niehaus Ryan Wong and currently is marketing communications manager at Topica. She is, she believes, typical of many young people in her field—her journalistic aspirations were undermined by the reality of the paychecks, and she was enticed to public relations as a way to get into the exploding technology industry. "Truth be told, I would not have gone into PR if it weren't for high-tech PR, and I wouldn't have stayed had I not liked the Net so much. It was the promise of being able to do something really new."

Alexander, along with many other of the women in public relations, insists that the predominance of women in the industry has nothing to do with gender issues. People choose the career out of intellectual curiosity, rather than because it's friendly to women, and the sheer number of females is an accident of education rather than ghettoization. But at the same time, it's hard to deny that public relations is where women are—as Birney puts it, "It's almost expected—it seems women are always in HR [human resources] and PR."

Taking that one step further, Brandt worries that the dominance of women in the industry may actually harm the prestige of public relations. "There have traditionally been industries throughout history where women have taken over and they become a ghetto—the pay goes down, the respect for the industry goes down, and it's stigmatized," he explains. "Will that happen in public relations? To some extent I think it might."

But that's still conjecture, and today it's difficult to determine whether PR truly is a ghetto. If the only women in the technology industry getting recognition are the public relations executives, is that a measure of where women are encouraged to be, or where the world is encouraged to look for women? A few plaudits from the media, after all, do not necessarily represent industry groupthink.

And there are, as Alexander points out, more women emerging in Silicon Valley as venture capitalists, journalists, financial officers, even chief technology officers. It's an evolutionary process, Alexander explains: "If you look at our educational system up until now, [the predominance of women in PR] is a reflection of how people were directed in their studies. I think if I or a lot of other women had gone to school 20 years later, we'd maybe have been encouraged in math and science more than we were."

As an upstart industry that prides itself in offbeat approaches, after all, Silicon Valley ought to be less grounded in gender stereotypes and glass ceilings than other industries. Maybe public relations is merely the first portion of that industry to witness some gender equity. In an information economy, where communication is increasingly vital, perhaps that's not such a bad place to start.

RELATED LINKS

- International Association of Business Communicators (http://www.iabc.com/homepage.htm)
- Public Relations Society of America (http://www.prsa.org)
- Public Relations Student Society of America (http://www.prssa.org)
- Women Executives in Public Relations (http://www.wepr.org)

FOR FURTHER RESEARCH

To find out more about the topics discussed in this reading, use InfoTrac College Edition. Type in keywords and subject terms such as "public relations," "glass ceiling," and "women and technology." You can access InfoTrac College Edition from the Wadsworth/Thomson Communication Cafe homepage: http://communication.wadsworth.com.

Reading 6-5

The Drug War's New Front

Mark Boal

EDITOR'S NOTE

Armed with a billion dollars, the White House Office of National Drug Control Policy (ONDCP) is going after the hearts and minds of America's youth with an aggressive antidrug campaign. With the help of advertising agencies, the ONDCP is waging an all-out integrated marketing campaign to change the way the mass media depict drug use. As this reading from Rolling Stone *explains, the government's antidrug efforts, which initially involved the review of TV scripts, has compromised the independence of the television networks and co-opted them for financial reasons into towing the government line.*

CONSIDER

1. How is the government's Office of National Drug Control Policy using integrated marketing techniques to spread the antidrug message?

2. Why were the television networks basically left with no option when it came to broadcasting antidrug messages from the government?

3. With regard to the script review scandal, what are the First Amendment issues raised by governmental interference in network programming?

The Office of National Drug Control Policy [ONDCP] was embarrassed in January 2000 when it was revealed that television executives were submitting scripts to the White House for approval and financial rewards. The storm, however, blew over quickly. The ONDCP denied that it was tampering with the actual content of TV shows; it claimed it was only seeking to determine whether a show met its antidrug guidelines. But *Rolling Stone* has learned that the ONDCP was, in fact, colluding with the TV industry through regular memos sent to TV producers. And during 1999, media–campaign director Alan Levitt held a series of thirty antidrug training meetings with TV executives and magazine editors. Shaping TV scripts is actually only a small part of a strategy, developed with the help of the best advertising agencies in the world, to change the way the mass media depict drug use. The plan is to hit 90 percent of the teen population with four antidrug messages per week. The message: Losers do drugs.

While the White House no longer reviews scripts prior to a show's airing, the policy shift is far too late: The networks have already realized how much money can be made by cooperating with the drug czar's office, and they continue to implant antidrug messages whenever possible.

Here's how the program works: The ONDCP buys commercial time to run one of its ads—Lauryn Hill or Art Alexakis talking about the evils of drug abuse. Under federal law, when the government buys space for a public service announcement, the network has to, in turn, donate ad time of comparable value. In essence, this gives the government a buy-one-get-one-free deal. It is not the kind of arrangement businesses appreciate, so the drug czar's office offered the networks a nearly irresistible compromise: To slip out of the deal, just insert antidrug messages in programming such as *ER* and *NYPD Blue*. The choice was either to become a handmaiden to the drug office and reap the profits, or to lose money. And when it comes to a hit show like *ER*, the extra revenue can run into the millions.

A recent episode of *Moesha* garnered the WB Network a $34,000 credit. In this particular show, ONDCP official Judi Kosterman suggested a revision to the plot.

Originally, the star and a pal were to attend a party, get blitzed on spiked punch, then kick off a jubilant Soul Train dance, winning laughter and applause. Kosterman's memo said, "Maybe rather than having onlookers laugh and applaud, we should have them maybe just laugh and point at them." The dance scene was revised so that in the version that aired, Moesha jerks around awkwardly without peer acclaim.

The program started in late 1997, when Congress approved $1 billion for the drug czar to spend on antidrug advertising. Most broadcast networks were willing to play ball, except for MTV, which opted out long before anyone else. When the White House first approached MTV, the channel tagged a plug for the Partnership for a Drug-Free America onto the end of a spring-break show. "It was a disaster," says a staffer at the ad agency Ogilvy & Mather, which is handling the media campaign for the ONDCP. "They had these kids drinking down in Jamaica, girls drinking beer out of guys' bellybuttons—many of them looked underage—and, okay, so there were no drugs, but please." He laughs. "Then they said, 'Brought to you by the Partnership for a Drug-Free America.' It was almost like they were trying to get us. It was that bad." After that, it was clear that MTV would not be participating.

At first, NBC refused to accept the terms of the deal. *Seinfeld* was the ratings king, and the last thing the cash-rich network wanted was to give away prime-time ad space. So at drug czar General Barry McCaffrey's personal request, President Clinton called Jack Welch, CEO of General Electric, NBC's parent company. That resulted in a call from Welch to Bob Wright, the network's president. "They didn't want to help us at all," says an Ogilvy employee. "But after the president's call, they were a lot more mortal." NBC started putting antidrug messages in some shows.

The youth-oriented WB Network was far more receptive from the outset. In only a year, WB went from having very few antidrug episodes to running almost as many as NBC and CBS combined. Thenetwork denies that it profited from the shift, but *Rolling Stone* has learned that the WB Network saw a more than fourfold increase in advertising dollars from the White House—from $1.2 million to $5 million—after producers boosted antidrug messages.

Long before this campaign began, TV writers knew that scripts showing drugs in an ambivalent or positive light would not be aired. For those who still don't get it, it takes just "a line on the script, a simple insertion" to fix, says NBC programming executive Kathy Talbert.

"You will never see a successful role model on TV smoking pot," explains Neal Baer, co-executive producer of *ER* and a supporter of the White House plan. "Even though that is something many people do"—indeed, it is a rite of passage for 50 percent of the teenage population, according to the ONDCP's own figures—"and even though you can show lots of other illegal acts."

In fact, the media have become an important new front in the War on Drugs, and Congress is giving the ONDCP its full support. At a recent Senate hearing on the script-review scandal, only a few senators expressed concern about the billion-dollar cash-for-credit program. And last November [1999], the Methamphetamine Anti-Proliferation Act passed the Senate unanimously. The bill attacks Web sites that offer instructions for making illegal drugs. Drug reformers worry that the language of the bill will suppress open discussion. Its wording lumps drug think tanks like the George Soros–funded Lindesmith Center together with magazines like *High Times* and Web sites featuring crank recipes.

The methamphetamine bill and the National Youth Antidrug Media Campaign are both attempts to hack the culture's software and delete the deviant code. The driving force of this new strategy is "integrated marketing." IM means deploying core messages across many so-called [media] platforms. "When you go to the movie theater, we are on the radio while you wait in line," explains Ogilvy's Dan Merrick, who oversees the campaign. "We have a logo on the cup and one on the popcorn bag. When you go to the bathroom, there's another ad in there. And just before the feature film, we hit you again. Not everybody sees every message, but it sinks in eventually."

Billboards, radio spots, and even comic books are buttressed by TV commercials scheduled for maximum impact. A baby-boom show like *Spin City* will run ads about the danger of drugs. At the same time, ads on shows like *Dawson's Creek* will say that drug use is uncommon. What's the intended result of this double-teaming? Johnny wakes up to white toast and OJ, asking whether drugs were popular back in Dad's heyday. Pop is prepped to answer, "Maybe, son, but the pot today is stronger than what we hippies had."

Will any of this work? Who knows? An evaluation of the White House's test campaign by 576 focus groups was reviewed by the Government Accounting Office and found to be unreliable, according to an advance copy of a report. So the campaign has no baseline with which to accurately monitor progress.

Meanwhile, critics abound. "This thing could backfire as easily as succeed," says Lynn Zimmer, a drug-policy expert at Queens College in New York. "Look at the 'Just Say No' campaign in the '80s. There was no group more bombarded with antidrug messages than those teens, and drug use went up. And look at how smoking rates went up *after* those ad campaigns."

The main effect of the campaign, she adds, is likely to be the strengthening of antidrug attitudes among those who already disapprove of drugs. Those at severe risk—10-year-olds with addict parents who leave heroin on the kitchen table—need far more than advertising.

Whether or not other kids buy its message, the ONDCP campaign has already become a model. The National Campaign to Prevent Teen Pregnancy is now clamoring for funding to push teen abstinence. Even acts that are legal and arguably benign—such as sex—could become targets of a government campaign.

"What concerns me is that being antidrug becomes a new surrogate for good citizenship and for patriotism," says Ethan Nadelmann, director of the Lindesmith Center. Of course, this is essentially what McCaffrey has in mind. Ever since the highly effective "Be All You Can Be" military recruiting campaign, he has "loved advertising," says a staffer. McCaffrey believes advertising can work the same magic for the drug war.

So it didn't surprise anyone in his office when, even after the deluge of negative publicity, McCaffrey would not budge. This media campaign is here to stay. After all, whether it works or not, it will be exceedingly difficult to attack. And now that the outer limits of media manipulation have been established, the rest of the government's plan looks oddly moderate. Some reformers predict the drug czar will argue that losing control over TV scripts was a blow that will require even more money to recover from. The scandal may be the best thing that ever happened to the drug warriors.

RELATED LINKS

- High Times Magazine (http://www.hightimes.com/welcome.tpl)
- The Media Awareness Project (http://www.mapinc.org)
- Office of National Drug Control Policy (http://www.whitehousedrugpolicy.gov)
- Partnership for a Drug-Free America (http://www.drugfreeamerica.org)

FOR FURTHER RESEARCH

To find out more about the topics discussed in this reading, use InfoTrac College Edition. Type in keywords and subject terms such as "war on drugs," "script review scandal," and "integrated marketing." You can access InfoTrac College Edition from the Wadsworth / Thomson Communication Cafe homepage: http://communication.wadsworth.com.

7

Media Concentration

Reading 7-1

The New Global Media:
It's a Small World of Big Conglomerates

Robert W. McChesney

EDITOR'S NOTE

This reading by Robert McChesney, a leading media historian, political economist, and analyst of press performance, discusses the transformation of the major American, European, and Japanese media conglomerates into a nascent global media system. As domestic markets become saturated and permit only incremental expansion, these large corporations are attempting to capitalize on growth from abroad. This often places global media at odds with local populations, especially, McChesney argues, if this growing corporate control comes with an implicit political bias in media content and the best journalism is geared toward the needs and prejudices of big business. McChesney's conclusion: rich media make for poor democracy.

CONSIDER

1. Why are the major media companies globalizing their operations and looking to international markets for new opportunities?

2. In what ways is the global commercial media system radical? Why, ultimately, is it politically and culturally conservative?

3. How might government subsidies and the local policies of different countries protect the culture industries abroad from American media domination?

The '90s have been a typical fin de siècle decade in at least one important respect: The realm of media is on the brink of a profound transformation. Whereas previously media systems were primarily national, in the past few years a global commercial-media market has emerged. "What you are seeing," says Christopher Dixon, media analyst for the investment firm Paine-Webber, "is the creation of a global oligopoly. It happened to the oil and automotive industries earlier this century; now it is happening to the entertainment industry."

Together, the deregulation of media ownership, the privatization of television in lucrative European and Asian markets, and new communications technologies have made it possible for media giants to establish powerful distribution and production networks within and among nations. In short order, the global media market has come to be dominated by the same eight transnational corporations, or TNCs, that rule U.S. media: General Electric, AT&T/Liberty Media, Disney, Time Warner, Sony, News Corporation, Viacom, and Seagram, plus Bertelsmann, the Germany-based conglomerate. At the same time, a number of new firms and different political and social factors enter the picture as one turns to the global system, and the struggle for domination continues among the nine giants and their closest competitors. But as in the United States, at a global level this is a highly concentrated industry; the largest media corporation in the world in terms of annual revenues, Time Warner (1998 revenues: $27 billion), is some fifty times larger in terms of annual sales than the world's fiftieth-largest media firm.

A few global corporations are horizontally integrated; that is, they control a significant slice of specific media sectors, like book publishing, which has undergone extensive consolidation in the late '90s. "We have never seen this kind of concentration before," says an attorney who specializes in publishing deals. But even more striking has been the rapid vertical integration of the global media market, with the same firms gaining ownership of content and the means to distribute it. What distinguishes the dominant firms is their ability to exploit the "synergy" among the companies they own. Nearly all the major Hollywood studios are owned by one of these conglomerates, which in turn control the cable channels and TV networks that air the movies. Only two of the nine are not major content producers: AT&T and GE. But GE owns NBC, AT&T has major media content holdings through Liberty Media, and both firms are in a position to acquire assets as they become necessary.

The major media companies have moved aggressively to become global players. Even Time Warner and Disney, which still get most of their revenues in the United States, project non-U.S. sales to yield a majority of their revenues within a decade. The point is to capitalize on the potential for growth abroad—and not get outflanked by competitors—since the U.S. market is well developed and only permits incremental expansion. As Viacom CEO Sumner Redstone has put it, "Companies are focusing on those markets promising the best return, which means overseas." Frank Biondi, former chairman of Seagram's Universal Studios, asserts that "99 percent of the success of these companies long term is going to be successful execution offshore."

Prior to the '80s and '90s, national media systems were typified by domestically owned radio, television, and newspaper industries. Newspaper publishing remains a largely national phenomenon, but the face of television has changed almost beyond recognition. Neoliberal free-market policies have opened up ownership of stations as well as cable and digital satellite TV systems to private and transnational interests, producing scores of new channels operated by the media TNCs that dominate cable ownership in the United States. The channels in turn generate new revenue streams for the TNCs: The major Hollywood studios, for example, expect to generate $11 billion from global TV rights to their film libraries in 2002, up from $7 billion in 1998.

While media conglomerates press for policies to facilitate their domination of markets throughout the world, strong traditions of protection for domestic media and cultural industries persist. Nations ranging from Norway, Denmark, and Spain to Mexico, South Africa, and South Korea keep their small domestic film production industries alive with government subsidies. In the summer of 1998 culture ministers from twenty nations, including Brazil, Mexico, Sweden, Italy, and Ivory Coast, met in Ottawa to discuss how they could "build some ground rules" to protect their cultural fare from "the Hollywood juggernaut." Their main

"The New Global Media: It's a Small World of Big Conglomerates." From *Rich Media, Poor Democracy: Communication Politics in Dubious Times* by Robert W. McChesney. Urbana, IL: University of Illinois Press, 1999. Copyright © 1999 by Robert W. McChesney. As edited and published by *The Nation*, November 29, 1999. Reprinted with permission.

recommendation was to keep culture out of the control of the World Trade Organization. A similar 1998 gathering, sponsored by the United Nations in Stockholm, recommended that culture be granted special exemptions in global trade deals.

Nevertheless, the trend is clearly in the direction of opening markets. Proponents of neoliberalism in every country argue that cultural trade barriers and regulations harm consumers, and that subsidies inhibit the ability of nations to develop their own competitive media firms. There are often strong commercial-media lobbies within nations that perceive they have more to gain by opening up their borders than by maintaining trade barriers. In 1998, for example, when the British government proposed a voluntary levy on film theater revenues (mostly Hollywood films) to benefit the British commercial film industry, British broadcasters, not wishing to antagonize the firms who supply their programming, lobbied against the measure until it died.

The global media market is rounded out by a second tier of four or five dozen firms that are national or regional powerhouses, or that control niche markets, like business or trade publishing. About half of these second-tier firms come from North America; most of the rest are from Western Europe and Japan. Each of these second-tier firms is a giant in its own right, often ranking among the thousand largest companies in the world and doing more than $1 billion per year in business. The roster of second-tier media firms from North America includes Dow Jones, Gannett, Knight-Ridder, Hearst, and Advance Publications, and among those from Europe are the Kirch Group, Havas, Mediaset, Hachette, Prisa, Canal Plus, Pearson, Reuters, and Reed Elsevier. The Japanese companies, aside from Sony, remain almost exclusively domestic producers.

This second tier has also crystallized rather quickly; across the globe there has been a shakeout in national and regional media markets, with small firms getting eaten by medium firms and medium firms being swallowed by big firms. Many national and regional conglomerates have been established on the backs of publishing or television empires, as in the case of Denmark's Egmont. The situation in most nations is similar to the one in the United States: Compared with 10 or 20 years ago, a much smaller number of much larger firms now dominate the media. Indeed, as most nations are smaller than the United States, the tightness of the media oligopoly can be even more severe. The situation may be most stark in New Zealand, where the newspaper industry is largely the province of the Australian-

American Rupert Murdoch and the Irishman Tony O'Reilly, who also dominates New Zealand's commercial radio broadcasting and has major stakes in magazine publishing. Murdoch controls pay television and is negotiating to purchase one or both of the two public TV networks, which the government is aiming to sell. In short, the rulers of New Zealand's media system could squeeze into a closet.

Second-tier corporations are continually seeking to reach beyond national borders. Australian media moguls, following the path blazed by Murdoch, have the mantra "Expand or die." As one puts it, "You really can't continue to grow as an Australian supplier in Australia." Mediaset, the Berlusconi-owned Italian TV power, is angling to expand into the rest of Europe and Latin America. Perhaps the most striking example of second-tier globalization is Hicks, Muse, Tate and Furst, the U.S. radio/publishing/TV/billboard/movie theater power that has been constructed almost overnight. In 1998 it spent well over $1 billion purchasing media assets in Mexico, Argentina, Brazil, and Venezuela.

Thus second-tier media firms are hardly "oppositional" to the global system. This is true as well in developing countries. Mexico's Televisa, Brazil's Globo, Argentina's Clarin, and Venezuela's Cisneros Group, for example, are among the world's sixty or seventy largest media corporations. These firms tend to dominate their own national and regional media markets, which have been experiencing rapid consolidation as well. They have extensive ties and joint ventures with the largest media TNCs, as well as with Wall Street investment banks. And like second-tier media firms elsewhere, they are also establishing global operations, especially in nations that speak the same language. As a result, they tend to have distinctly probusiness political agendas and support expansion of the global media market, which puts them at odds with large segments of the population in their home countries.

Together, the sixty or seventy first- and second-tier giants control much of the world's media: book, magazine, and newspaper publishing; music recording; TV production; TV stations and cable channels; satellite TV systems; film production; and motion picture theaters. But the system is still very much in formation. New second-tier firms are emerging, especially in lucrative Asian markets, and there will probably be further upheaval among the ranks of the first-tier media giants. And corporations get no guarantee of success merely by going global. The point is that they have no choice in the matter. Some, perhaps many, will falter as they accrue too much debt or as they enter unprofitable ventures. But the chances are that we are closer to the end of the process of establishing a stable global media market than to the beginning. And as it takes shape, there is a distinct likelihood that the leading media firms in the world will find themselves in a very profitable position. That is what they are racing to secure.

The global media system is fundamentally noncompetitive in any meaningful economic sense of the term. Many of the largest media firms have some of the same major shareholders, own pieces of one another, or have interlocking boards of directors. When *Variety* compiled its list of the fifty largest global media firms for 1997, it observed that "merger mania" and cross-ownership had "resulted in a complex web of interrelationships" that will "make you dizzy." The global market strongly encourages corporations to establish equity joint ventures in which the media giants all own a part of an enterprise. This way, firms reduce competition and risk—and increase the chance of profitability. As the CEO of Sogecable, Spain's largest media firm and one of the twelve largest private media companies in Europe, expressed it to *Variety,* the strategy is "not to compete with international companie but to join them." In some respects, the global media market more closely resembles a cartel than it does the competitive marketplace found in economics textbooks.

Global conglomerates can at times have a progressive impact on culture, especially when they enter nations that had been tightly controlled by corrupt crony media systems (as in much of Latin America) or nations that had significant state censorship over media (as in parts of Asia). The global commercial-media system is radical in that it will respect no tradition or custom, on balance, if it stands in the way of profits. But ultimately it is politically conservative, because the media giants are significant beneficiaries of the current social structure around the world, and any upheaval in property or social relations—particularly to the extent that it reduces the power of business—is not in their interest.

While the "Hollywood juggernaut" and the specter of U.S. cultural imperialism remains a central concern in many countries, the notion that corporate media firms are merely purveyors of U.S. culture is ever less plausible as the media system becomes increasingly concentrated, commercialized, and globalized. The global media system is better understood as one that advances corporate and commercial interests and values and denigrates or ignores that which cannot be incorporated into its mission. There is no discernible difference in the firms' content, whether they are owned by shareholders in Japan or Belgium or have corporate headquarters in New York or Sydney. Bertelsmann CEO Thomas Middelhoff bristled when, in 1998, some said it was improper for a German firm to control 15 percent of the U.S. book-publishing market. "We're not foreign. We're international," Middelhoff said. "I'm an American with a German passport."

As the media conglomerates spread their tentacles, there is reason to believe they will encourage popular tastes to become more uniform in at least some forms of media. Based on conversations with Hollywood executives, *Variety* editor Peter Bart concluded that "the world film-going audience is fast becoming more homogeneous." Whereas action movies had once been the only surefire global fare—and comedies had been considerably more difficult to export—by the late '90s comedies like *My Best Friend's Wedding* and *The Full Monty* were doing between $160 million and $200 million in non-U.S. box office sales.

When audiences appear to prefer locally made fare, the global media corporations, rather than flee in despair, globalize their production. This is perhaps most visible in the music industry. Music has always been the least capital intensive of the electronic media and therefore the most open to experimentation and new ideas. United States recording artists generated 60 percent of their sales outside the United States in 1993; by 1998 that figure was down to 40 percent. Rather than fold their tents, however, the five media TNCs that dominate the world's recorded-music market are busy establishing local subsidiaries in places like Brazil, where "people are totally committed to local music," in the words of a writer for a trade publication. Sony has led the way in establishing distribution deals with independent music companies from around the world.

With hypercommercialism and growing corporate control comes an implicit political bias in media content. Consumerism, class inequality, and individualism tend to be taken as natural and even benevolent, whereas political activity, civic values, and antimarket activities are marginalized. The best journalism is pitched to the business class and suited to its needs and prejudices; with a few notable exceptions, the journalism reserved for the masses tends to be the sort of drivel provided by the media giants on their U.S. television stations. This slant is often quite subtle. Indeed, the genius of the commercial-media system is the general lack of overt censorship. As George Orwell noted in his unpublished introduction to *Animal Farm,* censorship in free societies is infinitely more sophisticated and thorough than in dictatorships, because "unpopular ideas can be silenced, and inconvenient facts kept dark, without any need for an official ban."

Lacking any necessarily conspiratorial intent and acting in their own economic self-interest, media conglomerates exist simply to make money by selling light, escapist entertainment. In the words of the late Emilio Azcarraga, the billionaire head of Mexico's Televisa: "Mexico is a country of a modest, very fucked class, which will never stop being fucked. Television has the obligation to bring diversion to these people and remove them from their sad reality and difficult future."

It may seem difficult to see much hope for change. As one Swedish journalist noted in 1997, "Unfortunately, the trends are very clear, moving in the wrong direction on virtually every score, and there is a desperate lack of public discussion of the long-term implications of current developments for democracy and accountability." But there are indications that progressive political movements around the world are increasingly making media issues part of their political platforms. From Sweden, France, and India to Australia, New Zealand, and Canada, democratic left political parties are making structural media reform—breaking up the big companies, recharging nonprofit and noncommercial broadcasting and media—central to their agenda. They are finding out that this is a successful issue with voters.

At the same time, the fate of the global media system is intricately intertwined with that of global capitalism, and despite the self-congratulatory celebration of the free market in the U.S. media, the international system is showing signs of weakness. Asia, the so-called tiger of twenty-first-century capitalism, fell into a depression in 1997, and its recovery is still uncertain. Even if there is no global depression, discontent is brewing in those parts of the world and among those segments of the population that have been left behind in this era of economic growth. Latin America, the other vaunted champion of market reforms since the '80s, has seen what a World Bank official terms a "big increase in inequality." While the dominance of commercial media makes resistance more difficult, it is not hard to imagine widespread opposition to these trends calling into question the triumph of the neoliberal economic model and the global media system it has helped create.

RELATED LINKS

- Frontline: Media Giants (http://www.pbs.org/wgbh/pages/frontline/shows/cool/giants)
- Global Concentration: The Media Ownership Chart (http://www.mediachannel.org/ownership)
- The Media Borg Wants You (http://www.salon.com/tech/feature/2001/06/26/borg_intro/ind/ex.html)
- Media Space: Project on Global Media and Public Space (http://www.mediaspace.org)
- Robert McChesney (http://www.robertmcchesney.com)

FOR FURTHER RESEARCH

To find out more about the topics discussed in this reading, use InfoTrac College Edition. Type in keywords and subject terms such as "media concentration," "cultural imperialism," and "globalization." You can access InfoTrac College Edition from the Wadsworth/Thomson Communication Cafe homepage: http://communication.wadsworth.com.

Reading 7-2

Questions Abound as Media Influence Grows for a Handful

Laurence Zuckerman

EDITOR'S NOTE

Concerns over media concentration have been raised since the turn of the previous century. Recently, the issue has received renewed attention on account of a single sobering statistic: The number of companies that control most of what Americans read in print media and watch on television and at the movies has shrunk to six. However, the last two decades have also seen a burst of new information sources, from cable networks to the World Wide Web, enlarging the media landscape in new ways. Still, as the title of this reading suggests, questions abound as media influence grows for a handful of companies. Are the big entertainment conglomerates boring audiences with overwhelming sameness and are they smothering innovation, or do the economies of scale made possible by corporate efficiencies encourage ample creative expression? These questions are at the heart of debates over media concentration.

CONSIDER

1. Do you think that journalists, to avoid jeopardizing their careers, intentionally steer clear of certain issues and topics that challenge their corporate parents?

2. Is there a danger in the trend toward consolidation, where a small number of companies control most of what we read, listen to, or see in the media? Why or why not?

3. What is the counterargument—how do big media companies create new voices while preserving and amplifying others?

In 1983, Ben H. Bagdikian, a Pulitzer Prize–winning newspaperman, wrote in his book *The Media Monopoly* (Beacon Press) that a mere fifty companies controlled most of what Americans read in books, magazines, and newspapers and watched on television and at the movies.

For the book's sixth edition, published in March 2000, that number has shrunk to six.

"Every edition has been considered by some to be alarmist," Mr. Bagdikian said on Monday from his home in Berkeley, California, "and every edition ends up being too conservative."

Paradoxically, the public debate over the power of Big Media seems to have grown quieter since the 1980s, even as the industry has become increasingly concen-

trated. Critics cite the power of the media companies themselves to shape public debate on the issue, largely by ignoring it.

Critics also say that Wall Street is not likely to stop the trend since it, along with top media executives, profits handsomely from the corporate deals. And politicians in Washington are also unlikely to act, for fear of alienating large media owners and losing large campaign contributions.

But the issue is also filled with ambiguities that may have sapped many people's sense of outrage. For in addition to increased media concentration, the last two decades have also heralded an unprecedented proliferation of new information sources, from dozens of cable networks to the seemingly unlimited resources of the Internet.

And while some critics say that Big Media snuffs out new voices, others worry that small, independent purveyors of gossip on the Internet and in tabloids set the agenda for mainstream news organizations.

Is big always necessarily bad when it comes to media? To Mr. Bagdikian and other critics, the answer is yes. But it can also be argued that giants have the resources to create new voices and preserve others [see, for example, Reading 7-3]. Many of the best news and information sites on the World Wide Web are taking heavy losses but are subsidized by large media conglomerates.

It is hard to imagine many companies other than the Gannett Company, the giant newspaper chain, spending the millions of dollars it took to establish *USA Today,* now the largest newspaper in the country. New York 1, the local 24-hours cable news channel in New York City that is widely seen as a welcome new source of municipal coverage, required a large investment from its owner, Time Warner.

And then there is also the *New York Post,* where losses have been estimated at $20 million a year and it was considered close to death until Rupert Murdoch, the chief executive of the News Corporation, stepped in and bought it for a second time in 1993, thus preserving a conservative editorial voice in the city.

Critics argue that the bigger companies become, the more they will succeed in imposing their commercial agenda on the public, drowning out independent voices and placing the interests of the corporate parent over the journalism they practice.

"*Time* magazine is going to think twice about criticizing AOL if it is owned by Time Warner," said Ralph Nader, the consumer advocate.

Indeed, there are many examples of big media companies trimming their journalism to suit their corporate needs. A few years ago, [Murdoch's] News Corporation agreed to drop broadcasts of BBC World Service Television to China on Star TV, its Asian satellite network, after criticism from the Chinese government. The company's publishing arm later paid a substantial sum to the daughter of the Chinese leader Deng Xiaoping for a biography of her father.

At the height of the debate over a landmark telecommunications bill in 1995, CNN, which is owned by Time Warner—in turn, the second-largest cable television operation in the country—refused to run an ad by long-distance phone companies contending that cable TV rates would rise if the bill was adopted.

But, of course, the reason these and other such embarrassing episodes came to light is that they were pounced upon by competitors, often owned by rival conglomerates.

And, on numerous occasions, publications have written critically about their corporate cousins.

People magazine, owned by Time Warner, published an article highly critical of American Family Enterprises, the sweepstakes company, now bankrupt, that was 50 percent owned by Time Warner. And after Time Warner and Turner Broadcasting announced their merger in 1995, *Time* magazine wrote a story that referred to Mr. Levin as "the unsteady father" and Mr. Turner as "the unruly son."

On the other hand, it is impossible to know how many articles have not been pursued because journalists felt it could limit their careers to challenge their corporate parents.

Norman Pearlstine, the editor-in-chief of Time Inc., said editorial independence was related less to the size of the company than it was to whether the owners and editors were committed to editorial integrity.

"If a CEO is determined to have editors who don't cover him, or cover him as a house organ, then you are going to have bad journalism," he said.

"*Forbes* magazine is privately owned," he added, "but it still has never done a serious article on Malcom Forbes, or on Steve, who is running for president. It is not about business or concentration. It is about the mindset of the CEO."

Lewis D'Vorkin, *Forbes*' executive editor, said he was not certain how much coverage the Forbes family had received. But he said that a tribute to Malcom Forbes was featured on the magazine's cover after his death in 1990.

Critics argue that corporate interest will always skew the judgment of corporate officers. And even when it does not, they say, it is dangerous to have ever-larger media conglomerates run by small groups of people who may or may not believe in fostering honest journalism.

"AOL has a track record of dubious ethics," said Jeff Cohen, founder of Fairness & Accuracy in Reporting, a liberal-leaning media watch group in Manhattan. He cited a series of incidents in recent years, including America Online's use of controversial accounting methods and its banishing of some members from the online service because of comments they had made in chat groups.

When AOL was simply the largest of several online services offering access to the Internet, issues of censorship and privacy were mitigated by the fact that a user could simply switch to another service. But by virtue of its many cable systems that hold local monopolies, the future AOL Time Warner, as the proposed new company will be known, may be the only way to receive broadband access to the Internet in many areas of the country.

To critics, that means the commercialization of the Internet will rapidly increase. "It doesn't take an intricate deconstruction of what Steve Case and Gerald Levin said," Mr. Bagdikian commented, referring to the merger announcement by the chairmen of AOL and Time Warner. "What they were really looking forward to was creating the biggest shopping mall in the world."

But how much power do Mr. Case and Mr. Levin really have to shape what consumers see and hear? As the conglomerates grow larger, some argue that it becomes more difficult for top executives to wield influence.

"The chief executive officer hardly controls what goes on in the trenches," said James N. Rosse, who retired in October as chief executive of Freedom Communications, which owns the *Orange County Register* in California along with 25 other daily newspapers, eight television stations, and more than a dozen magazines. "I played an important leadership role in shaping the size and direction of the company. But I did not play any direct role in shaping the product itself. Nor should I have."

Many people who recall a golden age 30 or 40 years ago, when most newspapers and television stations were owned by small or family-owned companies, may be blinded by nostalgia. While many family-owned newspapers practiced exemplary journalism,

many were also beholden to local advertisers like car dealers, supermarket chains, and department stores. Reporters were sometimes barred from investigating local institutions in which the owner-publisher held an interest.

Newspaper chains, which bought many of these independent papers in the 1970s and 1980s, are often criticized for placing profits above journalism. But the distance of the new parent companies from local interests also created opportunities for strong local reporting.

The same can also be said today on a global scale. For example, Time Warner is now facing a $27 billion libel suit in Indonesia filed by former President Suharto. Though large media companies have also been known to cave in when their financial interests are threatened by foreign politicians, as News Corporation did in China, they also have the resources needed to stand up to such threats—if they so choose.

Much as critics like Mr. Bagdikian and Mr. Nader would like the government to curb the growth of media conglomerates, they say that the prospect of any action by Washington is thin. Indeed, the relaxation of regulations by Congress touched off the latest wave of media and telecommunications takeovers.

The biggest threat to the media giants, short of a revival of a "progressive movement" in this country, Mr. Nader said, are the products of the conglomerates themselves: "That they will just bore people to tears, that they will be so humdrum and bureaucratic that they will collapse under their own weight."

"But you don't want a society to rely on that," he said.

RELATED LINKS

- Center for Investigative Reporting (http://www.muckraker.org)
- Fairness & Accuracy in Reporting (http://www.fair.org)
- Frontline: Ben Bagdikian (http://www.pbs.org/wgbh/pages/frontline/smoke/interviews/bagdikian1.html)
- Investigative Reporters and Editors (http://www.ire.org)
- Project Censored (http://www.projectcensored.org/intro.htm)

FOR FURTHER RESEARCH

To find out more about the topics discussed in this reading, use InfoTrac College Edition. Type in keywords and subject terms such as "media monopoly," "editorial independence," and "media conglomerates." You can access InfoTrac College Edition from the Wadsworth/Thomson Communication Cafe homepage: http://communication.wadsworth.com.

Reading 7-3

Big Is Beautiful
Jack Shafer

EDITOR'S NOTE

Contrary to the previous two readings, this commentary contends that media mergers such as those between AOL and Time Warner and between AT&T and TCI (see Chapter 5) will have a positive effect on content diversity and government accountability. Instead of stifling innovation and hard-hitting news reporting, media mergers can free local outlets from the influence of local power holders and promote gutsy coverage while encouraging high standards. Corporate independence may be fading fast, but that doesn't automatically mean media quality has to suffer. Good journalism, this author argues, will survive AOL Time Warner, thanks to the rise of media criticism, and editorial quality just might equate with financial success.

CONSIDER

1. Was there ever a "golden era" of media? With the proliferation of new media today, are we experiencing a golden era of sorts now?

2. The more the press acts like a business, the less attention it pays to civic functions. Do you agree with this statement? Why or why not?

3. Is big media, as the author contends, the only institution powerful enough to hold big business and big government accountable?

When AOL and Time Warner announced their merger, the nation's media reporters autodialed the usual critics of media conglomeration: Robert McChesney, Tom Rosenstiel, Ben Bagdikian, and Mark Crispin Miller. Their collective complaint, known to every reader of *The Nation,* was duly recorded: Media conglomeration is bad for journalism and society.

"It's a business thing," McChesney said in the *New York Times.* "Good journalism is bad business and bad journalism is, regrettably, at times good business." In the *Miami Herald,* Bagdikian fretted that AOL Time Warner's devotion to the bottom line would injure democracy. Rosenstiel warned the *Washington Post* of the conflicts of interest posed by the purchase. Miller told NPR that the new conglomerate

would stuff Warner Bros. movies down our throats via AOL.

The McChesneyite critique of big media misses the long-term trend that started with Gutenberg and is accelerating with the Internet: As information processing becomes cheaper, so does pluralism and decentralization, which comes at the expense of entrenched powers—government, the church, the guild, nobility, and the magazines and TV stations that Big Media God Henry Luce founded. Do McChesney and company think we were better off in 1970, when there were three TV news networks, than we are today, when there are six or eight? Better off before the *New York Times* and *Wall Street Journal* became national newspapers? Before FM radio and cable? Evidentially so. McChesney obsesses about the nine global media companies, yet there are three dozen big media companies in the United States alone.

Critics of big media suffer from the Fallacy of the Golden Era. They think things were better in the past, but they never specify the status quo to which they want us to ante. Was small really small enough to be beautiful in 1898, when William Randolph Hearst ran the headline "How Do You Like the *Journal's* War?" How about 1944, when the White House press corps ignored the president's infirmities and poor health? Or the 1950s, when Scotty Reston carried official Washington's water?

From my vantage point, this is journalism's golden age—we just have a hard time detecting its luster because golden ages always shine more brightly from a distance. Another thing that tarnishes modern journalism is the recent proliferation of media critics, who bring brisk scrutiny to every ethical lapse. Editors and reporters of 20 years ago got a free ride compared with today's journalists.

As for McChesney's "good journalism is bad business" formula, I can only offer a horse laugh. Only a fool would say that the *New York Times,* the *Wall Street Journal,* the *Los Angeles Times,* and the *Washington Post* haven't paired editorial quality with financial success. Nor does McChesney acknowledge that as *USA Today* has become a better paper, it has become more viable as a business. Truth be told, the anticonglomerate conglomerate seems less vexed by conglomerate meddling in journalism—the *Los Angeles Times'* Staples Center scandal, *Time's* decision to put *Pokémon* (a Warner Bros. release) on its cover, and Rupert Murdoch's capitulation to the Chinese, who wanted the BBC off his satellite—than by the ultraevil the media conglomerates might do in the future.

Essentially, the McChesneyites have four beefs: (1) Consolidation reduces the number of voices. That's true only if you rig the tally, as McChesney does. (2) Global consolidation promotes cultural imperialism. Cultural imperialism isn't always bad, and new technology makes it easier for small cultures to export their voices. (3) The more the press acts like a business, the less attention it pays to its civic functions. See the previous note on golden ages. (4) Big media treats its audience like consumers, not citizens. Like WTO [World Trade Organization] critics, the McChesneyites hate anything that doesn't conform to their idea of democracy.

The critique of big media invariably romanticizes small, independent newspapers. But for every *Emporia Gazette* edited by a William Allen White, there's a *Manchester Union Leader* piloted by a William Loeb. As a reader, I care more about the newspaper I read than who owns it. Most of today's independents are family-operated companies blighted by the biological law of "regression to the mean," which dictates that heirs are rarely as bright or motivated as founders (look at the *San Francisco Chronicle*). So let's not reflexively mourn the gobbling of small media by big media.

Small, independently owned papers routinely pull punches when covering local car dealers, real estate, and industry, to whom they are in deep hock. The chains that buy up the *Podunk Banners* don't necessarily do a better journalistic job (look at Gannett), but they're not as beholden to the local powers that be as the "independents" are. What's more, if the owners (independent or corporate) of the *Podunk Banner* flinch from a story about contaminated groundwater or police brutality, the big media *New York Times* or *60 Minutes* can parachute in and do the story without fear or favor. Hurrah for big media!

Whatever its shortcomings—and these are many—only big media possesses the means to consistently hold big business and big government accountable. In the '80s, Exxon's brass visited the *Wall Street Journal's* top editors to complain about the paper's coverage. According to a reporter who was present, Exxon suggested that it might have to pull the company's advertising from the *Journal* in protest. At that point, Executive Editor Fred Taylor responded, "I didn't know advertising was one of Exxon's philanthropic activities." The Exxon threat proved hollow. As big as it was, it couldn't hurt the *Journal.* How would the *Podunk Banner* have fared against a similar threat from the area Chevrolet dealer?

If you don't believe big media has a leg up in making government behave, try this. Call Attorney General Janet Reno's office. Say that you're from the *Podunk Banner* and that you want to talk to her about some new policy. Then make a similar call posing as a reporter from the *Washington Post.* I needn't ask which call would get returned.

Fundamentally, the McChesney brigade worries more about AOL Time Warner's pulling journalistic punches than about any lost "independence." (Remember, they weren't Time Warner fans prior to the AOL deal.) But they exaggerate the propaganda power of Time Warner media. Not even a cover rave in *Time* for *Eyes Wide Shut*—a Warner Bros. release—could turn that plodding movie into a hit. (By the way, I believe the rave was genuine, and not ginned up to sell tickets.) Any sustained effort—conscious or unconscious—by a media conglomerate to slant the news in favor of its holdings will only damage the long-term value of its journalistic properties. Bad press is bad for anybody, but bad press is worse when it's directed at the press, as Disney learned when it killed a story by its ABC News subsidiary that criticized safety at Disney theme parks. Disney would have been better off letting the negative story run.

Some would have big media erect Fifth Columns within their walls, but navel-gazing doesn't automatically impress, as the Times-Mirror flagship *Los Angeles Times* learned after publishing a 30,000-word self-examination on the Staples Center scandal. One prominent critic called the story a "whitewash." What damaged the *Los Angeles Times* most after the initial revelations seeped out (from an alternative weekly that didn't exist 20 years ago, it's worth noting) was the beating it took from other big media. Big media strives to be ethical for the same reason big government and big business do: New technology prevents it from controlling information the way it used to, and being exposed by others hurts too much.

Media conglomeration runs in cycles, so the fish currently progressing through the bellies of the media kings may not stay there for long. In 1980, the media hysterics prophesied the end of literature when conglomerates bought the family-owned book publishers for their "synergy." RCA snared Random House. ITT took Bobbs-Merrill. CBS bought Holt, Rinehart, Winston, and other houses. A few years later, RCA, ITT, and CBS abandoned their "synergy" plans and sold their book divisions. Good publishing survived RCA. Good journalism will survive AOL.

(Full disclosure: The author draws his paycheck from Microsoft, which co-owns MSNBC with General Electric.)

RELATED LINKS

- Alliance for Better Campaigns (http://www.bettercampaigns.org)
- Committee of Concerned Journalists (http://www.journalism.org/ccj/index.html)
- NewsLab (http://www.newslab.org)
- Project for Excellence in Journalism (http://www.journalism.org/index.html)
- Society of Professional Journalists (http://www.spj.org)

FOR FURTHER RESEARCH

To find out more about the topics discussed in this reading, use InfoTrac College Edition. Type in keywords and subject terms such as "big media," "editorial pluralism," and "content diversity." You can access InfoTrac College Edition from the Wadsworth/Thomson Communication Cafe homepage: http://communication.wadsworth.com.

Reading 7-4

The Cultural Environment Movement
George Gerbner

EDITOR'S NOTE

In this reading about the Cultural Environment Movement, founder George Gerbner discusses the power of storytelling to structure society, socialize us into gender and class roles, and cultivate most of what we think, what we do, and how we conduct our affairs. Gerbner, the former dean of the Annenberg School for Communication at the University of Pennsylvania who now holds an endowed chair at Temple University, argues that the new globalized and consolidated media system requires active intervention if it is to remain open, vibrant, and responsive to the interests of the audience. The action agenda at the end of this reading summarizes several steps that can be taken to reshape the cultural mainstream.

CONSIDER

1. Gerbner discusses three distinct but related story types. How do stories of the third kind turn the lessons from the first two into action?

2. What are the lasting legacies and influences of the two major historical media eras (print and electronic) on Western culture?

3. Should schools in the United States, like schools in Canada, Australia, and Great Britain, be required to teach media literacy? What other CEM proposals have merit?

Most of what we know, or think we know, we have never personally experienced. We live in a world erected by the stories we hear and see and tell.

Unlocking incredible riches through imagery and words, conjuring up the unseen through art, creating towering works of imagination and fact through science, poetry, song, tales, reports, and laws—that is the true magic of human life.

Through that magic we live in a world much wider than the threats and gratifications of the immediate physical environment, which is the world of other species. Stories socialize us into roles of gender, age, class, vocation, and lifestyle, and offer models of conformity or targets for rebellion. They weave the seamless web of the cultural environment that cultivates most of what we think, what we do, and how we conduct our affairs.

The stories that animate our cultural environment have three distinct but related functions. They (1) reveal how things work; (2) describe what things are; and (3) tell us what to do about them.

Stories of the first kind, revealing how things work, illuminate the all-important but invisible relationships and hidden dynamics of life. They make perceivable the invisible and the hidden. Fairy tales, novels, plays, comics, cartoons, and other forms of creative imagination and imagery are the basic building blocks of human understanding. They show complex causality by presenting imaginary action in total situations, coming to some conclusion that has a moral purpose and a social function. You don't have to believe the "facts" of Little Red Riding Hood to grasp the notion that big bad "wolves" victimize old women and trick little girls—a lesson in gender roles, fear, and power.

Stories of the first kind build, from infancy on, the fantasy we call reality. I do not suggest that the revelations are false, which they may or may not be, but that they are synthetic, selective, often mythical, and always socially constructed.

Stories of the second kind depict what things are. These are descriptions, depictions, expositions, reports abstracted from total situations and filling in with "facts" the gaps in the fantasies conjured up by stories of the first kind. They are the presumably factual accounts, the chronicles of the past and the news of today.

Stories of what things are usually confirm some conception of how things work. Their high "facticity" (i.e., correspondence to actual events presumed to exist independently of the story) gives them special status in political theory and often in law. They give emphasis and credibility to selected parts of each society's fantasies of reality, and can alert it to certain interests, threats, and opportunities and challenges.

Stories of the third kind tell us what to do. These are stories of value and choice. They present things, behaviors, or styles of life as desirable (or undesirable), propose ways to obtain (or avoid) them, and the price to be paid for attainment (or failure). They are the instructions, cautionary tales, commands, slogans, sermons, laws, and exhortations of the day. Today most of them are called commercials and other advertising messages and images we see and hear every day.

Stories of the third kind clinch the lessons of the first two and turn them into action. They typically present a valued objective or suggest a need or desire, and offer a product, service, candidate, institution, or action purported to help attain or gratify it. The lessons of fictitious Little Red Riding Hoods and their realistic sequels prominent in everyday news and entertainment not only teach lessons of vulnerability, mistrust, and dependence but also help sell burglar alarms, more jails and executions promised to enhance security (which they rarely do), and other ways to adjust to a structure of power.

Ideally, the three kinds of stories check and balance each other. But in a commercially driven culture, stories of the third kind pay for most of the first two. That creates a coherent cultural environment whose overall function is to provide a hospitable and effective context for stories that sell. With the coming of the electronic age, that cultural environment is increasingly monopolized, homogenized, and globalized. We must then look at the historic course of our journey to see what this new age means for our children.

For the longest time in human history, stories were told only face to face. A community was defined by the rituals, mythologies, and imageries held in common. All useful knowledge is encapsulated in aphorisms and legends, proverbs and tales, incantations and ceremonies. Writing is rare and holy, forbidden for slaves. Laboriously inscribed manuscripts confer sacred power to their interpreters, the priests and ministers. As a sixteenth century scribe put it:

> Those who observe the codices, those who recite them. Those who noisily turn the pages of illustrated manuscripts. Those who have possession of the black and red ink and that which is pictured; they lead us, they guide us, they tell us the way. State and church ruled the Middle Ages in a symbiotic relationship of mutual dependence and tension. State, composed of feudal nobles, was the economic and political order; church its cultural arm.

The Industrial Revolution changed all that. One of the first machines stamping out standardized artifacts was the printing press. Its product, the book, was a prerequisite for all the other upheavals to come.

The book could be given to all who could read, requiring education and creating a new literate class of people. Readers could now interpret the book (at first the Bible) for themselves, breaking the monopoly of priestly interpreters and ushering in the Reformation.

When the printing press was hooked up to the steam engine the industrialization of storytelling shifted into high gear. Rapid publication and mass transport created a new form of consciousness: modern mass publics. Publics are loose aggregations of people who share some common consciousness of how things work, what things are, and what ought to be done—but never meet face to face. That was never before possible.

Stories can now be sent—often smuggled—across hitherto impenetrable or closely guarded boundaries of time, space, and status. The book lifts people from their traditional moorings as the Industrial Revolution uproots them from their local communities and cultures. They can now get off the land and go to work in faraway ports, factories, and continents, and have with them a packet of common consciousness—the book or journal, and later the motion picture (silent at first)—wherever they go.

Publics, created by such publication, are necessary for the formation of individual and group identities in the new urban environment, as the different classes and regional, religious, and ethnic groups try to live together with some degree of cooperation and harmony.

Publics are the basic units of self-government, electing or selecting representatives to an assembly trying to reconcile diverse interests. The maintenance and integrity of multiple publics makes self-government feasible for large, complex, and diverse national communities. People engage in long and costly struggles—now at a critical stage—to be free to create and share stories that fit the reality of their competing and often conflicting values and interests. Most of our assumptions about human development and political plurality and choice are rooted in the print era.

One of the most vital provisions of the of the print era was the creation of the only large-scale folk institution of industrial society, public education. Public education is the community institution where face-to-face learning and interpreting could, ideally, liberate the individual from both tribal and medieval dependencies and all cultural monopolies.

The second great transformation, the electronic revolution, ushers in the telecommunications era. Its mainstream, television, is superimposed upon and reorganizes print-based culture. Unlike the Industrial Revolution, the new upheaval does not uproot people from their homes but transports them in their homes. It retribalizes modern society and changes the role of education in the new culture.

For the first time in human history, children are born into homes where mass-mediated storytellers reach them on the average more than 7 hours a day. Most waking hours, and often dreams, are filled with their stories. Giant industries discharge their messages into the mainstream of common consciousness. The historic nexus of church and state is replaced by television and state.

These changes may appear to be a broadening and enrichment of local horizons, but they also mean a homogenization of outlooks and limitation of alternatives. For media professionals, the changes mean fewer opportunities and greater compulsions to present life in salable packages. Creative artists, scientists, humanists can still explore and enlighten and occasionally even challenge, but, increasingly, their stories must fit marketing strategies and priorities.

Despite being surrounded with sales messages, or perhaps because of it, a Consumer Federation of America survey concluded in 1990 that "Americans are not smart shoppers and their ignorance costs them billions, threatens their health and safety and undermines the economy."

Broadcasting is the most concentrated, homogenized, and globalized medium. The top 100 advertisers pay for two-thirds of all network television. Four networks, allied to giant transnational corporations—our private "Ministry of Culture"—control the bulk of production and distribution, and shape the cultural mainstream. Other interests, minority views, and the potential of any challenge to dominant perspectives lose ground with every merger.

The Cultural Environment Movement was launched in response to that challenge. Its Founding Convention was held in St. Louis, Missouri, March 15–17, 1996, in cooperation with Webster University. It was the most diverse representation of leaders and activists in the field of culture and communication that has ever met.[1]

The concepts that motivated us developed after 30 years of media research. It became clear that research is not enough. The new globalized and centralized cultural environment demanded a new active approach. Working separately on individual issues, rallying to meet each individual crisis, was not sufficient. Treating symptoms instead of starting to prevent the wholesale manufacturing of the conditions that led to those symptoms was self-defeating. Dealing with systemic connections requires coordination and organization. Individual effort, local action, and national and international constituencies acting in concert can, together, help to begin that long, slow, and difficult task. It involves:

- Building a new coalition involving media councils in the United States and abroad; teachers, students and parents; groups concerned with children, youth and aging; women's groups; religious and minority organizations; educational, health, environmental, legal, and other professional associations; consumer groups and agencies; associations of creative workers in the media and in the arts and sciences; independent computer network organizers and other organizations and individuals committed to broadening the freedom and diversity of communication.

- Opposing domination and working to abolish existing concentration of ownership and censorship (both of and by media), public or private. It involves extending rights, facilities, and influence to interests and perspectives other than the most powerful and profitable. It means including in cultural decision making the less affluent, more vulnerable groups who, in fact, are the majority of the population. These include the marginalized, neglected, abused, exploited, physically or mentally disabled, young and old, women, minorities, poor people, recent immigrants—all those most in need of a decent role and a voice in a freer cultural environment.

- Seeking out and cooperating with cultural liberation forces of other countries working for the integrity and independence of their own decision making and against cultural domination and invasion. Learning from countries that have already opened their media to the democratic process. Helping local movements, including in the most dependent and vulnerable countries of Latin America, Asia, and Africa (and also in Eastern Europe and the former Soviet Republics), to invest in their own cultural development; opposing aggressive foreign ownership and coercive trade policies that make such development more difficult.

- Supporting journalists, artists, writers, actors, directors, and other creative workers struggling for more freedom from having to present life as a commodity designed for a market of consumers. Working with guilds, caucuses, labor and other groups for diversity in employment and in media content. Supporting media and cultural organizations addressing significant but neglected needs, sensibilities, and interests.

- Promoting media literacy, media awareness, critical viewing and reading, and other media education efforts as a fresh approach to the liberal arts and an essential educational objective on every level. Collecting, publicizing, and disseminating information, research, and evaluation about relevant programs, services, curricula, and teaching materials. Helping to organize educational and parents' groups demanding preservice and in-service teacher training in media analysis, already required in the schools of Australia, Canada, and Great Britain.

■ Placing cultural policy issues on the social-political agenda. Supporting and, if necessary, organizing local and national media councils, study groups, citizen groups, minority and professional groups, and other forums of public discussion, policy development, representation, and action. Not waiting for a blueprint but creating and experimenting with ways of community and citizen participation in local, national, and international media policymaking. Sharing experiences, lessons, and recommendations and gradually moving toward a realistic democratic agenda.

The Cultural Environment Movement (CEM) is a coalition of independent organizations and supporters in every state of the United States and sixty-three other countries on six continents. Its over 150 affiliated and supporting organizations and its individual supporters represent a wide range of social and cultural concerns, united in working for freedom, fairness, diversity, responsibility, respect for cultural integrity, the protection of children, and democratic decision making in the media mainstream.

The Founding Convention was an invitational working assembly of 267 delegates and other supporters from fifteen countries gathered to consider the agenda for action. Keynote speakers had the same message: People must take control of their cultural environment and shape it to meet human needs. The program also featured storytellers, Native American dancers and musicians, Latin American singers and other artists, and representatives of women's, ethnic, labor, disabled persons', and other groups, giving live demonstrations of CEM's aim to have all liberating voices speak for themselves and to share stories that have something to tell instead of only things to sell.

The delegates debated and approved the Viewer's Declaration of Independence and an international People's Communication Charter. Meeting for a full day in fifteen working groups, the delegates also recommended an action program in various areas of con-

cern, including media monopoly, independent production, education and media literacy, health promotion, religion, technology and ecology, labor, cultural diversity and integrity, children and family, aging, women and gender issues, racial and ethnic diversity, media violence, storytelling, and problems of media reform and advocacy.

Documents available on the CEM Web site (www.cemnet.org) present the mandate of the Founding Convention. They form the basis of CEM's policies and programs. The Viewer's Declaration of Independence sets forth the compelling reasons for the coalition. The People's Communication Charter spells out standards for cultural policy making worldwide, and the Agenda for Action makes strategic recommendations.

NOTES

1. A pre-Convention event, the first International Broadcast Standards Summit, heard from Sophie Cathelineau of the Conseil de l'Audiovisuel, Paris, France; Friedrich Ebert, media researcher, Berlin, Germany; Jill Hills, professor of International Political Economy of City University, London, U.K.; Robert McChesney, historian at the University of Wisconsin; Matko Mestrovic, a consultant to Croatian radio and television; Colin Shaw, director of the Broadcast Standards Council of Great Britain; Keith Spicer, chair of the Canadian Radio-television and Telecommunications Council; Marc Raboy, professor of communication at the University of Montreal; and Janos Timar of the Hungarian National Committee on Radio and Television. The moderator was Jeffrey Cole, director of the Center for Communication Policy at UCLA, and the chair of a Summit panel was Mark Crispin Miller, professor of media studies at Johns Hopkins University.

   Keynote speakers at the Convention included Joan Brown Campbell, general secretary of the National Council of Churches; Riane Eisler, author and cultural historian; Fred W. Garcia, acting director of the White House Office of National Drug Control Policy; *Washington Post* columnist Dorothy Gilliam; Sumi Sevilla Haru, first national vice president of the Screen Actors Guild; Dr. Cees Hamelink, director of the Centre for Communication and Human Rights, Amsterdam, The Netherlands; Robert W. McChesney; writer and ecologist Bill McKibben; Colin Shaw, director of the Broadcasting Standards Council of Great Britain; and Keyan Tomaselli, University of Natal, South Africa.

RELATED LINKS

- Cultural Environment Movement (http://www.cemnet.org)
- Free the Media (http://past.thenation.com/issue/960603/0603mill.htm)
- A Twelve-Step Program for Media Democracy (http://past.thenation.com/issue/960603/0603step.htm)
- Media Access Project: Media Diversity Page (http://www.mediaaccess.org/programs/diversity/index.html)

FOR FURTHER RESEARCH

To find out more about the topics discussed in this reading, use InfoTrac College Edition. Type in keywords and subject terms such as "Cultural Environment Movement," "social construction of reality," and "commercial control." You can access InfoTrac College Edition from the Wadsworth / Thomson Communication Cafe homepage: http://communication.wadsworth.com.

New Technologies, the Self, and Social Life

This section explores issues involving new technologies, evolving conceptions of the self, and the changing nature of social life. Online, any number of activities and transactions are now becoming personalized, made possible by collaborative filtering software that compares Web users' purchasing history, stated preferences, and clickstreams (surfing patterns) with those of other users to generate custom offers. Yet despite its individualized character, online media use can also be characterized by a high degree of anonymity and ambiguity, as anyone with a misleading screen name knows (for example, *mumsquat* or *cockysqueeze*), raising questions about identity in the online environment. Notably, two emergent subcultures—game players and cyberpunks—have found ways to thrive amidst this ambiguity, fostering the values of competition, community, and cybernetic fusion. The readings in Chapter 8 dissect these issues at the bleeding edge of culture and technology, describing the range of meaningful experiences that can occur online. In Chapter 9, several readings take stock of the trend toward cultural acceleration. Movies, computer games, and TV shows are moving at an ever-quickening pace, holding our attention but perhaps diminishing satisfaction. Shortened attention spans, the pressing demands of modern life, and the ready availability of personal communications devices has led to the rise of multitasking—the microprocessor-like capacity to perform several tasks simultaneously—for a growing segment of the population. This juggling act is not without its consequences, however; the instant communication of e-mail, just one method of multitasking, threatens to drown computer users everywhere in a sea of inelegant prose, unwanted chain mail, bad jokes, and impatient requests.

8

At the Interface:
New Intimacies,
New Cultures

Reading 8-1

Love, Honor, Cherish. But Reveal My Password?
Joyce Cohen*

EDITOR'S NOTE

E-mail, a seemingly straightforward and efficient way of communicating, can sometimes complicate daily life more than simplifying it, raising issues of relational openness and trust. As this reading illustrates, many couples who share their whole lives with each other, from living space to friends and finances, have trouble sharing e-mail. More and more, e-mail is becoming one of the many things that must be negotiated in the delicate diplomacy of relationships. And as with other aspects of digital life, personal preferences and individual disclosure levels are bound to differ, making the transition from e-mail to "we mail" all the more nettlesome. Not surprisingly, many couples never even attempt it.

CONSIDER

1. How does e-mail add a layer of "instant intimacy" onto a close relationship, and what issues does it raise in terms of personal disclosure?

2. Would you be willing to fully share your account, including your e-mail address and password, with your partner? Why or why not?

3. How does e-mail, like medicine cabinets, credit card bills, and personal diaries, tempt the suspicious and distrustful?

Susan Fliess had been looking forward to receiving pictures of a friend's baby through e-mail. She never got the chance. The pictures arrived at fliess1@netscape.net, the e-mail address she shared with her husband, Kevin, but then: "Kevin was, like: 'What's this big, huge file? You know what their baby looks like,'" Ms. Fliess said. "The next thing I knew, he'd deleted it."

Ms. Fliess doesn't mind an overflowing inbox; her husband does. The Silicon Valley couple, married nearly 3 years, decided to deal with their different attitudes toward clutter by getting separate e-mail accounts.

The ascendancy of e-mail has opened a new arena to the delicate diplomacy of relationships. Couples can share many things—living space, secrets, friends, and finances. Should they share e-mail accounts, as well?

"A lot of things need to be negotiated, and e-mail is one of them," said JoAnn Magdoff, a psychotherapist in Manhattan who has written about the psychology of the Internet. "But e-mail has its own twists. It adds a layer of instant intimacy." A shared account "raises issues of how far you really want to go in terms of disclosure," Dr. Magdoff said.

People may want an individual e-mail address at home, but feel snubbed when their partners do, too. Or they may like the freedom to gripe to their friends without being fearful or self-conscious about what their partners might read.

One stay-at-home mother, who did not want her name used, said she resented that her husband had a private office address while she used their shared AOL address at home. "He can look at my mail," she said, "but I can't look at his."

Sometimes, he reads the mail and deletes it, so she doesn't see it at all. At other times, he uses AOL's "keep as new" function so she can't tell he has read the mail. And even when she has deleted her outgoing messages, her friends have occasionally incorporated them into their replies. Her husband was furious after finding out via an e-mail message sent to her that she had told a friend something she had kept from him.

A common mistake couples make is assuming that e-mail is like other, older forms of communication, Dr. Magdoff said. "People dash off e-mail where they wouldn't pick up the phone and certainly wouldn't pick up a pen," she said.

Home e-mail also affords much less privacy than, say, a home telephone. On the phone, callers assume that a couple share both a number and an answering machine; talkers almost always know if there is a chance they may be overheard.

It is not uncommon for couples to create a merged e-mail name, like romeoandjuliet@aol.com, or to announce their closeness with an address like wevegot eachother@aol.com. The inclusiveness of a merged name can be an appealing part of a relationship, said Lynn Harris, who dispenses relationship advice on the Breakup Girl Web site. She refers to joint e-mail addresses as "we-mail."

"I don't think people should share everything," Ms. Harris said. "Some things are your own stuff. With so much free Web-based e-mail, there's no need to share."

A couple's use of joint e-mail can reflect the way they function in the real world. For Rabbi Michael Beals, the leader of B'nai Tikvah Congregation in Los Angeles, and his wife, Elissa Green, a veterinarian, that means he handles the household correspondence.

"When we got married 5 years ago," Rabbi Beals said, "all the 'ugh' part of life Elissa delegated to me, like paying the bills and taking out the kitty litter. You should play to your strengths. My strength is communication, so I'm the one sending most of these messages out. We're a team. It's fine for me to speak in both of our names."

Their e-mail address, rabbivet@lafn.org, has caused some confusion, though, with people assuming the rabbi is a war veteran. Their signoff—"Michael, Elissa, Yofi and Shovas"—includes the dog and the cat. It expresses what is important to them, Rabbi Beals said, although some of their correspondents think both the address and the signoff are a little too cute.

Even people with their own accounts face a question: Should they reveal their passwords to their partners?

Ms. Harris believes that whatever conclusion a couple may reach, password sharing should not become another intimacy test in a relationship. "Some people are weird about sharing anything," Ms. Harris said. "They wouldn't give their mom food off their fork. You have to be careful about drawing relationship conclusions from other interpersonal weirdness. It might not be a matter of intimacy at all, but of what boundaries are comfortable."

The real red flag, Ms. Harris said, is online snooping. Like medicine cabinets, credit card bills and diaries, e-mail tempts the distrustful. Judging from Breakup Girl's advice seekers—and these are people in troubled partnerships, not harmonious ones—"the problem is there's enough suspicion to cause the snooping," Ms. Harris said.

And if that troubled partnership should dissolve, a shared e-mail address means yet another headache.

Four years ago, when Dina Robertson and her husband, Scott Robertson, got a home computer, "it didn't occur to me not to do something together," said Ms. Robertson, of Greenland, New Hampshire. So they combined everyone's initials, choosing SDDRobt @aol.com. (The second *D* is for their son, Douglass.)

A year ago, when her husband moved out, there was no dispute that Ms. Robertson, the coordinator for a children's advocacy group, would keep the address. She changed the password.

Now she is gradually reclaiming her maiden name, Dudarevitch. But she can't get rid of her husband's name on her e-mail.

"I am thoroughly involved with that address," she said. "If I changed it, it would affect hundreds of people. I feel locked into it. It really bothers me."

RELATED LINKS

- E-mail Communication and Relationships (http://www.rider.edu/users/suler/psycyber/emailrel.html)

- Help Me Harlan! (http://www.helpmeharlan.com)

- Delilah's Advice on Online Love (http://thriveonline.oxygen.com/sex/experts/delilah/delilah.online.html)

FOR FURTHER RESEARCH

To find out more about the topics discussed in this reading, use InfoTrac College Edition. Type in keywords and subject terms such as "we-mail," "e-mail privacy," and "relationship communication." You can access InfoTrac College Edition from the Wadsworth/Thomson Communication Cafe homepage: http://communication.wadsworth.com.

Reading 8-2
Identity Crisis
Sherry Turkle

EDITOR'S NOTE

In this reading from Life on the Screen, *Sherry Turkle describes the range of meaningful experiences that can occur online through virtual alteregos. Turkle, one of the foremost analysts of online identity, observes that as the stability of social life has eroded, "What matters most now is the ability to adapt and change—to new jobs, new career directions, new gender roles, new technologies." In cyberspace, identity is becoming more fluid and flexible. Virtual worlds, she asserts, provide ideal environments for gainfully exploring different aspects of the self.*

CONSIDER

1. What is the difference between experimenting with *multiplicity* and having the condition of *multiple personality disorder?*

2. Do you agree that psychological well-being will increasingly depend on giving up notions of a unitary self in favor of more flexible conceptions of self-identity?

3. How does the virtual reality of cyberspace function as a transitional space for many people?

Every era constructs its own metaphors for psychological well-being. Not so long ago, stability was socially valued and culturally reinforced. Rigid gender roles, repetitive labor, the expectation of being in one kind of job or remaining in one town over a lifetime, all of these made consistency central to definitions of health. But these stable social worlds have broken down. In our time, health is described in terms of fluidity rather than stability. What matters most now is the ability to adapt and change—to new jobs, new career directions, new gender roles, new technologies.

IDENTITY AND MULTIPLICITY

When people adopt an online persona they cross a boundary into highly charged territory. Some feel an uncomfortable sense of fragmentation, some a sense of relief. Some sense the possibilities for self-discovery, even self-transformation. Serena, a 26-year-old graduate student in history, says, "When I log on to a new MUD [Multi-User Dungeon] and I create a character and know I have to start typing my description, I always feel a sense of panic. Like I could find out something I don't want to know." Arlie, a 20-year-old undergraduate, says, "I am always very self-conscious when I create a new character. Usually, I end up creating someone I wouldn't want my parents to know about. It takes me, like, 3 hours. But that someone is part of me." In these ways and others, many more of us are experimenting with multiplicity than ever before.

With this last comment, I am not implying that MUDs or computer bulletin boards are causally implicated in the dramatic increase of people who exhibit

symptoms of multiple personality disorder (MPD), or that people on MUDs have MPD, or that MUDing is like having MPD. What I am saying is that the many manifestations of multiplicity in our culture, including the adoption of online personae, are contributing to a general reconsideration of traditional, unitary notions of identity.

The history of a psychiatric symptom is inextricably tied up with the history of the culture that surrounds it. When I was in graduate school in psychology in the 1970s, clinical psychology texts regarded multiple personality as so rare (perhaps one in a million) as to be barely worthy of mention. In these rare cases, there was typically one alter personality in addition to the host personality. Today, cases of multiple personality are much more frequent and typically involve up to sixteen alters of different ages, races, genders, and sexual orientations. In multiple personality disorder, it is widely believed that traumatic events have caused various aspects of the self to congeal into virtual personalities, the "ones" often hiding from the "others" and hiding too from that special alter, the host personality. Sometimes, the alters are known to each other and to the host; some alters may see their roles as actively helping others. Such differences led the philosopher Ian Hacking to write about a "continuum of dissociation."[1] These differences also suggest a way of thinking about the self in terms of a continuum of how accessible its parts are to each other.

At one extreme, the unitary self maintains its oneness by repressing all that does not fit. Thus censored, the illegitimate parts of the self are not accessible. This model would of course function best within a fairly rigid social structure with clearly defined rules and roles. At the other extreme is the MPD sufferer whose multiplicity exists in the context of an equally repressive rigidity. The parts of the self are not in easy communication. Communication is highly stylized; one personality must speak to another personality. In fact, the term "multiple personality" is misleading, because the different parts of the self are not full personalities.

They are split-off, disconnected fragments. But if the disorder in multiple personality disorder is the need for the rigid walls between the selves (blocking the secrets those selves protect), then the study of MPD may begin to furnish ways of thinking about healthy selves as nonunitary but with fluid access among their many aspects. Thus, in addition to the extremes of unitary self and MPD, we can imagine a flexible self.

The essence of this self is not unitary, nor are its parts stable entities. It is easy to cycle through its aspects and these are themselves changing through constant communication with each other. The philosopher Daniel Dennett speaks to the flexible self in his multiple drafts theory of consciousness.[2] Dennett's notion of multiple drafts is analogous to the experience of having several versions of a document open on a computer screen where the user is able to move between them at will. The presence of the drafts encourages a respect for the many different versions while it imposes a certain distance from them. No one aspect can be claimed as the absolute, true self. When [in France] I got to know French Sherry I no longer saw the less confident English-speaking Sherry as my one authentic self. What most characterizes the model of a flexible self is that the lines of communication between its various aspects are open. The open communication encourages an attitude of respect for the many within us and the many within others.

As we sense our inner diversity we come to know our limitations. We understand that we do not and cannot know things completely, not the outside world and not ourselves. Today's heightened consciousness of incompleteness may predispose us to join with others. The historian of science Donna Haraway equates a "split and contradictory self" with a "knowing self." She is optimistic about its possibilities: "The knowing self is partial in all its guises, never finished, whole, simply there and original; it is always constructed and stitched together imperfectly; and therefore able to join with another, to see together without claiming to be another."[3]

When identity was defined as unitary and solid it was relatively easy to recognize and censure deviation from a norm. A more fluid sense of self allows a greater capacity for acknowledging diversity. It makes it easier to accept the array of our (and others') inconsistent personae—perhaps with humor, perhaps with irony. We do not feel compelled to rank or judge the elements of our multiplicity. We do not feel compelled to exclude what does not fit.

VIRTUALITY AS TRANSITIONAL SPACE

In a journal published on the Internet, Leslie Harris speculates on how virtual experiences become part of the perceptual and emotional background "that changes the way we see things."[4] Harris describes an episode of *Star Trek: The Next Generation* in which Captain Picard plays Caiman, an inhabitant of the virtual world Catanh. On Catanh, Picard lives the experiences he had to forgo in order to make a career in Starfleet. He has a virtual experience of love, marriage, and fatherhood. He develops relationships with his community that are not possible for him as a Starfleet commander. "On" Catanh, the character Caiman "learns" to play the Ressiccan flute. Harris says, "He can eventually fall in love with a fellow crew member in his "real life" because he experienced the feelings of love, commitment, and intimacy 'on' Catanh." When in his real life Picard plays the flute with a fellow Starfleet officer he realizes that he is in love with her. Picard is aware that he has projected his desire for music and sensuality onto his virtual world. It is this awareness that lets him use music to link the "real" Captain Picard to the emotional growth he was able to experience as the virtual Caiman.

Here, virtuality is powerful but transitional. Ultimately, it is put in the service of Picard's embodied self. Picard's virtual Catanh, like the space created within psychoanalysis, operates in a time out of normal time and according to its own rules. In a successful psychoanalysis, the meetings between analyst and analysand come to an end, although the analytic process goes on forever. It is internalized within the person, just as Picard brought Catanh inside himself. Buddhists speak of their practice as a raft to get to the other shore, liberation. But the raft, like an analytic treatment, is thought of as a tool that must be set aside, even though the process of crossing the river is conceived of as neverending. Wittgenstein takes up a similar idea in *The Tractatus,* when he compares his work to a ladder that is to be discarded after the reader has used it to reach a new level of understanding.

In April 1995, a town meeting was held at MIT on the subject "Doing Gender on the Net." As the discussion turned to using virtual personae to try out new experiences, a 30-year-old graduate student, Ava, told her story. She had used a MUD to try out being comfortable with a disability. Several years earlier, Ava had been in an automobile accident that left her without a right leg. During her recuperation, she began to

MUD. "Without giving it a lot of advance thought," Ava found herself creating a one-legged character on a MUD. Her character had a removable prosthetic limb. The character's disability featured plainly in her description, and the friends she made on the MUD found a way to deal with her handicap. When Ava's character became romantically involved, she and her virtual lover acknowledged the "physical" as well as the emotional aspects of the virtual amputation and prosthesis. They became comfortable with making virtual love, and Ava found a way to love her own virtual body. Ava told the group at the town meeting that this experience enabled her to take a further step toward accepting her real body. "After the accident, I made love in the MUD before I made love again in real life," she said. "I think that the first made the second possible. I began to think of myself as whole again." For her, the Internet had been a place of healing.

Virtual reality gave Ava choices. She could have tried being one of this MUD's many Fabulous Hot Babes. If so, she might have never felt safe leaving the anonymity of the virtual world. But instead she was able to reimagine herself not as whole but as whole-in-her-incompleteness. Each of us in our own way is incomplete. Virtual spaces may provide the safety for us to expose what we are missing so that we can begin to accept ourselves as we are.

Virtuality need not be a prison. It can be the raft, the ladder, the transitional space, the moratorium that is discarded after reaching greater freedom. We don't have to reject life on the screen, but we don't have to treat it as an alternative life either. We can use it as a space for growth. Having literally written our online personae into existence, we are in a position to be more aware of what we project into everyday life. Like the anthropologist returning home from a foreign culture, the voyager in virtuality can return to a real world better equipped to understand its artifices.

CYBORG DREAMS

I have argued that Internet experiences help us to develop models of psychological well-being that are in a meaningful sense postmodern: They admit multiplicity and flexibility. They acknowledge the constructed nature of reality, self, and other. The Internet is not alone in encouraging such models. There are many places within our culture that do so. What they have in common is that they all suggest the value of approaching one's "story" in several ways and with fluid access to one's different aspects. We are encouraged to think of ourselves as fluid, emergent, decentralized, multiplicitous, flexible, and ever in process. The metaphors travel freely among computer science, psychology, children's games, cultural studies, artificial intelligence, literary criticism, advertising, molecular biology, self-help, and artificial life. They reach deep into the popular culture. The ability of the Internet to change popular understandings of identity is heightened by the presence of these metaphors.

For example, a *Newsweek* article [from April 1995] reports on a new narrative movement in psychotherapy, describing the trend as consistent with the "postmodernist idea that we don't so much perceive the world as interpret it." "The psyche," says *Newsweek,* "is not a fixed objective entity, but a fluid, social construct—a story that is subject to revision."[5] The new therapeutic movement described by *Newsweek* draws on deconstructionist literary criticism and on recent currents of psychoanalytic thought that emphasize conflicting narratives as a way of thinking about the analytic experience.[6]

The literary scholar Katherine Hayles, writing on the cultural resonances of chaos theory, has made the circulation of dominant metaphors a central theme of her work. She suggests that similarities arise in diverse scholarly disciplines and within popular culture "because of broadly based movements within the culture which made the deep assumptions underlying the new paradigms thinkable, perhaps inevitable, thoughts."[7] These assumptions carry a sense of the times that manifests itself in one place and then another, here as developmental psychology and there as a style of engineering, here as a description of our bodies and there as a template for corporate organization, here as a way to build a computer network and there as a manifesto of political ideals.

We are all dreaming cyborg dreams. While our children imagine "morphing" humans into metallic cyber-reptiles, our computer scientists dream themselves immortal. They imagine themselves thinking forever, downloaded onto machines. The AI [artificial intelligence] researcher W. Daniel Hillis says,

> I have the same nostalgic love of human metabolism that everybody else does, but if I can go into an improved body and last for 10,000 years I would do it in an instant, no second thoughts. I actually don't think I'm going to have that option, but maybe my children will.[8]

Hillis' musings exemplify the mythic side of cybernetics, apparent from its earliest days. Norbert Wiener, a pioneer in the field, once wrote, "This is an idea with which I have toyed before—that it is conceptually possible for a human being to be sent over a telegraph line."[9] Today, the cyborg, in which human and machine are one, has become a postmodern myth. The myth is fed by the extravagances of *Robocop, The Terminator,* and *Power Rangers* as well as by the everyday reality of children plugged into video games. When William Gibson was asked about his sources of inspiration for *Neuromancer,* he described the merging of human and machine as he watched a teenager playing a video game in a downtown arcade.

> Video games weren't something I'd done much, and I'd have been embarrassed to actually go into these arcades because everyone was so much younger than I was, but when I looked into one, I could see in the physical intensity of their postures how *rapt* these kids were. It was like one of those closed systems out of a Pynchon novel: you had this feedback loop, with photons coming off the screen into the kids' eyes, the neurons moving through their bodies, electrons moving through the computer. And these kids clearly *believed* in the space these games projected. Everyone who works with computers seems to develop an intuitive faith that there's some kind of *actual* space behind the screen.[10]

Thus, for Gibson, the video game player has already merged with the computer. The video game player is already a cyborg, an insight Gibson spun into a postmodern mythology. Over the past decade, such mythologies have been recasting our sense of collective identity.

For Will, a 37-year-old writer who has recently gone online, the Internet inspires a personal mythology in which he feels part of something far larger than himself: "The Internet is like a giant brain. . . . It's developing on its own. And people and computers are its neural net." This view puts human brains and computers in a provocative symmetry and together they contribute to a larger evolving structure. Will tells me that his new idea about the Internet as a brain made up of human and computer parts "felt like an epiphany." In an age where we feel fragmented as individuals, it is not surprising to see the emergence of popular mythologies that try to put the world back together again.

DWELLERS ON A THRESHOLD

In simulated science experiments, virtual chemicals are poured from virtual beakers, and virtual light bounces off virtual walls. In financial transactions, virtual money changes hands. In film and photography, realistic-looking images depict scenes that never took place between people who never met. And on the networked computers of our everyday lives, people have compelling interactions that are entirely dependent on their online self-representations. In cyberspace, hundreds of thousands, perhaps already millions, of users create online personae who live in a diverse group of virtual communities where the routine formation of multiple identities undermines any notion of a real and unitary self. Yet the notion of the real fights back. People who live parallel lives on the screen are nevertheless bound by the desires, pain, and mortality of their physical selves. Virtual communities offer a dramatic new context in which to think about human identity in the age of the Internet. They are spaces for learning about the lived meaning of a culture of simulation. Will it be a separate world where people get lost in the surfaces or will we learn to see how the real and the virtual can be made permeable, each having the potential for enriching and expanding the other? The citizens of MUDs are our pioneers.

As we stand on the boundary between the real and the virtual, our experience recalls what the anthropologist Victor Turner termed a liminal moment, a moment of passage when new cultural symbols and meanings can emerge.[11] Liminal moments are times of tension, extreme reactions, and great opportunity. In our time, we are simultaneously flooded with predictions of doom and predictions of imminent utopia. We live in a crucible of contradictory experience. When Turner talked about liminality, he understood it as a transitional state—but living with flux may no longer be temporary.

Multiple viewpoints call forth a new moral discourse. I have said that the culture of simulation may help us achieve a vision of a multiple but integrated identity whose flexibility, resilience, and capacity for joy comes from having access to our many selves. But if we have lost reality in the process, we shall have struck a poor bargain. In Wim Wenders' film *Until the End of the World,* a scientist develops a device that translates the electrochemical activity of the brain into digital images. He gives this technology to his family and closest friends, who are now able to hold small battery-driven monitors and watch their dreams. At first, they are charmed. They see their treasured fantasies, their secret selves. They see the images they otherwise would forget, the scenes they otherwise would repress. As with the personae one can play in a MUD, watching dreams on a screen opens up new aspects of the self.

However, the story soon turns dark. The images seduce. They are richer and more compelling than the real life around them. Wenders' characters fall in love with their dreams, become addicted to them. People wander about with blankets over their heads the better to see the monitors from which they cannot bear to be parted. They are imprisoned by the screens, imprisoned by the keys to their past that the screens seem to hold.

We, too, are vulnerable to using our screens in these ways. People can get lost in virtual worlds. Some are tempted to think of life in cyberspace as insignificant, as escape or meaningless diversion. It is not. Our experiences there are serious play. We belittle them at our risk. We must understand the dynamics of virtual experience both to foresee who might be in danger and to put these experiences to best use. Without a deep understanding of the many selves that we express in the virtual we cannot use our experiences there to enrich the real. If we cultivate our awareness of what stands behind our screen personae, we are more likely to succeed in using virtual experience for personal transformation.

NOTES

1. Ian Hacking, *Rewriting the Soul: Multiple Personality and the Sciences of Memory.* Princeton, NJ: Princeton University Press, 1995, p. 21.

2. Daniel C. Dennett, *Consciousness Explained.* Boston: Little, Brown, 1991.

3. Donna Haraway, "The Actors Are Cyborg, Nature Is Coyote, and the Geography Is Elsewhere: Postscript to 'Cyborgs at Large.'" In Constance Penley and Andrew Ross (Eds.), *Technoculture.* Minneapolis: University of Minnesota Press, 1991, p. 22.

4. Leslie Harris, "The Psychodynamic Effects of Virtual Reality," *The Arachnet Electronic Journal on Virtual Culture, 2,* 1 (February 1994).

5. Geoffrey Cowley and Karen Springen, "Rewriting Life Stories." *Newsweek,* April 17, 1995, p. 70.

6. See, for example, Barbara Johnson, *A World of Difference.* Baltimore: Johns Hopkins University Press, 1987; Donald P. Spence, *Narrative Truth and Historical Truth: Meaning and Interpretation in Psychoanalysis.* New York: W.W. Norton & Company, 1982; and Humphrey Morris (Ed.), *Telling Facts: History and Narration in Psychoanalysis.* Baltimore: Johns Hopkins University Press, 1992.

7. N. Katherine Hayles, *Chaos Bound: Orderly Disorder in Contemporary Literature and Science.* Ithaca, NY: Cornell University Press, 1990, p. 3

8. W. Daniel Hillis, quoted in Steven Levy, *Artificial Life: The Quest for a New Creation.* New York: Pantheon Books, 1992, p. 344.

9. Norbert Wiener, *God and Golem, Inc.: A Comment on Certain Points Where Cybernetics Impinges on Religion.* Cambridge, MA: MIT Press, 1964, p. 36.

10. Colin Greenland, "A Nod to the Apocalypse: An Interview with William Gibson," *Foundation, 36* (Summer 1986), 5–9.

11. Victor Turner, *The Ritual Process: Structure and Antistructure.* Chicago: Aldine, 1966.

RELATED LINKS

- Anonymity for Fun and Deception: The Other Side of "Community" (http://www.samizdat.com/anon.html)

- Identity Management in Cyberspace (http://www.rider.edu/users/suler/psycyber/identitymanage.html)

- Identity, Privacy, and Anonymity on the Internet (http://www.rewi.hu-berlin.de/Datenschutz/Netze/privint.html)

- Sherry Turkle's Home Page (http://web.mit.edu/sturkle/www)

FOR FURTHER RESEARCH

To find out more about the topics discussed in this reading, use InfoTrac College Edition. Type in keywords and subject terms such as "online identity," "postmodernism," and "multiplicity." You can access InfoTrac College Edition from the Wadsworth/Thomson Communication Cafe homepage: http://communication.wadsworth.com.

Reading 8-3

I Don't Know Who You Are, But (Click) You're Toast
Michel Marriott

EDITOR'S NOTE

The computer-based gaming industry now rivals Hollywood in its profitability and influence. This reading about online game playing explains the attractions of multiple-user immersive environments and the interactivity of competing with actual people (as opposed to software agents). Unlike games in real life, on the Internet there is always someone ready and willing to play. And, contrary to popular belief, not all computer gamers are young boys—on America Online, at least, a growing number of gamers are over 35 and slightly more than half the players are women.

CONSIDER

1. Why do computer-based games appeal to such diverse demographic groups? Are the attractions of computer games for women and older adults the same as they are for kids?

2. What is the difference between so-called "persistent universe" and "peer-to-peer" computer gaming?

3. In what other interactive, computer-based world did multiple-user games originate? How does this world differ from the newer, multimedia gaming environments?

Daniel Shiffman, a lanky 25-year-old who is a self-proclaimed computer geek, was never an athletic powerhouse. At the small private high school he attended in his native Baltimore, he was often "well down near the bottom of gym class," he recalled with a chuckle.

But when he is playing games online, sitting in a loft apartment in downtown Manhattan that he shares with three Net-smart roommates and sixteen computers, Shiffman, a financial planner and freelance computer consultant, is a nimble giant of a competitor. His opponents, all sitting at their own computers somewhere (anywhere, as long as they are connected to the

Internet), know only that he is a master player, capable of wielding a computer joystick with the alacrity of Wayne Gretzky on the ice and pounding his keyboard with such speed and accuracy that it might make boxing champ Evander Holyfield wince.

His game is Myth: The Fallen Lords, a world of magical characters, intricate strategies, and sudden death. Each player can play against all the other players or in teams. As many as sixteen can participate in a game session. The manufacturer of this wildly popular game, Bungie Software, offers advice that gives a glimpse into the game's free-for-all: "Kill your enemies. Kill your friends' enemies. Kill your friends."

"It's become an obsession of mine," Shiffman said happily during an interview at the Internet World conference in New York. "The novelty is that you are not playing yourself in a dark corner of a room somewhere, but you are interacting with actual people."

Shiffman has joined the swelling ranks of people who are finding greater challenges and just more downright fun by using their computers to play the cagiest opponents of them all: other people.

They are using the sophistication of Internet connections to play opponents all over the world in games like Myth and Ultima Online or to go full throttle in the cockpit of a MIG-29 fighter jet, matching wits and heat-seeking missiles against scores of other chairbound fighter pilots—in Manhattan, Denver, or anywhere—all in the same virtual space that appears on the computer screen as the airspace over central Africa.

In what might seem an odd turn, high-powered computers are also being called upon by people who want to play only old favorites, like Checkers, Scrabble, and Spades, with distant opponents.

Internet game players can, for example, fly World War II–era sorties over war-torn Europe, then reminisce later with fellow cyberaces in virtual lounges—if they survive their missions. Depending on the game, the talking is done in text-based chat or with full telephony that allows players to speak to one another as if they were on a conference call. All of that tends to make the games even more addictive, players, and people who criticize the games, say.

Using the Internet to play computer games, even aging ones better known for their single-player action, has in many cases lengthened the life of games in a genre well known for accelerated obsolescence. Total Annihilation, a futuristic action strategy game released in 1997, has flourished on the Internet, said John Uppendahl, a spokesman for Cavedog Entertainment, the California-based maker of the game. "You throw it out there to the world of the hundreds and thousands of people who have Total Annihilation and have so many perspectives, you give yourself hundreds of hours of extra game play by talking to different people and getting different ideas and ways to approach it."

Scott Wallin, senior director of online game development for Cavedog Entertainment, added that the community of game players the Internet fosters can just as easily make a game or kill it by spreading the word on its worthiness.

"What's really nice about the Web is the networking that it creates," he said.

Overall, computer-based games, including those for television-console systems like Nintendo and Sony PlayStation, have become a $5 billion industry, according to Forrester Research in Cambridge, Massachusetts, which studies Internet use and trends. Only 3 percent of that revenue is attributed specifically to computer games played over the Internet. But by 2002, Forrester forecasts, online gaming will account for close to a quarter of an estimated $8 billion computer game industry. Last year, a Forrester report noted that a poll of game developers found 76 percent had Internet games under development.

"People are becoming more familiar with PCs," said Seema Williams, a research analyst at Forrester. "More and more consumers have 6 months to 2 years of experience with them. They are more open now to playing games online."

In an April 1998 report, Ms. Williams noted that more than a million users of Microsoft's online Internet Gaming Zone had registered to play its most popular game, Spades.

America Online, which recently announced a redesign of its popular Games Channel, noted that more than 3.4 million individuals visited the channel in one month's time, logging more than 6 million hours of play.

America Online—the world's largest online service, with more than [20 million] members—also discovered that who is actually playing its online games defies widely accepted stereotypes. For example, 76 percent of AOL's players are 18 or older, 51 percent of them are 35 or older, and most surprisingly, given the commonly held conventions about computer gamers, slightly more than half of the gamers between 25 and 49 years old were women.

"Playing games online is one of the hottest new forms of entertainment," said Lawrence Schick, executive director of interactive entertainment for AOL.

"It's not just the kids who are playing. Mom and Dad are, too."

Ultimately, it is the human-to-human interaction that makes Internet games especially enticing, players say. IBM's silicon chess whiz, Big Blue, notwithstanding, playing against a computer simply cannot compare with using a computer to play against real people, Internet game makers say.

The makers of television-console game systems, like Nintendo and Sony PlayStation, have long known this. Many computer game experts said console games, a $2.6 billion industry, owe much of their success to the fact that people play such games against other people. But people play console games with people in the same room; none in the United States, as of this writing, are capable of linking players across the vastness of the Internet.

Even in the quicksilver world of computer innovation, the world of multiplayer Internet games is relatively new. The sonic boom in online gaming occurred only a couple of years ago, when smarter computers, programs, and fundamental improvements in the Internet itself made online games seem to come to life with dazzling graphics and blazing speed, explained John R. Taylor III, vice president for strategic development at the Kesmai Corporation.

"It is satisfying to see where things have evolved," said Taylor, who cofounded Kesmai, one of the oldest companies specializing in online multiplayer games, in 1982. The early Internet games took shape in a text-defined computer world of MUDs—Multi-User Dungeons, relatively primitive multiplayer programs— and Unix operating systems. Since then, games have progressed to the point of evoking convincing 3-D environments that offer movie-quality visuals with CD-quality soundtracks and sound effects. But oddly enough, with all the technology, what is most important is that they deliver real people as opponents.

"Even with all the sophistication that computers have, there is a trick or pattern to the way computers play," said David Campana, 30, an engineering manager. He said he much preferred playing the personal computer version of the action game Quake II against people rather than against his computer's integrated circuits.

"When you play against people, all bets are off," Campana said. "You never know how people are going to react. It's much better."

Actually, the Internet is not the only game in town. Many of the most advanced CD-ROM computer games can be played with multiple players on a local area network, or LAN, an in-house network in which the computers are wired to one another, as well as with players on the Internet. On a LAN, any computer on the local network that meets the game's minimal speed, space, and power requirements can usually be used to join the action.

Campana, who works for a technology company in Princeton, New Jersey, said that while he enjoyed playing action games online, he preferred to play his favorite game, Quake II, on a LAN at his office after hours. Sometimes more than a dozen of his coworkers stay late to play the game. On a LAN, all the players have identical connections to the in-house network, which is generally not true for players competing over the Internet.

Connections vary wildly on the Net, depending on modem speed, the computer's location, service provider, and whether some players have superfast connections like DSL, cable modems, and T1 lines. In-

variably, players with slow connections are at a disadvantage when drawing their weapons against players with faster connections. In the lexicon of online game players, slow players are often victims of what is called "latency." In Quake II, a game that can be won or lost on a hundredths-of-a-second response, a player with slow connections can appear practically arthritic.

But setting up and maintaining a LAN to play games is expensive and cumbersome. And some players can run into the same problem with LAN games that they run into in real-life games: finding someone to play with when you are ready to play.

On the Internet, that is seldom a problem. At any given time, millions are bustling from Web site to Web site, looking for someone to play. And the Web also offers the ancillary benefits of chat rooms, rankings, and message boards to compare strategy notes.

But to play on the Internet, players need an intermediary, what Ms. Williams at Forrester calls a "cyber-rec room." These services, called game centers, are proprietary online services, with names like Kesmai's Game Storm and Mplayer.com, that allow two or more players to compete electronically. Many of these centers also offer chat rooms and message boards to help players of similar interests and skill levels find one another for online games.

No two game centers are exactly alike. Some, like Mplayer, are free. Others charge a fee, like Game Storm (but games are free and can be downloaded from the Internet or from a disk that is mailed to members), and some, like America Online's Games Channel, which is exclusively for AOL members, has two rates for its more advanced games. On AOL, for example, Blackjack and Virtual Pool each cost 99 cents an hour to play, and Air Warrior II is $1.99 an hour.

Another major distinction among game centers is whether they provide something called a "persistent universe" or "massively multiplayer gaming." In a persistent universe, the computer-generated world is changed continuously as players enter, affect it in various ways, and exit. Such environments—like the mysterious medieval land of dragons and sorcerers of Ultima Online, a pay-for-play game—exist, almost organically, whether 5,000 people are playing or no one is playing.

"The characters' attributes are stored in the database," said Chris Holden, chief executive of Kesmai, based in Charlottesville, Virginia, explaining persistent-universe gaming. "So when a player comes back, he can pick up right where he left off."

Left the game and forgot to put your sword away? Ask another player still online to put it back in your castle for you. That is possible in persistent-universe gaming, which tends to be very expensive to maintain and support.

Other online games are in the peer-to-peer category. Devotees of persistent-universe games refer to these game centers disparagingly as "dating services." Services like TEN and Mpath are peer-to-peer, which means that they match up players for games that last only as long as the competitors are playing. When players lose or quit, ending the game, that particular computer world also dies.

Many of these companies, Ms. Williams said, are supported by advertisers that pitch anything from new computer games and computer-game magazines to M&M candies between matches to a mostly male audience of young adults.

Both kinds of online games have indirectly created an often unexpectedly strong sense of community, players and game makers say.

"It's all about social interaction," Holden said, "people talking and making friends—and enemies, for that matter. Anything that happens in real life when people gather can happen online."

Regular online players often organize themselves into teams, squadrons, or guilds, depending on the game. Some players meet off line to discuss the game or deepen friendships made online. Holden's colleague, Taylor, said he had met his wife while playing one of his company's Internet games.

Ms. Williams said the emerging Internet game world was "a new community and a new way to interact with that community."

Yet for Daniel Shiffman in his Manhattan apartment, his online Myth game is mostly just that: a game.

"But a really amazing one, a perfect combination of strategy and fighting," he said with a chuckle.

 SITE-SEEING: MULTIPLAYER GAMES

Many roads lead to the world of multiplayer games online, each offering a different approach. Here are some of the most popular game destinations:

- **Ultima Online**—*www.uo.com:* A fantasy role-playing game that was designed from the start by Origin Systems as a multiplayer game. Ultima is set in an ongoing world, with forests, castles, villages, and taverns, that continues to change even when you are off line. The only way to play is on the Internet. Ultima Online is, in essence, its own game center. To play, you must own a copy of the game and subscribe to Ultima's online gaming service.

- **Myth: The Fallen Lords**—*www.bungie.com:* An adventure role-playing game by Bungie Software that combines strategy and the hyperspeed of action games like Quake and Unreal. This game, much like Ultima Online, is set in an ongoing world, defined by magic and battle. Playing Myth on the Internet is free through Bungie.net.

- **Games Channel**—*www.aol.com:* A game center on America Online that is strictly for AOL members. Most of the most popular games, like the virtual card game Spades, can be played at no cost (not counting AOL's monthly membership fee). More advanced action and adventure games, which AOL groups under the rubric Xtreme Games, cost by the hour.

- **Game Storm**—*www.gamestorm.com:* A classic game center that offers a wide range of titles and has a monthly fee. Some games are original, like Aliens Online and Godzilla Online. The games are organized into categories like action, adventure, driving, sports, strategy, simulation, and puzzles and can be downloaded from the site at no additional cost.

- **Mpath Interactive's Mplayer.com**—*www.mplayer.com:* A free game center that permits thousands of players to compete with one another on the Internet while playing many of the most popular action and real-time strategy games, like Total Annihilation, Quake II, and Diablo. While Mplayer does not support games with ongoing universes (like Myth and Ultima), it encourages tournaments and chat rooms and ranks the best players.

FOR FURTHER RESEARCH

To find out more about the topics discussed in this reading, use InfoTrac College Edition. Type in keywords and subject terms such as "computer games," "immersive environments," and "interactivity online." You can access InfoTrac College Edition from the Wadsworth / Thomson Communication Cafe homepage: http://communication.wadsworth.com.

Reading 8-4

Cyberpunk!

Philip Elmer-Dewitt*

EDITOR'S NOTE

With virtual sex, smart drugs, and synthetic rock 'n roll gaining momentum, Time *magazine discovered in the early '90s that a new counterculture is surfing the dark edges of the computer age. If anything, the cyberpunk influence on popular culture has grown in recent years, with the success of technothriller movies like* The Matrix *and* Johnny Mnemonic, *bleeding-edge magazines like* Wired *and* Next Generation, *and industrial bands like Prodigy and the Chemical Brothers. Through the cyberpunk lifestyle, computer culture continues to offer advance glimpses of mainstream trends.* (**Boldface** *terms are defined in a glossary at the end of this reading.)*

CONSIDER

1. Why are the roots of cyberpunk as much literary as they are technological?

2. What are the four attitudes central to the idea of cyberpunk, and how do they conflict with traditional business values?

3. Of all the various technologies that cyberpunks embrace (e.g., brain implants, artificial life, virtual sex), which do you think will become mainstream over the next decade?

In the 1950s it was the beatniks, staging a coffeehouse rebellion against the "Leave It to Beaver" conformity of the Eisenhower era. In the 1960s the hippies arrived, combining antiwar activism with the energy of sex, drugs, and rock 'n roll. Now a new subculture is bubbling up from the underground, popping out of computer screens like a piece of futuristic **hypertext.**

They call it cyberpunk, a late-twentieth-century term pieced together from **cybernetics** (the science

---

"Cyberpunk! With Virtual Sex, Smart Drugs, and Synthetic Rock 'n Roll, a New Counterculture Is Surfing the Dark Edges of the Computer Age," by Philip Elmer-Dewitt. From *Time,* February 8, 1993, Cover Story, pp. 59–65. Copyright © 1993 Time, Inc. Reprinted with permission.

*Reported by David S. Jackson, San Francisco.

of communication and control theory) and **punk** (an antisocial rebel or hoodlum). Within this odd pairing lurks the essence of cyberpunk culture. It's a way of looking at the world that combines an infatuation with high-tech tools and a disdain for conventional ways of using them. Originally applied to a school of hard-boiled science fiction writers and then to certain semi-tough computer hackers, the word *cyberpunk* now covers a broad range of music, art, psychedelics, smart drugs, and cutting-edge technology. The cult is new enough that fresh offshoots are sprouting every day, which infuriates the hardcore cyberpunks, who feel they got there first.

Stewart Brand, editor of the hippie-era *Whole Earth Catalog,* describes cyberpunk as "technology with attitude." Science fiction writer Bruce Sterling calls it "an unholy alliance of the technical world with the underground of pop culture and street-level anarchy." Jude Milhon, a cyberpunk journalist who writes under the byline St. Jude, defines it as "the place where the worlds of science and art overlap, the intersection of the future and now." What cyberpunk *is* about, says Rudy Rucker, a San Jose State University mathematician who writes science fiction books on the side, is nothing less than "the fusion of humans and machines."

As in any counterculture movement, some denizens would deny that they are part of a "movement" at all. Certainly they are not as visible from a passing car as beatniks or hippies once were. Ponytails (on men) and tattoos (on women) do not a cyberpunk make—though dressing all in black and donning mirrored sunglasses will go a long way. And although the biggest cyberpunk journal claims a readership approaching 70,000 [*Wired* now has a circulation of 475,000], there are probably no more than a few thousand computer hackers, futurists, fringe scientists, computer-savvy artists and musicians, and assorted science fiction geeks around the world who actually call themselves cyberpunks.

Nevertheless, cyberpunk may be the defining counterculture of the computer age. It embraces, in spirit at least, not just the nearest thirtysomething hacker hunched over his terminal but also nose-ringed twentysomethings gathered at clandestine **raves,** teenagers who feel about the Macintosh computer the way their parents felt about Apple Records, and even preadolescent vidkids fused like Krazy Glue to their Super Nintendo and Sega Genesis games—the training wheels of cyberpunk. Obsessed with technology, especially technology that is just beyond their reach (like **brain implants**), the cyberpunks are future oriented to a fault. They already have one foot in the twenty-first century, and time is on their side. In the long run, we will all be cyberpunks.

The cyberpunk look—a kind of SF (science fiction) surrealism tweaked by computer graphics—is already finding its way into art galleries, music videos, and Hollywood movies. Cyberpunk magazines, many of which are 'zines cheaply published by desktop computer and distributed by electronic mail, are multiplying like cable-TV channels. The newest, a glossy, big-budget entry called *Wired,* premiered last week with Bruce Sterling on the cover and ads from the likes of Apple Computer and AT&T. Cyberpunk music, including **acid house** and **industrial,** is popular enough to keep several record companies and scores of bands cranking out CDs. Cyberpunk-oriented books are snapped up by eager fans as soon as they hit the stores.

(Sterling's latest, *The Hacker Crackdown,* quickly sold out its first hard-cover printing of 30,000.) A piece of cyberpunk performance art, *Tubes,* starring Blue Man Group, is a hit off-Broadway. And cyberpunk films such as *Blade Runner, Videodrome, Robocop, Total Recall, Terminator 2,* and *The Lawnmower Man* have moved out of the cult market and into the mall.

Cyberpunk culture is likely to get a boost from, of all things, the Clinton–Gore Administration, because of a shared interest in what the new regime calls America's "data highways" and what the cyberpunks call **cyberspace.** Both terms describe the globe-circling, interconnected telephone network that is the conduit for billions of voice, fax, and computer-to-computer communications. The incoming administration is focused on the wiring, and it has made strengthening the network's high-speed data links a priority. The cyberpunks look at those wires from the inside; they talk of the network as if it were an actual place—a **virtual reality** that can be entered, explored, and manipulated.

Cyberspace plays a central role in the cyberpunk worldview. The literature is filled with "console cowboys" who prove their mettle by donning virtual-reality headgear and performing heroic feats in the imaginary "matrix" of cyberspace. Many of the punks' real-life heroes are also computer cowboys of one sort or another. *Cyberpunk,* a 1991 book by two *New York Times* reporters, John Markoff and Katie Hafner, features profiles of three canonical cyberpunk hackers, including Robert Morris, the Cornell graduate student whose **computer virus** brought the huge network called the **Internet** to a halt.

But cyberspace is more than a playground for hacker high jinks. What cyberpunks have known for some time is that cyberspace is also a new medium. Every night on Prodigy, CompuServe, GEnie, and thousands of smaller computer bulletin boards, people by the hundreds of thousands are logging on to a great computer-mediated gabfest, an interactive debate that allows them to leap over barriers of time, place, sex, and social status. Computer networks make it easy to reach out and touch strangers who share a particular obsession or concern. "We're replacing the old drug-store soda fountain and town square, where community used to happen in the physical world," says Howard Rheingold, a California-based author and editor who is writing a book on what he calls **virtual communities.**

Most computer users are content to visit cyberspace now and then, to read their electronic mail, check the bulletin boards and do a bit of electronic shopping. But cyberpunks go there to live and play—and even die. **The WELL,** one of the hippest virtual communities on the Internet, was shaken 2½ years ago when one of its most active participants ran a computer program that erased every message he had ever left—thousands of postings, some running for many pages. It was an act that amounted to virtual suicide. A few weeks later, he committed suicide for real.

The WELL is a magnet for cyberpunk thinkers, and it is there, appropriately enough, that much of the debate over the scope and significance of cyberpunk has occurred. The question Is there a cyberpunk movement? launched a freewheeling online **flame-fest** that ran for months. The debate yielded, among other things, a fairly concise list of "attitudes" that, by general agreement, seem to be central to the idea of cyberpunk. Among them:

1. *Information wants to be free.* A good piece of information-age technology will eventually get into the hands of those who can make the best use of it, despite the best efforts of the censors, copyright lawyers, and **datacops.**

2. *Always yield to the hands-on imperative.* Cyberpunks believe they can run the world for the better, if they can only get their hands on the control box.

3. *Promote decentralization.* Society is splintering into hundreds of subcultures and designer cults, each with its own language, code, and lifestyle.

4. *Surf the edges.* When the world is changing by the nanosecond, the best way to keep your head above water is to stay at the front end of the Zeitgeist.

The roots of cyberpunk, curiously, are as much literary as they are technological. The term was coined in the late 1980s to describe a group of science fiction writers—and in particular **William Gibson,** a 44-year-old American now living in Vancouver. Gibson's *Neuromancer,* the first novel to win science fiction's triple crown—the Hugo, Nebula, and Philip K. Dick awards—quickly became a cyberpunk classic, attracting an audience beyond the world of SF. Critics were intrigued by a dense, technopoetic prose style that invites comparisons to Hammett, Burroughs, and Pynchon. Computer-literate readers were drawn by Gibson's nightmarish depictions of an imaginary world disturbingly similar to the one they inhabit.

In fact, the key to cyberpunk science fiction is that it is not so much a projection into the future as a metaphorical evocation of today's technological flux.

The hero of *Neuromancer,* a burned-out, drug-addicted street hustler named Case, inhabits a sleazy **Interzone** on the fringes of a megacorporate global village where all transactions are carried out in New Yen. There he encounters Molly, a sharp-edged beauty with reflective lenses grafted to her eye sockets and retractable razor blades implanted in her fingers. They are hired by a mysterious employer who offers to fix Case's damaged nerves so he can once again enter cyberspace, a term Gibson invented. Soon Case discovers that he is actually working for an AI (artificial intelligence) named Wintermute, who is trying to get around the restrictions placed on AIs by the **Turing police** to keep the computers under control. "What's important to me," says Gibson, "is that *Neuromancer* is about the present."

The themes and motifs of cyberpunk have been percolating through the culture for nearly a decade. But they have coalesced in the past few years, thanks in large part to an upstart magazine called **Mondo 2000.** Since 1988, *Mondo*'s editors have covered cyberpunk as *Rolling Stone* magazine chronicles rock music, with celebrity interviews of such cyberheroes as **Negativland** and **Timothy Leary,** alongside features detailing what's hot and what's on the horizon. *Mondo*'s editors have packaged their quirky view of the world into a glossy book titled *Mondo 2000: A User's Guide to the New Edge.* Its cover touts alphabetic entries on everything from virtual reality and wetware to designer aphrodisiacs and **techno-erotic paganism,** promising to make cyberpunk's rarefied perspective immediately accessible. Inside, in an innovative hypertext format, relatively straightforward updates on computer graphics, multimedia, and fiber-optics accompany wild screeds on such recondite subjects as **synesthesia** and **temporary autonomous zones.**

The book and the magazine that inspired it are the product of a group of brainy (if eccentric) visionaries holed up in a rambling Victorian mansion perched on a hillside in Berkeley, California. The MTV-style graphics are supplied by designer Bart Nagel, the over-caffeinated prose by Ken Goffman (writing under the pen name R. U. Sirius) and Alison Kennedy (listed on the masthead as Queen Mu, "domineditrix"), with help from Rudy Rucker and a small staff of freelancers and contributions from an international cast of cyberpunk enthusiasts. The goal is to inspire and instruct but not to lead. "We don't want to tell people what to think," says assistant art director Heide Foley. "We want to tell them what the possibilities are."

Largely patched together from back issues of *Mondo 2000* magazine (and its precursor, a short-lived 'zine called *Reality Hackers*), the *Guide* is filled with articles on all the traditional cyberpunk obsessions, from **artificial life** to **virtual sex.** But some of the best entries are those that report on the activities of real people trying to live the cyberpunk life. For example, Mark Pauline, a San Francisco performance artist, specializes in giant machines and vast public spectacles: sonic booms that pin audiences to their chairs or the huge, stinking vat of rotting cheese with which he perfumed the air of Denmark to remind the citizenry of its Viking roots. When an explosion blew the thumb and three fingers off his right hand, Pauline simply had his big toe grafted where his thumb had been. He can pick things up again, but now he's waiting for medical science and grafting technology to advance to the point where he can replace his jerry-built hand with one taken from a cadaver.

Much of *Mondo 2000* strains credibility. Does physicist Nick Herbert really believe there might be a way to build **time machines?** Did the **cryonics** experts at Trans-Time Laboratory really chill a family pet named Miles and then, after its near death experience, turn it back into what its owner describes as a "fully functional dog"? Are we expected to accept on faith that a **smart drug** called centrophenoxine is an "intelligence booster" that provides "effective anti-aging therapy," or that another compound, called hydergine, increases mental abilities and prevents damage to brain cells? "All of this has some basis in today's technologies," says Paul Saffo, a research fellow at the Institute for the Future. "But it has a very anticipatory quality. These are people who assume that they will shape the future and the rest of us will live it."

Parents who thumb through *Mondo 2000* will find much here to upset them. An article on house music makes popping MDMA (**ecstasy**) and thrashing all night to music that clocks 120 beats per minute sound like an experience no red-blooded teenager would want to miss. After describing in detail the erotic effects of massive doses of L-dopa, MDA, and Deprenyl, the entry on aphrodisiacs adds as an afterthought that in some combinations these drugs can be fatal. Essays praising the beneficial effects of psychedelics and smart drugs on the information-processing power of the brain sit alongside **rants** that declare, among other things, that "safe sex is boring sex" and that "cheap thrills are fun."

Much of this, of course, is a cyberpunk pose. As Rucker confesses in his preface, he enjoys reading and thinking about psychedelic drugs but doesn't really like to take them. "To me the political point of being pro-psychedelic," he writes, "is that this means being against consensus reality, which I very strongly am." To some extent, says author Rheingold, cyberpunk is driven by young people trying to come up with a movement they can call their own. As he puts it, "They're tired of all these old geezers talking about how great the '60s were."

That sentiment was echoed by a recent posting on The WELL "I didn't get to pop some 'shrooms and dance naked in a park with several hundred of my peers," wrote a cyberpunk wannabe who calls himself Alien. "To me, and to a lot of other generally disenfranchised members of my generation, surfing the edges is all we've got."

More troubling, from a philosophic standpoint, is the theme of **dystopia** that runs like a bad trip through the cyberpunk worldview. Gibson's fictional world is filled with glassy-eyed girls strung out on their Walkman-like **simstim decks** and young men who get their kicks from **microsofts** plugged into sockets behind their ears. His brooding, dehumanized vision conveys a strong sense that technology is changing civilization and the course of history in frightening ways. But many of his readers don't seem to care. "History is a funny thing for cyberpunks," says Christopher Meyer, a music-synthesizer designer from Calabasas, California, writing on The WELL. "It's all data. It all takes up the same amount of space on disk, and a lot of it is just plain noise."

For cyberpunks, pondering history is not as important as coming to terms with the future. For all their flaws, they have found ways to live with technology, to make it theirs—something the back-to-the-land hippies never accomplished. Cyberpunks use technology to bridge the gulf between art and science, between the world of literature and the world of industry. Most of all, they realize that if you don't control technology, it will control you. It is a lesson that will serve them—and all of us—well in the next century.

GLOSSARY

acid house   White-hot dance music that falls somewhere between disco and hip-hop.

artificial life   Inspired by the behavior of computer viruses, scientists are wondering how sophisticated a computer program or robot would have to be before you could say it was "alive." One computer software company, Maxis, has marketed a whole line of simulated animals, ant colonies, cities, train systems, and even a planetlike organism called Gaia.

brain implants   Slip a microchip into snug contact with your gray matter (a.k.a. wetware) and suddenly gain instant fluency in a foreign language or arcane subject.

computer virus   The cybernetic analog of AIDS, these self-replicating programs infect computers and can destroy data. There are hundreds loose in cyberspace, although few are as destructive as the Internet virus—which is now classified as a "worm" because the writer of the program did not mean to do damage.

cryonics   For a price, a terminally ill patient can be frozen—as in the movie *Forever Young*—until some future time when a cure has been discovered. Some people save on storage costs by having just their head frozen.

cybernetics   Norbert Wiener of MIT was designing systems for World War II antiaircraft guns when he realized that the critical component in a control system, whether animal or mechanical, is a feedback loop that gives a controller information on the results of its actions. He called the study of these control systems cybernetics (from *kybernetes,* the Greek word for "helmsman") and helped pave the way for the electronic brains that we call computers.

cyberspace   Science fiction writer William Gibson called it "a consensual hallucination . . . a graphic representation of data abstracted from the banks of every computer in the human system." You can get there simply by picking up the phone.

datacops   Any department or agency charged with protecting data security. Most notoriously: the U.S. Secret Service, whose 1990 Operation Sundevil launched constitutionally questionable predawn raids on computer hackers in a dozen U.S. cities and provoked international outrage in the cyberpunk community.

dystopia   Utopia's evil twin. Merriam-Webster defines it as "an imaginary place which is depressingly wretched and whose people lead a fearful existence."

ecstasy   Enthusiasts describe this New Age psychedelic, which heightens the senses, as "LSD without the hallucinations." The drug was outlawed in the United States in 1987.

flame-fest   Sociologists note that, without visual cues, people communicating online tend to flame: to state their views more heatedly than they would face to face.

William Gibson   Gibson knows precious little about cybernetic technology. When the success of *Neuromancer* enabled him to buy his own computer, he was surprised to discover that it had a disk drive. "I had been expecting an exotic crystalline thing. What I got was a little piece of a Victorian engine that makes noises like a scratchy old record player."

hypertext   In this article, words printed in bold are defined or expanded upon in this glossary. In a computer hypertext article, electronic footnotes like these actually pop up on the screen whenever you point your cursor at a "hot" word and click the button on your mouse.

industrial   Mixing rhythmic machine clanks, electronic feedback, and random radio noise, industrial music is "the sounds our culture makes as it comes unglued," says cyberpunk writer Gareth Branwyn.

Internet   The successor of an experimental network built by the U.S. Defense Department in the 1960s, the Internet links computers around the world. Users can connect to the Internet by phone to share information or tap into data banks.

Interzone   The wasteland setting of William Burroughs' novel *Naked Lunch* (1959) has become a favorite haunt for cyberpunk writers. It is here, in Gibson's words, that "the street finds its own uses for things," subverting cutting-edge technology to suit the needs of the underground.

Timothy Leary   Before his death in 1996, the ex-Harvard professor who encouraged a generation to "turn on, tune in, drop out" counted himself a cyberpunk. "The PC is the LSD of the 1990s," he said.

microsofts   Without apologies to the software company by the same name, Gibson has his fictional characters alter their reality by plugging into their brain these angular fragments of colored silicon, which house a read-only memory chip.

Mondo 2000   *Mondo* is Italian for "world"; 2000 is the year. Says editor R. U. Sirius: "I like the idea of a magazine with an expiration date."

Negativland   Better known for media pranks than records (*Helter Stupid*), this band canceled a tour in 1988 after a Minnesota teen axed his family to death. The band's press release said the family had been arguing about Negativland's song *Christianity Is Stupid*. The story was a hoax, but the press ran with it, turning the band into cyberpunk heroes.

punk   Cyberculture borrows heavily from the rebellious attitude of punk music, sharing with such groups as the Sex Pistols a defiance of mainstream culture and an urge to turn modern technology against itself.

rants   A hyperbolic literary form favored by cyberpunk writers, these extended diatribes make up in attitude what they lack in modesty.

raves   Organized on the fly (sometimes by electronic mail) and often held in warehouses, raves are huge, nomadic dance parties that tend to last all night, or until the police show up. Psychedelic mood enhancers and funny accessories (white cotton gloves, face masks) are optional.

simstim decks   These simulated stimuli machines are what television might evolve into. Rather than just watching your favorite characters on TV, you strap some plastic electrodes to your forehead and experience their thoughts and feelings—slightly edited, of course, to spare you the headaches and hangovers.

smart drugs   "Don't eat any of that stuff they say will make you smarter," says Bruce Sterling. "It will only make you poorer."

synesthesia   From the Greek *syn* ("union") and *esthesia* ("sensation"), synesthesia is a merging of sensory input in which sounds appear as colors in the brain or words evoke a specific taste or smell.

techno–erotic paganism   Sound intriguing? That's probably why the editors of *Mondo 2000* put the term on the cover of their book. Unfortunately, they never get around to explaining what it means.

temporary autonomous zones   These are the electronic analog of mountain fortresses and pirate islands, but they can be formed or dismantled in a flash, says cyberpunk essayist Hakim Bey. As political systems decay and networking becomes more widespread, he envisions a proliferation of autonomous areas in cyberspace: giant worker-owned corporations, independent enclaves devoted to data piracy, Green–Social Democrat collectives, anarchist liberation zones, etc.

time machines   Anyone who has read H. G. Wells or seen *Back to the Future* knows how these things are supposed to work. Certain obscure results of Einstein's relativity theory suggest that there could actually be shortcuts through the space–time continuum, but it's unlikely that a human could squeeze through them.

Turing police   British mathematician Alan Turing predicted in 1950 that computers would someday be as intelligent as humans.

virtual communities   Collections of like-minded people who meet online and share ideas on everything from politics to punk rock. The global village is full of tiny electronic subdivisions made up of cold-fusion physicists, white supremacists, gerontologists, and Grateful Deadheads. Like any other community, each has its own in-jokes, cliques, bozos, and bores.

virtual reality   An interactive technology that creates an illusion, still crude rather than convincing, of being immersed in an artificial world. The user generally dons a computerized glove and a head-mounted display equipped with a TV screen for each eye. Now available as an arcade game.

virtual sex   The way it would work, says Howard Rheingold, is that you slip into a virtual reality bodysuit that fits with the "intimate snugness of a condom." When your partner (lying somewhere in cyberspace) fondles your computer-generated image, you actually feel it on your skin, and vice versa. Miniature sensors and actuators would have to be woven into the clothing by a technology that has yet to be invented.

The WELL   Compared with 20 million-plus member networks such as America Online, the Northern California–based Whole Earth 'Lectronic Link is a tiny outpost in cyberspace. But its thousands of subscribers include an unusual concentration of artists, activists, journalists, and other writers. "It has a regional flavor," says cofounder Stewart Brand. "You can smell the sourdough."

RELATED LINKS

- The Cyberpunk Top 100 Sites (http://www.topsitelists.com/area51/cyberjunk/topsites.html)

- The Timothy Leary Home Page (http://www.leary.com/index_top.html)

- Resources on William Gibson (http://www.lib.loyno.edu/bibl/wgibson.htm)

- The WELL (http://www.thewell.org)

- *Wired* Magazine (http://www.wired.com/wired/current.html)

FOR FURTHER RESEARCH

To find out more about the topics discussed in this reading, use InfoTrac College Edition. Type in keywords and subject terms such as "cyberpunk," "computer culture," and "cyberspace." You can access InfoTrac College Edition from the Wadsworth/Thomson Communication Cafe homepage: http://communication.wadsworth.com.

9

Media Acceleration and the Increasing Velocity of Everyday Life

Reading 9-1

Prest-o! Change-o!

James Gleick

EDITOR'S NOTE

The remote control exemplifies the principle of unintended consequences, the tendency of new media and communication technologies to have social impacts that weren't anticipated. In this reading, writer James Gleick traces the acceleration of media, especially television and film, to the influence of the remote control and music television. Ironically, our antiboredom devices and ever-quickening production values often diminish program satisfaction, encouraging channel grazing and further reducing already shortened attention spans.

CONSIDER

1. What was the original problem that the remote control was meant to solve? Has it solved this problem, or has it only made things worse?

2. Is the accumulation of speed, and in particular the acceleration of media, a one-way street in cultural evolution, as Gleick claims?

3. What did NBC's 2000 Unit, and all the other TV networks, do to retain the drop-off in audience that would occur at the end of a typical show?

We have acquired various handheld antiboredom devices: chiefly, the "remote." Television watchers jump from channel to channel, and filmmakers copy that by jumping from scene to scene. The more we jump, the more we get—if not more quality, then at least more variety. Saul Bellow, naming our mental condition "an unbearable state of distraction," decided the remote control was a principal villain.

> Pointless but intense excitement holds us, a stimulant powerful but short-lived. Remote control switches permit us to jump back and forth, mix up beginnings, middles, and ends. Nothing happens in any sort of order. . . . Distraction catches us all in the end and makes mental mincemeat of us.[1]

When the first remote controls appeared in the 1950s, as luxury add-ons for television sets, they seemed like innocent devices that would save viewers occasional trips from the bed or sofa to the television set. They were pitched at the lazy or infirm. "Prest-o! Change-o! Remote control tuning with 'Lazy Bones' station selector," said a Zenith advertisement. "Amazing!" The inventors and marketers thought the primary purpose of their device would be to turn the set *off* as the user drifted toward sleep. Secondary uses, they thought, could include silencing commercials and, sure, changing channels, presumably once or twice an evening, when programs ended. (*Consumer Reports,* comparing the first models, sniffed that the magazine "did not test, though it recommends judicious use of, a simple built-in control device present on every television and radio set known as the 'off-switch.'"[2]) Marketers tried not-so-subtle appeals to masculine gun and control fetishism—users could "zap" with the "Flash-Gun" and "Space Commander." No one imagined the real power waiting in the remote control. The advertising and commentary of the '50s shows that it was not seen as a time-saving device in any sense. Nor did anyone think in terms of amplifying the television experience with dozens or thousands of channel changes per evening. Most households could get just three to five channels; how could they imagine the remote-meisters

waiting a generation up the road, using their wands to create on-the-go montages, nightly sound-and-light shows?

Now every television programmer works in the shadow of the awareness that the audience is armed. The remote control serves as an instant polling device, continually measuring dissatisfaction or flagging attention, if not for Nielsen's benefit then for your own. Possession of the device means that you have a choice to make every second. *Is this dull? Am I bored yet?*

The remote control is a classic case of technology that exacerbates the problem it is meant to solve. As the historian of technology Edward Tenner puts it: "The ease of switching channels by remote control has promoted a more rapid and disorienting set of images to hold the viewer, which in turn is leading to less satisfaction with programs as a whole, which of course promotes more rapid channel-surfing." If only the programmers could tie your hands . . . for your own good! Still, isn't possession of the remote a form of power? It does serve you, as a weapon against bad programming, even if the audience does not always use it wisely. Robert Levine, a social psychologist, cites studies that find "grazers" changing channels twenty-two times a minute. "They approach the airwaves as a vast smorgasbord, all of which must be sampled, no matter how meager the helpings," Levine writes.[3] He contrasts these frenetically greedy Westerners—Americans, mostly—with Indonesians, "whose main entertainment consists of watching the same few plays and dances, month after month, year after year," and with Nepalese Sherpas, who eat the same meals of potatoes and tea through their entire lives. The Indonesians and Sherpas are perfectly satisfied, Levine says.

Are they really? Will they spurn that remote control when it is offered? Or is the accumulation of speed, along with the accumulation of variety, along with the accumulation of wealth, a one-way street in human cultural evolution?

Broadcasters have to worry about this, and they believe it means they must be more efficient than ever in their use of time. Just as the technology of remote control has made it possible for you to run from boredom without leaving the couch, the Nielsen technologies have made it possible for television programmers to detect the first glimmerings of ennui, apathy, and listlessness almost before you yourself become aware of them. A minute is an ocean. At NBC, John Miller, executive vice president of advertising and promotion and event programming, explains just how fine-grained the decision making has become. "Every station looks at every second of air time and uses it to the best of their ability," he says. "We're all bound by the laws of physics. There are only 24 hours in a day and 60 minutes in an hour and 60 seconds in a minute. Everybody looks at their time with a microscope to get the best utilization they can. It is the only real estate we have." One piece of news turned up by NBC's research dismayed the programmers: as a typical show reached its end and the credits began to roll, one viewer in four, with a remote control presumably in hand, would give in to the urge to press the Channel Up or Channel Down button. A full 25 percent of the audience would start flipping around. That was clearly intolerable. A 25 percent drop in market share in return for gratifying the egos of the cast and crew? The NBC 2000 unit addressed this problem by creating what is known as the squeeze-and-tease: the credits are compressed into one-third of the screen (carefully tested for borderline readability) while the remaining two-thirds is used for "promotainment." You might see stars bantering about and around the peacock.

If you actually take in the screenwriter's name on the right *and* chuckle at the wisecrack on the left, you are multitasking. Anyway, every network has quickly adopted the same technique, because it is just enough, it seems, to hold your attention for the critical 10 or 30 seconds that would otherwise loom before you like an eternity.

The network's time obsession has changed the basic structure of standard shows like the 30-minute (23-minute, really) situation comedy. Network programmers feel they can no longer afford the batch of commercials that used to separate the end of one show from the beginning of the next. So those commercials have moved inside the shows, creating little islands of program at the beginning and the end, cut off by several minutes from the main body. Clever writers use these for stand-alone opening jokes and codas. "It's jokes and story right from the git-go—jump in and go," says Skip Collector, editor of *Seinfeld*. "That kind of relates to our lifestyle and our pace, everybody's rushing and going and that's what we're going to do." *Seinfeld* was one show that used the split-screen closing credit time for a final joke, rather than give it up for promotainment. It also dispensed with the traditional half-minute or so of opening titles: Mary Tyler Moore throwing her hat in the air week after week, or Cosby's family dancing around. More and more sitcoms just start with running story and flash a 3- to 5-second art card with the name of the show.

At least the major networks still program their airtime around the quaint assumption that viewers will arrive on the hour and half-hour and stay more or less in place. Many cable television channels have abandoned that idea. Like parents giving up on mealtime and leaving an assortment of snacks in the refrigerator, they design their programming for a perpetually restless clientele. E! Entertainment, for example, passes the minutes with a pastiche of clips, interviews, promotional tapes, and similar fare, all designed to be glittering enough to hold the attention of channel surfers whenever they happen to drop in. One of its features is *Talk Soup,* a compilation of brief moments from other networks' talk shows, as if talk shows weren't already in soundbite territory. We're reaching the level of distillation of an abridgement of a sampler of a *Reader's Digest*. Every meal a tasting menu. Sometimes the miniaturization is the joke. Nickelodeon's TV Land channel squeezed in Sixty-Second Sitcoms, complete with opening and closing credits, a tiny commercial, and time for, on average, two gags.

All these channels fill the gaps that used to be dead air by playing instances of a new miniature art form: "promos," "opens," "bumpers," and "channel IDs." NBC alone commissions 8,000 different promos a year. They range from 10 seconds to the "long form" 2 minutes, and they represent an astounding deployment of technical sophistication, products of a marriage between computers and the visual arts. In the early 1980s independent designers with new computer-graphics systems, a Paintbox and a Harry, could suddenly produce complex animated effects in an hour that had previously taken a full day. With the ability to compose effects frame by frame, to create multiple layers, images dissolving into new images, designers know that the viewer cannot always keep up. But they can't always help themselves. If the technology lets them add layers, they tend to add layers. Some of the power of these bits of video lies purely and simply in their speed—the length of time between cuts is steadily decreasing, to the point that we routinely absorb sequences of shots lasting eight frames, a third of a second, or less. For someone creating a 10-second channel ID that will be seen over and over again, an effect that cannot be parsed on first sight by a typical couch-bound viewer is not necessarily a bad thing. Designers sometimes don't know or care whether the viewers will actually see a four-frame image. It's an impression. Maybe they'll see more on the next viewing. A flashed image can be like a subtle allusion in a long poem, resonating just below the threshold of comprehension.

MTV ZOOMS BY

People who revile the evolution of a fast-paced and discontinuous cutting style—and, for that matter, people who like it—have a convenient three-letter shorthand for the principal villain: MTV. The most influential media consultant of modern times, Tony Schwartz, offers this doctrine of perception:

> The ear receives fleeting momentary vibrations, translates these bits of information into electronic nerve impulses, and sends them to the brain. The brain "hears" by registering the current vibration, recalling the previous vibrations, and expecting future ones. We never hear the continuum of sound we label as word, sentence, or paragraph. The continuum never exists at any single moment in time.[4]

Schwartz put his theories to work in some of the most famous political spots of the last generation, from the watershed 1964 anti-Goldwater commercial—a girl counting daisy petals juxtaposed with a nuclear explosion—to the fast-cut Read My Lips commercial that damaged George Bush in 1992. Schwartz sits now amid a treasure-house of aging tapes and memorabilia on the first floor of his Manhattan townhouse. He was one of the inventors of the supercompressed video montage—a 2- or 3-minute bit of film combining hundreds of nearly subliminal images of, say, the year in review. When the Cable News Network was new, its founder, Ted Turner, wanted shorter commercials to match the brisk pace of his 2-minute newscasts. The 30-second commercial, a bold innovation that had swept dizzyingly across the networks in 1971, somehow no longer seemed quite so swift. Turner hired Schwartz, who took a set of 30-second spots and cut them down to 8 seconds, 7 seconds, 5 seconds. Now Schwartz looks at his watch and says, "I could do a . . . let me see . . ." —apparently he is playing something back in his head—"3-second commercial that would outsell any of them." He feeds a cassette into one of a rack of videotape players and, sure enough, 3-second commercials: one or two quick images plus catchphrase. "Got a headache? Come to Bufferin." "You can see why Cascade's the better buy. Try Cascade." "As long as you've been taking pictures, you've trusted them to one film."

War and Peace it wasn't. But now even Schwartz is complaining about his up-to-date colleagues: "They see the stuff that's on MTV and they imitate that."

At MTV, the creative decision makers offer no apologies. A company fact sheet asserts, as a kind of slogan, "MTV zooms by in a blur while putting things in focus at the same time." Music Television began broadcasting in the summer of 1981, with the Buggles singing, appropriately enough, "Video Killed the Radio Star," followed by the Who, the Pretenders, Rod Stewart, and others in hybrid blends of music, images of musicians performing, and other rapidly intermixed images, real or surreal, related to the music or not, but always *cut* to the music. The basic MTV unit was a 3-minute movie created around a song. You might have been forgiven for thinking it was meant as a sort of wallpaper, something to put on in the background when you didn't want to watch television. Wasn't it really a descendant of television's Yule Log, burning away eternally at Christmas before a fixed camera while carols played on the audio track? Certainly the music video was premised on short attention spans. It is a 3-minute format within which no single shot is likely to last more than a second or two. MTV soon became one of the United States' foremost cultural exports, playing to 270 million households, including those reached by satellites over Southeast Asia, Mexico, and South America. Besides music videos—which evolved into a fantastically crisp and artful genre—the network has sent out its own talk shows, dance shows, pick-a-date game shows, and, most intriguingly, animated cartoons, like the famous, dim-witted, super-ironic *Beavis and Butthead*.

The not-so-hidden premise of *Beavis and Butthead* is that even music videos are slow paced and boring, so you need an overlay of comic commentary. In their own way, though, Beavis and Butthead are painfully slow—MTV going conventional and letting story, rather than music, dictate the pace. The MTV animation style is deliberately static; it makes the typical Disney feature look like a madcap action film. The dialogue staggers along as if through mud, and the comedy relies heavily on reaction shots (so standardized that the animators call them by name: Wide-Eyed 1, Wide-Eyed 2, This Sucks).

"We love pauses—pauses are like, hey!" says Yvette Kaplan, supervising director, as a bit of tape makes its way through the editing room, a segment involving an impotency clinic. "Oh, yeah," Butthead is saying in the sequence now running over and over again through the editor's screen. "Huh-huh. Me, too. Huh-huh. Maybe that place can help us score."

Of all the visual arts, animation takes the tightest control of every fraction of every second. On carefully diagrammed sheets, each consonant and vowel of each word is assigned to its precise one-twenty-fourth of a second frame. The characters' mouth movements have been reduced to an essential grammar of just seven or eight basic positions, enough to cover all English speech. This particular joke strikes the team in the editing room as . . . slow. There seems to be a lag in the line. "The pacing is everything," Kaplan says. "When it's flowing, it's just safer—you don't have time to drift away and miss the humor." They delete the "me, too" and nudge the pace forward a bit more by overlapping the final fraction of a second of the sound track with the visual track for the next scene. Alternatively, they might have jumped to the next scene's dialogue before cutting away visually, or they might have started the music for the next scene early—clever pacing techniques that viewers have learned to interpret automatically and unconsciously.

"The audience has gotten more sophisticated and you can take certain leaps without people scratching their heads," says Abby Terkuhle, president of MTV animation. And of course, we're starting young. "It's intuitive," he says. "Our children are often not thinking about A, B, C. It's like, okay, I'm there, let's go! It's a certain nonlinear experience, perhaps."

NOTES

1. Saul Bellow, "An Unbearable State of Distraction." Public address to the John F. Kennedy School of Government, Harvard University, November 9, 1989. [Available: http://mirror.shnet.edu.cn/harvard/www.ksg.harvard.edu/ksgpress/ksg_news/transcripts/bellow.htm]

2. *Consumer Reports,* November 1955, p. 53.

3. Robert Levine, *A Geography of Time: The Temporal Misadventures of a Social Psychologist.* New York: Basic Books, 1997, p. 45.

4. Tony Schwartz, *The Responsive Chord.* Garden City, NY: Anchor Press/Doubleday, 1974, p. 12.

RELATED LINKS

- *Faster* Web Site (http://www.fasterbook.com)
- James Gleick's Web Site (http://www.around.com)
- Remote Control Device (http://www.mbcnet.org/ETV/R/htmlR/remotecontro/remotecontro.htm)
- Zapping (http://www.mbcnet.org/ETV/Z/htmlZ/zapping/zapping.htm)

FOR FURTHER RESEARCH

To find out more about the topics discussed in this reading, use InfoTrac College Edition. Type in keywords and subject terms such as "NBC 2000 Unit," "squeeze and tease," and "media acceleration." You can access InfoTrac College Edition from the Wadsworth/Thomson Communication Cafe homepage: http://communication.wadsworth.com.

Reading 9-2

NoChores.com
Jared Sandberg*

EDITOR'S NOTE

Amazon.com and eBay brought online shopping into the mainstream. But a new wave of online delivery services promises to transform the way city dwellers take care of life's daily chores, from shopping for groceries to developing family photos to dropping off dry cleaning. Why hassle with a trip to the store when the store can come to you? Running "virtual errands" may cost a little more, but for those with room in their budgets, the extra expense can be offset by time saved. Newsweek *took note of this trend when it surfaced in the domestic landscape of urban environments in the summer of 1999, noting its time-saving appeal. Consolidation in the online delivery service market has since occurred with the dot-com bust, but many services have survived. Ordering a pizza has never been easier.*

CONSIDER

1. What household and convenience services is the Web well suited to provide? What services seem poorly suited for the Web?

2. Will the online world's dependence on the industrial world for transportation and delivery of goods ever change? Why or why not?

3. If online delivery services become popular in urban areas, how might that affect the character of big-city living?

New York City bike messengers face down death every day. Growling trucks threaten to flatten them. Taxis dart about them like sharks. None of this fazes Sasha Lowe, a 31-year-old film student who feints and dodges his way through the city dispensing videos. Riding a crummy 10-speed, he swerves around an opening car door and narrowly misses a bus lurching blindly from the curb. "If you think too much, you lose it," he says. And then it starts to rain.

Not exactly the work that springs to mind when you're talking about e-commerce and the Web. But Sasha is the bleeding edge of one of the fastest-growing segments of the Internet—the push to deliver services online, straight to the front door. We're not talking books and Amazon.com here. No, this is about the basic chores of daily life, taken off our hands by a galaxy of fresh digital start-ups like Kozmo.com. Feel like watching a movie tonight? Sit down at your keyboard and browse the virtual aisles of what amounts to your local video store, open until 1 A.M. Click a few keys, and within moments one of a hundred messengers like Sasha Lowe is speeding his way to you—guaranteeing delivery within an hour of anything from Casablanca to Austin Powers, all for $4.33.

And it's not just movies. These days, just about anyone living in a major city can get groceries delivered from Peapod. You can order ready-to-cook filet mignon from CookExpress. Streamline.com will do everything from pick up and repair your shoes to drop off your dry cleaning or get your family photos developed. No problem. Just let your fingers do the walking.

Of course, the real sales pitch here is convenience. Anything that can be delivered can be sold online, at least as these merchants of convenience see it. Online grocery store Webvan has moved into office supplies and beauty aids. Along with movies, Kozmo sells jumbo-size movie candy, popcorn, and Ben & Jerry's ice cream, not to mention a decent selection of books, magazines, and CDs. Future plans include beer and wine, sandwiches from New York's upscale Cosi eatery, and, God bless 'em, Krispy Kreme doughnuts. "I envision Kozmo as the Home Shopping Network on steroids," says Joseph Park, Kozmo's 27-year-old founder, sketching out a bazillionaire's vision as he peels the wrapper off an ice-cream bar.

Lots of folks expected biggies like Microsoft and AOL to grab this turf. Vying for the 80 percent of people's income that is spent locally, they poured hundreds of millions of dollars into developing digital "city guides" stuffed with restaurant and theater reviews. Only recently have they enabled people to buy tickets to a Broadway show instead of just reading about it. When it comes to the essence of e-commerce, says Boston Consulting Group's Michael Hansen, "they missed the boat." People don't want to surf the Web aimlessly, he argues. "They want convenience and commerce. They want the ability to get stuff done."

Microsoft and its ilk are pushing back into this arena. Obviously, taking the schlep out of shopping has immense appeal. If you're one of the 80 million Americans who sit in front of a computer every day, it's clearly easier to flit over to a Web site than drive to a store short on parking. By the time you get to the video store to rent *Shakespeare in Love,* the local chain is likely

---

"NoChores.com," by Jared Sandberg. From *Newsweek,* August 30, 1999, pp. 64–66. Copyright © 1999 Newsweek, Inc. All rights reserved. Reprinted with permission.

*With Bret Begun in New York.

out of stock. Online, you just order it in the morning (when the inventory is full) and ask for delivery that evening. At online supermarkets, you can shop from last week's saved grocery list. Or avoid shopping altogether by telling the store to automatically send you, say, toilet paper every week.

Done well, the results can be impressive. CookExpress.com, for instance, bills itself as the service that "shops, chops, minces, dices, and delivers." The San Francisco company ships out ready-to-cook meals for same-day delivery across the Bay Area—and overnight for the rest of the country. For $37.95, *Newsweek* tested it. Roughly 24 hours after we clicked in our order, a foam box packed with ice showed up at our door in Manhattan: an order of pan-roasted halibut for two in a tomato vinaigrette with roasted potatoes. It took about 20 minutes to heat up the carefully packaged ingredients. Verdict: not bad. Our next order, mustard chicken on spaetzle, was even better. The service even correctly transcribed the optional gift card, in German: Was ist das, der spaetzle? Company founder Darby Williams says the company searches for meals whose success depends on painstaking preparation of the sort that would make "your eyes glaze over." That way, CookExpress does the work. You take the credit.

It's not all wine and roses. Having to return some of this stuff isn't always easy. Sometimes you're at the mercy of glitchy technology. Katherine Pitta, a 25-year-old resident of Concord, California, likes the Webvan grocery store, but certain items from her orders sometimes don't show up. "They had server problems," she moans. And while the number of online delivery services swells in big cities, there aren't so many in the suburbs and fewer in small towns.

That will change. Streamline, for one, currently delivers only to people in Boston and its environs. Come fall, though, it will expand to Washington, DC, and to other regions after that. Like other services that are fast going regional, if not yet national, it is essentially an electronic homemaker. For $30 a month, the company sets up a dry storage box, partly refrigerated, in a subscriber's driveway. Every Wednesday or Friday, it stocks the box with whatever you've ordered, from groceries to videos to bottled water and meals from Boston's renowned Legal Seafood restaurants. Linda Godfrey, a 39-year-old mother of three in Needham, Massachusetts, loves it. Streamline provides her groceries every week—automatically sending stuff she always needs, like paper towels. It picks up and drops off her dry cleaning, delivers her Poland Spring water, sends her film to be processed, and even takes care of her recycling. It's not cheaper, but the service spares the stress of packing her kids along on errands. "It's just so peaceful," she says. If only the company would take her trash to the dump. "Once Streamline does that," she dreams aloud, "I'm set."

She may not have long to wait. Meantime, she could try www.trashpickup.com. Really.

RELATED LINKS

- Food.com (http://www.food.com)

- Grocery Delivery Services (http://www.zeal.com/Online_Shopping/Food___Drink/Markets/Grocery_Delivery_Services)

- RestaurantResults.com: Internet Delivery Service (http://restaurantresults.com/restaurants/003g.html)

- Webvan.com (http://www.webvan.com)

FOR FURTHER RESEARCH

To find out more about the topics discussed in this reading, use InfoTrac College Edition. Type in keywords and subject terms such as "online delivery services," "Web shopping," and "virtual errands." You can access InfoTrac College Edition from the Wadsworth/Thomson Communication Cafe homepage: http://communication.wadsworth.com.

Reading 9-3

Talk, Type, Read E-mail: Th

Amy Harmon

EDITOR'S NOTE

We all know the type, the friend who refuses to focus on one activity—or conversation—at a time, who must be occupied with multiple media simultaneously, who watches television while talking on the cell phone while fidgeting with a laptop, Palm Pilot, or Game Boy. As this reading explains, multitasking—the capacity of a microprocessor to keep several computer programs running at the same time—has lately become a way of life for a growing number of people. While multitaskers seem to thrive off their parallel diversions, adapting the rhythms of their own behavior to match that of their machines, their conduct places everyone else on the receiving end of a permanent call waiting. With technology, social behavior both fractures and accelerates; in the end, something more than time may be lost.

CONSIDER

1. What sorts of communications media seem to lend themselves to multitasking, and why?

2. To what extent is multitasking now a way of life for people who are "wired"? Can you think of any "quality of life" issues associated with constant multitasking?

3. Based on your personal experience, how many tasks can most people engage in at once and still be effective?

It's hard for Michael Redd to say just when doing one thing at a time became so deeply dissatisfying. His ratings with customers have certainly soared since he started responding to their e-mail as soon as it chimes in, no matter if he is on the phone or eating lunch or poring over a spreadsheet on some other screen.

But his fondness for multitasking is not limited to the workplace. Redd, a 30-year-old manager at McDonald's corporate office in Oak Ridge, Illinois, is happiest when his attention is most divided, like on a recent weekend afternoon when he watched a movie on television while talking to his sister and writing on his laptop. During commercial breaks, he flipped through his CD jukebox with a remote control, searching for a song whose name he had forgotten.

"I need to be able to do many things at once all the time," Redd said. "This may sound strange, but it makes me feel better."

Actually, it doesn't sound so strange. Multitasking—the word describes how a microprocessor keeps

lots of computer programs running at the same time—has lately become a way of life for many Americans. Inundated with more information than ever before and—perhaps perversely—prone to equate productivity with pleasure, many people are quietly adapting the rhythms of their own behavior to match that of their machines.

As a result, the number of tasks to which people are simultaneously applying themselves is multiplying like some mutant breed of postmodern rabbit. The shift is driven by the seductive suggestion implicit in the latest high-tech tools that they can be used not only for the pedestrian purposes of communication and information retrieval but also to swindle time.

Some, like Redd, thrill to the challenge of prying more minutes out of a day. Others decry the increasing fragmentation of mind and soul that the technology seems to demand. But as the trill of cellular phones and beepers and signals for arriving e-mail have grown more persistent, they have also become harder to ignore.

"You can't be as focused," said Adam Gwosdof, 31. When Gwosdof uses pay phones, he finds a bank of them where he can monopolize two lines at once—one to listen to his messages and one to call the people who have left them. "You feel like you're always trying

to c...
said.
time... ...hat it is. It's knowing I can't ever be done or shut things out."

Gwosdof runs a database design business in Manhattan and often finds himself being paged by one client while meeting with another and using the Internet to check on a third. He prefers to work on five projects at once so he can plug gaps of time that might otherwise be wasted. He insists that he can scan Internet newsgroups "subconsciously" while he talks to friends on the phone.

But Gwosdof has been rethinking the way his life is structured. He recently attended a seminar on time management, although he arrived late and left early.

"We can't just jump back and forth hundreds of times without it taking a toll on the psyche," he said, returning a reporter's page by using, he said, just one pay phone.

Inherently elastic and often covert, the true extent of human multitasking is difficult to measure, but anecdotal evidence abounds. "You know what, I have to go out, but I can do this from my car," said Toby Crabel, 43, preparing to respond to a reporter's inquiry on the subject. "I'll call you back in 3 minutes."

Crabel credits technology with allowing him to run a hedge fund out of his house in the middle of some cornfields northwest of Milwaukee. He has programmed his network of computers so that when he is reading to his daughter Kira, 8, he can be prompted by a digitized female voice that it is time to buy Treasury bonds.

Microsoft says the average office user of Windows 95 has more than three programs running at a time. At home, more than 10 million American households now have a television and a personal computer in the same room.

"This is not new, but it is accelerating," said John Robinson, director of a project at the University of Maryland devoted to gauging Americans' use of time. "You can't expand time, so what you try to do is deepen time by doing more things in the same period."

Less clear is multitasking's effects on the people who do it and those around them.

Consider the argument that erupts at least once a day between David Kohn and his fiancée, Natasha Lesser, who confer by phone from their respective Manhattan offices on such issues as what to have for dinner.

"It's the clicking sound that sets me off," said Kohn, 31. "Then she starts pausing between words."

Ms. Lesser, 29, an editor at Fodor's Travel Publications, said she has tried to restrain herself since it bothers him so much, but the fact is she has a lot of work to do. "Some of the things I have to do don't require me to think, so I feel, why can't I talk and do them at the same time? Otherwise I'd be here till 10 at night."

Nor is it entirely clear whether Kohn, who sits in front of a bank of sixteen televisions and a computer with a high-speed connection to the Internet for his job as a producer for the CBS Web site, is always as unwaveringly riveted to his conversations with Ms. Lesser as he makes out. The couple are still planning to get married in October. But both agree it is an ongoing problem. "We have discussed it," Kohn said. "At length."

To be sure, Americans are renowned for being obsessed with time, and multitasking was a time-honored human behavior well before Alt-Tab could zip you between, say, writing a newspaper article and reading up on a New York Police Department sex scandal in nary a microsecond. Women have long known about multitasking, as in the old song about bringing home the bacon, frying it up in a pan, and never, ever letting you forget you're a man. Some men have demonstrated a capacity to walk and chew gum at the same time. Others have not.

What is different now, modern multitaskers observe, is how closely human conduct is tied to our technological tools, particularly to the PC. The tasks we find ourselves attending to, however briefly, are often determined by what pops up on our screen. On either a PC or Macintosh, windows of one sort or another beg for us to open them. And since our computer manages to keep them all humming at the same time, why shouldn't we?

For one thing, computers do not actually do more than one thing at once. The genesis of computer multitasking was in the early 1960s, when John McCarthy, who was then a computer scientist at the Massachusetts Institute of Technology, suggested that instead of one person at a time feeding data from punch cards into a mainframe, fifty people could use the mainframe simultaneously. Every time a different user entered a command, the machine would stop what it was doing, store it, perform the new task—for perhaps a millisecond—and so on.

"The radical idea was that you could work at your own desk because the machine could tolerate constant interruption," said McCarthy, now a professor emeritus at Stanford University. "Even in those days, the machine could handle 100 instructions in 2.4 milliseconds so it was just a question of doing the arithmetic."

When mainframes shrank into PCs in the early 1980s, multitasking was temporarily forsaken. Until fairly recently, the most widely used computer operating systems did not allow more than one program to run at a time. But today PC's work on the same principle as the time-sharing schemes for the mainframe, albeit with only one user issuing many commands.

So while your computer seems to be downloading e-mail, spell-checking and playing solitaire with you at the same time, it is in fact doing each of them serially. It is, however, doing them really, really fast. A slow computer with a 100-megahertz processor can execute a million instructions between each pair of keystrokes by a very fast typist. And while a context switch—the computer term for saving one program in its current state while tending to another—requires a significant chunk of processing power, computers seem better able to weather the psychological toll of constant interruption.

"They switch faster than we do," said Earl Hunt, a professor of psychology and computer science at the University of Washington. "It's hard [for humans] to get around the forebrain bottleneck." It seems that although people can do some highly practiced tasks simultaneously, like juggling and riding a unicycle, in general they can pay attention to only one thing at a time without overtaxing short-term memory.

"Our brains function the same way the Cro-Magnon brains did, so technology isn't going to change that," Professor Hunt said. "You can do several tasks at once, but not all of them get done as well. That is why I feel that car phones are a bad idea."

Of course, not all jobs need to be done as well as others. One of the joys of multitasking, and perhaps one of its perils, is that it allows the blending of work and leisure in a way that was not possible before. Many multitaskers describe a sense of well-being that comes from the variety of tasks they are performing and the control they feel they exercise over which one comes first.

Ellen Ullman, author of *Close to the Machine,* about her life as a programmer [see Reading 11-3 for Ullman's view of Y2K], said she had tried to stop herself from sliding into the back-and-forth of multitasking on her computer at the expense of the softer-focus shifting of levels of attention more natural for humans.

"If you've ever watched someone who is a mother talk on the phone, feed the dog, bounce the baby, it's just astounding to see someone manage more or less well to do all those things," Ms. Ullman said. "But on a computer, multitasking is really binary. The task is either in the foreground or it's not. And now we are beginning to emulate the coarse-grain multitasking of computers that is a poor imitation of our own."

To the extent that multitasking depends on a certain prowess at filtering huge amounts of information without actually absorbing all of it, there is reason to believe that a generation that is growing up watching Celebrity Death Match on MTV while instant-messaging one another on America Online may be better at it than their elders. Observing the awesome multitasking skills of the younger traders at Bankers Trust, Marc Prensky, a vice president there, has advocated a new management approach for them.

"If people are really good at processing information from lots of different sources and you don't give it to them, you stifle them," said Prensky, an avid multitasker himself. "I think it's a real sea change. We should understand it first and then use it to our advantage."

For Jai Mani, an 11-year-old in Manhattan, it's all a bit simpler. The urge to multitask is like "a craving for food."

When he gets home from roller-blading camp, he wants to do three things. "Instead of listening to music for 30 minutes, watching TV for 30 minutes, and checking your e-mail for 30 minutes, you can do them all at the same time," said Jai, who has been known to watch television and keep an eye on his computer game in the high-gloss reflection of the piano while having a lesson. "It's just easier that way."

RELATED LINKS

- Americans' Use of Time Project (http://www.bsos.umd.edu/src/timeuse.html)

- Distractions of the Future (http://more.abcnews.go.com/sections/us/dailynews/distracteddriving010626.html)

- Multitasking Madness (http://www.contextmag.com/setFrameRedirect.asp?src=/archives/199809/InnerGameOfWork.asp)

■   PC-Webopaedia: Multitasking (http://www.pcwebopedia.com/TERM/M/multitasking.html)

 FOR FURTHER RESEARCH

To find out more about the topics discussed in this reading, use InfoTrac College Edition. Type in keywords and subject terms such as "multitasking," "time management," and "serial processing." You can access InfoTrac College Edition from the Wadsworth/Thomson Communication Cafe homepage: http://communication.wadsworth.com.

Reading 9-4

You Call This Progress? E-mail Has Become a Steady Drip of Dubious Prose, Bad Jokes, and Impatient Requests
Seth Shostak

EDITOR'S NOTE

Despite its many advantages, e-mail also has its downsides—and a growing number of detractors. In this reading, Seth Shostak, an astronomer at the SETI Institute in California, bemoans the "insistent arrogance" and "unstoppable proliferation" of e-mail messages that threaten to drown computer users everywhere in a sea of inelegant and unwanted communication. Masquerading as a better way to put everyone in touch, e-mail has instead morphed, in Shostak's view, into a steady drip of dubious prose, bad jokes, and impatient requests. Sometimes the phone seems like a better alternative.

CONSIDER

1. How does the "aggressive" nature of e-mail influence the pace, content, and tone of electronic messaging?

2. Do you agree with the author that e-mail has become "an incessant distraction, a nonstop obligation, and a sure source of stress and anxiety"? Why or why not?

3. On average, how much time do you spend writing and answering e-mail each day? Do you consider this time well spent?

It's as ubiquitous as winter damp, a pernicious miasma that brings rot and ruin to society's delicate underpinnings. I speak of e-mail, the greatest threat to civilization since lead dinnerware addled the brains of the Roman aristocracy.

A technical byproduct of the Internet, e-mail lets 10 million Americans pound out correspondence faster than you can say qwerty [the letters on the top left row of most keyboards]. One twitch of the finger is all it takes to dispatch missives to the next continent or the next cubicle at light speed. The result is a flood of what is loosely called "communication," a tsunami of bytes that is threatening to drown white-collar workers everywhere. Masquerading as a better way to put everyone in touch, e-mail has become an incessant distraction, a nonstop obligation, and a sure source of stress and anxiety. I expect that a public statement by the surgeon general is in the offing.

Mind you, e-mail started out cute and cuddly, an inoffensive spin-off from a government defense project. The technically inclined used it to send personal messages to colleagues without the need for a stamp or a wait. Only a small group of folks—mostly at universities—were plugged into this select network. The amount of traffic was manageable. E-mail was something to be checked every week or so. But technology marches on. Today access to the Internet is widespread, as common and accessible as a cheap motel. Everyone's wired, and everyone has something to say.

Unfortunately, this is not polite correspondence, the gentle art of letter writing in electronic form. E-mail is aggressive. It has a built-in, insistent arrogance. Because it arrives more or less instantaneously, the assumption is that you will deal with it quickly. "Quickly" might mean minutes, or possibly hours. Certainly not days. Failure to respond directly usually produces a second missive sporting the mildly critical plaint "Didn't you get my last e-mail?" This imperative for the immediate makes me yearn for old-style written communication, in which a week might lapse between inquiry and response. Questions and discussion could be considered in depth. A reply could be considered (or mentally shelved, depending on circumstance). Today, however, all is knee-jerk reaction.

In addition, there is the dismaying fact that electronically generated mail, despite being easy to edit, is usually prose at its worst. Of every ten e-mails I read, nine suffer from major spelling faults, convoluted grammar, and a stunning lack of logical organization—ASCII graffiti. For years I assumed this was an inevitable byproduct of the low student test scores so regularly lamented in newspaper editorials. Johnny can't read, so it's not surprising that he can't write either. But now I believe that the reason for all this unimpressive prose is something else: E-mail has made correspondents of folks who would otherwise never compose a text. It encourages messaging because it is relatively anonymous. The shy, the introverted, and the socially inept can all hunker down before a glowing computer and whisper to the world. This is not the telephone, with its brutally personal, audible contact. It's not the post, for which an actual sheet of paper, touched by the writer and displaying his imperfect calligraphic skills, will end up under the nose of the recipient. E-mails are surreptitiously thrown over an electronic transom in the dead of night, packaged in plain manila envelopes.

Still, it is not these esthetic debilities that make e-mail such a threat. Rather, it's the unstoppable proliferation. Like the brooms unleashed by the sorcerer's apprentice, e-mails are beginning to overwhelm those who use them. Electronic correspondence is not one to one. It is one to many, and that's bad news on the receiving end. The ease with which copies of any correspondence can be dispensed to the world ensures that I am "kept informed" of my coworkers' every move. Such bureaucratic banter was once held in check by the technical limitations of carbon paper. Now my colleagues just punch a plastic mouse to ensure my exposure to their thoughts, their plans, and the endless missives that supposedly prove that they're doing their jobs.

Because of e-mail's many-tentacled reach, its practitioners hardly care whether I'm around or not. I'm just another address in a list. So the deluge of digital correspondence continues irrespective of whether I'm sitting in my cubicle doing the boss's business or lying on the Côte d'Azur squeezing sand through my toes. Either way the e-mail, like a horde of motivated Mongolians, just keeps a-comin'. Vacations have lost their allure, and I hesitate to leave town. Consider: If I disappear for 2 weeks of rest and recreation, I can be sure of confronting screenfuls of e-mail upon my return. It's enough to make a grown man groan. The alternative is to take a laptop computer along, in the desperate hope of keeping up with e-mail's steady drip, drip, drip. Needless to say, there's something unholy about answering e-mails from your holiday suite. A friend recently told me that he can't afford to die: The e-mail would pile up and nobody could handle it.

Today I will receive fifty electronic messages. Of that number, at least half require a reply. (Many of the others consist of jokes, irrelevant bulletins, and important announcements about secret cookie recipes. I actually like getting such junk e-mails, as they allow the pleasure of a quick delete without guilt.) If I spend 5 minutes considering and composing a response to each correspondence, then 2 hours of my day are busied with e-mail, even if I don't initiate a single one. Since the number of Internet users is doubling about once a year, I expect that by the start of the new millennium, I—and millions like me—will be doing nothing but writing e-mails. The collapse of commerce and polite society will quickly follow.

I'm as much in favor of technology as the next guy. Personally, I think the Luddites should have welcomed the steam looms. But if you insist on telling me that e-mail is an advance, do me a favor and use the phone.

RELATED LINKS

- A Beginner's Guide to Effective E-mail (http://www.webfoot.com/advice/email.top.html)
- Internet Etiquette: Netiquette (http://www.udel.edu/interlit2/chapter5.html)
- The Online Disinhibition Effect (http://www.rider.edu/users/suler/psycyber/disinhibit .html)
- Test Your E-mail Etiquette (http://www.cnn.com/2000/TECH/computing/09/28/ email.manners.id g)
- Use Time Management to Reduce E-mail Madness (http://seattle.bcentral.com/seattle/ stories/2001/05/21/focus14.html)

FOR FURTHER RESEARCH

To find out more about the topics discussed in this reading, use InfoTrac College Edition. Type in keywords and subject terms such as "e-mail overload," "electronic correspondence," and "Internet relay chat." You can access InfoTrac College Edition from the Wadsworth/Thomson Communication Cafe homepage: http://communication.wadsworth.com.

SECTION IV

Social Impacts of Information and Communications Technologies

This section provides an overview of various social impacts of communication technology, focusing on the promises and paradoxes of networked computing as well as the criticisms of computer culture. The readings in Chapter 10 trace the development of the World Wide Web from its humble origins as a hypertext interface for research scientists in the early 1990s to the complex, multifaceted communication medium it has become today. When computers were introduced on a wide scale in business and in schools, it was hoped they would automatically solve efficiency problems and overcome educational hurdles. Instead, it took decades of investment and experimentation before economists started noticing real productivity gains from networked computing. Not surprisingly, improved productivity performance mirrors the growth and development of the World Wide Web. Businesses, it would appear, are finally reaping the benefits of distributed information technology. In schools, however, there still is no good evidence that most uses of computers significantly improve teaching and learning. The readings in Chapter 11 consider pessimistic, or dystopian, views of information technology that are critical of the "culture of computing." Perhaps no phenomenon better illustrates the perils of technological dependence than the Y2K computer scare, which resulted in minimal actual disruption but considerable pre-event anxiety. With information and data production at an all-time high, *information overload* persists as a contentious issue. Recent studies have also alleged that social pathologies are beginning to surface in cyberspace, notably the diagnosis of "Internet addiction" and the finding that substantial time spent online can lead to feelings of depression and loneliness. As these readings illustrate, there are no simple technological solutions to enduring social problems.

10

Networked Computing: Promises and Paradoxes

Reading 10-1

The World Wide Web Unleashed
John December

EDITOR'S NOTE

Since its introduction in the early '90s, the World Wide Web has revolutionized the media and personal communications landscape while transforming the way business is done. This reading from The World Wide Web Unleashed *by John December traces the origins of hypermedia, discusses the different forms that communication can take online, and describes the many communication functions the Web serves. Perhaps most importantly, December asserts, the Web gives people a way to develop new relationships with each other.*

CONSIDER

1. What were the proposals that led to the development of the Web, and who was associated with them?
2. Why does December consider the Web fundamentally to be a *communications* system as opposed to, say, a vast textual database or tool for commerce?
3. What are the different *levels* of communication that occur on the Web, and what distinct communication *functions* does the Web serve?

Few inventions in human history have captured as much attention as the World Wide Web. Emerging from technologies used in transmitting information over computer networks, the Web today is an important communication tool in the industrialized world. The Web is now part of world culture and commerce; companies use it, schools use it, governments use it, as do students, radicals, slackers, conservatives, teachers, poets, prisoners, the Pope, liberals, gardeners, cops, and even some dogs. To some, the Web represents a step toward the *information superhighway,* a phrase that up until 1994 had been full of hype and little substance.

Why has the Web assumed such a prominence in the communications landscape? Because people can use the Web to communicate with each other. It's not pure technology that drives the Web's success. The Web's possibilities as a communications system mean that you can use it to distribute information, communicate with others, and interact with other people or even software. There are those who love the bits and bytes of the technology that makes up the Web, but the Web involves much more. I don't think many people would put up with the expense and aggravation that it takes to participate in the Web—to spend the money on a computer, software, a modem, an Internet connection, and hours and hours of time—all in order to merely manipulate technology.

There's a lot to learn about the Web, but remember that the power of the Web all comes down to one word: communication. In this chapter, I want you to learn how the Web evolved and to appreciate the communication it makes possible.

WHAT IS THE WEB?

The Web is a communications system. Technically, the Web is a system for exchanging data over computer networks using special software. The Web can be used to transmit text and graphics. The Web gives people a chance to create and share information—to publish it, to broadcast it, and to accumulate it collaboratively with others. The Web thus gives people a way to create new relationships with each other.

The Web has become *the* way to organize the panoply of information, communication, and interaction on the global Internet. In fact, the Web has become so popular that many people forget that the Web is [simply] an application that uses the Internet for data communication.

The software that people use to browse and provide information on the Web has risen to such prominence that major software companies such as Microsoft consider Web software to be a key part of their strategic products and plans. The media content industry has similarly embraced the Web as a key part of its overall strategy for communicating with customers.

How has all this happened? If the Web is a communications system, where did it come from and why has it seemed to capture the imagination of many online technology users? Is there something compelling about the Web that will help it live beyond the hype it has experienced over the past years or will it burn out like the citizen's band radio craze of the 1970s? Or will it suffer the fate of the Picturephone, relegated to museums by the greater priorities of a new millennium?

WHERE DID THE WEB COME FROM?

Some say the Web started from a dream. Others say that its essential nature is nothing new and that humans have been communicating for centuries in the way the Web enables us to.

The technical origins of the system now known as the Web are in Switzerland. In March 1989, Tim Berners-Lee, a researcher at the Conseil Européen pour la Recherche Nucléaire (CERN) (European Laboratory for Particle Physics) in Geneva, Switzerland, proposed a system to enable efficient information sharing for members of the high-energy-physics community. Berners-Lee had a background in text processing, real-time software, and communications. He had previously developed a system that he called *Enquire* in 1980. Berners-Lee's 1989 proposal, called *HyperText and CERN,* circulated for comment. The important components of the proposal were the following:

- A user interface that would be consistent across all platforms and that would enable users to access information from many different computers

- A scheme for this interface to access a variety of document types and information protocols

- A specification for the storage of information in the form of documents with references, called "links," to other documents

By using the user interface, the user could follow these links and follow a variety of paths through the information. A set of documents organized this way is called *hypertext*. Berners-Lee was not the first person to propose hypertext, as you'll see.

By late 1990, an operating prototype of the Web ran on a NeXT computer, and a line-mode user interface (called *www*) was completed. The essential pieces of the Web were in place, although they were not widely available for network use.

In March 1991, the www interface was used on a network, and by May of that year it was made available on central CERN machines. The CERN team spread the word about their system throughout the rest of 1991, announcing the availability of the files in the Usenet newsgroup alt.hypertext on August 19, 1991, and to the high-energy-physics community through its newsletter in December 1991.

Berners-Lee's innovation didn't arise from a vacuum of ideas. Researchers had been working on hypertext systems for decades before 1989. In fact, it was Ted Nelson in 1965 who coined the term *hypertext* to characterize text that is not constrained to be sequential. Nelson's dream was Xanadu, a system to link all world literature with provisions for automatically paying royalties to authors. Key to the Xanadu system was the idea of linking information in nonhierarchical ways. These connections among information enable readers to follow links from one document to another, and document authors could create these links among existing documents.

BEFORE XANADU

Like Berners-Lee's idea of the Web, Nelson's idea of Xanadu was connected to previous ideas. The idea of associatively linking information via mechanical devices goes back to work done by the Director of the Office of Scientific Research who was responsible for the development of the first atomic bomb—Vannevar Bush. Having worked on calculating artillery firing tables, Bush knew the tediousness of routine calculations, and he proposed an analog computer. But Bush's main contribution to the roots of the Web was his July 1945 article, "As We May Think," in *The Atlantic*

Monthly (this article is available on the Web at http://www.isg.sfu.ca/~duchier/misc/bush/).

Bush called his system a *memex* (memory extension) and proposed it as a tool to help the human mind cope with information. Having observed that previous inventions had expanded human abilities to deal with the physical world, Bush wanted his memex to expand human knowledge in a way that took advantage of the associative nature of human thought. Bush's design for the memex involved technologies for recording information on film and mechanical systems for manipulation. Although the memex was never built, Bush's article defined, in detail, many concepts of associative linking within an information system.

However, the idea of presenting information in a fashion that is nonlinear did not start with the twentieth century or with computer scientists. The *Talmud*, an important document in the Jewish faith, includes commentaries and opinions of the first five books of the Bible. The *Talmud*'s organization contains commentary and commentaries on commentaries that extend from central paragraphs in the middle of the page. Also, footnotes as used in traditional paper texts have a relational, nonsequential quality that is similar to the spirit of hypertext. Certainly, fiction writers—everyone from James Joyce (*Finnegans Wake*), William Faulkner (*The Sound and the Fury*), and Julio Cortazar (*Hopscotch*)—have artistically represented the nonlinear nature of human experience in fiction.

One could argue that the Web reflects something more than just a technical ability to publish information globally or store and retrieve information. The Web might be another way to express the relatedness of ideas and words, something humans have been doing for thousands of years.

In the decades since Bush's 1945 article, ideas about the design of information systems as well as working computer systems emerged. In 1962, Doug Englebart began a project called Augment at the Stanford Research Institute. Augment's goal was to unite and cross-reference written material of many researchers into a shared document. One portion of the oN-Line System (NLS) included several hypertext features.

In 1965, Ted Nelson coined the term *hypertext* to describe text that is not constrained to be sequential. Hypertext, as described by Nelson, links documents to form a web of relationships that draws on the possibilities for extending and augmenting the meaning of a "flat" piece of text with links to other texts. Hypertext is thus more than just footnotes that serve as commentary or further information in a text; instead, hypertext extends the structure of ideas by making "chunks" of ideas available for inclusion in many parts of multiple texts.

Nelson also coined the term *hypermedia,* which is hypertext not constrained to be text. Hypermedia can include multimedia pictures, graphics, sound, and movies. In 1967, he proposed a global hypermedia system, Xanadu, that as mentioned above would link all world literature with provisions for automatically paying royalties to authors. Although Xanadu has never been completed, a Xanadu group did convene in 1979, and the project was bought and developed by Autodesk, Inc., from 1988 until the project was canceled in 1992. Afterward, Nelson reobtained the Xanadu trademark, and as of 1994 was working to develop the project further (see http://www.xanadu.net and Ted Nelson's home page at http://www.sfc.keio.ac.jp/~ted).

In 1967, a working hypertext system called Hypertext Editing System was operational at Brown University. Andries van Dam lead a team that developed the system, which was later used for documentation during the Apollo space missions at the Houston Manned Spacecraft Center. By 1985, another hypertext system, called Intermedia, came out of Brown University. It included bidirectional links and the possibility for different views of a hypertext, including a single node overview and an entire hypertext structure view called a web view.

In 1985, Xerox Palo Alto Research Center (PARC) (http://www.parc.xerox.com) introduced a system called NoteCards. Each node in NoteCards could contain any amount of information, and there were many types of specialized cards for special data structures.

Hypertext's stature as an important approach to information organization in industry and academia was marked in 1987, when the Association for Computing Machinery (http://www.acm.org) held its first conference on hypertext at the University of North Carolina. This was the same year that Apple Computer Corporation (http://www.apple.com) introduced its Hyper-Card system. Bundled free with each Macintosh computer sold, HyperCard became popular. Users organized the cards and stacks in HyperCard and took advantage of the possibilities for ordering the cards in various ways in the stack. Using HyperCard, people could quickly and easily create their own hypertext works. Because all other Macintosh users also had HyperCard, these works could be easily shared. This ease of creation and ease of sharing information la-

ter became important reasons why the Web became popular.

THE CONNECTION AT CERN
SPARKS AN IDEA IN THE USA

Many ideas from throughout history can converge in an inventor's mind. The ideas of Vannevar Bush, Ted Nelson, and others showed up in Tim Berners-Lee's proposal for the Web at CERN in 1989. This is when the Web was born; CERN was where most of the Web's character was formed—up until 1993.

In early 1993, a young undergraduate student at the University of Illinois at Urbana-Champaign named Marc Andreessen shifted attention to the United States. Working on a project for the National Center for Supercomputing Applications (NCSA), Andreessen led a team that developed an X Windows System browser for the Web called Mosaic. In alpha version, Mosaic was released in February 1993 and was among the first crop of graphical interfaces for the Web.

Mosaic—with its fresh look and graphical interface that presented the Web using a point-and-click design—fueled great interest in the Web. While Mosaic rose in popularity, Berners-Lee continued promoting the Web at CERN, presenting a seminar in February 1993 outlining the Web's components and architecture.

Communication using the Web continued to increase throughout 1993 as Mosaic's popularity increased. Data communication traffic from Web servers grew from 0.1 percent of the U.S. National Science Foundation Network (NSFNet) backbone traffic in March to 1 percent of the backbone traffic in September. Although it was not a complete measure of Web traffic throughout the world, the NSFNet backbone measurements give a sample of Web use. In September 1993, NCSA released the first (version 1.0) operational versions of Mosaic for the X Windows System, Macintosh, and Microsoft Windows platforms. By October, there were 500 known Web servers (versus 50 at the beginning of the year). During Mecklermedia's Internet World in New York City in 1993, John Markoff, writing on the front page of the business section of the *New York Times,* hailed Mosaic as the "killer app [application]" of the Internet. The Web ended 1993 with 2.2 percent of the NSFNet backbone traffic for the month of December.

In 1994, more commercial players got into the Web game. Companies announced commercial versions of

Web browser software, including Spry, Incorporated. Marc Andreessen and colleagues left the NCSA project in March to form, with Jim Clark (former chairman of Silicon Graphics), a company that later became known as Netscape Communications Corporation (http://home.netscape.com). By May 1994, interest in the Web was so intense that the first international conference on the World Wide Web, held in Geneva, overflowed with attendees. By June 1994, there were 1,500 known (public) Web servers.

By mid-1994, it was clear to the original developers at CERN that the stable development of the Web should fall under the guidance of an international organization. In July, the Massachusetts Institute of Technology (MIT) and CERN announced the World Wide Web Organization (which later became known as the World Wide Web Consortium, or W3C). Today, the W3C (http://www.w3.org) guides the technical development and standards for the evolution of the Web. The W3C is a consortium of universities and private industries, run by the Laboratory for Computer Science at MIT collaborating with CERN, the Institut National de Recherche en Informatique et en Automatique, and Keio University, with support from the U.S. Defense Advanced Research Projects Agency and the European Commission [Berners-Lee now serves as director of the W3C].

In 1995, the Web's development was marked by rapid commercialization and technical change. Netscape Communication's browser, called Netscape Navigator [and, later, Netscape Communicator], continued to include more Netscape-specific extensions of the Hypertext Markup Language (HTML), and issues of security for commercial cash transactions garnered much attention. By May 1995, there were more than 15,000 known public Web servers, a tenfold increase over the number from a year before. Many companies had joined the W3C by 1995, including AT&T, Digital Equipment Corporation, Enterprise Integration Technologies, FTP Software, Hummingbird Communication, IBM, MCI, NCSA, Netscape Communications, Novell, Open Market, O'Reilly & Associates, Spyglass, and Sun Microsystems.

THE SOCIAL EXPANSION OF THE WEB

Technical innovations throughout history have often failed because of their lack of social acceptance and use—for example, the picture phone and other technically "good ideas" that people simply never wanted and never used.

The Web doesn't seem doomed to the scrap heap. The Web appears to have caught on, at least among the technologically rich people and countries of the world, as part of the communications environment. From Wall Street (http://dowjones.com) to Wal-Mart (http://www.wal-mart.com), the Web has become part of communications culture. In the consumer world, the Web is routinely used to promote everything from Coca-Cola (http://www.cocacola.com) to movies (http://www.toystory.com).

Many businesses see the Web now as a key component of their work. As a key part of future business on the Web, the banking industry is gradually taking steps toward serving its customers online. Systems of "virtual cash" are in development that might create not only a widespread promotional market on the Web, but an actual market for trade. With financial payments, the Web is poised to become an even more important part of global communications and trade systems.

THE CULTURAL ROLE OF THE WEB

Neither Vannevar Bush's compulsively detailed description of the mechanics of his memex nor the gory technical details of the hypertext transport protocol reveal what the World Wide Web has brought to our culture. If you've not been living in a cave, you've heard and seen URLs (uniform resource locators), the naming scheme for referring to resources on the Web. If the cryptic syntax of URLs confuses you, you might have laughed along with David Letterman's fans when he satirically announced his own show's URL in an interview with Larry King as "WWW.com.com .com . . . . . com.com.diggedy.diggedy.dank .dot . . com.diggedy.www.com.Dave.com.com.DO" (actually, the uniform resource locator for David Letterman's *Late Show* on CBS is http://www.cbs.com/lateshow).

Letterman's satire of URLs and their ubiquity in many media is perhaps apt. The Web's URLs seem to appear everywhere—on T-shirts, hats, newspaper and magazine ads, radio spots, movie posters, television and radio commercials, promotional flyers, business cards, underwear, and tattoos. But the number of people who use the Web is a minority of the world's, and even the United States', population. Analysis by researchers at Vanderbilt University in 1996 put the number of Web users worldwide at around 20 million [today, there are an estimated 430 million users internationally, according to Nielsen Netratings]. Similarly, the face of the Web also isn't like the world's. The Georgia Tech surveys (http://www.cc.gatech.edu/gvu/user_surveys) reveal a Web that is mostly used by relatively old (average age 33 years), highly educated, white, American males.

The Web has opened up new cultural expressions, but these compete with all other forms of media for the scarcest resource on earth, the resource that no technology will ever make more of—human attention. The future of the Web will no doubt depend on its own value to people: If it doesn't provide compelling content, people won't use it, no matter what the flash of its technology.

WHAT GOOD IS THE WEB?

On the Web, you can read the current news, look up a book in a library catalog, check the weather, make airplane reservations, look at the current view of the Empire State Building, find college courses, read the *New York Times,* look up a word in a dictionary or thesaurus, locate stops on the Paris Metro, buy a book, incorporate a business, buy a CD, fall in love, dissect a frog, write to the President of the United States, sell advertising, look at cars, find out what's on CNN, look for a long-lost friend in phone directories, gamble, publish your own magazine, reserve a hotel room, rent a car, learn about Mediterranean architecture, find a job, or choose a college.

Today, many people find the Web a valuable way to connect to other people. Remember, the bottom line of the Web is *communication*. If you think about it just as a kind of vending machine, you won't see its full potential. The Web isn't just a publishing medium or a place to sell things, but a medium in which many kinds of communication contexts coexist simultaneously.

COMMUNICATION CONTEXTS
ON THE WEB

Communication on the Web can take many forms and can take place in many contexts. Different levels for communicating have evolved on the Web. These levels correspond, in many ways, to offline human communication contexts.

- *Interpersonal*. The Web enables users to create a home page, which typically conveys personal or professional information. The practice of creating a home page emerged from the technical necessity of defining the "default" page that a Web browser displays when you are requesting information from a Web server when only the host name or a host and directory name is given. Home pages are thus traditionally the top-level page for a server, organization, or individual. When created by individuals, home pages often reveal detailed personal information about their authors and are often listed in directories of home pages. Also, individuals often follow the tradition of linking to colleagues' or friends' pages, creating "electronic tribes." When used interpersonally, personal home pages offer one-to-one communication, although the technical operation of all pages on the Web is one-to-many.

- *Group*. Cliques of personal pages can define a particular Web "tribe" or group. Similarly, people can form associations on the Web that are independent of geography and focused on interest in a common topic. Subject-tree breakdowns of information on the Web often evolve from collaborative linking and the development of resource lists and original material describing a subject. Similarly, groups of people associate on the Web based on common interests in communication (a professional association, for example, that has a Web server to announce conferences or calls for participation in its publications). Web groups also can form around a focus on interaction based on social or professional discourse or symbolic exchange (perhaps nontextual) intended to define and indicate relationships in "play" systems, such as Web interfaces to Multiple User Dialogue/ Object-Oriented/Simulations (MU*s) or Web-based "chat" or conferencing systems.

- *Organizational*. Many servers appearing on the Web belong to an organization, not an individual, so the home page for a server often identifies the institution or organization that owns the server. In this way, the genre of the Campus-Wide Information System (CWIS) evolved on Web servers of educational institutions. Similarly, commercial, governmental, and nongovernmental organizations have followed the pattern established by CWIS to a large degree.

- *Mass.* Just as other media have been used for one-to-many dissemination of information (newspapers, radio, television), so too is the Web used for mass communication. Many commercial and noncommercial magazines and other publications are distributed through the Web. Moreover, as noted previously, all publicly available Web pages are potentially readable to anyone using the Web, and are thus potentially one-to-many communication.

The key concept to understand is that the Web as a communication system can be flexibly used to express many kinds of communication. The classification of the communication (in the categories listed previously) depends on who is taking part in the communication. The exact classification of any expression on the Web can be blurred by the potentially global reach of any Web page. Thus, a personal home page can be used interpersonally, but it can be accessed far more times on the Web than a publication created and intended for mass consumption. In addition to these contexts, the Web serves many communication functions.

- *Information Delivery.* A Web browser gives the user a "viewer" to "look into" data provided over networks. The structure of hypertext enables user selectivity because of the many ways that a user can choose to follow links in hypertext.
- *Communication.* People can use Web hypertext to create forums for sharing information and discussion and helping group members make contact with each other. With special interactive languages such as Java and Limbo, users can interact in real-time discussions.

- *Interaction.* Using special programming, a Web developer can build interactivity into an application, giving the user a way to receive customized information based on queries. Computer programs also can enable a user to change or add to an information structure.
- *Computation.* Using gateway programming or a language such as Java, the Web can be used to provide an interface to other applications and programs for information processing. Based on user selections, a Web application can return a computed or customized result.

SUMMARY

The Web emerged from ideas about the associative, nonlinear organization of information. Its protocols and technical standards were defined at the Conseil Européen pour la Recherche Nucléaire in the early 1990s. Subsequent development of graphical user interfaces to the Web in the United States has led to the widespread use of the Web in industry, education, government, and the general culture. Today, the Web is a hypertext information and communication system popularly used on the Internet. Communication on the Web can assume many forms and take place in many contexts, ranging from individual communication to group and mass communication.

RELATED LINKS

- Tim Berners-Lee Home Page (http://www.w3.org/People/Berners-Lee)
- December Communications (http://www.december.com)
- *Internet Literacy* Web Site (http://www.udel.edu/interlit2/contents.html)
- Internet Society (http://www.isoc.org)
- Network Solutions: Domain Name Registration (http://www.networksolutions.com)

FOR FURTHER RESEARCH

To find out more about the topics discussed in this reading, use InfoTrac College Edition. Type in keywords and subject terms such as "information superhighway," "Xanadu," and "hypermedia." You can access InfoTrac College Edition from the Wadsworth/Thomson Communication Cafe homepage: http://communication.wadsworth.com.

Reading 10-2

The Productivity Puzzle

Thomas K. Landauer

EDITOR'S NOTE

Since 1960 over $4 trillion has been spent computerizing the American workplace. And yet, until very recently, solid evidence that information technology leads to increased productivity was very hard to find. Economists refer to this conundrum—large investments in computers resulting in small gains for industry—as the productivity paradox. With the exception of telecommunications, the net impact of computers on productivity was quite disappointing through the mid-1990s. This reading, which should be read in conjunction with the next article, on the Internet's economic impact, explains why.

CONSIDER

1. What is the difference between phase one and phase two computing, according to Landauer?

2. Why does Landauer use the term "augmentation" to describe phase two computing?

3. Of all the industries that are computer intensive, why was telecommunications least affected by the productivity slowdown of the mid-1970s to mid-1990s?

I went into a department store to buy a cheap watch. The man ahead of me said to the salesclerk, "I really like this one."

"I can't find its stock number; I can't enter the sale."

The clerk went off to a backroom, where I heard her consulting one person, then another. A loudspeaker paged the manager. Eventually the clerk returned, apologizing, "It isn't in the book, and I can't find the manager."

"There's one right here. Can't I just pay for it?"

"I'm terribly sorry, I can't sell it without the number. Do you like this one? I have the number for it."

"I like the first one better."

"Well, let's wait for the manager. Gosh, I'm sorry."

"I don't have much time. Can't I just give you the money?"

"I'm really sorry. The manager should be along any minute."

After 5 minutes of fidgeting and apologies, the manager appeared. She said, "Did you look for the number on the box?"

From *The Trouble with Computers: Usefulness, Usability, and Productivity* by Thomas K. Landauer. Cambridge, MA: MIT Press, 1995. Copyright © 1995 The MIT Press. Reprinted with permission.

"Yes, but I didn't find it. And I asked the others. They didn't know either."

"I'll go look."

Off she went. Five minutes later the PA system spoke: "I can't find the number either, would the customer like a different watch?"

"No."

What's going on here? Computers are wonderful. Maybe, if you're like me a few years back, the very title of this book [*The Trouble with Computers*] would have puzzled you or made you mad. Trouble? Trouble indeed! Computers are fantastic, awesome. You love them; I love them. They're selling like hotcakes: maybe a little slower than they used to, but still they're the biggest bright spot in modern industry. Everyone wants one. Everyone uses them, one way or another. They're here, they're everywhere. Every accountant, author, secretary, scientist, businessperson, engineer has to have one. They're making new millionaires—no, billionaires—all over the place. Trouble? What trouble?

So finally it was my turn. By now I'd had plenty of time to select a watch and a couple of backups, just in case. No problem. My first pick had a number. So I gave the clerk my credit card. She put it in the machine for verification. The machine didn't take my card. She tried again, sliding the card faster. Again, slower. Again really fast. No go. Four more tries. Then she called across to the salesclerk at a nearby register. "What do I do when it won't accept the card?"

"Enter it with the keys."

"I tried." Dutifully, she tried again. Once. Twice. Three times. Then she called across: "Do you put in the first three numbers?"

"Yes."

"Six, three, eight?"

"No, four, seven, two for that machine."

"Oh, thanks."

The rest of the transaction went smoothly.

This sad but true example is not an isolated case. I suspect that everyone in America has run into computerized checkout machines that slow transactions and frustrate operators and customers alike. Many companies have had sorely disappointing experiences with the introduction of information technology, failing to realize the economies that they were expecting, often promised. Indeed, everywhere you look, some computer system is gobbling dollars while doing silly things and making life hard for its masters and servants alike. Millions of "micros" bought for homes end up in closets. Millions of PCs bought for white-collar workers gather dust. And it gets worse—wait and see.

Computers should make life easier and better. Computers are truly marvelous machines and getting more marvelous every year. Every day they get programmed to do astonishing new things. We're told over and over that we are in a computer revolution, that computers are leading us into a wonderful new Information Age. The computer and information revolution is widely predicted to be as consequential as the Industrial Revolution of the previous two centuries—throw in the printing press and agriculture as well. The money being invested in computers is probably comparable to the earlier investment in power-driven machines. "Muscle and movement" machines brought enormous increases in labor productivity. Solid evidence that the computer revolution has brought increased productivity, however, is very hard to find.

> The Internal Revenue Service invested over $50 million in PCs for its agents. The systems were supposed to help agents enter and look up data and make calculations more quickly and accurately. But the number of cases processed by each agent in a week went down by 40 percent.

I believe that computers are in deep trouble. Certainly they have had and continue to have amazing triumphs; they've helped put humans on the moon, to-

tally revised warfare, finally made it possible to solve centuries-old mathematics problems, led bursts of new scientific knowledge, taken over our bookkeeping and our telephone switches. Their raw power for calculation and storage continues to double every few years. But the promise that they would contribute to economics, to a vast improvement in standard of living, has not been kept. The nations, industries, and people who have invested in them heavily have not prospered proportionally (except those who sell computers). There is some sign that some corporations, usually very large ones, have had major successes with computers in the last few years, but it is not clear yet whether these successes were due to the computers themselves or to dramatic business revamping bred of recession pressures. We expected computers to bring across-the-board productivity help, work efficiency improvements for small and large alike. This they have not delivered.

> A major insurance underwriter spent $30 million on a computer system to streamline the operation of its dental insurance claims department. Within a year, the number of claims processed each day by its sixty-five employees increased by over 30 percent. And the total cost of each claims transaction went up from $3.50 to $5.00.[1]

Don't get me wrong. I'm a devoted software designer and a user and fan of computer systems. I'm an electronic mail devotee. It saves me hours of telephone tag, lets me keep work communications short and to the point and personal interactions tactful, and allows me and my correspondents to do our communicating when it's most convenient, not just when we're both available. But I'm a very critical fan. Like others, I have a love–hate relationship with the computer. I get twenty to fifty electronic messages each day—not instead of paper mail and telephone calls but *in addition*, and not all useful or entertaining.

My personal experience more or less captures the overall situation with computers: They do a lot of great things that could make us more efficient and they do a lot of stupid or unintended things that get in our way, and they're not cheap. The bottom line is pretty smudgy. Not only are the economic data equivocal on the productivity effects of computing, but more direct evaluations of their effects on work efficiency are pretty disappointing—much, much inferior to the hope and hype attached in the popular press and mind.

WHY? POOR USEFULNESS AND USABILITY DUE TO POOR EVALUATION, THAT'S WHY

So what's going on here? How did computer systems get this way? How come they aren't better than they are? Here's my overview of what has happened.

Since first leaving the research laboratories in the 1950s, computers as practical devices have been through two partly overlapping phases of evolution corresponding to two major realms of application. In the first phase, computers have been used for automation, to replace humans in the performance of tasks, either doing tasks that humans could do with no help or doing tasks no human would be capable of. All of these tasks involve the manipulation of numbers. The amazing feats that computers perform in mathematics and science all depend on doing well-known mathematical calculations that in principle could be done by humans with a pencil and paper. The difference, of course, is that computers do calculations millions of times as fast as people and with many fewer errors.

Computers can do anything that can be reduced to numerical or logical operations, and that includes a vast array of chores. Almost any process that science, engineering, and statistics have captured in their theories can be carried out by a properly instructed (programmed) computer. This has also meant that we could invent things like radar-directed gunfire, where data arrive in such volume and have to be acted upon so quickly that humans couldn't do the necessary additions and multiplication. It has made it possible to invent CAT scan X-ray and MRI machines that allow doctors to see our insides in glorious three-dimensional detail. Each picture takes billions of calculations. They have allowed us to build much bigger, faster, cheaper electronic means for connecting telephones to each other, replacing the switchboards and electromechanical devices of the not-so-distant past. Without these new computer-based switches, we'd need 2 million more telephone operators than we had in 1950 and would get much worse service at much higher prices. Computers have allowed us to build robots and electronically controlled lathes and milling machines and automatic process controllers for chemical plants and production lines. On the commercial front, their most important contribution has been the relief of bookkeepers. The endless, tedious copying, adding and subtracting, entering and retrieving of numbers on which

banks and other businesses depend has almost all been handed over to computers.

Phase one is now running out of steam. Most jobs that could be simply taken over by numerical processors have already been taken over. It's getting hard to think of useful new jobs to do by arithmetic. Certainly the excitement is not over; many more marvelous computer-based inventions will come our way. But the pace of gain from automation will be much slower. The easily reached fruits have been picked.

Phase two of computer application is augmentation, encompassing that wide range of things that people do that cannot be taken over completely by a numerical machine. Most of the things people do—talk, understand speech and language, write, read, create art and science, persuade, negotiate, decide, organize, administer, entertain, socialize—fall into this category. None of these things has yet been, or is likely soon to be, captured in a quantitative theory that can be executed as well by a computer as by a person. Although researchers are working busily, we're not nearly ready to replace humans with machines—even if we wanted to. Instead, computer systems have been designed and built to act as assistants, aids, and "power tools." It is here, in the design of these kinds of computer systems, that we have failed. Impressed with the successes of the automation machines, we have been eager to employ their offspring, the augmentation machines. And we have been paying good money for their services. But so far, they're just not working out. The evidence is that phase two helpers are not helpful enough to be worth their wages. Thus, the trouble with computers is that in their most recent applications—the jobs for which we now want them—they are not doing enough. Partly the problem is that they are still too hard to operate. Partly the problem is that they get misused, applied badly, and to the wrong jobs. Mostly the problem is that they don't yet do a sufficient number of sufficiently useful things.

THE EVIDENCE

For over 5 years a debate has been in progress about how much—or even whether—computers contribute to improved productivity. Economists, work sociologists, computer scientists, and other relevant experts have offered a variety of facts, analyses, and opinions. Many have concluded that computers have had very little positive effect on productivity. The bottom line, it has been variously asserted, is that while there are exceptions, most business investments in computers have yielded significantly lower returns than investments in bonds at market interest rates. Two analysts dissent from this view. Stanford University economist Timothy Bresnehan thinks there must be huge gains somewhere because there has been tremendous increase in the ratio of performance to price of computers themselves. Eric Brynjolfsson of MIT weighs in with a minority analysis purporting to show excellent results for heavy hardware investors among the Fortune 500 in recent years.[2] Others have examined the possibility of errors in the measurement of productivity or proposed alternative explanations for the facts.

What seems most striking about this debate is that it has occurred at all. Given the marvelous powers of modern computing, its reputation in the public mind, and the vast amounts of money spent on its application, its economic benefits should be manifest. The fact that many serious and competent scholars can conclude that there has been little net productivity gain attributable to this technology seems enough proof that something is wrong.

HISTORY

In the United States, computers first entered commercial use in a big way in the early 1960s. In 1950 the decennial census counted fewer than 900 computer operators in the entire United States. In 1960 there were still only 2,000. However, by 1970 there were 125,000 and by 1985 close to half a million (or, for comparison, about twice the number of telephone operators).[3] By 1985 computer and related information technology equipment purchases accounted for about 16 percent of total capital stock in the service sector, some $424 billion, up from 6 percent 15 years earlier.[4] By 1991, the annual equipment outlay was running over $100 billion.[5] And initial equipment costs are only the tip of the iceberg; the serious spending, which starts after the boxes arrive, at least triples the total. Operating and maintaining hardware costs as much as buying it. Software purchase or development adds another, approximately equal share; most of the major applications of computers have required new software customized for the business or firm. Finally, computer use eats a comparable large slice. Expensive specialized labor is needed to debug, repair, or modify software. Because systems are so complicated and hard to use, end users (those

whom the computer is intended to serve, as opposed to those who serve the computer) not only need extensive training but usually cannot use the computer fully by themselves; they need the assistance of systems analysts, consultants, trainers, or other intermediaries. Moreover, all of this needs supervision, organization, and management—whole electronic data processing and management information systems departments, not to mention the floor space and air-conditioning that they and their machines consume. Most of this outlay should be considered capital expense. It is all intended to make available a tool that is supposed to make other functions of production more efficient. Almost none of it is directly productive; almost none can be considered an input to production in the sense that raw material, energy, or most labor is.

Adding it all up, since 1960, something over $4 trillion (much more than an average year's GNP, or gross national product, during that period) has been spent on computing, and total current expenditures for the United States amount to around 10 percent of GNP. Although there was significant computerization, primarily of the phase one variety—complete automation, in which the machine replaces a human—in the '60s, the overwhelming amount of phase two computer investment—in which computers are used as aids in the mentally demanding jobs of information workers—occurred from the early '70s onward, at a time when the United States experienced much slower growth in productivity than in any previous period for which comparable data are available.[6]

Quantitative estimates of productivity are usually calculated as the amount of value added for each person-hour employed—so-called labor productivity—or as the number of dollars worth of output for each dollar spent on labor and capital combined—so-called multifactor productivity. Between 1948 and 1965, overall growth in productivity ranged between 2 percent and 7 percent for industrialized nations. From the end of World War II through the '60s, GNP, productivity, and the standard of living of industrial nations grew steadily.[7] Annual labor productivity gains were in the range of 2 percent (for the United States) to 7 percent (for Japan). From about 1970–1975 onward productivity gains have been much smaller, ranging from 0 to 1 percent for the United States, up to 2⅔ percent for Japan. Gains in productivity since 1948 have always been largest in farming and manufacturing, but before 1970, they were nearly as good in other industries as well. Since the early '70s, productivity in the nonfarm, nonmanufacturing sphere has been essentially flat, even declining in some years. During this same period, of course, manufacturing and farming have become smaller portions of the overall economy, so the slow growth of productivity in other areas has affected the overall picture even more strongly.

Phase one computer application had considerable impact on manufacturing. There were major early phase one computer applications in some nonmanufacturing, nonfarming segments as well, notably in banking, finance, and insurance, where computers were first used to automate record keeping, accounting, report generation, and billing. Some analysts have found healthy productivity growth for some periods in some segments of these businesses and for particular functions within them. For example, the insurance industry maintained normal labor productivity growth while its extensive bookkeeping, contract preparation, and arithmetic for figuring premiums were automated.[8] As a group, however, these closely related industries have registered declines in productivity growth since widespread adoption of electronic information processing beginning in the late '50s, despite a six-to-one increase in real (inflation-adjusted) investment per employee—largely in computers and other information technology. The number of bookkeepers and billing clerks even continued to grow briskly in U.S. industry as a whole as computers ostensibly took over all the record copying and arithmetic. The number of file clerks multiplied by two and a half between 1960 and 1970 as computers were reputedly replacing them. And although their increase was very modest in later years, file clerk jobs were still not on the endangered species list.[9]

With the important exception of telecommunications, the remaining nonfarm, nonmanufacturing industries, such as transportation, public utilities, trade, and services, have shown near flat productivity over the last two decades. These industries should be, and have been, the primary candidates for phase two computer applications. It is for them that word processors, PCs, laptops, spreadsheets, office automation machinery in general, electronic cash registers, inventory management, and management information systems have be designed.

While it would be rash to conclude solely from the recent stagnation of productivity that computers have no positive net effects on work efficiency, the historical trends in productivity certainly give no evidence of large improvements during the period when phase two computer use has been rapidly expanding.

The only major subclassification within nonfarm, nonmanufacturing that had nontrivial productivity gains between 1973 and 1987 was communications. Communications is composed primarily of television, radio, and telecommunications; the telephone companies are the biggest component, with total revenues over $100 billion a year. From more detailed data, it appears that the telephone business accounts for the superior productivity record of this category.

From 1973 to 1983, telephone company productivity increased over 6 percent annually. During the same period, there were productivity increases of just 1.5 percent in air transport, under 1 percent in retail food stores, and absolute declines in restaurants.[10] All of these, like the telephone business, are non-goods producing but have easily countable output. They are also industries that were using computers and in which one might have imagined computerization to be effective. However, telephone companies were the leading and largest users of both phase one and phase two computing, and they did well.

Most other service industries have also invested heavily in computers but have not done well at all. Probably the second-largest investors in phase two computing, as well of phase one application for record keeping, have been the brokerage, banking, and insurance businesses. Although there was apparently significant variation among subsectors, these businesses as a whole have shown a strong net decline in both labor and multifactor productivity since 1973.

There is no sign that industries that expanded their IT most rapidly improved their productivity the most; if anything, the opposite appears to be true.

NOTES

1. Shoshana Zuboff, *In the Age of the Smart Machine*. New York: Basic Books, 1988.

2. Timothy F. Bresnehan, "Measuring the Spillovers from Technological Advance: Mainframe Computers in Financial Services," *American Economic Review*, 76 (September 1986), 742–755; Erik Brynjolfsson and Lorin Hitt, *Is Information Systems Spending Productive? New Evidence and New Results*. Working paper. Cambridge, MA: Sloan School of Management, Center for Information Systems Research, MIT, 1993.

3. H. Allan Hunt and Timothy L. Hunt, *Clerical Employment and Technological Change*. Kalamazoo, MI: W. E. Upjohn Institute for Employment Research, 1986.

4. Stephen S. Roach, "America's Technology Dilemma: A Profile of the Information Economy," Memorandum. New York: Morgan Stanley, 1987.

5. Stephen S. Roach, *Inside the U.S. Economy*. New York: Morgan Stanley, 1992.

6. McKinsey Global Institute, *Service Sector Productivity*. New York: McKinsey and Co., 1992.

7. Martin Neil Baily and Alok K. Chakrabarti, *Innovation and the Productivity Crisis*. Washington, DC: Brookings Institution, 1988; Edward Fulton Denison, *Estimates of Productivity Change by Industry*. Washington, DC: Brookings Institution, 1989.

8. Heidi I. Hartmann, Robert E. Kraut, and Louise A. Tilly (Eds.), *Computer Chips and Paper Clips: Technology and Women's Employment*. Washington, DC: National Academy Press, 1986.

9. Roslyn L. Feldberg and Evelyn Nakano Glenn, "Technology and the Transformation of Clerical Work. In Robert E. Kraut (Ed.), *Technology and the Transformation of White Collar Work*. Hillsdale, NJ: Lawrence Erlbaum Associates, 1987, pp. 77–97.

10. U. S. Department of Labor, *Productivity Measures for Selected Industries, 1954–82*. Washington, DC: Government Printing Office, 1983.

RELATED LINKS

- Explaining the Productivity Paradox (http://www.neweconomyindex.org/productivity.html)

- The Productivity Paradox: A Reading List (http://averia.unm.edu/ITProductivity.html)

- Probing the Productivity Paradox (http://www.misq.org/archivist/vol/no18/issue2/edstat.html)

- The Productivity Paradox of Information Technology: Review and Assessment (http://ccs.mit.edu/papers/CCSWP130/ccswp130.html)

FOR FURTHER RESEARCH

To find out more about the topics discussed in this reading, use InfoTrac College Edition. Type in keywords and subject terms such as "productivity paradox," "computerization of industry," and "labor productivity." You can access InfoTrac College Edition from the Wadsworth/Thomson Communication Cafe homepage: http://communication.wadsworth.com.

Reading 10-3

Computer Age Gains Respect of Economists
Steve Lohr

EDITOR'S NOTE

After a two-decade lull, workplace productivity started to pick up in the mid- to late 1990s, prompting even the most hardened skeptics to reconsider technology's contribution to the economy. As this reading points out, economists are attributing this increase in productivity to the gains in speed and efficiency that the Internet and other information technologies make possible. Interestingly, improved productivity performance mirrors the growth and development of the World Wide Web. Businesses, it would appear, are finally reaping the benefits of information technology.

CONSIDER

1. In terms of increased workplace productivity, is the nation's massive investment in computers and communication technology finally paying off?

2. Which single information or communication technology, in your opinion, has had the greatest impact on improved productivity, and why?

3. In an information-age economy, do we need a broader definition of productivity and output that goes beyond the industrial-era concept of widgets coming off an assembly line? Is fundamental change afoot in the nature of economic output?

In a nation of technophiles, where Internet millionaires are minted daily, it seems heresy to question the economic payoff from information technology—the billions upon billions spent each year by companies and households on everything from computers to software to cell phones.

But for more than a decade, most of the nation's leading economists have been heretics. They have not been much impressed by the high-tech dogma—embraced by corporate executives, business school professors, and Wall Street alike—that regards the transformation of the economy through the magic of information technology as a self-evident truth.

"You can see the Computer Age everywhere," Robert Solow, a Nobel prizewinner at the Massachusetts Institute of Technology wrote, "but in the productivity statistics."

For years, even as the computer revolutionized the workplace, productivity—the output of goods and services per worker—stagnated, barely advancing 1 percent a year. So it is easy to see how Solow's pithy comment became the favorite punch line of the economic naysayers.

Yet today, even renowned skeptics on the subject of technology's contribution to the economy, like Solow, are having second thoughts. Productivity growth has picked up, starting in 1996, capped by a surge in the second half of 1998, after 8 years of economic expansion. That has drawn attention because past upward swings in productivity typically occurred early in a recovery as economic activity rebounded. Once companies increased hiring, it slowed again.

But something seems fundamentally different this time, something apparently having a lot to do with

the increased speed and efficiency that the Internet and other pervasive information-technology advances are bringing to the mundane day-to-day tasks of millions of businesses.

The question, posed by economists, is whether the higher productivity growth, averaging about 2 percent in the last 3 years, roughly double the pace from 1973 to 1995, is the long-awaited confirmation that the nation's steadily rising investment in computers and communications is finally paying off. The evidence is starting to point in that direction.

"My beliefs are shifting on this subject," said Solow. "I am still far from certain. But the story always was that it took a long time for people to use information technology and truly become more efficient. That story sounds a lot more convincing today than it did a year or two ago."

Another pillar in the pessimist camp was Daniel Sichel, an economist at the Federal Reserve. His work, along with another Fed economist, Stephen Oliner, in 1994, and on his own in 1997, found that computers contributed little to productivity growth. But recently, Sichel ran similar calculations for the last few years and came to a different conclusion.

In a paper recently published in the quarterly *Business Economics,* Sichel wrote that his new work points to "a striking step up in the contribution of computers to output growth." And the nation's improved productivity performance, he noted, is "raising the possibility that businesses are finally reaping the benefits of information technology."

The impact of information technology on the economy is more than an academic debate. If, as some experts assert, the technology dividend is a key reason for the nation's extraordinary run of high growth, rising wages, and low inflation, there are significant policy implications. If the recent gains are not just a temporary blip, it suggests that the Federal Reserve can be less fearful of inflation and keep interest rates stable rather than be forced to raise them to cool off what would otherwise be considered an overheated economy.

Alan Greenspan, the Fed chairman, seems to believe a fundamental change is under way. He told Congress early this year that the economy was enjoying "higher, technology-driven productivity growth."

Erik Brynjolfsson, an associate professor at the MIT Sloan School of Management, asserts that the economic value of speed, quality improvements, customer service, and new products is often not captured by government statistics. "These are the competitive advantages of information technology," he said. "We need a broader definition of output in this new economy, which goes beyond the industrial-era concept of widgets coming off the assembly line."

The government, after years of defending its figures, recently conceded that productivity growth may be understated. The core of the problem, government economists say, is the increasingly complex challenge of defining and measuring output in much of the economy's fast-growing service sector, which includes the vast reaches of banking, finance, health care, and education.

According to the official statistics, a bank today is only about 80 percent as productive as a bank in 1977. Yet that seems to take scant account of, say, 24-hour automated teller machines, which clearly benefit customers who no longer have to wait in lines to be served by human tellers during regular "bankers' hours."

Edwin Dean, chief of the productivity division of the Bureau of Labor Statistics, wrote in a research paper that the agency was increasingly concerned that its measurements did not "fully reflect changes in the quality of goods and services" or "capture the full impact of new technology on economic performance."

Still, the government's methods of measurement will not be overhauled any time soon. "These are tough, tough questions and we are not going to get instant solutions," Dean explained in an interview.

American corporations long ago made up their minds, voting for technology with their dollars. Investment in information technology—computing and telecommunications gear—has quadrupled over the last decade, rising as a share of all business spending on equipment, from 29 percent to 53 percent, according to the Commerce Department. And that is only the hardware. There have been similar surges in corporate spending on software, consulting, technical support, and training related to the field.

"The payoff from information technology is unquestionably there with individual companies and we're seeing it over and over again," said Chuck Rieger, a senior consultant at IBM's services division.

Of course, anecdotal evidence from individual companies is no proof of broad-based benefits in an $8.5 trillion economy. But what many experts find encouraging is that the rapid introduction of low-cost Internet technology means most companies can now afford to set up electronic links with customers and suppliers. For example, a recent survey of 2,500 manufacturing companies, conducted by Pricewaterhouse-Coopers, found that the number of factories with Internet links to customers and suppliers doubled in just one year.

At more and more companies, these Internet-based networks are already streamlining the mundane chores of business life like invoicing, purchasing, and inventory control. This is not the glamorous side of Internet commerce, occupied by Amazon.com and others selling consumer products. Yet if a technology dividend in productivity is at hand, the place to look is in the back offices of business. "That is where it will be," Solow, the MIT economist, said, "in the wholesale automation of corporate transactions."

This business-to-business commerce over the Internet is projected to jump from $48 billion in 1998 to $1.5 trillion by 2003, according to Forrester Research. During the same period, the research firm estimates that consumer sales over the Internet will rise from $3.9 billion to $108 billion.

The service sector of the economy is where productivity gains appear to have been especially sluggish and where experts are looking most closely for evidence of an efficiency payoff from technology.

In Chicago, banker Michael Rushmore speaks of how Internet computing has "fundamentally changed the way we do business" over the last 3 or 4 years. Take the way corporate loans are syndicated among many banks, notes Rushmore, a managing director of Nationsbanc Montgomery Securities, the securities arm of BankAmerica Corp.

Until a few years ago, syndicating a large corporate bank loan meant distributing a lengthy offering document, often running more than 200 pages, to 50 or 100 banks. It was, Rushmore recalled, a nightmarish, inefficient process that involved waves of overnight mail, constant faxing, and armies of messengers.

Today, much of that process is handled over the Internet on bank Web sites that other banks tap into to read and download the offering document, ask questions, and exchange views. Rushmore estimates that the Internet-based system trims 25 percent from the time it takes to close a deal, not just improving the ease of the transaction but also saving an immense number of hours of work.

About a year ago Booz Allen & Hamilton began using the Internet to bill several federal agencies that are its clients. Booz Allen estimates that it has saved $150,000 a year by eliminating the paper handling on its $10 million in monthly billings to the government. The greater speed and efficiency of electronic billing also means that the consulting firm is being paid 30 percent, or six business days per month, faster than before.

"Getting that money into the bank much more quickly is probably the biggest benefit," said Mark Arnsberger, an assistant controller for Booz Allen & Hamilton.

The rapid spread of Internet-based computing, experts say, promises to compress the time it takes for any new technology to enhance economic welfare in general. The classic study of the phenomenon, "The Dynamo and the Computer: An Historical Perspective on the Modern Productivity Paradox," by Paul David, an economic historian at Stanford University, was published in 1990.

The electric motor, David noted, was introduced in the early 1880s but did not generate discernible productivity gains until the 1920s. It took that long, he wrote, not only for the technology to be widely distributed but also for businesses to reorganize work around the industrial production line, the efficiency breakthrough of its day.

"The process takes longer than people think, but I still believe that we will get a revival of productivity growth led by the spread of computing," David said.

His is a misplaced faith, according to the dwindling band of technopessimists whose own beliefs remain unshaken. Sure, they concede, there has been surprisingly strong productivity growth as of late. Could this represent a break in the trend? Possibly, they grudgingly admit, but only a tiny shift at best, they insist.

The real problem, they explain, lies in the composition of the nation's vast service economy. More than half of all white-collar workers are what they term "knowledge workers"—managers, executives, and professionals like doctors, lawyers, teachers, even economists.

"The work they do does not lend itself to technology-driven improvements in productivity, and any gains are really difficult to eke out and are glacial," said Stephen Roach, chief economist at Morgan Stanley Dean Witter. "Paul David's electrical motor has nothing to do with the knowledge-intensive process of work in a service economy."

Paul Strassmann, former chief information officer at Xerox and the Pentagon, is a real technology cynic. Strassmann, author of *The Squandered Computer* (Information Economics Press, 1997), believes that corporate America's spending spree on information technology amounts to an "economic arms race," fueled by misguided management theories.

The recent improvement in productivity, according to Strassmann, is mainly attributable to the lower cost of capital because of low interest rates. His summary view, though at odds with those of technology optimists like Brynjolfsson of MIT, may also be received warmly by the Fed.

"The explanation for the productivity improvement is interest rates, not information technology," Strassmann said. "The hero here is not Bill Gates. It's Alan Greenspan."

Yet even Strassmann finds the technology undeniably useful, if not a productivity elixir. When asked a detailed question, he replied, "Just look it up on my Web site. It's a lot more efficient that way."

RELATED LINKS

- Beyond the Productivity Paradox (www.acm.org/pubs/articles/journals/cacm/1998-41-8/p49-brynjolfsson/p49-brynjolfsson.pdf)
- National Productivity Statistics (http://www.rich.frb.org/eq/pdfs/winter1998/webb.pdf)
- Perspectives on Productivity Growth (http://www.nabe.com/publib/be/990207.pdf)
- Bureau of Labor Statistics, U.S. Department of Labor (http://stats.bls.gov/blshome.htm)

FOR FURTHER RESEARCH

To find out more about the topics discussed in this reading, use InfoTrac College Edition. Type in keywords and subject terms such as "new economy," "productivity growth," and "benefits of information technology." You can access InfoTrac College Edition from the Wadsworth/ Thomson Communication Cafe homepage: http://communication.wadsworth.com.

Reading 10-4

The Computer Delusion
Todd Oppenheimer

EDITOR'S NOTE

The problem of documenting the computer's contribution to the economy also applies to the classroom. As noted in the original preface to this article in the Atlantic Monthly, *there is no good evidence that most uses of computers significantly improve teaching and learning, yet school districts are cutting such time-honored programs as music, art, and physical education—programs that demonstrably enrich children's lives—to make room for this dubious nostrum. The stated political goal of "computers in every classroom" may not be the panacea that rescues education from its current troubles.*

CONSIDER

1. Do you agree that music, art, and physical education classes ought to be cut when necessary to fund computer classrooms and technology coordinators? Why or why not?

2. In your opinion, why do politicians and school administrators put so much faith in computer technology?

3. According to child-development experts, what difference can hands-on learning make compared to computer learning, especially for young children?

In 1922 Thomas Edison predicted that "the motion picture is destined to revolutionize our educational system and . . . in a few years it will supplant largely, if not entirely, the use of textbooks." Twenty-three years later, in 1945, William Levenson, the director of the Cleveland public schools' radio station, claimed that "the time may come when a portable radio receiver will be as common in the classroom as is the blackboard." Forty years after that the noted psychologist

B. F. Skinner, referring to the first days of his "teaching machines," in the late 1950s and early 1960s, wrote, "I was soon saying that, with the help of teaching machines and programmed instruction, students could learn twice as much in the same time and with the same effort as in a standard classroom." Ten years after Skinner's recollections were published, President Bill Clinton campaigned for "a bridge to the twenty-first century . . . where computers are as much a part of the classroom as blackboards."

If history really is repeating itself, the schools are in serious trouble. In *Teachers and Machines: The Classroom Use of Technology Since 1920* (Teachers College Press, 1986), Larry Cuban, a professor of education at Stanford University and a former school superintendent, observed that as successive rounds of new technology failed their promoters' expectations, a pattern emerged. The cycle began with big promises backed by the technology developers' research. In the classroom, however, teachers never really embraced the new tools, and no significant academic improvement occurred. This provoked consistent responses: the problem was money, spokespeople argued, or teacher resistance, or the paralyzing school bureaucracy. Meanwhile, few people questioned the technology advocates' claims. As results continued to lag, the blame was finally laid on the machines. Soon schools were sold on the next generation of technology, and the lucrative cycle started all over again.

Today's technology evangels argue that we've learned our lesson from past mistakes. As in each previous round, they say that when our new hot technology—the computer—is compared with yesterday's, today's is better. "It can do the same things, plus," Richard Riley, the U.S. Secretary of Education, told me this spring.

How much better is it, really?

The promoters of computers in schools again offer prodigious research showing improved academic achievement after using their technology. The research has again come under occasional attack, but this time quite a number of teachers seem to be backing classroom technology. In a poll taken early last year U.S. teachers ranked computer skills and media technology as more "essential" than the study of European history, biology, chemistry, and physics; than dealing with social problems such as drugs and family breakdown; than learning practical job skills; and than reading modern American writers such as Steinbeck and Hemingway or classic ones such as Plato and Shakespeare.

In keeping with these views New Jersey cut state aid to a number of school districts this past year and then spent $10 million on classroom computers. In Union City, California, a single school district is spending $27 million to buy new gear for a mere eleven schools. The Kittridge Street Elementary School, in Los Angeles, killed its music program last year to hire a technology coordinator; in Mansfield, Massachusetts, administrators dropped proposed teaching positions in art, music, and physical education, and then spent $333,000 on computers; in one Virginia school the art room was turned into a computer laboratory. Ironically, a half dozen preliminary studies have recently suggested that music and art classes may build the physical size of a child's brain—and its powers for subjects such as language, math, science, and engineering—in one case far more than computer work did. Mean-

while, months after a New Technology High School opened in Napa, California, where computers sit on every student's desk and all academic classes use computers, some students were complaining of headaches, sore eyes, and wrist pain.

Throughout the country, as spending on technology increases, school book purchases are stagnant. Shop classes, with their tradition of teaching children building skills with wood and metal, have been almost entirely replaced by new "technology education programs." In San Francisco only one public school still offers a full shop program—the lone vocational high school. "We get kids who don't know the difference between a screwdriver and a ball-peen hammer," James Dahlman, the school's vocational department chair, told me recently. "How are they going to make a career choice? Administrators are stuck in this mindset that all kids will go to a 4-year college and become a doctor or a lawyer, and that's not true. I know some who went to college, graduated, and then had to go back to technical school to get a job." Last year the school superintendent in Great Neck, Long Island, proposed replacing elementary school shop classes with computer classes and training the shop teachers as computer coaches. Rather than being greeted with enthusiasm, the proposal provoked a backlash.

Interestingly, shop classes and field trips are two programs that the National Information Infrastructure Advisory Council, the Clinton Administration's technology task force, suggested reducing in order to shift resources into computers. But are these results what technology promoters really intend? "You need to apply common sense," Esther Dyson, the president of EDventure Holdings and one of the Advisory Council's leading school advocates, told me recently. "Shop with a good teacher probably is worth more than computers with a lousy teacher. But if it's a poor program, this may provide a good excuse for cutting it. There will be a lot of trials and errors with this. And I don't know how to prevent those errors."

The issue, perhaps, is the magnitude of the errors. Alan Lesgold, a professor of psychology and the associate director of the Learning Research and Development Center at the University of Pittsburgh, calls the computer an "amplifier" because it encourages both enlightened study practices and thoughtless ones. There's a real risk, though, that the thoughtless practices will dominate, slowly dumbing down huge numbers of tomorrow's adults. As Sherry Turkle, a professor of the sociology of science at the Massachusetts Institute of Technology and a longtime observer of children's use of computers, told me, "The possibilities of using this thing poorly so outweigh the chance of using it well, it makes people like us, who are fundamentally optimistic about computers, very reticent."

Perhaps the best way to separate fact from fantasy is to take supporters' claims about computerized learning one by one and compare them with the evidence in the academic literature and in the everyday experiences I have observed or heard about in a variety of classrooms.

Five main arguments underlie the campaign to computerize our nation's schools.

- Computers improve both teaching practices and student achievement.

- Computer literacy should be taught as early as possible; otherwise students will be left behind.

- To make tomorrow's workforce competitive in an increasingly high-tech world, learning computer skills must be a priority.

- Technology programs leverage support from the business community—badly needed today because schools are increasingly starved for funds.

- Work with computers—particularly using the Internet—brings students valuable connections with teachers, other schools and students, and a wide network of professionals around the globe. These connections spice the school day with a sense of real-world relevance, and broaden the educational community.

THE FILMSTRIPS OF THE 1990s

The Administration's vision of computerized classrooms arose partly out of the findings of the presidential task force—thirty-six leaders from industry, education, and several interest groups who have guided the Administration's push to get computers into the schools. The report of the task force, *Connecting K–12 Schools to the Information Superhighway* (produced by the consulting firm McKinsey & Co.), begins by citing numerous studies that have apparently proved that computers enhance student achievement significantly.

Unfortunately, many of these studies are more anecdotal than conclusive. Some, including a giant, oft-cited meta-analysis of 254 studies, lack the necessary scientific controls to make solid conclusions possible. The circumstances are artificial and not easily repeated,

results aren't statistically reliable, or, most frequently, the studies did not control for other influences, such as differences between teaching methods. This last factor is critical, because computerized learning inevitably forces teachers to adjust their style—only *sometimes* for the better. Some studies were industry-funded, and thus tended to publicize mostly positive findings. "The research is set up in a way to find benefits that aren't really there," Edward Miller, a former editor of the *Harvard Education Letter,* says. "Most knowledgeable people agree that most of the research isn't valid. It's so flawed it shouldn't even be called research. Essentially, it's just worthless." Once the faulty studies are weeded out, Miller says, the ones that remain "are inconclusive"—that is, they show no significant change in either direction.

Why are solid conclusions so elusive? Look at Apple Computer's "Classrooms of Tomorrow," perhaps the most widely studied effort to teach using computer technology. In the early 1980s Apple shrewdly realized that donating computers to schools might help not only students but also company sales, as Apple's ubiquity in classrooms turned legions of families into Apple loyalists. Last year, after the *San Jose Mercury News* (published in Apple's Silicon Valley home) ran a series questioning the effectiveness of computers in schools, the paper printed an opinion-page response from Terry Crane, an Apple vice president. "Instead of isolating students," Crane wrote, "technology actually encouraged them to collaborate more than in traditional classrooms. Students also learned to explore and represent information dynamically and creatively, communicate effectively about complex processes, become independent learners and self-starters, and become more socially aware and confident."

Crane didn't mention that after a decade of effort and the donation of equipment worth more than $25 million to thirteen schools, there is scant evidence of greater student achievement. To be fair, educators on both sides of the computer debate acknowledge that today's tests of student achievement are shockingly crude. They're especially weak in measuring intangibles such as enthusiasm and self-motivation, which do seem evident in Apple's classrooms and other computer-rich schools. In any event, what is fun and what is educational may frequently be at odds. "Computers in classrooms are the filmstrips of the 1990s," Clifford Stoll, the author of *Silicon Snake Oil: Second Thoughts on the Information Highway* (Anchor Books, 1995), told the *New York Times* last year, recalling his own school days in the 1960s. "We loved them because we didn't have to think for an hour, teachers loved them because they didn't have to teach, and parents loved them because it showed their schools were high-tech. But no learning happened." [See Reading 11–1 for Stoll's perspective on the culture of computing.]

Stoll somewhat overstates the case—obviously, benefits can come from strengthening a student's motivation. Still, Apple's computers may bear less responsibility for that change than Crane suggests. In the beginning, when Apple did little more than dump computers in classrooms and homes, this produced no real results, according to Jane David, a consultant Apple hired to study its classroom initiative. Apple quickly learned that teachers needed to change their classroom approach to what is commonly called "project-oriented learning." This is an increasingly popular teaching method, in which students learn through doing and teachers act as facilitators or partners rather than as didacts. (Teachers sometimes refer to this approach, which arrived in classrooms before computers did, as being "the guide on the side instead of the sage on the stage.") But what the students learned "had less to do with the computer and more to do with the teaching," David concluded. "If you took the computers out, there would still be good teaching there." This story is heard in school after school, including two impoverished schools—Clear View Elementary School in southern California, and the Christopher Columbus middle school in New Jersey—that the Clinton Administration has loudly celebrated for turning themselves around with computers. At Christopher Columbus, in fact, students' test scores rose before computers arrived, not afterward, because of relatively basic changes: longer class periods, new books, after-school programs, and greater emphasis on student projects and collaboration.

The value of hands-on learning, child-development experts believe, is that it deeply imprints knowledge into a young child's brain, by transmitting the lessons of experience through a variety of sensory pathways. "Curiously enough," the educational psychologist Jane Healy wrote in *Endangered Minds: Why Children Don't Think and What We Can Do About It* (Simon & Schuster, 1990), "visual stimulation is probably not the main access route to nonverbal reasoning. Body movements, the ability to touch, feel, manipulate, and build sensory awareness of relationships in the physical world, are its main foundations." The problem, Healy wrote, is that "in schools, traditionally, the senses have had little status after kindergarten."

Some computerized elementary school programs have avoided these pitfalls, but the record subject by subject is mixed at best. Take writing, where by all accounts and by my own observations the computer does encourage practice—changes are easier to make on a keyboard than with an eraser, and the lettering looks better. Diligent students use these conveniences to improve their writing, but the less committed frequently get seduced by electronic opportunities to make a school paper look snazzy. The easy "cut and paste" function in today's word processing programs, for example, is apparently encouraging many students to cobble together research materials without thinking them through. Reading programs get particularly bad reviews. One small but carefully controlled study went so far as to claim that Reader Rabbit, a reading program now used in more than 100,000 schools, caused students to suffer a 50 percent drop in creativity. (Apparently, after forty-nine students used the program for 7 months, they were no longer able to answer open-ended questions and showed a markedly diminished ability to brainstorm with fluency and originality.) What about hard sciences, which seem so well suited to computer study? Logo, the high-profile programming language refined by Seymour Papert and widely used in middle and high schools, fostered huge hopes of expanding children's cognitive skills. As students directed the computer to build things, such as geometric shapes, Papert believed, they would learn "procedural thinking," similar to the way a computer processes information. According to a number of studies, however, Logo has generally failed to deliver on its promises. Judah Schwartz, a professor of education at Harvard and a codirector of the school's Educational Technology Center, told me that a few newer applications, when used properly, can dramatically expand children's math and science thinking by giving them new tools to "make and explore conjectures." Still, Schwartz acknowledges that perhaps "99 percent" of the educational programs are "terrible, really terrible."

Even in success stories important caveats continually pop up. The best educational software is usually complex—most suited to older students and sophisticated teachers. In other cases the schools have been blessed with abundance—fancy equipment, generous financial support, or extra teachers—that is difficult if not impossible to duplicate in the average school. Even if it could be duplicated, the literature suggests, many teachers would still struggle with technology. Computers suffer frequent breakdowns; when they do work, their seductive images often distract students from the lessons at hand—which many teachers say makes it difficult to build meaningful rapport with their students.

HYPERTEXT MINDS

In schools throughout the country administrators and teachers demonstrate the same excitement, boasting about the wondrous things that children of 5 or 6 can do on computers: drawing, typing, playing with elementary science simulations and other programs called "educational games."

The schools' enthusiasm for these activities is not universally shared by specialists in childhood development. The doubters' greatest concern is for the very young—preschool through third grade, when a child is most impressionable. Their apprehension involves two main issues.

First, they consider it important to give children a broad base—emotionally, intellectually, and in the five senses—before introducing something as technical and one-dimensional as a computer. Second, they believe that the human and physical world holds greater learning potential.

The importance of a broad base for a child may be most apparent when it's missing. In *Endangered Minds,* Healy wrote of an English teacher who could readily tell which of her students' essays were conceived on a computer. "They don't link ideas," the teacher says. "They just write one thing, and then they write another one, and they don't seem to see or develop the relationships between them." The problem, Healy argued, is that the pizzazz of computerized schoolwork may hide these analytical gaps, which "won't become apparent until [the student] can't organize herself around a homework assignment or a job that requires initiative. More commonplace activities, such as figuring out how to nail two boards together, organizing a game . . . may actually form a better basis for real-world intelligence."

Others believe they have seen computer games expand children's imaginations. High-tech children "think differently from the rest of us," William D. Winn, the director of the Learning Center at the University of Washington's Human Interface Technology Laboratory, told *Business Week* in a cover story on the benefits of computer games. "They develop hypertext minds. They leap around. It's as though their cognitive strategies were parallel, not sequential." Healy argues the opposite. She and other psychologists think that the computer screen flattens information into narrow, sequential data. This kind of material, they believe, exercises mostly one half of the brain—the left hemisphere, where primarily sequential thinking occurs. The "right brain," meanwhile, gets short shrift—yet this is the hemisphere that works on different kinds of information simultaneously. It shapes our multifaceted impressions, and serves as the engine of creative analysis.

Opinions diverge in part because research on the brain is still so sketchy, and computers are so new, that the effect of computers on the brain remains a great mystery. "I don't think we know anything about it," Harry Chugani, a pediatric neurobiologist at Wayne State University, told me. This very ignorance makes skeptics wary. "Nobody knows how kids' internal wiring works," Stoll wrote in *Silicon Snake Oil,* "but anyone who's directed away from social interactions has a head start on turning out weird. . . . No computer can teach what a walk through a pine forest feels like. Sensation has no substitute."

This points to the conservative developmentalists' second concern: the danger that even if hours in front of the screen are limited, unabashed enthusiasm for the computer sends the wrong message—that the mediated world is more significant than the real one. "It's like TV commercials," Barbara Scales, the head teacher at the Child Study Center at the University of California at Berkeley, told me. "Kids get so hyped up, it can change their expectations about stimulation, versus what they generate themselves."

Faced with such sharply contrasting viewpoints, which are based on such uncertain ground, how is a responsible policymaker to proceed? "A prudent society controls its own infatuation with 'progress' when planning for its young," Healy argued in *Endangered Minds.*

Unproven technologies may offer lively visions, but they can also be detrimental to the development of the young, plastic brain. The cerebral cortex is a wondrously well-buffered mechanism that can withstand a good bit of well-intentioned bungling. Yet there is a point at which fundamental neural substrates for reasoning may be jeopardized for children who lack proper physical, intellectual, or emotional nurturance. Childhood—and the brain—have their own imperatives. In development, missed opportunities may be difficult to recapture.

The problem is that technology leaders rarely include these or other warnings in their recommendations. When I asked Dyson why the Clinton task force proceeded with such fervor, despite the classroom computer's shortcomings, she said, "It's so clear the world is changing."

REAL JOB TRAINING

Although projections are far from reliable, it's a safe bet that computer skills will be needed for a growing proportion of tomorrow's work force. But what priority should these skills be given among other studies?

Listen to Tom Henning, a physics teacher at Thurgood Marshall, the San Francisco technology high school. Henning has a graduate degree in engineering, and helped to found a Silicon Valley company that manufactures electronic navigation equipment. "My bias is the physical reality," Henning told me, as we sat outside a shop where he was helping students to rebuild an old motorcycle. "I'm no technophobe. I can program computers." What worries Henning is that computers at best engage only two senses, hearing and sight—and only two-dimensional sight at that. "Even if they're doing three-dimensional computer modeling, that's still a 2-D replica of a 3-D world. If you took a kid who grew up on Nintendo, he's not going to have the necessary skills. He needs to have done it first with Tinkertoys or clay, or carved it out of balsa wood." As David Elkind, a professor of child development at Tufts University, puts it, "A dean of the University of Iowa's School of Engineering used to say the best engineers were the farm boys," because they knew how machinery really worked.

Surely many employers will disagree and welcome the commercially applicable computer skills that today's high-tech training can bring them. What's striking is how easy it is to find other employers who share Henning's and Elkind's concerns.

Kris Meisling, a senior geological-research adviser for Mobil Oil, told me that "people who use computers a lot slowly grow rusty in their ability to think." Meisling's group creates charts and maps—some computerized, some not—to plot where to drill for oil. In large one-dimensional analyses, such as sorting volumes of seismic data, the computer saves vast amounts of time, sometimes making previously impossible tasks easy. This lures people in his field, Meisling believes, into using computers as much as possible. But when

geologists turn to computers for "interpretive" projects, he finds, they often miss information, and their oversights are further obscured by the computer's captivating automatic design functions. This is why Meisling still works regularly with pencil and paper—tools that, ironically, he considers more interactive than the computer, because they force him to think implications through.

"You can't simultaneously get an overview and detail with a computer," he says. "It's linear. It gives you tunnel vision. What computers can do well is what can be calculated over and over. What they can't do is innovation. If you think of some new way to do or look at things and the software can't do it, you're stuck. So a lot of people think, 'Well, I guess it's a dumb idea, or it's unnecessary.'"

I have heard similar warnings from people in other businesses, including high-tech enterprises. A spokeswoman for Hewlett-Packard, the giant California computer-products company, told me the company rarely hires people who are predominantly computer experts, favoring instead those who have a talent for teamwork and are flexible and innovative. Much the same perspective came from several recruiters in film and computer-game animation. In work by artists who have spent a lot of time on computers "you'll see a stiffness or a flatness, a lack of richness and depth," Karen Chelini, the director of human resources for LucasArts Entertainment, George Lucas's interactive-games maker, told me recently. "With traditional art training, you train the eye to pay attention to body movement. You learn attitude, feeling, expression. The ones who are good are those who as kids couldn't be without their sketchbook."

Some educators worry that as children concentrate on how to manipulate software instead of on the subject at hand, learning can diminish rather than grow. Simulations, for example, are built on hidden assumptions, many of which are oversimplified if not highly questionable. All too often, Turkle wrote in *The American Prospect,* "experiences with simulations do not open up questions but close them down." Turkle's concern is that software of this sort fosters passivity, ultimately dulling people's sense of what they can change in the world. There's a tendency, Turkle told me, "to take things at 'interface' value." Indeed, after mastering SimCity, a popular game about urban planning, a tenth-grade girl boasted to Turkle that she'd learned the following rule: "Raising taxes always leads to riots."

JUST A GLAMOROUS TOOL

It would be easy to characterize the battle over computers as merely another chapter in the world's oldest story: humanity's natural resistance to change. But that does an injustice to the forces at work in this transformation. This is not just the future versus the past, uncertainty versus nostalgia; it is about encouraging a fundamental shift in personal priorities—a minimizing of the real, physical world in favor of an unreal "virtual" world. It is about teaching youngsters that exploring what's on a two-dimensional screen is more important than playing with real objects, or sitting down to an attentive conversation with a friend, parent, or teacher. By extension, it means downplaying the importance of conversation, of careful listening, and of expressing oneself in person with acuity and individuality. In the process, it may also limit the development of children's imaginations.

Perhaps this is why Steven Jobs, one of the founders of Apple Computer and a man who claims to have "spearheaded giving away more computer equipment to schools than anybody else on the planet," has come to a grim conclusion: "What's wrong with education cannot be fixed with technology," he told *Wired* magazine in an interview last year. "No amount of technology will make a dent. . . . You're not going to solve the problems by putting all knowledge onto CD-ROMs. We can put a Web site in every school—none of this is bad. It's bad only if it lulls us into thinking we're doing something to solve the problem with education."

The solution is not to ban computers from classrooms altogether. But it may be to ban federal spending on what is fast becoming an overheated campaign. After all, the private sector, with its constant supply of used computers and the computer industry's vigorous competition for new customers, seems well equipped to handle the situation. In fact, if schools can impose some limits rather than indulging in a consumer frenzy, most will probably find themselves with more electronic gear than they need. That could free the billions [the Administration] wants to devote to technology and make it available for impoverished fundamentals: teaching solid skills in reading, thinking, listening, and talking; organizing inventive field trips and other rich hands-on experiences; and, of course, building up the nation's core of knowledgeable, inspiring teachers. These notions are considerably less glamorous than computers are, but their worth is firmly proved through a long history.

RELATED LINKS

- Connecting K–12 Schools to the Information Superhighway (http://www.uark.edu/mckinsey)

- Child Study Center, University of California at Berkeley (http://ihd.berkeley.edu/child.htm)

- Educational Technology Center, Harvard Graduate School of Education (http://www.gse.harvard.edu/~etc)

- Learning Research and Development Center (http://alan.lrdc.pitt.edu/lrdc)

- edtechnot.com's Jane Healy Links (http://www.edtechnot.com/nothealy.html)

- edtechnot.com's Todd Oppenheimer Links (http://www.edtechnot.com/notoppenheimer.html)

FOR FURTHER RESEARCH

To find out more about the topics discussed in this reading, use InfoTrac College Edition. Type in keywords and subject terms such as "technology education programs," "computerized classrooms," and "computer literacy." You can access InfoTrac College Edition from the Wadsworth / Thomson Communication Cafe homepage: http://communication.wadsworth.com.

11

Dystopian Views
of Information Technology

Reading 11-1

Further Explorations into the Culture of Computing
Clifford Stoll

EDITOR'S NOTE

Silicon Snake Oil, first published in 1995, is perhaps the most influential critique of the Internet lifestyle to appear in print. In this excerpt, author Clifford Stoll, an astrophysicist and avid computer user himself, discusses the limitations of network dependence and asserts that there are no simple technological solutions to enduring social problems. Rather than bringing us together, computer networks may instead isolate us from one another. What's missing from the ersatz neighborhood of online community, Stoll argues, is the very essence of a real neighborhood: a feeling of permanence and belonging, a sense of location, and the warmth that can only be derived from an understanding and appreciation of local history.

CONSIDER

1. Why does Stoll take issue with the technocratic belief that computers and information networks will make a better society?

2. Are computers merely tools for thinking, or do they alter our thinking processes to conform to their own idiosyncratic demands?

3. Stoll maintains that computer networks isolate us from one another, rather than bringing us together. Do you agree? Why or why not?

I just saw a video from Pacific Bell—I mean the Pacific Telesis Group—showing an imaginary couple buying a coat from Mongolia. We listen to them chat with a yak dealer; a computer interprets on the fly. In the background, children happily play with a three-dimensional game that teaches math.

The phone company wants me to believe that they'll invent automatic translation and worldwide videophones. And that virtual reality will be primarily used for teaching.

They might equally well show us a less benign future: boring corporate conferences held via satellite and big-screen music videos. Junk mail brought to us at the speed of light. Children avoiding their homework by playing shoot-'em-down, slash-'em-up games. Pornography downloaded into home computers. Credit companies sending dunning letters to a young couple via e-mail.

Now, I've also seen plenty of encouraging things over the networks: seventh-grade students exchanging poetry with friends. A shy woman who met her husband-to-be through the Usenet. International collaborations in sciences and humanities. Specialized mailings for nonprofit groups. Friendly support for a man whose child has leukemia. A family that used the Internet to get the latest research results on a disease. A retarded 25-year-old woman who used a children's math program to practice addition.

Those aren't eye-popping uses like computerized translators or three-dimensional virtual realities, but they're the blossoms in today's garden—much more real than the dreamland painted by network futurists.

In 1986, while managing a cluster of Unix workstations, I viewed networks mechanistically, as a collection of cables, connectors, and computers. After all, my job was to keep the system running, and the main ingredients are hardware. It hadn't occurred to me that the Internet, then so young, formed a community.

Experience dealing with people—not computers—changed my point of view. Other system operators and government agents went out of their way to help me out of a bind. Cooperating together—not only to link our computers, but to track down a rene-gade [chronicled in Stoll's 1989 book, *The Cuckoo's Egg,* published by Doubleday]—showed me that a computer network is, indeed, a community.

But what an impoverished community! One without a church, cafe, art gallery, theater, or tavern. Plenty of human contact, but no humanity. Cybersex, cybersluts, and cybersleaze, but no genuine, lusty, roll-in-the-hay sex.

And no birds sing.

Even ignoring everything palpable—children's laughter, plum jam, my sister Rosalie's green sports car—what's missing from this ersatz neighborhood? A feeling of permanence and belonging, a sense of location, a warmth from the local history. Gone is the very essence of a neighborhood: friendly relations and a sense of being in it together.

Oh—I hear you: It's only a metaphorical community. Much of what happens over the networks is a metaphor—we chat without speaking, smile without grinning, and hug without touching.

On my screen, I see several icons—a mailbox, a theater, a newspaper. These represent incoming messages, an entertainment video, and a news wire. But they're not the real thing. The mailbox doesn't clunk, the movie theater doesn't serve popcorn, and the newspaper doesn't come with a cup of coffee at the corner cafe.

How sad—to dwell in a metaphor without living the experience. The only sensations are a glowing screen, the touch of a keyboard, and the sound of an occasional bleep. All synthetic.

The common claim is that networks, like computers, are tools—utensils to get work done. I've heard this so often that I'm beginning to doubt it.

"A tool for what?" I ask my friends. Their replies are telling: It's a tool for thinking.

Ouch. We need a tool to spare us the effort of thinking? Is reasoning so painful that we require a labor-saving device? What is it we're trying to avoid?

Maybe we're obsessed with computers as tools because, as Thomas Carlyle wrote, man is a tool-using animal . . . without tools he is nothing, with tools he is all.

And so everything within our scope becomes a tool. Advertisements promote pens, dictionaries, and word processors as writing tools. I search in vain for something that isn't a tool: My shoes are personal-transportation tools; chewing gum is a relaxation tool; and the moon is a tool for telling time and illuminating the evening.

But I've never heard of a typewriter user's group, or schools spending thousands of dollars to put a radial-arm saw on every student's desk. Nor do I know of any screwdriver that inspires the same slavish infatuation as the Internet. The computer is a remarkably different kind of tool—one which can turn kids into reactive zombies, adults into frustrated bumblers.

Calling a computer a tool gives us a warm feeling that we're craftsmen, burgeoning with physical skills and manual dexterity. It imparts none of these.

Rather, the computer requires almost no physical interaction or dexterity, beyond the ability to type. And unlike a chisel, drill, or shovel, the computer demands rote memorization of nonobvious rules. You subjugate your own thinking patterns to those of the computer.

Using this tool alters our thinking processes. When Gutenberg invented the printing press, the prevailing style of writing changed, and again when the typewriter became common. Telegraphs, too, influenced literature. Stop. Think of the terseness of Hemingway. In turn, word processors change not just how but *what* we write. The handwritten bread-and-butter note gives way to an e-mail greeting.

Databases aren't just computer programs—there are other ways to organize information, like Rolodexes, address books, and manila folders in filing cabinets. These mechanical filing systems are intuitive, easy to use, and simple to set up. Yet the person deeply committed to a relational database system won't recognize opportunities where these physical devices might work better.

Nor is the computer the only tool for doing mathematics—analytic equations, calculus, approximations, and trigonometry have worked for centuries, if not millennia.

Simply by turning to a computer when confronted with a problem, you limit your ability to recognize other solutions. When the only tool you know is a hammer, everything looks like a nail.

Which is the tool: the computer or the user?

This leads to some important questions that I'm not smart enough to frame. When your thinking is strictly logical—when you're constrained to a digital mode of work—you lose the ability to leapfrog over conceptual walls.

The stiff-walled logic of computers rewards those who can rigorously follow strict-thought rules. These incentives include prestige and employment . . . our software and networks nourish drones.

At the same time, computers punish the imaginative and inventive by constraining them to prescribed channels of thought and action.

For example, we think that painting and drawing programs open up new vistas to graphic artists. But they strongly limit the artist's choices of colors, sizes, shapes, and textures. Moreover, the artist must strictly follow the program's rules. The artist working at a computer never lays a hand on media like origami, textiles, or alabaster.

When we find dance and music on computers, it seems so refreshingly delightful simply because the nature of computing is antithetical to flights of fancy.

And what of the person who can't follow instructions? Often he's the one who comes up with original solutions to problems. Yet this is the guy who cannot boot up without a snag. He has constant troubles with computers, simply because his thoughts are out of sync with the conventions of software designers. In a Darwinian manner, creative people are ill-adapted for survival around computers.

In short, the medium in which we communicate changes how we organize our thoughts. We program computers, but the computers also program us.

Marshall McLuhan divided media into hot and cool—movies and radio were hot, television and the telephone were cool. Hot media are low in participation; cool ones high in it. I'm not sure what he means, but on that scale the Internet, especially the Usenet, is certainly cool.

Think of these media as social interactions. Movies can be participatory, even if you don't get to choose who's on screen. Get a group of friends together to watch *Casablanca* at a campus cinema some weekend. There's gossip while waiting in line, along with the smell of popcorn, and the anticipation of seeing a classic film. You nudge each other during the good scenes, or perhaps put an arm around your sweetie. Or head over to *The Rocky Horror Picture Show,* and don't forget the toast.

Compare this to an intense night surfing the Internet—you have nobody to compare notes with, nobody to harmonize as you hum "As Time Goes By," nobody to spill popcorn on your favorite blanket. Your community disappears when your modem disconnects.

What's the nature of this networked community? It runs in all directions. Professorial, technocratic, punk. Sparks of intellect scattered across electronic fields, without coherent direction.

Listening to traffic crossing the Usenet, I hear a distinct libertarian political leaning: Stay off my back and let me do whatever I please.

It attracts extreme political positions and long-standing international feuds. They spill out of newsgroups frequented by Turks and Armenians, by Israelis and Palestinians, and by Serbs and Croats.

Thousands of Internet users will tell you that I'm giving but one side of a complex story. They'll point to hundreds of self-help groups that work as effectively as any neighborhood counseling organization. They'll show you the comp.risks forum, where anyone can read about the social implications of computing. They'll talk about the World Wide Web, where a click of a mouse will bring the latest news from London, Tokyo, or Berlin.

They're right. The Usenet is a community where hundreds of thousands engage in friendly banter. From across the Net and across the ocean, I hear the latest jokes on rec.humor.funny, reports on travel adventures on rec.travel, and listings of jobs on misc.jobs.offered. Before checking out an old Dracula film, I check into rec.arts.movies.

If I were being fair to the Usenet, I'd have to mention the experts who thanklessly help newcomers on such forums as comp.unix.questions, news.answers, and news.newusers.questions. I'd probably have to include some of the lesser-known watering holes, like rec.arts.books, where book-folk congregate, and alt.best-of-usenet, where every day I read gaffes by newcomers as well as exceptionally creative flames.

Don't get me wrong: There's lots of good things happening online. I've seen bulletin boards for cancer survivors, bagpipers, and cave explorers. A carpenter's union in New York state gets the news out over a bulletin board.

Another way to spread the word is through electronic mailing lists. These lists let exclusive groups thrive over the networks, whether medieval English scholars, feminist authors, or Japanese animation addicts.

Mailing lists are universally available over e-mail. To get on the mailing list for postcard collectors, just send mail to postcardrequest@bit.listserv.postcard, with the subject line of *subscribe*. They're simple, too: A user sends mail to one site, and everyone down the line gets a copy.

The neatness of these mailing lists extends beyond their simplicity and wide availability. It's a great way to make a closed discussion, say for sensitive topics like gender issues or recovery groups. There's a place for folk dancers to compare steps and accordion players to exchange notes. Around San Francisco, book fanatics send mail to ead@netcom.com to get the latest scoop on bookstore happenings.

But mailing lists almost guarantee mailbox overflow. When the comet crashed into Jupiter, I picked up fifty messages from the Net; another 100 fell into the bitbucket. And mailing-list traffic, like Usenet newsgroups, often has little content.

Virtually everything is debated on the Usenet: whether computers are best left on at night, if cats can be fed a vegetarian diet, if abortion should be legal.

Predictable replies—maybe, maybe, and maybe, but each with more stridency. Plenty of opinions, but not much informed dialogue, and even less consensus.

Of course, since there are no easy answers, arguments over the Usenet are seldom resolved. They'll degenerate into name-calling; eventually one of the participants figuratively walks away, and a new debate begins.

Now, recurrent debates aren't bad—they're just circular and tedious. Next time I have to spend a week in traction, I'll check into the Usenet. One of the joys of computers is how they're great at wasting time that might otherwise be difficult to waste.

A UNIVERSAL PANACEA, OR SILICON SNAKE OIL?

Imagine driving from Yankee Stadium in the Bronx to Jones Beach on Long Island. You'd likely take the Cross Bronx Expressway, the Throgs Neck Bridge, the Cross Island Parkway, the Long Island Expressway, and the Meadowbrook State Parkway. Say thanks to Robert Moses—he created these public works.

From 1930 to 1970, Robert Moses built roads, bridges, parks, and housing projects. Nothing stopped him—not politicians, community leaders, urban planners, neighborhoods. Quite the contrary: He bribed politicians, intimidated community leaders, hired the urban planners, and plowed under the neighborhoods. Anyways, in 1955 only a reactionary Luddite would possibly oppose highway construction. The automobile was clearly the key to the future.

Your imaginary trip across the Cross Bronx Expressway won't show you the thousands of people evicted from their homes, the old brownstone apartments paved over, the diverse neighborhoods cleaved by noisy traffic arteries. Robert Moses did more to destroy New York City than any one individual.

Moses disdained anyone who couldn't afford a car, so he built parkways with low overpasses that blocked buses. No walkways or bike paths, either. In a similar way, computer mavens shun the technophobes, so they write manuals that can't be understood by novices. Internet merchants want government subsidies to build ever-faster links, but they won't offer lower connect rates for the poor.

Today's Internet hustlers invade our communities with computers, not concrete. By pushing the Internet as a universal panacea, they offer a tempting escape from this all-too-mundane world. They tell us that we need not get along with our neighbors, heck, we needn't even interact with them. Won't need to travel to a library either; those books will come right to my desk. Interactive multimedia will solve classroom problems. Fat paychecks and lifelong employment await those who master computers.

They're well meaning, of course. They truly believe in virtual communities and electronic classrooms. They'll tell you how the computer is a tool to be used, not abused. Because clearly, the computer is the key to the future.

The key ingredient of their silicon snake oil is a technocratic belief that computers and networks will make a better society. Access to information, better communications, and electronic programs can cure social problems.

I don't believe them. There are no simple technological solutions to social problems. There's plenty of distrust and animosity between people who communicate perfectly well. Access to a universe of information cannot solve our problems: We will forever struggle to understand one another. The most important interactions in life happen between people, not between computers.

Computer networks isolate us from one another, rather than bring us together. We need only deal with one side of an individual over the Net. And if we don't like what we see, we just pull the plug. Or flame them. There's no need to tolerate the imperfections of real people. It's the same intolerance found on the highway, where motorists direct intense anger at one another.

By logging on to the networks, we lose the ability to enter into spontaneous interactions with real people.

Evening time is now spent watching a television or a computer terminal—safe havens in which to hide. Sitting around a porch and talking is becoming extinct, as is reading aloud to children.

The Internet puts me in touch with thousands of people across the country. But it's more important to spend time with my friends and neighbors. Karen Anderson, the penguin keeper at San Francisco's Steinhart Aquarium, puts it this way: "The people who are right close to me are the most important ones in my life. Why should I get excited about personal relationships on some computer network?"

Karen told me of the work of Dr. Luis Baptista, the curator of ornithology at the California Academy of Sciences. This guy knows his birds—he can whistle the songs of doves and sparrows. Jeez, he did his dissertation on the dialects of these birds.

Well, to see how birds learn songs, he raised white-crowned sparrows. When they left the nest, Dr. Baptista placed single fledglings in a special cage where they could see and hear an Asian strawberry finch. The young birds could also hear several dialects of their own sparrow songs in the same room, but they couldn't see those sparrows.

The fledgling sparrows didn't learn their own songs. Instead, they matured, singing the songs of the Asian finches with whom they socially interacted. And later, as parents, these sparrows taught their young to sing Chinese songs, too. Sparrows learn from living teachers, not from machines.

In the same way, the isolation of computers and on-line networks causes us to sing others' songs. Children, raised with less social interaction, adopt the ways of the first people they come in close contact with. It encourages a divorce from parental values and the dominance of peer culture. Kids that interact with computers rather than their parents miss out on the most important part of growing: being close to their families.

Think I'm exaggerating? One teenager in Berkeley began using a computer when he was 3 years old; today, he's utterly fluent in getting around the Internet, but can't converse with an adult. I know several computer wizards who can tell you details of their computer's disk cache, but don't know when their family immigrated to America. And I've met dozens of high school students who can proficiently use a word processor, but have never written a thank-you letter.

RELATED LINKS

- Clifford Stoll Topic Page (http://users.hub.ofthe.net/~rpmcint/clfstoll.htm)
- Cyberspace, Hypertext, and Critical Theory (http://landow.stg.brown.edu/cpace/cspaceov.html)
- edtechnot.com's Clifford Stoll Links (http://www.edtechnot.com/notstoll.html)
- edtechnot.com's Neil Postman Links (http://www.edtechnot.com/notpostman.html)

FOR FURTHER RESEARCH

To find out more about the topics discussed in this reading, use InfoTrac College Edition. Type in keywords and subject terms such as "information superhighway," "technological utopia," and "technorealism." You can access InfoTrac College Edition from the Wadsworth/Thomson Communication Cafe homepage: http://communication.wadsworth.com.

Reading 11-2

The First Law of Data Smog
David Shenk

Information, once rare and cherished like caviar, is now plentiful and taken for granted like potatoes.

EDITOR'S NOTE

In this reading from Data Smog, *author David Shenk suggests that the character of information, and the way we think about it, has fundamentally changed since the development of computer technology. As we have accrued more and more data and information, they have become a commodity—as well as a pollutant. Until the mid-twentieth century, more information was generally seen as a good thing; now we produce information much faster than we are able to process it. With information and data production at an all-time high, Shenk argues that* information overload *has surfaced as a contentious social, political, and even emotional problem.*

CONSIDER

1. What are some of the personal, societal, and professional implications of the first law of data smog (above)?
2. Why has information production not only increased, but also accelerated, in the period following World War II?
3. What are some possible ways of counteracting the incessant barrage of information characteristic of a message-dense society?

Still, the concept of *too much information* seems odd and vaguely inhuman. This is because, in evolutionary-historical terms, this weed in our information landscape has just sprouted—it is only about 50 years old.

Up until then, more information was almost always a good thing. For nearly 100,000 years leading up to this century, information technology has been an unambiguous virtue as a means of sustaining and developing culture. Information and communications have made us steadily healthier, wealthier, more tolerant. Because of information, we understand more about how to overcome the basic challenges of life. Food is more abundant. Our physical structures are sturdier, more reliable. Our societies are more stable, as we have learned how to make political systems function. Our citizens are freer, thanks to a wide dissemination of information that has empowered the individual. Dangerous superstitions and false notions have been washed away: Communicating quickly with people helps to overcome our fear of them and diminishes the likelihood of conflict.

Then, around the time of the first atomic bomb, something strange happened. We began to produce information much faster than we could process it.

This had never happened before. For 100,000 years the three fundamental stages of the communications process—production, distribution, and processing—had been more or less in synch with one another. By and large, over our long history, people have been able to examine and consider information about as quickly as it could be created and circulated. This equipoise lasted through an astonishing range of communications media—the drum, smoke signal, cave painting, horse, town crier, carrier pigeon, newspaper, photograph, telegraph, telephone, radio, and film.

But in the mid-twentieth century this graceful synchrony was abruptly knocked off track with the introduction of computers, microwave transmissions, television, and satellites.[1] These hyperproduction and hyperdistribution mechanisms surged ahead of human processing ability, leaving us with a permanent processing deficit, what Finnish sociologist Jaako Lehtonen calls an "information discrepancy."[2]

In this way, in a very short span of natural history, we have vaulted from a state of information scarcity to one of information surplus—from drought to flood in the geological blink of an eye. In 1850, 4 percent of American workers handled information for a living;[3] now *most* do, and information processing (as opposed to material goods) now accounts for more than half of the U.S. gross domestic product.[4] Data has become more plentiful, more speedy (computer processing speed has doubled every 2 years for the last 30 years),[5] and more dense (from 1965 to 1995, the average network television advertisement shrunk from 53.1 seconds to 25.4 seconds and the average TV news "sound bite" shrunk from 42.3 seconds to 8.3 seconds; meanwhile, over the same period, the number of ads per network TV minute increased from 1.1 to 2.4).[6]

Information has also become a lot cheaper—to produce, to manipulate, to disseminate. All of this has made us information rich, empowering Americans with the blessings of applied knowledge. It has also, though, unleashed the potential of information gluttony.

Just as fat has replaced starvation as this nation's number-one dietary concern, information overload has replaced information scarcity as an important new emotional, social, and political problem. "The real issue for future technology," says Columbia's Eli Noam, "does not appear to be production of information, and certainly not transmission. Almost anybody can *add* information. The difficult question is how to *reduce* it."[7]

Action photographers often use a machine called a "motor drive" that attaches to 35mm cameras. The motor drive allows a photographer to shoot many separate exposures in any given second just by keeping his or her finger on a button. *Click-click-click-click-click . . .*

What an elegant metaphor for our age: With virtually no effort and for relatively little cost, we can capture as much information as we want. The capturing requires very little planning or forethought, and in fact is built right into the design of our machines. With a thumb and index finger, we effortlessly Copy and Paste sentences, paragraphs, books. After writing e-mail, we "carbon copy" it to 1 or 100 others. The same goes for the photocopy machine, onto which we simply enter whatever number of copies we desire. *Would you like those collated and stapled? It's no bother.*

Only as an afterthought do we confront the consequences of such a low transaction cost. "E-mail is an open duct into your central nervous system," says Michael Dertouzos, [the former] director of MIT's Laboratory for Computer Science, exaggerating playfully to make a serious point. "It occupies the brain and reduces productivity."[8]

With information production not only increasing, but *accelerating* [see Reading 9-1], there is no sign that processing will ever catch up. We have quite suddenly mutated into a radically different culture, a civilization that trades in and survives on stylized communication. We no longer hunt or gather; few of us farm or assemble. Instead, we negotiate, we network, we interface. And as we enjoy the many fruits of this burgeoning information civilization, we also have to learn to compensate for the new and permanent side effects of what sociologists, in an academic understatement, call a "message dense" society.

Audio buffs have long been familiar with the phrase *signal-to-noise ratio*. It is engineering parlance for measuring the quality of a sound system by comparing the amount of desired audio signal to the amount of unwanted noise leaking through. In the Information Age, *signal-to-noise* has also become a useful way to think about social health and stability. How much of the information in our midst is useful, and how much of it gets in the way? What is our signal-to-noise ratio?

We know that the ratio has diminished of late, and that the character of information has changed: As we have accrued more and more of it, information has emerged not only as a currency, but also as a pollutant.

- In 1971 the average American was targeted by at least 560 daily advertising messages. Twenty years later, that number had risen sixfold, to 3,000 messages per day.[9]

- In the office, an average of 60 percent of each person's time is now spent processing documents.[10]

- Paper consumption per capita in the United States tripled from 1940 to 1980 (from 200 to 600 pounds), and tripled again from 1980 to 1990 (to 1,800 pounds).[11]

- In the 1980s, third-class mail (used to send publications) grew thirteen times faster than population growth.[12]

- Two-thirds of business managers surveyed report tension with colleagues, loss of job satisfaction, and strained personal relationships as a result of information overload.[13]

- More than 1,000 telemarketing companies employ 4 million Americans, and generate $650 billion in annual sales.[14]

Let us call this unexpected, unwelcome part of our atmosphere "data smog," an expression for the noxious muck and druck of the Information Age. Data smog gets in the way; it crowds out quiet moments, and obstructs much-needed contemplation. It spoils conversation, literature, and even entertainment. It thwarts skepticism, rendering us less sophisticated as consumers and citizens. It stresses us out.

Data smog is not just the pile of unsolicited catalogs and spam arriving daily in our home and electronic mailboxes. It is also information that we pay handsomely for, that we *crave*—the seductive, mesmerizing quick-cut television ads and the 24-hour up-to-the-minute news flashes. It is the faxes we request as well as the ones we don't; it is the misdialed numbers and drippy sales calls we get during dinnertime; but it is also the Web sites we eagerly visit before and after dinner, the pile of magazines we pore through every month, and the dozens of channels we flip through whenever we get a free moment.

The blank spaces and silent moments in life are fast disappearing. Mostly because we have asked for it, media is everywhere. Televisions, telephones, radios, message beepers, and an assortment of other modern communication and navigational aids are now as ubiquitous as roads and tennis shoes—anywhere humans can go, all forms of media now follow: onto trains, planes, automobiles, into hotel bathrooms, along jogging paths and mountain trails, on bikes and boats . . .

Information and entertainment now conform to our every orientation: Giant television screens adorn stadiums and surround theatrical stages; more ordinary-size TVs hang from ceilings in bars and airport lounges; mini-TVs are installed in front of individual seats in new airliners. Cellular telephone conversation creates a new ambiance for sidewalks and hallways. Beepers and laptop computers follow us home and come with us on vacation.

Meanwhile, the flavor of the information has also changed. It's no longer a matter of mono *versus* stereo or black and white *versus* color. TV and computer screens have been transformed into a hypnotic visual sizzle that MTV aptly calls "eye candy." With hypermedia, "dense TV," and split-screens providing a multiplicity of images at once, straining our attention has become one of our most popular forms of entertainment.

We've heard a lot lately about the moral decay evident in our entertainment packaging. But it isn't so much the content of the messages that should worry us as much their ubiquity, and it is critical to realize that information doesn't have to be unwanted and unattractive to be harmful.

Take advertising (please). Though the bulk of today's commercial messages are esthetically appealing and can each be considered relatively harmless, in aggregate they have crept into every nook and cranny of our lives—onto our jackets, ties, hats, shirts, and wristbands; onto bikes, benches, cars, trucks, even tennis nets; onto banners trailing behind planes, hanging above sporting and concert events, and now, in smaller form, bordering Web pages; onto the sides of blimps hovering in the sky. Magazine ads now communicate not only though color and text but also through smell and even sound.

The smog thickens from the insidious blurring of editorial content and commercial messages in "advertorials" and product placements, to the point where it often becomes impossible to determine whether someone is trying to tell you something or merely sell you something. Increasingly, our public spaces are up for rent. "Is it crass?" asks the official marketer for the city of Atlanta, Joel Babbitt, who has designs to sell high-tech advertising on city sidewalks, streets, parks, and garbage trucks. "Yes, but so is the Blockbuster Bowl. So is Michael Jordan wearing a Nike cap on the bench and getting a million dollars for it . . . If it brings in money that helps our citizens, what's the harm?" [15]

What is the harm of an incessant barrage of stimuli captivating our senses at virtually every waking moment? Providing a thorough answer to that question is one of the most important things we can do in our message-dense society.

Challenge. Third Annual Colloquium, June 16–17, 1995. Frankfurt am Main: Schaffer-Poeschel Verlag Stuttgart, 1995, p. 21.

2. Jaako Lehtonen, "The Information Society and the New Competence," *American Behavioral Scientist,* November/December 1988, pp. 104–111.

3. Louise Sweeney, *The Christian Science Monitor,* January 26, 1978, p. 26.

4. Orrin Klapp, *Overload and Boredom.* New York: Greenwood Press, 1986, p. 7.

5. Robert E. Calem, *New York Times* on the Web, February 14, 1996. "We'll be at 1 million times faster [than ENIAC] in 6 years if Moore's Law continues to hold true, which it always has," said Prof. Mitchell Marcus, chairman of the University of Pennsylvania's Computer and Information Science Department.

6. *TV Dimensions 1995* and *Magazine Dimensions 1995.*

7. Noam, "Visions of the Media Age," pp. 18–19.

8. Michael Dertouzos, *Technology Review,* August/September 1994.

9. Noam, "Visions of the Media Age," p. 28.

10. Patrick Ames, *Beyond Paper.* Indianapolis: Hayden Press, 1993.

11. Jeff Davidson, "The Frantic Society," *Business and Society Review 83* (September 22, 1992), 4; Noam, "Visions of the Media Age," p. 22.

12. Noam, "Visions of the Media Age," pp. 20–24.

13. David Lewis, "Dying for Information? An Investigation into the Effects of Information Overload in the U.K. and Worldwide." *Reuters Business Information,* October 1996.

14. Cristina Rouvalis, "Charm, Persistence, and a Telephone." *Pittsburgh Post-Gazette,* May 25, 1997.

15. Petter Applebome, "How Atlanta's Adman Pushes the City to Sell Itself," *New York Times,* February 9, 1993, p. A16.

NOTES

1. Eli M. Noam, "Visions of the Media Age: Taming the Information Monster." In *Multimedia: A Revolutionary*

RELATED LINKS

- www.davidshenk.com (http://www.technorealism.org/dshenk/homepage.html)
- Technorealism (http://www.technorealism.org)

- Change and Information Overload: Negative Effects (http://pespmc1.vub.ac.be/CHINNEG.html)

- Deep Thinking and Deep Reading in an Age of Info-Glut, Info-Garbage, Info-Glitz, and Info-Glimmer (http://www.nbps.k12.wi.us/district/StaffDev/Workshops/Searching/deep_thinking_and_deep_reading_in_an_age_of_infoglut.htm)

- A Few Thoughts on Cognitive Overload (http://icl-server.ucsd.edu/~kirsh/Articles/Overload/published.html)

FOR FURTHER RESEARCH

To find out more about the topics discussed in this reading, use InfoTrac College Edition. Type in keywords and subject terms such as "information overload," "information discrepancy," and "information society." You can access InfoTrac College Edition from the Wadsworth/Thomson Communication Cafe homepage: http://communication.wadsworth.com.

Reading 11-3

The Myth of Order. The Real Lesson of Y2K Is That Software Operates Just Like Any Natural System: Out of Control

Ellen Ullman

"Bugs are an unintended source of inspiration. Many times I've seen a bug in a game and thought, 'That's cool—I wouldn't have thought of that in a million years.'"
—Will Wright, creator of SimCity and chief game designer at Maxis

"I've fixed about 1,000 bugs in my life. How many have I created? Undoubtedly more."
—Patrick Naughton, executive vice president of products, Infoseek

EDITOR'S NOTE

After years of media hype, the Year 2000 (Y2K) computer problem, known to many as the "millennium bug," resulted in only minimal disruption of a few systems. Perhaps the worst glitch was experienced by the Pentagon, which quietly endured three days of malfunctioning spy satellites. In the months before the millennial transition, concern over possible power grid and transportation disruptions prompted the banking industry to reassure nervous customers through television ads, publications like the Utne Reader *to issue a 120-page Y2K Citizen's Action Guide, and the American Red Cross to recommend that the public have enough food and supplies on hand to last several days to a week. In this reading, writer and computer programmer Ellen Ullman draws on her 20 years of programming experience and concludes that the real lesson of Y2K is that software operates just like any natural system: beyond the control of any individual. Y2K also illustrates the importance of advanced planning and disaster prevention—an estimated $250 billion was spent on Y2K-related repairs worldwide—in an era of growing complexity and technological dependence.*

CONSIDER

1. What was the origin of the Y2K problem, and what could have been done to prevent it from becoming such a pressing issue?

2. How do inevitable design flaws or system defects such as the "millennium bug" cause us to rethink the reliability and trustworthiness of information technology?

3. As a cultural phenomenon, what does society's reaction to the Y2K episode say about our reliance on computer hardware and software?

Y2K has uncovered a hidden side of computing. It's always been there, of course, and always will be. It's simply been obscured by the pleasures we get from our electronic tools and toys, and then lost in the zingy glow of technoboosterism. Y2K is showing everyone what technical people have been dealing with for years: the complex, muddled, bug-bitten systems we all depend on, and their nasty tendency toward the occasional disaster.

It's almost a betrayal. After being told for years that technology is the path to a highly evolved future, it's come as something of a shock to discover that a computer system is not a shining city on a hill—perfect and ever new—but something more akin to an old farmhouse built bit by bit over decades by nonunion carpenters.

The reaction has been anger, outrage even—how could all you programmers be so stupid? Y2K has challenged a belief in digital technology that has been almost religious. But it's not surprising. The public has had little understanding of the context in which Y2K exists. Glitches, patches, crashes—these are as inherent to the process of creating an intelligent electronic system as is the beauty of an elegant algorithm, the satisfaction of a finely tuned program, the gee-whiz pleasure of messages sent around the world at light speed. Until you understand that computers contain both of these aspects—elegance and error—you can't really understand Y2K.

Technically speaking, the "millennium bug" is not a bug at all, but what is called a design flaw. Programmers are very sensitive to the difference, since a bug means the code is at fault (the program isn't doing what it was designed to do), and a design flaw means it's the designer's fault (the code is doing exactly what was specified in the design, but the design was wrong or inadequate). In the case of the millennium bug, of course, the code was designed to use two-digit years.

The problem comes if computers misread the two-digit numbers—00, 01, et cetera. Should these be seen as 1900 and 1901, or as 2000 and 2001? Two-digit dates were used originally to save space, since computer memory and disk storage were prohibitively expensive. The designers who chose to specify these two-digit "bugs" were not stupid, and perhaps they were not even wrong. By some estimates, the savings accrued by using two-digit years will have outweighed the entire cost of fixing the code for the year 2000.

But Y2K did not even begin its existence as a design flaw. Up until the mid-1980s—almost 30 years after two-digit years were first put into use—what we now call Y2K would have been called an "engineering trade-off," and a good one. A trade-off: to get something you need, you give up something else you need less urgently; to get more space on disk and in memory, you give up the precision of the century indicators. Perfectly reasonable. The correct decision. The surest sign of its correctness is what happened next: two-digit years went on to have a long, successful life as a "standard." Computer systems could not work without standards—an agreement among programs and systems about how they will exchange information. Dates flowed from program to program, system to system, from tape to memory to paper, and back to disk—it all worked just fine for decades.

Though not for centuries, of course. The near immortality of computer software has come as a shock to programmers. Ask anyone who was there: We never expected this stuff to still be around.

Bug, design flaw, side effect, engineering trade-off—programmers have many names for system defects, the way Eskimos have many words for snow. And for the same reason: They're very familiar with the thing and can detect its fine gradations. To be a programmer is to develop a carefully managed relationship with error. There's no getting around it. You either make your accommodations with failure, or the work will become intolerable. Every program has a bug; every complex system has its blind spots. Occasionally, given just the right set of circumstances, something will fail spectacularly. There is a Silicon Valley company, formerly called Failure Analysis (now Exponent),

"The Myth of Order. The Real Lesson of Y2K Is That Software Operates Just Like Any Natural System: Out of Control," by Ellen Ullman. From *Wired,* April 1999, pp. 126–129, 183–184. Copyright © 1999 by Ellen Ullman. Reprinted with permission of the author.

whose business consists of studying system disasters. The company's sign used to face the freeway like a warning to every technical person heading north out of Silicon Valley: Failure Analysis.

In the popular imagination, the programmer is a kind of traveler into the unknown, venturing near the margin of mind and meatspace. Maybe. For moments. On some extraordinary projects, sometimes—a new operating system, a newly conceived class of software. For most of us, though, programming is not a dramatic confrontation between human and machine; it's a confused conversation with programmers we will never meet, a frustrating wrangle with some other programmer's code.

Most modern programming is done through what are called application programming interfaces, or APIs. Your job is to write some code that will talk to another piece of code in a narrowly defined way using the specific methods offered by the interface, and only those methods. The interface is rarely documented well. The code on the other side of the interface is usually sealed in a proprietary black box. And below that black box is another, and below that another—a receding tower of black boxes, each with its own errors. You can't envision the whole tower, you can't open the boxes, and what information you've been given about any individual box could be wrong. The experience is a little like looking at a madman's electronic bomb and trying to figure out which wire to cut. You try to do it carefully but sometimes things blow up.

At its core, programming remains irrational—a time-consuming, painstaking, error-stalked process, out of which comes a functional but flawed piece of work. And it most likely will remain so as long as we are using computers whose basic design descends from ENIAC, a machine constructed to calculate the trajectory of artillery shells. A programmer is presented with a task that a program must accomplish. But it is a task as a human sees it, full of unexpressed knowledge, implicit associations, allusions to allusions. Its coherence comes from knowledge structures deep in the body, from experience, memory. Somehow all this must be expressed in the constricted language of the API, and all of the accumulated code must resolve into a set of instructions that can be performed by a machine that is, in essence, a giant calculator. It shouldn't be surprising if mistakes are made.

There is irrationality at the core of programming, and there is irrationality surrounding it from without. Factors external to the programmer—the whole enter-

prise of computing, its history and business practices—create an atmosphere in which flaws and oversights are that much more likely to occur.

The most irrational of all external factors, the one that makes the experience of programming feel most insane, is known as "aggressive scheduling." Whether software companies will acknowledge it or not, release schedules are normally driven by market demand, not the actual time it would take to build a reasonably robust system. The parts of the development process most often foreshortened are two crucial ones: design documentation and testing.

Even if programmers were given rational development schedules, the systems they work on are increasingly complex, patched together—and incoherent. Systems have become something like Russian nesting dolls, with newer software wrapped around older software, which is wrapped around software that is older yet. We've come to see that code doesn't evolve; it accumulates.

The problem of old code is many times worse in a large corporation or a government office, where whole subsystems may have been built 20 or 30 years ago. Most of the original programmers are long gone, taking their knowledge with them—along with the programmers who followed them, and ones after that. The code, a sort of *palimpsest* by now, becomes difficult to understand. Even if the company had the time to replace it, it's no longer sure of everything the code does. So it is kept running behind wrappers of newer code—so-called middleware, or quickly developed user interfaces like the Web—which keeps the old code running, but as a fragile, precious object. The program runs, but is not understood; it can be used, but not modified. Eventually, a complex computer system becomes a journey backward through time. Look into the center of the most slick-looking Web banking site, built a few months ago, and you're bound to see a creaky database running on an aged mainframe.

Adding yet more complexity are the electronic connections that have been built between systems: customers, suppliers, financial clearinghouses, whole supply chains interlinking their systems. One patched-together wrapped-up system exchanges data with another patched-together wrapped-up system—layer upon layer of software involved in a single transaction, until the possibility of failure increases exponentially.

It's from deep in there—somewhere near the middlemost Russian doll in the innermost layer of software—that the millennium bug originates. One system sends it on to the next, along with the many bugs and problems we already know about, and the untold numbers that remain to be discovered. One day— maybe when we switch to the new version of the Internet Protocol, or when some router somewhere is replaced—one day the undiscovered bugs will come to light and we'll have to worry about each of them in turn. The millennium bug is not unique; it's just the flaw we see now, the most convincing evidence yet of the human fallibility that lives inside every system.

It's hard to overstate just how common bugs are. Every week, the computer trade paper *Info World* prints a little box called The Bug Report, showing problems in commonly used software, some of them very serious. And the box itself is just a sampling from www .bugnet.com, where one day's search for bugs relating to "security" yielded a list of sixty-eight links, many to other lists and to lists of links, reflecting what may be thousands of bugs related to this keyword alone. And that's just the ones that are known about and have been reported.

If you think about all the things that can go wrong, it'll drive you crazy. So technical people, who can't help knowing about the fragility of systems, have had to find some way to live with what they know. What they've done is develop a normal sense of failure, an everyday relationship with potential disaster.

One approach is to ignore all thoughts about the consequences—to stay focused on the code on your desk. This is not that difficult to do, since programmers get high rewards for spending large amounts of time in front of a computer workstation, where they're expected to maintain a very deep and narrow sort of concentration.

If you can't stay focused on your code, another approach is to develop an odd sort of fatalism, a dark, defensive humor in the face of all the things you know can go wrong. Making fun of bugs is almost a sign of sophistication. It shows you know your way around a real system, that you won't shy back when things really start to fall apart. A friend of mine once worked as a software engineer at a Baby Bell. He liked to tell people how everyone in the company was amazed to pick up a handset and actually get a dial tone. It was almost a brag: Ha ha, my system's so screwed up you wouldn't believe it.

Now here comes a problem that's no joke. Technical people can't help hearing about the extreme consequences that will come down on the world if they don't find all the places problems like Y2K are hiding. And

they simultaneously know that it is impossible to find all the problems in any system, let alone in ones being used long beyond their useful life spans.

"Y2K is a sort of perverse payback from the universe for all the hasty and incomplete development efforts over the last 10 years," said the Y2K testing lead for a midsize brokerage. Also speaking on condition of anonymity, Lawrence Bell (a pseudonym) said it like an I-told-you-so, a chance for him to get back at every programmer and programming manager who ever sent him junky software.

Bell is a tall, impeccably groomed young man whose entire workday consists of looking for bugs. He's in QA, quality assurance, the place where glitches are brought to light, kept on lists, managed, prioritized, and juggled—a complete department devoted to bugs. He has the tester's crisp manner, the precision of the quality seeker, in whom a certain amount of obsessive fussiness is a very good thing.

The only thing about Y2K that was really bothering Bell was the programmers. There is a classic animosity between programmers and testers—after all, the tester's role in life is to find everything the programmer did wrong. But Y2K and its real-world time pressures seem to have escalated the conflict.

The source of the hostility is documentation: Programmers are supposed to make a record of the code they've written. Documentation is how quality assurance people know what the system is supposed to do, and therefore how to test it. But programmers hate to write documentation, and so they simply avoid doing it. "The turnover is high," said Bell, "or the programmers who have been here a long time get promoted. They don't want to go back to this project they wrote 10 years ago—and get punished for not documenting it."

Programmers have fun and leave us to clean up their messes, is Bell's attitude. They want to go off to new programs, new challenges, and the really annoying thing is, they can. "They say, 'I want to do something new,'" said Bell, truly angry now, "and they get away with it."

"No more programmers working without adult supervision!"

This was declaimed by Ed Yardeni, chief economist for Deutsche Bank Securities, before a crowded hotel ballroom. On the opening day of the Year 2000 Symposium, August 10, 1998 (with cameras from *60 Minutes* rolling), Yardeni explained how the millennium bug would bring about a world recession on the order of the 1973–1974 downturn, and this would occur because the world's systems "were put together over 30 to 40 years without any adult supervision whatsoever." Blame the programmers. The mood at the conference was like that of a spurned lover: All those coddled boys in T-shirts and cool eyewear, formerly fetishized for their adolescent ways, have betrayed us.

It has become popular wisdom to say that Y2K is the result of "shortsightedness." It's a theme that has been taken up as a near-moral issue, as if the people who created the faulty systems were somehow derelict as human beings.

In fact, some of the most successful and long-lived technologies suffer from extreme shortsightedness. The design of the original IBM PC, for example, assumed there would never be more than one user, who would never be running more than one program at a time, which would never see more than 256K of memory. The original Internet protocol, IP, limited the number of server addresses it could handle to what seemed like a very large number at the time, never imagining the explosive growth of the Web.

I once worked on a Cobol program that had been running for more than 15 years. It was written before the great inflation of the late 1970s. By the time I saw it, in 1981, the million-dollar figure in all dollar amounts was too large for the program's internal storage format, and so multiple millions of dollars simply disappeared without a trace.

We are surrounded by shortsighted systems. Right at this moment, some other program is surely about to burst the bounds of its format for money or number of shares traded or count of items sold. The Dow Jones Industrial Average will one day break 20,000, the price of gas will top $9.99, the systems we're renovating now may live long enough to need renovation again. Some system designer, reacting to the scarce computer resource of our day—not memory but bandwidth—is specifying a piece of code that we will one day look back on as folly.

At the Year 2000 Symposium where Yardeni spoke, there was a technical workshop about creating a "time machine"—a virtual time environment for testing "fixed" Y2K programs. One of the presenters, Carl Gehr of the Edge Information Group, patiently explained that, when designing the test environment, "you have to specify an upper limit" for the year. While everyone scribbled notes, an awful thought occurred to me. "But what upper limit?" I said out loud. "Should we be worrying about the year 9000? 10,001?"

Gehr stopped talking, heads came up from their notes, and the room went quiet. It was as if this were the first time, in all the rush to fix their systems, the attendees had been able to stop, reflect, think about a faraway future. Finally, from the back of the room came a voice: "Good question."

Things can go very, very wrong and still not be the end of the world. Says Bell: "It's just a big user test."

Gehr glanced over at his colleague, Marilyn Frankel, who was waiting to talk about temporary "fixes" for Y2K-affected code. "Marilyn will address that later, I'm sure," he said.

RELATED LINKS

- Salon.com Directory: Ellen Ullman (http://www.salonmag.com/directory/topics/ellen_ullman)

- *Wired*'s Y2K Archive (http://www.wired.com/wired/archive/y2k)

- Year 2000 Crisis: Resources (http://www.bladecomputing.com/y2k/resources.htm)

- The Year 2000 Problem (http://www.nytimes.com/library/tech/reference/millennium-index.html)

- Y2K Citizen's Action Guide (http://www.utne.com/y2k/Y2KbookMain.pdf)

FOR FURTHER RESEARCH

To find out more about the topics discussed in this reading, use InfoTrac College Edition. Type in keywords and subject terms such as "Y2K," "millennium bug," and "technological failure." You can access InfoTrac College Edition from the Wadsworth/Thomson Communication Cafe homepage: http://communication.wadsworth.com.

Reading 11-4

Researchers Find Sad, Lonely World in Cyberspace

Amy Harmon

EDITOR'S NOTE

Although it was roundly criticized on methodological grounds by Net enthusiasts and members of the research community alike, the Carnegie Mellon HomeNet study of long-term Internet use—the first of its kind—documented a disturbing trend: Spending a lot of time online can lead to feelings of depression and loneliness. The results, as this reading discusses, suggest that the interactive medium of cyberspace may be no more socially healthy than traditional media and run contrary to the expectations of the researchers who designed the study and many of the organizations—including computer companies—that financed it. Interestingly, the study's authors stress that the negative effects of Internet use they found were not inevitable.

CONSIDER

1. Why did the researchers conclude that relationships maintained over long distances through the Internet erode personal security and happiness?

2. If avid Internet use really does lead to a decline in normal levels of social involvement and psychological well-being, what should be done about it—anything?

3. On what grounds can the study be criticized or its findings questioned? Do you agree or disagree with what the study found?

In the first concentrated study of the social and psychological effects of Internet use at home, researchers at Carnegie Mellon University have found that people who spend even a few hours a week online experience higher levels of depression and loneliness than they would have if they used the computer network less frequently.

Those participants who were lonelier and more depressed at the start of the 2-year study, as determined by a standard questionnaire administered to all the subjects, were not more likely to use the Internet. Instead, Internet use itself appeared to cause a decline in psychological well-being, the researchers said.

The results of the $1.5 million project ran completely contrary to expectations of the social scientists who designed it and to many of the organizations that financed the study. These included technology companies like Intel Corp., Hewlett-Packard, AT&T Re-

search, and Apple Computer, as well as the National Science Foundation.

"We were shocked by the findings, because they are counterintuitive to what we know about how socially the Internet is being used," said Robert Kraut, a social psychology professor at Carnegie Mellon's Human Computer Interaction Institute. "We are not talking here about the extremes. These were normal adults and their families, and on average, for those who used the Internet most, things got worse."

The Internet has been praised as superior to television and other "passive" media because it allows users to choose the kind of information they want to receive and, often, to respond actively to it in the form of e-mail exchanges with other users, chat rooms, or electronic bulletin board postings.

Research on the effects of watching television indicates that it tends to reduce social involvement. But the new study, titled "HomeNet," suggests that the interactive medium may be no more socially healthy than older mass media. It also raises troubling questions about the nature of "virtual" communication and the disembodied relationships that are often formed in the vacuum of cyberspace.

Participants in the study used inherently social features like e-mail and Internet chat more than they used passive information gathering like reading or watching videos. But they reported a decline in interaction with family members and a reduction in their circles of friends that directly corresponded to the amount of time they spent online.

At the beginning and end of the 2-year study, the subjects were asked to agree or disagree with statements like "I felt everything I did was an effort," and "I enjoyed life" and "I can find companionship when I want it." They were also asked to estimate how many minutes each day they spent with each member of their family and to quantify their social circle. Many of these are standard questions in tests used to determine psychological health.

For the duration of the study, the subjects' use of the Internet was recorded. For the purposes of this study, depression and loneliness were measured independently, and each subject was rated on a subjective scale. In measuring depression, the responses were plotted on a scale of 0 to 3, with 0 being the least depressed and 3 being the most depressed. Loneliness was plotted on a scale of 1 to 5.

By the end of the study, the researchers found that 1 hour a week on the Internet led, on average, to an increase of 0.03, or 1 percent, on the depression scale, a loss of 2.7 members of the subject's social circle, which averaged 66 people [in size], and an increase of 0.02, or four-tenths of 1 percent, on the loneliness scale.

The subjects exhibited wide variations in all three measured effects, and while the net effects were not large, they were statistically significant in demonstrating deterioration of social and psychological life, Kraut said.

Based on these data, the researchers hypothesize that relationships maintained over long distances without face-to-face contact ultimately do not provide the kind of support and reciprocity that typically contribute to a sense of psychological security and happiness, like being available to baby-sit in a pinch for a friend, or to grab a cup of coffee.

"Our hypothesis is there are more cases where you're building shallow relationships, leading to an overall decline in feeling of connection to other people," Kraut said.

The study tracked the behavior of 169 participants in the Pittsburgh area who were selected from four schools and community groups. Half the group was measured through 2 years of Internet use, and the other half for 1 year. The findings will be published this week by *The American Psychologist*, the peer-reviewed monthly journal of the American Psychological Association.

Because the study participants were not randomly selected, it is unclear how the findings apply to the general population. It is also conceivable that some unmeasured factor caused simultaneous increases in use of the Internet and decline in normal levels of social involvement. Moreover, the effect of Internet use varied depending on an individual's life patterns and type of use. Researchers said that people who were isolated because of their geography or work shifts might have benefited socially from Internet use.

Even so, several social scientists familiar with the study vouched for its credibility and predicted that the findings would probably touch off a national debate over how public policy on the Internet should evolve and how the technology itself might be shaped to yield more beneficial effects.

"They did an extremely careful scientific study, and it's not a result that's easily ignored," said Tora Bikson, a senior scientist at RAND, the research institution. Based in part on previous studies that focused on how local communities like Santa Monica, California, used computer networks to enhance civic participation, RAND has recommended that the federal government provide e-mail access to all Americans [see Reading 12-4].

"It's not clear what the underlying psychological explanation is," Ms. Bikson said of the study. "Is it because people give up day-to-day contact and then find themselves depressed? Or are they exposed to the broader world of the Internet and then wonder, 'What am I doing here in Pittsburgh?' Maybe your comparison standard changes. I'd like to see this replicated on a larger scale. Then I'd really worry."

Christine Riley, a psychologist at Intel Corp., the giant chip manufacturer that was among the sponsors of the study, said she was surprised by the results but did not consider the research definitive.

"For us, the point is there was really no information on this before," Ms. Riley said. "But it's important to remember this is not about the technology, per se; it's about how it is used. It really points to the need for considering social factors in terms of how you design applications and services for technology."

The Carnegie Mellon team—which included Sara Kiesler, a social psychologist who helped pioneer the study of human interaction over computer networks; Tridas Mukophadhyay, a professor at the graduate business school who has examined computer-mediated communication in the workplace; and William Scherlis, a research scientist in computer science—stressed that the negative effects of Internet use they found were not inevitable.

For example, the main focus of Internet use in schools has been gathering information and getting in touch with people from faraway places. But the research suggests that maintaining social ties with people in close physical proximity could be more psychologically healthy.

"More intense development and deployment of services that support pre-existing communities and strong relationships should be encouraged," the researchers write in their article. "Government efforts to wire the nation's schools, for example, should consider online homework sessions for students rather than just online reference works."

At a time when Internet use is expanding rapidly—nearly [170 million] adult Americans are online, according to Nielsen Media Research—social critics say the technology could exacerbate the fragmentation of U.S. society or help to fuse it, depending on how it is used.

"There are two things the Internet can turn out to be, and we don't know yet which it's going to be," said Robert Putnam, a political scientist at Harvard University whose book, *Bowling Alone* (Simon & Schuster, 2000) chronicles the alienation of Americans from each other since the 1960s. "The fact that I'm able to communicate daily with my collaborators in Germany and Japan makes me more efficient, but there are a lot of things it can't do, like bring me chicken soup."

Putnam added, "The question is, how can you push computer-mediated communication in a direction that would make it more community friendly?"

Perhaps paradoxically, several participants in the Internet study expressed surprise when they were informed of the study's conclusions by a reporter.

"For me it's been the opposite of depression; it's been a way of being connected," said Rabbi Alvin Berkun, who used the Internet during the study for a few hours a week to read the *Jerusalem Post* and communicate with other rabbis across the country.

But Berkun said his wife did not share his enthusiasm for the medium. "She does sometimes resent when I go and hook up," he said, adding after a pause, "I guess I am away from where my family is while I'm on the computer."

RELATED LINKS

- HomeNet Project (homenet.andrew.cmu.edu/progress/)

- Human-Computer Interaction Institute, Carnegie Mellon University (www.cs.cmu .edu/~hcii/)

- *American Psychologist* (www.apa.org/journals/amp.html)

- The Psychology of Cyberspace Web Site (http://www.rider.edu/users/suler/psycyber/ psycyber.html)

FOR FURTHER RESEARCH

To find out more about the topics discussed in this reading, use InfoTrac College Edition. Type in keywords and subject terms such as "Internet addiction," "online media use," and "virtual community." You can access InfoTrac College Edition from the Wadsworth/Thomson Communication Cafe homepage: http://communication.wadsworth.com.

SECTION V

New Technologies and the Public Sphere

This section addresses the relationship between new communication technologies and the public sphere, with articles that analyze the role of electronic media in democratic processes as well as the problem of unequal access to information technology, a circumstance referred to as the "Digital Divide." The readings in Chapter 12 document the rise of a new breed of civic animal, the "netizen," who scours the Net for political information, engages in spirited electronic discussions, organizes around issues and causes, and participates in bona fide political actions—all online. In the view of some observers, the 1996 election—the first presidential contest to feature campaign Web pages—heralded the birth of a "Digital Nation" celebrating the right of the individual to speak and be heard, a cornerstone idea of American media and democracy. By the 2000 election, any major candidate campaigning out there on the stump most surely maintained a Web presence as part of his or her overall campaign strategy. From unprecedented online donations to candid candidate interactions and grassroots citizen actions, cyberpolitics has clearly arrived. But, as the readings in Chapter 13 highlight, access to computer technology remains problematic for many people. Despite recent gains, high-income white households tend to have far greater access to the Internet than minority and rural households at the lowest income levels. One proposal to help overcome the digital divide, presented in a report by the RAND Corporation, involves providing nearly universal access to e-mail to all U.S. residents, along the lines of universal telephone service. The authors of the report maintain that the unique properties of e-mail allow citizens to engage in an active civic dialog, fostering interactive communication and providing significant social and political benefits in the process.

12

Electronic Democracy

Reading 12-1

Birth of a Digital Nation

Jon Katz

EDITOR'S NOTE

For some, the 1996 election featuring the humdrum presidential contest between Bill Clinton and Bob Dole was about the slow death of the current political system. For media observer Jon Katz, on the other hand, 1996 marked the rise of a new civic animal, the "netizen," and witnessed the birth of a Digital Nation. In Katz's view, the interactivity inherent in online media is at the core of netizenship. Whereas traditional one-way information systems restrict feedback from the audience, "the new digital world celebrates the right of the individual to speak and be heard—one of the cornerstone ideas behind American media and democracy." Political opinions, Katz finds, almost never remain static on the Web.

CONSIDER

1. According to Katz, how does the nascent Digital Nation differ from the traditional world of offline politics? Do you agree with what he says?

2. In what ways are members of the Digital Nation not representative of the population as a whole? What are some of their "postpolitical" core values?

3. How can the Internet, and the online community it affords, be thought of as revolutionary in a social and political sense?

FIRST STIRRINGS

On the Net last year, I saw the rebirth of love for liberty in media. I saw a culture crowded with intelligent, educated, politically passionate people who—in jarring contrast to the offline world—line up to express their civic opinions, participate in debates, even fight for their political beliefs.

I watched people learn new ways to communicate politically. I watched information travel great distances, then return home bearing imprints of engaged and committed people from all over the world. I saw positions soften and change when people were suddenly able to talk directly to one another, rather than through journalists, politicians, or ideological mercenaries.

I saw the primordial stirrings of a new kind of nation—the Digital Nation—and the formation of a new "postpolitical" philosophy. This nascent ideology, fuzzy and difficult to define, suggests a blend of some of the best values rescued from the tired old dogmas—the humanism of liberalism, the economic opportunity of conservatism, plus a strong sense of personal responsibility and a passion for freedom.

I came across questions, some tenuously posed: Are we living in the middle of a great revolution, or are we just members of another arrogant élite talking to ourselves? Are we a powerful new kind of community or just a mass of people hooked up to machines? Do we share goals and ideals, or are we just another hot market ready for exploitation by America's ravenous corporations?

And perhaps the toughest questions of all: Can we build a new kind of politics? Can we construct a more civil society with our powerful technologies? Are we extending the evolution of freedom among human beings? Or are we nothing more than a great, wired babble pissing into the digital wind?

Where freedom is rarely mentioned in mainstream media anymore, it is ferociously defended—and exercised daily—on the Net.

Where our existing information systems seek to choke the flow of information through taboos, costs, and restrictions, the new digital world celebrates the right of the individual to speak and be heard—one of the cornerstone ideas behind American media and democracy.

Where our existing political institutions are viewed as remote and unresponsive, this online culture offers the means for individuals to have a genuine say in the decisions that affect their lives.

Where conventional politics is suffused with ideology, the digital world is obsessed with facts.

Where our current political system is irrational, awash in hypocritical god-and-values talk, the Digital Nation points the way toward a more rational, less dogmatic approach to politics.

The world's information is being liberated, and so, as a consequence, are we.

MY JOURNEY

Early in 1996, writer John Heilemann and I set out on parallel media journeys for HotWired's *The Netizen,* originally created to explore political issues and the media during the election year. One concept behind *The Netizen*—a conceit, perhaps—was that we would watch the impact of the Web on the political process in the first "wired" election. Heilemann was to cover the candidates, the conventions, and the campaigns. I would write about the media covering them.

Things didn't turn out quite as we'd expected at *The Netizen.* The year of the Web was not 1996—at least not in terms of mainstream politics. [For a perspective on the 2000 election, see Reading 12-2.] The new culture wasn't strong enough yet to really affect the political process. The candidates didn't turn to it as they had turned in 1992 to new media like cable, fax, and 800 numbers.

And the election was shallow from the beginning, with no view toward the new postindustrial economy erupting around us and no vision of a digital—or any other kind of—future. By spring '96, it seemed clear to me that this campaign was a metaphor for all that doesn't work in both journalism and politics. I couldn't bear the *New York Times* pundits, CNN's politico-sports talk, the whoring Washington talk shows, the network stand-ups.

Why attend to those tired institutions when what was happening on the monitor a foot from my nose seemed so much more interesting? Fresh ideas, fearsome debates, and a brand-new culture were rising out of the primordial digital muck, its politics teeming with energy. How could a medium like this new one have a major impact on a leaden old process like that one? By focusing so obsessively on Them, we were missing a much more dramatic political story—Us.

So I mostly abandoned Their campaign, focusing instead on the politics of Ours—especially interactivity and the digital culture. I was flamed, challenged, and stretched almost daily. The Web became my formidable teacher, whacking me on the palm with a ruler when I didn't do my homework or wasn't listening intently enough; comforting me when I got discouraged or felt lost.

I argued with technoanarchists about rules, flamers about civility, white kids about rap, black kids about police, journalists about media, evangelicals about sin. I was scolded by scholars and academics for flawed logic or incomplete research. I was shut down by "family values" e-mail bombers outraged by my attacks on Wal-Mart's practice of sanitizing the music it sells.

I saw the strange new way in which information and opinion travel down the digital highway—linked to Web sites, passed on to newsgroups, mailing lists, and computer conferencing systems. I saw my columns transformed from conventional punditry to a series of almost-living organisms that got buttressed, challenged, and altered by the incredible volume of feedback suddenly available. I lost the ingrained journalistic ethic that taught me that I was right, and that my readers didn't know what was good for them. On the Web, I learned that I was rarely completely right, that I was only a transmitter of ideas waiting to be shaped and often improved upon by people who knew more than I did.

Ideas almost never remain static on the Web. They are launched like children into the world, where they are altered by the many different environments they pass through, almost never coming home in the same form in which they left.

All the while, I had the sense of [fellow *Netizen* writer] Heilemann cranking along like the Energizer Bunny, responsibly slugging his way through the torturous ordeal of campaign coverage, guiding the increasingly exasperated people who actually wanted to follow the election. What Heilemann learned and relayed was that the political system isn't functioning. It doesn't address serious problems, and the problems it does address are not confronted in a rational way. It doesn't present us with the information we need or steer us toward comprehension—let alone solution.

Over the course of 1996, the ideologies that shape our political culture seemed to collapse. Liberalism finally expired along with the welfare culture it had inadvertently spawned. Conservatism, reeling from the failure of the so-called Republican revolution, was exposed as heartless and rigid. The Left and the Right—

even on issues as explosive as abortion and welfare—appeared spent. While they squabbled eternally with one another, the rest of us ached for something better. In 1996, we didn't get it.

The candidates didn't raise a single significant issue, offer a solution to any major social problem, raise the nation's consciousness, or prod its conscience about any critical matter. The issues the candidates did debate were either false or manipulative, the tired imperatives of another time.

"Nineteen ninety-six was the year that Old Politics died," wrote Heilemann. "For outside this bizarre electoral system that's grown and mutated over the past 40 years—this strange, pseudo-meta-ritual that, experienced from the inside, feels like being trapped in an echo chamber lined with mirrors—there are profound, paradigm-shifting changes afoot."

There *are* paradigm-shifting changes afoot: The young people who form the heart of the digital world are creating a new political ideology. The machinery of the Internet is being wielded to create an environment in which the Digital Nation can become a political entity in its own right.

By avoiding the campaign most of the time, I ended up in another, unexpected place. I had wandered into the nexus between the past and the future, the transition from one political process to a very different one.

While Heilemann came to believe he was attending a wake, I began to feel I was witnessing a birth—the first stirrings of a powerful new political community.

THE NASCENT NATION

All kinds of people of every age and background are online, but at the heart of the Digital Nation are the people who created the Net, work in it, and whose business, social, and cultural lives increasingly revolve around it.

The Digital Nation constitutes a new social class. Its citizens are young, educated, affluent. They inhabit wired institutions and industries—universities, computer and telecom companies, Wall Street and financial outfits, the media. They live everywhere, of course, but are most visible in forward-looking, technologically advanced communities: New York, San Francisco, Los Angeles, Seattle, Boston, Minneapolis, Austin, Raleigh. They are predominantly male, although female citizens are joining in enormous—and increasingly equal—numbers.

The members of the Digital Nation are not representative of the population as a whole: They are richer, better educated, and disproportionately white. They have disposable income and available time. Their educations are often unconventional and continuous, and they have almost unhindered access to much of the world's information. As a result, their values are constantly evolving. Unlike the rigid political ideologies that have ruled America for decades, the ideas of the postpolitical young remain fluid.

Still, some of their common values are clear: They tend to be libertarian, materialistic, tolerant, rational, technologically adept, disconnected from narrow labels like liberal or conservative and from conventional political organizations like the Republican or Democratic parties. They are not politically correct, rejecting dogma in favor of sorting through issues individually, preferring discussions to platforms.

The digital young are bright. They are not afraid to challenge authority. They take no one's word for anything. They embrace interactivity—the right to shape and participate in their media. They have little experience with passively reading newspapers or watching newscasts delivered by anchors.

Although many would balk at defining themselves this way, the digital young are revolutionaries. Unlike the clucking boomers, they are not talking revolution; they're making one. This is a culture best judged by what it does, not what it says.

In *On Revolution* (Viking Press, 1963), Hannah Arendt wrote that two things are needed to generate great revolutions: the sudden experience of being free and the sense of creating something. The Net is revolutionary in precisely those ways. It liberates millions of people to do things they couldn't do before. Men and women can experiment with their sexual identities without being humiliated or arrested. Citizens can express themselves directly, without filtering their views through journalists or pollsters. Researchers can get the newest data in hours, free from the grinding rituals of scientific tradition. The young can explore their own notions of culture, safe from the stern scrutiny of parents and teachers.

There's also a sense of great novelty, of building something different. The online population of today has evolved dramatically from the hackers and academics who patched together primitive computer bulletin boards just a few years ago—but the sensation of discovery remains. People coming online still have the feeling of stepping across a threshold. Citizenship in this world requires patience, commitment, and determination—an investment of time and energy that often brings the sense of participating in something very new.

It's difficult to conceive of the digital world as a political entity. The existing political and journalistic structures hate the very thought, since that means relinquishing their own central place in political life. And the digital world itself—adolescent, self-absorbed—is almost equally reluctant to take itself seriously in a political context, since that invokes all sorts of responsibilities that seem too constraining and burdensome.

This is a culture founded on the ethos of individuality, not leadership. Information flows laterally, or from many to many—a structure that works against the creation of leaders.

Like it or not, however, this Digital Nation possesses all the traits of groups that, throughout history, have eventually taken power. It has the education, the affluence, and the privilege that will create a political force that ultimately must be reckoned with.

SOME POSTPOLITICAL CORE VALUES

Out of sight of the reporters, handlers, spin-masters, and politicians of the presidential campaign, a new political sensibility took shape in 1996. It brought fresh ideas. It brought real debates about real issues.

The postpolitical ideology draws from different elements of familiar politics. The term *postpolitical* gets tossed around in various circles, but here it refers to a new kind of politics beyond the traditional choices of left/right, liberal/conservative, Republican/Democrat. Although still taking shape, this postpolitical ideology combines some of the better elements of both sides of the mainstream American political spectrum.

From liberals, this ideology adopts humanism. It is suspicious of law enforcement. It abhors censorship. It recoils from extreme governmental positions like the death penalty. From conservatives, the ideology takes notions of promoting economic opportunity, creating smaller government, and insisting on personal responsibility.

The digital young share liberals' suspicions of authority and concentration of power but have little of their visceral contempt for corporations or big business. They share the liberal analysis that social problems like poverty, rather than violence on TV, are at the root of crime. But, unlike liberals, they want the poor to take more responsibility for solving their own problems.

The postpoliticos can outdo liberals on some fronts. They don't merely embrace tolerance as an ideal; they are inherently tolerant. Theirs is the first generation for whom pluralism and diversity are neither controversial nor unusual. This group couldn't care less whether families take the traditional form or have two moms or two dads. They are nearly blind to the color and ethnic heritage of the people who enter their culture.

On the other hand, the digital young's intuitive acceptance of tolerance and diversity doesn't prevent them from rejecting liberal notions like affirmative action. And they are largely impervious to victim-talk, or politically correct rhetoric, or the culture of complaint celebrated in the liberal media coverage of many minority issues.

This culture is no less averse to the cruel and suffocating dogma of the Right. The postpolitical young embrace the notion of gender equality and are intrinsically hostile to any government or religious effort to dictate private personal behavior. While conservatism has become entwined with an evangelical religious agenda, the digital young are allergic to mixing religion and politics.

If liberals say, "Here's the tent: we have to get everyone inside," and conservatives say, "Here's the tent: we don't want it to get too crowded inside," the postpolitical young say, "Here's the tent: everyone is welcome—but everyone has to figure out how to get inside on his or her own." [For another perspective on the rise of a merit-based ethos, see Reading 13-3.]

One of the biggest ideas in the postpolitical world is that we have the means to shape our lives, and that we must take more responsibility for doing so. This ascending generation believes its members should and will control their destinies. A recent survey in *American Demographics* magazine studied young Americans and called them self-navigators. "In a fast-changing and often hostile world, self-navigation means relying on oneself to be the captain of one's own ship and charting one's own course," wrote the Brain Waves Group, the survey's developers. Those characteristics also describe many citizens of the Digital Nation.

This group values competence and hard work, the survey found. Traditional formulas for success carry little weight since college degrees no longer guarantee

jobs, getting a job doesn't guarantee you'll keep it, retirement may never be possible, and marriages can fail. Despite such caution, this group—in sharp contrast to its boomer parents—sees a future of great opportunity. The Digital Nation is optimistic about its own prospects.

Although these ideas work well for them now, as the postpolitical young of the digital world grow older, they will confront a new range of problems, from developing careers to raising children to preparing for old age. Their ideology will, of necessity, develop and change.

As they raise children, they will face issues such as neighborhood safety, maintaining parks, and improving the educational system. As they buy homes, they will encounter bread-and-butter political issues like taxation and zoning. Faced with developing a new political agenda in a radically different world, they will inevitably find themselves face-to-face with the ghosts of the old one.

A NEW FORM OF LIBERTARIANISM

The closest thing the digital world has to dogma is its ingrained libertarianism, its wholehearted commitment to political and economic freedom, its fierce opposition to constraints on individual expression—from the chilling [liberal] fanaticism of the politically correct to the growing [conservative] movement to censor popular culture.

The online world is the freest community in American life. Its members can do things considered unacceptable elsewhere in our culture. They can curse freely, challenge the existence of God, explore their sexuality nearly at will, talk to radical thinkers from all over the world. They can even commit verbal treason.

The Internet is still a wild frontier. The hackers and geeks who founded and shaped it believed that there should be no obstacles between people and information, and there are still vibrant, almost outlaw communities that enforce this notion: cypherpunks who act as technoanarchists, flamers who challenge punditry, hackers who breech the barriers constantly being thrown up by government and business.

The single dominant ethic in this community is that information wants to be free. Many of those online know that this idea is antithetical to the history of media, to the nature of politics and capitalism. Corporations do not believe that information should be free—they believe they should control it and charge for it. Government doesn't believe that information should be free—witness the fiasco of the Communications Decency Act. Religious organizations, educators, and many parents don't believe information ought to be liberated, either. The realization that children have broken away from many societal constraints and now have access to a vast information universe is one of the most frightening ideas in contemporary America.

These new libertarian notions are often misunderstood. While some longstanding political groups associated with libertarianism are profoundly hostile to government, the digital young are not so much paranoid about government as frustrated by its lack of effectiveness. They don't see government conspiring to take over their lives as much as they consider it an outdated means of solving problems. It's widely acknowledged in online discussions, for example, that traditional drug policies have been catastrophic failures and that radical new ideas—legalization, perhaps—should be considered.

The digital young, from Silicon Valley entrepreneurs to college students, have a nearly universal contempt for government's ability to work; they think it's wasteful and clueless. On the Net, government is rarely seen as an instrument of positive change or social good. Politicians are assumed to be manipulative or ill-informed, unable to affect reform or find solutions, forced to lie to survive. The Digital Nation's disconnection from the conventional political process—and from the traditional media that mirror it—is profound.

Both politics and journalism tend to refer to this alienation as a civic disorder, brought on by new media and new culture and a decline in literacy and civilization. The young must be disinterested because they are distracted by music or coarsened by too much TV. But in their own way, the young are saying something different: The political system doesn't work, so why bother to pay attention to it?

This very sense of alienation has planted the seeds of more civil notions of politics and community. Although online culture is widely perceived as hostile and chaotic, the stereotype is superficial. Writing for *The Netizen,* I noticed a recurring phenomenon that speaks both to that sense of alienation and to the potential for community.

Months of these exchanges have convinced me that alienation online—and perhaps offline as well—is not ingrained, that it comes from a reflexive assumption that powerful political and media institutions don't care, won't listen, and will not respond. Proven wrong, many of the most hostile flamers became faithful correspondents, often continuing to disagree—but in a civil way. I found myself listening more to them as well.

We were forming a new sort of media culture. In small ways, over time, we were moving beyond the head-butting that characterizes too many online discussions (offline ones, too) and engaging in actual dialog, the cornerstone of any real political entity. We were finding that interactivity could bring a new kind of community, new ways of holding political conversations.

Of all the prospects raised by the evolution of digital culture, the most tantalizing is the possibility that technology could fuse with politics to create a more civil society. It's the possibility that we could end up with a media and political culture in which people could amass factual material, voice their perspectives, confront other points of view, and discuss issues in a rational way.

JUST THE BEGINNING

The digital world is often disconnected from many of the world's problems by virtue of its members' affluence and social standing. Founded in the bedrooms of suburban hackers and the classrooms of prestigious institutions, it has often been derided as self-absorbed. It has yet to respond to any political or social crisis that doesn't directly concern it.

The digital young do need to develop coherent philosophies for responding to the very problems that the exhausted current system fails to address: limited economic opportunity, endemic underclass problems, never-ending racial hostility. The Digital Revolution eventually needs to offer solutions for eradicating poverty, ignorance, and war in radical and hopeful ways.

Here is a growing élite in control of the most powerful communications infrastructure ever assembled. The people rushing toward the millennium with their fingers on the keyboards of the Information Age could become one of the most powerful political forces in history. Technology is power. Education is power. Communication is power. The digital young have all three. No other social group is as poised to dominate culture and politics in the twenty-first century.

It's not clear what they're going to make of such advantages, whether they will choose to remain a technologically obsessed subculture in pursuit of the Next

Big Thing, or whether they will decide to meet the world head on and recognize their responsibilities as citizens of a new era.

The ascending young citizens of the Digital Nation can, if they wish, construct a more civil society, a new politics based on rationalism, shared information, the pursuit of truth, and new kinds of community.

If they choose to form a political movement, they could someday run the world. If they choose to develop a common value system, with a moral ideology and a humane agenda, they might even do the world some good.

RELATED LINKS

- "Cyberdemocracy and the Public Sphere" (http://slashdot.org/features/00/10/17/1848204.shtml)

- "The Digital Citizen" (http://hotwired.lycos.com/special/citizen)

- MediaChannel Issue Guides: Cyberdemocracy (http://www.mediachannel.org/atissue/cyber)

- *Netizens: An Anthology* (http://www.columbia.edu/~rh120)

- The Netizen Links (http://hotwired.lycos.com/netizen/netizenlinks/96/39/index3a.html)

FOR FURTHER RESEARCH

To find out more about the topics discussed in this reading, use InfoTrac College Edition. Type in keywords and subject terms such as "electronic democracy," "cyberpolitics," and "digital culture." You can access InfoTrac College Edition from the Wadsworth/Thomson Communication Cafe homepage: http://communication.wadsworth.com.

Reading 12-2

A Candidate on the Stump Is Surely on the Web
Tina Kelley

EDITOR'S NOTE

Since the advent of the World Wide Web—the Internet's graphical interface—in the early 1990s, each political election has promised to bring online media into the mainstream of civic life. As this reading from the preprimary season points out, the 2000 presidential contest appears to have sealed the deal. From unprecedented online donations and citizen involvement— Senator John McCain, for example, received approximately $810,000 in online contributions and attracted some 7,000 new volunteers to his campaign within 48 hours of winning the New Hampshire primary—to candid candidate–citizen interactions and grassroots Net activism, cyberpolitics has arrived. From here on out, a candidate on the stump must surely be on the Web.

CONSIDER

1. Which political candidates seemed to have effective Internet strategies during the 2000 election, and which didn't? What distinguished the good sites from the bad?

2. Do you think the Internet's growing campaign role is a positive development for American politics? Why or why not?

3. How can a well-designed Web site help a campaign organize its ground troops—campaign volunteers and political activists—offline?

The modern campaign headquarters is no longer a rented storefront decorated with bumper stickers, bunting, and empty soda cans. Increasingly it has an annex open any hour of the day or night, at an address starting with www.

If in 1996 a candidate could prove hipness simply by posting an electronic version of a campaign brochure on the World Wide Web, White House hopefuls for 2000 are learning to use their Internet sites to raise money and rally troops. The Web page is the new whistle-stop, a way for candidates to carry their messages daily to more people than they can reach on the campaign trail.

By posting everything from their baby pictures (as George W. Bush has done) to their favorite Bible stories (an offering from Elizabeth Dole), candidates are using the Internet as a fireside chat room, to portray themselves as just plain folks.

The sites also provide a new conduit for cash: Bill Bradley has towered over the opposition in online fund-raising, while the Steve Forbes campaign created a way for Web surfers to crash a recent $1,000-a-plate gala—for a small fee, of course.

No one is suggesting that the Internet has come of age as a medium of political influence, as television did most notably with the Kennedy–Nixon debates of 1960. But with 67 million Americans online [as of 1999], up from 7.5 million 4 years ago, it has become a new variable in campaign calculus.

"It used to be said the candidate had to have a good message, a good ground game, and enough money to wage a good air game on TV," said Rick Segal, the Internet strategy adviser to Mr. Forbes. "This is the first cycle that it can be proven that a candidate needs to have a good online game as well."

That game includes producing fill-in-the-blank e-mail that backers can send to all their friends in support of the candidate, and gathering campaign contributions requiring just a few mouse clicks.

And for all that, the sites are a relative bargain—Mr. Bush spent $57,000 on his over the last 7 months—with candidates hiring Web consultants, contracting with private companies, or allowing volunteers to create and maintain them.

Lately the sites have not only conveyed the campaigns' messages but also made news: Governor Bush became the first presidential candidate to make updated lists of campaign donors available online, and Senator John McCain of Arizona got under the skin of fellow Republicans by using his site to single out examples of Congressional pork.

Howard Opinsky, Mr. McCain's press secretary, affirmed the Internet's growing campaign role, saying it was "almost like the fifty-first state."

"It has no boundaries," Mr. Opinsky said. "The Internet has progressed from a billboard to a two-way street, and I think it's probably good in the end for the political process."

To be sure, Web pages—unlike television or radio commercials, which to the public can seem unavoidable—depend on the initiative of people to look for them. But such surfers are valuable visitors: Mr. Bradley's campaign says that on an average day his site brings in about $7,000 and is seen by 5,000 people, more than he might encounter in a day on the campaign trail.

Mr. Bradley's campaign workers try to drum up traffic to his site by displaying the address on every lectern he uses. And Mr. Segal has worked to make sure the Forbes site is indexed in Internet search engines, thereby increasing the probability of surfers' stopping by, and is placing advertisements on news and financial Web sites.

At the same time, as the Internet grows in popularity, candidates are cutting down on printed campaign literature. The Forbes campaign, for example, says it is sending out fewer newsletters than it would have in pre-Internet campaigns, because the Internet is a faster and less expensive medium.

And more than in a television advertisement, the candidates are able to convey their personalities through their pages. The aura of digital friendliness that results can either charm or repel prospective supporters.

Mr. Bradley's site, for example, includes recipes for dishpan cookies, oatmeal icebox cookies and butter-

---

horns, from Rosalie Dunker, Dede Herrell, and Em Aubuchon, who baked for his campaign kickoff in Crystal City, Missouri. Governor Bush has baby pictures of himself and his daughters on his site and mentions his family's dog, Spot, and three cats, India, Cowboy, and Ernie.

One presidential hopeful even sells his gospel recordings on line, at www.hatchmusic.com (a site separate from that of his campaign), where one can download snippets of Senator Orrin G. Hatch singing "The Cross Before the Crown."

At www.AlGore2000.com, technologically savvy voters are rewarded with a message from the vice president that is embedded in the source code, the programming blueprints of a site.

"Thanks for checking out our source code!" the candidate—or a group of Gore techies—writes, describing plans to improve the code. "The fact that you are peeking behind the scenes at our site means you can make an important difference to this Internet effort."

In another innovative move, the Forbes campaign blended virtual reality with real reality by inviting 400 computer users to an online version of a $1,000-a-plate bash at the Waldorf-Astoria in New York. For $10 each, plugged-in supporters saw live video of the festivities, and typed messages back and forth with Mr. Forbes and others in attendance. Later that night his address was seen on a free Webcast by about 1,800 people, 600 more than at the live event.

In many respects, the partnership between established candidates and the wild, wild Web is uneasy as they plumb the possibilities of this new technology.

"Campaigns are a tight, disciplined, focused message delivered in a focused way, reducing chance, variables, and conflict to a minimum," said Phil Noble, president of PoliticsOnline of Charleston, South Carolina, a company offering Internet expertise. "The Internet is about millions of voices colliding, all at the same time, about all kinds of things in a near-chaotic pattern."

But candidates recognize that the Internet is an effective way to get their messages across and to keep the prospective voter's attention. Studies have shown that campaigns can usually get 45 seconds of a voter's attention by phone or 30 seconds in a television advertisement, compared with 8 minutes through a Web site, said Emilienne Ireland, president of Campaign Advantage, an Internet campaign-services company in Bethesda, Maryland.

And more than ever before, the candidates' pages are used to bring in contributions. Mr. Bradley's campaign says it has raised over $770,000 through his site, 4 percent of its total contributions. (According to a survey by PoliticsOnline, Mr. McCain raised $260,000 on the Internet through September; no other candidate had brought in more than $100,000 through the Net.)

Of the half-million people who have visited the Bradley site since last December, 14.4 percent have filled out a form to get involved, and 1 percent have brought out their credit cards or checkbooks to contribute, said Lynn Reed, a consultant to the campaign.

"The Bradley campaign has been real effective in the overall strategic use of the Net," said Jonah Seiger, cofounder and principal of Mindshare Internet Campaigns, consultants in Washington. "They raised a great deal of money and a great deal of press attention, suggesting they clearly have a better strategic sense of the Net than the Gore campaign does, considering that Gore is so identified with the Net. Here they're doing something that is really going to hit Gore where it hurts."

But Andrew Sather, senior vice president at Sapient, Internet consultants in Cambridge, Massachusetts, who redesigned the official White House Web site, cited the Gore campaign's use of the Web to let visitors interact with the candidate, through electronic town halls, where people can pose questions about anything from class size to the income gap.

The Bush campaign has used its site to gain credentials for the Texas Governor as a Net-savvy candidate, notably with the decision to post a list of all his contributors, even those who gave less than $200.

"This gives Americans the opportunity to look for themselves at the broad-based support Governor Bush is receiving," said Scott McClellan, a campaign spokesman. About 100,000 people had dipped into the 1,750-page listing as of October 1999, he said.

At the same time, just as readers of Web pages get more information about their candidate, the candidate gets more information about them, helping a campaign organize its ground troops. Several Web watchers pointed to what the Forbes campaign calls electronic precincts as a canny use of the Internet: In a political version of multilevel marketing, a campaign volunteer brings in a handful of other volunteers, who in turn bring in more. The first volunteer, the e-precinct captain, is rewarded with special briefings, online video presentations, a chance to meet the candidate, and real-world recognition.

"It's something that's growing in its own viral kind of way," said Mr. Segal, the Forbes adviser, who added that the campaign had about 5,000 e-precincts, a few with as many as 5,000 members each.

The Forbes campaign keeps tabs on where its e-volunteers live and what kind of volunteering they would like to do. Using similar information, the Bradley campaign was able to send e-mail to 5,000 supporters in the Northeast, encouraging them to take part in a weeklong canvass [voter outreach effort] in New Hampshire this summer.

"We were able to get 300 folks, free," Ms. Reed said. "If you had to make phone calls for the same return, it might not be worth it."

With all those electronic addresses and zip codes flowing in from supporters to Web masters, some Internet experts have become concerned about what is done with this information. To reassure supporters, the Gore site posts this disclaimer: "We do not share our volunteer lists with any other site or any other entity."

Chuck Todd, managing editor of *The Hotline,* a daily Web-based political newsletter published by the *National Journal,* predicts that the watershed event of the Internet's new power will most likely occur in a primary campaign, in a small or particularly well-wired state. "The way, in the past, there was a last-minute TV barrage, there will be a huge Internet campaign to swing votes toward a candidate," he said.

Some analysts say the Internet may not show its full potential as a political tool until 2004 at the earliest, when high-speed Internet connections become more common and zapping messages to particular groups of voters has been refined to an art.

"The potential watershed moment will be when [a candidate like] Al Gore can make sure his pro-choice abortion ads are only seen by moderate, pro-choice women," Mr. Todd said. "That's what the Internet allows, targeting and identifying voters by household."

RELATED LINKS

- Campaign Scoop (http://hotlinescoop.com/web/content/campaignscoop)
- The Internet Archive (http://www.archive.org)
- The Internet and Politics (http://www.nytimes.com/library/tech/reference/index-campaign.html)
- Politics1.com (http://www.politics1.com)
- PoliticsOnline (http://www.politicsonline.com)

FOR FURTHER RESEARCH

To find out more about the topics discussed in this reading, use InfoTrac College Edition. Type in keywords and subject terms such as "cyberpolitics," "electronic precincts," and "Net activism." You can access InfoTrac College Edition from the Wadsworth / Thomson Communication Cafe homepage: http://communication.wadsworth.com.

Reading 12-3

Disinformocracy
Howard Rheingold

EDITOR'S NOTE

Net enthusiast and virtual community pioneer Howard Rheingold is a passionate champion of the potential for online media to transform social and political life. But as this prescient reading from his book The Virtual Community *reveals, he is cautious about overplaying the claims for new technology. Keeping democracy responsive requires constant vigilance. And with the growing commercialization of the public sphere, the need for citizens to remain active has never been more vital. One must not mistake consumer behavior for authentic communication, this excerpt warns, whether in our personal or political lives. "People who use computers to communicate, form friendships that sometimes form the basis of communities," Rheingold comments, "but you have to be careful to not mistake the tool for the task and think that just writing words on a screen is the same thing as real community."*

CONSIDER

1. What implications does "the commodification of the public sphere" have for democracy, and how might computer networks reinvigorate civic discourse and public life?

2. Why is Rheingold cautious about declaring that computer networks are inherently democratizing?

3. If traditional broadcast media tend to centralize power, will decentralized computer networks over time redistribute existing power arrangements?

Virtual communities could help citizens revitalize democracy, or they could be luring us into an attractively packaged substitute for democratic discourse. A few true believers in electronic democracy have had their say. It's time to hear from the other side. We owe it to ourselves and future generations to look closely at what the enthusiasts fail to tell us, and to listen attentively to what the skeptics fear.

The telecommunications industry is a business, viewed primarily as an economic player. But telecommunications gives certain people access to means of influencing certain other people's thoughts and perceptions, and that access—who has it and who doesn't have it—is intimately connected with political power. The prospect of the technical capabilities of a near-ubiquitous high-bandwidth Net in the hands of a small number of commercial interests has dire political implications. Whoever gains the political edge on this technology will be able to use the technology to consolidate power [see also Reading 5-4].

There might be a fork in the road of technology-dependent civilization, forced by the technical capabilities of the Net. Two powerful and opposed images of the future characterize the way different observers foresee the future political effects of new communications technology. The utopian vision of the electronic agora, an "Athens without slaves" made possible by telecommunications and cheap computers and implemented through decentralized networks like Usenet, has been promoted by enthusiasts, including myself, over the

past several years. I still believe that this technology, if properly understood and defended by enough citizens, does have democratizing potential in the way that alphabets and printing presses had democratizing potential.

Those who see electronic democracy advocates as naive—or worse—point to the way governments and private interests have used the alluring new media of past technological revolutions to turn democratic debate into talk shows and commercials. Why should this new medium be any less corruptible than previous media? Why should contemporary claims for computer-mediated communication as a democratizing technology be taken any more seriously than the similar-sounding claims that were made for steam, electricity, and television?

The political process, according to this school of critics, has been turned into a commodity—something to be packaged, marketed, and sold—resulting in the commodification of the public sphere. The public sphere is what these social critics claim we used to have as citizens of a democracy, but have lost to the tide of commercialization. The public sphere is also the focus of the hopes of online activists, who see computer-mediated communication as a way of revitalizing the open discussions among citizens that feed the roots of democratic societies.

THE SELLING OF DEMOCRACY: COMMODIFICATION AND THE PUBLIC SPHERE

There is an intimate connection between informal conversations, the kind that take place in communities

"Disinformocracy." From *The Virtual Community: Homesteading on the Electronic Frontier* by Howard Rheingold. Cambridge, MA: The MIT Press. 2000. Copyright © 2000 The MIT Press. Reprinted with permission.

and virtual communities, in coffee shops and computer chat rooms, and the ability of large social groups to govern themselves without monarchs or dictators. This social-political connection shares a metaphor with the idea of cyberspace, for it takes place in a kind of virtual space that has come to be known by specialists as the public sphere.

Here is what the preeminent contemporary writer about the public sphere, social critic and philosopher Jürgen Habermas, had to say about the meaning of this abstraction:

> By "public sphere," we mean first of all a domain of our social life in which such a thing as public opinion can be formed. Access to the public sphere is open in principle to all citizens. A portion of the public sphere is constituted in every conversation in which private persons come together to form a public. They are then acting neither as business or professional people conducting their private affairs, nor as legal consociates subject to the legal regulations of a state bureaucracy and obligated to obedience. Citizens act as a public when they deal with matters of general interest without being subject to coercion; thus with the guarantee that they may assemble and unite freely, and express and publicize their opinions freely.[1]

In this definition, Habermas formalized what people in free societies mean when we say "The public wouldn't stand for that" or "It depends on public opinion." And he drew attention to the intimate connection between this web of free, informal, personal communications and the foundations of democratic society. People can govern themselves only if they communicate widely, freely, and in groups—publicly. The First Amendment of the U.S. Constitution's Bill of Rights protects citizens from government interference in their communications—the rights of speech, press, and assembly are communication rights. Without those rights, there is no public sphere. Ask any longtime citizen of Prague, Budapest, or Moscow.

Because the public sphere depends on free communication and discussion of ideas, as soon as your political entity grows larger than the number of citizens you can fit into a modest town hall, this vital marketplace for political ideas can be powerfully influenced by changes in communications technology. According to Habermas,

When the public is large, this kind of communication requires certain means of dissemination and influence; today, newspapers and periodicals, radio and television are the media of the public sphere. . . . The term "public opinion" refers to the functions of criticism and control or organized state authority that the public exercises informally, as well as formally during periodic elections. Regulations concerning the publicness (or publicity [Publizitat] in its original meaning) of state-related activities, as, for instance, the public accessibility required of legal proceedings, are also connected with this function of public opinion. To the public sphere as a sphere mediating between state and society, a sphere in which the public as the vehicle of publicness— the publicness that once had to win out against the secret politics of monarchs and that since then has permitted democratic control of state activity.

Ask anybody in China about the right to talk freely among friends and neighbors, to own a printing press, to call a meeting to protest government policy, or to run a bulletin board service. But brute totalitarian seizure of communications technology is not the only way that political powers can neutralize the ability of citizens to talk freely. It is also possible to alter the nature of discourse by inventing a kind of paid fake discourse. If a few people have control of what goes into the daily reporting of the news, and those people are in the business of selling advertising, all kinds of things become possible for those who can afford to pay.

The idea that public opinion can be manufactured and the fact that electronic spectacles can capture the attention of a majority of the citizenry damages the foundations of democracy. According to Habermas,

> It is no accident that these concepts of the public sphere and public opinion were not formed until the eighteenth century. They derive their specific meaning from a concrete historical situation. It was then that one learned to distinguish between opinion and public opinion. . . . Public opinion, in terms of its very idea, can be formed only if a public that engages in rational discussion exists. Public discussions that are institutionally protected and that take, with critical intent, the exercise of political authority as their theme have not existed since time immemorial.

The public sphere and democracy were born at the same time, from the same sources. Now that the public sphere, cut off from its roots, seems to be dying, democracy is in danger, too.

The concept of the public sphere as discussed by Habermas and others includes several requirements for authenticity that people who live in democratic societies would recognize: open access, voluntary participation, participation outside institutional roles, the generation of public opinion through assemblies of citizens who engage in rational argument, the freedom to express opinions, and the freedom to discuss matters of the state and criticize the way state power is organized. Acts of speech and publication that specifically discuss the state are perhaps the most important kind protected by the First Amendment to the U.S. Constitution and similar civil guarantees elsewhere in the world. Former Soviets and Eastern Europeans who regained it after decades of censorship offer testimony that the most important freedom of speech is the freedom to speak about freedoms.

In eighteenth century America, the Committees of Correspondence were one of the most important loci of the public sphere in the years of revolution and constitution-building. If you look closely at the roots of the American Revolution, it becomes evident that a text-based, horseback-transported version of networking was an old American tradition. In their book *Networking,* Jessica Lipnack and Jeffrey Stamps describe these committees as

> a communications forum where homespun political and economic thinkers hammered out their ideological differences, sculpting the form of a separate and independent country in North America. Writing to one another and sharing letters with neighbors, this revolutionary generation nurtured its adolescent ideas into a mature politics. Both men and women participated in the debate over independence from England and the desirable shape of the American future. . . .

During the years in which the American Revolution was percolating, letters, news-sheets, and pamphlets carried from one village to another were the means by which ideas about democracy were refined. Eventually, the correspondents agreed that the next step in their idea exchange was to hold a face-to-face meeting. The ideas of independence and government had been debated, discussed, discarded, and reformulated literally

hundreds of times by the time people in the revolutionary network met in Philadelphia.

Thus, a network of correspondence and printed broadsides led to the formation of an organization after the writers met in a series of conferences and worked out a statement of purpose—which they called a Declaration of Independence. Little did our early networking grandparents realize that the result of their youthful idealism, less than two centuries later, would be a global superpower with an unparalleled ability to influence the survival of life on the planet.[2]

As the United States grew and technology changed, the ways in which these public discussions of "matters of general interest," as Habermas called them—slavery and the rights of the states versus the power of the federal government were two such matters that loomed large—began to change as well. The text-based media that served as the channel for discourse gained more and more power to reshape the nature of that discourse. The main communications media of the nineteenth century, penny press newspapers, were the first generation of what has come to be known as the mass media. At the same time, the birth of advertising and the beginnings of the public relations industry began to undermine the public sphere by inventing a kind of buyable and sellable phony discourse.

The simulation (and therefore destruction) of authentic discourse, first in the United States and then spreading to the rest of the world, is what Guy Debord would call the first quantum leap into the "society of the spectacle" and what Jean Baudrillard would recognize as a milestone in the world's slide into hyperreality.[3] Mass media's colonization of civil society turned into a quasi-political campaign promoting technology itself when the image-making technology of television came along. ("Progress is our most important product," said General Electric spokesman Ronald Reagan, in the early years of television.) And in the twentieth century, as the telephone, radio, and television became vehicles for public discourse, the nature of political discussion has mutated into something quite different from anything the framers of the Constitution could have foreseen.

A politician is now a commodity, citizens are consumers, and issues are decided via sound bites and staged events. The television camera is the only spectator that counts at a political demonstration or convention. According to Habermas and others, the way the new media have been commodified through this evolutionary process from hand-printed broadside to telegraph to penny press to mass media has led to the radical deterioration of the public sphere. The consumer society has become the accepted model both for individual behavior and political decision making. Discourse degenerated into publicity, and publicity used the increasing power of electronic media to alter perceptions and shape beliefs.

The consumer society, the most powerful vehicle for generating short-term wealth ever invented, ensures economic growth by first promoting the idea that the way to be is to buy. The engines of wealth depend on a fresh stream of tabloids sold at convenience markets and television programs to tell us what we have to buy next in order to justify our existence. What used to be a channel for authentic communication has become a channel for the updating of commercial desire.

Money plus politics plus network television equals an effective system. It works. When the same packaging skills that were honed on automobile tail fins and fast foods are applied to political ideas, the highest bidder can influence public policy to great effect. What dies in the process is the rational discourse at the base of civil society. That death manifests itself in longings that aren't fulfilled by the right kind of shoes in this month's color or the hot new prime-time candidate everybody is talking about. Some media scholars are claiming a direct causal connection between the success of commercial television and the loss of citizen interest in the political process.

Neal Postman, in his book *Amusing Ourselves to Death,* pointed out that Tom Paine's *Common Sense* sold 300,000 copies in 5 months in 1776.[4] The most successful democratic revolution in history was made possible by a citizenry that read and debated widely among themselves. Postman argued that the mass media, and television in particular, has changed the mode of discourse itself, by substituting fast cuts, special effects, and sound bites for reasoned discussion or even genuine argument.

The various hypotheses about commodification and mode of discourse focus on an area of apparent agreement among social observers who have a long history of heated disagreements.

When people who have become fascinated by computer networks start spreading the idea that such networks are inherently democratic in some magical way, without specifying the hard work that must be done in real life to harvest the fruits of that democra-

tizing power, they run the danger of becoming unwitting agents of commodification. First, it pays to understand how old the idea really is. Next, it is important to realize that the hopes of technophiles have often been used to sell technology for commercial gain. In this sense, Net enthusiasts run the risk of becoming unpaid, unwitting advertisers for those who stand to gain financially from adoption of new technology.

The critics of the idea of electronic democracy have unearthed examples from a long tradition of utopian rhetoric that James Carey has called "the rhetoric of the 'technological sublime.'" He put it this way:

> Despite the manifest failure of technology to resolve pressing social issues over the last century, contemporary intellectuals continue to see revolutionary potential in the latest technological gadgets that are pictured as a force outside history and politics. . . . In modern futurism, it is the machines that possess teleological insight. Despite the shortcomings of town meetings, newspaper, telegraph, wireless, and television to create the conditions of a new Athens, contemporary advocates of technological liberation regularly describe a new postmodern age of instantaneous daily plebiscitary democracy through a computerized system of electronic voting and opinion polling.[5]

Carey was prophetic in at least one regard—he wrote this years before Ross Perot and William Clinton both started talking about their versions of electronic democracy during the 1992 U.S. presidential campaign. If the United States is on the road to a version of electronic democracy in which the president will have electronic town hall meetings, including instant voting-by-telephone to "go directly to the people" (and perhaps bypass Congress?) on key issues, it is important for American citizens to understand the potential pitfalls of decision making by plebiscite. Media-manipulated plebiscites as political tools go back to Joseph Goebbels, who used radio so effectively in the Third Reich. Previous experiments in instant home polling and voting had been carried out by Warner, with their Qube service, in the early 1980s. One critic, political scientist Jean Bethke Elshtain, called the television-voting model an

> interactive shell game [that] cons us into believing that we are participating when we are really simply performing as the responding "end" of a

prefabricated system of external stimuli. . . . In a plebiscitary system, the views of the majority . . . swamp minority or unpopular views. Plebiscitism is compatible with authoritarian politics carried out under the guise of, or with the connivance of, majority views. That opinion can be registered by easily manipulated, ritualistic plebiscites, so there is no need for debate on substantive questions.[6]

What does it mean that the same hopes, described in the same words, for a decentralization of power, a deeper and more widespread citizen involvement in matters of state, a great equalizer for ordinary citizens to counter the forces of central control, have been voiced in the popular press for two centuries in reference to steam, electricity, and television? We've had enough time to live with steam, electricity, and television to recognize that they did indeed change the world, and to recognize that the utopia of technological millenarians has not yet materialized.

An entire worldview and sales job are packed into the word *progress,* which links the notion of improvement with the notion of innovation, highlights the benefits of innovation while hiding the toxic side effects of extractive and lucrative technologies, and then sells more of it to people via television as a cure for the stress of living in a technology-dominated world. The hope that the next technology will solve the problems created by the way the last technology was used is a kind of millennial, even messianic, hope, apparently ever latent in the breasts of the citizenry. The myth of technological progress emerged out of the same Age of Reason that gave us the myth of representative democracy, a new organizing vision that still works pretty well, despite the decline in vigor of the old democratic institutions. It's hard to give up on one Enlightenment ideal while clinging to another.

I believe it is too early to judge which set of claims will prove to be accurate. I also believe that those who would prefer the more democratic vision of the future have an opportunity to influence the outcome, which is precisely why online activists should delve into the criticisms that have been leveled against them. If electronic democracy advocates can address these critiques successfully, their claims might have a chance. If they cannot, perhaps it would be better not to raise people's hopes. Those who are not aware of the history of dead ends are doomed to replay them, hopes high, again and again.

The idea that putting powerful computers in the hands of citizens will shield the citizenry against totalitarian authorities echoes similar, older beliefs about citizen-empowering technology. As Langdon Winner put it in his essay "Mythinformation,"

> Of all the computer enthusiasts' political ideas, there is none more poignant than the faith that the computer is destined to become a potent equalizer in modern society. . . . Presumably, ordinary citizens equipped with microcomputers will be able to counter the influence of large, computer-based organizations.
>
> Notions of this kind echo beliefs of eighteenth century revolutionaries that placing firearms in the hands of the people was crucial to overthrowing entrenched authority. In the American Revolution, French Revolution, Paris Commune, and Russian Revolution the role of "the people armed" was central to the revolutionary program. As the military defeat of the Paris Commune made clear, however, the fact that the popular forces have guns may not be decisive. In a contest of force against force, the larger, more sophisticated, more ruthless, better equipped competitor often has the upper hand. Hence, the availability of low-cost computing power may move the baseline that defines electronic dimensions of social influence, but it does not necessarily alter the relative balance of power. Using a personal computer makes one no more powerful vis-à-vis, say, the National Security Agency than flying a hang glider establishes a person as a match for the U.S. Air Force.[7]

The great power of the idea of electronic democracy is that technical trends in communications technologies can help citizens break the monopoly on their attention that has been enjoyed by the powers behind the broadcast paradigm—the owners of television networks, newspaper syndicates, and publishing conglomerates. The great weakness of the idea of electronic democracy is that it can be more easily commodified than explained. The commercialization and commodification of public discourse is only one of the grave problems posed by the increasing sophistication of communications media. The Net that is a marvelous lateral network can also be used as a kind of invisible yet inescapable cage. The idea of malevolent political leaders with their hands on the controls of a Net raises fear of a more direct assault on liberties.

Virtual communitarians, because of the nature of our medium, must pay for our access to each other by forever questioning the reality of our online culture. The land of the hyperreal begins when people forget that a telephone only conveys the illusion of being within speaking distance of another person and a computer conference only conveys the illusion of a town hall meeting. It's when we forget about the illusion that the trouble begins. When the technology itself grows powerful enough to make the illusions increasingly realistic, as the Net promises to do within the next 10 to 20 years, the necessity for continuing to question reality grows even more acute.

What should those of us who believe in the democratizing potential of virtual communities do about the technological critics? I believe we should study what the historians and social scientists have to say about the illusions and power shifts that accompanied the diffusion of previous technologies. Computer-mediated communication and technology in general has real limits; it's best to continue to listen to those who understand the limits, even as we continue to explore the technologies' positive capabilities. Failing to fall under the spell of the "rhetoric of the technological sublime," actively questioning and examining social assumptions about the effects of new technologies, reminding ourselves that electronic communication has powerful illusory capabilities, are all good steps to take to prevent disasters.

If electronic democracy is to succeed, however, in the face of all the obstacles, activists must do more than avoid mistakes. Those who would use computer networks as political tools must go forward and actively apply their theories to more and different kinds of communities. If there is a last good hope, it will come from a new way of looking at technology. Instead of falling under the spell of a sales pitch, or rejecting new technologies as instruments of illusion, we need to look closely at new technologies and ask how they can help build stronger, more humane communities—and ask how they might be obstacles to that goal. The late 1990s may be seen in retrospect as a narrow window of historical opportunity, when people either acted or failed to act effectively to regain control over communications technologies. Armed with knowledge, guided by a clear, human-centered vision, governed by a commitment to civil discourse, we the citizens hold the key levers at a pivotal time. What happens next is largely up to us.

NOTES

1. Jürgen Habermas, *The Theory of Communicative Action.* Vol. 1, *Reason and the Rationalization of Society.* Translated by Thomas McCarthy. Boston: Beacon Press, 1984; discussion of the Habermasian public sphere also appears in *New German Critique 3* (Fall 1974), 45–55.

2. Jessica Lipnack and Jeffrey Stamps, *Networking: The First Report and Directory.* Garden City, NY: Doubleday, 1982.

3. Guy Debord, *Comments on the Society of the Spectacle.* London: Verso, 1992; Jean Baudrillard, *Selected Writings.* Edited by Mark Poster, Stanford, CA: Stanford University Press, 1988.

4. Neal Postman, *Amusing Ourselves to Death: Public Discourse in the Age of Show Business.* New York: Viking Penguin, 1985.

5. James Carey (with John J. Quirk), "The Mythos of the Electronic Revolution." In *Communication as Culture: Essays on Media and Society.* Winchester, MA: Unwin Hyman, 1989.

6. Jean Bethke Elshtain, "Interactive TV—Democracy and the QUBE Tube." *The Nation,* August 7, 1982, p. 108.

7. Langdon Winner, *The Whale and the Reactor.* Chicago: University of Chicago Press, 1986, p. 112.

RELATED LINKS

- Popcultures.com: Jean Baudrillard (http://www.popcultures.com/theorists/baudrillard.html)

- Cyberdemocracy: Internet and the Public Sphere (http://www.hnet.uci.edu/mposter/writings/democ.html)

- Guy Debord (http://www.nothingness.org/SI/debord.html)

- Howard Rheingold's Home Page (http://www.rheingold.com)

- The Unfinished Project of Enlightenment: The Critical Social Theory of Jurgen Habermas (http://www.flash.net/~oudies/habermas.htm)

FOR FURTHER RESEARCH

To find out more about the topics discussed in this reading, use InfoTrac College Edition. Type
in keywords and subject terms such as "public sphere," "electronic democracy," and "commodification." You can access InfoTrac College Edition from the Wadsworth/Thomson Communication Cafe homepage: http://communication.wadsworth.com.

Reading 12-4

Universal Access to E-mail

Robert H. Anderson, Tora K. Bikson, Sally Ann Law, and Bridger M. Mitchell*

EDITOR'S NOTE

*This 1995 report from the respected RAND think tank, a best-seller among policy proposals, outlines the rationale for guar-
anteeing nearly universal access to e-mail in the United States, along the lines of universal telephone service. The authors
maintain that the unique properties of e-mail allow individuals to engage in an active civic dialog, fostering interactive communication among citizens and delivering significant social and political benefits in the process. Though e-mail began as a means
of information interchange for small, select groups, its regular use has important social, political, and economic implications.
Like the telephone, e-mail has evolved into a social utility. But the challenge remains in connecting everyone to the network,
an issue that may require societal intervention.*

CONSIDER

1. Despite the arguments in favor of universal access, do you think providing e-mail accounts to nearly all U.S.
   citizens is a desirable and feasible idea?

2. In your view, will increased access to e-mail help reduce feelings of alienation that many citizens harbor
   and revitalize the involvement of ordinary citizens in the political process?

3. What are some of the disadvantages of making e-mail universally accessible, and why?

Over the last 15 years, the burgeoning use of personal
computers has popularized a number of new information services, including in particular electronic mail or
"e-mail." E-mail is a form of information interchange
in which messages are sent from one personal computer

*With Christopher Kedzie, Brent Keltner, Constantijn Panis,
Joel Pliskin, and Padmanabhan Srinagesh.

(or computer terminal) to another via modems and a
telecommunications system. The use of e-mail began
on the ARPAnet (the precursor of the Internet) in the
1960s and 1970s in the United States, gradually spread
along with the use of mainframe- and minicomputer-
based local nets in the 1970s, and "exploded" along
with the rapid growth of personal computers (PCs) and
the Internet in the 1980s. E-mail began as a means of
information interchange for small, select groups; its
use has spread to encompass millions of people in the
United States and all over the world. E-mail has given
rise to the formation of many "virtual communities"—
groups of individuals, often widely separated geograph-
ically, who share common interests. The interpersonal

linkages and loyalties associated with these virtual communities can be real and powerful.

E-mail has unique properties that distinguish it from other forms of communication; for example, it supports true interactive communication among many participants. For the first time in human history, we would assert, the means of "broadcasting" or "narrowcasting" are not confined to the few with printing presses, TV stations, money to buy access to those scarce resources, and the like. E-mail is also, unlike telephone calls (with the exception of voice mail and answering machines), asynchronous, so that communication does not depend on the simultaneous availability and attention of sender and recipient. Generalizing greatly, e-mail increases the power of individuals, permitting them to be active participants in a dialog extended in both time and space, rather than passive recipients of "canned" programming and prepackaged information. These characteristics give rise to the question: Can e-mail's novel properties address society's most compelling problems? If so, by what means?

PROBLEM STATEMENT

It is now possible to imagine the arrangement or construction of systems in which nearly universal access to e-mail within the United States could become feasible within a decade—indeed, that is one aspiration of the U.S. National Information Infrastructure (NII) initiative. Since e-mail use is growing rapidly (e.g., within individual corporations, CompuServe, America Online, Internet, and Bitnet systems and on numerous dial-in electronic bulletin boards), the question may be asked: "Why bother? It's happening anyway." Three important answers to this question are: (1) In spite of the growth of these e-mail systems, the majority of U.S. residents probably will continue to lack access to e-mail well into the next century without societal intervention; (2) there is today a significant lack of active participation by many citizens in the dialog that forms the basis for the U.S. democratic process[1]; and (3) some citizens, such as inner-city minorities and the rural poor, are relatively disenfranchised and constitute groups that will be the last to be reached by commercial e-mail systems that evolve in private markets. Because the properties of e-mail allow individuals to engage in an active civic dialog, with informative and affiliative dimensions, universal e-mail might provide significant benefits in creating interactive communication among U.S. citizens and residents.

The problem, then, is achieving active, responsive citizen participation in our national dialog for all citizens—participation not only in national politics but in local affairs, job markets, educational systems, health and welfare systems, international discourse, and all other aspects of our society.

There are hints that the distinctive properties of electronic mail systems (including access to, and the ability to post and retrieve messages from, various electronic bulletin boards) may well be relevant to this re-enfranchisement of all citizens. Civic networks exemplify these opportunities.

It is also clear that widespread citizen access to an e-mail system could have profound economic implications that might provide new sources of business and revenue to entrepreneurs providing new services; for example, installation of the French Programme Télétel system resulted in a flourishing of electronic services available to virtually all French citizens (and, for that matter, many visitors—through terminals available in hotel rooms and public sites).

It is important to note, however, that the Minitel terminal used by Télétel was not originally conceived of as access to an e-mail system but rather as an "electronic telephone directory." As is often the case, when some facility for communication becomes possible within a system (e.g., ARPAnet, Télétel, and to a growing extent the Dialog system within the United States), its convenience and empowerment of individuals quickly cause e-mail to become an important form of usage. Lack of true e-mail capabilities may be a major contributor to the failure of other electronic service ventures such as teletext experiments, although too many factors may be involved to confirm this assessment.

UNIVERSAL E-MAIL

The initial forays into widespread availability of electronic mail, such as the ARPAnet (and now Internet) experience, Télétel, and growing Prodigy, CompuServe, and America Online usage, lead to an intriguing question: What about "universal e-mail"? What about providing all residents of the United States with access to e-mail service, just as they now all (or almost all) have access to telephone service and postal service? What would be involved in such an undertaking? What are the pros and cons? What are the advantages and disadvantages? Could this have beneficial effects for U.S. society? Greater cohesion? Reduced alienation? Increased participation in the political process? Influence national security? What about beneficial effects for the U.S. economy? Or other productive side effects? And who would pay for the infrastructure and its usage?

More specific questions arise immediately regarding the services and functions to be provided by a universal e-mail system: the required degree of access to such a "universal" service; the provision of privacy; alternative system architectures and implementation schemes; the cost of such a system/service and the method of payment; the likely social and international effect of universal e-mail; and finally, public versus private roles in creating and operating such a service. This report describes our initial study of these and related issues over a 2-year period and presents the results of our analyses.

SOME DEFINITIONS

Electronic Mail

For the purposes of this report, we have adopted a definition of electronic mail provided in an earlier RAND report (Anderson et al., 1989):

An electronic mail system:

1. Permits the asynchronous electronic interchange of information between persons, groups of persons, and functional units of an organization; and

2. Provides mechanisms supporting the creation, distribution, consumption, processing, and storage of this information.

The words in this definition all have significance. Key among them are the following:

- *Asynchronous:* One defining attribute of e-mail is the ability to send a message when the recipient is not at that moment logged in; the message is placed in an "inbox" for later inspection by the recipient at his or her convenience.

- *Electronic:* The message travels over telecommunications systems at the speed of electricity in copper, of light in a fiber-optic cable, or of microwave or a satellite link (plus additional switching delays). Although some system "gateways" buffer messages for periodic transmission, the result still has a dynamic fundamentally different from postal mail, newspapers, and other traditional media.

- *Interchange of information:* Anyone within the system can send as well as receive messages.

- *Between persons, groups of persons, and functional units of an organization:* Messages may be sent to "mailboxes" representing individuals or groups; "aliases" may be established representing a number of individual addresses, so that a message may be sent to a group of individuals in one action; mailboxes such as "purchasing@abc.com" or "president@whitehouse.gov" may be established that represent a function, to be used by whomever is presently handling that function.

- *Mechanisms supporting the creation, distribution, consumption, processing, and storage:* It must be possible to create messages, send and receive them, store them for future inspection and re-use, and "process" them (e.g., copy portions and paste them into later messages, forward them to others, modify their contents, and reuse them in other applications).

By the above definition, multipart messages containing embedded formatted word-processing documents, video clips, bitmapped pictures, sound clips, and the like are certainly e-mail. Faxes sent from one dedicated fax machine to another, appearing only on output paper are not (because they are not processable in a useful manner), but a "fax" sent from one PC to another meets the definition (because it may be stored for later retransmission, and its contents may be "processed"—e.g., by character-recognition or graphics-enhancement programs; in fact, some recipients may never get it in paper form. Similarly, using a personal computer to interact with "chat" groups and MUDs[2] usually qualifies as a form of e-mail, because most communication programs through which this interaction is carried out allow the transcript of the interaction to be saved, processed, reused, and so on.

We have tried to use a rather narrow definition of e-mail to focus this report on electronic mail, although it will be clear that most e-mail users will also have facilities at hand to browse the World Wide Web, participate in multiuser simulations and games, and so forth.

Universal Access

The other key concept in this report is "universal access." By this, we simply mean e-mail facilities and services that are:

- Available at modest individual effort and expense to (almost) everyone in the United States in a form that does not require highly specialized skills; or,

■ Accessible in a manner analogous to the level, cost, and ease of use of telephone service or the U.S. Postal Service.

We do not, therefore, envision that every single person will have access, but that e-mail can achieve the same ubiquity that telephones (including the availability of payphones) and TVs have. Table 1 shows the penetration of related technologies into U.S. households, for comparison.

Note that the above percentages are not distributed uniformly across various sectors of our society. For example, a recent report (Mueller & Schement, 1995) describes telephone access in Camden, New Jersey, by family income, ethnicity, age, and other demographic factors. The report indicates that, overall, only 80.6 percent of households in Camden have telephones; notable disparities include families on Food Stamps, who lag 20.4 percentage points behind households not on Food Stamps. For many households, "universal access" means traveling to the nearest working payphone (where receiving incoming messages is sometimes precluded either socially or by the technology). Similarly, universal access to e-mail for many may require using public terminals in shared spaces such as libraries and schools (but where barriers to message reception can readily be eliminated).

ADVANTAGES OF UNIVERSAL E-MAIL

E-mail services can be used both for "telephone-type" messages and for other, usually longer, messages or documents that might otherwise be sent using facsimile or hard-copy postal services, both public and private. Compared with the telephone system, one primary advantage of an e-mail service is that it eliminates "telephone tag." It also provides a content record of the interactions that can be retrieved, printed, studied, selectively forwarded, and in general reused. Other advantages are that it permits (but certainly does not require) more deliberative and reflective, but still interactive, conversational dialogs, as well as one-to-many and many-to-many conversations. These features have led to many new social, commercial, and political groupings of people: the "virtual communities" mentioned above, using e-mail as the linkage. It provides a common context among a set of participants.

Table 1. Availability of Related Technologies in U.S. Households

Technology	Percentage of Households
Television	95
Telephone	93
Videocassette recorder	85
More than one TV	66
Cable TV	64
Pay-per-view service	51
Videogame system	40
Video camera	28
Fax	6

SOURCE: *Times Mirror* (1994).

Compared with postal services, an e-mail service offers much faster mail delivery—usually minutes between any two locations in the United States (although currently, delays up to a day occur with some Internet access providers), compared with one to several days for postal systems. E-mail systems also afford much more flexibility (both locational and temporal) in that delivery. In the current postal system, a person's mail is delivered to one or two (or at most a few) fixed addresses (e.g., home or office). In most e-mail systems, a person with the proper (portable) terminal equipment can log in to his or her "mailbox" from any location that has electronic access to the system. Today, this means that people can pick up their e-mail from their office, their home, their hotel rooms, another office (perhaps in another city) they are visiting, or any site with a phone jack.[3] In the future, as terminal equipment gets smaller and cellular telephones become more ubiquitous, one will be able to pick up or send e-mail while traveling in a car and flying in an airplane. This results in more geographic independence (*where* one gets mail) and temporal flexibility (*when* one gets mail).

These advantages are available in any e-mail system. The additional advantage of a universal e-mail system is that since everyone belongs to the system, a user can send e-mail to anyone, not just a limited group, and receive e-mail from anyone. This makes the special advantages of e-mail available for all of one's correspondence, not just a subset. If the costs of such a service permit attractive pricing, it could take over a significant portion of the business of current postal services[4]—especially when next-generation e-mail systems allow the transmission and viewing of multimedia messages containing high-resolution color pictures, "movie clips" of image sequences, and sound, which could, among other things, support a variety of "electronic commerce."

DISADVANTAGES OF UNIVERSAL E-MAIL

The concept of universal e-mail raises serious concerns as well. For example, individual users could get "flooded" with messages, unless some means of "filtering" incoming message traffic is provided. Also, some virtual communities enabled by e-mail could be bad for U.S. society, rather than good; they could conceivably lead to a less cohesive society, rather than a more cohesive one. It is also clear that within any e-mail system, some users will be "more equal" than others; they will be able to purchase more powerful equipment, giving them more power over their electronic communication. Some will become more knowledgeable in the features and facilities of the system—permitting them, for example, to assemble tailored mailing lists for broadcast of their messages—allowing them to take advantage of those features for their own personal benefit or gain. Special-interest groups may in particular be motivated to become further empowered by use of these communication tools. Some (but not all) would also consider it a disadvantage that national borders become more transparent to international commerce and influences (Ronfeldt et al., 1993).

MOTIVATIONS FOR UNIVERSAL E-MAIL

The apparent advantages of universal e-mail, despite the possible side effects and disadvantages, lead to a number of possible motivations for establishing such a service in the United States, ranging across the spectrum from the utilitarian to the idealistic. At the utilitarian end is efficiency. Electronic mail uses modern information and telecommunications technology to provide a much faster and more efficient means of conveying information from one point to another than current postal systems, which rely on "technologies"— letters written on paper, put in sealed envelopes, and physically transported from sender to receiver—over two millennia old. The increased speed and efficiency of information delivery by e-mail could have many commercial and economic benefits, contributing to increased U.S. economic competitiveness.

At the idealistic end of the spectrum of motivations, the hypothesis is made that electronic mail makes possible much more egalitarian, deliberative, and reflective dialogs among individuals and groups (see Sproull & Kiesler, 1991, for supporting evidence). It might therefore lead to new social and political linkages within U.S. society, reduce the feelings of alienation that many individuals in the United States feel and give them a new sense of "community," revitalize the involvement of the common citizen in the political process, etc., and in general strengthen the cohesion of U.S. society.

Different motivations across this spectrum will appeal to different elements of U.S. society. To achieve widespread appeal—and political/economic support—a U.S. universal e-mail service should satisfy a broad spectrum of these motivations, whether the system is "designed" to meet these objectives (e.g., with heavy U.S. government involvement) or evolves through private initiative and entrepreneurship subject to constraints, incentives, or standards that encourage universal access.

NOTES

1. Documentation about the decline in U.S. "social capital" and its effect on the performance of representative government may be found in Putnam (1993) and Putnam (1995). Among the data cited in his 1995 article: U.S. voter turnout has declined by nearly a quarter from the early 1960s to 1990; Americans who report they have "attended a public meeting on town or school affairs in the past year" declined from 22 percent in 1973 to 13 percent in 1993; participation in parent–teacher organizations dropped from more than 12 million in 1964 to approximately 7 million today; since 1970, volunteering is off for Boy Scouts by 26 percent and for the Red Cross by 61 percent.

2. A MUD is variously defined as Multiple User Domain, Multiple User Dimension, Multiple User Dungeon, or Multiple User Dialogue. It is a computer program allowing users to explore and help create an online environment. Each user takes control of a computerized persona/avatar/ incarnation/character. The user can walk around, chat with other characters, explore dangerous monster-infested areas, solve puzzles, and even create his or her very own rooms, descriptions, and items.

3. E-mail can also be forwarded automatically to an alternative mailbox (e.g., closer to a vacation spot or sabbatic location).

4. In this regard, it should be noted that the current U.S. postal services deliver two things: information (e.g., letters) and bulk material (e.g., packages). A universal e-mail system should, in principle, be able to take over much of the information delivery functions; it obviously cannot handle the bulk material delivery functions. However, some bulk material consists of catalogs and advertising that may, in fact, increasingly become accessible electronically.

REFERENCES

Anderson, R. H., Shapiro, N. Z., Bikson, T. K., & Kantar, P. H. (1989). *The Design of the MH Mail System.* Santa Monica, CA: RAND, N-3017-IRIS.

Klein, H. K. (1995). "Grassroots Democracy and the Internet: The Telecommunications Policy Roundtable—Northeast USA (TPR-NE)." Internet Society: INE '95 Proceedings. Available at http://inet.nttam.com/HMP/PAPER/164/txt/paper.txt.

Lynch, D., & Rose, M. (1993). *The Internet System Handbook.* Reading, MA: Addison-Wesley.

Mueller, M., & Schement, J. R. (1995). *Universal Service from the Bottom Up: A Profile of Telecommunications Access in Camden, New Jersey.* Rutgers University Project on Information Policy, Rutgers University School of Communication.

Putnam, R. D. (1995). "Bowling Alone: America's Declining Social Capital." *Journal of Democracy, 6*(1).

Putnam, R. D. (1993). *Making Democracy Work: Civic Traditions in Modern Italy.* Princeton, NJ: Princeton University Press.

Ronfeldt, D., Thorup, C., Aguayo, S., & Frederick, H. (1993). *Restructuring Civil Society Across North America in the Information Age: New Networks for Immigration Advocacy Organizations.* Santa Monica, CA: RAND, DRU-599-FF.

Sproull, L., & Kiesler, S. (1991). *Connections: New Ways of Working in the Networked Organization.* Cambridge, MA: MIT Press.

Times Mirror (1994). *Technology in the American Household.* Los Angeles, CA: Times Mirror Center for The People & The Press.

RELATED LINKS

- December.com: Tools (http://www.december.com/net/tools)
- E-mail Guide (http://www.emailaddresses.com/email_guide.htm)
- *Internet Literacy:* Electronic Mail (http://www.udel.edu/interlit2/chapter6.html)
- Universal Access to E-mail Web Site (http://www.rand.org/publications/MR/MR650)
- Universal E-mail: (http://backofficesystems.com/tips/paper/univ-e-m.htm)

FOR FURTHER RESEARCH

To find out more about the topics discussed in this reading, use InfoTrac College Edition. Type in keywords and subject terms such as "universal service," "universal e-mail," and "civic participation." You can access InfoTrac College Edition from the Wadsworth/Thomson Communication Cafe homepage: http://communication.wadsworth.com.

13

The Digital Divide

Reading 13-1

Mind the Gap: The Digital Divide as the Civil Rights Issue of the New Millennium

Andy Carvin

EDITOR'S NOTE

In his 2000 State of the Union address, then-President Clinton brought the issue of the "Digital Divide"—the tendency of high-income white households to have far greater access to the Internet than minority and rural households at the lowest income levels—to national prominence. Now the government, concerned that anyone without access is in danger of being shut out of the Information Revolution, is teaming up with private industry and community organizations such as the Digital Divide Network with the goal of making Internet access as widespread as phone service. In this reading, Andy Carvin, a senior associate at the Benton Foundation, argues that the Digital Divide is an important civil rights issue that can't be solved by access to technology alone.

CONSIDER

1. Why can't the Digital Divide be solved by increased access to technology alone? What other factors are important to consider, according to the author?

2. Should we open our schools and libraries to the community so that no computer lab or training room sits idle during evening and weekend hours?

3. What are some potential long-term consequences of the Digital Divide, and why is it one of the most important civil rights issues facing information societies?

The Digital Divide is one of the most important civil rights issues facing our modern information economy.

In the years since the start of the Internet Revolution, the American public has been exposed to more than its fair share of overused catchphrases. Way back in the early 1990s, then-Senator Al Gore spoke of an Information Superhighway that would connect the country's citizens to an overwhelming variety of telecommunications opportunities. We read about the near-Messianic coming of a 500-channel universe in which we'll be able to relish a mind-numbing array of programming options, from The Jack Russell Terrier Channel to Ex!, The Ex-Convicts Network. Countless Web sites and multimedia products boast about their "interactivity" when in truth the only interactivity they offer is in choosing which hyperlink to press next. And consider the phrase "click here"—before the advent of the Internet it would have been seen as a completely baffling command. Now it's the Cyber Age equivalent of a welcome mat: Click here and enter the Web site of your dreams.

But despite the media's penchant for beating to death anything to do with the Internet, a new phrase has recently entered the public's online lexicon, one that actually carries significant societal ramifications: the "Digital Divide." In the most basic sense, the Digital Divide is the ever-growing gap between those people and communities who have access to information technology and those who do not (in other words, the haves and have-nots). The Digital Divide has been on the radar screens of those of us in the policy world for a while now, but over the course of 1999 its profile was raised as more political leaders took an interest in the subject.

The Digital Divide may seem like an intangible concept to some, but studies have begun to articulate it in no uncertain terms. Consider these statistics from the U.S. Department of Commerce:

- Households earning incomes over $75,000 are over twenty times more likely to have home Internet access than those at the lowest income levels.

- Only 6.6 percent of people with an elementary school education or less use the Internet.

- In rural areas, those with college degrees are eleven times more likely to have a home computer and twenty-six times more likely to have home Internet access than those with an elementary school education.

- People with college degrees or higher are ten times more likely to have Internet access at work as persons with only some high school education.

Such statistics should not be taken lightly. The Digital Divide is one of the most important civil rights issues facing our modern information economy. As telecommunications increasingly entwines itself with educational, social, financial, and employment opportunities, those communities lacking access will find themselves falling further behind the rest of society. The Internet has the potential to empower its users with new skills, new perspectives, new freedoms, even new voices; those groups who remain sequestered from the technology will be further segregated into the periphery of public life.

In schools, we've seen the Digital Divide tackled head-on with the implementation of the E-Rate program. Each year tens of thousands of schools receive over $2 billion in federal telecommunications subsidies to help support classroom Internet access. Though some schools still haven't felt the benefits of the E-Rate, many others have: Over 50 percent of classrooms nationwide now have Internet access. Real progress is being made.

Whether the issue is in schools or in communities, the Digital Divide is finally beginning to receive the attention it deserves. But as we try to develop a long-term strategy for combating the divide, it begs an important question: *Is the Digital Divide essentially an access issue?* In one sense, the question is a no-brainer. There is a widening gap between those who have access to information technology and those who don't; therefore, when dealing with the Digital Divide we need to concentrate on giving more people Internet access.

But giving people access doesn't instantly solve the manifold woes of our communities and schools. If it did, every kid with Internet access would be getting straight A's and every adult with access would be gainfully employed and prosperous. It's just not that simple. Technology access is only one small piece of a much larger puzzle, a puzzle that if solved might help raise the quality of life for millions of people. None of us can rightfully say we've found all the individual pieces yet, but some of the pieces are obvious enough that we can begin to put the Digital Divide puzzle together:

The Digital Divide is about content. The value of the Internet can be directly correlated to the value of its content. If all you can find online is shopping, Poké-mon trading clubs, and porn, you could make a pretty good argument that it's not very important to give people access to the Internet. As anyone who has used it knows, the Internet can offer a wealth of opportuni-ties for learning and personal enhancement, but we've only scratched the surface in terms of its potential. As more underprivileged and disenfranchised communi-ties gain access, the Internet itself must provide the right tools so people are able to take advantage of and use the online medium for more varied purposes, more learning styles, more languages and cultures. The In-ternet may feel like a diverse place, but when compared with the wealth of diversity and knowledge reflected by humanity in the real world, it's still pretty weak. Until the Net contains content that has true value to all of its potential users it will remain a place for the elite.

The Digital Divide is about literacy. As much as we hate to admit it, functional illiteracy amongst adults is one of America's dirty little secrets. Millions of adults struggle to fill out forms, follow written instructions, or even read a newspaper. A National Adult Literacy Survey conducted in the early 1990s suggested that as many as 44 million American adults—almost one out of every four—were functionally illiterate, while an-other 50 million adults were plagued by limited liter-acy. We often talk about the importance of information literacy when it comes to using the Internet. Informa-tion literacy is an obviously vital part of the equation, but how can we expect to address and conquer the Digital Divide when nearly half of all American adults can't even process written information competently? Literacy must be tackled at the most basic level in or-der to afford more people the opportunity to use tech-nology effectively.

The Digital Divide is about pedagogy. Internet access in schools isn't worth a hill of beans if teachers aren't prepared to take full advantage of technology. Research has shown that educators who are resistant to construc-tivist, or participatory, teaching practices are less likely to utilize the Internet in their lessons, while educators who are more comfortable with constructivist prac-tices are more likely to do so. Teachers who employ more real-world interaction are thus more inclined to employ online interaction. How can professional de-velopment be reformed to take these differences into account?

The Digital Divide is about community. One of the greatest strengths of the Internet is in its facility for fos-tering community. Communities often appear in the most low-tech of places: You can surf the Web until your knuckles implode and yet not feel like you've ac-tually bonded with anyone, but you can subscribe to a simple e-mail listserv and join a gathering of people who have been enjoying each others' wisdom for years. It's paramount for people coming to the Internet for the first time to have opportunities to join existing communities and forge new communities of their own. Public spaces must be preserved online so that people can gather without feeling like direct marketing or more popular and powerful voices are crowding them out. If people can't build meaningful relationships on-line, how can they be expected to gravitate to it?

These five puzzle pieces—access, content, literacy, pedagogy, and community—may not be enough to complete the entire Digital Divide puzzle, but they go a long way in providing a picture of what's at stake. Giving people access to technology is important, but it's just one of many issues that need to be considered. Schools, libraries, and community centers are taking that first step in getting wired, but they must also con-sider the needs of the learners, the teachers, and the communities that support them.

We must continue fighting the scourge of illiter-acy—among students, their parents, and among the community—by expanding formal and informal op-portunities that improve reading and critical-thinking skills. We must demand engaging content from on-line producers and refuse to buy into mediocre content when it doesn't suit our teaching needs. We must en-courage all learners to be creators as well, sharing their wise voices both online and offline. And we must open our schools and libraries to more connections with our communities—no computer lab or training room should sit idle during evening and weekend hours. These are but a few examples of what the education community can do.

The Digital Divide is real, and it will only get worse if we ignore it. Click here to change the world.

RELATED LINKS

- Digital Divide Network: http://digitaldividenetwork.org
- The Benton Foundation (http://www.benton.org)
- Closing the Digital Divide (http://www.digitaldivide.gov)
- The Digital Divide: A Resource List (http://www.gseis.ucla.edu/faculty/chu/digdiv)
- Digital Divide Links (http://www.pbs.org/digitaldivide/links.html)

FOR FURTHER RESEARCH

To find out more about the topics discussed in this reading, use InfoTrac College Edition. Type in keywords and subject terms such as "Digital Divide," "Internet access," and "functional illiteracy." You can access InfoTrac College Edition from the Wadsworth/Thomson Communication Cafe homepage: http://communication.wadsworth.com.

Reading 13-2

Computer Haves and Have-Nots in the Schools

Debra Nussbaum

EDITOR'S NOTE

The Digital Divide presents the nation's classrooms with a new challenge: to educate and equally stimulate students who are familiar with computers and those who aren't, the computer haves and have-nots. As this reading calls attention to, computer literacy begins in the home. Students with access to home computers have a decided advantage over those who don't. Even though experts disagree over the extent to which computers should be used in the early grades, the playing field is clearly not level for the child who does not have technology close at hand.

CONSIDER

1. How are teachers addressing the problem of differing levels of computer literacy—some students knowing a lot about computers, others little or nothing—in their classrooms?

2. Should computers be used extensively in elementary school, or should students learn the basics first without the aid of technology?

3. If having a computer at home improves a child's chances for academic success, should the government offer subsidies for families that can't afford a new machine?

When William Yokoyama started seventh grade, he had already been using a home computer for more than

"Computer Haves and Have-Nots in the Schools," by Debra Nussbaum. From the *New York Times,* October 22, 1998, p. G1. Copyright © 1998 The New York Times Company. Reprinted with permission.

6 years. He could easily use it as a word processor, to surf the Internet, draw pictures, make charts and graphics, and write simple game programs.

The first week of computer classes in his middle school "they were teaching how to power up," recalled William, 14, of Chula Vista, California, who is now in the ninth grade. The class goal was to learn how to type a business letter. William wanted more of a challenge.

Some of his equally computer-literate friends stayed in the class because "they thought it was an easy A," he said. "I'd rather have fun while I'm trying to get an A."

Teachers at his school, Bonita Vista Middle School, agreed with William and his father, Irv Yokoyama, and moved William into a course where he could use the computer as a research tool to study subjects like the environment and atomic energy.

Such is the new national classroom challenge faced daily by teachers and parents, now that computers are common in schools and in most homes where there are children: how to teach and stimulate both the computer haves and the have-nots?

Those students who have access to home computers go to the classroom with skills far beyond those who don't, most of whom need several lessons just on booting up and operating the mouse.

As America continues its romance with technology, the issue is arising more often among educators.

While not all educators agree that there is a problem, or even that computers should be used extensively by grade-school pupils, many say that the playing field is clearly not level for the child who does not have technology as close as the bedroom or the family room.

"Any student who has a computer in the home has a decided advantage over kids who don't," said Ken Tobin, a science education professor at the University of Pennsylvania and the director of teacher education at the university.

The computer has become such a key communication and research tool in education that many students will use the Internet well before going to the library, said Paul Myers, associate professor of computer science at Trinity University in San Antonio. In 13 years of teaching his class on Computers and Society, he has found that he no longer needs to spend the first two weeks giving instructions on using the keyboard, because usually every student knows how.

The balance has now tipped to the point where Professor Myers says educators are encouraging students to visit the library so that they don't forget how valuable a resource books are for research.

"I think there is an issue here—the issue of the haves and have-nots," said David Tremblay, senior industry analyst for ZD Market Intelligence, a market research company based in La Jolla, California. "Lower-income households are much less likely to have personal computers. You can't assume everyone has a computer."

Morton Sherman, schools superintendent for Cherry Hill, New Jersey, a Philadelphia suburb, doesn't see children without PCs at home as the top issue in education. But "it's a growing issue," he said, adding: "And it's not just a matter of having or not having, but whether they are being used. We have a responsibility to support these kids. There are also teachers who are haves and have-nots.

"There were kids in the '70s and '80s who didn't have calculators. Technology is an essential tool—it's not a luxury. For those who do not have it, the gap is getting wider."

Income is certainly a factor. Of households with annual incomes of $75,000 or more, 68 percent have computers. Of households with annual incomes of $20,000 or less, only 19 percent do.

But at the same time, there are also more computers available in school buildings, according to Quality Education Data, a private education research company in Denver. There are now 85,900 public schools with computers, out of a total of 87,200 in the United States.

While some technologically astute people are starting to question the need for computers in the schools at all, educators like Professor Tobin and many school administrators and teachers advocate granting access to computers after school hours at libraries, community centers, and the schools themselves.

Nearly 80 percent of the students in the affluent Cherry Hill district have home computers, said John Scarinci, the district technology director. He compares not having a computer at home to not having an *Encyclopedia Britannica* in the 1960s.

"It's less convenient," he said, for students without home computers. But he added that students could get access at the library or at a friend's house, much as he did growing up without an encyclopedia at home.

Parents also seem to be feeling more pressure to buy computers for their children, and as prices drop, more families can afford them.

A new basic computer system can now be had for less than $1,000. Web TV and similar systems that provide Internet access can be purchased for $200 or less with discounts, and used computer equipment is only $300 to $500, Mr. Scarinci said. "It's the price of a television set."

Chip and Daisy Gilliland of Port Richey, Florida, whose three children range from a baby to a second-grader, are shopping for their first personal computer.

"A lot of other kids do have computers," Mrs. Gilliland said. "They feel bigger and smarter using the computer. With all the technology, we want to get the kids used to using the computer. We wouldn't have thought of it just for ourselves."

Matthew Fusfield, a college freshman who graduated from Cherry Hill High School East, agrees that students do better with computers at home. He got his first computer in fourth grade and helped the district set up its computerized bulletin board system when he was in high school.

"The computer is an advantage in education," he said. "It's a tool. It's not an absolute necessity, but research is much quicker."

Mr. Fusfield said he had often helped others learn about computers during class. Educators see this trend of students with experience helping other students as changing the dynamics of the classroom and sometimes the philosophy of teaching.

Students not only teach other students but sometimes they even teach the teacher.

"It changes a lot of the power pieces in the classroom," said Judith McGonigal, a teacher in the Haddonfield school district in southern New Jersey. "The kids that have more experience become the coteacher in the classroom. You are the colearners with the kids."

Still, because of the cost of computer equipment and the constant changes and upgrades required, many rural and urban districts can't afford to keep up with more affluent suburban districts. And even in districts like Cherry Hill, the gap between haves and have-nots could grow as the school opens up an interactive message system for teachers, administrators, and students called Cherry Hill Live. The district tries to accommodate all students by giving them computer time in the classroom and in labs.

Recently Cherry Hill stopped using computer teachers to teach technology skills in elementary school; instead, the regular classroom teacher takes children to the computer lab once a week.

"We are moving away from technology as a subject and using it as a tool," Mr. Scarinci said.

Ellen Specter, a kindergarten teacher at Cherry Hill, says that the students who gravitate to the computers during free time are often those who have computers at home. In her morning class, fifteen of the twenty-three students have computers. In the afternoon class, seventeen out of twenty do.

Every class starts with Mrs. Specter giving instructions to point to the monitor, point to the keyboard, point to the mouse. Some children point to a rabbit icon on the screen instead.

Students have to find the yellow notepad icon on the Student Writing Center software made by The Learning Company of Fremont, California. They get a list of words to click on and can change the border on their screen.

Soon, the children can be heard saying things like "Mrs. Specter, mine's stuck!" and "Something happened, Mrs. Specter." But there are also voices saying, "Cool!" and "Look!"

"Some students are not used to moving the mouse," she said. "I see a wide range of skills depending on whether they have a computer at home and whether they are allowed to use it."

Rita Mitchell, a computer teacher at Lindenwold Elementary in southern New Jersey, said that about half the children in her classes come from homes without computers. She sees a gap when teaching in a small room off the school library.

"Where I find the biggest difference is in third grade," she said. "The kids who have it at home know a whole lot more about computers than those who don't. Their drawings are more sophisticated. I have to make sure that I keep all the children on task and that I'm not losing them."

Sometimes she will let more advanced students try out new software to keep them occupied while others get used to handling the mouse.

With sixteen Macintosh computers in her lab, she divides the classes of about thirty students roughly in two. In one group she places those who have computers at home along with those who may not have computers but who follow directions well. In the other group, she puts students who don't have computers and who may have more trouble learning next to children who have a computer and can help them.

Finding and creating a curriculum that allows students to learn at their own pace is the solution for many teachers. It is the same approach used for years to encourage readers who need extra help while also challenging students who read above their grade level.

"The term is *differentiation*," said Mrs. McGonigal, who has taught for 30 years. "Each learner goes into it where they are. You're not teaching everyone the same thing."

When students reach the fourth or fifth grade and start doing more research on the Internet for class projects that may involve complex graphics and color charts, teachers see even more advantages for those who have home computers.

"When it gets to the Internet I see more expertise," said Ginger Hovenic, executive director of the Harborside School in downtown San Diego and a consultant to the Classroom in the Future Foundation, which trains teachers to use technology. "You can see the kids who have spent a lot of time exploring things. That's when I see the big gap begin to happen."

Some schools, like Robert Smalls Middle School in Beaufort, South Carolina, have a program under which students' parents can lease a laptop, in this case for $15 a month, for the child if they cannot afford to buy one.

Melissa McFeely is a teacher who believes in the program. Last year, out of twenty-one students in her homeroom, nineteen were from low-income families. All but three of those nineteen students leased a laptop. "More and more families are going to give up other things to have computers in the home," she said.

Peer pressure may also force the issue of getting a computer at home. It's now "cool" to be good at the computer, but that status may make the kids who do not have the technological tools at home feel even more uncomfortable—and left behind.

Karen Marshall, a New Jersey mother of four who used to work as a computer classroom aide, said she felt that students were sometimes embarrassed to say they did not have a computer or they did not have the skills other children had on the computer.

"I had some kids who had never touched a computer but didn't want to admit it," she said. "There's a lot of [social] pressure to be computer literate and the majority of kids don't want to admit it if they can't do it. If these issues aren't addressed in education, the gap could widen between the kids who have the knowledge and the kids who don't."

RELATED LINKS

- The Digital Divide's New Frontier (http://www.childrenspartnership.org/pub/low_income)
- NetDay Digital Divide Initiative (http://www.netday.org/dd.htm)
- PBS Digital Divide Series Home (http://www.pbs.org/digitaldivide)
- PowerUp Home Page (http://www.powerup.org/index.shtml)

FOR FURTHER RESEARCH

To find out more about the topics discussed in this reading, use InfoTrac College Edition. Type in keywords and subject terms such as "computer literacy," "classroom computing," and "educational technology." You can access InfoTrac College Edition from the Wadsworth/Thomson Communication Cafe homepage: http://communication.wadsworth.com.

Reading 13-3

The Rise of the Overclass: How the New Elite Scrambled Up the Merit Ladder—and Wants to Stay There Any Way It Can

Jerry Adler*

EDITOR'S NOTE

In 1984 Newsweek marked the arrival of a new species of successful American—the yuppie, or upwardly mobile professional. A decade later, the magazine took stock of another breed of upwardly mobile achievers and declared that "we are witnessing an epochal moment in American sociology"—the birth of a new elite of highly paid high-tech strivers somewhat ominously dubbed "the overclass." They might not send their kids to private schools and they might not even think of them-selves as members of an overclass, but, as writer Jerry Adler notes, they are technologically savvy and they are pulling away from the rest of America in some ways too important to ignore.

CONSIDER

1. How does membership in the overclass differ from inheriting wealth or an aristocratic title?

2. What distinguishes and defines members of the overclass? What are their common cultural and professional interests, as well as lifestyle choices?

3. Unlike the word "yuppie," which was widely used to describe overachievers in the 1980s, the term "over-class" never quite caught on. Why do you suppose this is?

You've probably never heard of the overclass, which is just how its members like it; they have a lot to answer for. They are the people who put Jim Carrey on mag-azine covers, who renamed blue-green "teal," and keep loaning money to Donald Trump—not out of any sin-ister conspiracy to ruin the country but because, well, it's their job. As "professionals" and "managers" they lay claim to an increasing share of the national income, but they wind up spending most of it at mirror-walled restaurants where they have to eat $10 arugula salads. They're famous for having opinions, but it's hard to know what these are, since they never call talk-radio shows. If they didn't exist we'd have to invent them, because otherwise we'd have no answer to the ques-tion, *whatever happened to all those yuppies we used to see running around, anyway?*

We are witnessing an epochal moment in Amer-ican sociology, the birth of a new class. There is, obvi-ously, nothing new in the fact that some people in America have more money, influence, and prestige than others. But designating them "the overclass" is not just another way for journalists to package the squeal of the skewered bourgeoisie. When "the poor" became "the underclass" it meant no longer thinking of them as just "a lot of people without money," but as the in-heritors of a "culture of poverty." Similarly, the over-

class refers to a group with a common culture and in-terests, with the obvious difference from the underclass that nobody is trying to get *out* of the overclass.

Important discoveries like this always galvanize the national dialogue. Michael Lind, who gives a neo-Marxian analysis of the overclass in his book *The Next American Nation* (The Free Press, 1995), was being at-tacked last week from both the left and the right, even as the *Atlantic Monthly* was arriving in mailboxes with a cover story by Nicholas Lemann on "The Structure of Success in America." Lind puts more emphasis on race and parentage, while Lemann dwells more on the role of SAT tests in determining who gets the goodies in American society. But they're talking about the same people, who are also part of the IQ elite described in last year's [controversial and disputed] best-seller *The Bell Curve* (The Free Press, 1994).

And this same insight resonates throughout society. Marketing consultants are already whacking the over-class into demographic slices so thin that they can peel off the Lexus segment from that for Infinitis. Political consultants study how to covertly appeal to the newly identified bloc, while simultaneously attacking their opponents for pandering to it. Bashing an elite is always great political sport. But somehow the people derided by the Left as "corporate America" and by the Right as the "liberal establishment" seldom find their real inter-ests seriously threatened.

Who *is* the overclass? It is hard to talk about class in America, a country in which 90 percent of adults in defiance of statistics and common sense identify them-selves to pollsters as "middle class." What distinguishes the overclass, in fact, is precisely its effort to distance itself *from* the middle class, rather than lay claim to it. If the overclass is hard to define, it's because it is a state of mind *and* a slice on the income curve. But it is not a ruling class: Bill Clinton seems to belong, but Newt

---

*With John McCormick in Chicago, Andrew Murr in Los Angeles, Rich Thomas and Thomas Rosenstiel in Washington, Nina Biddle in New York, Daniel Glick in Seattle, Debra Rosenberg in Nantucket, and Ginny Carroll in Houston.

Gingrich clearly doesn't; Bill Gates does, but probably not the chairman of Dow Chemical. The overclass obviously is affluent, but how much is that in dollars? Lind refers to families in the top "quintile," or 20 percent, of household income, because most government statistics are kept that way. But that implies a cutoff of only about $67,000 a year. Any figure is necessarily arbitrary, but it seems more logical to speak of a class consisting of the top 5 percent in household income, roughly 12.5 million people with incomes starting at $113,182.

That figure—more than three times the median household income—probably seems extravagant to most Americans, but *Fortune* magazine recently proclaimed on its cover the alarming news that the new standard for executive pay is "four times your age"—in other words, $120,000 at the age of 30. The fact is that no matter how many Danielle Steel novels we read most of us have only the vaguest idea of the lives of people much richer (or poorer) than we are. Mark Mellman, a Democratic pollster, once asked voters to imagine what it would be like to have dinner with their member of Congress. Overwhelmingly they described a meal out of an Edith Wharton novel, with liveried servants and string quartets. Congress members make $133,600 a year.

But money is not the only entry requirement. Inherited wealth doesn't count for much, unless you're actively investing it yourself, preferably in something creative like a yogurt plant in Kazakhstan, nor does income from a local business like a fast-food franchise. (Owning a Cajun or Tuscan restaurant is okay, though, even if it loses money.) The overclass is national, or even transnational, in outlook, although its members mostly cluster on both coasts. It judges people, itself included, mainly on "merit," a quality that can be demonstrated only by a continual and strenuous accumulation of academic and professional credentials. Even more than money, it values competitive achievement: books published, screenplays produced, products launched, elections won. Of course, those things generally translate into money in the end anyway.

You might think that anyone would be proud to be associated with such a productive and successful class, but somehow that's not the case. The overclass, in fact, is one of the most anguished and self-doubting oligarchies in history, a habit of mind that began in the first act that defined it as a generation, its resistance to being drafted for Vietnam. "We've kept our compact with *ourselves*," says Chicago novelist and lawyer Scott Turow. "We know the unexamined life is not worth living, we're good parents, we recycle. But what have we done for anybody else? That's the question people of this class will ask when their kids are grown." Who wants to be in that position? *Not I,* says Eric Redman, a partner in a big Seattle law office, with a corner office on the sixty-first floor of Seattle's tallest building. Also a Rhodes scholar, a Harvard Law graduate, and a member of the Harvard class of 1970—of whom nearly 30 percent, responding to an anonymous survey for their twenty-fifth reunion, reported a net worth of more than $1 million. But Redman describes himself as just a "glorified hourly wage slave. . . . My broker told me the really big money isn't being made in salaries, but real estate and stock options." So count him out. What about Faith Popcorn, the endlessly quotable president of a marketing firm called BrainReserve, who lives and works in her own townhouse in the most expensive part of Manhattan? Not her either. "I'm not psychologically like those rich people," she says. "I lived in a studio apartment for 25 years before I bought my brownstone, and my cottage in Wainscott [a fashionable section in the Hamptons] is only 750 square feet."

Perhaps they just don't realize that the overclass is not the old-fashioned, discredited, morally bankrupt aristocracy. "They're the first wave of people who went to Ivy League schools on their merits, did well, and are still hustling to do well," says Nelson W. Aldrich, Jr.—himself a scion of an old aristocratic family and the author of *Old Money.* The overclass was made possible by the transformation in the 1950s and 1960s of the Ivy League from a closed network dedicated to serving the least disreputable offspring of the WASP elite into a great machine for identifying future national leaders. A degree from an Ivy League or equivalent school is an almost indispensable credential of overclass membership—and not only because it presumes that you learned something while getting it. "At the highest levels," Lind says, "everyone was a roommate in college." Turow, who has degrees from Amherst, Stanford, *and* Harvard, says friends sometimes ask him whether their children really need $100,000 worth of higher education to get ahead in life. "If you're asking me whether an Ivy League graduate will have access in ways that don't exist to graduates of otherwise outstanding schools like the University of Illinois," he tells them, "the answer is yes."

The overclass leads a distinctive lifestyle, which basically reflects yuppie tastes updated to take into account its increased affluence, sophistication, and of course weight—often a simple matter of substituting a Mercedes SL320 for a 10-speed bicycle. It is a lifestyle founded on privilege—on the premise, according to Stan Schultz, a cultural historian at the University of Wisconsin, that "we are terribly busy souls doing important things that no one else can do . . ." *so of course we have to fly business class, we need a full-time nanny instead of day care, we eat out four nights a week instead of trying to make our own risotto with squid ink.* The widespread belief that yuppies as a class would perish from Brie-cheese poisoning turned out to be overoptimistic. They're still at it, according to the consumer-research wizards of Claritas, Inc., who have identified a specific segment of the overclass, comprising mostly urban singles and couples without children, whose members eat Brie cheese at *more than five times the national average.*

Politically, the overclass exists in a state of perpetual tension between its economic interests, which lie with the Republicans, and its psychological affinity for the Democrats. "One trait that comes through the data is the economic conservatism of this group," says Tom W. Smith of the National Opinion Research Center at the University of Chicago. "They don't like to give money away." But their values are libertarian and cosmopolitan—typically pro-choice on abortion, pro-NAFTA on trade, environmentally aware. And at odds, therefore, with the Republican social agenda, which is driven by groups like the Christian Coalition (founded by Yale Law School alumnus Pat Robertson) and The Family Research Council, which actively loathe everything about the overclass, except its money. "If you're making six figures, Republicans aren't hurting you," said Diana Sperraza, a TV news producer vacationing on Nantucket Island this summer. "You don't want to think about it," she says. "You have a foot in each camp, really."

It's likely those tendencies described by Sperraza actually cancel each other out. As far as political power goes, individual members of the overclass naturally serve in high positions—such as the presidency—in both parties. But except for those whose careers are actually in politics or journalism, they don't seem to wield extraordinary influence. "These people want access and power," says Maria Cantwell, a former Democratic congresswoman who represented Seattle's East Side, home to many Microsoft millionaires. "But they're too busy to use it. They're too used to the fast track to make things happen. That's not government."

One of Lind's most controversial points is that the overclass has used its money and access to manipulate public policy, enriching itself at the expense of everyone else. But the money and access that count in Congress are wielded by institutions, not "classes" composed of disparate individuals. Much has been made of the reduction in marginal tax rates since 1980. But over the same period many loopholes were closed, so that while tax burdens were shifted around some among individuals, as a group the top 5 percent paid 31 percent of all federal income taxes last year—up from 27.8 percent in 1977. It is true that the gap in after-tax income between the richest Americans and all the others has been growing. But economists now agree that the government's consumer price index, which is used to adjust income statistics, overstates the effect of inflation on people's wages. By other measures, middle-class income is growing—slowly—the poor are stagnating, and the rich are getting richer, very rapidly.

If it lacks a distinctive political interest, the overclass nevertheless has an ideology, the ideology of "merit." Its success validates its intelligence and effort. Other oligarchies in the past have made similar assertions, of course, but the overclass is the first that is able to demonstrate superiority mathematically, with the help of SAT scores. "They believe they create their job, their opportunity, and their wealth," says Edward Blakely, dean of urban planning at the University of Southern California. The attitude he describes may account for the peculiar reaction the overclass has to failure, such as the loss of a job. Its members decline to acknowledge it. "Their view," says Peter Meder, who runs an executive-search firm in the Chicago suburb of Deerfield, "is still one of total entitlement. . . . The opening line is, 'I'm networking right now. I'm taking some time off to evaluate my options.' Can you imagine a factory worker or a retail-store manager getting fired and saying, 'I'm taking time off to evaluate my options'?"

In the abstract, "merit" is a wonderful ideal, and a far more efficient way to allocate rewards in a modern society than, say, primogeniture [ancestry]. Of course, in the real world luck plays a role in everyone's life; some people go to high school in Beverly Hills and some in East St. Louis. But people who believe that all rewards flow from merit tend not to have much sympathy for life's failures. "As you do well, you convince yourself that anyone can do well," says Stephen Klineberg, a sociologist at Rice University. "They don't feel particularly connected to the plight of the working class," says Blakely. When a factory worker loses his job, the overclass isn't hostile, just uncomprehending, he says: "It's a case of 'What's wrong with them? Why can't they go back to school?'"

Failure just is not an option for the overclass. Elise Gunter, a successful Hollywood lawyer, recently had dinner with an investment banker friend, who explained his theory that America is becoming a two-tier society. One class will have the autonomy to live where and how it wants; the other will be increasingly constrained and shut out. Pedigree and power, money and education will make the difference, and so he had set out to become as rich and successful as possible. "You couldn't imagine anyone saying that 10 or 15 years ago," she said with a shudder. "But he said it matter-of-factly, as if to say, 'Of course that's the way it is.' On the one hand it was disturbing, but part of me agrees with that."

Gunter's friend had an extreme case, verging on paranoia, of a more general overclass anxiety. "You could call them scared to death, leading lives of quiet desperation," says Aldrich. "Or not-so-quiet desperation. They talk about their desperation while eating out." This belief in the coming triumph of the smart and rich helps explain why the overclass is so driven to reject so vehemently middle-class values and tastes. Is health the only reason so few of them smoke? Or is it also a way of choosing sides with the winners? "*We are the talented few,*" says Schultz. "*We wouldn't think of going to Las Vegas, except once to be able to comment on how tacky America is.*" Can anyone doubt that arugula would quickly be seen for the bitter, stringy vegetable it actually is if Burger King began offering it on sandwiches?

Of course, salad vegetables don't have much significance, even symbolically. But other personal choices, such as where to live and send children to school, very much do. Increasingly the overclass is choosing to live in ways that minimize its mixing with the middle class (which is doing the same, of course, with respect to the poor). Sometimes it just moves farther out into the suburbs, or higher up the high-rise. But increasingly often it chooses to live in a walled and gated community guarded by private security forces. "It becomes a matter of status not to have contact [with strangers]," observes Mike Davis, a perceptive critic of Los Angeles society. "Physical isolation is a luxury." In Laguna Niguel, a wealthy Orange County beach town, a group of homeowners won permission to put gates at their entry roads—guarding not just the 250 homes, but a

public park right in the middle of their subdivision. The plan is being challenged in court by another resident of the town.

No issue is more fraught with desperation for the overclass than schools. Their conviction that they rose to their eminence in one generation on "merit" leads inescapably to the conclusion that their own kids might not make it, or deserve to. But few are willing to put that proposition to the test; instead, they maneuver frantically to get their offspring into the best possible private schools, starting (in highly competitive environments such as Manhattan) with preschool before the age of 3. "Those who believe in public education as a democratic ideal," says Pearl Kane, an authority on independent schools at Columbia University Teachers College, "move to Greenwich, Connecticut, and pay a million dollars for their homes." Those who don't are like one well-to-do Los Angeles mother, a former public-school teacher herself, who says bluntly that the problem with the public schools is having children of different social classes, where "they don't have the same values in their home. . . . If I'm working hard to push my child I want to make sure the other parents are, too." One residential development soon to be built in California has hit on the perfect overclass solution: a gated community with a private school inside.

And let's wish the future residents long and happy lives, in contented ignorance of people like Michael Brennan, a union electrician from Arlington Heights, Illinois. He had a few years of college, intending to be a teacher, but lost interest. When a friend from college derided people with "dead-end jobs," Brennan thought to himself, "Hey, some people just want to feed their kids and meet their responsibilities." He's working now on a job at a big Chicago law firm, and when he shows up at 2 A.M. to shut off the power, he finds lawyers still at their desks from 18 hours before, even on weekends. Some of them probably feel sorry for or even contemptuous toward him. They probably think, if they think about it at all, that he envies them. They're very wrong. "Some of these people I feel sorry for," he says. "You wonder if they've sold their souls. Life's pretty short." Even for the overclass.

RELATED LINKS

- A Kinder, Gentler Overclass (http://www.theatlantic.com/unbound/interviews/ba2000-06-15.htm)
- *Silicon Alley Reporter* Top 100 (http://www.siliconalleyreporter.com/sar100)

- *Time* Digital Archive: Cyber Elite (http://www.time.com/time/digital/cyberelite/list.html)
- To Have and to Have Not (http://www.hartford-hwp.com/archives/45/006.html)
- Who Are the Digerati? (http://www.edge.org/digerati)

FOR FURTHER RESEARCH

To find out more about the topics discussed in this reading, use InfoTrac College Edition. Type in keywords and subject terms such as "overclass," "upwardly mobile professionals," and "meritocracy." You can access InfoTrac College Edition from the Wadsworth/Thomson Communication Cafe homepage: http://communication.wadsworth.com.

Reading 13-4

Tech Savvy: Educating Girls in the New Computer Age
Sherry Turkle, Patricia Diaz Dennis, and associates

EDITOR'S NOTE

One of the lesser discussed aspects of the Digital Divide is gender related: the disparity between women and men in attitudes toward, and mastery of, new technologies. In high school, girls represent just 17 percent of computer science "AP" test takers. In college, women receive less than a third of computer science degrees awarded. And in the workforce, women represent just one in five information technology professionals. This report, sponsored by the American Association of University Women Educational Foundation, concludes that the way information technology is used, applied, and taught in the nation's classrooms must change to resolve the digital gender divide.

CONSIDER

1. How does the report define information technology fluency—what three kinds of knowledge does technological fluency consist of?

2. Do you agree with the report's key recommendations? Which recommendation should be implemented first, and why? Can you think of any other steps that should be taken?

3. Sherry Turkle, one of the report's authors, argues that girls are not so much computer-phobic as they are critical of computer culture. How could computer culture become more inviting for girls?

In contemporary culture, the computer is no longer an isolated machine: It is a centerpiece of science, the arts, media, industry, commerce, and civic life. Information technology is transforming every field, and few citizens are unaffected by it. The commission has chosen to use the terms "computers" and "computer technology" to refer to this larger "e-culture" of information and simulation, and has focused its inquiries, discussion, and recommendations on computers and education.

The question is no longer whether computers will be in the classroom, but how computers can be used to enhance teaching and learning—ideally, in ways that promote the full involvement by girls and other groups currently underrepresented in many computer-related endeavors. The commission's themes and recommendations, while focused on girls in schools, would, if addressed, improve the quality of the computer culture for all students.

KEY THEMES

1. Girls have reservations about the computer culture—and with good reason. In its inquiries into gender issues in computers and education, the commission found that girls are concerned about the passivity of their interactions with the computer as a "tool"; they reject the violence, redundancy, and tedium of computer games; and they dislike narrowly and technically focused programming classes. Too often, these concerns are dismissed as symptoms of anxiety or incompetence that will diminish once girls "catch up" with the technology.

The commission sees it differently: In some important ways, the computer culture would do well to catch up with the girls. In other words, girls are pointing to important deficits in the technology and the culture in which it is embedded that need to be integrated into our general thinking about computers and education. Indeed, girls' critiques resonate with the concerns of a much larger population of reticent users. The commission believes that girls' legitimate concerns should focus our attention on changing the software, the way computer science is taught, and the goals we have for using computer technology.

2. Teachers in grades K–12 have concerns—and with good reason. Teachers, three-fourths of whom are women, critique the quality of educational software; the "disconnect" between the worlds of the curriculum, classroom needs, and school district expectations; and the dearth of adequate professional development and timely technical assistance. Even those teachers technologically savvy enough to respond to the commission's online survey had incisive criticisms of the ways that computer technology has come into the classroom, and of the ways that they are instructed and encouraged to use it.

Often, teachers' concerns are met with teacher bashing: "Teachers are not measuring up" to the new technology, is our frequent response. Again, the commission sees it differently. Rather than presume teachers' inadequacies, the commission believes that teachers need opportunities to design instruction that takes advantage of technology across all disciplines. Computing ought to be infused into the curriculum and subject areas that teachers care about in ways that promote critical thinking and lifelong learning.

3. Statistics on girls' participation in the culture of computing are of increasing concern, from the point of view of education, economics, and culture. Girls are not well represented in computer laboratories and clubs, and have taken dramatically fewer programming and computer science courses at the high school and postsecondary level. Therefore, girls and women have been labeled as computer-phobic.

The commission sees it differently: It interprets such behavior not as phobia but as a choice that invites a critique of the computing culture. We need a more inclusive computer culture that embraces multiple interests and backgrounds and that reflects the current ubiquity of technology in all aspects of life. As this report describes, girls assert a "we can, but I don't want to" attitude toward computer technology: They insist on their abilities and skills in this area even as they vividly describe their disenchantment with the field, its careers, and social contexts. Although some of this attitude may be defensive, it is important to take a hard look at what these girls are feeling defensive about.

4. Girls' current ways of participating in the computer culture are a cause for concern. A common alternative to computer science courses—and a common point of entry for girls into the computer world—has been courses on computer "tools," such as databases, page layout programs, graphics, online publishing, and other "productivity software."

The commission believes that while mastery of these tools may be useful, it is not the same thing as true technological literacy. To be "technologically literate" requires a set of critical skills, concepts, and problem-solving abilities that permit full citizenship in contemporary e-culture. Girls' grasp of specific computer tools—use of the Internet and e-mail, and competency with productivity software such as PowerPoint or page layout programs—may have satisfied an older standard of computer literacy and equity; the new definition of computer literacy and equity described in this report is a broader one (see below).

The new standard of "fluency" assumes an ability to use abstract reasoning; to apply information technology in sophisticated, innovative ways to solve problems across disciplines and subject areas; to interpret vast amounts of information with analytic skill; to understand basic principles of programming and other computer science fundamentals; and to continually adapt and learn new technologies as they emerge in the future. It is our job as a society to ensure that girls are just as competent as their male peers in meeting these standards.

When they began their deliberations, commissioners explored various ways of defining what it would mean to achieve "gender equity" in the computer culture. Some commissioners emphasized concrete suggestions to get more girls into the "pipeline" to computer-related careers and to participate in these disciplines as they are presently constituted. Other commissioners emphasized ways that the computer culture itself could be positively transformed through the integration of girls' and women's insights, concentrating on the "web" of cultural associations that women's greater participation might create.

The commission does not view the two perspectives as dichotomous or competing. They are mutually reinforcing. One of the values in getting more girls and women in the computer pipeline is that their greater presence may transform the computer culture overall; by the same token, changes in the e-culture itself—the ways technology is discussed, valued, and applied—would invite more girls and women to participate fully in that culture.

WHAT IS FLUENCY WITH INFORMATION TECHNOLOGY?

What "everyone should know" about technology cannot be a static list of prescriptions to use word processing programs or e-mail. Instead, fluency goals must allow for change, enable adaptability, connect to personal goals, and promote lifelong learning. Like language fluency, information technology fluency should be tailored to individual careers and activities.

As described by a National Research Council report, fluency with information technology[1] requires the acquisition of three kinds of interdependent knowledge that must be taught in concert: skills, concepts, and capabilities. Skills are necessary for job preparedness, productivity, and other aspects of fluency. They include such things as using the Internet to find in-

formation, or setting up a personal computer. Skills change as technology advances: Using the Internet became essential in the past 5 years, and designing a home page will be essential soon. Concepts explain how and why information technology works. Capabilities, essential for problem solving, include managing complex systems as well as testing solutions.

Fluency is best acquired when students do coherent, ongoing projects to achieve specific goals in subjects that are relevant and interesting to them.

A project for biology students might be: Design an information system to track HIV testing and notification; communicate the design to potential participants; and convince users that privacy will be maintained. In this example, students would need content knowledge about HIV testing and about notification practices. They would use fluency skills such as organizing a database and communicating with others, and fluency concepts such as algorithmic thinking and an understanding of personal privacy concerns. To complete the project, students would use fluency capabilities such as sustained reasoning, testing solutions, and communicating about information technology.

A project for German language learners might be: Critique a program that translates directions for using a cellular phone by researching alternative cellular phone interfaces; devise tests of the program; evaluate the translation with potential users; and design a presentation to communicate recommendations to program designers. Students would need content knowledge of contemporary German language, such as referring to a cellular phone as a "handy," as well as appreciation of the diverse cellular phone interfaces. Students would need fluency skills, such as using the Internet to find information and using a graphic or artwork package to create illustrations. They would use fluency concepts, such as algorithmic thinking and awareness of the social impact of information technology. To complete the project, they would use fluency capabilities, such as testing solutions, managing complex systems, and thinking about information technology abstractly.

The commission has reviewed existing research, considered research that the AAUW Educational Foundation commissioned on the topic, talked with researchers, and listened to girls' and teachers' observations about computing. The commissioners urge immediate action on the following recommendations to ensure social equity as well as a more thoughtful integration of technology in education and our lives.

KEY RECOMMENDATIONS

- **Compute across the curriculum.** Computers can no longer be treated as a "set-aside," lab-based activity. Computation should be integrated across the curriculum, into such subject areas and disciplines as art, music, and literature, as well as engineering and science. This integration supports better learning for all, while it invites more girls into technology through a range of subjects that already interest them.

- **Redefine computer literacy.** Computer literacy needs to be redefined to include the life-long application of relevant concepts, skills, and problem-solving abilities. What does this mean? Students must be trained to be literate citizens in a culture increasingly dependent on computers. Students—especially females, who predominate in clerical and service occupations—must be educated to move beyond word processing and presentation software to solve real-life problems with technology. While a tally of girls in computer science classes is a convenient benchmark, empowering girls and other nontraditional users to mine computer technology for sophisticated, innovative uses requires a mastery of these literacies and abilities, not quickly outdated programming skills alone.

- **Respect multiple points of entry.** Different children will encounter different entry points into computing—some through art, for example, some through design, some through mathematics. These multiple entry points need to be respected and encouraged, while we remain sensitive to activities and perspectives that are appealing to girls and young women.

- **Change the public face of computing.** Make the public face of women in computing correspond to the reality rather than the stereotype. Girls tend to imagine that computer professionals live in a solitary, antisocial, and sedentary world. This is an alienating—and incorrect—perception of careers that will rely heavily on computer technology and expertise in this century.

- **Prepare tech-savvy teachers.** Schools of education have a special responsibility: They need to develop teachers who are able to design curricula that incorporate technology in a way that is inclusive of all students. Schools of education also

must be able to assess "success" for students and teachers in a tech-rich classroom. The focus for professional development needs to shift from mastery of the hardware to the design of classroom materials, curricula, and teaching styles that complement computer technology.

- **Begin a discussion on equity for educational stakeholders.** A more equitable and inclusive computer culture depends on consciousness-raising within schools about issues of gender, race, and class. School districts should put in place institutional mechanisms that will facilitate such conversations in partnership with parents, community leaders, and representatives from the computer and software industry.

- **Educate students about technology and the future of work.** Schools have a message to communicate about the future of work: All jobs, including those in the arts, medicine, law, design, literature, and the helping professions, will involve more and more computing. Conversely, technological careers will increasingly draw on the humanities, social science, and "people skills." It is especially important that girls not bound immediately for college understand career options in computer and network support, and the impact of new technologies on more traditional fields.

- **Rethink educational software and computer games.** Educational software and games have too often shown significant gender bias. Girls need to recognize themselves in the culture of computing. Software should speak to their interests and girls should be treated as early as possible as designers, rather than mere end users, of software and games.

- **Support efforts that give girls and women a boost into the pipeline.** Create and support computing clubs and summer school classes for girls, mentoring programs, science fairs, and programs that encourage girls to see themselves as capable of careers in technology.

NOTES

1. The term *fluency* and its description are adapted from the National Research Council, Computer Science and Telecommunications Board, *Being Fluent with Information Technology* (Washington, DC: National Academy Press, 1999).

RELATED LINKS

- American Association of University Women (http://www.aauw.org/home.html)
- Being Fluent with Information Technology (http://stills.nap.edu/html/beingfluent)
- *Multimedia Literacy* Web Site (http://www.mhhe.com/cit/hofstetter/multilit3e/student/contents.html)
- *Tech-Savvy* Web Page (http://www.aauw.org/2000/techsavvy.html)

FOR FURTHER RESEARCH

To find out more about the topics discussed in this reading, use InfoTrac College Edition. Type in keywords and subject terms such as "information technology fluency," "computer culture," and "educational software." You can access InfoTrac College Edition from the Wadsworth/Thomson Communication Cafe homepage: http://communication.wadsworth.com.

Policing the Electronic World: Issues and Ethics

This section takes up the thorny issues involved in policing the electronic world, including copyright protection, privacy and surveillance, computer hacking, and the threat of cyberterrorism. The readings in Chapter 14 examine the implications of copyright protections, which are designed to discourage unauthorized copying and distribution of intellectual property. In the case of the MP3 music format, however, many people think that charging a fee—in essence penalizing the consumer—is the wrong answer to the question of file-sharing over the Web and that free copies of individual songs may actually increase music sales in the long run. If artists enter into a more interactive (i.e., low-cost file-sharing) relationship with audiences, the argument goes, audiences in return may decide to reward artists by becoming loyal fans—and paying customers. Another area of electronic concern pertains to privacy and the new technology. Due to the rise of computerized tracking software, biometrics, and miniaturized recording devices, individual privacy has come increasingly under siege. As the readings in Chapter 15 point out, the proliferation of surveillance technologies may help vanquish crime but at the expense of unprecedented monitoring of public spaces and private places. Surfing the edges of the e-world are virus writers and virus-exchange groups who reveal the vulnerabilities of online communication systems, notably by hacking high-profile Web sites. VXers, as they are known, claim they perform a public service by highlighting the security defects of new software releases, forcing advances in the virus protection industry. Antivirus watchdogs, on the other hand, argue that virus writers represent a terrorist threat. The readings in Chapter 16 discuss how the stereotype of the lone computer hacker is giving way to the more alarming trend of "hacker collectives" and the advent of organized cyberinsurgency. Computer reliance has left business and government highly exposed, and the very nature of open networked systems has created loopholes for backdoor opportunists worldwide.

14

Copyright

Who Will Own Your Next Good Idea?

Charles C. Mann

EDITOR'S NOTE

Intellectual property, the legal term for any idea, piece of knowledge, or expression in tangible form that has an owner, is the primary product of the Information Age. Copyright laws are designed to discourage illegal copies of someone else's intellectual property from being made. With the rise of digital media, however, such "leakage"—the unauthorized reproduction and distribution of copyrighted works—threatens to turn into an unstoppable flow. A distinction should perhaps be drawn between file-sharing, where no money is exchanged, and piracy, where copyrighted works are sold for a profit. Artists are understandably miffed when unauthorized copies of their works are sold without their permission, but efforts to restrict digital file-sharing raise as many questions as they answer. Moreover, as this article from the Atlantic Monthly *points out, when electronic media are exported internationally, the laws that govern copyright in the United States don't always apply. Widespread pirating of software, music, and videos, made simple by the introduction of digital technology, costs U.S. firms as much as $20 billion a year. Depending on your perspective, digitized expression can be a convenience or a curse.*

CONSIDER

1. Do you agree with John Perry Barlow of the Electronic Frontier Foundation that digitized expression makes traditional notions of copyright outmoded and irrelevant? Why or why not?

2. In your view, is the threat of piracy and counterfeiting of digital media as real and damaging as industry representatives claim? Why or why not?

3. How do digital technologies lower the reproduction and distribution costs of pirated media content?

About 12 years ago I walked past a magazine kiosk in Europe and noticed the words *temple des rats* on the cover of a French magazine. Rat temple! I was amazed. A few months before, a friend of mine had traveled to northwestern India to write about the world's only shrine to humankind's least favorite rodent. The temple was in a village in the Marusthali Desert. That two Western journalists should have visited within a few months of each other stunned me. Naturally, I bought the magazine.

The article began with a Gallic tirade against the genus *Rattus*. *Le spectre du rat, le cauchemar d'humanité! Quel horreur!*—that sort of thing. Then came the meat: an interview, in Q&A form, with a "noted American journalist" who had just gone to the rat temple. The journalist, who was named, was my friend. No such interview had occurred: The article was a straight translation, with fake interruptions by the "interviewer" such as *Vraiment?* and *Mon Dieu!*

I was outraged. To my way of thinking, these French people had ripped off my friend. I telephoned him immediately; he had the same reaction. Expletives crackled wildly across the Atlantic. Reprinting his copyrighted article without permission or payment was the same, we decided, as kicking down his door and stealing his CD player.

We were wrong. Although the magazine had done my friend wrong, what was stolen was not at all like a CD player. CD players are physical property. Magazine articles are *intellectual* property, a different matter entirely. When thieves steal CD players, the owners no longer have them, and are obviously worse off. But when my friend's writing was appropriated, he still had the original manuscript. What, then, was stolen? Because the article had been translated, not one sentence in the French version appeared in the original. How could it be considered a copy? Anomalies like this are why intellectual property has its own set of laws.

Intellectual property is knowledge or expression that is owned by someone. It has three customary domains: copyright, patent, and trademark (a fourth form, trade secrets, is sometimes included). Copyrighted songs, patented drugs, and trademarked soft drinks have long been familiar denizens of the American landscape, but the growth of digital technology has pushed intellectual property into new territory. Nowadays one might best define intellectual property as anything that can be sold in the form of zeroes and ones. It is the primary product of the Information Age.

All three forms of intellectual property are growing in importance, but copyright holds pride of place. In legal terms, copyright governs the right to make copies of a given work. It awards limited monopolies to creators on their creations: For a given number of years no one but Walt Disney can sell Mickey Mouse cartoons without permission. Such monopolies, always valuable, are increasingly lucrative. For the past 20 years the copyright industry has grown almost three times as fast as the economy as a whole, according to the International Intellectual Property Alliance, a trade group representing film studios, book publishers, and the like. Last year, the alliance says, copyrighted material contributed more than $400 billion to the national economy and was the country's single most important export.

These figures may actually understate the value of copyright. Today it is widely believed that personal computers, cable television, the Internet, and the telephone system are converging into a giant hose that will spray huge amounts of data—intellectual property—into American living rooms. As this occurs, according to the conventional scenario, the economic winners will be those who own the zeroes and ones, not those who make the equipment that copies, transmits, and displays them. Because copyright is the mechanism for establishing ownership, it is increasingly seen as the key to wealth in the Information Age.

At the same time, the transformation of intellectual property into electronic form creates new problems. If the cost of manufacturing and distributing a product falls, economic forces will drive down its price, too. The Net embodies this principle to an extreme degree. Manufacturing and distribution costs collapse almost to nothing online: Zeroes and ones can be shot around the world with a few clicks of a mouse. Hence producers of digital texts, music, and films will have trouble charging anything at all for copies of their works—competitors can always offer substitutes for less, pushing the price toward the vanishing point.

In addition, creators must deal with piracy, which is vastly easier and more effective in the digital environment. People have long been able to photocopy texts, tape-record music, and videotape television shows. Such leakage, as copyright lawyers call it, has existed since the first day a reader lent a (copyrighted) book to a friend. With the rise of digital media, the leakage threatens to turn into a gush. To make and distribute a dozen copies of a videotaped film requires at least two videocassette recorders, a dozen tapes, padded envelopes and postage, and considerable patience. And because the copies are tapes of tapes, the quality suffers. But if the film has been digitized into a computer file, it can be e-mailed to millions of people in minutes; because strings of zeroes and ones can be reproduced with absolute fidelity, the copies are perfect. And online pirates have no development costs—they don't even have to pay for paper or blank cassettes—so they don't really have a bottom line. In other words, even as digital technology drives the potential value of copyright to ever greater heights, that same technology threatens to make it next to worthless.

How real is the threat of piracy? Very real, according to Jack Valenti, of the Motion Picture Association of America. The world, in his view, is a "heartbreaking," "devastating," "pirate bazaar" in which counterfeiters with "no sense of morality" steal billions from America's moviemakers. In December the MPAA estimated that piracy, chiefly in the form of illegal videocassettes, costs the U.S. motion picture industry more than $2.5 billion a year.

Movies are not the only losers. Publishers complain that pirates knock off expensively produced textbooks in fields ranging from business management and computer science to medicine and English. Music companies hire a firm called GrayZone to hunt down bootleg-CD makers and Web-site pirates around the globe. In some countries—Russia and China, for example—more than 90 percent of all new business software is pirated, according to the Business Software Alliance and the Software Publishers Association, the two major trade associations in the field. The International Intellectual Property Alliance claims that foreign copyright infringement alone costs U.S. firms as much as $20 billion a year.

Critics charge that these huge figures are absurd, and not only because of the obvious difficulty of measuring illicit activity. While researching this article I obtained a CD-ROM called "CAD Xpress" for about $30 ("CAD" is the acronym for "computer-assisted design"). It contained a copy of the current version of AutoCAD, the leading brand of architectural-drafting software, which has a list price of $3,750. According to the Software Publishers Association, my copy of CAD Xpress represents a $3,750 loss to Autodesk, the man-ufacturer of AutoCAD. This assumes, of course, that I, and every other buyer of CAD Xpress, would otherwise pony up thousands of dollars for AutoCAD.

More important, in the view of Stanley Besen, an economist at Charles River Associates, a consulting firm in Washington, DC, the huge estimates of piracy losses don't take into account the copyright owners' responses to copying. "Suppose I know that people are going to copy Lotus 1-2-3," he said to me. "So I sell it for $500, knowing that four people will make copies of each program, whereas I might sell it for only $100 if all five users purchased programs for themselves." The price takes copying into account, and no loss occurs.

JAMES BROWN HAS A PROBLEM

If there is a totemic example of the vexations of copyright infringement, it's James Brown, the Godfather of Soul. Now 65, Brown was born horribly poor and raised by his aunt in a Georgia brothel. As a child, he shilled for the brothel by singing and dancing in the streets. He was caught stealing clothes from cars and was sent away for several years when still in his teens. But rather than slide into full-fledged delinquency, Brown emerged to begin a 50-year music career that shaped the course of gospel, rhythm and blues, rock and roll, disco, and funk (which he more or less invented). Spinning, falling on his knees, dropping into splits, he climaxed shows with an exuberant fake heart attack, after which he was carried offstage on a cape and "resurrected" by screaming fans. Brown was one of the first African American pop singers to wrest control of his career—including the copyright to his songs—from the white music establishment.

In the 1980s Brown's commercial star dimmed. But his music was heard more than ever before, because rappers by the dozen built their songs around recorded snippets—"samples," in the jargon, which are "looped," or played over and over—of such Brown hits as "Cold Sweat" and "Get on the Good Foot." Thirty years after the release of "Say It Loud (I'm Black and I'm Proud)," Brown's black-power anthem from 1968, bits and pieces of the song are still all over the airwaves. "It is impossible to listen to more than 15 minutes of rap radio on any given night in Boston without hearing a back beat, a guitar hook, or a snatch of vocals from 'Say It Loud,'" Mark Costello and David Foster Wallace wrote in *Signifying Rappers,* a critical study of the genre.

What does Brown think of his place on the cutting edge of intellectual-property regulation? I called him to find out. A receptionist patched me through to a cell phone. Brown was in a car and somewhat distracted; he had discerned clues to a fellow driver's mental condition and unwholesome fondness for his mother from his behavior at the wheel. I knew that the unlicensed copying of Brown's music had been curtailed in the aftermath of a 1991 court decision, which prevented the rapper Biz Markie from distributing a record that sampled the singer Gilbert O'Sullivan without permission. I wanted to know what Mr. Please, Please, Please thought of the new software that allows people to put entire albums on the World Wide Web. The previous night, for instance, I had downloaded part of his landmark 1963 album, "The James Brown Show Live" at the Apollo, from a computer in Finland. "This technology," he said, "I hate it. Hate it!" Then he hung up.

In the age of the Internet, Xerox PARC researcher Mark Stefik argues, the only way to foil piracy—indeed, the only way to charge for intellectual property—will be to equip all televisions, telephones, computers, music players, and electronic books with chips that regulate the flow of copyrighted material. "Kind of like having V-chips for copyright," he says. When I download *The Sound and the Fury* into my electronic book, the ©-chip will register the transaction, speeding my payment to the copyright owner and invisibly encoding the record in my copy of the text. If I lend the novel to my sister by e-mailing her a copy, my e-book will erase the original copy, so that only one is in circulation. The software won't permit my sister to dump the text into any e-book without a ©-chip, so the copy will always remain within a closed circle. Similar rules will apply to videos, music, journalism, databases, photographs, and broadcast performances—any configuration of zeroes and ones that can be sold and delivered by wire. Current, if primitive, examples of what Stefik calls "copyright boxes" include Nintendo machines, whose proprietary hardware is meant to ensure that only Nintendo-approved games work on them, and digital audio tape (DAT) recorders, which contain a chip that prevents the copying of previously copied tapes.

Copyright boxes could let copyright owners subdivide usage rights, creating new markets for information. If I want to download music by James Brown, for example, I could negotiate the terms at the Web site of his company, James Brown Enterprises. By paying a little extra, I could obtain the right to send a copy of "Say It Loud" to my sister without deleting it from my computer. By paying a little less, I could rent the music for a party next week, with the ©-chip expunging the music the morning after. I might buy a site license, so that everyone in the family could listen to "Say It Loud." I might acquire only the right to listen myself, typing in a password to prove my identity every time I wanted to hear the Hardest-Working Man in Show Business. Copyright boxes, Stefik says, "open up a lot of possibilities."

These possibilities, he concedes, will not be easy to achieve: "I don't see this as a debate about next week." People may find ways to circumvent ©-chips; others may regard the chips as unworkably inconvenient. But perhaps the greatest obstacle, Stefik thinks, is attitude. A small but significant group of technophiles scoffs at the whole idea of copyright boxes, believing that the Internet changes the role of intellectual property so much that the chips will be useless. Some Web denizens believe that the change is profound enough that efforts to safeguard copyright in the digital world actually work against the interests of a democratic society.

FREE SOFTWARE

Perhaps the most widely known copyright skeptic is John Perry Barlow, who cofounded the Electronic Frontier Foundation, a civil liberties group for cyberspace. Intellectual-property law "cannot be patched, retrofitted, or expanded to contain digitized expression," Barlow declared in a widely read manifesto from 1994. "These towers of outmoded boilerplate will be a smoking heap sometime in the next decade." Barlow's idea derives from his experiences writing for the Grateful Dead. Unlike most bands, the Dead allowed fans to record concerts and trade the tapes, which ended up increasing their audience. "Not that we really planned it, but it was the smartest thing we could have done," Barlow told me recently. "We raised the sales of our records considerably because of it."

Experiences like his, he said, show that copyright is not so much wrong as outmoded: "Copyright's not about creation, which will happen anyway—it's about distribution." In Barlow's view, copyright made sense when companies had to set up elaborate industrial processes for "hauling forests into Waldenbooks or encapsulating music on CDs and distributing them to Tower Records." To make such investments feasible, unauthorized copying had to be stopped—that's why the Dead let fans trade homemade tapes of concerts but sent "nasty lawyers" after counterfeiters who duplicated and sold official recordings. In the future, Barlow told me, people will be able to download music and writing so easily that they will be reluctant to take the trouble to seek out hard copies, let alone want to pay for them. Musicians or writers who want to be heard or read will have to thumbtack their creations onto the Web for fans to download—free, Barlow insisted. Because distributing material on the Internet costs next to nothing, there will be no investment in equipment and shipping to protect. Record companies and publishers will be obviated, and the economic justification for copyright will vanish.

Some people may still try to control their works with copyright boxes, concedes Esther Dyson, a cyberpundit who puts out *Release 1.0,* an insider's newsletter about technology. But they will have a tough time. Even if creators can use ©-chips to forestall piracy, they will still have to compete for an audience with everyone else posting material on the Net—that is, with the entire world. Like television stations on cable systems with hundreds of channels, writers and musicians on the Internet will be so desperate for audiences that, Dyson says, they will be glad to be copied, because their increased notoriety will translate into lucrative personal-appearance fees. "It's a new world," Dyson says. "People will have to adjust."

CLICKWRAP WORLD

David Nimmer has a story. Imagine the year 2010, he says. The last Barnes & Noble-Walden-Borders-Broadway store in the United States has just closed. Now no offline book, music, or video stores remain, except for a replica bookstore in Disneyland. Anyone who wants to obtain poems, essays, or novels must download them from the Internet into an electronic book. Anyone who wants to watch a movie, listen to recorded music, or look at a reproduction of a painting must download it into the appropriate copyright box. But before getting books, music, and films, people must first click on the "OK" button to accept the terms of the ubiquitous standard download contract—the "Gates from Hell Agreement," Nimmer and two coauthors call it in an article in the *California Law Review.*

The agreement prohibits the contractee from letting anyone else view the copyrighted material. If problems surface, the agreement authorizes private police officers to descend on users' houses to check for il-

licit printouts and copies. Should search victims whine about unwarranted search and seizure, the courts reply that they freely signed away those Fourth Amendment rights by clicking the "OK" button.

"Crazy, isn't it?" Nimmer says of this scenario. "But that's what they're talking about." A former federal prosecutor, Nimmer is now at the Los Angeles firm of Irell and Manella, and is an author, with his late father, of *Nimmer on Copyright,* a widely cited treatise. A lawyer who represents entertainment, publishing, and technology companies, Nimmer is an advocate for the rights of copyright holders. Yet he is greatly distressed by some of the proposed legislation. "You're talking not about copyright but about an attack on copyright," he says. "I'm extremely bothered by where we might be heading."

Because the copyright industry has energetically campaigned for protection against illicit copying, Congress is knee-deep in copyright bills. One of the most important would bring this country into conformity with a treaty adopted in 1996 by the World Intellectual Property Organization. WIPO administers the Berne Convention, an international-copyright agreement enacted in 1887. The WIPO treaty, which is universally lauded, asks signatory nations to "provide adequate legal protection . . . against the circumvention of effective technological measures" against piracy. To implement this request, the Clinton Administration and many prominent Republicans have backed legislation that bans making or using any device that can evade any method of copy protection. In making the vague language of the treaty harshly specific, the Administration set off an explosion of protest.

When these proposals appeared, last year, they aroused violent opposition from what Barlow proudly calls "a ragtag assembly of librarians, law professors, and actual artists." He adds, "This will sound hyperbolic, but I really feel that the copyright industry, its congressional supporters, and the Clinton Administration were trying to propose that if you read a book, you were making a copy in your memory and should therefore pay a proper license." The underlying legislative problem is that "the movement is all in one direction," says James Boyle, a copyright specialist at the Washington College of Law at American University. "There's no movement [in the other direction] to contract copyright terms or increase fair use."

Microsoft Agent is a program that makes cute little animated figures. The license not only tells customers they can't "rent, lease or lend" the program but also informs them that they have no right to make the figures "disparage" Microsoft. McAfee VirusScan, the leading antivirus software, has a license term that is every writer's dream: nobody may publish a review of the program "without prior consent" from the company. But even that is surpassed by Digital Directory Assistance, maker of PhoneDisc, a CD-ROM containing millions of phone numbers and addresses. According to the license, the software can't be "used . . . in any way or form without prior written consent of Digital Directory Assistance, Inc."

If agreements like these govern electronic books in the future, the ©-chip inside will not permit the text to be transmitted unless the customer first accepts the clickwrap license. Because current licenses typically forbid copying or lending intellectual property, Nimmer fears that copyright owners will end up with all the protections of copyright while the public is forced to surrender its benefits—especially the right to lend privately or copy within the limits of fair use the expressions of others. Any reader who wants to challenge the licenses for overreaching copyright will be forced into litigation—a situation that inevitably redounds to the benefit of large companies that can afford to pay legal fees. "It's an end run around copyright," Nimmer says. "It provides a mechanism to put a stranglehold on information, and that in itself is a bad idea."

I submit that it is even worse than he thinks. Copyright, according to Martha Woodmansee, an English professor at Case Western Reserve University, is implicitly based on the "romantic notion of the author." During the Renaissance, she explains in *The Author, Art, and the Market,* writers generally considered themselves vehicles for divine inspiration, and thus not entitled to benefit personally from their work. "Freely have I received," Martin Luther said of his writing, "freely given, and want nothing in return." In the eighteenth century the book trade grew; some writers changed their minds about making a living from the pen. Justifying the switch, the German philosophers Johann Fichte and Immanuel Kant evolved the image of the artist as a sovereign being who creates beauty out of nothing but inspiration.

This picture, though lovely, is incomplete. Artists often combine the materials around them into new forms—inconveniently for copyright, which assumes solitary originality. As the critic Northrop Frye put it, "Poetry can only be made out of other poems; novels out of other novels." Shakespeare derived some of the language in *Julius Caesar* from an English translation of a French translation of Plutarch; he followed a printed history so closely for *Henry V* that scholars believe he had the book open on his desk as he wrote. In this century Eugene O'Neill gleaned *Mourning Becomes Electra* from Aeschylus. Charles Ives was an inveterate borrower; in his Fourth Symphony the second movement alone quotes at least two dozen tunes by other composers. Andy Warhol filled galleries with reproductions of Brillo boxes, Campbell's soup cans, and photographs of Marilyn Monroe. And so on.

Warhol's place in art history is uncertain, but in one respect he was right on target. In a time increasingly dominated by corporate products and commercial media, the raw materials out of which art is constructed seem certain to include those products and media. In the 1940s little girls bonded emotionally with anonymous dolls and had elaborate self-transformative fantasies about Cinderella, whose story they might have heard from their parents. Today girls bond with Barbie™ and dream of the broadcast exploits of Sabrina the Teenage Witch™. Fans fill the Internet with homemade stories about Captain Kirk, Spiderman, and Special Agent Fox Mulder—skewed, present-day versions of the folktales our forebears concocted about Wotan, Paul Bunyan, and Coyote the Trickster. Five hundred channels watched 6 hours a day—how can art that truly reflects the times ignore it?

Copyright should not impede artistic efforts to explain our times. Nor should we let it interfere with the relation between producers and consumers of art. Any work of art is a gift, at least in part—something done not purely from motives of calculation. Knowing this, people approach works of art in a more receptive state than they do, say, advertisements. The same people who would unhesitatingly copy Microsoft Word at their jobs, the novelist Neal Stephenson said to me recently, "would no more bootleg a good novel than they would jump the turnstile at an art museum." Stephenson, the author of *The Diamond Age,* a witty, imaginative science fiction novel about pirating an electronic book, believes that in the long run this relationship of respect and trust is the only safeguard that works of art have. It is also the reason they are worth safeguarding. What will the act of reading be like if every time I open a book I must negotiate the terms under which I read it? The combined changes in copyright law could lead us closer to what Michael Heller, a law professor at the University of Michigan, calls "the tragedy of the anticommons," in which creators and writers cannot easily connect, because they are divided by too many gates and too many toll-keepers.

It seems unlikely that in the foreseeable future all ties will be severed. But opposing pressures from the Internauts who want to open copyright up and the software companies and publishers who want to clamp it shut presage major change in the way our culture is created and experienced. Unfortunately, as Hal Varian points out, we will be changing laws today to fit a to-morrow we can as yet only guess at. The likelihood of guessing correctly now, he says, is "close to minimal." Yet it's easy to feel the pressure to make—and force—decisions right away. As I write this, knowing that I am close to finished, I realize what will be one of the first questions my editors ask: whether they can put this article on the Web.

RELATED LINKS

- *The Atlantic Monthly* Digital Edition (http://www.theatlantic.com/)
- Copyright and Related Issues for Multimedia and Online Entrepreneurs (http://www.medialawyer.com/lec-copy.htm#III)
- Indiana University Online Copyright Tutorial (http://www.iupui.edu/~copyinfo/online_tutorial.html)
- International Intellectual Property Alliance (http://www.IIPA.com)
- U.S. Copyright Office (http://lcweb.loc.gov/copyright)

FOR FURTHER RESEARCH

To find out more about the topics discussed in this reading, use InfoTrac College Edition. Type in keywords and subject terms such as "intellectual property," "copyright infringement," and "software pirating." You can access InfoTrac College Edition from the Wadsworth/Thomson Communication Cafe homepage: http://communication.wadsworth.com.

Reading 14-2

The Next Economy of Ideas

John Perry Barlow

> *An invasion of armies can be resisted, but not an idea whose time has come.*
>   —Victor Hugo

EDITOR'S NOTE

Napster, perhaps the third "killer application" of the Internet (the first being e-mail and the second being the graphical Web browser), has taken the music-sharing community by storm. But the popular file-sharing program has enraged the recording industry and supporters of existing copyright law. In the view of John Perry Barlow, a former songwriter for the Grateful Dead and opinionated cofounder of the Electronic Frontier Foundation, noncommercial distribution of information through programs such as Napster actually increases the sale of commercial work. File-sharing, Barlow asserts, allows artists to enter into a more interactive relationship with audiences. In return, audiences may reward artists by becoming loyal fans—and consumers. In this reading, a follow-up to his influential 1994 Wired *essay "The Economy of Ideas," Barlow boldly asserts that copyright won't survive the Napster bomb—but creativity will.*

CONSIDER

1. Why does Barlow think that the free proliferation of expression does not decrease its commercial value? Do you agree?

2. If great artists throughout history produced and authored works without royalties and copyright protections, why do we consider them so essential today?

3. Why is the Recording Industry Association of America convinced that the easy accessibility of freely downloadable commercial songs will bring about an economic apocalypse?

The great cultural war has broken out at last.

Long awaited by some and a nasty surprise to others, the conflict between the industrial age and the virtual age is now being fought in earnest, thanks to that modestly conceived but paradigm-shattering thing called Napster.

What's happening with global, peer-to-peer networking is not altogether different from what happened when the American colonists realized they were poorly served by the British Crown: The colonists were obliged to cast off that power and develop an economy better suited to their new environment. For settlers of cyberspace, the fuse was lit last July [2000], when Judge Marilyn Hall Patel tried to shut down Napster and silence the cacophonous free market of expression, which was already teeming with more than 20 million directly wired music lovers.

Despite an appeals-court stay immediately granted the Napsterians, her decree transformed an evolving economy into a cause, and turned millions of politically apathetic youngsters into electronic Hezbollah. Neither the best efforts of Judge Patel—nor those of the Porsche-driving executives of the Recording Industry Association of America [RIAA], nor the sleek legal defenders of existing copyright law—will alter this simple fact: No law can be successfully imposed on a huge population that does not morally support it and possesses easy means for its invisible evasion.

To put it mildly, the geriatrics of the entertainment industry didn't see this coming. They figured the Internet was about as much of a threat to their infotainment empire as ham radio was to NBC. Even after that assumption was creamed, they remained as serene as sunning crocodiles. After all, they still "owned" all that

stuff they call "content." That it might soon become possible for anyone with a PC to effortlessly reproduce their "property" and distribute it to all of humanity didn't trouble them at all.

But then along came Napster. Or, more to the point, along came the *real* Internet, an instantaneous network that endows any acne-faced kid with a distributive power equal to Time Warner's. Moreover, these were kids who don't give a flying byte about the existing legal battlements, and a lot of them possess decryption skills sufficient to easily crack whatever lame code the entertainment industry might wrap around "its" goods.

Practically every traditional pundit who's commented on the Napster case has, at some point, furrowed a telegenic brow and asked, "Is the genie out of the bottle?" A better question would be, "Is there a bottle?" No, there isn't.

Which is not to say the industry won't keep trying to create one. In addition to ludicrously misguided (and probably unconstitutional) edicts like the Digital Millennium Copyright Act, entertainment execs are placing great faith in new cryptographic solutions. But before they waste a lot of time on their latest algorithmic vessels, they might consider the ones they've designed so far. These include such systems as the pay-per-view videodisc format Divx, the Secure Digital Music Initiative (SDMI), and CSS, aka the Content Scrambling System—the DVD encryption program, which has sparked its own legal hostilities on the Eastern front, starting with the New York courtroom of Judge Lewis Kaplan [see Reading 14-3].

Here's the score: Divx was stillborn. SDMI will probably never be born owing to the wrangling of its corporate parents. And DeCSS (the DVD *decryptor*) is off and running, even though the Motion Picture Association of America (MPAA) has prevailed in its lawsuit aimed at stopping Web sites from posting—or even linking to—the disc-cracking code. While that decision is appealed, DeCSS will keep spreading: As the Electronic Frontier Foundation was defending three e-distributors inside Kaplan's court last summer, nose-ringed kids outside were selling T-shirts with the program silk-screened on the back.

The last time technical copy protection was widely attempted—remember when most software was copy-protected?—it failed in the marketplace, and failed miserably. Earlier attempts to ban media-reproduction technologies have also failed. Even though entertainment execs are exceptionally slow learners, they will eventually realize what they should have understood long ago: The free proliferation of expression does not decrease its commercial value. Free access *increases* it, and should be encouraged rather than stymied.

The war is on, all right, but to my mind it's over. The future will win; there will be no property in cyberspace. Behold DotCommunism. (And dig it, ye talented, since it will enrich you.) It's a pity that entertainment moguls are too wedged in to the past to recognize this, because now they are requiring us to fight a war anyway. So we'll fatten lawyers with a fortune that could be spent fostering and distributing creativity. And we may be forced to watch a few pointless public executions—Shawn Fanning's [Napster's inventor] cross awaits—when we could be employing such condemned genius in the service of a greater good.

Of course, it's one thing to win a revolution, and quite another to govern its consequences. How, in the absence of laws that turn thoughts into things, will we be assured payment for the work we do with our minds? Must the creatively talented start looking for day jobs?

Nope. Most white-collar jobs already consist of mind work. The vast majority of us live by our wits now, producing "verbs"—that is, ideas—rather than "nouns" like automobiles or toasters. Doctors, architects, executives, consultants, receptionists, televangelists, and lawyers all manage to survive economically without "owning" their cognition.

I take further comfort in the fact that the human species managed to produce pretty decent creative work during the 5,000 years that preceded 1710, when the Statute of Anne, the world's first modern copyright law, passed the British parliament. Sophocles, Dante, da Vinci, Botticelli, Michelangelo, Shakespeare, Newton, Cervantes, Bach—all found reasons to get out of bed in the morning without expecting to own the works they created.

Even during the heyday of copyright, we got some pretty useful stuff out of Benoit Mandelbrot, Vint Cerf,

Tim Berners-Lee, Marc Andreessen, and Linus Torvalds, none of whom did their world-morphing work with royalties in mind. And then there are all those great musicians of the last 50 years who went on making music even after they discovered that the record companies got to keep all the money.

Nor can I resist trotting out, one last time, the horse I rode back in 1994, when I explored these issues in a *Wired* essay called "The Economy of Ideas." The Grateful Dead, for whom I once wrote songs, learned by accident that if we let fans tape concerts and freely reproduce those tapes—"stealing" our intellectual "property" just like those heinous Napsterians—the tapes would become a marketing virus that would spawn enough Deadheads to fill any stadium in America. Even though Deadheads had free recordings that often were more entertaining than the band's commercial albums, fans still went out and bought records in such quantity that most of them went platinum.

My opponents always dismiss this example as a special case. But it's not. Here are a couple of others closer to Hollywood. Jack Valenti, head of the MPAA and leader of the fight against DeCSS, fought to keep VCRs out of America for half a dozen years, convinced they would kill the film industry. Eventually that wall came down. What followed reversed his expectations (not that he seems to have learned from the experience). Despite the ubiquity of VCRs, more people go to the movies than ever, and videocassette rentals and sales account for more than half of Hollywood's revenues.

The RIAA is unalterably convinced that the easy availability of freely downloadable commercial songs will bring on the apocalypse, and yet, during the 2 years since MP3 music began flooding the Net, CD sales have *risen* by 20 percent.

Finally, after giving up on copy protection, the software industry expected that widespread piracy would surely occur. And it did. Even so, the software industry is booming. Why? Because the more a program is pirated, the more likely it is to become a standard.

All these examples point to the same conclusion: Noncommercial distribution of information *increases* the sale of commercial information. Abundance breeds abundance.

This is precisely contrary to what happens in a physical economy. When you're selling nouns, there is an undeniable relationship between scarcity and value. But in an economy of verbs, the inverse applies. There is a relationship between familiarity and value. For ideas, fame *is* fortune. And nothing makes you famous faster than an audience willing to distribute your work for free.

All the same, there remains a general and passionate belief that, in the absence of copyright law, artists and other creative people will no longer be compensated. I'm forever accused of being an antimaterialistic hippie who thinks we should all create for the Greater Good of Mankind and lead lives of ascetic service. If only I were so noble. While I do believe that most genuine artists are motivated primarily by the joys of creation, I also believe we will be more productive if we don't have to work a second job to support our art habit. Think of how many more poems Wallace Stevens could have written if he hadn't been obliged to run an insurance company to support his "hobby."

Following the death of copyright, I believe our interests will be assured by the following practical values: relationship, convenience, interactivity, service, and ethics.

Before I explain further, let me state a creed: Art is a service, not a product. Created beauty is a relationship, and a relationship with the Holy at that. Reducing such work to "content" is like praying in swear words. End of sermon. Back to business.

The economic model that supported most of the ancient masters was patronage, whether endowed by a wealthy individual, a religious institution, a university, a corporation, or—through the instrument of governmental support—by society as a whole.

Patronage is both a relationship and a service. It is a relationship that supported genius during the Renaissance and supports it today. Da Vinci, Michelangelo, and Botticelli all shared the support of both the Medicis and, through Pope Leo X, the Catholic Church. Bach had a series of patrons, most notably the Duke of Weimar. I could go on, but I can already hear you saying, "Surely this fool doesn't expect the return of patronage."

In fact, patronage never went away. It just changed its appearance. Marc Andreessen was a beneficiary of the "patronage" of the National Center for Supercomputer Applications when he created Mosaic [the first graphical Web browser]; CERN was a patron to Tim Berners-Lee when he created the World Wide Web. DARPA was Vint Cerf's benefactor; IBM was Benoit Mandelbrot's.

"Aha!" you say, "but IBM is a corporation. *It* profited from the intellectual property Mandelbrot created." Maybe, but so did the rest of us. While IBM would patent air and water if it could, I don't believe it ever attempted to patent fractal geometry.

Relationship, along with *service,* is at the heart of what supports all sorts of other modern, though more anonymous, "knowledge workers." Doctors are economically protected by a relationship with their patients, architects with their clients, executives with their stockholders. In general, if you substitute "relationship" for "property," you begin to understand why a digitized information economy can work fine in the absence of enforceable property law. Cyberspace is *un*-real estate. Relationships are its geology.

Convenience is another important factor in the future compensation of creation. The reason video didn't kill the movie star is that it's simply more convenient to rent a video than to copy one. Software is easy to copy, of course, but software piracy hasn't impoverished Bill Gates. Why? Because in the long run it's more convenient to enter into a relationship with Microsoft if you hope to use its products in an ongoing way. It's certainly easier to get technical support if you have a real serial number when you call. And that serial number is not a thing. It's a contract. It is the symbol of a relationship.

Think of how the emerging digital conveniences will empower musicians, photographers, filmmakers, and writers when you can click on an icon, upload a cyberdime into their accounts, and download their latest songs, images, films, or chapters—all without the barbaric *inconvenience* currently imposed by the entertainment industry.

Interactivity is also central to the future of creation. Performance is a form of interaction. The reason Deadheads went to concerts instead of just listening to free tapes was that they wanted to interact with the band in meatspace. The more people knew what the concerts sounded like, the more they wanted to be there.

I enjoy a similar benefit in my current incarnation. I'm paid reasonably well to write, despite the fact that I put most of my work on the Net before it can be published. But I'm paid a lot more to speak, and still more to consult, since my real value lies in something that can't be stolen from me—my point of view. A unique and passionate viewpoint is more valuable in a conversation than the one-way broadcast of words. And the more my words self-replicate on the Net, the more I can charge for symmetrical interaction [i.e., interactivity].

Finally, there is the role of *ethics*. (I can hear you snickering already.) But hey, people actually *do* feel inclined to reward creative value if it's not too inconvenient to do so. As Courtney Love said recently, in a brilliant blast at the music industry: "I'm a waiter. I live on tips." She's right. People want to pay her because they like her work. Indeed, actual waitpeople get by even though the people they serve are under no legal obligation to tip them. Customers tip because it's the right thing to do.

I believe that, in the practical absence of law, ethics are going to make a major comeback on the Net. In an environment of dense connection, where much of what we do and say is recorded, preserved, and easily discovered, ethical behavior becomes less a matter of self-imposed virtue and more a matter of horizontal social pressure.

Besides, the more connected we become, the more obvious it is that we're all in this together. If I don't pay for the light of your creation, it goes out and the place gets dimmer. If no one pays, we're all in the dark. On the Net, what goes around comes around. What has been an ideal becomes a sensible business practice.

Think of the Net as an ecosystem. It is a great rain forest of life-forms called ideas, which, like organisms—those patterns of self-reproducing, evolving, adaptive information that express themselves in skeins of carbon—require other organisms to exist. Imagine the challenge of trying to write a song if you'd never heard one.

As in biology, what has lived before becomes the compost for what will live next. Moreover, when you buy—or, for that matter, "steal"—an idea that first took form in my head, it remains where it grew and you in no way lessen its value by sharing it. On the contrary, my idea becomes *more* valuable, since in the informational space between your interpretation of it and mine, new species can grow. The more such spaces exist, the more fertile is the larger ecology of mind.

I can also imagine the great electronic nervous system producing entirely new models of creative worth where value resides not in the artifact, which is static and dead, but in the real art—the living process that brought it to life. I would have given a lot to be present as, say, the Beatles grew their songs. I'd have given even more to have participated. Part of the reason Deadheads were so obsessed with live concerts was that

the audience *did* participate in some weird, mysterious way. They were allowed the intimacy of seeing the larval beginnings of a song flop out onstage, wet and ugly, and they could help nurture its growth.

In the future, instead of bottles of dead "content," I imagine electronically defined venues, where minds residing in bodies scattered all over the planet are admitted, either by subscription or a ticket at a time, into the real-time presence of the creative act.

I imagine actual storytelling making a comeback. Storytelling, unlike the one-way, asymmetrical thing that goes by that name in Hollywood, is highly participatory. Instead of "the viewer" sitting there, mouth slack with one hand on a Bud while the TV blows poisonous electronics at him, I imagine people actually engaged in the process, and quite willing to pay for it.

This doesn't require much imagination, since it's what a good public speaker encourages now. The best of them don't talk at the audience, but *with* them, creating a sanctuary of permission where something is actually *happening*. Right now this has to happen in meatspace, but the immense popularity of chat rooms among the young natives of cyberspace presages richer electronic zones where all the senses are engaged. People will pay to be in those places—and people who are good at making them exciting will be paid a lot for their conversational skills.

I imagine new forms of cinema growing in these places, where people throw new stuff into the video stew. The ones who are good enough will be paid by the rest of us to shoot, produce, organize, and edit.

People will also pay to get a first crack at the fresh stuff, as Stephen King is proving by serializing novels on the Web. Charles Dickens proved the same thing long ago with his economic harnessing of serialization. Though Dickens was irritated that the Americans ignored his British copyright, he adapted and devised a way to get paid anyway, by doing public readings of his works in the U.S. The artists and writers of the future will adapt to practical possibility. Many have already done so. They are, after all, creative people.

It's captivating to think about how much more freedom there will be for the truly creative when the truly cynical have been dealt out of the game. Once we have all given up regarding our ideas as a form of property, the entertainment industry will no longer have anything to steal from us. Meet the new boss: no boss.

We can enter into a convenient and interactive relationship with audiences, who, being human, will be far more ethically inclined to pay us than the moguls ever were. What could be a stronger incentive to create than that?

We've won the revolution. It's all over but the litigation. While that drags on, it's time to start building the new economic models that will replace what came before. We don't know exactly what they'll look like, but we do know that we have a profound responsibility to be better ancestors: What we do now will likely determine the productivity and freedom of twenty generations of artists yet unborn. So it's time to stop speculating about when the new economy of ideas will arrive. It's here. Now comes the hard part, which also happens to be the fun part: making it work.

RELATED LINKS

- The Berkman Center for Internet and Society, Harvard Law School (http://cyber.law
  .harvard.edu)

- The Economy of Ideas (http://www.wired.com/wired/archive/2.03/economy.ideas.html)

- Electronic Frontier Foundation (http://www.eff.org)

- Fair Use Online (http://cyber.law.harvard.edu/fairuse)

- Selling Wine Without Bottles: The Economy of Mind on the Global Net (http://www
  .eff.org/pub/Publications/John_Perry_Barlow/idea_economy.article)

FOR FURTHER RESEARCH

To find out more about the topics discussed in this reading, use InfoTrac College Edition. Type in keywords and subject terms such as "Napster," "file-sharing programs," and "peer-to-peer networking." You can access InfoTrac College Edition from the Wadsworth/Thomson Communication Cafe homepage: http://communication.wadsworth.com.

Reading 14-3

Copyright Questions in a Digital Age
Raju Chebium

EDITOR'S NOTE

Even though history shows that new technologies help expand their markets, the entertainment industries have their own history of pursuing legal action against inventors and other media entrepreneurs who facilitate the unauthorized distribution of media content. Two high-profile cases, one against the popular file-sharing Web site Napster and the other against the publisher of a journal for hackers, 2600, demonstrate the industry's resolve and aversion to ceding control. As this reading from the CNN.com Law Center points out, society is being asked to determine how copyright protections apply at a time when creative works are widely available in cyberspace and digital technology has made copying words, sounds, and images far easier than ever before. Until the copyright issues surrounding its operation are fully played out in federal court, the future of Napster remains clouded. In the meantime, the company has formed an alliance with German publishing giant Bertelsmann as part of an effort, according to a company press release, "to transform Napster into a membership-based service that preserves the Napster experience."

CONSIDER

1. What type of expression is entitled to copyright protection? What is the main criterion for determining whether a given work deserves such protection?

2. Should *all* file-sharing and music-swapping be illegal, or should some information be free regardless of who created it and holds the copyright?

3. In the case of the DeCSS descrambling program, is it fair to hold the person who merely posted the source code legally liable for its distribution?

For more than 200 years, the United States has had copyright laws to protect the ownership rights of the creators of expressive works of fiction, music, and art, and to ensure that the creators are compensated adequately when the work is used by others.

With the advent of the Internet and the digital age, society is being asked to determine how copyright protections apply at a time when creative works are widely available in cyberspace and the technology to access such material improves nearly daily.

Experts say the high-tech context in which copyright questions are being raised—as exemplified by the Napster case in California and a DVD-encryption case out of New York—also shows that the law is always a few steps behind technology.

Of the two, the Napster case has received the most publicity because it involves highly popular software that millions of people around the world use to share music for free by dipping into someone else's hard drive.

The Recording Industry Association of America filed a lawsuit against Napster in December 1999, accusing the company of encouraging the illegal copying and distribution of copyrighted music on a massive scale.

The case, *A&M Records v. Napster,* pits the $40 billion music industry against a California company established by a teenager, 19-year-old whiz kid Shawn Fanning, a former student turned digital entrepreneur. The case raises fundamental questions about freedom of information on the Internet and what copyright protections musicians and composers have in cyberspace.

For those and other reasons, legal experts point to the Napster case as crucial to the future of cyber-

"Copyright Questions in a Digital Age," by Raju Chebium. From CNN.com, August 7, 2000. Copyright © 2000 CNN.com. This article first appeared in the CNN.com Law Center, at http://www.cnn.com/LAW. An online version remains in the CNN archives. Reprinted with permission.

space and copyright law in the United States, the world's leader in high-tech issues. But will the Napster case make new law? Experts say that is not likely.

The case "underscores the need for companies using Internet technology to understand that they can't simply ignore existing intellectual property laws," said Steven Lieberman, a Washington copyright attorney. "This Napster case doesn't make new law. It applies longstanding law to a new technology."

Michael Madison, a copyright scholar who teaches at the University of Pittsburgh law school, notes that copyright applies to creative works, such as books, plays, movies, and music—any work where someone had to exercise their powers of creativity and imagination.

While fiction is an obvious example of creativity, the courts generally will extend copyright protections to any work where even a slender element of creativity was involved.

"One consequence of that [legal recognition] is that almost all computer software is protected by copyright law, even though many people regard software as the electronic version of a machine. And since the Internet is constituted entirely of software, the Internet, among other things, amounts to an enormous aggregation of copyrighted works," Madison said.

U.S. copyright law gives control over the distribution of copyrighted work to the copyright holder, whether that is the work's originator or a publisher, movie studio, or record label to which the originator has assigned copyright.

THE NAPSTER CASE
AND ITS IMPLICATIONS

The 9th U.S. Circuit Court of Appeals in San Francisco is charged with deciding if Napster Inc. can be held liable as a contributor to copyright infringement by those who use its software. In July 2000 the appeals panel granted Napster's request for a stay of an order that would have effectively shut down the site. [But in February 2001 the Circuit Court ordered that an injunction be issued barring Napster from allowing the trading of copyrighted songs on its service.]

The future of Napster remains clouded until the copyright issues surrounding its operation are fully heard in court.

At its core, copyright law says that the creators of certain literary and artistic works have the right to ensure that their works are not used without permission, which typically means without paying for it. However, copyright holders can give up their exclusive right (literally, to "copy" the work) to publishers or other authorized entities on a limited or all-inclusive basis.

Legislation and court rulings have held that consumers, audiences, and scholars have a significant right to make use of exceptions within the copyright law to avoid lawsuits.

At the heart of the Napster case is whether Napster Inc. is facilitating personal and fair use of the music by giving people the means to download music for free or whether Napster is knowingly contributing to large-scale and unlawful copyright infringement by its users.

The music industry went after Napster partly because of Napster's high profile and partly because it was impractical to go after the millions of Napster users individually.

Adam Powell, vice president of technology and programs at the Freedom Forum in Arlington, Virginia, said Napster had become so popular and visible that it had become an icon of sorts. By suing Napster, the music industry was setting an example to Napster-like sites everywhere.

Napster has "almost become a common noun, like Kleenex or Xerox," Powell said.

THE DVD CASE

The DVD case, *Universal v. Reimerdes* (c. 2000), pits eight Hollywood movie studios against cyberjournalist Eric Corley, who edits the online hacker journal *2600*. At issue is Corley's publication of computer code that makes it possible for computer users to descramble DVD encryption software—known as the Content Scrambling System, or CSS—designed to prevent digital versatile discs from being copied.

Using the descrambling program, called DeCSS, users can copy movies from DVDs to computer hard drives or other recording devices.

First Amendment rights were raised during the trial, with Carnegie Mellon computer science professor David Touretzky arguing that blocking the publication of existing computer code, a type of language and form of expression, was tantamount to prior restraint and would have a "chilling effect" on his ability as a computer scientist to express himself and conduct research.

The DVD case, the first test of the Digital Millennium Copyright Act passed by Congress in 1998, centers less on traditional copyright issues (distribution without permission) than on *who* can be held liable for enabling someone else to make illegal copies.

THE DOCTRINE OF FAIR USE

Both of these high-profile cases involve the concept of "fair use," which came into being in the nineteenth century, when the *Folsom v. Marsh* (c. 1841) case weighed the consumer's right to information against the copyright holder's need for profit.

The doctrine essentially states that people have the right to use copyrighted material under certain circumstances that constitute a fair, one-time, noncommercial, personal use of the material. Students, for instance, are not penalized for making copies of a few pages of a textbook for studies because that constitutes a fair use of the material.

But if someone makes multiple copies of the entire textbook and tries to sell it at the street corner, courts would likely view that as a clear copyright infringement because the original work was duplicated without permission and used for profit, without the copyright owner getting a cut of the spoils.

The Napster and DVD cases pose questions as to how the fair use doctrine relates to the First Amendment.

The mass use of the Internet since the early 1990s has made it possible for people to access and sometimes copy entire books, movies, stories, dramatic works, and other intellectual property directly through their computers—not just once but many times, for free, as is the case with Napster software—and redistribute it (or merely make it available) without permission.

Do MP3 downloads from other people's computers constitute fair use, or do they, as the entertainment industry says, equate with massive copyright infringement by users? This question is at the heart of the Napster case. [For other perspectives on these issues, see Readings 14-1 and 14-2.]

FACTS ABOUT COPYRIGHT

The first copyright law was adopted in the United States in 1790.

The basis of current copyright law is the Copyright Act of 1976, an intricately complicated piece of legislation.

In a case considered the legal predecessor for the Napster case, *Sony v. Universal* (c. 1984), the movie industry sued the Sony Corp. in an unsuccessful attempt to control home recording of audiovisual materials. Hollywood claimed that Sony's Betamax video cassette recorders allowed people to engage in copyright infringement by enabling them to record television programs for later viewing.

But the Supreme Court ruled in 1984 that such "time shifting"—taping programs on VCRs for personal viewing at a later time—is not a violation of copyright.

In 1992, Congress passed the Audio Home Recording Act, which allowed people to make copies of music for personal use. The law was passed in response to the introduction of digital audio tape (DAT) recorders, just before the Internet revolution.

The law assured consumers that they could not be sued for copy infringement for making noncommercial copies of recordings for their personal use. The Audio Home Recording Act was an attempt to modify copyright protections to what at that time was a new technology, experts said.

In 1998, Congress passed the Digital Millennium Copyright Act to address the complex issue of copyright protections in a digital environment. An important aspect of the act is anticircumvention protection, which makes it a crime to manufacture or "offer to the public" a way of circumventing encryption and other security technology designed to prevent access to copyrighted works without permission.

The law, which is applicable in the DVD case, allows copyright holders to take legal action against unauthorized copying of movies in digital format. The key issue in the DVD trial, however, is that the law now makes it illegal not only to copy and sell a copyrighted movie, but also simply to tell *someone else* how to play and copy that work without the movie studio's permission.

Both the Napster and DVD cases raise free speech, fair use, and copyright issues, which makes them important to future legal and legislative action in the high-tech arena. And Napster has spawned a host of other music-swapping and file-sharing sites, increasing the scope of such peer-to-peer networking activity.

The First Amendment protects people against governmental intrusion into what and how they speak, think, write, or act. Copyright law could be construed as placing limits on those freedoms by saying people have to pay to use some creative material, Madison said.

The dilemma of copyright and intellectual property law rests in figuring out ways to balance the sometimes competing free speech and fair use doctrines.

"If you, in the course of exercising First Amendment rights, have some occasion to make use of some material that is protected by copyright, you do not want to be accused of infringement of copyright," Madison said. "The key in both [the Napster and DVD] cases is that the technology of First Amendment expression is also the technology of copyright infringement."

RELATED LINKS

- Motion Picture Association of America (http://www.mpaa.org)
- Recording Industry Association of America (http://www.riaa.com)
- Napster (http://www.napster.com)
- MP3.com (http://www.mp3.com)
- *2600: The Hacker Quarterly* (http://www.2600.com)

- Music on the Internet (http://www.nytimes.com/library/tech/reference/index-music.html)
- Digital Video (http://www.nytimes.com/library/tech/reference/index-video.html)

FOR FURTHER RESEARCH

To find out more about the topics discussed in this reading, use InfoTrac College Edition. Type in keywords and subject terms such as "MP3 format," "copyright laws," and "digital music distribution." You can access InfoTrac College Edition from the Wadsworth/Thomson Communication Cafe homepage: http://communication.wadsworth.com.

15

Privacy and Surveillance

Reading 15-1

In Defense of the Delete Key

James M. Rosenbaum

EDITOR'S NOTE

The computer Delete key doesn't really do its job. Files allegedly erased are merely removed from sight, not from your hard drive. As a result, a growing number of individuals and corporations, from Monica Lewinsky to Microsoft, are finding themselves liable for acts never committed, only expressed. Once expressed electronically, however, ideas and desires seem to take on a life of their own—oftentimes well beyond the author's actual intent. In this short but eloquent plea, James M. Rosenbaum, a federal district court judge for the District of Minnesota, argues that because we are not free to make mistakes online or retract messages once sent, we are gradually enforcing "a dangerous self-censorship over our ideas and expressions."

CONSIDER

1. Do you agree with Judge Rosenbaum that the computer Delete key represents an "elaborate deception"? Should anything be done to change its operation?

2. How would individuals and companies be protected if the courts recognized cybertrash, "the stuff which, in less electronic times, would have been wadded up and thrown into a wastebasket"?

3. What is lost, in a digital age, when an increasing number of passing comments uttered electronically are forever archived?

It is becoming widely known that a computer's Delete key represents an elaborate deception. The deception is pure, and inheres in the key's name: When the Delete key is used, nothing is deleted.[1] It is now clear that relatively simple devices can recover almost everything that has been "deleted." This durability of computerized material compounds itself, because once a computer file is generated—let alone disseminated—internal and external copies proliferate. And each is impervious to deletion.

In practice, this once-arcane fact has spawned a new legal industry: the mining of e-mails, computer files, and especially copies of hard drives to obtain deleted material.

Knowing these facts leads me to two thoughts: One, we have now placed an electronic recording device over every office door; and two, we should not stand for it. Finally, I suggest a possible remedy.

THE ELECTRONIC RECORDER

There was a time when people spoke casually "off the record" amongst themselves. That time has passed. At this earlier time, two people could easily say something—even, perhaps, something politically incorrect—simply between themselves. They might even have exchanged nasty notes between themselves. And when they had moved past this tacky, but probably innocent, moment, it was truly gone.

Their words either vanished into the air, or the note was wadded up and thrown into a wastebasket. From there, the note was removed to a "delete" device called an incinerator. Once there, it was destroyed forever. The computer, and its evil spawn the e-mail, have ended this earlier time forever. For many of us, e-mail and the computer now substitute for those doorway conversations and those idle notes. But unlike those notes, they are not easily thrown away.

In the computer, the conversation lingers, and the note persists. In my view, this is wrong.

A PRECEPT AND SOME THOUGHTS ON THE LAW

None of us is perfect. But the preservation and persistence of evidence of our imperfections does not prove we are wrong, vile, venal, or even duplicitous. It just proves we are human—perhaps even farther beneath the angels than we might have wished—but lower nonetheless.

Today, legal discovery deep-sea fishes for snippets of deleted e-mails and deleted files in search of proof of imperfections. And the fish which are caught are thrown, as proof, into courtrooms throughout the land. In my view, they are just fish, and as valueless as the same fish might be if allowed to rot as long as the finally-recovered file has been deleted.

Sometimes people just have bad ideas, or might just pass an idle—if imperfect—thought. This does not mean the person is vile. Mere evidence that a person who has done "A," but once expressed "B," does not prove that the person is lying or deceitful. The fallacy in the "truth" of the recovered e-mail or computer file is that it might just have been a bad idea, properly rejected, and consigned to an imperfectly labeled wastebasket. The problem is that on the computer's hard drive, it looks like more.

The second part of the fallacy is the almost universal—and I argue almost universally wrong—idea that finding this deleted material is the electronic equivalent of finding the inculpatory "second set of books." The evil of the second set of books lies not in the fact of their conception, but that they were used. The fact that one conceives of something—even something improper—does not necessarily mean it was acted upon.

The preservation and discovery of computer-deleted material has forced companies and prudent individuals to severely curtail the practice of using e-mails for all but the most innocuous materials. Any other course of action subjects the computer user to long-term liability for idle thoughts.

THE LARGER RISK

In some ways, the greater risk in the preservation and discovery of computerized material lies in the knowledge that things will not be expressed, and ideas will not be exchanged, out of a pernicious—but valid—

fear that their mere expression will be judged tantamount to the act. This is dangerous indeed.

One of the United States Constitution's many geniuses lies in its lofty protection of free speech. Legally,
it protects the speaker only from state rather than private regulation. But the Constitution's words express a
higher ideal: The First Amendment's premise is that a
society is freer and in less danger when the wrong, the
venal, the potentially evil is expressed and subjected
to the light of day and to the "marketplace of ideas."
Conversely, but importantly, is the negative concept:
The marketplace of ideas and expression is impoverished and demeaned when it is deprived of ideas which
may be discussed and tested, and ultimately, perhaps,
rejected. Knowledge of the computer's awesome power
to always remember, and never forget, a bad idea once
expressed erodes and endangers this powerful concept.

People who recognize that whatever you say on a
computer "can and will be used against you," prudently
avoid saying anything "dangerous" via computer. But
does anyone believe that people are "thinking" more
perfect thoughts simply because they are increasingly
reluctant to express them? I seriously doubt it.

We are, instead, enforcing a dangerous self-censorship over our ideas and expressions. And we do not restrict this censorship to ourselves. Businesses and organizations regularly adopt restrictions on the words
and ideas which can be input into the company's or organization's computers. Why? Because of the intersection of legal developments and technology.

Once upon a time, liability was based on objective
acts done or omitted. Did the person threaten violence
(assault); did he or she strike a victim (battery); did he
or she fail to act reasonably under the circumstances
(negligence)? If so, the actor was liable for the consequent act. Unless the actor's intentions were objectively manifest, however, no liability accrued. In the
1950s, the song "Standing on the Corner" was correct:
"Brother, you can't go to jail for what you're thinking,
or for the 'oooh' look in your eye. You're only standing on the corner, watching all the girls go by."

This is, unquestionably, a new century. And since
the end of the last, the song's proposition has been
somewhat modified. At least in some cases, there has
been a shift to subjective proof. In these areas, courts
and the law consider the recipient's perception of the
actor's behavior. But even here, purely subjective views
do not alone suffice—there must be some outward
manifestation of the impure thoughts.

Into this classic legal environment comes the
computer. It never forgets, and never forgives. An idle
thought "jotted" onto a calendar, a tasteless joke passed
to a once-trusted friend, a suggestive invitation directed at an uninterested recipient, if done electronically, will last forever. Years later, it can subject its author to liability.

A PROPOSAL

While recognizing the difficulties inherent in such a
suggestion, I recommend a cyber statute of limitations.
This limitation recognizes that even the best humans
may have a somewhat less than heavenly aspect. It acknowledges that anyone is entitled to make a mistake
and to think a less than perfect thought. I suggest that,
barring a pattern of egregious behavior, or an objective
record of systematic conduct—absent, if you will, a
real "second set of books"—that the courts recognize
the existence of cybertrash. This is the stuff, which, in
less electronic times, would have been wadded up and
thrown into a wastebasket. This is what the Delete button was meant for, and why pencils still have erasers.

The length of this cyber statute of limitations can
be set as arbitrarily as any other. In light of the free expression risks I perceive, I suggest the length should be
short—perhaps 6 months for an isolated message. If an
idea was merely a lousy one, or was an isolated cyber-
utterance, and the actor/author did not objectively
manifest some untoward behavior, he or she would
be considered presumptively human, and—at least for
the law's purposes—Delete would mean delete. If,
to the contrary, there was an objective continuation
of the challenged conduct, or a continuing pattern of
wrongful acts, the cyber statute of limitations would be
tolled as any other.

This suggestion is feasible. Computers internally
record the date on which a "document" was created.
Once the limitations period has passed, documents
should be legally consigned to the cyberwastebasket.

My solution is imperfect. But so are humans.
If perfect recall defines perfection, computers have
achieved it. But their operators have not achieved it
with them, and humans are unlikely to do so. A legal
system which demands human perfection, and which
penalizes a momentary failing, cannot operate in the
real world.

THE ULTIMATE FLAW

This suggestion recognizes that the computer is, itself, flawed. Its permanent memory is a flaw which undermines its value and endangers its users. Its inability to forget weakens and undermines the very ideas it permanently holds. The real flaw is that the computer lies: It lies when it says Delete. This mechanical lie ought not to debase and degrade the humans who are, and ought to be, its master.

NOTES

1. For those with little knowledge, and less interest, a computer's Delete key acts somewhat like a thief who steals a card from the old library's card file. When the card was in place, the librarian could decode the library's filing system and find the book. If the card was gone, or unreadable, the book was still in the library, but it could no longer be found amidst the library's stacked shelves. In a computer, the "lost" book can be found with very little effort.

RELATED LINKS

- Daemon Seed: Old E-mail Never Dies (http://www.wired.com/wired/archive/7.05/email.html)
- "Deleted" Computer Files Don't Die Easily (http://www.sacbee.com/ib/tech/wiredlife/wired121800.html)
- *The Green Bag: An Entertaining Journal of Law* (http://www.greenbag.org)
- PC-Webopaedia: Delete Key (http://webopedia.internet.com/TERM/D/Delete_key.html)
- Send Those Computer Files to the Shredder (http://www.law.com/professionals/automated_lawyer/tech_reviews.html)

FOR FURTHER RESEARCH

To find out more about the topics discussed in this reading, use InfoTrac College Edition. Type in keywords and subject terms such as "Delete key," "e-mail lawsuits," and "digital evidence." You can access InfoTrac College Edition from the Wadsworth/Thomson Communication Cafe homepage: http://communication.wadsworth.com.

Reading 15-2

Privacy and the New Technology: What They Do Know Can Hurt You

Simson Garfinkel

EDITOR'S NOTE

Privacy is under siege from all sides. Over the next 50 years we will see new types of privacy invasions that find their roots in advanced technology and unbridled information exchange, including the selling of medical records and biological information. That's the assessment of Simson Garfinkel in this excerpt from Database Nation: The Death of Privacy in the 21st Century. *Threats to privacy can be tamed, he argues, by being careful and informed consumers, involving government in the privacy fight, and stepping up our personal privacy protection efforts.*

CONSIDER

1. Why does Garfinkel think the term "privacy" falls short of conveying the myriad ways in which technology undermines individual autonomy and self-integrity?

2. Many people today say that in order to enjoy the benefits of modern society, we must give up some degree of personal privacy. Do you agree? Why or why not?

3. Should government get involved in the privacy fight and, if so, how? Or would it be better to leave issues of individual freedom to individual citizens?

You wake to the sound of a ringing telephone—but how could that happen? Several months ago, you reprogrammed your home telephone system so it would never ring before the civilized hour of 8 A.M. But it's barely 6:45. Who was able to bypass your phone's programming?

You pick up the receiver, then slam it down a moment later. It's one of those marketing machines playing a recorded message. What's troubling you now is how this call got past the filters you set up. Later on you'll discover how: The company that sold you the phone created an undocumented "back door"; last week, the phone codes were sold in an online auction.

Now that you're awake, you decide to go through yesterday's mail. There's a letter from the neighborhood hospital you visited last month. "We're pleased that our emergency room could serve you in your time of need," the letter begins. "As you know, our fees (based on our agreement with your HMO) do not cover the cost of treatment. To make up the difference, a number of hospitals have started selling patient records to medical researchers and consumer-marketing firms. Rather than mimic this distasteful behavior, we have decided to ask you to help us make up the difference. We are recommending a tax-deductible contribution of $275 to help defray the cost of your visit."

The veiled threat isn't empty, but you decide you don't really care who finds out about your sprained wrist. You fold the letter in half and drop it into your shredder. Also into the shredder goes a trio of low-interest credit-card offers. Why a shredder? A few years ago you would never have thought of shredding your junk mail—until a friend in your apartment complex

had his identity "stolen" by the building's superintendent. As best as anybody can figure out, the super picked one of those preapproved credit card applications out of the trash, called the toll-free number, and picked up the card when it was delivered. He's in Mexico now, with a lot of expensive clothing and electronics, all at your friend's expense.

On that cheery note, you grab your bag and head out the door, which automatically locks behind you.

This is the future—not a far-off future but one that's just around the corner. It's a future in which what little privacy we now have will be gone. Some people call this loss of privacy "Orwellian," harking back to *1984*, George Orwell's classic work on privacy and autonomy. In that book, Orwell imagined a future in which a totalitarian state used spies, video surveillance, historical revisionism, and control over the media to maintain its power. But the age of monolithic state control is over. The future we're rushing toward isn't one in which our every move is watched and recorded by some all-knowing Big Brother. It is instead a future of a hundred kid brothers who constantly watch and interrupt our daily lives. Orwell thought the Communist system represented the ultimate threat to individual liberty. Over the next 50 years, we will see new kinds of threats to privacy that find their roots not in Communism but in capitalism, the free market, advanced technology, and the unbridled exchange of electronic information.

WHAT DO WE MEAN BY PRIVACY?

The problem with this word *privacy* is that it falls short of conveying the really big picture. Privacy isn't just about hiding things. It's about self-possession, autonomy, and integrity. As we move into the computerized world of the twenty-first century, privacy will be one of our most important civil rights. But this right of privacy isn't the right of people to close their doors and pull down their window shades—perhaps because they want to engage in some sort of illicit or illegal activity. It's the right of people to control what details about their lives stay inside their own houses and what leaks to the outside.

Most of us recognize that our privacy is at risk. According to a 1996 nationwide poll conducted by Louis Harris & Associates, 24 percent of Americans have "personally experienced a privacy invasion." In 1995 the same survey found that 80 percent felt that "consumers have lost all control over how personal information about them is circulated and used by companies." Ironically, both the 1995 and 1996 surveys were paid for by Equifax, a company that earns nearly $2 billion each year from collecting and distributing personal information.

Today the Internet is compounding our privacy conundrum—largely because the voluntary approach to privacy protection advocated by the Clinton Administration doesn't work in the rough-and-tumble world of real business. For example, a study just released by the California HealthCare Foundation found that nineteen of the top twenty-one health Web sites have privacy policies, but most sites fail to follow them. Not surprisingly, 17 percent of Americans questioned in a poll said they do not go online for health information because of privacy concerns.

But privacy threats are not limited to the Internet: Data from all walks of life are now being captured, compiled, indexed, and stored. For example, New York City has now deployed the Metrocard system, which allows subway and bus riders to pay their fares by simply swiping a magnetic-strip card. But the system also records the serial number of each card and the time and location of every swipe. New York police have used this vast database to crack crimes and disprove alibis. Although law enforcement is a reasonable use of this database, it is also a use that was adopted without any significant public debate. Furthermore, additional controls may be necessary: It is not clear who has access to the database, under what circumstances that access is given, and what provisions are being taken to prevent the introduction of false data into it. It would be terrible if the subway's database were used by an employee to stalk an ex-lover or frame an innocent person for a heinous crime.

"New technology has brought extraordinary benefits to society, but it also has placed all of us in an electronic fishbowl in which our habits, tastes, and activities are watched and recorded," New York State Attorney General Eliot Spitzer said in late January, in announcing that Chase Manhattan had agreed to stop selling depositor information without clear permission from customers. "Personal information thought to be confidential is routinely shared with others without our consent."

THE ROLE OF TECHNOLOGY

Today's war on privacy is intimately related to the recent dramatic advances in technology. Many people today say that in order to enjoy the benefits of modern society, we must necessarily relinquish some degree of privacy. If we want the convenience of paying for a meal by credit card or paying for a toll with an electronic tag mounted on our rearview mirror, then we must accept the routine collection of our purchases and driving habits in a large database over which we have no control. It's a simple bargain, albeit a Faustian one.

This trade-off is both unnecessary and wrong. It reminds me of another crisis our society faced back in the '50s and '60s—the environmental crisis. Then, advocates of big business said that poisoned rivers and lakes were the necessary costs of economic development, jobs, and an improved standard of living. Poison was progress: Anybody who argued otherwise simply didn't understand the facts.

Today we know better. Today we know that sustainable economic development *depends* on preserving the environment. Indeed, preserving the environment is a prerequisite to the survival of the human race. Without clean air to breathe and clean water to drink, we will all die. Similarly, in order to reap the benefits of technology, it is more important than ever for us to use technology to protect personal freedom.

Blaming technology for the death of privacy isn't new. In 1890 two Boston lawyers, Samuel Warren and Louis Brandeis, argued in the *Harvard Law Review* that privacy was under attack by "recent inventions and business methods." They contended that the pressures of modern society required the creation of a "right of privacy," which would help protect what they called "the right to be let alone." Warren and Brandeis refused to believe that privacy had to die for technology to flourish. Today, the Warren/Brandeis article is regarded as one of the most influential law review articles ever published.

Privacy-invasive technology does not exist in a vacuum, of course. That's because technology itself exists at a junction between science, the market, and society. People create technology to fill specific needs and desires. And technology is regulated, or not, as people and society see fit. Few engineers set out to build systems designed to crush privacy and autonomy, and few businesses or consumers would willingly use or purchase these systems if they understood the consequences.

FIGHTING BACK

How can we keep technology and the free market from killing our privacy? One way is by being careful and informed consumers. Some people have begun taking simple measures to protect their privacy, measures like making purchases with cash and refusing to provide their Social Security numbers—or providing fake ones. And a small but growing number of people are speaking out for technology *with* privacy. In 1990 Lotus and Equifax teamed up to create a CD-ROM product called Lotus Marketplace: Households, which would have included names, addresses, and demographic information on every household in the United States, so small businesses could do the same kind of target marketing that big businesses have been doing since the '60s. The project was canceled when more than 30,000 people wrote to Lotus demanding that their names be taken out of the database.

Similarly, in 1997 the press informed taxpayers that the Social Security Administration was making detailed tax-history information about them available over the Internet. The SSA argued that its security provisions—requiring that taxpayers enter their name, date of birth, state of birth, and mother's maiden name—were sufficient to prevent fraud. But tens of thousands of Americans disagreed, several U.S. senators investigated the agency and the service was promptly shut down. When the service was reactivated some months later, the detailed financial information in the SSA's computers could not be downloaded over the Internet.

THE ROLE OF GOVERNMENT

But individual actions are not enough. We need to involve government itself in the privacy fight. The biggest privacy failure of the U.S. government has been its failure to carry through with the impressive privacy groundwork that was laid in the Nixon, Ford, and Carter administrations. It's worth taking a look back at that groundwork and considering how it may serve us today.

The 1970s were a good decade for privacy protection and consumer rights. In 1970 Congress passed the Fair Credit Reporting Act, which gave Americans the previously denied right to see their own credit reports and demand the removal of erroneous information. Elliot Richardson, who at the time was President Nixon's Secretary of Health, Education, and Welfare, created a commission in 1972 to study the impact of computers on privacy. After years of testimony in Congress, the commission found all the more reason for alarm and issued a landmark report in 1973.

The most important contribution of the Richardson report was a bill of rights for the computer age, which it called the Code of Fair Information Practices. The Code is based on five principles:

- There must be no personal data record-keeping system whose very existence is secret.

- There must be a way for a person to find out what information about the person is in a record and how it is used.

- There must be a way for a person to prevent information about the person that was obtained for one purpose from being used or made available for other purposes without the person's consent.

- There must be a way for a person to correct or amend a record of identifiable information about the person.

- Any organization creating, maintaining, using, or disseminating records of identifiable personal data must assure the reliability of the data for their intended use and must take precautions to prevent misuse of the data.

The biggest impact of the Richardson report wasn't in the United States but in Europe. In the years after the report was published, practically every European country passed laws based on these principles. Many created data-protection commissions and commissioners to enforce the laws. Some believe that one reason for Europe's interest in electronic privacy was its experience with Nazi Germany in the 1930s and 1940s. Hitler's secret police used the records of governments and private organizations in the countries he invaded to round up people who posed the greatest threat to German occupation; postwar Europe realized the danger of allowing potentially threatening private information to be collected, even by democratic governments that might be responsive to public opinion.

But here in the United States, the idea of institutionalized data protection faltered. President Jimmy Carter showed interest in improving medical privacy, but he was quickly overtaken by economic and political events. Carter lost the election of 1980 to Ronald Reagan, whose aides saw privacy protection as yet another failed Carter initiative. Although several privacy-protection laws were signed during the Reagan/Bush era, the leadership for these bills came from Congress, not the White House. The lack of leadership stifled any chance of passing a nationwide data-protection act. Such an act would give people the right to know if their name and personal information is stored in a database, to see the information and to demand that incorrect information be removed.

In fact, while most people in the federal government were ignoring the cause of privacy, some were actually pursuing an antiprivacy agenda. In the early 1980s, the government initiated numerous "computer matching" programs designed to catch fraud and abuse. Unfortunately, because of erroneous data these programs often penalized innocent people. In 1994 Congress passed the Communications Assistance to Law Enforcement Act, which gave the government dramatic new powers for wiretapping digital communications. In 1996 Congress passed two laws, one requiring states to display Social Security numbers on driver's licenses and another requiring that all medical patients in the United States be issued unique numerical identifiers, even if they pay their own bills. Fortunately, the implementation of those 1996 laws has been delayed, thanks largely to a citizen backlash and the resulting inaction by Congress and the executive branch.

Continuing the assault, both the Bush and Clinton administrations waged an all-out war against the rights of computer users to engage in private and secure communications. Starting in 1991, both administrations floated proposals for use of "Clipper" encryption systems that would have given the government access to encrypted personal communications. Only recently did the Clinton Administration finally relent in its 7-year war against computer privacy. President Clinton also backed the Communications Decency Act (CDA), which made it a crime to transmit sexually explicit information to minors—and, as a result, might have required Internet providers to deploy far-reaching monitoring and censorship systems. When a court in Philadelphia found the CDA unconstitutional, the Clinton Administration appealed the decision all the way to the Supreme Court—and lost.

PROTECTING PRIVACY

One important step toward reversing the current direction of government would be to create a permanent federal oversight agency charged with protecting privacy. Such an agency would:

- Watch over the government's tendency to sacrifice people's privacy for other goals and perform governmentwide reviews of new federal programs for privacy violations before they're launched.

- Enforce the government's few existing privacy laws.

- Be a guardian for individual privacy and liberty in the business world, showing businesses how they can protect privacy and profits at the same time.

- Be an ombudsman for the American public and rein in the worst excesses that our society has created.

Some privacy activists scoff at the idea of using government to assure our privacy. Governments, they say, are responsible for some of the greatest privacy violations of all time. This is true, but the U.S. government was also one of the greatest polluters of all time. Today the government is the nation's environmental police force, equally scrutinizing the actions of private business and the government itself.

At the very least, governments can alter the development of technology that affects privacy. They have done so in Europe. Consider this: A growing number of businesses in Europe are offering free telephone calls—provided that the caller first listens to a brief advertisement. The service saves consumers money, even if it does expose them to a subtle form of brainwashing. But not all these services are equal. In Sweden both the caller and the person being called are forced to listen to the advertisement, and the new advertisements are played during the phone call itself. But Italy's privacy ombudsman ruled that the person being called could not be forced to listen to the ads.

The Fair Credit Reporting Act was a good law in its day, but it should be upgraded into a Data Protection Act. Unfortunately, the Federal Trade Commission and the courts have narrowly interpreted the FCRA. The first thing that is needed is legislation that expands it into new areas. Specifically, consumer-reporting firms should be barred from reporting arrests unless those arrests result in convictions. Likewise, consumer-reporting firms should not be allowed to report evictions unless they result in court judgments in favor of the landlord or a settlement in which both the landlord and tenant agree that the eviction can be reported. Companies should be barred from exchanging medical information about individuals or furnishing medical information as part of a patient's report without the patient's explicit consent.

We also need new legislation that expands the fundamental rights offered to consumers under the FCRA. When negative information is reported to a credit bureau, the business making that report should be required to notify the subject of the report—the consumer—in writing. Laws should be clarified so that if a consumer-reporting company does not correct erroneous data in its reports, consumers can sue for real damages, punitive damages, and legal fees.

Further, we need laws that require improved computer security. In the '80s the United States aggressively deployed cellular-telephone and alphanumeric-pager networks, even though both systems were fundamentally unsecure. Instead of deploying secure systems, manufacturers lobbied for laws that would make it illegal to listen to the broadcasts. The results were predictable: dozens of cases in which radio transmissions were eavesdropped. We are now making similar mistakes in the prosecution of many Internet crimes, going after the perpetrator while refusing to acknowledge the lia-

bilities of businesses that do not even take the most basic security precautions.

We should also bring back the Office of Technology Assessment, set up under a bill passed in 1972. The OTA didn't have the power to make laws or issue regulations, but it could publish reports on topics Congress asked it to study. Among other things, the OTA considered at length the trade-offs between law enforcement and civil liberties, and it also looked closely at issues of worker monitoring. In total, the OTA published 741 reports, 175 of which dealt directly with privacy issues, before it was killed in 1995 by the newly elected Republican-majority Congress.

Nearly 40 years ago, Rachel Carson's book *Silent Spring* helped seed the U.S. environmental movement. And to our credit, the silent spring that Carson foretold never came to be. *Silent Spring* was successful because it helped people to understand the insidious damage that pesticides were wreaking on the environment, and it helped our society and our planet to plot a course to a better future.

Today, technology is killing one of our most cherished freedoms. Whether you call this freedom the right to digital self-determination, the right to informational autonomy, or simply the right to privacy, the shape of our future will be determined in large part by how we understand, and ultimately how we control or regulate, the threats to this freedom that we face today.

RELATED LINKS

- Center for Democracy and Technology (http://www.cdt.org)
- Echelon Watch (http://www.aclu.org/echelonwatch/index.html)
- Global Internet Liberty Campaign (http://www.gilc.org)
- Internet Privacy Resources (http://www.privacyrights.org/netprivacy.htm)
- MSNBC Technology: Online Privacy (http://www.msnbc.com/news/TECHPRIVACY_front.asp)
- "Privacy in the Digital Age" (http://www.nytimes.com/library/tech/reference/index-privacy.html)
- "The Reinvention of Privacy" (http://www.theatlantic.com/issues/2001/03/lester-p1.htm)

FOR FURTHER RESEARCH

To find out more about the topics discussed in this reading, use InfoTrac College Edition. Type in keywords and subject terms such as "privacy invasion," "electronic databases," and "privacy protection." You can access InfoTrac College Edition from the Wadsworth/Thomson Communication Cafe homepage: http://communication.wadsworth.com.

Reading 15-3

The Challenge of an Open Society

David Brin

You're wondering why I've called you here. The reason is simple. To answer all your questions. I mean—all. This is the greatest news of our time. As of today, whatever you want to know, provided it's in the data-net, you can know. In other words, there are no more secrets.
　　—John Brunner, *The Shockwave Rider*, 1974

EDITOR'S NOTE

Fifteen minutes into the future, society faces a dilemma. The proliferation of surveillance cameras and recording equipment—so-called "snoop technology"—has vanquished crime but at the expense of unprecedented monitoring of public spaces and private places. Early in the twenty-first century, writes David Brin in this excerpt from The Transparent Society, *we will confront a troubling choice: Live free but under constant scrutiny on the one hand, or retain our supposed privacy while relying on the authorities to responsibly monitor society on the other.*

CONSIDER

1. Given the choice between Brin's two mythical cities, which would be a more desirable place to live, and why?

2. What central issue will the citizens of countless twenty-first century communities have to confront, according to Brin?

3. Why does Brin consider accountability to be the keystone of Western civilization's success?

This is a tale of two cities. Cities of the near future, say 10 or 20 years from now.

Barring something unforeseen, you are apt to be living in one of these two places. Your only choice may be which one.

At first sight, these two municipalities look pretty much alike. Both contain dazzling technological marvels, especially in the realm of electronic media. Both suffer familiar urban quandaries of frustration and decay. If some progress is being made in solving human problems, it is happening gradually. Perhaps some kids seem better educated. The air may be marginally cleaner. People still worry about overpopulation, the environment, and the next international crisis.

None of these features is of interest to us right now, for we have noticed something about both of these twenty-first century cities that is radically different. A trait that marks them as distinct from any metropolis of the late 1990s.

Street crime has nearly vanished from both towns. But that is only a symptom, a result.

The real change peers down from every lamppost, every rooftop and street sign.

Tiny cameras, panning left and right, survey traffic and pedestrians, observing everything in open view.

Have we entered an Orwellian nightmare? Have the burghers of both towns banished muggings at the cost of creating a Stalinist dystopia?

Consider city number one. In this place, all the myriad cameras report their urban scenes straight to Police Central, where security officers use sophisticated image processors to scan for infractions against public order—or perhaps against an established way of thought. Citizens walk the streets aware that any word or deed may be noted by agents of some mysterious bureau.

Now let's skip across space and time.

At first sight, things seem quite similar in city number two. Again, ubiquitous cameras perch on every vantage point. Only here we soon find a crucial difference. These devices do not report to the secret police. Rather, each and every citizen of this metropolis can use his or her wristwatch television to call up images from any camera in town.

Here a late-evening stroller checks to make sure no one lurks beyond the corner she is about to turn.

Over there a tardy young man dials to see if his dinner date still waits for him by a city fountain.

A block away, an anxious parent scans the area to find which way her child wandered off.

Over by the mall, a teenage shoplifter is taken into custody gingerly, with minute attention to ritual and rights, because the arresting officer knows that the entire process is being scrutinized by untold numbers who watch intently, lest her neutral professionalism lapse.

In city number two, such microcameras are banned from some indoor places . . . but not from police headquarters! There any citizen may tune in on bookings, arraignments, and especially the camera control room itself, making sure that the agents on duty look out for violent crime, and only crime.

Despite their initial similarity, these are very different cities, representing disparate ways of life, completely opposite relationships between citizens and their civic guardians. The reader may find both situations somewhat chilling. Both futures may seem undesirable. But can there be any doubt which city we'd rather live in, if these two make up our only choice?

TECHNOLOGY'S VERDICT

Alas, they do appear to be our only options. For the cameras are on their way, along with data networks that will send myriad images flashing back and forth, faster than thought.

In fact, the future has already arrived. The trend began in Britain a decade ago, in the town of King's Lynn, where sixty remote-controlled video cameras were installed to scan known "trouble spots," reporting directly to police headquarters. The resulting reduction in street crime exceeded all predictions; in or near zones covered by surveillance, crime dropped to one-seventieth of the former rate. The savings in patrol

costs alone paid for the equipment in a few months. Dozens of cities and towns soon followed the example of King's Lynn. Glasgow, Scotland, reported a 68 percent drop in crime citywide, while police in Newcastle fingered over 1,500 perpetrators with taped evidence. (All but seven pleaded guilty, and those seven were later convicted.) In May 1997, Newcastle soccer fans rampaged through downtown streets. Detectives studying video tapes picked out 152 faces and published 80 photographs in local newspapers. In days, all were identified.

Today, over 300,000 cameras are in place throughout the United Kingdom, transmitting round-the-clock images to a hundred constabularies [police stations], all of them reporting decreases in public misconduct. Polls report that the cameras are extremely popular with citizens, though British civil libertarian John Wadham and others have bemoaned this proliferation of snoop technology, claiming, "It could be used for any other purpose, and of course it could be abused."

Visitors to Japan, Thailand, and Singapore will see that other countries are rapidly following the British example, using closed-circuit television (CCTV) to supervise innumerable public areas.

This trend was slower coming to North America, but it appears to be taking off. After initial experiments garnered widespread public approval, the City of Baltimore put police cameras to work scanning all 106 downtown intersections. In 1997, New York City began its own program to set up 24-hour remote surveillance in Central Park, subway stations, and other public places.

No one denies the obvious and dramatic short-term benefits derived from this early proliferation of surveillance technology. That is not the real issue. In the long run, the sovereign folk of Baltimore and countless other communities will have to make the same choice as the inhabitants of our two mythical cities. *Who will ultimately control the cameras?*

Consider a few more examples.

How many parents have wanted to be a fly on the wall while their child was at day care? This is now possible with a new video monitoring system known as Kindercam, linked to high-speed telephone lines and a central Internet server. Parents can log on, type www.kindercam.com, enter their password, and access a live view of their child in day care at any time, from anywhere in the world. Kindercam will be installed in 2,000 day care facilities nationwide by the end of 1998.

Mothers on business trips, fathers who live out of state, even distant grandparents can all "drop in" on their child daily. Drawbacks? Overprotective parents may check compulsively. And now other parents can observe your child misbehaving!

Some of the same parents are less happy about the lensed pickups that are sprouting in their own workplaces, enabling supervisors to tune in on them in the same way they use Kindercam to check up on their kids.

That is, if they notice the cameras at all. At present, engineers can squeeze the electronics for a video unit into a package smaller than a sugar cube. Complete sets half the size of a pack of cigarettes were recently offered for sale by the Spy Shop, a little store in New York City located two blocks from the United Nations [see http://www.w2.com/docs2/z/spyshop .html]. Meanwhile, units with radio transmitters are being disguised in clock radios, telephones, and toasters, as part of the burgeoning "nannycam" trend. So high is demand for these pickups, largely by parents eager to check on their baby-sitters, that just one firm in Orange County, California, has recently been selling from 500 to 1,000 disguised cameras a month. By the end of 1997, prices had dropped from $2,500 to $399.

Cameras aren't the only surveillance devices proliferating in our cities. Starting with Redwood City, near San Francisco, several police departments have begun lacing neighborhoods with sound pickups that transmit directly back to headquarters. Using triangulation techniques, officials can now pinpoint bursts of gunfire and send patrol units swiftly to the scene, without having to wait for vague telephone reports from neighbors. In 1995 the Defense Department awarded a $1.7 million contract to Alliant Techsystems for its prototype system SECURES, which tests more advanced sound pickup networks in Washington and other cities. The hope is to distinguish not only types of gunfire but also human voices crying for help.

So far, so good. But from there, engineers say it would be simple to upgrade the equipment, enabling bored monitors to eavesdrop through open bedroom windows on cries of passion, or family arguments. "Of course we would never go that far," one official said, reassuringly.

Consider another piece of James Bond apparatus now available to anyone with ready cash. Today, almost any electronics store will sell you night vision goggles using state-of-the-art infrared optics equal to those issued by the military, for less than the price of a video camera. AGEMA Systems, of Syracuse, New York, has sold several police departments imaging devices that can peer into houses from the street, discriminate the heat given off by indoor marijuana cultivators, and sometimes tell if a person inside moves from one room to the next. Military and civilian enhanced-vision technologies now move in lockstep, as they have in the computer field for years.

In other words, even darkness no longer guarantees privacy.

Nor does your garden wall. In 1995, Admiral William A. Owens, then vice chairman of the Joint Chiefs of Staff, described a sensor system that he expected to be operational within a few years: a pilotless drone, equipped to provide airborne surveillance for soldiers in the field. While camera robots in the $1 million range have been flying in the military for some time, the new system will be extraordinarily cheap and simple. Instead of requiring a large support crew, it will be controlled by one semiskilled soldier and will fit in the palm of a hand. Minuscule and quiet, such remote-piloted vehicles, or RPVs, may flit among trees to survey threats near a rifle platoon. When mass-produced in huge quantities, unit prices will fall.

Can civilian models be far behind? No law or regulation will keep them from our cities for very long. The rich, the powerful, and figures of authority will have them, whether legally or surreptitiously. And the contraptions will become smaller, cheaper, and smarter with each passing year.

So much for the supposed privacy enjoyed by sunbathers in their own backyards.

Moreover, surveillance cameras are the tip of the metaphorical iceberg. Other entrancing and invasive innovations of the vaunted Information Age abound. Will a paper envelope protect the correspondence you send by old-fashioned surface mail when new-style scanners can trace the patterns of ink inside without ever breaking the seal?

Let's say you correspond with others by e-mail and use a computerized encryption program to ensure that your messages are read only by the intended recipient. What good will all the ciphers and codes do, if some adversary has bought a "back door" password to your encoding program? Or if a wasp-sized camera drone flits into your room, sticks to the ceiling above your desk, inflates a bubble lens, and watches every keystroke that you type?

In late 1997 it was revealed that Swiss police had secretly tracked the whereabouts of mobile phone users via a telephone company computer that records billions of movements per year. Swisscom was able to locate its mobile subscribers within a few hundred meters. This aided several police investigations. But civil libertarians expressed heated concern, especially since identical technology is used worldwide.

The same issues arise when we contemplate the proliferation of vast databases containing information about our lives, habits, tastes, and personal histories. The cash register scanners in a million supermarkets, video stores, and pharmacies already pour forth a flood of statistical data about customers and their purchases, ready to be correlated. (Are you stocking up on hemorrhoid cream? Renting a daytime motel room? The database knows.) Corporations claim this information helps them serve us more efficiently. Critics respond that it gives big companies an unfair advantage, enabling them to know vastly more about us than we do about them. Soon, computers will hold all your financial and educational records, legal documents, and medical analyses that parse you all the way down to your genes. Any of this might be examined by strangers without your knowledge, or even against your stated will.

As with those streetlamp cameras, the choices we make regarding future information networks—how they will be controlled and who can access the data—will affect our own lives and those of our children and their descendants.

A MODERN CONCERN

The issue of threatened privacy has spawned a flood of books, articles, and media exposes—from Janna Malamud Smith's thoughtful *Private Matters* and Ellen Alderman and Caroline Kennedy's erudite *Right to Privacy* all the way to shrill, paranoic rants by conspiracy fetishists who see Big Brother lurking around every corner. Spanning this spectrum, however, there appears to be one common theme. Often the author has responded with a call to arms, proclaiming that we must become more vigilant to protect traditional privacy against intrusions by faceless (take your pick) government bureaucrats, corporations, criminals, or just plain busybodies.

That is the usual conclusion—but not the one taken here.

For in fact, it is already far too late to prevent the invasion of cameras and databases. The *djinn* [genie] cannot be crammed back into its bottle. No matter how many laws are passed, it will prove quite impossible to legislate away the new surveillance tools and databases. They are here to say.

Light *is* going to shine into nearly every corner of our lives.

The real issue facing citizens of a new century will be how mature adults choose to live—how they can compete, cooperate, and thrive—in such a world. A transparent society.

Our civilization is already a noisy one precisely because we have chosen freedom and mass sovereignty, so that the citizenry itself must constantly argue out the details, instead of leaving them to some committee of sages.

What distinguishes society today is not only the pace of events but the nature of our tool kit for facing the future. Above all, what has marked our civilization as different is its knack for applying two extremely hard-won lessons from the past.

> *In all of history, we have found just one cure for error— a partial antidote against making and repeating grand, foolish mistakes, a remedy against self-deception. That antidote is criticism.*

Scientists have known this for a long time. It is the keystone of their success. A scientific theory gains respect only by surviving repeated attempts to demolish it. Only after platoons of clever critics have striven to come up with refuting evidence, forcing changes, do a few hypotheses eventually graduate from mere theories to accepted models of the world.

If neo-Western civilization has one great trick in its repertoire, a technique more responsible than any other for its success, that trick is accountability. Especially the knack—which no other culture ever mastered—of making accountability apply to the mighty. True, we still don't manage it perfectly. Gaffes, bungles, and inanities still get covered up. And yet, one can look at any newspaper or television news program and see an eager press corps at work, supplemented by hordes of righteously indignant individuals (and their lawyers), all baying for waste or corruption to be exposed, secrets to be unveiled, and nefarious schemes to be nipped in the bud. Disclosure is a watchword of the age, and politicians have grudgingly responded by passing the Freedom of Information Act (FOIA), truth-in-lending laws, open meeting rules, and codes to enforce candor in real estate, in the nutritional content of foodstuffs, in the expense accounts of lobbyists, and so on.

Although this process of stripping off veils has been uneven, and continues to be a source of contention, the underlying moral force can clearly be seen pervading our popular culture, in which nearly every modern film or novel seems to preach the same message—suspicion of authority. The phenomenon is not new to our generation. Schoolbooks teach that freedom is guarded by constitutional "checks and balances," but those same legal provisions were copied, early in the nineteenth century, by nearly every new nation of Latin America, and not one of them remained consistently free. In North America, constitutional balances worked only because they were supplemented by a powerful mythic tradition, expounded in story, song, and now virtually every Hollywood film, that any undue accumulation of power should be looked on with concern.

Above all, we are encouraged to distrust government.

The late Karl Popper pointed out the importance of this mythology in the dark days during and after World War II, in *The Open Society and Its Enemies*. Only by insisting on accountability, he concluded, can we constantly remind public servants that they *are* servants. It is also how we maintain some confidence that merchants aren't cheating us, or that factories aren't poisoning the water. As inefficient and irascibly noisy as it seems at times, this habit of questioning authority ensures freedom far more effectively than any of the older social systems that were based on reverence or trust.

And yet, another paradox rears up every time one interest group tries to hold another accountable in today's society.

Whenever a conflict arises between privacy and account-ability, people demand the former for themselves and the latter for everybody else.

The rule seems to hold in almost every realm of modern life, from special prosecutors investigating the finances of political figures to worried parents demanding that lists of sex offenders be made public. From merchants anxious to see their customers' credit reports to clients who resent such snooping. From people who "need" caller ID to screen their calls to those worried that their lives might be threatened if they lose telephone anonymity. From activists demanding greater access to computerized government records in order to hunt patterns of corruption or incompetence in office to other citizens who worry about the release of personal information contained in those very same records.

In opposing this modern passion for personal and corporate secrecy, I should first emphasize that I *like*

privacy! Outspoken eccentrics need it, probably as much or more than those who are reserved. I would find it hard to get used to living in either of the cities described in the example at the beginning of this chapter. But a few voices out there have begun pointing out the obvious. Those cameras on every street corner are coming, as surely as the new millennium.

Oh, we may agitate and legislate. But can "privacy laws" really prevent hidden eyes from getting tinier, more mobile, and cleverer? In software form they will cruise the data highways. "Antibug" technologies will arise, but the resulting surveillance arms race can hardly favor the "little guy." The rich, the powerful, police agencies, and a technologically skilled elite will always have an advantage.

In the long run, as author Robert Heinlein prophesied years ago, will the chief effect of privacy laws simply be to "make the bugs smaller"?

The [original] subtitle of this book—*Will Technology Force Us to Choose Between Privacy and Freedom?*—is intentionally provocative. I think such a stark choice can be avoided. It may be possible to have both liberty and some shelter from prying eyes.

But suppose the future *does* present us with an absolute either-or decision, to select just one, at the cost of the other. In that case, there can be no hesitation.

Privacy is a highly desirable *product* of liberty. If we remain free and sovereign, we may have a little privacy in our bedrooms and sanctuaries. As citizens, we'll be able to demand some.

But accountability is no side benefit. It is the one fundamental ingredient on which liberty thrives. Without the accountability that derives from openness—enforceable upon even the mightiest individuals and institutions—how can freedom survive?

In the Information Age to come, cameras and databases will sprout like poppies—or weeds—whether we like it or not. Over the long haul, we as a people must decide the following questions:

Can we stand living exposed to scrutiny, our secrets laid open, if in return we get flashlights of our own that we can shine on anyone who might do us harm—even the arrogant and strong?

Or is an illusion of privacy worth any price, even the cost of surrendering our own right to pierce the schemes of the powerful?

There are no easy answers, but asking questions can be a good first step.

RELATED LINKS

- David Brin's Web Page (http://www.kithrup.com/brin)
- EarthCam: Webcam Network (http://www.earthcam.com)
- HotSeat: The Transparent Society (http://hotwired.lycos.com/packet/hotseat/97/22/transcript4a.html)
- Surveillance Camera News (http://www.mediaeater.com/cameras/news.html)
- Video Surveillance (http://www.privacyinternational.org/issues/cctv)

FOR FURTHER RESEARCH

To find out more about the topics discussed in this reading, use InfoTrac College Edition. Type in keywords and subject terms such as "surveillance," "snoop technology," and "transparent society." You can access InfoTrac College Edition from the Wadsworth/Thomson Communication Cafe homepage: http://communication.wadsworth.com.

Reading 15-4

Europe to U.S.: No Privacy, No Trade
Simon Davies

EDITOR'S NOTE

United States privacy protections for personal information are lax compared to those being enforced by the European Union. Now the European Union wants every country that member nations do business with to adhere to its stringent privacy code, including the United States. But the message from Washington is clear—the United States will not play ball with European notions of privacy—raising the likelihood of protracted international confrontation over the ways that consumer data are used.

CONSIDER

1. In what ways do European notions of information and personal privacy differ from American notions?
2. Each country in the European Union will soon have a high-level data protection commissioner. Should the United States create a similar position?
3. Why in the United States are attempts to pass comprehensive privacy laws typically met with failure?

As marketers in the United States lay the groundwork necessary to transform mountains of consumer-profile data into nuggets of gold, the European Union is preparing to make that task even more difficult by launch-

"Europe to U.S.: No Privacy, No Trade," by Simon Davies. From *Wired,* May 1998, pp. 135–136, 187–188. Copyright © 1998 by Simon Davies. Reprinted with permission of the author.

ing the biggest privacy gambit in history. If the European plan succeeds, every country on earth will soon adhere to a global privacy code. If it fails, the United States and Europe could end up in the throes of an ugly trade war over the international transfer of personal information.

Beginning October 25, 1998, a group of Brussels bureaucrats (known locally as "Eurocrats") oversees the implementation of a new privacy policy throughout Europe. Under this régime, known as the European

Data Protection Directive, any country that trades personal information with the U.K., France, Germany, Spain, Italy, or any of the other ten E.U. states will be required to embrace Europe's strict standards for privacy protection.

NO PRIVACY, NO TRADE

The new rules will oblige every country within the European Union to conform to a common set of standards that bind all governments and corporations to a rigorous system of privacy protection. Under the directive, European citizens are guaranteed a bundle of rights, including the right of access to their data, the right to know where the data originated, the right to have inaccurate data rectified, the right of recourse in the event of unlawful processing, and the right to withhold permission to use their data for direct marketing.

Enforceability lies at the heart of the directive. In seeking to guarantee that its citizens have privacy rights that are enshrined in explicit rules, the E.U. has set up procedures that will allow individuals to appeal to a legal authority if their rights are violated. Every European country will have a privacy commissioner or agency to enforce the law. The E.U. will expect the countries with which it does business to do the same — and that includes the United States.

The sting on the tail is contained in Article 25 of the directive. European countries will not be allowed to send personal information to countries that do not maintain adequate standards of privacy. Thus, a French company that wants to send credit card information to a data-processing company in China will not be able to do so. China has no privacy law, and no interest in privacy.

The United States, likewise, has few guaranteed privacy protections for the private sector. As a result, the U.S. may soon find itself unable to access personal data relating to almost half of the developed world.

Unless a way forward is found, a huge chunk of business between the world's two biggest economic blocs may hit the buffers. At stake is the future of banking, travel, credit card transactions, electronic commerce, and government business. In cyberspace, the European rules may create new headaches for Web sites that use cookies or profiling systems such as Aptex Software's SelectCast. "If the data collected by a cookie or profile links to the name of a specific European individual, it can trigger the directive," says Peter P. Swire, a law professor at Ohio State University.

The cost of implementing the European directive will be high. The United Kingdom estimates that compliance will cost British companies roughly £1.4 billion (about U.S. $2.3 billion)—which suggests that the combined European figure will add up to the equivalent of $15 billion to $20 billion.

For U.S. companies, the transition will be awkward. Consider one example: In November 1994 Citibank concluded a cobranding agreement with the German National Railway that was to form the basis of the biggest credit card project in German history. It soon emerged, however, that personal data on millions of German citizens would be processed in the U.S. The news triggered a public outcry, and German data-protection authorities bluntly told Citibank and the railway that the arrangement would be prohibited unless the two companies could devise an acceptable way to protect the privacy of cardholders. The benchmark laid down by local authorities was even stricter than the E.U. directive's — Citibank must guarantee privacy standards at least equal to those that exist under German law.

After 6 months of intense negotiations, the companies signed a contractual agreement that required both parties to institute a wide range of privacy protections. The agreement was applauded in Europe as a huge step forward, but it also required Citibank to make significant changes in the way it manages customer information.

Lawyers in the U.S. and Europe have been scrambling to find ways to reduce the potential havoc. Nevertheless, governments on both sides of the Atlantic appear to be spoiling for a fight.

The message from Washington, DC, has been consistent and unequivocal: The U.S. will not play ball with European notions of privacy, nor will it allow privacy laws to become a barrier to trade. As White House technology adviser Ira Magaziner recently told the National Press Club, "If we have to go to the World Trade Organization about it, we will."

For its part Brussels has been single-minded in its determination to pursue the privacy directive's goals. Germany's Spiros Simitis, the world's first data protection commissioner, told an audience in Washington, "Don't imagine for a moment that you can get away with paying lip service to privacy. Europe requires a régime of real protection. That is the new global position."

CULTURE CLASH

Ulf Brühann is sitting in his office in 200 Rue de la Loi, Brussels, contemplating the impact of the directive. As head of the E.U. unit responsible for its implementation, he is anxious to ensure that the world takes him seriously.

Brühann wants the U.S. to understand that Europe is committed to the directive and will fight for it. Last year he told a meeting of government privacy commissioners from twenty-five countries that the E.U. will insist that its trading partners embrace data-protection policies that not only guarantee data security and the "transparency" of data-processing procedures, but which also give citizens comprehensive access to their files.

Brühann was clear about the sort of privacy policy he expected other countries to establish: "Appropriate institutional and enforcement mechanisms must be in place to ensure that rules are complied with in practice, that support and help is available to individuals who do have problems, and that ultimately a remedy is available to individuals so that breaches of the rules can be put right and compensation paid if appropriate."

Numerous non-E.U. countries have already responded to the directive by instituting tough privacy laws. Canada's federal government, for example, has proposed a new privacy régime to control private-sector activities. But in the U.S., the history of efforts to pass omnibus privacy laws is replete with failure. Direct marketers, credit card companies, and representatives from the U.S. finance industry have consistently mobilized opposition, warning of imminent financial woes should strict privacy rules become law. The subtext to the corporate threat is the notion that the public has become weary of expensive federal agencies. According to Jim Tobin, vice president of public affairs for American Express in Europe, "The market can develop privacy solutions. No one needs another cumbersome government regulator."

According to Brühann, the key question now facing the European authorities is not whether action should be taken to enforce the directive, but "how far do we need to go?"

SABRE RATTLING

Sweden has already tested the waters. In what could well be a sign of things to come, Sweden's privacy watchdog, Anitha Bondestam, instructed American Airlines in 1997 to delete all health and medical details on Swedish passengers after each flight unless "explicit consent" could be obtained. These details (information about allergies, asthma notification, dietary needs, disabled access, and so on) are routinely collected, but Bondestam's order meant that American would be unable to transmit the information to its SABRE central reservation system in the U.S.

The airline appealed to Stockholm's District Administrative Court, arguing it was "impractical" to obtain consent. American further argued that people would be inconvenienced if they had to repeat the information each time they flew. The court was unconvinced. Inconvenience, it concluded, does not constitute an exemption from legal rules for the protection of data. American launched a second action in the Administrative Court of Appeal, but the airline lost this case, too, and the matter now rests before Sweden's Supreme Administrative Court. In the meantime, the export and processing of medical data to American's reservation system has been suspended.

Under the privacy directive, any of the E.U.'s 350 million-plus citizens will be able to file a claim over abuse of personal data that can be pursued all the way to the European Court of Human Rights—one of the E.U.'s highest judicial authorities. At any point during this arduous process, business contracts can be suspended, injunctions can halt data flows, and compensation can be claimed. The publicly funded privacy watchdog of each E.U. nation is required by law to act on behalf of citizens whose rights have been violated. If the national watchdog—or, indeed, Brussels itself—fails in this duty, the European court system can be invoked. Procedure, in other words, must be followed.

While this prospect has sent shivers down the spines of U.S. businesses that trade with Europe, the Clinton administration has taken a hard line on the question of appointing a government privacy watchdog. "We don't recognize the validity of that approach," says Magaziner. "We would say the U.S. has equivalent privacy protection. I don't believe it is lesser. I believe it is different."

THE AMERICAN WAY

Brussels is baffled by the U.S. position, but the White House believes that European demands can be met by a mix of privacy friendly business-to-business contracts, self-regulation schemes, and technology-based privacy-protection systems.

U.S. businesses are eager to find nonlegislative solutions. Last December Ron Plesser, a Washington, DC, lobbyist, announced the release of a self-regulatory code of conduct for individual reference services such as Metromail, CDB Infotek, and Lexis-Nexis's P-Trak. The code limits the use and collection of personal information, while relying on independent auditors to monitor compliance.

At the same time, U.S. technologists are working to build privacy mechanisms such as P3P and TRUSTe into the architecture of cyberspace. Developed by the World Wide Web Consortium, P3P—the Platform for Privacy Preferences Project—allows Internet users to set default preferences for the collection, use, and disclosure of personal information on the Web. TRUSTe, on the other hand, is more like a seal of approval—it uses a standardized icon to link to a company's privacy practices and indicate that these practices are monitored by outside auditors.

None of these options is perfect. To date, market acceptance of technological tools like P3P and TRUSTe has been limited. Ron Plesser's code of conduct for reference services has been widely criticized as a ploy to stave off government regulation while not going nearly far enough to protect personal privacy.

Meanwhile, the man responsible for the evolution of Citibank's contract with the German National Railway—Berlin deputy privacy commissioner Alexander Dix—believes that the contract model offers only a partial answer for U.S. businesses. Small and medium-size companies, he warns, may not be able to afford complex contracts. "Contractual standard setting by private corporations can only complement and support—but never replace—national legislation," he says.

The process might well be endless, paralyzing deals and complicating intricate multilevel negotiations. In hopes of avoiding such an outcome, several U.S. banks and other companies are working to develop "model" contracts that could be used in cookie-cutter fashion. The mere existence of such potential solutions means that for the moment, at least, few people in Europe want to talk openly about a trade war with the U.S.

But there's still a long way to go before the E.U. will be satisfied. The view from Brussels is that no current U.S. self-regulation system would be acceptable to a European privacy commissioner. The White House has called for submissions on what it calls "effective self-regulation," but U.S. industry will be required to review the fundamentals of its current business practices if it wants to get anywhere in transactions across the Atlantic.

In the long term, the E.U.'s goal is to create a global privacy arrangement similar to the intellectual property treaty now being pushed by the World Intellectual Property Organization. For the U.S., accustomed to leadership in such global matters and eager to promote e-commerce, the E.U.'s new privacy stance is proving difficult to comprehend.

 RELATED LINKS

- EU and the US: The Efficacy of Data Protection Legislation and the Anonymous Alternative (http://www.zeroknowledge.com/company/policy.asp)
- Europa: The European Union Online (http://europa.eu.int/index_en.htm)
- European Union Directive on Data Protection (http://www.privacy.org/pi/intl_orgs/ec/eudp.html)
- Platform for Privacy Preferences (P3P) Project (http://www.w3.org/P3P)
- Privacy International (http://www.privacy.org/pi)
- TRUSTe (http://www.truste.org)

FOR FURTHER RESEARCH

To find out more about the topics discussed in this reading, use InfoTrac College Edition. Type in keywords and subject terms such as "European Data Protection Directive," "privacy protection," and "privacy laws and policies." You can access InfoTrac College Edition from the Wadsworth / Thomson Communication Cafe homepage: http://communication .wadsworth.com.

16

Hacking and the
Digital Underground

Reading 16-1

Notes from the Virus Underground

Kim Neely

EDITOR'S NOTE

Much of success of the new Web-based economy hinges on the performance and dependability of the computer servers and networks that make up the Internet. By spreading both harmless and data-destroying parasite programs that embed themselves into other programs and "reproduce," virus writers and virus-exchange groups reveal the vulnerabilities of this relatively open and dynamic communication system. VXers, as they are known, claim they perform a public service by highlighting the security defects of new software releases, forcing advances in the virus-protection industry. Antivirus watchdogs, on the other hand, argue that computer viruses represent a terrorist threat. Rolling Stone *writer Kim Neely tracked the exploits of one virus-exchange group and came back with this inside story of who creates computer viruses and why.*

CONSIDER

1. In the language of the virus community, what is the difference between a computer virus with a "malicious payload" compared to one that merely "replicates"? Should we be concerned about either?

2. Should virus-exchange groups writing at the "state of the art" be allowed to introduce new computer viruses to compel the industry to remain ever vigilant in its virus-protection efforts?

3. How is it that computer viruses like the Melissa virus can reproduce and infect host computers so rapidly on individual machines that are spread across vast networks?

It's three in the morning on the Internet Relay Chat channel *#codebreakers* and Opic is waiting. It has taken a week of cryptic e-mail missives, bounced around the world and back again via a chain of anonymous remailers, to arrange this meeting, but the enigmatic 21-year-old is here when he said he would be. "Sorry about all the confusion," he types. His welcome appears on the screen after a slight lag, a symptom of the proxy servers he's routing himself through to cloak the address of his Internet service provider.

Opic is a "coder," part of a ten-man Internet virus-exchange (VX) group known as CodeBreakers. He writes computer viruses. In and of itself this isn't a pursuit that would require anyone to go into hiding. Writing viruses is perfectly legal in the United States.

Intentionally spreading a virus to unwitting computer users though—that's a prosecutable offense. Especially if that virus turns out to be the fastest-spreading piece of self-replicating code in history. You wouldn't want to be linked to someone even suspected of pulling a stunt like that. This is why Opic and the other members of CodeBreakers have been so skittish lately.

Computer viruses are small parasitic programs that attach themselves to other programs and reproduce. They've been around since the mid-'80s but the general public didn't become aware of them until 1992 when the data-gobbling Michelangelo became the first "celebrity" virus. Ten years ago there were only about thirty known computer viruses. Today according to Symantec and Network Associates, the top antivirus-software companies in the United States, there are some 40,000 viruses in existence.

Anything that a virus does besides replicate is called its payload. Some viruses contain no payload at all and can reside on a PC for years without being detected. Others display jokey screen messages, print text, or play music. Some viruses cause gradual insidious corruption of data files; others lie dormant throughout the year and then destroy files or reformat hard drives when a certain date rolls around.

Viruses that permanently wipe out files or erase hard drives are the least common type. Still, virus researchers contend that there is no such thing as a truly benign virus. Even some "nonmalicious" viruses are so

"Notes from the Virus Underground," by Kim Neely. From *Rolling Stone,* September 16, 1999, pp. 65–67, 130. Copyright © 1999 Rolling Stone LLC. All rights reserved. Reprinted with permission.

sloppily programmed that they result in software malfunctions, crashes, and file corruptions not intended by their authors. Theoretically, if a virus was buggy enough to disrupt the day-to-day operations of a crucial machine or network—say that of a hospital or an air traffic–control system—and happened to hit on a day when that organization's backup system was down, even the most harmless virus would have the potential to be life-threatening.

This spring, Microsoft users everywhere met Melissa, a technically harmless—it contained no data-destroying payload—but alarmingly prolific Word 97 macro virus. Among the viruses known to be actively spreading today, macro viruses are the most common. They are written in the Visual Basic for Applications programming language included in the popular software package Microsoft Office—the user-friendliness of which makes viruses fairly easy for even nonprogrammers to create—and travel via infected Microsoft Word or Excel documents.

Melissa upped the ante for virus spreading. Instead of relying on users themselves to transfer the infected documents from machine to machine via disk or e-mail, the virus operated like a chain letter from hell, corrupting Word documents and, if Microsoft's Outlook e-mail software was installed on an infected machine, peeking into the user's address book and sending e-mails—each with an infected document attached—to the first fifty addresses found.

Melissa clogged e-mail gateways, panicked PC users, and sparked an FBI manhunt that at least initially pointed to a retired member of CodeBreakers known as VicodinES. Vic, as he's known in the clannish virus underground, was first linked to Melissa when similarities were discovered between Melissa and an earlier virus, PSD2000, that he had created and that was available for download on his Web site. The FBI began sniffing around the CodeBreakers a few days after Melissa surfaced, shutting down two Web sites containing viruses written by VicodinES: Codebreakers.org, the group's own site, and SourceofKaos.com, a domain that hosted Vic's personal site. Working from logs provided by America Online, investigators later traced the Usenet post that triggered Melissa's joy ride to a 30-year-old Aberdeen, New Jersey, programmer named David L. Smith. Smith now faces charges that could carry a maximum penalty of 40 years in prison and $480,000 in fines.

Authorities have yet to reveal whether Smith and VicodinES are one and the same. The CodeBreakers have maintained from the beginning that Melissa was neither written nor spread by Vic. Rather, they say, Smith simply cobbled Melissa together out of two earlier viruses, one of them Vic's PSD2000. This is entirely possible: Files containing viruses are swapped like trading cards on the Internet, and coders often modify existing viruses to create their own new mutations.

Interest in the group on the part of law enforcement appears to have cooled in the months since Smith's arrest. So aside from the precautions they take to protect their identities, the CodeBreakers have returned to business as usual. They're still writing viruses, still making them available to anyone who cares to download them via an electronic 'zine, *CodeBreakers VX Zine*, edited by Opic. "After much internal dialogue," he explained in the 'zine's first post-Melissa issue, the CodeBreakers had simply decided to "continue doing what they have always done: find new, innovative, and interesting viral techniques."

Opic has agreed to this late-night chat not because he is eager to rehash the Melissa sordidness but because he was approached with what for him must have been a powerful lure: genuine curiosity about why he—or anyone—writes viruses.

Sarah Gordon, an antivirus researcher with IBM who has been studying virus writers for nearly a decade, says it's impossible to tell how many coders are currently practicing, because many never tell anyone about their activities. She conservatively estimates that there are several hundred writers with a presence on the Net and that they make up roughly fifteen active, findable VX groups. Of those writers, only a small minority are very prolific.

Coders come in all different stripes, and their motivations and ethics vary widely. For every stereotypical 15-year-old bully who writes nothing but data-destroying code that he e-mails to his enemies, there's also a middle-aged Silicon Valley exec who downloads a virus from the Internet, plays around with it out of idle curiosity, and accidentally infects his firm's network.

Opic would seem to fall somewhere between those two extremes. A college student who focuses on the arts, he's been writing viruses for 2 years. He has no formal computer training; he's entirely self-taught. He usually reveals his interest in viruses to his girlfriends (if only to explain the long hours he spends at the keyboard), but his parents and other relatives don't know about it.

Opic got his start by hacking into local university systems with a friend. Once he began learning about viruses, he was hooked. "I found it fascinating that I could actually make this [computer] do what I wanted," he types, "that I could write something that would travel from computer to computer. It's a classical art concept: playing God and all."

According to Gordon, many coders see what they do as a creative endeavor. At least one virus writer with whom she has had extensive contact, a Bulgarian coder known as Dark Avenger, channels his emotions into his code the way an artist would channel them into a painting.

"There was a certain frantic yet very deliberate way that he wrote his programs," Gordon remembers. "Some of the things that he'd put in the source code would just lead you around and around through this maze. And then there would be this part where the code was very calm, laid out very methodically. It was really interesting to see that during the times when things were really confusing in his life, he was writing code that, if you looked at it, was like looking at a pile of spaghetti."

Opic is more imaginative than most coders. Instead of the requisite Iron Maiden lyrics or "Too bad, lamer!" brag messages, he salts his viruses with Fugazi lyrics and snippets of his own poetry ("There is a path to the transcendence of the dollar: Embark rich beggars . . ."). Opic doesn't write data-destroying viruses; a user whose PC is infected by one of his programs is more likely to be annoyed by pesky text messages that appear on a given day of the month or to be haunted by a printer with a mind of its own. "I'm into making points through ambiguity, rather than the tried-and-true 'in your face' method," he says.

Most of the viruses he's writing these days are "proof of concept" programs, created to shine a big, embarrassing spotlight on software vulnerabilities. One such virus is Caligula, the bit of code for which Opic is most widely known. A Word macro virus, Caligula searches for the file containing a user's private encryption key—the key that enables users of the popular Pretty Good Privacy (PGP) utility to decode their encrypted documents and e-mail—and uploads it to Opic's FTP site.

Opic says he had no intention of using the files to gain access to anyone's encoded documents. "I had no interest in impersonating or violating anyone or debunking PGP, which is a great asset to myself and millions of others," he says. "But it was vulnerable due to

Microsoft's platform and some lazy or non-security-conscious programmers. Had I not coded it, it's possible that someone with more malicious intentions would have."

Gordon says she's heard that argument from virus writers before. She views it as an attempt to legitimate irresponsible behavior. "If that's what you have in mind," says Gordon, "there are more responsible ways of working toward solving such problems rather than just posting something on the Internet and saying, 'Oh, here's a new problem,' so that everybody in the world can go out and exploit it."

Opic concedes that in making their viruses available to anyone who's curious enough to seek them out, VXers do play a role in any damage caused by programs that fall into the hands of individuals with malicious intentions. But, he counters, it's "an indirect role—in the same manner that gun manufacturers play a role in thousands of murders each year." Still, why wouldn't Opic consider contacting a software manufacturer directly when he's written a virus aimed at vulnerabilities in that vendor's product?

"Ever tried it?" he asks. "That's obviously the least intrusive route, but it doesn't work. The world is overrun by bureaucracy." He points to Caligula as an example. "What I did was nothing new," he says. "Many have known it was possible; many people, in fact, have written and published papers on the problem. But no one did anything about it until I illustrated the point."

Rob Rosenberger—a security expert whose Web site, Vmyths.com, attempts to educate consumers about hoaxes and media hype related to viruses—says he believes that a small minority of virus writers do ultimately contribute to the greater good. "This is a controversial opinion," says Rosenberger, "but I really think the guys who are writing at the state of the art should be left alone to do what they do, because they also force an advancement in the antivirus world. They make the world more secure."

Not all viruses are inspired by security holes. Sometimes personal politics turn up between the lines of code. One of Opic's favorite creations, Koyyanisqati [sic], was a macro virus that launched a "ping flood" attack—a barrage of data packets that overloads servers and disrupts Internet connections—on four different Web sites. Two of the sites were devoted to kiddie porn; the other two were racist hangouts. Koyyanisqati [sic], Opic says, was his "attempt at a 'good' virus." Still, he can understand why someone like Sarah Gordon wouldn't see it as an achievement. "I suspect she would agree with my feelings in this case, but not my methods," he says.

There's no question that the antivirus-software industry—which has retail sales that are predicted to reach $3 billion by 2002—stands to gain from nurturing virus hysteria. Anytime the threat of an especially sexy virus surfaces, the antivirus companies race to develop fixes, issue "virus alerts," and bend the ears of quote-hungry reporters. And invariably, after a virus outbreak that receives national media attention, there is a subsequent spike in antivirus-software sales: According to the Reston, Virginia, computer industry market research firm PC Data Inc., virus-protection software sales increased by more than 67 percent between March 28 and April 3, 1999, at the height of the Melissa scare. Most users know so little about the reality of viruses that it's easy for AV vendors to indulge in gloomy hyperbole to gain an edge.

"The threat of virus infection is now greater than ever!" claims the product Web page for VirusScan at McAfee.com. "The need to protect your PC has become vital, as there are now over 40,000 known computer viruses, with more than 300 new viruses being created each month"

Figures like that strike fear into the heart of PC users. What most of them don't realize is that of the estimated 40,000 viruses in existence, only about 150 are currently known to be actively spreading. The rest are cooped up in antivirus research labs. And while AV firms often incorporate terms like *deadly, dangerous,* and *malicious* into their sales literature, only a small minority of viruses pose any real threat to a user's data. A quick look at the WildList, a monthly tabulation of viruses known to be "in the wild," provides a more realistic picture. Total number of viruses known to be actively spreading as of this writing: 132. And of the eighteen most common viruses reported in the most recent WildList, only three—CIH, ExploreZip, and One_Half—destroy data.

There's an interesting symbiosis between VXers and AVers. The members of each group generally profess to despise the members of the other, but both groups, in a sense, are dependent on each other. Virus writers need the antivirus industry to challenge them as well as to provide them with notoriety. In VX circles, having the antidote to your latest virus turn up in a new release of Norton AntiVirus or McAfee VirusScan entitles you to major bragging rights. In turn, virus writers are fond of pressing the notion that they keep an entire industry employed.

The friction between the two groups can be intense; frequent bickering matches erupt on Usenet newsgroups such as alt.comp.virus and comp.virus. The AVers' favorite ploy is to hit coders in the ego, accusing them of shoddy programming skills. Every once in a while, a coder strikes back. Nick Fitzgerald, a consulting editor for *Virus Bulletin* magazine, once made the mistake of publicly scorning a virus writer for his "pathetic" programming abilities and later found himself on the receiving end of a creation called ColdApe, a.k.a. the Love Monkey virus. Users infected by ColdApe unwittingly sent e-mails to Fitzgerald's address at *Virus Bulletin,* informing him that they wanted to make "hot monkey love" to him. Fitzgerald says that ColdApe cost him and *Virus Bulletin* "hundreds of hours" of work.

"If you did make this virus, then first off, damn you," reads a June 2 Usenet post by one Marcin Mirski. "And second, how can I get my infected files back?"

Messages like this turn up fairly often in the alt .comp.virus newsgroup. Mirski has come to the group to ask about the happy faces that keep showing up on his screen when he's using Windows 98. The happy faces, he reported in an earlier post, are accompanied by a message reading, "Oops! I've got such terrible munchies. TERMiTE v1.0 RAiD [Slam]."

Within 24 hours, Mirski's query has been answered with a post by RAiD, the proud papa of TERMiTE, a.k.a HLLP.5000. "Isn't he kewl?" asks RAiD in his response. "Have you seen my graphical payload yet? Does it look like crawling termites to you? Have you seen my other payload yet? You're still here, so I guess not."

Other posters add to the thread, explaining to Mirski the steps he needs to follow to get rid of TERMiTE before it launches the randomly triggered second payload, which will wipe his hard drive. In the midst of the advice giving, David Chess, a highly respected antivirus researcher with IBM, pointedly addresses TERMiTE's author: "Just out of curiosity, RAiD, did you feel any impulse whatever to apologize to Mr. Mirski for having written a damaging virus in the first place?"

"None whatsoever," RAiD fires back. "I'm rather proud of that virus. Why on earth would I apologize for something it was designed to do? Mind you, I didn't expect it to get as far as it has. But that's neither here nor there."

A member of the VX group Slam and one of the loudest, most unrepentant coders on the Net, RAiD is the kind of virus writer who makes antivirus workers—and often other virus writers—gnash their teeth in frustration. He's the guy who pops into the mind of PC users as they nervously scan their disks with AV software. Not only does he write viruses with malicious payloads, he also takes a fairly obvious measure of delight in watching them spread.

What drives coders like RAiD? During an informal late-night Internet Relay Channel chat, he offered several clues. While his buddies—guys with handles like CyberYoda and VirusBust and Knowdeth—were standoffish, RAiD was clearly itching for a piece of the spotlight. He expressed doubt about whether his comments would be accurately reported, writing that "the media have made us out to be villains," but he couldn't seem to resist sharing his views anyway. "Personally, I'm interested in exploits," he wrote, "and new ways to infect things. If it can be infected, I want to infect it."

"Not to cause harm to people," he added, "but to see if I can."

According to Opic, RAiD is in the minority of virus writers today, one of a small number who are unapologetic about "opening [Pandora's] box and loving it." From what she's seen of RAiD's activities, Sarah Gordon agrees. "He's not very representative at all of the current crop," she says.

"There are malicious people out there, but they're not accepted around us," says Evul, a 29-year-old coder from the group Ultimate Chaos, whose members frequently associate with the CodeBreakers. "With me, it's about creating and sharing your creativity, as opposed to maliciously or subversively using it on somebody." SPooky, 17, one of Opic's compatriots in CodeBreakers, quit writing last spring when he examined the log files sent back to him by one of his viruses, Marker, and learned that it had infected organizations like Blue Cross–Blue Shield. "There have to be limits, and I think I have found mine," he explained on his Web site at the time.

Most people find it surprising that virus writers have *any* moral or ethical boundaries. When Gordon presents her research on VXers at industry conventions, she says, most of her audiences view virus writers as "antisocial kids with no girlfriends." They're shocked to learn that in tests of ethical development, coders are usually within the norms for their ages. "A lot of the people who do this are, in all aspects, normal, decent people," says Gordon.

Virus writers who do happen to witness firsthand the human pain and problems wrought by a digital catastrophe often become ex-writers very quickly. "On a computer, you don't have contextual clues," Gordon explains. "People lose touch, and they don't realize the impact they're having on another person. It's very possible that sometimes when virus writers say, 'Viruses don't really hurt people,' they believe that. They haven't seen that other person crying because they lost their thesis."

Nick Fitzgerald claims that maliciousness in virus-writing circles—or, as he puts it, the "screw them over and trash their data" ethic—has become increasingly common within the last 2 or 3 years. But to Opic and his friends, the public image of the "typical" virus writer as a cyberterrorist hell-bent on inflicting harm is just plain passé. According to Opic, few of the writers he knows are still interested in creating viruses that destroy data; the wave of the future is programs that *collect* it. The PGP key-stealing capabilities of Caligula, he says, merely scratch the surface in terms of what is possible.

Virus writers, he points out, would not be such a threat to the computing public if it weren't for the constant dumbing-down of PC technology—a result of the ever-increasing consumer demand for more-automated, user-friendly software and the eagerness of companies like Microsoft to meet it. There are a number of unsettling advances on the horizon that play into this dynamic. The VX community is now exploring viruses that propagate via programming languages like HTML and Java, which are commonly used to write Web pages. Executable code can be embedded into HTML files, and because some newer communications programs automatically execute HTML when it's found in an e-mail, it's conceivable that viruses could be spread simply by users' viewing their mail. Java, says Opic, presents the possibility of "remote and automatic infection"—i.e., visit a Web site containing infected Java files, now you're infected. New Internet languages create the possibility, Opic says, for "global infection in hours. A virus can spread to millions of computers before anyone even suspects there's a problem."

Asked if he can understand why most people find that idea scary, Opic says they *should* find it scary. Still, he contends that virus writers and their creations are only a symptom; the problem itself is the "overall development mentality"—namely, the low priority given to security issues by software manufacturers like Microsoft—that allows them to flourish. [For another perspective on this issue, in relation to the Y2K phenomenon, see Reading 11-3.] As long as there are operating systems and software programs with vulnerabilities that can be exploited, virus writers are going to exploit them—sometimes for no better reason than the fact that they can.

It's five in the morning, and lines of text are still marching across the screen. "Humans are almost forced to open Pandora's box at times," Opic writes. A few seconds later, a server message appears in the chat window: "Opic has set the topic on channel #*codebreakers* to 'Curiosity Killed the Cat.'"

RELATED LINKS

- The Codebreakers: Cryptanalysis and Steganalysis (http://ise.gmu.edu/~njohnson/Security/cryptanalysis.htm)

- Hackers at Large International Conference (http://www.hal2001.org)

- How a Computer Virus Works (http://www.cnn.com/2000/TECH/computing/10/23/virus.works.idg)

- How to Become a Hacker (http://www.tuxedo.org/~esr/faqs/hacker-howto.html #WHAT_IS)

- *Virus Bulletin* Magazine (http://www.virusbtn.com)

FOR FURTHER RESEARCH

To find out more about the topics discussed in this reading, use InfoTrac College Edition. Type in keywords and subject terms such as "computer virus," "malicious payload," and "virus-exchange group." You can access InfoTrac College Edition from the Wadsworth/Thomson Communication Cafe homepage: http://communication.wadsworth.com.

Reading 16-2

Hunting the Hackers
Steven Levy and Brad Stone*

EDITOR'S NOTE

For three days in February 2000 a coordinated denial of service, or "ping flood," attack overwhelmed several high-profile Web sites, including Yahoo!, Excite, Amazon.com, eBay, E*Trade, Datek, CNN.com, Buy.com, and ZDNet, preventing legitimate users from gaining access. As this Newsweek *article noted at the time, the attacks were a wake-up call to the fragility of the Internet and highlighted the need for preventative security—an aspect of e-commerce that online companies ignore at their peril.*

CONSIDER

1. What are denial of service, or DOS, attacks, and why are they so threatening to the online community?

2. What options do Internet service providers have for preventing and responding to denial of service attacks?

3. What did these coordinated attacks reveal about the security of the Internet's infrastructure?

Hell week for e-commerce began at just about latte time last Monday morning. At around 10:20 A.M. Pacific time, the brisk pace of the Yahoo! portal—a Gladstone bag of digital services including e-mail, news, fantasy sports leagues, and a renowned Web directory—slowed precipitously. Net surfers accustomed to an average page-loading time of 1.7 seconds were confronted by an annoying 6-second World Wide Wait. Then it got really bad. By 10:30 almost half of those attempting to jack into the Web's second-most-popular site were finding nothing but error messages.

Yahoo's operations team, four engineers led by cofounder David Filo (with an $8 billion stake in the company, surely the richest repairman in the world), got on the horn with GlobalCenter, the Sunnyvale, California-based service that hosts Yahoo's machines. At first the nerd squad figured that a router had failed. But analyzing the flow of bits, they discovered what Global's exec VP Laurie Priddy called "a huge tidal wave of data." Millions of meaningless digital pack-

ets—short, anonymous "pings" that ranged from simple diagnostic messages to requests for page views—were descending on the once-pastoral setting of the Yahoo! server farm like a plague of bit-locusts. "The volume was massive," says Priddy. "It was coming, seemingly, from everywhere." By 11 A.M. less than 10 percent of Yahoo's customers could access a page, according to Keynote Systems, which monitors Web traffic, and even for them it took more than 20 seconds to load it up, no matter how fast the connection.

Yahoo! was under attack, the first of several sites that would dramatically expose cyberspace's dirty secret: Though the Internet is an amazing creation that has boosted our economy and provided lots of cheeky Super Bowl ads, it is still a work in progress that can be knocked silly with surprising ease. Even the e-commerce giants are no sturdier than the respective houses of Little Pigs No. 1 and 2. Instead of a stiff huff from a wolf's lungs, all it takes is a well-directed "denial of service" attack to blow away the edifices, at least on a temporary basis. And when you try to track the culprit, it turns out that all you can find is sheep's clothing—the dummy computers through which the cybervandal laundered his poisonous computer code.

So by 10:30, when Yahoo! president Jeff Mallett was alerted, the engineers had concluded they were indeed victims of a denial of service attack. This is a de-

*With Jared Sandberg and Thomas Hayden in New York and Gregory Vistica and Donatella Lorch in Washington.

liberate attempt to shut down a network operation by overloading it—like shooting a fire hose of bits into a virtual glass of water. What's more, as the team began tracing the traffic, they discovered that the attack was launched through at least fifty locations, a sure sign that their nemesis was using someone else's machines to launch a distributed attack. This is done by first planting software "slaves" in innocent third-party computers, or "zombies." At a given time, those rogue slave programs use the processing power of their hosts to send a flood of destructive messages to the actual target servers.

Filo and the team started redirecting Yahoo's traffic to an unaffected server on the East Coast. By 1:15 in the afternoon, at least half of its customers could answer positively to the "Do you Yahoo?" question, and by 3 P.M. the service was running normally. Just around then, the bad data stopped flowing. "Pretty much once we blocked it, it appeared they figured it out and stopped," says Priddy.

Actually, they just moved. On Tuesday, the Yahoo! folks got a panic call from the popular auction site eBay, asking for advice. They're baa-aack. Not only eBay, but CNN.com and the flagship of e-commerce, Amazon.com, got DOSed. Perhaps the cruelest twist was the attack on the cyberstore Buy.com. When CEO Gregory Hawkins heard that his site was buried in bits, he was standing on the Nasdaq trading floor, celebrating his IPO and waiting to tape a cable television segment. Despite the attack, Buy.com stock rose from an opening $13 to $25. Love that bubble.

On Wednesday, the hit list spread to computer-journalism site ZDNet and stock brokerages E*Trade and Datek.

By the time Attorney General Janet Reno held a press conference vowing an all-out FBI dragnet to stop the technoperps, the message had sunk in: Toto, we're not in Wal-Mart anymore. An hour after Reno pounded the lectern, the portal Excite@Home became the ninth DOS victim of the week. "Massive amounts of data overloaded our connections," says Excite's Joe Minarik. "It's as if you've got a phone line that can handle 100 calls, and they drive 1,000 to it."

The shame of it is that more than 2 years ago, the Computer Emergency Response Team began warning the Net community about DOS incursion—obviously rarely heeded warnings. To be fair, it's devilishly difficult to prevent such an attack. On the day of the Yahoo! blitz, Steve Bellovin, an AT&T security guru, was coincidentally giving a speech at an Internet service provider. One of his PowerPoint slides read, What are the strong defenses? The next slide: There aren't any. Indeed, eBay spokesperson Kevin Pursglove admits that there's no assurance that tomorrow's bidding wars on Pokémon holofoils won't be muddied by pinging tsunamis. "We can't promise our users that this will go away in the short term," he says.

The key appears to be protecting all of cyberspace from predatory programs that recruit dozens, even hundreds, of unsuspecting machines in a DOS attack. Internet service providers could install filters on the data they ship, to sift out evil pings. Several security firms hope to introduce "zombie agents" that sniff out unwanted scripts. Another company, RSA Security, claims it has created a method that, when an attack is sensed, requires visiting computers to solve cryptographic "puzzles"—a task that will overwhelm the attacking machines.

While the Net tries to get its act together—and waits for the zombies to rise again—the action is shifting to the FBI geek hunt. The first clue: Part of the attack on CNN was funneled through a computer at the University of California, Santa Barbara. Stanford and UCLA also confirmed that their computers were used in the attacks. By the end of the week the FBI was seeking subpoenas to search computers in California and Oregon. But that probably won't get the authorities significantly closer to the real culprits, who certainly didn't leave valid return addresses. The best hope is that by painstakingly examining the logs of the routers that direct Internet traffic, investigators might discover clues to the actual origin of the attack.

Another approach is to examine the "magic packets" directed toward the target computers, in hopes that they contain snippets of text or code that will implicate the perpetrators. "It's a snowball rolling down a hill," says a law enforcement official. "These investigations are time-consuming, tedious, and immense." The FBI isn't exactly overloaded with Internet infrastructure gurus (a situation made worse by defections to the lucrative private sector), so it is relying heavily on outside consultants, some of whom have moved operations to the bureau's Pennsylvania Avenue headquarters for the investigation. The consultants have written specialized software to speed the excruciating high-tech search.

If the attackers were extremely careful, that "digital forensics" approach won't work. Then the FBI would have to rely on more traditional detective work to nab the service deniers. "They are probably using their numerous informants through the computer underground to try to gain intelligence on who might be behind these attacks," guesses former hacker Kevin Mitnick, who was recently released from prison. "If their motive is bragging rights, eventually their tale will be told to an informant—that's the FBI's best chance at finding out who's behind this."

Who will be found at the end of the digital trail? If caught and convicted, the perps face up to 10 years in the pokey, with fines that could reach a quarter-million bucks each. Janet Reno admitted that the FBI not only doesn't know who they are, but is unsure of their motives. Some investigators, techies and digital rubberneckers, though, have ventured several theories on who might be behind it:

- *Malicious hackers.* Launching an assault on someone's computer or Web site without an apparent financial gain is a hallmark of "black hat" hackers, who get their chips off by using a crummy laptop machine to ruin the days of e-commerce moguls like Jeff Bezos. (These are not to be confused with the "white hat" hackers, who cross over to work for security firms—for the money.) These could be garden-variety teenage geeks ("Aaron, come to dinner!" "Not now, Mom, I'm bringing E*Trade to its knees!") or a more exotic form of technovandal, the noirish Euro-thug who fires digital missiles from a cybercafe in Sofia or Amsterdam. Since the software programs, or scripts, necessary to launch a denial-of-service attack are readily available for download [see Reading 16-1], even a relatively dim "packet monkey" or "script bunny" could be behind one or more of these Web meltdowns. "Sometimes kids walk down the street snapping car antennas and [slashing] tires," says AT&T's Bellovin, "and sometimes they take out Yahoo! and CNN."

- *Profiteers.* On the other hand, maybe there is a financial component to all this. *Newsweek* has learned that the FBI has been alerted to the possibility that the attacks might have been an effort to goose the price of computer-security stock—which leapt skyward this week in the wake of a near panic about the future of e-commerce. "You don't do this without money involved," says one source involved in the investigation. "One attack is cute, but seven times?" But so far there's no evidence that the security companies

are the twenty-first century equivalent of hook-and-ladder arsonists. In fact, they're paranoid about getting hit themselves. "We were worried all week and we're still worried," says Zach Nelson of the Network Associates division MyCIO.com.

- *Net purists.* Not too long ago, the Internet was the last, best hope for an altruistic renaissance of personal expression and political speech, embracing the extremes of human experience. Now it's largely viewed as a mega shopping mall, with virtual Bal Harbours, Brimfields, and banks—all to the benefit of instant billionaires. "This was in some ways comparable to what happened in Seattle at the WTO [antiglobalism protests]," says Kalle Lasn, editor of the Vancouver-based magazine *Adbusters*.

- *Adbusters.* Could it be that the DOS was launched as a culture jam to rouse the credit card crowd from what Lasn calls "a consumer trance"? Ray Thomas, who has helped organize DOS attacks with the Web-activist group RTmark, doubts it. "These DOS attacks could fit in with some of our tactics, but we always attach a clear message," he says. Still, it's interesting to note that while Yahoo's commercial ventures were snuffed, the company's Geocities sites, which host just-plain-folks home pages, were left alone.

In a strange way, whoever was behind last week's invasion was doing us all a favor. The damage was relatively minor. "What's the economic impact here?" asks terrorism expert Gary Richter of Sandia National Labs. "For an hour or two people couldn't do their day trades, or buy some books. Well, 5 years ago, you couldn't do those things anyway." (As for the revenues lost by the e-commerce sites, figure it this way: Since dot-coms typically lose money on every sale they make, they might have come out ahead.) But of course the day is approaching when Net access will be a lifeblood, and denial of service will be less like having a lollipop confiscated and more like having the lights doused and the pantry cleaned out. If the lessons learned last week result in a collective effort to seriously address the wimpy security of the Internet infrastructure—with everyone from government to Web sites to service providers to institutions and plain-vanilla users with cable modems working together—then the minor setbacks will be the best investment since Yahoo! stock on the day it went public.

What doesn't kill the Net will make it stronger.

CLOSED DOORS

The trouble began on Monday, when hackers brought Web giant Yahoo! to its knees. Over the next 3 days other victims suffered traffic jams and service breaks.

- Yahoo!: First hit Monday morning, the portal was immobilized for 3 hours; at times availability ranged from zero to 10 percent.

- Buy.com: Next down was this e-commerce site, hit on Tuesday morning; it never went totally black, but availability dropped to a low of 9.4 percent.

- eBay: The auction house was almost totally incapacitated for hours Tuesday afternoon; a second attack was thwarted the next day.

- CNN.com: Late Tuesday afternoon, the site was crippled from 4:45 to 5:30 P.M., when less than 5 percent of users could reach the home page.

- Amazon.com: Early Tuesday evening the bookseller was slammed; from 5:00 to 5:45 P.M.; it took users 6 minutes, 20 seconds to connect to the home page.

- ZDNet.com:. Wednesday brought a new round of attacks, starting with this media outlet; its home page was unreachable for almost 2 hours, from 4:15 to 6:15 in the morning.

- E*Trade: The next attack was directed at the online trading house; on Wednesday the site's home page lagged between 5:00 and 7:00 A.M.

- Datek: The brokerage was difficult to reach for only 30 minutes on Wednesday morning; the site denies it was attacked by hackers.

- Excite: The last attack hit Excite on Wednesday night. The home page was slow for 2 hours; from 7:15 to 7:30, availability was 42.9 percent.

MISSION: TOTAL OVERLOAD

Investigators and computer-security experts aren't certain how the attacks were carried out, but the hackers likely used a variation of a so-called "ping flood" assault like this:

1. The hacker scans the Internet for vulnerable "server" or "host" computers operated by businesses and universities.

2. The hacker then breaks into the weak computers and secretly stashes a "slave" software program that will await his instructions to begin the attack.

3. He issues the signal and the slaves begin to broadcast a "ping" request to their locally connected computers, asking whether they are "alive," that is, online and working.

4. Their replies aren't directed back to the hacker; instead, the hacker forges the "return address," directing replies to the ultimate victim, in this case, Amazon.com.

5. Amazon.com is so flooded with bogus replies from hundreds, if not thousands, of machines that legitimate attempts to get through never make it to the victimized site.

Last week's cybervandals will be difficult to nab. They could have mounted the assaults from anywhere in the world. And they used multiple computers belonging to others to cover their tracks.

HOW TO KEEP FROM GETTING HACKED

If you're connected to the Internet, you're vulnerable to intruders. But there are ways to keep your data safe.

1. Use antivirus software and update it often to keep destructive programs off your computer.

2. Don't allow online merchants to store your credit card information for future purchases.

3. Use a hard-to-guess password that contains a mix of numbers and letters, and change it frequently.

4. Use different passwords for different Web sites and applications to keep hackers guessing.

5. Use the most up-to-date version of your Web browser, e-mail software, and other programs.

6. Send credit card numbers only to secure sites; look for a padlock or key icon at the bottom of the browser to confirm it is a secure site.

7. Confirm the site you're doing business with. Watch your typing; it's amazon.com, not amozon.com.

8. Use a security program that gives you control over "cookies" that send information back to Web sites.

9. Install "firewall" software to screen traffic if you use DSL or a cable modem to connect to the Net.

10. Don't open e-mail attachments unless you know the source of the incoming message.

RELATED LINKS

- Alliance for Internet Security (http://www.trusecure.com/html/partners/alliance.shtml)
- Computer Emergency Response Team Coordination Center (http://www.cert.org)
- Denial of Service (DoS) Attack Resources (http://www.denialinfo.com)
- How Not to Be a Zombie in the Hacker Wars (http://www.nytimes.com/library/tech/00/02/circuits/articles/17pete.html)
- Security of the Internet (http://www.cert.org/encyc_article/tocencyc.html)

FOR FURTHER RESEARCH

To find out more about the topics discussed in this reading, use InfoTrac College Edition. Type in keywords and subject terms such as "denial-of-service attack," "malicious hackers," and "Internet security." You can access InfoTrac College Edition from the Wadsworth/Thomson Communication Cafe homepage: http://communication.wadsworth.com.

Reading 16-3

Organized Exploitation of the Information Superhighway

Leah James and Jestyn Cooper

EDITOR'S NOTE

Hacker attacks and computer viruses are becoming a regular, if not disconcerting, feature of the cyberlandscape. Government agencies and major corporations alike (including even Microsoft) remain vulnerable to electronic intrusion and disruption. As this reading from Jane's Intelligence Review *points out, the stereotype of the lone computer hacker is giving way to the more alarming trend of "hacker collectives" and the advent of organized cyberinsurgency. Computer reliance has left organizations highly exposed, and the very nature of open networked systems has created loopholes for backdoor opportunists worldwide.*

CONSIDER

1. While the popular stereotype of a cyberattacker is a nerdy teenager, who actually represents the biggest security concern for senior managers in industry?

2. How have the very qualities that made government and business so dependent on new information technology—ease, access, and low cost—also made them vulnerable?

3. Do hacker attacks and the spread of computer viruses on a mass scale provide adequate justification for regulating the Internet?

Chernobyl came and went; Melissa caused some consternation, but it was not until the arrival of "I Love You" that the virus phenomenon made a deep impression on computer users around the world. Within 36 hours of its impact being registered, the so-called "Love Bug" had infected an estimated 5 million machines. It was not that this was the most damaging virus to date, or the most innovative, but it did succeed in drawing unprecedented attention to the dangers associated with the Internet and e-mail.

The "Love Bug" was accredited to a single, disenchanted Filipino computer student. Given the extent of the chaos he created, could not similar means be employed, perhaps to even greater effect, by criminals, terrorists, or even rogue states, such as Libya or North Korea? How prepared are law enforcement agencies around the world to meet this potential threat? Despite several years of progress, the capabilities of the hacker are undeniably superior.

THE LONE HACKER

It has long been held that, in terms of a threat to IT [information technology] systems, the protagonist would be an individual, skilled and knowledgeable, but at odds with the society surrounding him: typically, a college-educated, twentysomething male who found the challenge of accessing otherwise-secure IT networks motivation enough. To complete the stereotype, these young, alienated "hackers" would invariably be complemented by less opportunistic and more idealistic computer experts, whose disruptive tendencies were but an expression of the computer users' commitment to the freedoms of information and speech.

To a greater or lesser extent, each of these classic hacker definitions probably account for the majority of those engaged in such activities today. The proliferation of do-it-yourself manuals, both online and in hard

copy, offering guidance on a variety of techniques to disrupt even apparently sophisticated networks, has only increased the attractiveness of their domain. Despite the release of over 200 viruses each month in the U.S. alone, the hacker's propensity for expensive mischief remains little more than that. Lacking coordination, they rarely cause anything more than a headache for businesses and the IT security firms that protect them.

The greater danger comes from those with more experience, determination, and guile, to whom notoriety (or, as has been alleged in certain instances, financial reward) is often the primary goal. Kevin Mitnick is regarded as a martyr to hackers. A spate of attacks on some of the largest Internet sites, including Amazon.com and CNN, followed the end of a case against him that covered twenty-five counts of computer and wire fraud. David Smith, a computer programmer and the source of the Melissa virus, faces up to 10 years imprisonment and a $100,000 fine. Their exploits encourage those with more malicious intent.

To an extent, they also provide succor to the growing number of vengeful downsized or just frustrated employees in the U.S., Western Europe, and elsewhere. These represent the biggest security concern for 90 percent of senior managers in the U.S., not least because, prior to surrendering passwords and access codes, they have the opportunity to exact some form of revenge. It has been said that, while "people think of cyberattackers as nerdy teenagers, . . . most [damage] is done against business by junior employees and subcontractors."

Despite the prominence of Smith, Mitnick, and others, the character of hacking today is interlinked and communal. There is a near-constant exchange of information throughout what must now be regarded as a movement in its own right, and these sources relate as much to tactics as they do to the inherent weaknesses of leading government and commercial Web sites.

With the emergence of numerous "hacker collectives" around the world, an unprecedented degree of organization is becoming evident in their work. One such group, Hacking for Girlies, claim to "have planned not just for the day the FBI comes, we've even

---

planned for a hostile raid where the Feds actually plant evidence."

The innocuous-sounding name disguises the fact that they once forced the *New York Times* to suspend their online publications for a costly 9 hours. Members of another collective, L0pht, testified before a Congressional investigation that they could halt all Internet activity within 30 minutes. The coordinated expertise found within these groups is beginning to acquire a political dimension and become even more disruptive, as many authorities attempt to inhibit their activities, typically through the introduction of a more substantial regulatory regime for the Internet.

THE ADVENT OF CYBERINSURGENCY

The very assets that have made government and businesses so dependent upon the new information technology—ease, access, and low cost—are also what makes them so vulnerable. The Internet provides activists, from the protester to the hardened terrorist, with the means to apply a full range of tactics, including protest and blockade, disruption and destruction, potentially leading to the loss of life. The "cyberoption" not only enhances the traditional roles and traits of terrorism, but also offers new forms of attack and a range of targets hitherto unavailable.

Almost since its inception, the Internet has been adopted by nongovernmental organizations to mobilize support. In Seattle during November 1999 and Washington, DC, in April 2000 it was a decisive tool that enabled the convergence of various protestors.

The Internet offers the terrorist, guerrilla, or activist a means of reaching a huge audience at relatively little cost. Anyone with a computer and a modem can read daily updates of Hezbollah activity in southern Lebanon; Sendero Luminoso in Peru; Pakistani-backed separatists in Kashmir; or animal rights organizations in Europe. In the past, underground organizations have been forced to rely on traditional media sources, which remain far easier for the authorities to shut down.

In 1998 a U.S. Senate subcommittee heard evidence confirming that insurgent groups of all sizes were successfully using the Internet to promote their message. Much of the material is anti-Western and anti-Israeli. However, there is little that can be done to prevent such activity, for groups like the Sri Lankan Tamil Tigers avoid domestic restrictions by establishing foreign-based Web sites. U.S. intelligence reports indicate that as far back as 1996, the Kandahar headquarters of Osama bin Laden were furnished with state-of-the-art computer and communications equipment.

The Internet is a vital tool for those who aim to coordinate activities with like-minded groups in inaccessible places. Bin Laden's use of cyberspace has been helped by the presence of IT-trained Egyptian nationals who were veterans of the war in Afghanistan. E-mail, chat rooms, and electronic bulletin boards help keep Bin Laden's al-Qaida network in touch with Hamas and Hezbollah.

THE DEATH OF DISTANCE

The World Wide Web offers the insurgent organization much more that just a bulletin board to get their message across and means of communicating with supporters.

Online terrorism not only gives the perpetrator the opportunity to attack targets globally, it allows them to operate without the physical presence of bombers, assassins, or kidnappers. The "Love Bug" came from the Philippines, although its origins are alleged to have been found in Germany. There is no reason why cyberattacks against the U.S. and Europe could not be launched from terrorist bases in Lebanon, Yemen, or Sudan.

One of the unique qualities of cyberinsurgency as a form of terrorism is that it can cause widespread economic damage without harming life (the concept of "bloodless terrorism"). But that would not be the case if the PKK (of Turkey), the ETA (of Spain), or the PIRA (of Ireland) used viruses or hacking to attack emergency services, air traffic control systems, or defense systems; they are just three groups believed to be working on such a capability.

Whereas many terrorist groups believe that mass loss of life damages their cause, that cannot be said for extremist organizations such as al-Qaida or the Tamil Tigers, for example. After all, a computer attack by Islamists on a networked medical referral service, perhaps causing devastating loss of life, is surely just a modern version of the 1983 suicide attack on the U.S. Marine Corps barracks in Lebanon or the 1993 World Trade Center bombing [and destruction in 2001].

In August 1999 the East Timorese leader, José Ramos-Horta, warned the Indonesian government that if it failed to honor the results of the forthcoming referendum on independence, a "cyberarmy" of teenagers around the world would hack into vital government, defense, and banking computer systems. The cause of East Timorese independence was popular amongst many in the West, and a number of small-scale online incidents in previous years against Indonesia may have laid some groundwork for a larger offensive.

THE ANONYMOUS TERRORIST

The advent of the anonymous terrorist is a relatively new phenomenon. It does not necessarily suit the purposes of anarchists and religious extremists to publicize their activities, and they can capitalize from the anonymity and ambiguity provided by the Internet.

Left-wing groups in the 1970s and early 1980s who sought to bring down capitalism and Western imperialism attempted to do so through disruption and undermining public confidence in the government. Today, the anarchist wanting to attack globalization, the International Monetary Fund (IMF), or the World Bank can do so by hitting capitalist targets electronically with even greater effect than protesting on the streets of Seattle, London, or Washington.

What damage could the cyberterrorist really do? There are pitfalls for the perpetrator. Intelligence agencies are improving their capability not only to defend from online attack, but also to track down group members. Even so, dependence on computer technology in the U.S. leaves the world's only superpower highly exposed.

Whereas few may wish to challenge the might of the U.S. military on the battlefield, the Pentagon has admitted to having had its information technology assets targeted on many occasions, particularly since the mid-1990s. These attacks have increased when there has been a buildup of Western forces in the Gulf and in the Balkans. Following the [purportedly accidental] NATO bombing of the Chinese embassy in Belgrade in May 1999 during the Kosovo conflict, numerous U.S. government Web sites reported a rise in hacker attacks.

The origins of such incidents are difficult to uncover. Supported by other intelligence reports, the Emergency Response and Research Institute claimed in 1998 that information warfare classes were being taught by extremist religious foundations in Pakistan. Official denials from Islamabad aside, rumors are rife that Pakistani trained, anti-U.S. cyberterrorists have links with Afghani groups and sympathetic organiza-

tions in Western Europe. The Pakistan based "Hackerz Club" is reported to have regularly attacked Indian and U.S. Web sites, replacing images with "Free Kashmir" slogans. Among those sites to be hit are a U.S. Air Force base in Texas and the Department of Energy in New Mexico.

While online terrorism does not necessarily need state sponsorship, there are suspicions that Iran, Iraq, Libya, and Syria may support cyberinsurgency, possibly through sponsorship of bright young graduates attending IT training programs.

POTENTIAL FOR DAMAGE

It is difficult to gauge the extent of the online threat, in part because established criminal and terrorist organizations are interspersed with a disparate array of smaller activist groups and individuals. Ultimately, there is little difference between the dangers each presents. A lone Swedish hacker managed in 1996 to disable the Florida 911 emergency services network. A similar attack could have been achieved by Cuban dissidents in light of the Elian Gonzales incident, Islamist groups operating under the auspices of Bin Laden, or any number of disgruntled groups with grievances against the U.S.

The private sector is understandably averse to the bad publicity that can be generated by disclosure of a successful attack on an IT system or Web site. At present, there is no legal requirement to report such an incident. Anything that draws attention to the vulnerabilities of businesses such as Amazon.com, eBay, or newly wired firms of the old economy such as IBM and Citibank can have serious financial consequences. Many major corporations, therefore, trust no one [and reveal as little as possible], demonstrating a level of paranoia similar to that of the hackers who attempt to disrupt their operations.

The building of trust between companies and law enforcement agencies in this area has been central to recent reforms in the U.S. The creation of "flexible, evolutionary approaches that span both the public and private sectors" was called for in May 1998 under the aims of Presidential Decision Directive 63.

While the Information Sharing and Analysis Centers that will facilitate the confidential transfer of ideas and expertise between industry and government take shape, the task of strengthening the relationship has been entrusted to law enforcement officials. Businessmen remain far from convinced. According to one: "What matters to a business is ensuring continuity of operations . . . but catching the bad guy is all that the FBI cares about."

NO RULES

The Federal Bureau of Investigation and other agencies in the U.S. and worldwide have yet to gain a credible track record in combating online crime, terrorism, or the universal menace of hacking attacks. Although certain individuals have at times been apprehended— the FBI was remarkably quick in leading the Philippine authorities to "Love Bug" suspect Reonel Ramones— the rarity of prosecution creates little disincentive or deterrent.

In appointing the FBI as the lead agency in this field, the U.S. government seems to have accepted that, in the main, threats to the Internet relate to law enforcement, not questions of national security. In doing so, this has enabled the necessary process of legislative reform to begin in earnest.

Most countries in the world, however, are yet to reach this stage. As the FBI discovered in the Philippines, international computer crimes are too modern for [many countries'] archaic laws. Ramones was instead arrested on a charge more usually seen during instances of credit card fraud.

Even countries that have been at the forefront of efforts to protect online trade and commerce concede that they are unlikely to regain the upper hand. The Netherlands uncovers around 14 percent of "black," or underground, Internet transactions and yet is able to bring about a prosecution in just 0.5 percent of cases. Organized crime syndicates have long exploited these shortcomings, not least as part of complex, multinational schemes that enable money to be laundered with remarkable speed and anonymity.

Law enforcement also is often placed at a significant disadvantage by its structure and lack of adequate resources. While the U.S. may be a pioneer in addressing the online threat, it reportedly still takes an average of 49 months for government agencies to order, acquire, and install IT equipment. Moreover, the FBI may represent the lead agency, but they are not alone and the potential for duplicative law enforcement efforts complicates matters. As Frank Ciluffo of the Center for Strategic and International Studies has remarked: "Anything where you have fifty-plus cooks in one kitchen, it gets very difficult."

The situation is similar in the U.K. Despite the creation of a National Infrastructure Security Coordination Centre, which draws upon the expertise of the Government Communications Headquarters and British intelligence agency MI5, these two in turn compete for responsibility with HM Customs and Special Branch.

In light of the problems encountered at the national level, it is not surprising that a combined, transnational legislative response resembles little more than an idea. In May 2000, a panel of over 300 computer-security experts gathered at the G8 summit in Paris. They called for the development of "a global text so there cannot be 'digital havens.'"

Nevertheless, the principle of state sovereignty is an insurmountable obstacle, one that may accommodate extremists, criminals, money launderers, and terrorists, but which forms the basis of the international system. Therefore the initiative will remain with individual countries and their respective law enforcement agencies, leaving information sharing and bilateral technical assistance the best means by which to promote a joint approach to regulating of the Internet.

In the absence of a sufficient legal typology, many governments have instead resorted to the increased monitoring of online activity. In this regard, one program in particular has caused alarm around the world. The Echelon network began in 1948 as a method by which the U.S., U.K., Canada, Australia, and New Zealand could intercept the military and diplomatic communications of the Soviet Union and its allies. With the end of the Cold War, however, Echelon was directed towards the collection of more commercial information from all corners of the globe. The European Union alleges that this has been used by companies such as Boeing, Raytheon, and AT&T to the disadvantage of international firms, including Airbus, Thomson-CSF, and NEC.

The European parliament contends that "all fax, e-mail, and telephone messages are routinely intercepted" at a rate of 3 million messages per minute. The main proponents of Echelon have countered that the information gathered is used only if bribery or a breach of U.N. sanctions is suspected.

The French Director Générale de Sécurité Extérieure is not beyond reproach. Their similar, but less sophisticated, system (dubbed "Frenchelon" by the

Central Intelligence Agency) is also accessed by the German authorities. The furor over the Echelon network has only served to mask the introduction of more pervasive domestic Internet monitoring regimes in the U.S. and U.K.

PROSPECTS FOR ONLINE SECURITY

The very nature of the computer systems that companies spend so much money and manpower trying to protect creates another set of problems. Although it has become very popular of late to blame Microsoft for a host of Windows-based concerns, in this instance there is an element of justification. The dominance of their software and operating systems only adds to the ease with which these systems may be exploited. This has been borne out by the most successful viruses of recent years, which have invariably manipulated the widespread reliance on Microsoft products [see Reading 16-1].

By comparison, users of Macintosh and Linux systems have had far fewer problems, although Linux is now becoming a target for hackers.

That the situation will continue to deteriorate is inevitable. Internet usage is growing horizontally and vertically, with penetration rates rising rapidly in the developing world, and with ever more innovative methods of access being introduced.

Instead of just having a personal computer succumb to a virus, the vulnerability of personal digital assistants is soon likely to be exposed. The Timofonica virus recently targeted Spanish mobile telephone networks with a derivative of the "I Love You" virus. Moreover, the growth of online commerce presents new problems. During 1998 consumers in Western Europe spent £2.6 billion via the Internet, and an estimated 1.05 million users held bank accounts online. The opportunities for an individual or group determined to wreak havoc rise in line with this trend.

Consequently, demands for the enhanced regulation of Internet and e-mail traffic will only increase, albeit in the face of ever more vociferous complaints from libertarians. Whether national governments can ever regain the advantage over the online interests of hackers, criminals, and terrorists is debatable. With that in mind, the threat can only be managed through a greater sense of security consciousness amongst all those who use the Internet. In that respect, the sharp prompt offered by the "Love Bug" may not have been so devastating after all.

RELATED LINKS

- Crime on the Internet (http://www.nytimes.com/library/tech/reference/index-cybercrime.html)
- Cybercrime.gov (http://www.cybercrime.gov)
- Cybercrime...Cyberterrorism...Cyberwarfare... (http://www.csis.org/pubs/cyberfor.html)
- The Information Warfare Site: Cyberterrorism (http://www.iwar.org.uk/cyberterror)
- Jane's Intelligence Review (http://jir.janes.com)

FOR FURTHER RESEARCH

To find out more about the topics discussed in this reading, use InfoTrac College Edition. Type in keywords and subject terms such as "computer virus," "hacker," and "cyberterrorism." You can access InfoTrac College Edition from the Wadsworth/Thomson Communication Cafe homepage: http://communication.wadsworth.com.

Index